A LITERARY HISTORY OF LATIN & ENGLISH POETRY

Victoria Moul's groundbreaking study uncovers one of the most important features of early modern English poetry: its bilingualism. The first guide to a forgotten literary landscape, this book considers the vast quantities of poetry that were written and read in both Latin and English from the sixteenth to the eighteenth century. Introducing readers to a host of new authors and drawing on hundreds of manuscript as well as print sources, it also reinterprets a series of landmarks in English poetry within a bilingual literary context. Ranging from Tottel's miscellany to the hymns of Isaac Watts, via Shakespeare, Jonson, Herbert, Marvell, Milton and Cowley, this revelatory survey shows how the forms and fashions of contemporary Latin verse informed key developments in English poetry. As the complex, highly creative interactions between the two languages are revealed, the work reshapes our understanding of what 'English' literary history means.

VICTORIA MOUL is Associate Professor in Early Modern Latin and English at University College London and is a leading expert on the relationship between Latin and English poetry. She is the author of *Jonson, Horace and the Classical Tradition* (Cambridge University Press, 2010) and the editor of *A Guide to Neo-Latin Literature* (Cambridge University Press, 2017). She has published widely on classical, early modern and modernist poetry alike.

A LITERARY HISTORY OF LATIN & ENGLISH POETRY

Bilingual Verse Culture in Early Modern England

VICTORIA MOUL
University College London

CAMBRIDGE
UNIVERSITY PRESS

University Printing House, Cambridge CB2 8BS, United Kingdom

One Liberty Plaza, 20th Floor, New York, NY 10006, USA

477 Williamstown Road, Port Melbourne, VIC 3207, Australia

314–321, 3rd Floor, Plot 3, Splendor Forum, Jasola District Centre, New Delhi – 110025, India

103 Penang Road, #05–06/07, Visioncrest Commercial, Singapore 238467

Cambridge University Press is part of the University of Cambridge.

It furthers the University's mission by disseminating knowledge in the pursuit of education, learning, and research at the highest international levels of excellence.

www.cambridge.org
Information on this title: www.cambridge.org/9781107192713
DOI: 10.1017/9781108131667

© Victoria Moul 2022

This publication is in copyright. Subject to statutory exception and to the provisions of relevant collective licensing agreements, no reproduction of any part may take place without the written permission of Cambridge University Press.

First published 2022

A catalogue record for this publication is available from the British Library.

Library of Congress Cataloging-in-Publication Data
NAMES: Moul, Victoria, 1980– author.
TITLE: A literary history of Latin & English poetry : bilingual verse culture in early modern England / Victoria Moul, King's College London.
Other titles: A literary history of Latin and English poetry
DESCRIPTION: Cambridge ; New York : Cambridge University Press, 2022. | Includes bibliographical references and index.
IDENTIFIERS: LCCN 2022008897 (print) | LCCN 2022008898 (ebook) | ISBN 9781107192713 (hardback) | ISBN 9781316642634 (paperback) | ISBN 9781108131667 (epub)
SUBJECTS: LCSH: English poetry–Early modern, 1500-1700–History and criticism. | English poetry–18th century–History and criticism. | Latin poetry, Medieval and modern–England–History and criticism. | Latin poetry, Medieval and modern–Appreciation–England. | Latin poetry, Medieval and modern–Translations into English–History and criticism. | BISAC: LITERARY CRITICISM / European / English, Irish, Scottish, Welsh | LCGFT: Literary criticism.
CLASSIFICATION: LCC PR531 .M68 2022 (print) | LCC PR531 (ebook) | DDC 821.009–dc23/eng/ 20220414
LC record available at https://lccn.loc.gov/2022008897
LC ebook record available at https://lccn.loc.gov/2022008898

ISBN 978-1-107-19271-3 Hardback

Cambridge University Press has no responsibility for the persistence or accuracy of URLs for external or third-party internet websites referred to in this publication and does not guarantee that any content on such websites is, or will remain, accurate or appropriate.

In memory of my father, Dennis Moul, who first said poems to me.

Contents

List of Figures		*page* ix
Acknowledgements		x
List of Abbreviations		xii

Introduction   1

PART I SHORTER VERSE

1 Anglo-Latin 'Moralizing Lyric' in Early Modern England   25
2 Metrical Variety and the Development of Latin Lyric Poetry in the Latter Sixteenth Century   68
3 Buchanan, Beza and the Genre of the Sidney Psalter   96
4 Formal Panegyric Lyric in England, 1550–1650   136
5 Abraham Cowley and Formal Innovation: Verse Sequences, Inset Lyrics, Pindarics and Free Verse   183
6 Religious and Devotional Epigram and Lyric   223
7 Epigram Culture and Literary Bilingualism in Early Modern England   271
8 Satire, Invective and Humorous Verse   320

PART II LONGER VERSE

9 Panegyric Epic in Early Modern England   355
10 Latin Style and Late Elizabethan Poetry: Rethinking Epyllia   406

11	Palingenian Epic: Allegory, Ambition and Didacticism	447
Afterword		497

Metrical Appendix: Latin Metres   499
Bibliography A: Manuscripts   504
Bibliography B: Early Printed Books   516
Bibliography C: Secondary Literature   533
Index   565

Figures

1 Theodorus Beza [Theodore de Bèze], *Psalmorum Davidis et aliorum prophetarum, libri quinque* (London: Thomae Vautroullerij & impensis Herculis Francisci, 1580), pp. 4–5 (Psalm 2). By permission of the Master and Fellows of St John's College, Cambridge. *page* 102
2 St John's College, Cambridge, MS O.65, pp. 1–2. By permission of the Master and Fellows of St John's College, Cambridge. 253
3 Payne Fisher, *Irenodia Gratulatoria* (London: T. Newcomb, 1652), frontispiece engraving. By permission of The Warden and Fellows of All Souls College, Oxford. 390

Acknowledgements

I am grateful to many friends, colleagues and students who have read or discussed parts of this book, from the initial proposal onwards. These include James Corke-Webster, Bianca Facchini, Sophie Lunn-Rockliffe, Richard Maber, Fiachra Mac Góráin, Gesine Manuwald, Anthony Ossa-Richardson, Nigel Smith, Chris Stamatakis, Edward Taylor and Blair Worden as well as the anonymous readers for Cambridge University Press, both of the initial proposal, and, especially, of the submitted manuscript. I am particularly grateful to Elizabeth Scott-Baumann and Edward Holberton, who have been unstintingly generous with their interest, enthusiasm and encouragement over the entire course of the project.

Portions of the book were originally presented in various talks and seminars, and I am grateful to audiences in Oxford, Cambridge, Berkeley, St Andrews, Birmingham, Trondheim, Gothenburg, Warwick and London. The archival work on which the book partly depends would have been impossible without the assistance of archivists and librarians across the country: I am particularly grateful to Suzanne Paul of Cambridge University Library, Jess Nelson at the National Archives and Isabel Sullivan at Surrey History Centre for their interest and support.

A full picture of early modern Latin poetry in either print or manuscript is still many years off; for the chance to make a start on such a survey, however, and incorporate some of the early findings in this book I am enduringly grateful to the Leverhulme Trust for funding 'Neo-Latin Poetry in English Manuscript Verse Miscellanies' (2017–21), and to the excellent team of doctoral students and post-doctoral researchers who have worked with me on the project: Bianca Facchini, Sharon van Dijk, Raffaella Colombo and Edward Taylor. Supervising their research and reading their publications has been a constant pleasure and stimulation, and without their work examining, transcribing, describing and translating manuscript material the project would have been vastly smaller in scope. Although I have made every effort to acknowledge them individually

Acknowledgements

where a particular poem only came to my attention because of their work, there are many other cases where the argument of this book rests upon a range of material encompassable only by a team project. For institutional support, I am grateful to both King's College London and University College London, and especially to my head of department in Greek & Latin at UCL, Gesine Manuwald.

During the latter stages of writing this book, I was working also on an edited volume on C. H. Sisson, alongside my colleague John Talbot. The editorial conversations I have had with John, focused on Sisson but ranging far beyond him, have proved some of the most stimulating exchanges I have had about poetry, how it works and what it means. Though there is none of Sisson in this book, the two projects have been complementary.

This is a book about poetry, born of a love of poetry of all kinds. Most of what I have learnt about poetry I have learnt from those who spoke it to me and read it with me. Of these, I would like to mention in particular Lea Chambers, James Engell, Denis Feeney, Eivind Kahrs, Jonathan Katz, Charles Low, Chris Minkowski, Andrew Mylne and John Smith as well as the Reverend Peter Bustin and my father, Dennis Moul.

Finally but not least, for their love and distraction, my husband, David, and our young sons, Joseph and Felix. I first conceived of this project shortly after Felix was born and the book has absorbed, I hope, a little of the boys' mischief and exuberance.

Abbreviations

BL	British Library
Bod.	Bodleian Library
CELM	Peter Beal (ed.), *Catalogue of English Literary Manuscripts 1450–1700* (https://celm-ms.org.uk)
CUL	Cambridge University Library
EEBO	Early English Books Online
ESTC	English Short Title Catalogue (http://estc.bl.uk)
NLPEM	Neo-Latin Poetry in English Manuscript Verse Miscellanies
ODNB	Oxford Dictionary of National Biography

Journals

AN&Q	American Notes and Queries
Anglia	Anglia – Zeitschrift für Englische Philologie
Arion	Arion: A Journal of Humanities and the Classics
BHR	Bibliothèque d'humanisme et Renaissance
C&L	Christianity and Literature
CA	Classical Antiquity
CFCEL	Cuadernos de filología clásica. Estudios Latinos
CL	Comparative Literature
CQ	Cambridge Quarterly
CRCL	Canadian Review of Comparative Literature
EJ	English Journal
ELH	English Literary History
ELR	English Literary Renaissance
EMS	English Manuscript Studies
ES	English Studies
ESMEA	Essays and Studies by Members of the English Association
G&R	Greece and Rome
GHJ	The George Herbert Journal

HJ	Historical Journal
HL	Humanistica Lovaniensia
HLB	Harvard Library Bulletin
HLQ	Huntington Library Quarterly
HTR	Harvard Theological Review
HU	History of Universities
IJCT	International Journal of the Classical Tradition
IR	Innes Review
JDJ	John Donne Journal
JEGP	Journal of English and Germanic Philology
LC	Literature Compass
Logos	Logos: A Journal of Catholic Thought and Culture
MLN	Modern Language Notes
MLR	The Modern Language Review
MP	Modern Philology
MSN	Marvell Society Newsletter
N&Q	Notes and Queries
P&P	Past and Present
PBSA	Papers of the Bibliographical Society of America
PLL	Papers in Language and Literature
PQ	Philological Quarterly
QCTC	Quaderni di cultura e di tradizione classica
R&R	Renaissance and Reformation / Renaissance et réforme
RES	Review of English Studies
RPL	Res publica litterarum
RQ	Renaissance Quarterly
RS	Renaissance Studies
SEL	Studies in English Literature, 1500–1900
SJ	Sidney Journal
SLI	Studies in the Literary Imagination
SP	Studies in Philology
SQ	Shakespeare Quarterly
SR	Studies in the Renaissance
SUP	Studi umanistici piceni
T&L	Translation and Literature
TAPA	Transactions of the American Philological Association
TCBS	Transactions of the Cambridge Bibliographical Society
TCO	The Classical Outlook
TCS	Transactions of the Cymmrodorion Society
TLS	The Times Literary Supplement

TSLL	Texas Studies in Literature and Language
UBHJ	University of Birmingham Historical Journal
WRM	Wolfenbütteler Renaissance-Mitteilungen
YES	Yearbook of English Studies

In quotations of original material, standard abbreviations such as tildes and 'q;' for '-que' have been silently expanded.

Introduction

The literary culture of early modern England was bilingual; literature of all kinds, including poetry which is the focus of this book, was read and written in both English and Latin throughout the whole of the period that we call Renaissance or early modern.[1] Both the overlap and the *lack* of overlap between Latin and English poetry makes a difference to our understanding of this literary culture. It matters that so many apparently innovative moves in English poetics – including the fashion for epyllia, epigrams and Cowley's 'irregular' Pindaric odes – can be traced back to continental Latin poetry: that is, to 'neo-' Latin rather than primarily classical verse. It is important that so many popular poems circulated bilingually, in both Latin and English versions, or with answers or ripostes in the other language. But it also matters that there are some forms – such as sonnets in English and (until Marvell's 'First Anniversary') short panegyric epic in Latin – that were a characteristic feature of verse in one language but not the other.

The quantity of neo-Latin poetry in surviving manuscript and print sources from early modern England is vast, and to a large extent still unmapped and unexplored.[2] Most first-line indexes of poetry do not

---

[1] Poetry was, of course, also read and (less often) written in England in other languages, especially French, Italian, Dutch, ancient Greek and Hebrew. But both the consumption and the output of poetry in all these languages put together is dwarfed by the activity in Latin.

[2] The only surveys are Binns, *Intellectual Culture* (covering Elizabethan and Jacobean material only, and with minimal coverage of manuscript sources) and Bradner, *Musae Anglicanae* (only very partial coverage of print, and almost none of manuscript; omits discussion of the Protectorate altogether). This book draws on data from a large project I have been running since 2017, conducting the first survey of post-medieval ('neo-') Latin verse in early modern English manuscripts ('Neo-Latin Poetry in Early Modern English Manuscripts, c.1550–1700', generously funded by the Leverhulme Trust). At the time of writing, the project has identified 28,080 probably or certainly post-medieval items of Latin verse in 1,237 manuscripts held in 40 archives and collections. This is far from a complete survey even of English holdings. The knowledge I have gained from this project has transformed what this book has been able to cover, and I am very grateful to the Leverhulme Trust for their support.

include any Latin.[3] Indeed, the vast majority of scholarship on the (English) poetry of this period is written as if contemporary Latin poetry simply did not exist.[4] This book outlines some of the ways in which developments in Latin poetry were related to – both influencing and influenced by – the landmarks of English poetry with which scholars, students and lovers of English literature are familiar. In so doing, it attempts to chart some of the vast and largely unknown field of Latin poetry that was read and written in early modern England between around 1550 and 1700 in a way that is both accessible and, I hope, engaging to readers who have no Latin themselves: to convey something of the particular pleasures and expectations of this poetry, of how it works, what it is like to read, and how and why it was enjoyed. But I aim also to demonstrate how English verse culture as a whole looks, feels, sounds and makes sense differently if we stop pretending that all that Latin is not there.

Landmark works and authors recontexualised by this 'bilingual' approach include Tottel's *Songs and Sonnets* (Chapter 1); the Elizabethan interest in quantitative metrics (Chapters 2 and 3); the Sidney psalter (Chapter 3); the so-called 'Ovidian' epyllia of the 1590s (Chapter 10); Marvell's 'Horatian Ode' (Chapter 4); his 'First Anniversary' and Dryden's *Annus Mirabilis* (Chapter 9); Jonson's and Cowley's experiments in Pindaric lyric (Chapter 5); the unclassical tradition of didactic and allegorical epic (Chapter 11), including Fletcher's *Purple Island*; Herbert's *Temple* and the development of religious lyric through to the hymns of Isaac Watts (Chapters 3 and 6); Jonson's *Epigrams* (Chapter 7); and the conception and practice of satiric, humorous and invective verse (Chapter 8).

Other surprises relate to the *lack* of obvious contact: there are no sonnets in Latin, and no 'standard' way of translating a sonnet in Latin emerges at any stage; conversely, the extraordinary popularity of Latin 'free verse' and 'literary inscriptions' in the later seventeenth century, though connected to the increasingly 'free' Pindarics produced in the latter part of that period in English, has no direct English analogue (Chapter 5). It is hard to imagine any serious English poem attempting, as David Kinloch's *De hominis procreatione* does, a detailed description not only of sexual

---

[3] The exceptions are the first-line index to the Nottingham Portland manuscripts, and Hilton Kelliher's addendum to the index of verse in British Library manuscripts. The latter covers only manuscripts acquired between 1894 and 2009, and excludes a single manuscript containing over 700 Latin epigrams (BL MS Add. 73542).

[4] This is unfortunately mostly true even of scholarship focusing on classical reception. A recent exception is Wong, *Poetry of Kissing*.

intercourse but also of all the various ways in which sex may fail to lead to conception, a rather startling literalization of the frustrated erotics of the Elizabethan epyllion to which Kinloch's poem is closely related in style (Chapter 10); or, as in the second book of Cowley's *Plantarum Libri Sex* (dating from c.1660), to stage a debate between personified herbs on the causes of female menstruation and the ethics of abortion (Chapter 11).

Such an approach is not intended to denigrate the poetry of the sixteenth, seventeenth and early eighteenth century written in English. On the contrary, I consider the period stretching from Spenser to Pope to be uncontroversially the most brilliant 150 years of English poetic history. This is poetry that I love and know well and have been reading since childhood. But it is also poetry which arises from, draws upon and feeds back into a wider literary culture that was intensely bilingual: it is not just that enormous quantities of Latin verse were both read and written, often by the same poets whose English verse we still read and teach, but that the Latin and the vernacular poetry are in constant conversation. The book arises from a strong desire to understand better where that English poetry comes from as much as it does from my enthusiasm for the Latin poetry of the period.

Education and Readership

Educated early modern men (and some women) wrote, read and circulated Latin verse intensively because they had been trained to do so: Latin was central to both secondary and tertiary education not only because Latin literature was the main subject of study at school (though this is certainly true), but also because Latin was the medium of education. Boys and young men at grammar school and university – in modern terms, from upper-primary to the end of secondary school age – were educated *in* Latin.[5] There are obvious parallels with the use of 'world' languages (such as English or French) in secondary and tertiary education today in many parts of the world where they are not a mother tongue.

Latin literary dexterity – including multiple modes of transformation between languages and forms, such as the rendering of themes in both prose and verse, or recasting an hexameter extract into a lyric, as well as

---

[5] Though some students matriculated at 18, most were younger. The average undergraduate in early modernity was (in modern terms) of upper secondary rather than university age, and some were younger still: Andrew Marvell, for instance, matriculated at Cambridge aged 13; John Donne at Oxford aged only 12.

translation into English and back into Latin (so-called 'double translation') – was central to educational success.[6] While there is little evidence that schoolboys were regularly asked to compose English poetry as such, especially before the mid-seventeenth century, there is no question that anyone who had completed secondary education (regardless of university experience) had been required not only to read but also to compose a considerable quantity of Latin verse.[7] The small proportion of girls who were educated were probably instructed in similar ways to boys, though perhaps with a lesser emphasis upon active oral and written skills as opposed to passive comprehension.[8]

Due to the almost exclusive focus upon Latin, early modern schoolboys read a great deal more Latin than even students specialising in the classics do today, and in particular the chronological range of the Latin texts studied was much wider than ours.[9] Too much scholarship on 'classical reception' in early modern England has assumed, implicitly or explicitly, that 'the classics' of the Renaissance schoolroom were, more or less, those of a good Classics BA degree today. This is a particularly distorting assumption in a British context, since the British 'Classics' curriculum has been and to a significant extent remains one of the narrowest in the world. Of course early modern schoolboys read a great deal of Cicero, Livy, Ovid, Virgil and Horace. But this was far from all they read in Latin

---

[6] On the importance of oral Latin proficiency and performance, see Knight, 'Neo-Latin Literature and Early Modern Education'.

[7] Charles Hoole, *A New Discovery of the old Art of Teaching Schoole* (1661) is the earliest example of which I am aware that recommends verse composition in *English* as part of the standard chain of translation, paraphrase and retranslation. Existing studies, which have drawn largely upon surviving statutes and curricula, are a good source for what school and university students were reading, but less informative on composition (though see e.g. Hale, *Milton's Cambridge Latin*). For school composition, surviving manuscript records represent a largely untouched trove of evidence. I am aware of surviving examples of verse exercises or collections from the following institutions: Blundell's School; Bristol Grammar School; Bromley School; Dorchester School; Durham Cathedral School; Eton College; Kingston Grammar School; Ludlow School; Merchant Taylors' School; Newport School (Essex); Nottingham School; Saffron Walden School; Stamford School (Lincolnshire); St Paul's School (London); Tavistock School (Devon); Westminster School; Winchester College; Witney School; Witton Grammar School; Woodstock School (Oxfordshire). For discussion of the teaching of Latin metre and the prizing of metrical variety, see Chapter 2.

[8] Some highly educated women, such as Queen Elizabeth, plainly had excellent active Latin. The number of women who had a reading (that is, passive) knowledge of the language has perhaps been underestimated, given the very large number of Latin poems addressed to women throughout the period. In a handful of cases, surviving Latin exercises by girls suggest a similar approach to that taken with boys (see for example the discussion of Ann Loftus' Latin epigrams in Chapter 7). See also Stevenson, *Women Latin Poets*.

[9] This is particularly true of modern Anglophone classical teaching and scholarship. Latin teaching elsewhere in Europe, for instance in Germany and the Netherlands, has traditionally been much more likely to include at least some examples of medieval and early modern Latinity.

and in most cases it wasn't what they read first, either: many children, for instance, read Mantuan's Christian eclogues, the *Adulescentia*, before they read the Virgilian original. Mantuan (1447–1516) was a Carmelite monk whose work was popular in the northern European schoolroom because it is easy to construe, highly quotable and excerptable, and conveniently hostile to the papal Curia. Other works known to have been widely read in the late sixteenth- and seventeenth-century classroom include Palingenius' (fl. c.1530) *Zodiacus Vitae* (an extraordinary philosophical epic, composed in deceptively straightforward hexameters, discussed in Chapter 11) and the so-called *Disticha Catonis* (*Cato's Distichs*), a late antique work consisting entirely of moralizing epigrams in single hexameter couplets (discussed in Chapter 7). Indeed, two of only a handful of Latin texts that we can be sure Shakespeare knew – because he refers to them in his early work – are Palingenius and Mantuan.[10] These are two enormously influential Latin works which most modern Latinists have not even heard of, let alone read.[11] Extracts of both these poems, alongside some other works commonly read at school, are found very frequently in manuscript commonplace books and personal notebooks, including those of adults as well as schoolboys, suggesting that they were remembered, read and revisited into adult life.[12]

What early modern readers and poets meant by and expected from 'epigram' and '(didactic) epic' were shaped by works in the tradition of *Cato's Distichs* and Palingenius' *Zodiacus Vitae* as much as they were by Martial or Lucretius. Whereas a modern classicist associates dactylic hexameter exclusively with medium to long works, such as epic, satire and verse epistle, medieval and early modern readers encountered hexameters initially as the medium of moralizing and mnemonic verse, frequently in single couplets. What difference it makes if we read early modern poetry in these genres with this in mind is explored in Chapters 11 (for didactic epic) and 7 (for epigram).

Mantuan and Palingenius were both writing what would now usually be termed 'neo-' (that is, post-medieval) Latin, but early modern schoolboys also often read late antique and early Christian material such as works by

---

[10] Palingenius: *As You Like It* II.7; Mantuan: *Love's Labours Lost* IV.2. Mantuan's *Adulescentia* is a model for Spenser's *Shepherds' Calendar*. The influence of Palingenius, and to a lesser extent Mantuan, is discussed in Chapter 11.
[11] *ESTC* records 11 printings of Palingenius in Britain between 1536 and 1638, and 28 of Mantuan before 1682. Both were also printed repeatedly elsewhere in Europe; Palingenius was particularly popular in France (Beckwith, 'A Study of Palingenius' *Zodiacus Vitae*').
[12] On the manuscript evidence for the reading of Mantuan and Palingenius, see further Chapter 11.

Ausonius, Claudian, Prudentius and Augustine (not to mention *Cato's Distichs*), which are now rarely read even at university in the Anglophone world. In the commonplace book prepared by the future Charles I as a gift to his father James I, for instance, Claudian is the sixth most frequently excerpted author, with 44 quotations (more than Virgil with 41), and Ausonius the ninth (not far below Virgil, with 27).[13] Finally, there are several works – such as the *Satires* of Persius or the poetry of Statius and Silius Italicus – which we would recognise as 'classical' but which held a more prominent place in early modern education than they do in typical Latin literature survey courses today.

Early modern readers were encouraged to think of the full range of Latin – and indeed Greek, Hebrew and vernacular – literature in relation to one another, as valuable in large part for their consonances and similarities, rather than in terms of their stylistic uniqueness or diverse historical contexts. The pervasive habit of 'commonplacing' contributed strongly to this type of reading, since collating material from a variety of texts under the same heading (such as 'the brevity of life') tends to reinforce the ways in which works resemble rather than differ from one another. Some surviving commonplace books attest to this very dramatically: one unusually well-filled example, made almost certainly in the mid-1630s, repeatedly juxtaposes the compiler's favourite classical authors (particularly Horace, Ovid, Juvenal, Pindar, Seneca and Boethius) with modern extracts drawn especially from the Latin drama of George Buchanan (1506–82), the Latin lyric verse of Casimir Sarbiewski (1595–1640) and (in English) Robert Burton's *Anatomy of Melancholy* (first published 1621) and the poetry of Michael Drayton (1563–1631).[14]

The level of practical Latinity produced by the early modern education system was no doubt variable, but it is obvious from its widespread use even for relatively informal purposes such as letters, diary entries, jokes, comic songs and private prayers, that it was a living language for a large number of people, and at least accessibly comprehensible for many more. This is not least because Latin literacy – like learning an international language today – was the gateway to almost all advanced knowledge, including the learning of other languages. The journal of Bulstrode Whitelocke (1605–75) reports that following his parents' move to London around 1615, he joined

---

[13] BL MS Royal 12 D VIII. The three most frequently quoted are Ovid, Seneca and Horace. Excerpts from Ovid are dominated, as is typical, by the exile poetry (*Tristia* and *Ex Ponto*).

[14] CUL MS Dd. IX. 59. It also includes extracts from Donne and Shakespeare, the latter without attribution. Entries in this manuscript are not recorded in *CELM*.

Merchant Taylors' school aged 11 (having previously been briefly at Eton); that at 13, during a period of heated and violent rivalry between the boys of Merchant Taylors' and those of St Paul's, he made a Latin oration on the miseries of Civil War and the benefits of peace; and that in 1619, aged probably still only 14, he went up to St John's College, Oxford, already excellent in Latin and Greek and well versed in Hebrew.[15] Grammars and elementary texts in both Greek and Hebrew at this period were in Latin. Similarly, when Bartholus Herland, a Danish Latin poet, moved to London in the early 1660s, his notebook records his study of English grammar, with a particular focus upon English strong verbs. Even though the English verbal system is linguistically close to that of Danish, and certainly much more so than to Latin, all of Herland's notes on English grammar and even his glosses of English vocabulary are in Latin, not in Danish.[16] As Hans Helander has put it: 'Up to the eighteenth century, educated people learnt *nearly everything they knew* by means of literature written in Latin.'[17] Ann Moss has written of Latin in this period as a 'verbal environment in which to live': no-one's mother tongue, but not what we mean today by a 'dead' language either.[18]

Given the intense Latinity of educational and professional institutions, and the status of Latin as the international language of scholarship and science, it is unsurprising that a large number of Latin books were published in Britain throughout early modernity.[19] But the great majority of Latin works available in England had not been printed there: whereas almost all works in English were printed in Britain (and are therefore recorded in the *ESTC*), most modern Latin works by authors elsewhere in Europe, as well as a fair number by British authors – that is, the great majority of neo-Latin works overall – were read in England in imported

---

[15] BL MS Add. 53726, fols. 7ʳ–8ᵛ. Spalding, 'Whitelocke, Bulstrode'.
[16] BL MS Sloane 2870, fols. 148ʳ–50ᵛ. Joe Moshenska has mentioned this manuscript, which includes correspondence with Sir Kenelm Digby, as evidence of Digby's international contacts; in fact the Digby material belongs to the part of the manuscript dating from after Herland was already in London (*A Stain in the Blood*, 521).
[17] Helander, *Neo-Latin Literature in Sweden*, 13 (italics original).
[18] Moss, *Renaissance Truth*, 3 and *passim*.
[19] Books catalogued by the *ESTC* as Latin works comprise between 49 per cent and 3 per cent of the total printed Latin and English output between the start of the sixteenth century and first decades of the eighteenth. The overall trend in this period is a decrease in the proportion of Latin works, though an increase in the numbers of Latin items (from 168 in 1500–9 to over 800 a year in the first decades of the eighteenth century). This data does not include the many works with some Latin sections, such as Latin dedicatory or paratextual material to an essentially English work, or verse anthologies including some Latin poems.

8   Introduction

continental editions.[20] Even where particularly popular continental Latin works were eventually printed in England, the date of those English printings is often misleading. Hils' 1646 selection of the Polish poet Casimir Sarbiewski's (1595–1640) Latin verse, with facing translation, for instance, and the 1657 London edition of Angelin Gazet's (1568–1653) comic verse collection, *Pia Hilaria*, both significantly postdate the increase in the popularity of those works: that is, they are a response to market demand, and reflect an existing readership relying initially on continental editions.[21]

For this reason, surviving library lists and booksellers' catalogues, as well as careful analysis of commonplace books, manuscript miscellanies and patterns of allusion and reference, are better guides to the modern Latin works that were read than the *ESTC*. From such data, the cultural importance of certain works of recent or contemporary Latin become clear: even small or largely non-literary libraries in the early seventeenth century, for instance, typically included a copy of the Latin psalm paraphrases of George Buchanan (1506–82), sometimes bound with those of the French Calvinist Théodore de Bèze (1519–1605); the epigrams of John Owen (c.1564–c.1622); and, very often, one or both of the Latin novels of the Franco-Scot John Barclay (1582–1621).[22] These three works

---

[20] See Roberts, 'The Latin trade'. Only 26 per cent of Ben Jonson's largely Latin library, for instance, was printed in Britain (London, Oxford, Cambridge or Edinburgh). Jonson's library, as traced today, included 38 works of classical Latin, 25 works of classical Greek (mostly with parallel Latin translations) and 88 volumes of post-classical Latin (66 prose, 20 verse, 2 drama). In contrast, he owned only 12 volumes of English poetry (five of them translations of classical works), 19 of English prose and a single volume of English drama (McPherson, 'Ben Jonson's Library'). Most Latin texts printed in Britain were school texts, or works by British neo-Latin authors, such as John Owen and George Buchanan (though in both cases their works were also printed frequently elsewhere in Europe). Even some of the most influential works of British neo-Latin, such as the *Delitiae Poetarum Scotorum* (Amsterdam, 1637), were however not printed in Britain.

[21] *Pia Hilaria* was first published in Amsterdam in 1618; Donne's 'Vota Amico Facta' is a translation of one of the poems. Sarbiewski's poetry began to appear in print in 1624; as the Cambridge commonplace book mentioned above demonstrates, it was certainly known in England by the 1630s.

[22] The library list of Lincoln's Inn in 1646, for instance (BL MS Harley 7363), is limited largely to works of law, divinity and philosophy; of only around 20 'literary' titles, most are classical, but include the (Latin) epigrams of Owen and Huntingdon as well as Barclay's *Argenis*. A probably late seventeenth-century book list (BL MS Harley 6396), focused on science, mathematics and theology, contains no English poetry at all apart from Milton's *Paradise Lost*, but includes the verse of Buchanan and Sarbiewski, the *Adagia* and *Moriae Encomium* of Erasmus, and Barclay's *Argenis*. Barclay's novels lie largely beyond the scope of this book, though it is very striking how often his novels are excerpted, sometimes very extensively, in commonplace books of the early to mid-seventeenth century. In William Brackston's commonplace book (CUL MS Dd. VIII. 28, c.1630), extracts from Barclay's *Argenis* stand first under many headings; another fragmentary commonplace book from around the same time (CUL MS Dd. XI. 80) consists almost entirely of

are without doubt among the most widely read works of contemporary literature in Jacobean England, and not only in England: they are also the works that would be cited by any educated contemporary elsewhere in Europe if you asked them to name a famous British author.

Buchanan, Owen and Barclay are figures who have dropped almost completely out of English literary history, although without them major English literary developments – including, for instance, Jonson's *Epigrams* (1616); the tradition of English hymnody (an early eighteenth-century development deriving in large part from psalm paraphrase); and the English novel – would have developed quite differently, if at all. We may notice that, with their inclusion, British literary history looks strikingly more European than we are used to, and less centred either on England or on London: Buchanan and Barclay are Scots, though Barclay was educated by Jesuits in France and was culturally French, and Buchanan spent time in France, where he taught Montaigne as a boy; Owen was a Welshman educated in England, who became a schoolmaster in Warwickshire.

Moreover, these are British authors who – unlike any writers writing in English at this period – were influential across Europe: in the seventeenth century Latin, much like English today, was an international language. A good deal of important recent work has explored the relationship between English poetry and that of other European vernaculars, especially French, Italian and Dutch.[23] But vastly more people in early modernity could read Latin than any vernacular language and very few educated readers of the period would have read French or Italian more easily than they read Latin: there is very little evidence for the systematic teaching of any modern language at school until the late seventeenth century at the earliest, and, as Peter Davidson has pointed out, contemporaries who spoke several European languages well were singled out for their prodigious achievement.[24] It makes no sense to try to map the European-wide

---

extracts from Barclay's *Satyricon* alongside several references to Palingenius. Barclay's works were considered as serious objects of study and as a source of improving as well as amusing extracts.

[23] See e.g. Smith, 'Cross-Channel Cavaliers'.

[24] Davidson, *Universal Baroque*, 30; Southampton grammar school, which educated two future translators of Du Bartas in the 1570s, Josuah Sylvester and Robert Ashley, very unusually specialized in French under the mastership of Hadrianus Saravia, a Belgian Protestant émigré. The dissenting academies were some of the first to teach modern foreign languages systematically, though still in curricula in which the classical languages dominated. Hoole's guide for schoolmasters (*New Discovery*, 1661) makes no mention of instruction in any language other than English, Latin, Greek and Hebrew.

exchange and cross-fertilization of poetic styles and forms without putting Latin at the heart of any such study.

English poets were, then, steeped in Latin poetry from their schooldays on, and by 'Latin poetry' I mean the Latin poetry of all periods, including their own. Any poet who wished to achieve – as, for instance, Milton did – a European-wide reputation naturally wrote in Latin, and just as many poets of the period, like Hoskyns, Campion, Herbert, Crashaw, Marvell, Milton, Cowley, Addison or Watts, produced work in both languages, so too were there many (now forgotten) poets who made their careers largely or entirely in Latin. Alongside Owen, we could mention in this category Scipio Gentili, Giles and Phineas Fletcher, Thomas Watson, William Gager, Elizabeth Jane Weston, Payne Fisher, Raphael Thorius, Maurice Ewens, William Hogg, William King and Anthony Alsop. Several major figures, such as Andrew Melville and Théodore de Bèze, remembered today for their achievements in other fields, were famous at the time for their Latin verse. Indeed, Calvinists of many nations produced a great deal of innovative Latin poetry in the latter sixteenth and early seventeenth century in their attempt to craft a Protestant Latin poetics. Even poets like Ben Jonson, who, unusually for their period, wrote in adulthood only in the vernacular, were undoubtedly *reading* widely in Latin.

Most students and even scholars of early modernity, if they are aware of Latin literary culture at all, think of Milton, the only poet whose Latin work has received sustained attention. This makes Milton's Latinity appear unique. Milton's Latin verse is unusually *good*; but in its existence, range, choice of forms and genres and in its relationship to his vernacular poetry it is on the contrary typical and even rather conservative. There is nothing in Milton's Latin corpus as original, for instance, as Herbert's Latin verse sequence on the death of his mother, *Memoriae Matris Sacrum* (1627).

Whereas we would tend to distinguish sharply between classical and post-classical Latin, and often even between classical and late antique Latin literature, early modern teachers and readers alike did so much less: for them Latin literature was a going concern, a matter of fashion and innovation as much as of tradition and the ancient world. If we want to understand Anglo-Latin poetry as a living literature interacting with other Latin and vernacular poetry across Europe, we have to set aside an assumption that (our conception of) the 'classical' was always the most highly valued or most carefully imitated, as well as the distorting tendency of the still limited quantity of specialist criticism on 'neo-Latin' to treat all post-medieval Latin literature as monolithic. Poets writing Latin verse in the 1550s, just like those writing English or French verse at the same time, naturally did so quite differently from those doing so in the 1650s, even if they were composing a poem on the same topic.

Indeed, the very term 'neo-' Latin, often defined specifically in relation to the stylistic imitation of the Augustan classics, is unhelpful here. The great majority of the Latin verse actually produced in early modern England was not particularly classical either in form or in style, especially if by 'classical' we mean like Virgil rather than, say, Claudian; and some of it, such as the ongoing composition of rhyming Latin verse throughout the sixteenth and seventeenth centuries, was markedly not. This period saw widespread innovation in Latin poetry, both in the creation of new forms and in the application of existing forms to new contexts. Equally, several genres which loom large in any survey of classical literature – including full-scale mythological epic, love elegy and (before the eighteenth century) hexameter verse satire – were relatively rarely composed by Latin poets in England. If we approach early modern Latin poetry assuming that the style and form of what we find will closely track the classical canon as it is taught today, we will tend hugely to overemphasize the significance of some types of verse, and to be blind even to the existence of other sorts of great cultural importance and high fashion.

For these reasons I have where possible avoided the term 'neo-Latin', preferring the more neutral if cumbersome 'post-medieval' Latin or, best of all, just 'Latin' alone. No early modern readers spoke of 'neo-Latin' style, and though they do sometimes divide lists of authors or works between 'ancient' and 'modern', such distinctions frequently reflect how works were experienced and understood, and the context in which they were encountered, more than they do historical reality: in one such list, for instance, Palingenius, a shadowy figure but certainly active in Italy during the 1530s, appears among the classical authors – presumably because, as an authoritative text encountered in the early years at school, his *Zodiacus Vitae* 'felt' like a classic.[25]

For scholars and students of classical 'reception', this book should function, I hope, as testimony to the enormous importance of Latin literature in early modern England, but also as a note of caution. Most studies of classical reception take the 'classical' texts from which they begin for granted, without considering what was actually read in early modernity, or how. It makes a difference to what 'pastoral' means if you read Virgil's *Eclogues* only after Mantuan's *Adulescentia*; to your conception of epigram

---

[25] BL MS Add. 28010, fol. 66ʳ, in a list of recommended authors dated 1627. On Palingenius, see Chapter 11.

if you encounter a (carefully expurgated) selection of Martial's epigrams alongside Owen's *Epigrammata* after a year spent memorising *Cato's Distichs*; and to your sense of lyric if your metrical handbook refers you to Buchanan's Latin *Psalms* alongside the *Odes* of Horace. Even amongst classical authors, several of the stylistic and generic models that emerge as particularly significant in early modern England are unlikely to be familiar to modern Anglophone classicists: prominent among these are Boethius, Prudentius and, above all, Claudian, the influence of whose work is tracked especially in Chapters 9 (panegyric epic) and 10 (epyllion and epithalamia).

Scripture, Religion and Paraphrase in Early Modern Education and Literary Culture

Boethius, Prudentius and Claudian were valued for their distinctive style, and because they offered a range of formal and generic models not found in earlier classical poetry, but above all for their (supposed) Christianity.[26] This is a book about early modern poetry, but no such book can succeed if it is not also concerned with religious belief and devotion, in an age in which faith and practice permeated culture and education. The Bible as a literary resource is as foundational for all these poets, whether writing in Latin or English, as classical texts, if not considerably more so; alongside the Bible stand liturgical and devotional material, such as the prayer book and catechism, which were also regularly paraphrased in Latin prose or verse, or alluded to in original compositions. The interrelationship of Latin poetry and religion in sixteenth- and seventeenth-century England was just as important for Protestants as it was for Catholics: Calvinism as an international movement, for instance, was grounded in the major *Latin* texts it produced, and if Latin poetry of passionate personal devotion is traditionally associated with Catholic literary style and education (and the Jesuits in particular), biblical paraphrase was of particular importance to Protestants. In practice, the influence flowed continuously in all directions: the great dissenter poet Isaac Watts reaches a mature style via the lasting influence of the baroque devotional verse of Casimir Sarbiewski, a Polish Jesuit whose marriage of scriptural paraphrase and Horatian poetics was

---

[26] The question of Claudian's religious affiliations is now contentious, but early modern scholars believed him to have been a Christian. Several explicitly Christian poems attributed to Claudian in early modernity are no longer believed to be his, though his authorship of one is still generally accepted, on which see Chapter 9.

read avidly by poets in England from the second third of the seventeenth century onwards, and who was as influential upon Andrew Marvell and Abraham Cowley as he was upon more obviously sympathetic poets such as Richard Crashaw.

If the Renaissance and the resultant flood of critical editions of classical works renewed poets' sense of what they could do with the poetry of the ancient world, so too did the scholarly results of the Reformation inspire them with a fresh sense of the literary possibilities of the Bible. Almost all the great wealth of serious scriptural scholarship produced in this period, extending even to editions of the Talmud and grammars of Syriac and Aramaic, was produced in Latin. From the publication of Junius and Tremellius' Protestant Latin Bible in 1576, most of the people who were writing Latin poetry would also have encountered scripture very often (though of course far from always) in Latin.[27] Latin continued to be used, for instance, for school and university worship throughout this period. If early modern Latin poetry tends to be overlooked by literary scholars and critics, however, so too does scriptural literature – and the huge quantities of scriptural verse in Latin are thereby at a kind of double disadvantage.

One of the most commonly produced – and generally ignored – modes of scriptural verse was the scriptural 'paraphrase', a literary practice that could range from the versifying of scripture with as few changes as possible through to meditational or imaginative pieces based only loosely on the passage to which they were attached. Verse paraphrase (rather than 'translation') is perhaps the single most characteristic activity of early modern Latin literary culture. Early modern paraphrase, as I am using the term here, is best understood as the recasting of an authoritative text – whether classical, biblical, doctrinal or canonical in another way – into a new form. This can include translation from one language into another – Dryden uses the word in this way when he employs it as the 'middle term' (between 'metaphrase' and 'imitation') in his famous discussion of translation – but does not necessarily do so. Nor does it necessarily imply, as 'paraphrase' usually does in everyday modern English, that the original text is shortened or simplified: indeed Dryden is clear that for him paraphrase involves 'amplifying' though not 'altering' the sense of the original.[28]

---

[27] On the widespread use of the Latin Bible by Protestants, and the much-reduced association between the Latin Bible and Catholicism in the late sixteenth and seventeenth century, see Killeen, *Political Bible*, 15.

[28] Dryden, 'The Preface to Ovid's Epistles', in *Ovid's Epistles, Translated by Several Hands* (1680), sig. A8ʳ.

Indeed, many examples of paraphrase operate within a single language, and produce longer texts than the original: examples include such standard exercises as the recasting of the Lord's Prayer in Latin into elegiac couplets, or of Aesop's fables (read in simple Latin prose in the early years of a grammar school education) into Latin verse. In these instances, the transformation is primarily a formal one, with a transition from prose into verse. Other kinds of paraphrase may be prose–prose or verse–verse: Augustine Richardson's paraphrase of Virgil's first eclogue into sapphic stanzas dates probably from around 1600, and resembles examples given in school textbooks throughout the period.[29]

Paraphrase of all kinds was of great educational and wider cultural importance. Both the use of paraphrases and the production of them was central to school experience: early modern school editions of canonical classical texts made frequent use of Latin–Latin paraphrase to aid comprehension, providing for instance a running prose version alongside Virgil's *Aeneid*, and similar tools were commonly provided also for adult use: in Chapter 3 we see how Beza's 1580 edition of the psalms, used by Mary Sidney in preparing her English versions, provided first a literal translation of the Hebrew into Latin, then (as a parallel text) a somewhat expanded 'paraphrase', followed by a more detailed commentary and discussion, and finally, as the fourth element for each psalm, Beza's verse paraphrases.

Teachers assumed that the versification even of complex material made it more rather than less memorable, and as a result versified Latin renderings of even densely technical subjects are one of the stranger features of early modern culture: we find Latin verse treatises on, for instance, Hebrew grammar, and the so-called 'Westminster' grammar, an introduction to ancient Greek written in Latin hexameters, was still being used in the nineteenth century.[30] 'Lily', the (somewhat misleadingly named) standard Latin grammar prescribed for use in English schools makes extensive use of Latin verse summaries, which were frequently quoted: when the schoolboy William in Shakespeare's *Merry Wives of Windsor* (IV.1) recites

---

[29] *Ecloga Virgilii prima Sapphico carmine* (c.1600), single surviving copy now in the Folger Shakespeare Library. Richardson was born in 1569 or 1570.

[30] Busby, *Rudimentum Grammaticae Graeco-Latinae Metricum*. Busby was a legendary headmaster at Westminster School for 57 years between 1638 and 1695. The work was very frequently emended and reprinted. An entertainingly scathing essay in *The Edinburgh Review* indicates that Westminster was still making routine use of Busby's grammatical verse for teaching Latin and Greek as late as 1831 ([Anon.], 'Art. III').

grammatical rules from memory, he is quoting from the verse summary in Lily, not the prose text.[31]

Religious and linguistic educational aims were frequently combined in paraphrases produced for school use: elementary textbooks for the youngest boys contained simple Latin verse paraphrases of key texts, such as the Lord's Prayer and catechism; more advanced versions include John Harmar's *Hymnus ad Christum, Historia de Christo Metrica* (1658), retelling the story of the Christ in parallel Latin and ancient Greek verse, with each line numbered for classroom use.[32] This kind of essentially mnemonic use of Latin verse is found widely also in material for adults: versified Latin tags for recalling legal or ecclesiastical rules are found frequently in manuscript. Some items of this kind made it into print: John Glanville's *Articuli Christianae fidei* (1613) is a Latin verse paraphrase of the 39 Articles of 1563. Indeed, Latin verse was so prominent a feature not only of what boys read at school, and of what they had to produce, but also of how they memorized what they needed to know, that the association between Latin poetry and education in general must have been very strong for all those who had experienced a grammar school education, as well as those men and (many fewer) women who had received a similar education via private tuition at home.[33]

Standard school exercises relied upon paraphrase of various kinds, including both what we would recognize as 'translation' back and forth into English but also, extremely frequently, within Latin but between forms. Ben Jonson himself notes how he was taught by Camden to render a theme first in prose and then in verse.[34] Hundreds of instances of exercises of this type survive, with a moral tag or proverbial topic the starting point for a composition first in Latin prose and then in verse.

---

[31] Other quotations or allusions to Lily in Shakespeare are found at *Titus Andronicus* IV.2; *Henry IV Part I* II.2 and *Much Ado About Nothing* IV.1; see also e.g. Marston, *What You Will* (1601), II.2.907–8. Two works, a more elementary Latin grammar in English (*Shorte Introduction*) and a more advanced work in Latin (*Brevissima Institutio*, which contains the grammatical verse) are referred to as 'Lily', though both works were in practice produced by a committee commissioned by Henry VIII and include material prepared by Colet and Erasmus as well as Lily himself. See Smith, 'Lily, William' and Gwosdek, *Lily's Grammar*. On the use of grammatical verse, see Moul, 'Grammar in Verse'.

[32] Harmar, *Hymnus ad Christum* (1658). *Preces matutinae* (1578), versified prayers and school rules for use at Lord Williams's Grammar School in Thame, are an example of a common basic type of this sort of text.

[33] BL MS Sloane 2287, for instance, is a commonplace book mostly in English, all in a single hand, which includes several pages of Latin grammatical verse accompanied by translations (fols. 102^r–3^v), apparently notes made by a woman, Dorothy Dolman, whose signature appears on fol. 103^v. The date 1689 is found at the start of the volume.

[34] Donaldson (ed.), 'Informations to Drummond', 378.

CUL MS Add. 8861/2 is a typical example, containing prose paragraphs on two different *sententiae* (*Pectora nostra duas non admittentia curas*, 'Our hearts do not admit of two concerns at the same time', and *Inter amicos nè sis arbiter*, 'Do not act as a judge between friends'), each followed by a short Latin poem on the same theme in elegiac couplets.[35] We see this pattern of work reproduced in adult life: hundreds of letters from adults as well as university students offer praise and make a polite request first in prose and then in Latin verse. The collection of letters addressed to Archbishop Whitgift in the late sixteenth century, for instance, includes 33 Latin poems from a range of correspondents including a schoolmaster in Croydon and a fellow of New College, Oxford as well as various clergymen.[36]

Early modern schoolchildren did not have their literary or rhetorical understanding of a text assessed by essay questions or written commentaries as modern students might. They both acquired and demonstrated mastery of authoritative texts almost exclusively in two ways: by oral examination at all levels (from the classroom to public performances) and, in written work, by paraphrase broadly understood. That such paraphrastic ability was considered a marker of educational achievement is clear both from surviving textbooks and from the many instances of presentation volumes containing 'fine copies' of the best such work. In his published *Progymnasmata* of 1590, John Brownswerd (c.1540–89), schoolmaster in Macclesfield, demonstrates the kind of thing that must have been commonplace: his volume of exemplary exercises opens with the rendering of a single scriptural episode (here the story of David and Goliath from 1 Samuel 17) into four Latin versions, each in a different metre.[37] The book also includes an example of verse–verse Latin paraphrase, in this instance of Horace *Odes* 1.1 into elegiac couplets.[38] Sixty years later, Nicholas Grey's *Parabolae evangelicae* (1650), written for use at Tonbridge school, works in much the same way: though misleadingly catalogued by the *ESTC* as a Latin grammar, the volume is in fact a set of verse paraphrases of the Gospel parables in a wide variety of Latin verse

---

[35] CUL MS Add. 8861/2, item b, fols. 1ʳ–2ᵛ, papers removed from Add. MS 8861/1, Miles Stapylton's commonplace book at Oxford, dating from between 1677 and 1684.
[36] BL MS Harley 6350, letters dated between c.1584 and 1604.
[37] A copy of this volume was owned by William Camden (1551–1623), headmaster of Westminster School, now Westminster Abbey CB 7 (10).
[38] Brownswerd, *Progymnasmata*, 52–4.

forms, effectively a textbook of the New Testament and of Latin verse composition simultaneously.[39]

A manuscript now in Staffordshire County Record Office is a presentation copy of Latin and English verse paraphrases of the first ten of Aesop's fables, following the order in which they appear in the many late sixteenth-century editions of this text used at school. Dating probably from the latter sixteenth century, the volume is dedicated 'To that uniquely best and most wise man, Master Bagot, Esquire, patron of letters, for whom Nicholas Fox, Edward Sprott and all his pupils at Bromley earnestly desire the greatest possible happiness and success in all his endeavours'.[40] Aesop's fables are not themselves Christian texts, but they are strongly moralizing, and readily assimilable to Christian teaching. In the first fable, a cock finds a jewel amid the dung, but not knowing what it is, he wishes he had found a barleycorn instead. The story recalls the Gospel expression 'pearls before swine', and the unrecognized 'jewel' may be interpreted generally as wisdom, more specifically as Christian truth, or, as in the case of several school editions, as the acquisition of humanist learning itself. Such an interpretation makes it a particularly appropriate text for the early years of grammar school, and this gloss is reflected in the paraphrases offered by the boys from Bromley:

MORAL

As Cockes so gemmes: so rustick clownes
    Do all good artes disdayne
And being rude, and wanting arte
    Artes they accounte but vayne.
By pretious stone each wiser one
    May arte heare vnderstand
By coke a blocke who learning lothes
    & learned men withstande.[41]

By far the longest poem in a remarkable collection of Latin verse presented to Queen Elizabeth in 1563 by Eton schoolboys is Giles Fletcher's 314-line 'eclogue': in fact an extended verse paraphrase of a passage from Livy,

---

[39] Grey (1592–1660) was headmaster, successively, of Charterhouse, Merchant Taylors', Eton and Tonbridge.
[40] Staffordshire County Record Office, MS D(W)1721/3/248, fol. 1^r. Translation of Latin dedication.
[41] Staffordshire County Record Office, MS D(W)1721/3/248, fol. 2^v. The bilingualism is unusual for the period, in which Latin–Latin paraphrase is much more typically found. Latin verse paraphrases of Aesop were a common school exercise. See examples in Corpus Christi College, Oxford, MS 324 (c.1560), fol. 126^{r-v}; BL MS Sloane 1466 (c.1623–33), fols. 379–82; Bod. MS Lat. misc. e. 32 (c.1630–40), fols. 95^r–6^r; Cheshire Archives, MS DBC 2309/2/3 (1665), fol. 7^r.

Ab Urbe Condita IX, telling of the humiliating Samnite victory over the Romans at the Caudine Forks in 321 BC. This poem is somewhat oddly – even, we might think, tactlessly – offered to the Queen as consolation for the defeat of the English at Le Havre earlier in 1563.[42] Over a hundred years later, a Dutch school manuscript from the 1680s, now in the British Library, contains many examples, such as the paraphrase of an Horatian ode in honour of Agrippa into Latin hexameters in praise of King William III.[43]

For adults educated in this way, paraphrase is the *standard* way of engaging closely with the most authoritative texts. Early modern 'paraphrase culture' of this kind, though encompassing examples we would describe as translation, has crucial differences from literary translation as it is usually understood today. We tend to assume that vernacular translations of the classics, for instance, exist to allow those who cannot read the language of the original to access such literature. Although there are of course examples of literary translation into both English and Latin for this kind of purpose in early modernity, the majority of 'translations' in manuscript sources, and a significant proportion of 'translations' also in print, are not translations in this modern sense: they are instances of the wider category of paraphrase. That is, they are not replacements for an original text aimed at those who cannot read it; on the contrary, such material assumes knowledge of the source text. This point about what paraphrase is 'for' is emphasized by the habit, particularly striking in the later seventeenth and eighteenth centuries, of producing Latin versions of well-known English poems, a phenomenon discussed briefly in Chapter 7.

While scriptural paraphrase in English, especially by women and especially in the seventeenth century, has attracted some distinguished critical attention, the parallel Latin phenomenon has, with the limited exception of psalm paraphrases, been almost entirely ignored.[44] There is not, to my knowledge, any available scholarly survey or list of such works published or produced in Latin in early modern England. This neglect is particularly surprising given the obvious relevance of the practice, especially the

---

[42] BL MS Royal 12 A XXX, fols. 37ʳ–49ᵛ. Discussed also in Dijk, 'Eclogues of Giles Fletcher the Elder', 55–64.

[43] BL MS Sloane 2832, fol. 50ᵛ.

[44] E.g. Ross, 'Epic, Meditation, or Sacred History?'; Auger, *Du Bartas' Legacy*; Green, 'Poetic Psalm Paraphrases'; Wilcher, 'Lucy Hutchinson and Genesis'; Campbell, *Divine Poetry*. The list of English works given by Lily Campbell remains particularly full and includes several works which have still been barely considered. The English genre might have maintained a higher profile had Spenser's version of the Song of Songs and Ecclesiastes survived.

Protestant practice, of scriptural paraphrase to the 'biblical epic' projects of Cowley's *Davideis*, Milton's *Paradise Lost*, and indeed the kind of satirical biblical allegory of Dryden's *Absalom and Achitophel*, which uses the story of a rebellion against King David to tackle the Exclusion Crisis of 1679–81. For all the emphasis upon classical Latin and Greek texts in the early modern school, boys began and ended their days with prayer and the study of scripture, not of the ancients. Charles Hoole's suggestions for how to make this framing encounter with scripture educational point to the fundamental importance of paraphrase: he has his sixth formers (the most senior class) begin their day by translating the Greek New Testament into Latin or English and the English or Latin Bible into Greek; as part of their study of Hebrew, he recommends double-translation from the psalter (and subsequently Proverbs, Ecclesiastes and Job) into Latin and back into Hebrew.[45]

Scriptural verse paraphrase is a constant feature of early modern Anglo-Latin verse, both in print and in manuscript. Poetry of this kind is found throughout the period – from Walter Haddon's (1516–72) collection of New Testament and psalm paraphrases published in 1555, through to the popular Latin verse paraphrases by William Hogg (or Hog, b. 1652) in the final years of the seventeenth century, which included Latin verse renderings of Job, Proverbs and the Song of Songs as well as of several of Milton's English poems.[46] It includes work by well-known authors who wrote in many genres (such as Walter Haddon, Andrew Melville and Thomas Drant); 'specialist' poets who published mainly or only scriptural paraphrase, such as Alexander Julius and Jakob Falckenburg; and very large numbers of minor poets who included scriptural verse paraphrases within miscellaneous verse collections.[47]

---

[45] Hoole, *New Discovery* (1661), 191 and 193.

[46] Haddon, *Oratio Iesu Christi* (1555); Hog, *Paraphrasis in Jobum* (1682; 2nd edn 1683); Hog, *Satyra Sacra Vanitatem Mundi* (1685), including also paraphrases of inset songs in the Old Testament, Deuteronomy 32, Exodus 15 and Judges 5; Hog, *Paraphrasis poetica*, paraphrase of *Paradise Lost*, *Paradise Regained* and *Samson Agonistes* (1690); Hog, *Comoedia Joannis Miltoni*, Latin version of Milton's *Comus* (1698); Hog, *Solomonis Cantici Canticorum Paraphrasis Poetica*, verse paraphrase of Song of Songs (1699); Hog, *Cato Divinus; sive Proverbia Solomonis* (1699).

[47] Printed works (excluding collections of psalm paraphrases, discussed in Chapter 3) include: Drant (c.1540–78), *In Selomonis regis ... Ecclesiasten* (1571); Vaughan, *Erotopaignion pium* (1597), contains paraphrase of the Song of Songs and various psalms); Bridges, *Sacro-sanctum Novum Testamentum* (1604); Johnstoun, *Canticum Salomonis* (1633); Dawson, *Summa moralis theologiae* (1639; paraphrase of Proverbs, Ecclesiastes and the Song of Songs). Some authors produced multiple works in this genre, including Jakob Falckenburg (multiple Old Testament books between 1609 and 1614) and Alexander Ross (from 1619, all Virgilian centos, with many subsequent editions). Several of these are mentioned briefly in Binns, *Intellectual Culture*, 81–3. Some of the many mid-seventeenth-century examples of scriptural verse paraphrase are discussed in Chapter 11.

English readers naturally also read many examples of Latin scriptural paraphrase made by authors outside England, such as those of the French Protestant Latin poet Paul Thomas (1565–1636), whose work went through multiple editions in the first half of the seventeenth century: Ben Jonson owned a copy of Thomas' *Poemata*, in which the volume of *Silva sacra* is composed almost entirely of scriptural paraphrase.[48] While most such works were read in imported editions, a handful of the most popular, such as Beza's paraphrase of Job, were printed in England, and some English authors of scriptural paraphrase had a reputation elsewhere in Europe.[49] In manuscript, we find a similar variety, ranging from large-scale professional presentation manuscripts to dozens of examples made apparently for purely personal satisfaction or very limited circulation, and hundreds if not thousands of scriptural Latin poems in private notebooks and miscellanies.[50] Popular scriptural verse included also versified summaries of scripture, either as continuous verse or as sequences of epigrams.[51]

Works as various as Haddon's Lord's Prayer in sapphics; Ross' Virgilian cento of the Old Testament; Du Bartas' *Septmaines*; Herbert's *The Temple*, with its close links to the psalters of Philip and Mary Sidney, Beza and Buchanan; Milton's *Paradise Lost*; Lucy Hutchinson's *Order and Disorder* and the many versions of and responses to the Song of Songs, by authors as theologically diverse as Beza, Crashaw, Marvell, Du Moulin and Watts, all arise from, belong to and are legible within essentially the same approach to scriptural authority rooted in paraphrase. I have discussed the practice of paraphrase here in the introduction because the centrality of paraphrase as a literary practice is relevant to all the chapters that follow, and because it is

[48] Editions in 1617, 1627, 1633, 1640. See McPherson, 'Ben Jonson's Library', no. 189.
[49] Beza, *Iobus* (1589). Alexander Ross' scriptural paraphrases in the form of Virgilian centos were very popular across Europe. His *Christiados libri XIII* (London, 1634; reprinted in significantly expanded form, 1638, and again in 1659 and 1769) was also printed in Rotterdam (1653), Zurich (1664) and Debrecen (1684).
[50] See for instance James Calfhill's paraphrase of the Book of Wisdom, dated 1559 and dedicated to Queen Elizabeth I (BL MS Royal 2 D II); Andrew Melville's verse paraphrases of the Letter to the Romans (Bod. MS Cherry 1, fols. 135ʳ–70ᵛ) and the Letter to the Hebrews (BL MS Harley 6947, fols. 34ʳ–54ᵛ); John Bridges' Latin verse paraphrases of the Old Testament (BL MSS Royal 2 D XIV–XIX, c.1604–18); and a large number of examples of lyric paraphrases of the Song of Songs (e.g. St John's College, Cambridge, MS O.65; Nottingham University Library, MS PwV 1456).
[51] William Smith's 1598 *Gemma fabri* (1598), a summary of the biblical books in Latin verse, was borrowed in part from a work written by John Shepreve before his death in 1542, though not published until 1586 (*Summa et synopsis Novi Testamenti*). Shepreve's work was reprinted yet again as a part of John Shaw's *Bibliorum summula* in 1623. Prudentius' *Dittochaeon* (*Scenes from History*), a work consisting of 49 quatrains divided into eight books each dealing with a separate incident from the Old and New Testament, offered an important model for non-continuous scriptural paraphrase. Henry Dethick's *Feriae Sacrae* (1577) belongs to this model, as do the versified parables produced by Nicholas Grey for use at Tonbridge school (described briefly above).

in my view a more helpful model for understanding much (though of course not all) of the poetry with which this book is concerned than 'translation', 'allusion', 'intertextuality' or even 'imitation'. George Herbert, one of the handful of poets to whom this book returns most frequently, describes prayer as 'the soul in paraphrase':

> Prayer the church's banquet, angel's age,
> God's breath in man returning to his birth,
> The soul in paraphrase, heart in pilgrimage,
> The Christian plummet sounding heav'n and earth
> ('Prayer (I)', 1–4)

There is nothing basic, boring or purely instrumental about paraphrase in early modernity. Here Herbert associates the concept with constant movement and activity ('returning', 'in pilgrimage', 'plummet'); as Brian Cummings has pointed out, Herbert's sonnet is itself continuously in motion. A single sentence with no main verb, he describes it as a poem which 'stops without ending'.[52] Any individual piece of paraphrase, likewise, has a first and last sentence or line; but paraphrase itself is a continuous conversation. In Chapter 1, we see how a distinct and enduringly popular but critically neglected type of poem, the 'moralizing lyric', emerges from this 'culture of paraphrase', in which poets and readers do not distinguish sharply or consistently between the translation, response and imitation of a series of similar texts by authors far removed in time; and how our tendency to insist on these distinctions occludes rather than reveals a meaningful generic category.

---

[52] Cummings, *Literary Culture of the Reformation*, 327.

PART I

Shorter Verse

CHAPTER I

Anglo-Latin 'Moralizing Lyric' in Early Modern England

The type of poem referred to in this chapter as the 'moralizing lyric' has been produced continuously in English at least from the time of Tottel's miscellany down to the present day; it is the tradition to which Kipling's enduringly popular, if critically unfashionable and easily pastiched poem, 'If –' belongs:

> If you can keep your head when all about you
>   Are losing theirs and blaming it on you,
> If you can trust yourself when all men doubt you,
>   But make allowance for their doubting too;
> If you can wait and not be tired by waiting,
>   Or being lied about, don't deal in lies,
> Or being hated, don't give way to hating,
>   And yet don't look too good, nor talk too wise:
>
> ...
>
> If you can talk with crowds and keep your virtue,
>   Or walk with Kings—nor lose the common touch,
> If neither foes nor loving friends can hurt you,
>   If all men count with you, but none too much;
> If you can fill the unforgiving minute
>   With sixty seconds' worth of distance run,
> Yours is the Earth and everything that's in it,
>   And—which is more—you'll be a Man, my son![1]

Both Latin and English poetry in this tradition was popular in early modernity: several pieces of this type are among the most widely circulated poems of the period, including Walter Raleigh's (c.1552–1618) 'E'en such is time' and Henry Wotton's (1568–1639) 'The Character of a Happy Life', the latter of which I give below:

---

[1] Kipling, *Collected Poems*, 605. The poem was voted the nation's favourite in a 1995 survey and according to Gary Dexter remains in or near the top slot (Dexter, *The People's Favourite Poems*).

> How happy is he born and taught
> That serveth not another's will;
> Whose armour is his honest thought,
> And simple truth his utmost skill!
>
> Whose passions not his masters are;
> Whose soul is still prepared for death,
> Untied unto the world by care
> Of public fame or private breath;
>
> Who envies none that chance doth raise,
> Nor vice; who never understood
> How deepest wounds are given by praise;
> Nor rules of state, but rules of good;
>
> Who hath his life from rumours freed;
> Whose conscience is his strong retreat;
> Whose state can neither flatterers feed,
> Nor ruin make oppressors great;
>
> Who God doth late and early pray
> More of His grace than gifts to lend;
> And entertains the harmless day
> With a religious book or friend;
>
> —This man is freed from servile bands
> Of hope to rise or fear to fall:
> Lord of himself, though not of lands,
> And having nothing, yet hath all.

The great popularity of poems of this kind in early modernity is demonstrated primarily by manuscript circulation – Wotton's poetry was not published until 1651 but was circulating very widely in manuscript in the preceding decades. Peter Beal's *Catalogue of English Literary Manuscripts* (*CELM*) records 63 copies of 'The Character of a Happy Life' and a huge 116 copies of Raleigh's 'E'en such is time'.[2] In seventeenth-century manuscripts, the single most widely excerpted poem by George Herbert, a poet appreciated today for his devotional lyrics, is the long didactic poem 'The Church-Porch', written in 77 highly quotable stanzas.[3] The poem ends:

---

[2] These are certainly not complete counts in either case. *CELM* does not for instance include the copy of 'E'en such is time' found in Charles Caesar's commonplace book (BL MS Add. 43410, fol. 163ᵛ).
[3] Ray, 'Herbert Allusion Book', v. Ray records 52 allusions to this poem, more than to any other (176).

> In brief, acquit thee bravely; play the man.
> Look not on pleasures as they come, but go.
> Defer not the least virtue: life's poor span
> Make not an ell, by trifling in thy woe.
> > If thou do ill; the joy fades, not the pains:
> > If well; the pain doth fade, the joy remains.

Lyrics of this sort deal in the concise, memorable, rousing and often beautiful expression of conventional wisdom: that riches do not bring happiness or real freedom; that worldly fame and importance are transitory; that virtue is its own reward.

I have chosen to begin with poetry of this sort for several reasons: unlike some other poetic forms discussed in subsequent chapters, which have a discernible 'vogue' and then fall out of fashion or evolve to a significant degree, lyrics of this kind were consistently popular throughout the whole of the period covered by this book – and indeed remain so. They represent a very stable poetic form, in which key examples, composed between the 1530s and the early eighteenth century, from Wyatt to Watts (and indeed well beyond that, far beyond the scope of this book), recognizably belong together. The impersonal tone and moral seriousness of these lyrics set them apart from shorter-lived poetic trends, such as Petrarchan romance, 'metaphysical' wit or Restoration satire, even where they borrow stylistically from the fashions of their day; and though several of the most popular examples were associated with specific events – such as Raleigh's 'E'en such is time', widely believed to have been composed immediately before his execution – they have a 'generalizing' authority which does not depend upon the identity or circumstances of authorship. Indeed, they frequently circulated anonymously or under a range of attributions. Finally, though far from least important, these poems include some of the best lyric poetry of the sixteenth and seventeenth centuries, and many of them retain their power to console nearly five centuries later.

Such poetry has not attracted a great deal of critical comment and has barely been discussed at all in terms of wider literary traditions. As Arthur Marotti has remarked, the poems found most frequently in manuscript collections form 'an interesting combination of texts that it would be difficult to anticipate from the printed volumes of the period or from the literary histories that are based on the products of print culture': a polite way of pointing to the disjunction between the early modern literature we write about, and what was actually read.[4] (Marotti in his turn largely

---

[4] Marotti, *Manuscript, Print*, 126. In his brief discussion of three particularly popular types, Marotti describes as his second category 'poems that express general cultural beliefs or moral truisms or both', and mentions in passing several of the poems discussed in this chapter (129–30).

ignores Latin poetry; and this book, likewise, has set aside several not insignificant genres, such as secular love poetry.) The 'plain' style of most of these poems perhaps strikes many readers as neutrally, almost transparently 'English', and has contributed to critical neglect.[5] But this most ostensibly English of forms has its roots in the translation and imitation of classical poetry, and emerged in the sixteenth century in both Latin and English, with influence moving in both directions. As a starting point for this book, it demonstrates what can be learnt by a serious attention to literary bilingualism: repeatedly, it is the Latin versions of this form, including translations of the best-known English examples *into* Latin, which point to the classical texts that underpin these poems, and the (broadly) Latin lyric context to which they were understood to belong by contemporary readers.

Poems of this kind have connections both with devotional or religious verse (including scriptural paraphrase), and with the tradition of didactic monostichs, distichs and epigrams, though they form a distinct category of their own.[6] They are longer than the average epigram, typically ranging from around 10 to 50 lines. Latin examples are often (though far from always) in lyric metres; they are not usually part of a sequence or 'conversational' exchange of poems as epigrams often were; they typically do not refer explicitly to specific contemporary events or individuals, though they may well have implicit contemporary purchase and in manuscript sources are quite often given sharper historical force by details of titling or attribution; unlike the typical epigram, they are not characterized by a single 'point' (whether satiric, topical or moralizing), even though they do have a clear didactic message; in terms of classical models, they look towards the long and complex tradition of 'Horatian' lyric rather than to the epigrammatic tradition represented, in early modernity, by the twin streams of Martial and Cato (discussed in Chapter 7).

---

[5] Though see Yvor Winters' very important series of articles on the 'plain style' in sixteenth-century English lyric ('16th Century Lyric in England', Parts I, II and III). Winters identifies a non-Petrarchan 'school' of English verse in the latter sixteenth century, characterized by what he describes as 'aphoristic' lyrics, such as those of Gascoigne and Raleigh. Though Winters is describing a broader phenomenon than the 'moralizing' lyric with which this chapter is concerned, and does not discuss translation or classical influence directly, he remarks that he considers the best poems of this type to be 'among the most perfect examples of the classical virtues to be found in English poetry' (Part I, 263–4).
[6] Devotional and religious verse is discussed in Chapters 3 (psalm paraphrase) and 6 (devotional lyric and scriptural epigram); longer scriptural paraphrase also features in Chapter 11. The link between the seventeenth-century vogue for literary epigram (such as those of Jonson and Owen) and the tradition of short moralizing and didactic verse such as the so-called *Disticha Catonis* is discussed in Chapter 7.

This enduringly popular mode of verse has its roots in classical poetry, but classical poetry grouped in ways which are not standard for modern classicists, and are therefore barely represented in modern classical scholarship or (more problematically) in recent work on 'classical reception'. In early modern England, a cluster of models, centred around Horace but extending well beyond him, were understood to 'belong' together thematically: these included Horace's moralizing lyrics, especially *Odes* 2 and the second epode, and sometimes incorporating extracts from the satires, epistles or the epodes condemning civil war; several of Seneca's tragic choruses; the lyric portions ('metra') of Boethius' prosimetric work *De consolatione philosophiae*; some of the longer and non-satiric of Martial's epigrams (especially 10.47); and a few single poems such as Claudian's 'Old Man of Verona' (*Carmina Minora* 20). In the seventeenth century, this set of classical and late antique texts was increasingly augmented by contemporary Latin authors, especially (in England from the 1630s onwards) the Horatian Latin lyric of the Polish Jesuit poet, Casimir Sarbiewski. In practice, this set of texts often also included scriptural verse paraphrase, most often of key psalms (such as Psalm 1).[7] A 'reception history' or history of translation of any single classical author, even where such exists, is likely to miss the cultural importance – the contemporary *obviousness* – of a cluster of this sort, where the similarities between the texts, rather than the differences in style, tone or historical context, are what lends them authority.

Of the relevant classical authors, Horace has attracted by far the greatest critical attention. The modern perception of Horace, however, tends to be one of a lyric poet of evanescent pleasure, of 'wine, women, and song,' and of a distinctively dispassionate and sometimes ironic tone.[8] Although there are traces of this Horace in early modern English poetry, Horatian imitation in this period is dominated by a quite different version of the Roman poet – as above all a great moralist, both in lyric (the *Odes* and *Epodes*) and hexameter (*Satires* and *Epistles*), and a moralist rooted strongly in the everyday realities of courtly life, the demands of patronage, and the pleasures and compromises of panegyric.[9] Though it is barely mentioned in most modern accounts, a large number of Horace's odes are technically

---

[7] On the poetics of psalm paraphrase, see Chapters 2 and 3.
[8] See for example Harrison, 'Reception of Horace'.
[9] Burrow, 'Wyatt and Sixteenth Century Horatianism' and Moul, *Jonson, Horace*, esp. 9–12. The *Epistles* and *Odes* Book 2, with its moral and philosophical themes, and Book 4, with an emphasis upon panegyric, are accordingly particularly popular in early modern translations and imitations; whereas modern criticism has tended to find those collections less rewarding than Books 1 and 3.

classifiable as hymns, or contain hymnic passages, and the association of Horace with lyric address to the divine, though not central to this chapter, is of the utmost importance in early modernity, linking him closely with the psalmist David: this aspect of the Latin lyric tradition is discussed in Chapters 3 (on psalm paraphrase), 4 (on the development of formal panegyric lyric) and 6 (on devotional lyric).

Moralizing Lyric in Tottel's Miscellany

Richard Tottel's *Songes and Sonettes* (often referred to as 'Tottel's miscellany'), first printed in 1557, was a publishing sensation, and proved profoundly influential.[10] The collection itself is so heterogeneous that it has been described by some critics as 'disorienting', though this is arguably much less the case for anyone accustomed to reading personal manuscript miscellanies: Tottel resembles a print version of such collections.[11] The poetry of Henry Howard, Earl of Surrey and of Thomas Wyatt, both of whom were writing in the 1530s and 1540s, is significantly represented in the anthology; and though Mary Thomas Crane has rightly stressed the 'uniform moral message' of the collection as a whole, criticism has focused on Surrey's and Wyatt's contributions, with the majority of attention devoted to their sonnets and love lyrics.[12]

Neither the moralizing verse of Tottel's miscellany, nor its substantial element of translation and imitation (that is, of paraphrase broadly understood), has received much critical regard. In practice, however, these two elements – of moralizing verse, and of verse which reworks an existing poem – frequently overlap: *Songes and Sonettes* includes no fewer than three versions of *Odes* 2.10 on the 'golden mean', probably the most famous of all Horace's moralizing odes. None of the three versions, however, is titled with reference to Horace, but only in general moralizing terms: 'Praise of mean and constant estate' (no. 32), 'Of the golden mean'

---

[10] Tottel's miscellany was printed twice in 1557. The first edition, in June, contained 271 poems, expanded to 280 poems. Richard Tottel was the printer, not the editor, of the work. The volume contained many poems by Henry Howard, Earl of Surrey and (especially) by Thomas Wyatt, as well as unattributed pieces. The collection was reprinted in 1559 (twice), 1565, 1567, 1574, 1585 and 1587, with further editions quite likely lost, and is mentioned by Slender in Shakespeare's *The Merry Wives of Windsor* (1.i.188). A series of similar anthologies followed, including *The Passionate Pilgrim* (1599), *England's Helicon* (1600) and *A Poetical Rhapsody* (1602). For Tottel's influence upon mid-Tudor verse, see Heale, *Autobiography and Authorship in Renaissance Verse*, ch. 1; on the complex textual history of the anthology, see Powell, 'Network behind *"Tottel's" Miscellany*'.
[11] Wall, *Imprint of Gender*, 24   [12] Crane, *Framing Authority*, 169.

(no. 253), and 'The mean estate is to be accounted the best' (no. 163).[13] A fourth poem with an almost identical title, 'Of the meane and sure estate' (no. 128), is not in fact another version of *Odes* 2.10 but rather Wyatt's translation of the final part of the second chorus from Seneca's *Thyestes*, on how true kingship lies not in power but in self-government and virtuous obscurity:

> Stond who so list upon the slipper wheele,
> Of hye astate and let me here rejoyce.
> And use my life in quietnesse eche dele [*all the time; every bit*],
> Unknowen in court that hath the wanton toyes,
> In hidden place my time shal slowly passe
> And when my yeres be past withouten noyce
> Let me dye olde after the common trace
> For gripes of death doth he to hardly passe
> That knowen is to all: but to him selfe alas
> He dyeth unknowen, dased with dreadfull face.[14]

> Stet quicumque volet potens
> aulae culmine lubrico:
> me dulcis saturet quies.
> obscuro positus loco
> leni perfruar otio,
> nullis nota Quiritibus
> aetas per tacitum fluat.
> sic cum transierint mei
> nullo cum strepitu dies,
> plebeius moriar senex.
> illi mors gravis incubat
> qui, notus nimis omnibus,
> ignotus moritur sibi.
>
> (Seneca, *Thyestes*, 391–403)

---

[13] All are presented anonymously, although no. 32 is known to be by Henry Howard, Earl of Surrey. For a fuller discussion, see Moul, 'Horace'. The miscellany also includes Wyatt's Horatian epistles (nos. 134, 135 and 136) and a translation of Horace, *Odes* 4.4 ('All worldly pleasures vade', no. 166). Other poets translated or imitated (though without explicit acknowledgement) include Lucretius, Seneca, Martial, Boethius, Ausonius, Petrarch, Bonifacio, Serafino, Sannazaro, Collinutio, Beza, Haddon, Scaliger and Muret. On Grimald's translations of Beza, see Hudson, 'Grimald's Translations'. On the role of translation in this and similar collections, see Greene, 'The Lyric'. Numeration as in Holton and MacFaul (eds.), *Tottel's Miscellany*.

[14] All quotations from Tottel are from Holton and MacFaul (eds.), *Tottel's Miscellany*. An alternative version of the same poem, beginning 'Stond who so list upon the Slipper toppe', is found in Arundel Castle, MS Harington 311; see Hughey (ed.), *Arundel Harington Manuscript*. For other English translations of this chorus, see Gillespie, 'Seneca ex Thyestes'.

The overlap in titles reflects connections between the texts. Seneca's moralizing choruses are dependent upon and consciously reminiscent of Horace in metre, theme and often also in specific allusions.[15] In Tottel, the similar titles and thematic overlap point to an 'Horatio-Senecan' zone of classical imitation which would have been obvious to early modern readers, but is far removed from mainstream scholarly perspectives on either Horace or Seneca today.[16]

The title given to Wyatt's poem, 'Of the meane and sure estate', points towards two meanings of the word 'mean': 'lowly' and 'middle' (as in the 'golden mean' of Horace *Odes* 2.10).[17] The overlap reflects a 'blurring' of the source texts too. Horace *Odes* 2.10 uses imagery of the tall pine tree, towers and mountaintops:

> Auream quisquis mediocritatem
> diligit, tutus caret obsoleti
> sordibus tecti, caret invidenda
>   sobrius aula.
>
> Saepius ventis agitatur ingens
> pinus et celsae graviore casu
> decidunt turres feriuntque summos
>   fulgura montis.
>   (*Odes* 2.10.5–12)

> *Whoever loves the golden mean*
> *Safely avoids the grime*
> *Of a shabby hovel, and soberly does without*
>   *An enviable palace.*
>
> *The great pine is more often rocked*
> *By winds, and lofty towers collapse*
> *With a heavier fall, and lightning strikes*
>   *The mountain tops.*

Several of the imitations in Tottel expand upon the social and political connotations of this imagery, as in Poem 163 ('The meane estate is to be accompted the best') which comments explicitly: 'The higher hall the

---

[15] Compare for instance the combination of 'golden mean' and sailing imagery (indebted to Horace, *Odes* 2.10) in *Oedipus* 882–914 and *Medea* 599–606, and the substantial borrowings from Horace, including *Odes* 1.1 and *Epodes* 2, in *Hercules Furens* 125–204.
[16] See further Moul, 'Horace, Seneca'.
[17] See Holton and MacFaul (eds.), *Tottel's Miscellany*, 449. Other examples of poems in praise of poverty or simplicity of life (a 'mean estate') include 'Of the meane and sure estate written to John Poins' (no. 134, by Wyatt), 'They of the meane estate are happiest' (no. 140), and 'The meane estate is best' (no. 160).

greater fall / such chance have proude and lofty mindes' (19–20).[18] In poems of this kind, the imagery is informed by the tradition of interpretation and response to Horace, including Seneca's chorus. The line 'The higher hall the greater fall' uses a Senecan commonplace to make explicit what is only hinted at in Horace. Similarly, several of the poems on the benefits of virtuous obscurity over wealth and high office – the essential theme of Seneca's kingship chorus – introduce imagery of sailing influenced by Horace.[19]

The theme of Seneca's chorus is perhaps the single most common one for moralizing lyric of this kind: there are multiple examples in Horace, the most widely imitated of which is *Epodes* 2, often interpreted in early modernity without reference to its ironizing conclusion, and it is also the central message of Claudian's much imitated poem, 'The Old Man of Verona' (*Carmina Minora* 20), of Martial 10.47, and of several of the lyric portions of Boethius' *Consolation of Philosophy*.[20] Indeed, Surrey's version of Martial 10.47 is included in Tottel under the title 'The meanes to attain happy life' (no. 31):

> Martial, the things that do attain
> The happy life, be these, I finde.
> The richesse left, not got with pain:
> The frutefull ground: the quiet minde:
> The egall frend, no grudge, no strife:
> No charge of rule, nor governance:
> Without disease the healthful life:
> The household of continuance:
> The meane diet, no delicate fare:
> Trew wisdom joyned with simplenesse:
> The night discharged of all care,
> Where wine the wit may not oppresse:
> The faithfull wife, without debate:
> Such slepes, as may begile the night:
> Contented with thine own estate,
> Ne wish for death, ne feare his might.[21]

---

[18] Compare also Wyatt, 'Who lyst his welth and eas Retayne', in which the first two verses and ominous Latin refrain ('circa regna tonat') come from Seneca's *Phaedra*. The poem incorporates imagery of lofty mountains and steersmanship.

[19] As in no. 169 quoted below: 'they saile in Scillas cost, / Remainying in the stormes tyll shyp and al be lost'; see also no. 160, 'The meane estate is best', 13–18.

[20] On the reception of *Epodes* 2 see Røstvig, *Happy Man*. On versions of this poem in English, see Sullivan, 'Some Versions of Martial'.

[21] First published at the end of Book III in Baldwin, *A treatise of Morall phylosophie* (1547/8). Discussed in Evans, 'The Text of Surrey's "The Meanes to Attain Happy Life"'; McGaw, 'The

In a near-contemporary manuscript now in the British Library, a copy of this same poem, Surrey's translation of Martial, is titled 'The Noble Table of A Quiet Lieff written & made by Martiall the Poet worthy to bee set fourthe in golden verses in eny Mans howse', alongside improving quotations from Euripides (in Latin), Seneca and Cassiodorus.[22] Contemporary or later seventeenth-century translations of Martial 10.47 include those by Ben Jonson, Thomas Randolph, Charles Cotton, Abraham Cowley and John Evelyn, as well as a host of amateur and anonymous poets.[23]

Another of Wyatt's poems in Tottel, titled (possibly with particular reference to Henry VIII) 'He ruleth not though he raigne over realms that is subject to his own lustes' (no. 122), deals overall with the same subject as Seneca's 'kingship' chorus, though it is in fact derived not from Seneca but from the verse portions of Boethius' *Consolation of Philosophy*: the first stanza corresponds to Boethius 3.5, the second 3.6 and the third 3.3. The poem demonstrates that Power, Glory and Riches are all false goods, with no real value.[24]

> If thou wilt mighty bee, flee from the rage
> Of cruel will, and see thou kepe thee free
> From the foule yoke of sensuall bondage,
> For though thyne empyre stretche to Indian sea,
> And for thy feare trembleth the fardest Thylee,
> If thy desire have over thee the power,
> Subject then art thou and no governour.
> (No. 122, 1–7; first stanza, corresponding to Boethius 3.5)

Text of Surrey's "The Meanes to Attain Happy Life" – A Reply' and Edwards, 'Surrey's Martial Epigram'.

[22] BL MS Egerton 2642, fol. 246ʳ. This copy of the poem is not noted in *CELM*. The great majority of this large collection, made by Robert Commaundre, Rector of Tarporley, co. Chester, dates to the latter half of the sixteenth century, with some additions in the early seventeenth. It includes poems on the deaths of Lady Jane Grey, Cranmer, Ridley and Latimer; anti-Papal verse; and several dated items referring to events of the 1570s. Quotations are drawn from a wide range of classical, late antique, patristic, medieval and contemporary Latin texts, including extracts from Gower, Mantuan, Sannazaro and Walter Haddon, and Greek literature in Latin translation. This collection is discussed in more detail in Chapter 7.

[23] For several examples, see Gillespie, *Newly Recovered English Classical Translations*, EP71–EP83. Gillespie's is far from a complete list: this is a very frequently translated poem in the seventeenth century.

[24] Wyatt has changed the order of topics from that found in Boethius, and omits *metrum* 3.4, on Honours, perhaps because in its specific denunciation of Nero it is less generalizing than the others. Wyatt's poem is often considered to be indebted primarily to Chaucer's *Boece*, though this has been contested (see Thomson, 'Wyatt's Boethian Ballade').

Both content and the structure of this poem can be frequently paralleled in later lyrics. Compare for instance Poem 91 in Fulke Greville's *Caelica*, on the illusory rewards of nobility and fame:

> Rewards of earth, Nobilitie and Fame,
> To senses Glorie, and to conscience woe,
> How little be you, for so great a name?
> Yet lesse is he with men that thinks you so.
> > *For earthly Power, that stands by fleshly wit,*
> > *Hath banish'd that Truth which should governe it.*
>
> *Nobilitie, Powers golden fetter is,*
> Wherewith wise Kings subjection doe adorne,
> To make man thinke her heavy yoke, a blisse,
> Because it makes him more than he was borne.
> > Yet still a slave, dimm'd by mists of a Crowne,
> > Lest he should see, what riseth, what puls downe.
>
> *Fame*, that is but good words of evill deeds,
> Begotten by the harme we have, or doe,
> *Greatest farre off, least ever where it breeds,*
> We both with dangers and disquiet wooe.
> > And in our flesh (*the vanities false glasse*)
> > We thus deceiv'd adore these Calves of brasse.[25]

Just as Seneca is indebted to the moralizing portions of Horace, so is Boethius dependent upon Horace and Seneca. The lyrics of these three are united by form as well as content: all wrote primarily in lyric metres, and the majority (though not all) of the lyric metres of Seneca and Boethius are borrowed from Horace. Boethius (c.477–524 AD) is a good example of a poet rarely read by classicists today who had a much more central place in the early modern canon: his poetry was frequently excerpted and translated in manuscript miscellanies.[26] The thematic collection of classical Latin verse extracts prepared by the future Charles I as a gift for his father, for instance, includes two extracts of Boethius 3 *met.* 12 alongside Claudian's 'Old Man of Verona' (*Carmina Minora* 20) under the heading 'De

---

[25] Greville, *Certaine Learned and Elegant Workes* (1633), 238. *Caelica* was not published until 1633, though was probably completed by 1618 and elements may date from much earlier. See Parker, 'Fulke Greville and Proportional Form', chap. 2 of *Proportional Form*.

[26] Typical examples include BL MS Egerton 2642 (latter sixteenth century); BL MS Harley 3910 (probably 1620s, discussed below); BL MS Add. 15228 (1630s, discussed below); Bod. MS Eng. poet. f. 16 (1650s); CUL MS Add. 24 (D) (1645); CUL MS Add. 11 (1652); Leeds University Library, MS BC Lt 71 (1690s). On the citation of Boethius as an authority for Latin lyric metres not found in Horace, see Chapter 2.

Felicitate' ('On Happiness').[27] Richard Fanshawe's verse translations, dating from the 1630s, include 21 verse translations from Horace's *Odes* and *Epodes*, but also translations of almost the complete sequence of the metrical portions of Boethius, thirteen of Martial's epigrams, and Psalm 45.[28] Similarly, Phineas Fletcher's *The Purple Island* (1633) includes two translations from the metrical portions of Boethius as well as six English psalm paraphrases.[29]

In Tottel, similar generalizing titles are given for translations and expansions of Horace, Seneca, Boethius and Martial, as well as pieces such as Grimald's 'Prayse of measurekepying' (no. 108), in fact a translation of Beza's *Elegia* 2 (that is, a contemporary Latin poem in the same tradition), or 'The pore estate to be holden for best' (no. 169), which incorporates an acrostic on the name of Edward Somerset, who had fallen from power in 1549 and was executed in 1552:

> **E** xperience now doth shew what God us taught before,
> **D** esired pompe is vaine, and seldome doth it last:
> **W** ho climbes to raigne with kinges, may rue his fate full sore.
> . . .
> **S** uch as with oten cakes in poore estate abides,
> **O** f care have they no cure, the crab with mirth they rost,
> **M** ore ease fele they then those, that from their height down slides
> **E** xcesse doth brede their wo, they saile in Scillas cost,
> **R** emainyng in the stormes tyll shyp and al be lost.
> **S** erve God therefore thou pore, for lo, thou lives in rest,
> **E** schue the golden hall, thy thatched house is bes **T**.[30]

The last line of this poem alludes to *Odes* 2.10, but the sustained and explicit moralizing is closer in tone to Seneca or Boethius.

Hudson, noting how the translation of contemporary (neo-)Latin verse shaped Grimald's 'epigrammatic' English style, remarks that 'these qualities belong to the Latin sources from which he translates; and we are pointed to sixteenth-century Latin poetry as a factor in some of the most important tendencies in English poetry in the early Renaissance'.[31] This perceptive comment has not been taken up by subsequent scholarship, but the moralizing verse which is such a marked element of Tottel's miscellany

---

[27] BL MS Royal 12 D VIII, fols. 37ʳ–8ʳ. Three further quotations of Boethius 3.9 and 3.12 are under 'De Deo' (fols. 27ᵛ–9ᵛ).
[28] BL MS Add. 15228; Davidson (ed.), *Poems and Translations of Sir Richard Fanshawe*.
[29] Fletcher, *Purple Island* (1633).
[30] The last letter of the poem is capitalised to indicate the final letter of the acrostic-telestic, spelling out 'Edward Somerset'.
[31] Hudson, 'Grimald's Translations', 394.

was certainly a popular Latin form. For a near-contemporary Anglo-Latin example we could turn, for instance, to Walter Haddon's poem 'Perpetua est mutatio tum animi tum corporis', printed in his *Lucubrationes* (1567):

> Lubricus incertis iactatur motibus orbis,
> Posteriora nouos apportant tempora casus.
> Ipse homo, diuinum, solers, ratione refertum
> Est animal, partes & circumspectat in omnes.
> Sydereis mens lapsa polis, est numine plena.
> Iungitur humorum concordi semine corpus,
> Ordine membrorum praestans, formaeque decore.
> Tempora sed tacitis praeterlabentia pennis.
> Forma ruit, vires languent, artusque fatiscunt.
> ...
>
> Ergò deus mentes nobis, & corpora iunxit,
> Per quae continui fluxus, motusque peragrant.[32]
>
> (1–2)

> *The slippery world is tossed by unpredictable motion*
> *As later ages bring new kinds of disaster.*
> *Man himself is a divine animal, intelligent, filled with reason*
> *And he looks around himself carefully on all sides.*
> *His mind, fallen from the starry heavens, is filled with god.*
> *His body is assembled by the seeds of the humours in harmony,*
> *Pre-eminent in the arrangement of its parts, and in the beauty of its form.*
> *But time slides past on silent feathers.*
> *Beauty is lost, strength fades, limbs totter.*
> [...]
> *Therefore god joined our minds and our bodies,*
> *Through which flows continuously flux and motion.*

Haddon's poem begins with that tell-tale Senecan word 'lubricus' ('slippery'), linking it to the kingship chorus of the *Thyestes* ('Stet quicumque uolet potens / aulae culmine **lubrico**', 391–2; 'Stond who so list upon the slipper wheele, / Of hye astate').

Poems of this sort were an enduringly popular kind of early modern lyric, representing some of the most widely circulated poems in manuscript miscellanies; they are closely related to the classical tradition, as the overlap between translation and looser imitation in Tottel's volume demonstrates, but they have barely been considered in terms of classical reception because they do not fit well into the models of classical imitation which have been most influential in recent years. By paying attention to how poems of this

---

[32] Haddon, *Lucubrationes*, 'Poemata', 61–3.

sort were composed in (or translated into) Latin as well as English, we can see how they were understood at the time in relation to the classical Latin lyric tradition derived from Horace.

Classical Allusion and Translation

Analyses of allusion and intertextuality usually work by breaking a poem down into constituent and contributing elements, often emphasizing, at least in the more interesting readings, a sophisticated 'conversation' or even competition created between distinct allusions. Such an approach has been influential in the study of both classical Latin poetry and the reception of classical poetry in early modern literature.[33] It works well for a great deal of classicizing literature, but it is not a satisfactory model for poetry of the sort discussed in this chapter. What is effective and memorable about these generalizing lyrics is not usually their allusive structure: in most cases, there is no real sense of an allusive 'dialogue' between elements derived from Horace, Seneca, Martial, Claudian, Boethius and scriptural or contemporary sources. The power of these poems derives rather from the force of their authority, an impression created by the very familiarity of the theme: a sense of multiple overlapping precedents, each in themselves morally as well as aesthetically authoritative. This 'conventional' mode of literary authority is augmented, in some instances, by the counterpoint between general sentiments and the specific contexts in which such poems were placed not only (or even mostly) by their authors, but also by those who read, transcribed and circulated them.

The congruence of the translation and imitation of Horace, Seneca, Boethius, Martial, Claudian and contemporary or near-contemporary Latin poetry such as that of Beza and Haddon has attracted little critical attention partly because it is found most obviously in the kind of widely circulated lyrics which, though appearing in multiple print and manuscript miscellanies, have not often been included in modern anthologies; but also because our modern patterns of education and scholarship, both in classics

---

[33] Greene, *Light in Troy*, for instance, focuses upon the tension created by 'dialectical' imitation; this concept is linked to Pigman's 'eristic' imitation (Pigman, 'Versions of Imitation'). These readings, in which an individual poet grapples with and outdoes authoritative earlier texts, stress authorial personality and individual 'self-fashioning'. (Pigman's discussion of his other categories of imitation, 'transformative' and 'dissimulative', still tends to emphasize an author's unique response to one specific – even if concealed – model.) This approach works well for many early modern poets, including Ben Jonson, discussed at length by Greene, *Light in Troy*, 264–93 (see also Moul, *Jonson, Horace*).

and English literature, make the existence of a substantial zone of 'Horatio-Senecan-Boethian' lyric, and the links between this kind of poem and the psalms – a point which must have been obvious to the point of banality to educated early modern readers – hard to discern. There are several reasons for this. First, the elements of Horatian lyric least popular today, both in teaching and scholarship – hymns, moralizing, and panegyric lyric – map almost exactly onto the most widely appropriated poems in sixteenth- and seventeenth-century England. Second, Seneca's drama is no longer a centrepiece of early classical education, as it was in early modernity; and work on Seneca's influence upon the development of Renaissance drama has paid relatively little attention to the lyric qualities of the Senecan chorus, or the frequency with which such passages were excerpted and translated.[34] Late antique Latin poetry is rarely taught by Anglophone classics departments, so both Boethius and Claudian are unfamiliar to many classically educated readers of English poetry.

Moreover, studies of English poetic culture in the sixteenth and seventeenth centuries have largely ignored neo-Latin verse, despite the great quantity of Latin material found in both print and manuscript sources of the period. This refusal to engage with what we actually find in early modern literary sources helps to obscure the classical roots of the 'moralizing' lyric: time and again, a resonant English lyric which does not look or sound markedly 'Horatian' or 'Senecan', especially to the reader who associates Seneca with drama (not lyric) and Horace with erotic or sympotic (not moralizing or political) verse, is found in contemporary manuscripts accompanied by a Latin version, or Latin companion poem, which, whether by metre or diction or both, makes the associations of the piece with the classical tradition of moralizing lyric quite plain.

The cultural centrality of paraphrase – discussed in the introduction – is key to this phenomenon. Tottel makes no distinction between translations, freer imitations, and 'original' poems. None of the titles in the volume indicates that the poem is or is not a translation, imitation, or response. Both print and manuscript sources of the sixteenth and seventeenth centuries reflect this: translations, imitations, responses or

---

[34] Particularly important here is the influence of popular contemporary anthologies of extracts such as Mirandula, *Illustrium Poetarum Flores* (1507) (influential revised edn, 1538); Maior, *Sententiae veterum poetarum* (1534); Dornavius, *Amphitheatrum sapientiae* (1619); Langius, *Anthologia* (1625). On Seneca's use of Horace, see Spika, *De imitatione Horatiana*; Degl'Innocenti Pierini, '*Aurea mediocritas*'; Stevens, 'Seneca and Horace'. On Boethius and Horace, see Tarrant, 'Ancient Receptions of Horace'. Gillespie, *Newly Recovered English Classical Translations*, includes sections on both Horace and Seneca.

sequences of such poems frequently appear in volumes alongside moralizing lyrics which belong to the same tradition, and are presented as such, but which are in modern terms 'original' rather than versions of existing poems.

Sequences and Clusters of Moralizing Lyric in Manuscript Sources: BL MS Harley 3910

British Library Harley MS 3910 is a typical example from the middle of the period covered by this book; a small paper book of 147 leaves, it contains a large variety of English and Latin poetry in various hands, with many examples of bilingual presentation of both classical and contemporary Latin verse.[35] None of the entries is dated, although the poems included, and events referred to, suggest that it dates from the 1620s.[36] The sequence most relevant to this chapter begins on fol. 76^v, with an eight-line extract from the opening of Horace, *Odes* 3.3, accompanied on the facing page (fol. 77^r) by an English translation:

> A Just and setled man, resolued aright;
> Not Ciuicke rage forcing to things vnfitt,
> Not cruell'st Tyrants terrifying sight
> Nor feircest stormes wch the swolne ocean splitt;
> Nor Thundring Joues high hand can e're affright
> Or shake his solid mind from her fix't plight
> Yea, though the shatter'd world in peeces fall,
> The ruines strike him, not appall'd at all.

This portion of Horace is very commonly excerpted and translated in miscellanies of the period.[37] The following double-page spread (fols. 77^v–8^r)

---

[35] For instance, a Latin poem by William Alabaster with an English translation by Hugh Holland (fols. 51^v–2^r); Latin epigrams with English translations (fols. 56^{r-v}); a Latin song from John Barclay's *Euphormio* (first published 1605) with an English translation on the facing page (fols. 75^v–76^r). The consistent bilingualism, in which Latin texts are accompanied by English versions, is a feature of manuscript culture from around the second quarter of the seventeenth century onwards, a development discussed further in Chapter 11. This is a relatively early example of systematic translation into English.

[36] See the entry for this manuscript in *CELM*. The final section of the volume contains many poems in Latin and English commemorating the death of Thomas Murray, Secretary to Charles, Prince of Wales, who died in 1623. This sequence is the subject of a recent article (Doelman, 'Daring Pen of Sorrow'). Stuart Gillespie dated two of the translations in this manuscript to the early eighteenth century (Gillespie, 'Seneca ex Thyestes') but personal correspondence with him has confirmed that this was based on a transcription error. He now concurs with a dating from around 1620; this is reflected in Gillespie, *Newly Recovered English Classical Translations*.

[37] Compare for instance a translation of the same passage in CUL MS Dd. XIV. 8, fol. 25^v.

contains the Latin text, with facing translation, of the section from the 'kingship' chorus of Seneca's *Thyestes* already discussed above: indeed, the opening eight lines of *Odes* 3.3 is one of the identifiable sources for Seneca's chorus, as the sequence of entries here suggests.[38] This notebook, however, records not one but two distinct versions of the Senecan chorus, the first considerably longer than the second (thirty-two compared to twelve lines), though both apparently indebted to Wyatt's version.[39]

These three classical translations – one of *Odes* 3.3 and two of the 'kingship' chorus – are in fact only the beginning of a sequence, all with facing Latin text, of passages from Seneca, Horace, Martial and Boethius, namely: the second chorus of Seneca's *Medea*; the first chorus of the *Agamemnon*; *Phaedra* 483–558; Horace, *Odes* 2.3, 2.14, 2.15, 3.23, 4.7, 4.9; Martial 9.17, 10.47 and 11.40; Boethius, *De consolatione philosophiae* 1.4 and 3.6.[40] There is an obvious thematic coherence to this selection; compare for instance the translation of the first chorus of the *Agamemnon* (fol. 84[r], translating lines 57–74), which begins:

> O deceitfull kingdomes Fate,
> In their greatest, and best estate
> Placing their high-crested state
> Doubtfully, precipitate.
> Scepters n'ere in quiet sway
> Nor e're kept their certaine day
> Care on care doth them perplex
> And new stormes their minds still vexe:
> Not the Lybicke sea so raues
> Rowling roaring waues on waues;
> Nor the Euxine so turmoiles
> Or from his huge depth so boiles
> When the frosty neighbour-Pole

---

[38] Compare Horace, *Odes* 3.3.1–8 and Seneca *Thyestes*, 348–64. For discussion of the Horatianism of this chorus, see Tarrant (ed.), *Seneca's Thyestes*, 137.

[39] BL MS Harley 3910, fols. 77[v]–9[r]. Both of these are printed in Gillespie's recent short anthology of translations just of this passage (Gillespie, 'Seneca ex Thyestes'). I have not been able to identify the author of these poems. Translations of this passage survive by many English poets; Gillespie also prints examples by Jasper Heywood, Robert Sidney, Abraham Cowley, Matthew Hale, Andrew Marvell, John Wright, John Norris of Bemerton, Robert Dobbins, John Rawlet, Richard Bulstrode, Daniel Baker, George Granville, Thomas Morrell, John Cotton, Richard Polwhele and Goldwin Smyth, as well as several anonymous versions.

[40] BL MS Harley 3910, fols. 76[v]–99[r]. Boethius, *Cons.* 3 met. 6 is incorporated into Wyatt's 'He ruleth not though he raigne over realms that is subject to his own lustes' (no. 122), discussed above. Some further translations (e.g. of Catullus 63 and Horace, *Odes* 4.7) appear in the more varied material (including a large amount of contemporary Latin verse) elsewhere in the volume, outside this thematically coherent sequence.

> Doth his freer course countroul
> As the state & port of kings
> Fortune wheeling, headlong flings
> To be feared they feare, desire,
> Night to them no safe retyre ...

with the version of Boethius, *Cons.* 1.4 (fol. 93ʳ):

> He that is still, in setled state
> And vnderfoote hath trode proud Fate,
> And either Fortune can behold
> with an undaunted looke & bold,
> Him, no seas rage, nor threatning surge
> Wᶜʰ from the bottome stirr'd doth vrge
> Nor mountaines casting smoake & fire,
> from horrid riftes, wᶜʰ all admire,
> Nor feircest lightnings from aboue,
> vsd to strike highest towres, shall moue
> why doe fond men so much admire,
> Madd Tyrants rage, & strengthlesse ire?
> Lay by vaine Hope, & Feare, & then
> Thou shalt disarme the rage of men.
> But he that feares, or wishes; hee
> Being vnsetled, and not free,
> Hath Lost his sheild, & place; and knitt
> A Chaine, to be drag'd-on by itt./

and that of Horace, *Odes* 2.3 (fol. 94ʳ), beginning:

> Still keepe an euen mind in thy distresse,
> And temper'd from loose mirth in good successe;
> Thou art to Dye, whether in discontent
> And wasting sadnes all thy tyme be spent ...

In this series, the original Latin texts have significant overlaps in theme and tone, but these are emphasized and augmented by the translations, which reuse certain words and phrases ('And so **precipitate** with all', translating Seneca, *Thyestes* 341–2; 'Doubtfully, **precipitate**', translating Seneca, *Agamemnon* 58; 'He that is **still**, in **setled state**', Boethius, *Cons.* 1.4.1; '**Still** keepe an even mind', Horace, *Odes* 2.3.1; 'Meane **estat's** doe longer last', translating *Agamemnon* 102; 'In their greatest and best **estate**', translating *Agamemnon* 57). The Latin that stands behind these overlapping translations is often quite different: towards the end of the version of the *Agamemnon* chorus, for instance, the English line 'Meane estat's doe longer last' (fol. 86ʳ) translates the Latin line *modicis rebus longius aevum est* (fol. 85ᵛ, *Agamemnon* 102). Here 'estat's' translates Latin *rebus* ('things,' 'matters,' 'situation'). At the beginning of the same poem, the line 'In their greatest, and best estate' (fol. 84ʳ) uses the same English word ('estate') to translate the Latin phrase *magnis ... bonis* (*Agaememnon* 57) , which means literally 'great goods'. The sense of ethical coherence is intensified by the close relationship between the English words 'estate' and 'state', both of which had a different and wider range of meanings in early modern English than they do today.[41] The word 'state' recurs particularly frequently in the sequence: the phrase 'setled state', for instance, appears both in the translation of Boethius, *Cons.* 1.4.1 – 'He that is still, in setled state' translating *Quisquis composito serenus aevo* (fols. 92ᵛ–3ʳ) – and in the translation of Horace, *Odes* 4.9 ('From her right and setled state', fol. 98ʳ), linking by vocabulary two ostensibly rather different poems.[42]

These repeated words and phrases have a cumulative force, partly by virtue of their recurrence in the sequence, and partly by their ethical and literary resonance, reaching back, via Jonson, to Elizabethan and Tudor lyric, and indeed (as in 'Meane estat's doe longer last') to Tottel's miscellany itself. The translations are also quite substantial expansions, as the *mise-en-page* of the manuscript makes clear. Some pages have as few as 8 lines on the left (Latin) side against 23 on the right, and the translation is most expansive in the moralizing passages most closely related to the 'theme' of the collection: in the translation of the *Agamemnon* chorus, for instance, the memorable phrase 'as the state & port of kings' (15) expands the much less striking *regnum casus* (*Agamemnon* 71). The line from the translation of Horace, *Odes* 4.9, 'From her right and setled state' (fol. 98ʳ), already discussed above, is also a significant expansion: the only Latin word to which the phrase corresponds directly is the single adjective *rectus* ('upright', *Odes* 4.9.36). In this way, a set of ancient poems which already share elements of theme and tone are brought further together by details of translation. Whereas modern readers and scholars might tend to stress the *individuality* of authors – emphasizing for instance the differences in style, tone and political context of Horace and Seneca, and the

---

[41] See for instance *OED* 'state,' obsolete usages related to wealth, status, and the natural or proper condition of something, often with an overlap with 'estate': I.1.b. (b), 2.a., 5.a., 5.b., 6.a., 6.b., 7.a., and II.15, 18, 19, 22, 23. The word could even mean the royal throne itself (II.17.a.).

[42] The author of this sequence may have been influenced by Ben Jonson in particular, in whose work 'state' recurs frequently and with a resonant and ethically significant range of meaning (see Moul, *Jonson, Horace,* 190 and n42). Compare Vaughan's similar opening to his translation of Boethius, *Cons.* 1 *met.* 4: 'Whose calme soule in a settled state / Kicks under foot the frowns of Fate', published in *Olor Iscanus* (1651), 46.

role of Seneca's lyrics as dramatic choruses – the typical early modern reader values the sense of a common purpose and a moral consensus, and translates or excerpts accordingly.

Several of these translations are successful English poems in their own right, though the parallel text format (which is maintained throughout) and the inclusion of some lines, such as 'Doubtfully, precipitate', which are hard to follow without reference to the Latin, imply a close relationship with the original. Such sequences, found commonly in seventeenth-century miscellanies, demonstrate the shared literary associations which linked lyrics by Horace, Seneca, Boethius and a selection of other individual pieces, such as Martial 10.47, Claudian's 'Old Man of Verona' and versions of the Psalms. (In sixteenth-century sources, such thematic sequences are equally common, but less frequently include parallel translation.) Verse translation, however, is not a very fashionable area of literary study, and where such material has been discussed, it is usually in reference to individual authors (whether classical or early modern). Stuart Gillespie's recent *Newly Discovered Classical Translations*, for instance, restores to visibility a great wealth of forgotten translations, many of very high quality, but is (understandably) organized by classical author; similarly, the scattered classical translations of well-known English poets, such as Jonson or Wyatt, are edited for inclusion in collected works, leaving little sense of the original manuscript context in which they are often found surrounded not by other poems by the same author, but by thematically related items from a wide chronological range: such excerpting and editing of translations makes it harder to see how individual poems, authors or, as here, 'types' of poems were commonly associated by readers, translators and imitators in early modernity.

Where such sequences are found in sources dating from the Civil War period, the selection of translated material often reflects the political upheaval: John Polwhele's (c.1606–72) notebook, for instance, begins with a typical 1630s blend of tributes to Ben Jonson and George Herbert alongside Horatian translations (*Odes* 1.1, 2.14, and a fragment of the *Ars poetica*) before, apparently in direct response to the events of 1649, breaking suddenly into an extraordinary sequence of heavily revised and explicitly politicized versions of Horace (*Odes* 1.14 [twice], 1.33, 4.9; *Epodes* 5, 7 and 16; *Epistles* 1.18) and Boethius (*Cons.* 1, *met.* 2–7; 2, *met.* 1–8; 3, *met.* 1–6, twenty translations).[43] In a typical example, Polwhele

---

[43] Stuart Gillespie is preparing an edition of the Horatian translations ('John Polwhele's Horatian Translations').

expands and elaborates four rather generalizing lines in *Cons.* 1. *met.* 5 on the injustice of fortune:

> Premit insontes
> Debita sceleri noxia poena,
> At perversi resident celso
> Mores solio sanctaque calcant
> Iniusta vice colla nocentes.
> Latet obscuris condita virtus
> Clara tenebris iustusque tulit
> Crimen iniqui.
>
> (29–36)

The innocent endure the pains that are properly the punishments for wickedness; evil practices occupy the lofty throne and wicked men trample underfoot sacred necks, in an unjust reversal of fortune. The clear brightness of virtue lies hidden in darkness, and the righteous man is charged for the crime of the wicked.

In an otherwise fairly straightforward and little-corrected translation, Polwhele has revised these lines intensely, with a confusing series of further possibilities added at the end; a semi-diplomatic transcription gives a sense of the intensity of revision, and of how the patterns of expansion and reworking are politically inflected:

> the Gothes, & Vandalls tread vppon
> most sacred necks to mounte the throne
> Barbarian Gothes mounte on the throne
> behead the Lords annointed one
> Patritians in exile hide
> att home true Patriotts haue dyed
> for treason
> The <ostro>=Gothes <doe> ^ and Vandals tread vppon
> most sacread necke & mounte the throne[44]

Such a version bears only a remote resemblance to the original. Nothing in the Latin corresponds to 'behead the Lords anointed one', which obviously refers to the execution of Charles I.

In the early eighteenth century, the poetry composed by Reverend Daniel Baker (d. 1722) and collected after his death by his nephew, reflects changed literary fashions – he looks to Cowley as well as Herbert as a model, and many of his English poems are in Cowleian Pindarics – but also substantial continuity. The second item in the collection, 'The

---

[44] Bod. MS Eng. poet. f. 16, fol. 18^v.

Retreat', is a standard moralizing poem on the benefits of obscurity, indebted to both Claudian and Horace, with a marginal reference to Martial 2.90:

> Pardon me, Friend, that I so soon
> Forsake this great tumultuous town:
> And on the sudden hasten down.
>
> That I preferment court no more
> But all my hopes and cares give o'er
> While I'm young, and while I'm poor.
>
> . . .
>
> Thus, Oh! Thus let me obscurely lie!
> Thus let my well-spent Hours slide by!
> Thus let me live! Thus let me Die![45]

Baker's large collection of classical translations includes 5 pieces of Horace, 16 of Martial's epigrams and (yet again) a translation of the kingship chorus from Seneca's *Thyestes*.

The thematically coherent sequences of moralizing translations in the notebooks of Fanshawe, Polwhele, Baker and the anonymous compiler of British Library Harley MS 3910 all consist mainly of translations made apparently by the compiler themselves; many similar sequences, however, either incorporate or depend largely upon the poems and translations of others: Bod. MS Rawl. poet. 173, for instance, dating from about 1705, contains several of Dryden's translations of Horace alongside John Glanville's version of the *Thyestes* chorus.

Beyond Translation

The popularity of the 'moralizing lyric' can also be traced beyond the (porous) boundaries of translation, whether of individual pieces or in sequences, and into the larger realm of English lyric, both in printed collections and in manuscript sources. In a few cases, the classical roots are obvious: Michael Drayton's *Odes* are an ambitious early attempt to import the Horatian (or rather neo-Horatian and humanist) lyric 'book' into English.[46] Drayton's work is discussed in more detail in Chapter 4,

---

[45] BL MS Add. 11723, fols. 7ᵛ–8ʳ.
[46] On the humanist verse 'book', compared to the later sixteenth- and seventeenth-century tendency towards mixed collections, see Chapter 2.

but his fourth ode, though not a translation or imitation of any specific model, is a good example of the moralizing lyric:

> Uppon this sinfull earth
> if man can happy be
> and higher then his birth
> (Frend) take him thus of me:
>
> Whome promise not deceiues
> that he the breach should rue,
> nor constant reason leaues
> opinion to pursue.
>
> ...
>
> Noe man can be so free
> though in imperiall seate
> nor Eminent as hee
> that deemeth nothing greate.
> (1–8, 37–40)[47]

Drayton's interesting preface acknowledges the role of moralizing verse within the overall economy of what he describes as Horatian 'mixed' lyric: that is, a lyric collection which, like those of Horace, incorporates both the grandest panegyric lyric of the Pindaric kind, as well as the lighter mode of erotic or love lyric associated in Greek with Anacreon.[48]

Where passages of conventional moralizing verse appear within larger works, they have often been marked by early readers, probably for the purposes of excerpting into commonplace books. The twelfth and final Canto of Phineas Fletcher's *Purple Island*, for instance, opens with a moralizing poem on the blessedness of a simple rural existence. In the British Library copy of this work (which has been digitized by *EEBO*), the whole of this song (stanzas 2–6) has been pointed as gnomic in the margin.[49]

Lyrics of this sort are not usually well represented in modern anthologies of Renaissance poetry, but they are ubiquitous in early modern manuscript miscellanies. Bod. MS Rawl. poet. 31, dating from c. 1620–33, is a typical example: identified authors include Sir John Harington, Henry Wotton, Ben Jonson, John Donne and Edward Herbert, and the material by

---

[47] Drayton, 'To my worthy frend; Master Iohn Sauage of the Inner Temple', from *Poemes Lyrick and Pastorall* (1606), sig. B6ᵛ–B7ᵛ.
[48] Drayton, *Poemes Lyrick and Pastorall*, 'To the Reader', no signature.
[49] Fletcher, *Purple Island*, 159–60. BL 239.i.23.(1.).

Donne and Jonson in particular has attracted scholarly attention.[50] This manuscript collection includes, on adjacent pages, two examples of the tradition we are tracing here: Henry Wotton's popular poem, 'How happy is he born and taught' (fol. 5[r], quoted above) and Thomas Campion's 'The man of life upright' (fol. 5[v]), the latter of which I give below:

> The man of life upright,
>   Whose guiltless hart is free
> From all dishonest deedes,
>   Or thought of vanitie,
>
> The man whose silent dayes
>   In harmless joyes are spent,
> Whome hopes cannot delude,
>   Nor sorrow discontent,
>
> That man needes neither towers
>   Nor armour for defence,
> Nor secret vautes to flie
>   From thunders violence.
>
> Hee onely can behold
>   With unafrighted eyes
> The horrours of the deepe,
>   And terrours of the Skies.
>
> Thus, scorning all the cares
>   That fate, or fortune brings,
> He makes the heav'n his booke,
>   His wisedome heev'nly things,
>
> Good thoughts his onely friendes,
>   His wealth a well-spent age,
> The earth his sober Inne,
>   And quiet Pilgrimage.[51]

Campion's poem takes its cue (and, in manuscript versions, often its title, 'Integer Vitae') from Horace, *Odes* 1.22, which begins 'Integer vitae

---

[50] Several of the pieces by Jonson or his associates (e.g. Jonson's translation of Horace, *Epodes* 2; 'To Sir Robert Wroth,' a related poem; and a partial translation of Horace, *Epistles* 1.18) have a moral force and belong more broadly to this tradition, though their longer length, the sharpness of their allusive relationship with Horace in particular, and their use of prominent named addressees, represent a distinct, albeit related, kind of poem. Jonson's poems of this kind are some of the best-studied moralizing verse of this period, but they are not 'moralizing lyrics' of the generalizing (and often anonymous) type considered here.

[51] Text cited from Davis (ed.), *Works of Thomas Campion*. Campion's poem was first published as no. 18 in his *Booke of Ayres* (1601).

scelerisque purus' ('The man whose life is wholesome and free of wickedness'). The opening four stanzas of Campion's poem loosely paraphrase the first eight lines of the Horatian ode (similar to the relationship between Seneca, *Thyestes* 348–64 and Horace, *Odes* 3.3.1–8, noted above). But the focus and unity of Campion's lyric are quite different from the Horatian ode which (typically for Horace) moves after line 8 from the idea that the good man is safe from harm, to a related but distinct suggestion that the lover in the grip of his obsession is equally protected even in the harshest of environments. The irony is augmented by Horace imagining *himself* (not Fuscus, the addressee of the poem) as the preoccupied lover:

> Integer vitae scelerisque purus
> non eget Mauris iaculis neque arcu
> nec venenatis gravida sagittis,
>   Fusce, pharetra,
> sive per Syrtis iter aestuosas
> sive facturus per inhospitalem
> Caucasum vel quae loca fabulosus
>   lambit Hydaspes.
> Namque me silva lupus in Sabina,
> dum meam canto Lalagen et ultra
> terminum curis vagor expeditis,
>   fugit inermem . . .
> Horace, *Odes* 1.22.1–12

> *The man of upright life and free from sin*
> *requires no Moorish spear nor bow*
> *and quiver laden with poisoned*
> *   arrows, Fuscus,*
> *whether his route lies through*
> *the sweltering Syrtes or inhospitable*
> *Caucasus or regions the fabulous*
> *   Hydaspes laps.*
> *For as I wandered free from care*
> *singing of Lalage in Sabine*
> *woods, unarmed, beyond my bounds,*
> *   there fled a wolf.*[52]

The tone of these two poems is quite different: there is nothing arch about Campion's account of what the good man might hope to escape, whereas Horace's list (2–8) is markedly over-the-top – both this passage and a subsequent description of exotic wanderings (17–24), are probably

---

[52] Translation Shepherd, *Horace: Complete Odes and Epodes*, 89.

indebted to Catullus 11.1–12; and Horace's poem is also linked metrically to Catullus 11 and 51 (the latter itself a version of an earlier poem by Sappho). Two of Catullus' most famous poems about Lesbia, these have often been read as the beginning and end of the 'Lesbia cycle'.[53] The alert reader discerns literary self-consciousness, a suggestion of erotic adventure and a degree of irony in Horace's poem well before its explicit 'turn' to the erotic from line 10 onwards. Campion's popular poem, by contrast, raises no such uncertainties of tone, and in both form and content has links to later hymnody. Indeed, *Odes* 1.22 was often associated with the first psalm: as we have seen, psalm paraphrases are frequently found included in sequences of 'moralizing lyric'.[54] The tonal stability and moral seriousness of Campion's poem, despite its obvious debt to Horace, are not ultimately particularly Horatian: but both those characteristics *are* typical of Senecan choruses, the metrical portions of Boethius and the broadly (but not precisely) 'Horatian' tradition of moralizing lyric indebted to all three. This type of verse draws heavily upon Horace metrically, lexically and thematically, but has a quite different tone and 'feel' from anything that Horace actually wrote.

John Ashmore's *Certain Selected Odes of Horace, Englished* (1621), often cited as the first collection of English translations of Horatian lyric, demonstrates both the moral associations of the *Odes* at this period, and the sense of a moralizing subgenre of poems on how to live well, of which Horace himself is only a part. The subtitle of the book continues: *With Poems (Antient and Modern) of divers Subjects, Translated. Whereunto are added, both in Latin and English, sundry new Epigrammes, Annagramms, Epitaphes*, and the work is in fact divided into four parts: the translations and imitations of Horace (1–28); a section of mostly contemporary epigrams, presented in Latin and English (29–79, by far the longest); a section entitled 'The Praise of a Country Life' (81–7) including poems and extracts by Martial and Virgil as well as neo-Latin examples; and a final section 'Of a Blessed Life' (91–6), once again a mixture of ancient and modern pieces.

The selection of Horace's lyric that Ashmore chooses to translate is typical of the period in its emphasis upon moral themes, and the relative

---

[53] Ancona, *Time and the Erotic*, 113–21 and 168 (n33).
[54] On links between Psalm 1 and *Odes* 1.22, see Hamlin, *Psalm Culture*, 67–8. On psalm paraphrase in general, see Chapter 3. There is evidence of Campion's poem influencing translations of Horace's ode: the translation of *Odes* 1.22 by 'Sir T. H.' printed in Alexander Brome's *Poems of Horace* (1666), for instance, alludes to Campion's poem in its opening line ('Who lives upright, and pure of heart', p. 30), though the tone of the translation as a whole is much closer to that of Horace.

prominence of odes from Books 2 and 4.[55] (In contrast to modern critics and teachers, who tend to prefer *Odes* 1 and 3.) He also includes *Epodes* 2. In this way his selection of Horatian translations sets up the moralizing themes of the final two sections, on the 'Country Life' and the 'Blessed Life'. The latter of these, 'Of a Blessed Life', includes an English lyric with a Latin title, 'Lipsii laus, & vota Vitae beatae' ('Lipsius' praise and prayer for a blessed Life'):

> He's like the gods, and higher then
> The rest-less Race of mortall Men,
> That wisheth not, or (in despaire)
> The doubtfull Day of Death doth feare.
> In whom Ambition doth not raigne,
> That is not vext with hope of Gaine,
> That trembles not at Threats of Kings,
> Nor Darts that angry *Iove* down flings:
> But, firmly seated in one Place,
> Vulgar Delights doth scorne, as base:
> That of his Life one *Tenor* keeps;
> Secure that wakes, secure that sleeps.
>   If I might live at mine owne pleasure,
> I would no Office seek, nor Treasure;
> Nor captive Troups should me attend,
> As to my Charret I ascend
> Drawne by white Steeds, with Shouts and Cries;
> A Spectacle to gazing Eyes.
>   In Places I remote would be:
> Gardens and Fields should solace me:
> There, at the bubbling waters noyse,
> I with the Muses would reioyce.
>   So, when my *Lachesis* hath spun
> The thread of Life, she well drew on;
> Not unto any man a Foe,
> I full of Years from hence would goe,
>   And Date my dayes in quiet state,
>   As my good *Langius* did of late.[56]

This is, as the title suggests, a translation of a Latin poem by Justus Lipsius:

---

[55] The Horatian translations are *Odes* 1.1, 5, 13, 22, 23, 26; 2.10, 14, 15, 16, 18; 3.9, 30; 4.3, 7, 8 and *Epodes* 2. *Odes* 2 has the largest number of moralizing odes; *Odes* 4, written ten years after *Odes* 1–3, has the largest number of grand panegyric odes, and is a particularly important model for political panegyric in early modernity, as discussed in Chapter 4.
[56] Ashmore, *Certain Selected Odes of Horace*, 94–5.

Ille est par superis Deis,
Et mortalibus altior
Qui fati ambiguum diem
Non optat levis, aut timet.
 Quem non ambitio impotens
Non spes sollicitat lucri:
Quem non concutiunt metu
Regum praecipites minae
Non telum implacidi Iovis.
Uno sed stabilis loco   10
Vulgi ridet inania:
Securoque oritur dies,
Securo cadit & dies.
 Vitam si liceat mihi
Formare arbitriis meis:
Non fasces cupiam aut opes,
Non clarus niveis equis
Captiva agmina traxerim:
 In solis habitem locis,
Hortos possideam atque agros,   20
Illic ad strepitus aquae
Musarum studiis fruar.
 Sic cum fata mihi ultima
Pernerit Lachesis mea;
Non ulli gravis aut malus,
Qualis Langius hic meus,
Tranquillus moriar senex.

Lipsius' lyric was very popular: in Ben Jonson's copy of Lipsius, the entire poem is underlined, and other translations are found in manuscript.[57] Despite a witty Catullan allusion in the opening line, it is derived in particular from Seneca. Indeed, a contemporary work, Philip Camerarius' *Operae horarum subcisivarum*, quotes Lipsius' poem (which is reproduced in full) in a chapter, titled 'Commendatio privatae vitae' ('Praise of a private life') which begins by quoting Seneca, *Phaedra* 483–95 (p. 341) and then comments explicitly on the links between Lipsius' lyric and the metrical portions of Boethius (p. 342).[58] Lipsius' phrase *ambitio*

---

[57] Bryan and Evans, 'Jonson's Response to Lipsius', notes that this is one of the most heavily marked pages. Other translations in manuscript circulation include Bod. MS Rawl. poet. 62, fols. 41^v–2^r, a manuscript dating from between 1627 and 1643 and apparently belonging to someone in Cambridge; the translation is not the one found in Ashmore.

[58] *Operae horarum subcisivarum, sive meditationes historicae*, first published in Nuremburg in 1591, with several further editions. The page numbers refer to the 1609 Frankfurt edition of this work. Translations were produced in French (1610), English (1610) and German (1625–30).

impotens ('powerless ambition', 5) is borrowed from the same chorus of the *Thyestes* so often translated and imitated at this period ('quem non **ambitio impotens**', 350). Lipsius' poem transforms the 'never stable' popular favour of Seneca's chorus into the true stability of the wise man ('uno sed stabilis loco', 10; 'firmly seated in one Place'); while the fickleness of the mob in Seneca ('vulgi praecipitis') is transferred to the unpredictability and violence of royal power ('regum praecipites minae', 8; 'Threats of Kings'). There are several further parallels between Lipsius' poem and the final two choruses of Seneca's *Oedipus*, which themselves draw on Horace: *Oedipus* 882–910 is written in the same unusual stichic glyconic metre used here by Lipsius (which is also the single most frequent metre in Boethius), and the subject of the *Oedipus* chorus is fate and the virtues of the 'middle path'.[59] Ashmore's collection points to a bilingualism in moralizing lyrics typical of the seventeenth century: original Latin and English poems stand alongside English translations from both classical and neo-Latin.

Indeed, the Latin 'feel' and associations of English lyrics in this tradition, far from obvious to the modern reader, are reflected in the contemporary habit of translating English poems of this type into (almost, as it were, 'back' into) Latin verse. Henry Wotton (1568–1639), for instance, whose ubiquitous 'The Character of a Happy Life' has already been mentioned, was one of the masters of the suggestive moralizing lyric in the late sixteenth and early seventeenth centuries. His works have largely slipped out of the lyric 'canon', but copies appear in manuscript collections throughout the seventeenth century – the *CELM* lists 63 copies of 'The Character of a Happy Life' – and many Latin translations of his poems are also found in manuscript sources.[60]

---

[59] On the glyconic metre and the 'golden mean' in *Oedipus* 882–914 see Geiger, 'Horatian and Senecan Metrics', 177–8, and Tarrant, '*Custode rerum Caesare*'. The metre is used by Boethius at 1.6, 2.8, 3.12, 4.3 and 5.4. For a seventeenth-century example, see George Herbert, *Musae responsoriae* 25. *Oedipus* 980–97 is not in the same metre but includes many of the same tropes. I am grateful to Kathrin Winter for pointing out the links to the *Oedipus* here.

[60] On the manuscript transmission of this poem see Main, 'Wotton's "The Character of a Happy life"' and Pebworth, 'New Light on Sir Henry Wotton's "The Character of a Happy Life"'. Maren-Sofie Røstvig's *Happy Man* is an invaluable study of one particular (though broadly interpreted) version of the 'happy life' lyric, focused on or at least incorporating a rural setting. She looks only at examples from 1600 onwards and does not consider sixteenth-century texts such as those included in Tottel's miscellany. She also does not consider the relationship of these poems to the broader class of 'moralizing' lyrics, in both English and Latin, though her work deserves much more credit than it has received for insisting upon the importance of neo-Latin as well as classical and English authors.

Perhaps the most striking example of the translation of English into Latin lyric concerns Wotton's fine poem, found in many manuscripts with varying titles, and published posthumously in Izaak Walton's *Reliquiae Wottonianae* of 1651 in the following form:

Upon the sudden Restraint of the Earle of Somerset, then falling from favor.

> Dazel'd thus, with height of place,
> Whilst our hopes our wits beguile,
> No man markes the narrow space
> 'Twixt a prison, and a smile.
>
> Then, since fortunes favours fade,
> You, that in her armes doe sleep,
> Learne to swim, and not to wade;
> For, the Hearts of Kings are deepe.
>
> But, if Greatness be so blind,
> As to trust in towers of Aire,
> Let it be with Goodness lin'd,
> That at'least, the Fall be faire.
>
> Then though darkned, you shall say,
> When Friends faile, and Princes frowne,
> *Vertue* is the roughest way,
> But proves at night a *Bed of Downe*.[61]

This poem was probably written, as the title in this edition indicates, about the spectacular fall in 1616 of Robert Carr, the Earl of Somerset; a royal favourite for around a decade, he was charged and convicted of the murder by poison of Sir Thomas Overbury, who had opposed his marriage to his wife Frances. Extant examples of the poem in both print and manuscript, however, often give it either a generic title ('On the sudden restraint of a favourite') or link the poem to the fall of another prominent individual, such as Walter Raleigh (imprisoned for marrying without the Queen's permission in 1591; later executed for treason in 1618); Francis Bacon (found guilty of taking bribes in 1621); George Villiers, Duke of Buckingham (impeached in 1626, eventually assassinated in 1628); and even William Davison (secretary to Queen Elizabeth I, who was made the

---

[61] Wotton, *Reliquiae Wottonianae*, 522.

scapegoat for the execution of Mary, Queen of Scots, in 1587).[62] In some instances, the poem is in fact attributed to the unfortunate favourite, as in one Bodleian manuscript where it is titled 'By ye moste Illustrious Prince George Duke of Buckingham &c.', or a copy in the Leeds Archives which ascribes the poem to Sir Walter Raleigh.[63]

This is a lovely and memorable poem, which is at once timelessly imprecise and politically highly suggestive. It belongs recognizably to the kind of politico-moral 'generalizing lyric' under discussion. Nevertheless, there is nothing very obviously Horatian about the English poem, especially from the perspective of a modern classicist: it is not a translation, or even a close imitation, and it has no marked classicizing touches. In the only existing article dedicated to the poem, Ted-Larry Pebworth does not relate it in any way to the classical tradition.[64] But contemporary readers *did* read the poem as part of that broadly Horatian tradition of moralizing lyric which is the subject of this chapter. 'Dazel'd thus, with height of place' is found in at least five manuscripts (to my knowledge) accompanied by multiple Latin translations, and in each case the choice of metre and vocabulary, as well as specific allusions, make the association with Horace and Seneca explicit. I give below an edited transcription of one stanza, alongside the Latin translations which accompany it in four of the five sources. The Latin on the right is in sapphic stanzas, on the left in alcaics.[65]

---

[62] The two copies relating the poem to 'Secretary Davison' are both in the same manuscript in the Bradford Archives (MS 32D86/17, fols. 26ᵛ and 124ᵛ). For full details of the various ascriptions of the poem, see Pebworth, 'Sir Henry Wotton's "Dazel'd Thus"'.

[63] Bod. MS Rawl. poet. 166, p. 83. West Yorkshire Archive Service, MS 156/237, fol. 56ᵛ.

[64] Pebworth, 'Sir Henry Wotton's "Dazel'd Thus"'.

[65] Four sources reproduce the poems in this format, with essentially the same Latin texts (bar minor differences in spelling and punctuation) (BL MS Harley 6038, fol. 44ʳ⁻ᵛ; BL MS Harley 1221, fol. 110ʳ; BL MS Add. 72439, fol. 149ʳ and Nottingham University Library, MS PwV 518). The fifth manuscript (Bod. MS Rawl. poet. 166, p. 82) contains a further three (different) Latin translations, two of which include 'alternative' translations for one stanza (in one case the first stanza, in another the last). This probably reflects some kind of informal translation competition among friends. Several of Wotton's other poems are also found translated into Latin at this period; these include his 'Ode to the King' (Bod. MS Sancroft 89, pp. 57–8) and his widely-circulated poem on the Queen of Bohemia (Bod. MS Douce 357, fol. 19ʳ; BL MS Add. 47111, fol. 24ᵛ; Folger Shakespeare Library, MS V.a.103, Part I, fol. 53ʳ⁻ᵛ; The Family Album, Glen Rock, Pennsylvania, [Wolf MS], p. 3). It is likely that others are extant but unidentified, given the limited indexing of Latin verse. All five manuscripts add a fifth stanza, not reproduced here, but discussed by Pebworth, 'Sir Henry Wotton's "Dazel'd Thus"', 161–3, who considers it a later addition.

> Then though darkened he may say
> While friends sinke & princes frowne
> Vertue is the hardest way
> Yet at night a bed of Downe

Tunc lapsus alto culmine gloria	Tunc amicorum fugiat corona
Dum cauta fallit turba clientium	Et necem princeps rigido minetur
Et rex minatur; dura, cantet,	Ore, cantabit, placidum est cubile
Dulce parat pietas cubile.	Ardua virtus.[66]

The striking *mise-en-page* of these double translations, with the sapphic and alcaic versions of the poem set alongside one another in the same way in all four manuscripts, immediately suggests a markedly Horatian interpretation of the poem. Indeed, the Latin versions are full of echoes of Horace: in this section, the phrase *turba clientium* ('crowd of clients', 2 on the left) is borrowed from *Odes* 3.1.13, which is also in alcaics. But these lines are forcefully Senecan as well: the phrase *tunc lapsus alto culmine gloriae* ('then fallen from the high gable of glory', 1 on the left) borrows from the same much-imitated passage, the second chorus of Seneca's *Thyestes*, with which this chapter began: *stet quicumque volet potens | aulae **culmine lubrico*** (391–2, 'Stond who so list upon the slipper wheele, / Of hye astate'). The translator at this point has in fact conflated two separate passages of the *Thyestes*, blending the second chorus – which implies but does not explicitly state the possibility of falling from high office (*culmine lubrico*, 'on the slippery gable') – with Thyestes' speech near the end of the play, where he describes himself as *ex alto culmine lapsum* ('fallen from a high gable', 927). The translation in this way combines Horace's non-specific disdain for popular favour with a much sharper reference to the memorably horrific evocation of personal disaster in the *Thyestes*. (Thyestes ends up unwittingly eating his own children.) The Latin translation of Wotton's poem reflects the origin of the 'moralizing lyric' in the translation of these classical texts, while also suggesting the personalized force of a poem widely interpreted at the time as being about (or even by) a particular victim of spectacular political misfortune.

---

[66] The text here is based on Harley MS 6038, with minor emendations based on the other witnesses. Pebworth notes only the two Harley manuscripts and does not discuss the Latin translations. The Latin versions are anonymous, though may be the work of Georg Weckherlin (1584–1653), a German poet resident in London. Reasons for this possible attribution are discussed in Moul, 'Dazel'd Thus with Height of Place'.

This oscillation between specific and generalizing effect is a feature of many of the poems belonging to this tradition that were written and published, especially by royalist authors, under pressure of the English Civil War (1642–51) and its immediate aftermath. Verse collections by Robert Herrick (*Hesperides*, 1648), Mildmay Fane (*Otia Sacra*, 1648), Richard Lovelace (*Lucasta*, 1649 and *Posthume Poems*, 1659) and Henry Vaughan (*Silex Scintillans*, 1650 and *Olor Iscanus*, 1651) all reflect an engagement with this tradition, sharpened by circumstance. Robert Herrick's 'His Age: Dedicated to his Peculiar Friend, Mr John Wickes, under the name of Postumus', first published in *Hesperides*, is one example of this kind of poem which is found in contemporary manuscript miscellanies as well as in print: *CELM* records ten copies. In common with many of the longer lyric poems of the period – such as Lovelace's 'The Grasse-hopper', 'Advice to my best Brother' and even (though to very different political effect) Marvell's 'Horatian Ode' – Herrick's poem has a well-recognized Horatian base: the opening lines follow Horace, *Odes* 4.7 (the ode to Postumus), though Herrick continues by imitating a series of Horace's moralizing passages, both lyric (*Odes* 2.16 and 2.18) and hexameter (*Satires* 2.6 and *Epistles* 1.10).[67]

Observations of this sort, however, are of limited help in understanding the strength and success of the English poem: for all the scholarly satisfaction in 'spotting' the Horatian allusions, the overall effect of Lovelace's poem is not very much like reading Horace at all. None of Horace's *Odes* are devoted so uniformly to moralizing, and the moralizing sentiments which in Herrick's poem are piled up, one after another, are found individually in Horace, often at the beginning or the end of a given poem, and almost always distanced or complicated by what follows or precedes. Moreover, the handful of Horace's *Odes* which are of anything close to the length of Herrick's poem are his grandest panegyric celebrations of public office and achievement. Formally, the closest analogues for this almost obsessive appropriation of Horatian motifs are found outside Horace himself: Herrick's poem is indebted stylistically to the more insistently moralizing Horatianism of Seneca and Boethius and their sixteenth-century imitators (such as the Lipsius lyric discussed above) but also, most proximately, to the mid-seventeenth-century vogue for extended

---

[67] The most important Horatian sources are *Odes*, 1.4, 2.14 and 4.7, with elements derived also from *Satires* 2.6, *Epistles* 1.10, and *Odes* 2.16 and 2.18; see the fine discussion in Martindale, 'Best Master'. Lovelace, 'Advice to my best Brother' is based loosely upon *Odes* 2.10, a poem which probably also stands behind Mildmay Fane's 'How to ride out a Storm' (*Otia Sacra*, 161–3).

philosophical and moralizing 'Horatian' poems exemplified by the Latin odes of the enormously popular Jesuit poet Casimir Sarbiewski (1595–1640).[68]

Similar observations can be made about Richard Lovelace's 'The Grasshopper. To my Noble Friend, Mr. Charles Cotton. Ode', first published in *Lucasta* (1649). This well-known and still frequently anthologized poem has often been described as Horatian, and does indeed have an Horatian core: the two stanzas addressed directly to Cotton (21–8) are based on Horace, *Odes* 1.9 and perhaps also *Epodes* 13.1–8, and the whole poem, as Joanna Martindale puts it, 'suggests' the Soracte ode.[69] Scholars have been quick to note that the opening twelve lines on the grasshopper are based not upon Horace but rather a poem from the Greek *Anacreontea* 43.[70] Except that, as Martindale pointed out in passing, Lovelace's model is almost certainly not directly Anacreon, but rather Sarbiewski's own Anacreontic grasshopper poem, *Odes* 4.23, given here with a translation by John Chatwin dating from the early 1680s:

> O quae populeâ summa sedens comâ,
> Caeli roriferis ebria lacrymis,
>   Et te voce, Cicada,
>   Et mutum recreas nemus.
>
> Post longas hiemes, dum nimium breuis
> Aestas se leuibus praecipitat rotis,
>   Festinos, age, lento
>   Soles excipe jurgio.
>
> Vt se quaeque dies attulit optima,
> Sic se quaeque rapit: nulla fuit satis
>   Vmquam longa voluptas,
>   Longus saepiùs est dolor.

---

[68] On Sarbiewski, see Schäfer (ed.), *Sarbiewski*. His odes appeared from 1625; the first published English translations are in G. H[ils], *Odes of Casimire* (1646), though English enthusiasm demonstrably precedes this publication by at least a decade. Hils' selection prints 25 odes, 3 epodes and 6 epigrams, all with facing translations. A prefatory English poem imagines Horace and Sarbiewski seated together upon the summit of the Muses' hill. Quotations of the Latin in this chapter are from Sarbiewski, *Lyricorum Libri IV* (1634).

[69] Martindale, 'Best Master', 74. Don Cameron Allen sensitively remarks: 'The remedy for the moment is provided by the doctrine of Horace [i.e. in stanzas 6–7], although the inner conviction of an infinite present, once satisfaction is procured, is totally Christian' (*Image and Meaning*, 154). Allen does not mention Sarbiewski, but his remark applies equally well to Sarbiewski's verse.

[70] See McDowell, *Poetry and Allegiance*, 128; Allen, *Image and Meaning*, 80–92. Abraham Cowley's 'The Grasshopper,' is an imitation of the Greek lyric, on which see Mason, 'Abraham Cowley and the Wisdom of Anacreon'. On the vogue for the Anacreontea, see O'Brien, *Anacreon Redivivus*.

> Thrice happy Thou! Who on the Poplar's Boughs,
> Sit'st drunk with Heav'n's Ambrosial Dews.
> And with thy Notes thyself, dost please,
> And all the num'rous Throng of list'ning Trees.
>
> After long Colds and odious Winters past,
> On nimble Wheels the Summers hast;
> Blame its unkindness, gently say –
> The Sun too soon withdraws his chearing Ray.
>
> As ev'ry happy Day itself does show,
> So in a trice it leaves us too,
> No pleasure over long remains
> For short-liv'd joys We meet with lasting pains.[71]

Lovelace's image of the grasshopper drinking the tears of dew, which has been described as an original elaboration on his part, in fact comes directly from Sarbiewski (*Caeli roriferis ebria lacrymis*, 'drunk with the dew-bearing tears of heaven', 2). Most relevant to this chapter, however, is the blend of elements in the final stanza of the poem:

> Thus richer than untempted Kings are we,
>   That asking nothing, nothing need:
> Though Lord of all what Seas imbrace; yet he
>   That wants himselfe, is poore indeed.

The first couplet here, as Scodel has noted, is close to three lines from that most ubiquitous of models, the kingship chorus of Seneca's *Thyestes*: *Rex est qui metuet nihil, / rex est qui cupiet nihil: / hoc regnum sibi quisque dat* ('He is king who shall fear nothing, / He is king who shall desire nothing: / Each man grants this kingdom to himself', 388–90), itself a popular trope (compare for instance Sarbiewski *Odes* 4.3, 'Regnum sapientis', 'The Kingdom of the wise man').[72] But Lovelace's conclusion combines Seneca not, as we might have expected, with Horace directly, but rather with lines drawn once again from the 'Polish Horace', Sarbiewski (here given with Hils' translation):

---

[71] Bod. MS Rawl. poet. 94, fols. 223–6. One of six English translations printed in Fordoński and Urbański (eds.), *Casimir Britannicus*, 112.
[72] Scodel, *Excess and the Mean*, 232. Modern scholarship considers lines 388–9 to be possible interpolations (Tarrant (ed.), *Seneca's Thyestes*, 146); they were accepted as authentic, however, by the poets and translators under discussion.

> Pauper est, qui se caret; & superbè
> Ipse se librans, sua rura latam
> Addit in lancem, socioque fallens
>   Pondus in auro,
> Ceteris paruus, sibi magnus vni,
> Ipse se nescit . . .
>   (*Odes* 4.34.9–14)
>
> *He's poore that wants himselfe, yet weighs*
> *Proudly himselfe; in this scale layes*
> *His lands, in th'other broad one, by,*
> *The false weight of his gold doth lye,*
> *Great to himselfe; to others small,*
> *That never knows himselfe at all.*[73]

The importance of Sarbiewski's lyrics to English poets of the seventeenth and eighteenth centuries has been noted several times, usually in reference to the strikingly large number of English translations from this period. Poets of the mid-seventeenth century who engaged directly with Sarbiewski, in translation or imitation, include Mildmay Fane, Henry Vaughan, Abraham Cowley, Sir Edward Sherburne, Edward Benlowes and Andrew Marvell as well as Lovelace and Herrick.[74] But the stylistic influence of Sarbiewski extends well beyond specific translations or imitations: Sarbiewski's odes are markedly Horatian in their metre and diction – they are inconceivable without Horace; but Sarbiewski himself cited Martial and Seneca as his most important influences after Horace, and

---

[73] The combination of Seneca and Sarbiewski at the end of the poem is discussed briefly by McDowell, *Poetry and Allegiance*, 138. Neither Scodel nor McDowell notes the existence of Sarbiewski's 'grasshopper' poem, perhaps because *Ode* 4.23 is not one of those printed and translated in George Hil's 1646 English edition. McDowell claims 'the first three stanzas [of Lovelace's poem] are derived from *Anacreontea* 43' (128). He also suggests that Lovelace's poem is a response to Stanley's version of *Anacreontea* 43, published in 1647, which he discusses at some length (128–30).

[74] Seven paraphrases were published in Vaughan's *Olor Iscanus* (1651); seven also in Sherburne, *Poems and Translations* (1651). There are at least seven English versions of Sarbiewski, *Odes* 2.5, including versions by Abraham Cowley and Isaac Watts. Lovelace, *Lucasta* (1649) includes a translation of *Odes* 4.13 ('To his Deare Brother Colonel F. L.', 110–11), a poem also translated, among English poets alone, by Vaughan, Watts and Thomas Yalden (on which see Arens, 'Sarbiewski's Ode Against Tears'). John Hall's 1649 elegy for Henry, Lord Hastings, published in *Lachrymae Musarum*, is also an adaptation of Sarbiewski's *Ode* 4.13 (see Clarke, 'Royalists Write the Death of Lord Hastings'). On Sarbiewski and English poetry, see, briefly but effectively, Davidson, *Universal Baroque*, 31–2; Røstvig, *Happy Man* and 'Benlowes, Marvell, and the Divine Casimire'; Fordoński and Urbański (eds.), *Casimir Britannicus*; Gömöri, 'Polish Swan Triumphant'; Money, 'Aspects of the Reception of Sarbiewski'; Birrel, 'Sarbiewski, Watts and the Later Metaphysical Tradition'; Brown, 'Towards an Archaeology of English Romanticism' (on Coleridge and Sarbiewski). The influence of Sarbiewski is discussed further in Chapter 6.

his critical writings make considerable use of Seneca.[75] Sarbiewski's odes are on average significantly longer than those of Horace, and in their meditative circling around a given ethical point resembles Seneca's moralizing choruses more than any of Horace's own lyrics. They are much more consistently moralizing than Horace, both in the proportion of poems devoted to moral themes, and in the lack of any tendency to turn aside from or aslant to the moral which is so distinctive of Horace's own lyric output.[76] His explicitly Christian and often devotional lyrics repeatedly start from Horace, but also seek to augment and sometimes directly confront the pagan poet, as in his third epode, 'Palinodia. Ad secundam libri Epodon Odam Q. Horatii Flacci. Laus otii Religiosi' ('Palinode. On the second ode in Horace's book of Epodes. Praise of religious leisure') which rewrites *Epodes* 2, beginning: *At ille, Flacce, nunc erit beatior, / Qui mole curarum procul / Paterna liquit rura, litigantium / Solutus omni iurgio* ('But that man, Flaccus, will now be even more blessed / Who far removed from weight of cares / Leaves his ancestral lands, released / From all the quarrels of litigants'). In other words, both the Horatian and un-Horatian elements of his style closely resemble the similar points made above about Herrick and Lovelace.

Sarbiewski's *Ode* 3.4, for instance, bears the kind of generalizing title typical of Tottel's miscellany: 'Ad Egnatium Nollium. Aequo semper rectoque animo adversus Fortunae inconstantiam standum esse', translated by Hils as 'To Egnatius Nollius. That we ought to be of an even and upright mind, against the inconstancy of fortune.' It is a very beautiful but typically 'one-note' poem that draws extensively and recognizably upon Horace and the wider 'Horatian' lyric tradition but which, in its unironized moralizing, rhetorical structure and marked use of alliteration in the final stanza, is closer to Kipling than to Horace himself:

> Siue te molli vehet aura vento,
> Siue non planis agitabit vndis;
> Vince Fortunam, dubiasque NOLLI,
>   Lude per artes.
> Riserit? vultum generosus aufer.
> Fleuerit? dulci refer ora risu:
> Solus, & semper tuus esse quouis
>   Disce tumultu.

---

[75] See Li Vigni, *Poeta quasi creator*; Stawecka (ed.), *Sarbiewski. Dii Gentium Bogowie Pogan*, e.g. 176, 190, 280.

[76] 'The lyrics of the "divine Casimire" single out *beatus ille* motifs with much greater frequency than had previously been the case and also fuse them more fervently with Christian ideas' (Røstvig, *Happy Man*, 14).

> Ipse te clausam modereris vrbem
> Consul aut Caesar; quoties minantûm
> Turba Fatorum quatient serenam
>   Pectoris arcem.
> Cum leues visent tua tecta Casus,
> Laetus occurres: praeeunte luctu
> Faustitas & Pax subeunt eosdem
>   Saepe penates.
> Dextra sors omnis gerit hoc sinistrum,
> Quod facit molles: habet hoc sinistra
> Prosperum, quem non ferit, imminentes
>   Durat in ictus.
> Ille qui longus fuit, esse magnus
> Desinit moeror. facilem ferendo
> Finge Fortunam; levis esse longo
>   Discit ab vsu.

Again with Hils' translation:

> Art thou blow'n on, with gentle gale,
> Or in rough waters forc'd to sayle?
> Still conquer Fortune, make but sports
> Of her, and her uncertain Arts.
> Laughs shee? turne bravely away thy face.
> Weeps she? bring't back, with smiling grace:
> When shee's most busie, be thou than
> Retyr'd, and alwayes thine own man.
> Thus close shut up, thine owne free state
> Thou best mayst rule, chiefe Magistrate;
> When the fierce Fates shall most molest,
> The serene palace of thy brest.
> When light mischance, thy sort, or thee
> Shall visit; meet it merrily:
> Good luck, and peace, in that house stay
> Where mourning, first, hath led the way.
> In dext'rous chance, this hurt we see,
> It makes us soft: Extremity –
> This, prosperous hath, wheresoe're it hits,
> It hardens, and for danger fits.
> The griefe that hath been of such length,
> Doth 'bate its violence and strength.
> By bearing much, make fortune free;
> Shee learnes, by custome, light to be.

An enormous commonplace book, now in Cambridge University Library, demonstrates exhaustively which Latin poets seemed to readers in the mid-seventeenth century to 'belong' together. The anonymous compiler repeatedly draws upon various combinations of Horace, Boethius, Seneca and 'Casimir' (i.e. Sarbiewski) under moralizing headings.[77] The page for 'Aequabilitas, aequanimitas' ('Equanimity'), for instance, contains four main entries, two of which are accompanied by further cross-references.[78] The first is an extract from Horace, *Odes* 2.3: *Aequam memento rebus in arduis / Seruare mentem, non secus ac bonis / Ab insolenti temperatam / Laetitia* ('Remember to keep a level head, / In difficult times, and in good ones restrain / Yourself from intemperate joy'), with a cross-reference to *Odes* 2.10, on the golden mean. A further cross-reference, without quotations, refers us to Sarbiewski's *Odes* 3.4 (given above) and 4.13. The next extract is also from Horace (though not attributed to him) – this time from the *Epistles*, the most systematically philosophizing of all Horace's works. The third is from Boethius *Cons.* 1 met. 4: *Quisquis composito serenus aeuo / fatum sub pedibus &c.* ('He who has ground proud fate beneath his heel / Calm in his own well-ordered life', translated in BL MS Harley 3910 and discussed above). This is accompanied by further references, without quotations, to Boethius *Cons.* 2. pros. 2, and Sarbiewski *Odes* 2.6, 4.3 and 4.13: Sarbiewski 4.13 is the same poem to which Horace *Odes* 2.3 was also linked. The final extract under this heading is a five-line quotation from Seneca's *Herc. Oet.*

The order of entries suggests that the compiler of this manuscript, having already begun a commonplace book, at some point read Sarbiewski with great enthusiasm, and set about adding cross-references from Sarbiewski, as on this page, to many of the existing entries.[79] Here we have a vivid glimpse of what it was like to encounter Sarbiewski for the first time in England in the seventeenth century, and with which earlier poets and texts he was naturally associated by his readers. Indeed, Sarbiewski's lyrics – and especially the subset of them most often translated or imitated

---

[77] CUL MS Dd. IX. 59. The catalogue describes the manuscript as c.1700, but this is misleading (a paper slip available in the manuscripts room describes it more accurately as 'seventeenth century'). Though mostly in Latin, the commonplace book includes extracts also in Greek and English. Identifiable printed sources include a large number from between the late 1620s and mid-1630s, though none datable definitely to after 1635. It was therefore very probably put together in the mid-1630s. Drayton is the most frequently cited poet in English; Sarbiewski and Buchanan are the most frequently cited post-classical Latin poets.

[78] CUL MS Dd. IX. 59, fol. 10ᵛ.

[79] Similar discernible 'layers' of entries are drawn from Buchanan's Latin verse drama and from Thomas Farnaby's collection of Greek epigrams, *Florilegium epigrammatum Graecorum* (1629), in which each Greek epigram is accompanied by a Latin verse translation (many by Farnaby himself). The compiler of the manuscript has copied both Greek and Latin passages and adds the attributions of the Latin as in the printed text.

in England – fit precisely within the blended tradition of Latin moralizing lyric which is the subject of this chapter, a point which no doubt partly explains their great popularity. Sarbiewski offered English readers a 'Christian Horace' who accorded more closely than Horace himself with the most influential aspects of the 'Horatian' tradition at the time.

Just as Lovelace's 'Grasse-hopper' ends with a highly conventional quatrain which sounds (and indeed in a sense is) broadly 'Horatian' but which in its details is drawn most directly from Seneca and Sarbiewski (that is, a Christianized Horatianism), so in several collections of this period we find Sarbiewski standing in for Horace in sequences of translation: Henry Vaughan's *Olor Iscanus* (1651), for instance, juxtaposes translations of Ovid's exile poetry, Boethius and Sarbiewski.[80] Such sequences demonstrate how the stock of popular poems of this general type is updated over time.

We find the same phenomenon in relation to original poems as well as translations. First published as the closing song of his 1650s play *The Contention of Ajax and Ulysses*, James Shirley's (1596–1666) 'The glories of our blood and state' quickly circulated widely as a lyric in this tradition:

> The glories of our blood and state
>   Are shadows, not substantial things;
> There is no armour against Fate;
>   Death lays his icy hand on kings:
>   Sceptre and Crown
>   Must tumble down,
> And in the dust be equal made
> With the poor crooked scythe and spade.
>
> Some men with swords may reap the field,
>   And plant fresh laurels where they kill:
> But their strong nerves at last must yield;
>   They tame but one another still:
>   Early or late
>   They stoop to fate,
> And must give up their murmuring breath
> When they, pale captives, creep to death.

---

[80] Four translations from Ovid's *Tristia* and *Ex Ponto*; twelve of the metrical portions of Boethius; seven of Sarbiewski. Boethius' work had particular resonance in the 1650s: both Sir Edward Spencer's summary and commentary (1654) and Theodor Poelman's complete edition (1655) were published in this decade in London.

> The garlands wither on your brow;
>   Then boast no more your mighty deeds!
> Upon Death's purple altar now
>   See where the victor-victim bleeds.
>   Your heads must come
>   To the cold tomb:
> Only the actions of the just
> Smell sweet and blossom in their dust.[81]

Though composed a century later, Shirley's poem plays upon the suggestive ambiguity of 'state' in the same way as the moralizing lyrics in Tottel's miscellany.

Like Wotton's lyric before it, Shirley's poem was also translated into Latin. Leeds Brotherton Collection MS Lt 55, a miscellany of mainly satiric verse from the 1670s, includes a double translation of Shirley's poem first into hexameters, and then into rather effective sapphic stanzas, two per English verse. The final English stanza is translated as follows:

> Frontibus marcent virides coronae
> Temperent se facta loqui superbi
> En jacet mortis tepidum piamen
>   Victor in aras
> Frigidas omnes veniunt ad urnas
> Facta sed justi generosa solum
> Post necem fragrant, vegetoque semper
>   Pulvere florent.[82]

As in the Latin translations of Wotton's 'Dazel'd thus with height of place', the choice of sapphic stanzas points towards the Latin lyric history of the form, and inserts Shirley's poem as it were 'back' into the nexus of classical and classicizing models from which it emerges. If the form is similar to the Wotton translations of the 1620s, however, the style of the Latin is quite different: the Latin poem shares with its English model a metaphorical boldness typical of its period. In this way we see how the striking continuities of the moralizing lyric form, in terms of tone and content, run alongside changes in style.

Such 'fashionable' iterations of the moralizing lyric extend also to matters of form. A collection of verse assembled by one John Watson

---

[81] Shirley, *Contention of Ajax and Ulysses* (1659), end of Act III; Gifford and Dyce (eds.), *Dramatic Works and Poems*, vol. VI, 369–97. *CELM* records 41 copies, some accompanied by music, in manuscripts dating from the 1660s to the late eighteenth century.

[82] Leeds University Library, MS BC Lt 55, fol. 10ʳ. The *CELM* entry for this manuscript (ShJ 163.5) recognizes that the Latin poem in hexameters is a translation of Shirley's poem (which follows it), but not that this sapphic ode is also a translation of it.

between 1667 and 1673 preserves a Latin translation of Shirley's poem into rhyming, stress-based stanzas rather than classical quantitative metre:

> Natalium Lux et Magnificentia
> Res sunt umbraticae Minimèque Entia ;
> Nil contra Fatum praevalent Arma
> Aurea nec Reges proteget Parma,
>   Sceptra & Caesariae Trabeae
>   Invasae dirâ Mortis rabie
> Plebi jungentur et inanes
> Amborum capiet Urna manes.
> (lines 1–8, corresponding to the first English stanza)[83]

The use of end rhyme obviously recalls the English poem, though it does not precisely reproduce the rhyme scheme of Shirley's original (ABABCCDD): instead, the Latin poem consistently groups the rhyming words together (AABBCCDD; in the first stanza only, AA and BB also rhyme, though more weakly). Though generally associated with medieval Latin verse, rhyming Latin poetry and songs were produced throughout early modernity, a point discussed further in Chapter 8, and indeed appear to have been particularly popular in the latter part of the seventeenth century, the period to which this manuscript belongs. This is also the period in which we find the greatest quantity of Latin poems which are translated from English. In both these respects, then, Watson's manuscript reflects the fashions of its day.

Half a century later, Isaac Watts, a dissenting poet and the first of the great English hymn-writers, turns to Sarbiewski, a Polish Jesuit, alongside and in some respects more readily than to Horace himself. Watts made many translations of Sarbiewski, and his early English poetry includes dozens of pieces which belong clearly to the tradition traced in this essay, such as this extract from his poem 'To Mr. John Lock Retired from The World of Business':

> He that has Treasures of his own
> May leave the Cottage or the Throne,
> May Quit the Globe, and dwell alone
>   Within his spacious Mind.[84]

Indeed, by the mid-eighteenth century Watts himself had been assimilated into sequences of moralizing verse in manuscript miscellanies: a Latin and

---

[83] BL MS Add. 18220, fol. 47ʳ, one of several instances of Latin verse translations of English poetry in this manuscript.
[84] Watts, *Horae Lyricae* (1706), 118. *Horae Lyricae*, Watts' first published collection, went through many subsequent editions and contains some Latin as well as (mostly) English poetry. On Watts and Latin religious verse, see Chapter 6.

English collection by the Quaker John Kelsall (1683–1743) includes a paraphrase of Horace, *Odes* 2.10 (on the golden mean), four English psalm paraphrases translated from Buchanan's Latin, several original moralizing poems ('On Obedience' and 'On Contentment') in both English and Latin versions, and an English paraphrase of one of Watt's own hymns ('On Parting with carnal Joys. Paraphras'd from Watt's Hymn 10 Book 2').[85]

Wotton's 'Dazel'd thus' is a beautiful example of a type of poem which is immediately recognizable to any sensitive and experienced reader of English poetry, a mode of verse which has persisted relatively unchanged through successive waves of poetic fashion: this is not the poetry of Elizabethan sonneteers or love elegists; nor is it 'metaphysical' verse or Augustan satire. Poetry of this kind has an enduring, if enduringly unfashionable, role in English literature: Kipling's poem 'If –', quoted at the start of this chapter, is an expansion of the theme – of consistent virtue and restraint in the face of both good and ill fortune – which is the subject of Seneca's most widely translated chorus (*Thyestes* 336–403) as well as the opening lines of Horace, *Odes* 4.9, and indeed Sarbiewski's *Odes* 2.1. 'If –' was voted Britain's favourite poem in a 1995 BBC opinion poll; Wotton's 'How happy is he born and taught' was apparently George Washington's favourite hymn; and the hymns of Watts and Wesley are still sung regularly in Christian churches of many denominations around the world.[86]

Kipling is almost as out of fashion as Wotton and Watts, but he was a fine reader of Horace, and his memorable immortalization of a peculiarly English brand of stoicism descends directly, via Jonson, Wotton and the English hymn book, from Horace.[87] Recent classical criticism has shown little interest in Horace's moral and philosophical lyrics (less so than in the philosophical content of his hexameter verse), and has done almost nothing with Horace as a religious poet, although many of his odes are formally hymns, a point of great importance for his early modern readers. This hymnic element of Horatian lyric forms the foundation for its use in psalm paraphrase, to which the next two chapters turn. But to gain a sense of the moralizing tradition of 'Horatian' lyric, we do best to read not the criticism of our own day, but poetry: the poetry of Seneca and Boethius, but also of Wyatt, Wotton, Sarbiewski, Lovelace, Vaughan and Watts.

---

[85] Society of Friends Archive, MS Vol S 193/5. [86] Spann and Williams, *Presidential Praise*, 5–8.
[87] Kipling wrote several poems titled as odes from 'Book V' of Horace; on Kipling's Horace, see Medcalf, 'Horace's Kipling'.

CHAPTER 2

Metrical Variety and the Development of Latin Lyric Poetry in the Latter Sixteenth Century

The lively late Elizabethan debate about the decorum of rhyme and the role of quantitative metrics is well known.[1] But the intense interest in metrical matters at this period, which culminates in the metrical variety and pronounced innovation of the Sidney psalter and, ultimately, in the achievement of Herbert's *Temple*, sits within, and emerges from, a geographically wider and chronologically precedent Latin phenomenon. It is not that poets and theorists such as Roger Ascham, Gabriel Harvey, Richard Stanyhurst, George Puttenham, Abraham Fraunce, Thomas Campion, Fulke Greville and Philip and Mary Sidney began to wrestle with the question of how classical quantitative metres might be transferred to English verse for no particular reason. They were thinking about these matters because the contemporary use of *Latin* metre underwent very rapid change in the second half of the sixteenth century, leading to an explosion in the possibilities especially of Latin lyric, as well as a series of technical guides and handbooks.

Relatively few modern readers have a good grasp even of basic classical Latin metres; this is considerably complicated in the case of neo-Latin verse, which uses a wider range of metres than those typically encountered by classics students today, and in which new metrical forms were often created. Several of the quantitative metres found in the Latin verse of the later sixteenth century have no standard scholarly descriptor (although, unlike some of the Latin poetry of the seventeenth century, their constituent parts can almost always be identified in classical terms). Although it has passed almost unnoticed by scholarship, metrical creativity is one of the most astonishing features of the Latin poetry of this period, and it is nowhere more evident than in the collections of psalm paraphrases. We cannot begin to appreciate the literary excitement caused by this

---

[1] See Attridge, *Well-Weighed Syllables*; Hardison, *Prosody and Purpose*; Schmidt, 'Realigning English Vernacular Poetics'.

work – and by its vernacular imitations, such as the remarkable metrical display of the Sidney psalter – without understanding something of the music of Latin metre, and of the pace of Latin metrical innovation in the latter sixteenth century.

This section of the book seeks therefore to do two related things: first, in this chapter, to offer a 'big picture' overview of Latin metrical innovation and experiment, as it reached and was received and taught in England, in the latter half of the sixteenth century; and then, in the chapters that follow, to trace the effect of these innovations as they played out in both Latin and English poetry. Chapter 3 places the greatest English lyric achievement of Elizabethan England, the Sidney psalter, within the wider and largely Latin tradition of psalm paraphrase to which it belongs, and sets out an argument for the close relationship between the Sidney psalter and its primary (but almost entirely neglected) literary models, the Latin psalm paraphrase collections of George Buchanan and Théodore de Bèze (Beza).[2] The final part of Chapter 3 continues this story into the seventeenth century, while the further development of religious and devotional lyric between George Herbert and Isaac Watts is the subject of Chapter 6. Chapter 4 turns from scriptural and religious lyric to the related, but more gradual, emergence of the formal panegyric ode in English, and places that development in the context of the evolution of the Latin ode in England between the mid-sixteenth and the mid-seventeenth century. Chapter 5, on the relationship between the English and Latin traditions of Pindaric odes and related experimental forms, also begins in the latter sixteenth century, with the impact upon English literary culture of the Latin and French Pindaric experiments of that period. In this way, we see how a whole series of landmarks in English poetry – from the Sidney psalter, to Herbert's *Temple*, the odes of Jonson and of Cowley, Marvell's 'Horatian Ode' and even the work of the first of the great eighteenth-century hymn-writers, Isaac Watts – represent different facets of the working out in English poetry of the extraordinary period of Latin formal and metrical innovation in the latter half of the sixteenth century. This story of rapid waves of formal innovation stands alongside the account given in Chapter 1 of the enduring popularity throughout this period of a type of verse, the moralizing lyric, characterized by its tone and content rather than its form.

---

[2] For clarity, I have throughout this book referred to Théodore de Bèze as 'Bèze' if referring to his works in French, and as 'Beza' when referring to his works in Latin.

The story of the development of new Latin lyric metres in the latter sixteenth century has not been told; in several instances, as noted above, even the requisite technical vocabulary has not been fully established, or is used inconsistently.[3] As a result, this chapter is unusually technical. This is, I think, unavoidable: these *are* technical matters, which were taught technically in sixteenth-century England from an early age. Readers who are unfamiliar with the quantitative principles of Latin poetry might wish to start with the brief appendix on Latin metre. We should not, however, overemphasize the difficulty. All words in both Latin and English can be described in terms of quantity (some syllables typically take longer to pronounce than others) as well as stress (some syllables are typically emphasized more than others, a particularly important feature of English pronunciation). Though most Latin metres are based on the patterns created by different quantities, and most English metres are based on the patterns created by stress, anyone can learn to listen for both, and in practice the best poetry in either language makes use of both these elements to various degrees.

The essential principles of quantitative metre, and an outline of the most common patterns, were an element of even the most basic Latin grammars. In a period in which Latin verse was encountered from the start of education, in which much didactic material was in Latin verse, and it was widely assumed that the versifying of knowledge made it easier, not harder, to remember, matters of metre probably seemed a good deal less daunting than they do even to experienced readers of Latin today. A surprisingly wide range of early modern readers, including some women as well as any men who had had a grammar school education, would have been familiar with metrical terms which are now the province only of specialists – this is clear, for instance, from the metrical notes typically provided in the editions of both Buchanan's and Beza's psalters (and indeed routinely in editions of Buchanan for more than a century), and from the metrical comments in surviving school notebooks. But these matters are not *merely* technical. We should always remember that metrical terms describe sound. The great expansion in metrical options for Latin poets and readers in this period transformed the 'soundscape' of Latin lyric verse. In order to give some sense of this aural transformation, I have where possible in this chapter used

---

[3] For instance, the various ways of numbering the asclepiad metres used by Horace is particularly unhelpful when attempting to use these terms to describe neo-Latin variations and innovations upon an aeolic base.

examples of quantitative metres (or their approximations) in English, both from early modern and more recent sources.

Latin Psalm Paraphrase and Humanist Practice

The metrical variety typical of Latin psalm paraphrase collections, and of latter sixteenth-century Latin verse experiments more generally, is both profoundly unclassical and also distinct from humanist practice. For readers and scholars without specialist training, it is easy to assume that all neo-Latin verse is statically classical, simply revisiting, albeit in different cultural, political and religious contexts, forms and genres established in Augustan Rome. This is not straightforwardly true of any aspect of Renaissance and early modern Latin poetry, and it is particularly misleading in the case of psalm paraphrase, which is unclassical both in its metrical innovation and in its formal variety, as well as in the (biblical) texts on which it is founded.

The standard model for the publication of humanist Latin verse composition involved 'books' of poems organized by genre and metre, many of which were (broadly speaking) classical, though others were not: George Buchanan's (1506–82) work, for instance, includes a book of elegies, a book of hendecasyllables, three books of epigrams and one of iambics, and a didactic poem (*De Sphaera*) in five books, as well as a miscellaneous volume of *Silvae*, and his psalm paraphrases.[4] In this, Buchanan is typical of Latin poets from the early humanists to his own contemporaries and beyond – compare the similar arrangements of the verse of, for instance, Giovanni Pontano (1426–1503), Jacopo Sannazaro (1458–1530), and indeed Beza's (1519–1605) own 1548 *Juvenilia* (containing elegies, epitaphs, epigrams and a *Silva* collection).[5] Other possible 'books' with a classical basis included dedicated collections of odes, eclogues (as in Mantuan, *Adulescentia* or Spenser's *Shepherds' Calendar*), love elegy (such as Christoforo Landino's *Xandra* or Pontano's *De amore coniugali*), satire, verse epistles, *Heroides* and epic. Non-classical forms which were

---

[4] These are broadly, though not purely, classical categories. There are no classical books of hendecasyllables as such (though Catullus wrote many poems in this metre). The very popular Renaissance *Silvae* collections have a single classical model (the *Silvae* of Statius).

[5] Pontano's volumes of verse include the *Parthenopeus* (love poetry in elegiac and lyric metres), *Eclogues*, *Lyra* (in Horatian lyric metres), *De tumulis* (elegiac imaginary tomb inscriptions), *Baiae* (hendecasyllables) and *De laudibus divinis* (hymns) as well as didactic poetry and two other collections of elegiac love poetry (*De amore coniugali* and *Eridanus*); Sannazaro published an epic poem (*De partu virginis*), piscatory eclogues (*Piscatoria*) as well as many elegies and epigrams published posthumously as three volumes each of *Elegiae* and *Epigrammata*.

frequently the basis of entire verse books in the latter sixteenth century include *Tumuli* (imagined verse inscriptions for those who have died, a form invented by Pontano), *Urbes* (poems on famous cities, such as those by Julius Caesar Scaliger and by John Johnston, some of the latter of which were included by Camden in *Britannia*), *Anacreontea* (poems modelled on the 'anacreontic' verse in the Greek Anthology, a vogue initiated by Henri Estienne's *Carmina Anacreontica* published in 1554) and *Aenigmata* (verse riddles, such as those by Scaliger and Hadrianus Junius). Two particularly influential volumes of Latin verse in 1580s England were the collections of odes and elegies by the German poet Paulus Melissus (Paul Schede, 1539–1602), and the Latin odes of the Dutchman Janus Dousa (1545–1604), accompanied by a collection of *Silvae*.[6] Dousa also published two books of Latin elegies and a book of epigrams. Many generically organized collections of this sort appeared also in the vernacular: Ronsard composed collections of *Odes*, *Hymnes* and *Amours* as well as an (unfinished) epic poem; Michael Drayton (1563–1631) published books of eclogues, *Heroides* and odes in the 1590s and first decades of the seventeenth century; Milton published a 'first' book of Latin elegies, though never produced a second. Ben Jonson's *Epigrams*, *Forest* and *Underwoods* are similarly intended to recall the humanist 'book categories' of *Silvae* (meaning literally 'woods') and *Epigrammata*. Many similar projects are extant only in manuscript.

In practice, some degree of 'unclassical' variety was common within these parameters. Books of Latin elegies quite frequently include the occasional poem in a lyric metre as, for instance, in Petrus Lotichius Secundus' *Elegiarum liber* (1551). The same is true of epigram collections. Both Jonson's *Epigrams* and George Herbert's Latin epigram collection, *Lucus*, for instance, contain one very long poem; Campion's first book of *Epigrammata* includes several poems in lyric metres.[7] Though modelled on Statius' five books of *Silvae*, the *silva* collection was a much more important element of Renaissance and early modern Latin poetry than it is in any classical canon. Although a *silva* collection is

---

[6] Melissus, *Schediasmata poetica* (1586); Dousa, *Odarum Britannicarum Liber* (1586). Every one of Melissus' nine books of odes and five books of elegies begins with a poem to Queen Elizabeth I. Dousa's *Odes* includes a poem addressed to Melissus and was owned by Camden (Westminster Abbey CB 7 (8). For the Latin political ode, see Chapter 4.

[7] The second edition of Campion's epigrams (*Epigrammatum Libri* II, 1619), reorganized and with additional material, is much less metrically varied. This reflects the changing Latin literary fashions of the early seventeenth vs. the late sixteenth century, and specifically the enormous influence upon Latin epigram of John Owen (on which see Chapter 7).

by definition mixed, and these books often (as in the case of Statius and Jonson) included a few poems in lyric metres, the term suggests a collection of verse written for various specific occasions, assembled after the fact, and without any claim to particular coherence: it is a much less 'grand' and ambitious form than the stand-alone lyric collections of Horace or Pindar, and *silva* collections typically contain at most only a handful of poems in lyric metres.[8]

The verse collection of Catullus, written mainly in elegiac couplets and hendecasyllables, also contains a small number of lyric and iambic metres, and two long poems in hexameter. The intense metrical variety of the *Odes* and *Epodes* of Horace are, however, the closest single classical model for the psalm paraphrase collections: in early modernity, the *Epodes* were often considered a fifth book of *Odes*, and the psalms are also traditionally divided into five books, strengthening the connection. When Buchanan first published in 1565/6 a complete psalter that incorporated in a single poetic work not only lyric and iambic metres, but also elegiac couplets and hexameters (indeed, Buchanan's first psalm is in hexameter), he was doing something technically audacious and, in literary terms, highly ambitious; but he was also making a strong 'completist' claim for the psalter as a work of literature: a book of poetry (and, by extension, a holy poet, King David) which includes within it all that is poetic.[9] In this way, the psalmist becomes a kind of ultra-classical poet: a master not only (like Horace, Pindar or Orpheus with whom he is most often associated) of technically challenging and aurally beautiful lyric forms, but also of forms associated with epic, love poetry and even satire and invective.[10] As George Wither

---

[8] The modesty topos may of course be disingenuous. Recent criticism on Statius' *Silvae* has emphasized thematic and political coherence, and similar arguments could certainly be made about many of the neo-Latin *silva* collections.

[9] Buchanan's psalter contains 30 separate metres in the earliest editions; then, following some revision, 29 in all subsequent ones. Buchanan continued to revise his psalms until his death in 1582. The polymetric quality of Buchanan's psalter is probably inspired in particular by the psalm paraphrases of Jean Macrin (published in his three books of lyric *Hymni*, 1537–40) and of Marc Antonio Flaminio (published in 1548), both of whom used Horatian metres. Neither however produced a complete psalter. Green, *Poetic Paraphrase*, 33 points out that Buchanan's metrical diversity surpasses that of Ausonius, Prudentius and Boethius as well as Horace and almost all earlier neo-Latin poets.

[10] Buchanan did not, however, use hendecasyllables for any of the psalms. This was a very common metre at the time, and indeed one in which he had composed an entire book of Latin verse. This was probably out of a sense of decorum due to the association of hendecasyllables with Catullus, and perhaps specifically because many early humanists used hendecasyllables for erotically explicit verse, such as Pontano's *Pruritus* (1449), *Parthenopeus* (1457) and *Baiae* (c.1500), and the hugely popular *Basia* of Johannes Secundus (1511–36).

put it in his 1619 *Preparation to the Psalter*: 'these holy *Hymnes* are not written all in one kinde of *Poesie*, but the Prophet hath made use almost of all sorts.'[11]

Though the complete set of Buchanan's Latin psalm paraphrases was widely available in continental editions from 1566 onwards, the first edition to be printed in England dates from 1580.[12] In this volume, a metrical appendix identifies each of the metres, and provides a metrical diagram. In most cases, the metres are also keyed to a specific model: several of his most common metres were borrowed from late antique (and, importantly, Christian) rather than classical poets, such as Prudentius and Boethius; a further handful had no ancient precedent.[13] Beza in his turn much extended this project by using an even larger number of metres for his psalter (47), including many which have no classical or late antique model, and which are probably his own invention; Beza also brought to Latin psalm paraphrase both a distinctively Protestant scriptural literalism, and styles and forms far removed from classical poetry, such as elements of rhyme and varied stanza structures. The element of innovation in these psalm paraphrase collections meant that they were quickly treated as metrical authorities in their own right.[14]

The impact of these collections depends upon an understanding of classical Latin metres and their associations: but as a project it is profoundly *unclassical*, cutting across the established formal and generic conventions of both classical and neo-classical, humanist verse. Buchanan and Beza were motivated by their conviction of the unrivalled excellence and completeness of the psalter as poetry, which should be reflected in its Latin literary form. But they were also responding – and in both cases significantly contributing – to a distinctive feature of contemporary Latin literary culture.

---

[11] Wyther [Wither], *Preparation to the Psalter*, 77.

[12] Buchanan, *Paraphrasis Psalmorum*. Further editions were published, also in London by Thomas Vautrollerius, in 1583 and 1592. Further editions were printed in Edinburgh in 1611, 1615 and 1621, and in London in 1620, 1640 and 1648. For a full account of the enormously frequent reprinting of Buchanan's psalms across Europe into the nineteenth century, see Green, *Poetic Paraphrase*, 26–32.

[13] Metrical appendix on pages 305–11. Aside from Horace, the poets cited as models for specific metres are Prudentius (three times), Boethius (also three times) and Claudian (once). The remaining metres have no classical authority: some are found elsewhere in neo-Latin poetry, others may have been Buchanan's own invention. For a fuller discussion of the metrical practice of Buchanan and Beza, see Chapter 3.

[14] The use of Buchanan as a metrical authority is discussed further in Chapter 3.

The Music of Anglo-Latin Poetry in the Latter Sixteenth Century: Metrical Variety

In England, the final third of the sixteenth century (closely followed by the first part of the seventeenth) is marked out from the periods that precede and follow it by the extraordinary pursuit of Latin metrical variety, not only in the psalm paraphrases, but in the writing of Latin poetry in general. Despite (and in part perhaps because of) the great wealth of surviving material, however, the neo-Latin metrical practice of England in the later sixteenth century has not been the subject of any previous dedicated scholarship.[15] This chapter offers a first attempt at a 'field guide' to the metrical fashions, and their associations, of the Latin poetry of this period.

Until the 1560s, both published and manuscript Latin verse in England was metrically conservative, dominated by hexameters (used frequently, and unclassically, for short, moralizing and didactic verse as well as longer items), elegiacs and, where we find lyric verse, mostly by end-stopped sapphic stanzas. The volume of Walter Haddon's scriptural verse paraphrases published in 1555, for instance, is limited to hexameter and elegiacs; John Seton's volume for the accession of Mary in 1553 contains only elegiacs and sapphics; Thomas Wilson's 1551 memorial volume for the Brandon brothers is one of the most metrically various of this period, containing also iambic dimeters and phalaecian hendecasyllables, but no Horatian lyric metres other than sapphic stanzas.[16]

The 'unclassical' Latin poetry most frequently found in mid-sixteenth-century manuscripts is in fact rhyming Latin verse of various kinds, including 'leonine' hexameters, a popular medieval form in which the end of the line rhymes with the middle, as well as poems written in end-rhymed stress-based metres. Although Buchanan, like most of the French and Italian humanist poets, avoids medieval forms of this kind, examples

---

[15] Many useful observations can be found in passing in Binns, *Intellectual Culture*, but he is more interested in genre than metre as such and includes no systematic survey of metrical matters. Some useful work exists on specific trends in wider neo-Latin verse in this period (usually with limited if any discussion of Anglo-Latin examples), such as O'Brien, *Anacreon Redivivus*, and Laurens, 'La réussite tardive d'un Anacréon latin' on the fashion for anacreontics following the publication of Estienne's *Carmina Anacreontica* (1554). The relationship between the metrical innovation of Ronsard and the Pléiade poets and contemporary Latin practice, for instance, deserves further investigation, though see Schmitz, 'L'ode latine'. It would be particularly interesting to know to what extent metrical trends were passing between countries.

[16] Walter Haddon, *Oratio Iesu Christi* (1555) containing paraphrases of Matthew 5–7, the Epistle of St James, and Psalm 103; John Seton, *Panegyrici* (1553). The development of the sapphic in the latter half of the sixteenth century is discussed separately in Chapter 4. For a modern edition of Haddon's verse, see Lees (ed.), *Poetry of Walter Haddon*.

of both medieval and contemporary Latin poems in rhyming forms are found frequently in English manuscript sources of the sixteenth and seventeenth centuries. Willes' 1573 handbook of verse composition includes two examples of rhyming Latin verse, and many of Beza's psalm paraphrases – as discussed in Chapter 3 – have rhyming elements. The ongoing production and cultural role of rhyming Latin verse in early modern England is discussed in Chapter 8.

Though nineteen psalms had been published in 1556, Buchanan's complete Latin psalter was published for the first time in late 1565 or early 1566, and rapidly went through a large number of editions in several countries.[17] In England, it is in this decade that we begin, more generally, to see the stirrings of greater metrical experiment, especially in relation to Latin iambic and lyric metres. The remarkable Eton College collection for Queen Elizabeth is a particularly impressive early example.[18] Dating from 1563, its 77 poems contain 17 different metres, several of them found only very rarely even in neo-Latin poetry; many of the poems are also acrostics.[19] One of the poems is in alternating lines of sapphic hendecasyllables and the lesser asclepiad (choriambic tetrameter), a combination I have, so far, not encountered in any other Latin poem:

---

[17] On the dating of this (undated) edition and the print history of Buchanan's psalms, see Green, *Poetic Paraphrase*, 26–32.

[18] BL MS Royal 12 A XXX. This collection has been published with a parallel translation and brief notes by David Money, in Goldring *et al.* (eds.), *Progresses and Public Processions*, 259–368; see also Money, 'Musarum Pueritia'. Most other presentation volumes of manuscript verse from around this period remain metrically fairly conservative: compare for instance BL MS Royal 12 A XXXIII (complimentary verses to Edward VI by the boys of Winchester College, 1552), 43 poems, all elegiacs and hexameters apart from four in phalaecian hendecasyllables and two in stichic iambic dimeters; BL MS Lansdowne 388, item 13 (marking the visit of Cardinal Pole to Cambridge in 1557), 39 poems, all elegiacs or hexameter bar three odes in sapphics; BL MS Royal 12 A XLVII (1566 Oxford collection for the Queen's visit to Woodstock), 20 Latin poems, all in elegiacs apart from two in sapphics and one in stichic adoneans; BL MS Lansdowne 388, item 3 (1573 Winchester College collection for the Queen), 45 poems, all hexameter or elegiac apart from two in iambic trimeters and one each of iambic distichs, sapphics and dactylic tetrameter. The Eton collection appears in this respect ahead of its time, and more typical of the metrical diversity found in school manuscript collections in the final quarter of the century. Whether there are similar examples of such metrical variety in school presentation volumes made in France or the Netherlands in the mid-sixteenth century, I do not know, though I hope to extend this research to wider European collections in due course.

[19] The complete list of metrical forms is as follows: elegiacs, alcaics, hexameter, sapphic stanzas, sapphic hendecasyllables, phalaecian hendecasyllables, iambic trimeter, iambic dimeter, iambic distichs, stichic lesser asclepiad (as in *Odes* 1.1), two types of asclepiad stanza, stichic adonean, first archilochean, couplets composed of: (a) a sapphic hendecasyllable followed by an adonean; (b) a phalaecian hendecasyllable followed by a sapphic hendecasyllable (as in Boeth. 3.10); (c) a sapphic hendecasyllable followed by a lesser asclepiad. It would be interesting to know whether the headmaster, William Malym, or one of the other teachers was responsible for encouraging such variety.

> Eugè raucarum sonitus tubarum,
>   O Vindsora, meis perstrepit auribus.
> Audio certé peditum cateruam,
>   Hinnitum & tremulum quadrupedantium.
> Ne sit hostilis vereor caterua,
>   Quae Vindsora parat nos popularier.[20]
>
> *Hurrah for the sound of the raucous trumpets,*
>   *O Windsor, that echoes in my ears.*
> *I am sure that I hear a crowd of footsoldiers,*
>   *And the tremulous whinnying of horses.*
> *I am afraid that the crowd might be hostile,*
>   *A Windsor crowd which is preparing to lay waste to us.*

The quantitative patterns here are as follows:

– U – – – U U – U – –
– – – U U – – U U – U –[21]

Both lines are marked aurally by the succession of three long syllables, such as 'raūcārūm' and 'Ō Vīndsōr-', and a central single or double choriamb – U U –), as in '-ūm sonitūs' and '-sōra, meīs'. Three adjacent long syllables are easier to achieve in Latin than in English – over half of Latin syllables are long – but it is nevertheless an ear-catching tag. These distinctive aural elements – of repeated long syllables and one or more choriambs – are found in both of these lines as well as in several of the other standard choriambic lines used in asclepiad metres (discussed further below).

Though I am unaware of any late antique or medieval model for the specific combination used here, the English modernist poet Basil Bunting uses an English quantitative version at the opening of his *Odes* 1.9, giving the reader unused to Latin a sense of the aural effect:

> Dear be still! Time's start of us lengthens slowly.
> Bright round plentiful nights ripen and fall for us.[22]

---

[20] Royal 12 A XXX, Eton collection, 1563, fols. 27ʳ–8ʳ (quotation at 27r); ascribed to one 'Kinge', who contributed three poems in total. One of the schoolboy poets in this collection is Giles Fletcher, aged about 15 in 1563.

[21] This metrical combination, though apparently unique, is perhaps modelled on the similar combination of a sapphic hendecasyllable and a glyconic (that is, a choriambic trimeter rather than tetrameter) found once in Boethius (*Cons.* 2. *met.* 3) and four times in Buchanan (Psalms 33, 70, 121 and 142) .

[22] Bunting, *Complete Poems*, 105. Bunting's comments upon the role of quantity in English poetry are exemplary (Makin (ed.), *Basil Bunting on Poetry*, 26–30), and his own poetry is metrically among the most accomplished in English of any period.

Bunting makes a theme of the unusual 'fullness' of the lines, slowed by the pile-up of long syllables ('still! Time's start'; 'Bright round plent-'). The impression of luxuriating slowness suggests the erotic anticipation and relish which is the theme of the poem. The Eton piece describes the unexpected noise heralding the Queen's arrival: Windsor goes on to reassure Eton, alarmed by the sound, that it does not portend any civil war, but is only a sign that the Queen herself is approaching. The poem perhaps alludes in this way to the unusual 'sound' of the metre itself. Though not typical of the period – most other presentation volumes from the early 1560s are metrically much more conservative – the 1563 Eton manuscript is nevertheless not unique: two Cambridge collections of 1564, though not as ambitious as the Eton collection, also show an interest in metrical variety.[23]

As so often, practice precedes theory. Richard Willes' *Poematum liber*, published by Tottel in 1573, offers a partial guide to the new poetics. The volume is most memorable for its enthusiastic demonstration of the flashier kinds of poetic experiment, including acrostics, anagrams, chronograms, and even figure (picture) poems of the kind later made famous in English by George Herbert.[24] These kinds of 'mannerist' techniques, which we tend to associate with the English poetry of the early or mid-seventeenth century, are typical in Latin verse of the latter part of the century before.[25] But forms such as pattern poems or anagram epigrams, however sophisticated, are only the showiest and in many ways least interesting manifestation of a much wider fascination with formal and especially metrical variety: though Willes' collection is organized by type (form and occasion) of poems, rather than their metre, it incorporates a good deal of metrical variety, and Willes even claims to have invented one

---

[23] CUL MS Mm. IV. 39, containing 77 poems in 8 different metres, including a pattern poem; CUL MS Add. 8915, containing 270 poems also in 8 different metres, including a polymetric poem.

[24] The figure poems demonstrated by Willes (4–11) include an altar, a sword, wings and an egg. Herbert's figure poems include wings ('Easter-wings') and an altar ('The Altar'). The collection also demonstrates a Virgilian cento, macaronic poems using multiple languages, and examples of rhyming verse. Willes includes a short treatise on poetry, and prose notes (also in Latin) on all the forms he demonstrates. The book is discussed in Binns, *Intellectual Culture*, 50–9.

[25] Other late sixteenth-century examples of 'figure' poems include a poem in the shape of a column in the Oxford University collection commemorating Sir Christopher Hatton (*Oxoniensium στεναγμος*, 1592, sig. B1ʳ) and several figure poems in Willet, *Sacrorum emblematum centuria una* (1592?), a popular emblem book in Latin and English, republished in 1596. Some of the many examples in presentation manuscripts are to be found in Bod. MSS Add. A. 276, Ashmole 1730; Lat. misc. e. 23 (12 examples); Rawl. poet. 63; BL MSS Add. 74231; Royal 12 A LV (three examples); Royal 14 B XVI; Society of Antiquaries (London), MS SAL 437. Jonson's poem 'An Execration upon Vulcan' contains a memorable critical dismissal of such effortful 'hard trifles' (35).

metrical form himself (discussed further below). The following year Julius Caesar Scaliger, already famous for the much-cited *Poetices libri septem* (1561), published his own huge volume of Latin verse, which includes compositions in almost every known classical metre, even such unusual forms as galliambics, as well as entire books of *anacreontica*, *aenigmata* and *logogriphi*.[26]

Whereas Willes' work in the 1570s was intended (like Scaliger's *Poetices*) to demonstrate various genres and forms, with metrical variety only incidental to that aim, John Brownswerd's *Progymnasmata quaedam poetica*, published in 1589, focuses upon metrical variation.[27] The volume begins by demonstrating how a single poem on a suitable biblical theme (in this case, the battle of David and Goliath from 1 Samuel 17) can be recast in four different Latin metres: hexameter, 'asclepiadaeum' (i.e. stichic lesser asclepiad, as in Horace, *Odes* 1.1), 'phaleucium' (i.e. phalaecian hendecasyllables) and 'sapphicum' (sapphic stanzas). There are many manuscript examples of this kind of self-conscious metrical variation: BL MS Sloane 1768, for instance, contains in its first half the verse translations, mostly into Latin, of Francis Thorius (de Thoor; Thorie), a Flemish Protestant and doctor who spent time in London and who was friends with Daniel Rogers, a member of Philip Sidney's circle.[28] This sequence includes 23 poems by Ronsard, of which all but one is a sonnet.[29] Sonnets are of course highly conventional and easily recognizable in formal terms; but in his Latin versions Thorius does not settle on a single metrical form. He starts with a translation into elegiac couplets – which we might consider the obvious choice, given the association with Latin love elegy – then switches to hexameter for the next thirteen translations. Over the final eleven versions, however, he tries out six different metrical forms: two more elegiacs, another in hexameter, one in asclepiads, three in iambic trimeter, one in phalaecian hendecasyllables and one in an unusual 'reverse iambic distich' (an iambic dimeter followed by an iambic

---

[26] Scaliger, *Poemata* (1574).
[27] Brownswerd, *Progymnasmata* (1589, reissued 1590). A copy is in William Camden's collection, bound in the same volume as Dousa's odes discussed above (Westminster Abbey CB 7).
[28] His son, Raphael Thorius, whose poetry occupies the second half of the manuscript, was better known as a Latin poet than his father, and his *Hymnus Tabaci* (written 1610; published 1626) was a popular success in the seventeenth century.
[29] The exception is one poem of 18 lines. Prescott, 'From "Amours" to *Amores*', points out that some of the sonnets attributed to Ronsard in the manuscript are not in fact by him; Devos, 'François Thorius (Thooris) et son fils Raphaël' and Bergmans, 'Les Poésies manuscrites de François et Raphaël Thorius'.

trimeter, rather than the other way around), a form very close to one used by Beza in his psalm paraphrases.[30]

Metrical Sequences and Transitions

Another mode of metrical variety is created by juxtaposing two or more metres within a single poem. Classical parallels are rare, though some of Seneca's choruses incorporate changes of metre, and the early humanist poet Francesco Filelfo (1398–1481) composed many polymetric Latin hymns. Scaliger's 1574 verse collection reflects the fashion for this kind of experiment, including a poem or verse sequence incorporating no fewer than 33 different metres.[31] In English manuscripts, the largest number of polymetric sequences date from the latter sixteenth century: such sequences may themselves have been influenced by psalm paraphrase, perhaps especially the practice followed by Beza (and the Sidney psalter) of using a different metre for each of the 22 sections of the enormously long Psalm 119.[32]

Several later sixteenth-century manuscripts preserve examples of what appears to have been an established, though short-lived, polymetric form: a poem in hexameters or elegiacs with a closing 'tag' of either one or (sometimes) two sapphic stanzas. One of the few print examples of this form appears in Drant's *Medicinable Morall* (1566), one of a sequence of poems on the death of Frances, Duchess of Suffolk (1517–59). In this brief poem, a single elegiac couplet (a dactylic hexameter followed by a pentameter) is followed by a final hexameter line, and then a sapphic stanza:

> Hiis ita digestis, premitur tractabile caelum,
>   Et scissae coiere viae, clausere meatus.
> Tum nostro lentum carmen sic creuit ab ore.
> Euge, ter faelix, quarter ô beata,
> Senties faelix, gemino marito,
> Stirpe ter faelix, hominum voluptas,
>   Cura deorum.[33]

---

[30] Beza, Psalm 41, in which the first line of each couplet is an iambic dimeter catalectic (with the final syllable missing).

[31] Scaliger, *Poemata*, 291–306; outdoing Filelfo's *Odes* 3.8, with 13 changes of metre. On lyric sequences see Ijsewijn and Sacré, *Companion to Neo-Latin Studies, Part II*, 428.

[32] Of 107 neo-Latin verse items in early modern English manuscript sources identified as polymetric, 38 (36 per cent) are datable to the final third of the sixteenth century (1567–1600), compared to only 5 to the mid-sixteenth century and 29 to the early seventeenth century; in the corpus as a whole, 31.1 per cent of verse items are datable to the early seventeenth century, compared to 11.4 per cent to the late sixteenth.

[33] Drant, *Medicinable Morall*, sig. Liii^{r-v}.

> *Matters being as they are, the yielding heaven is pressed shut,*
> *And the torn paths have closed, the openings sealed.*
> *Thus has our gentle song grown from our mouth.*
> *Oh well done! thrice happy, oh four times blessed woman,*
> *You shall feel blessed, with your two husbands,*
> *Thrice blessed with offspring, the delight of men,*
> *The care of the gods.*

The change of metre marks a change of tone and register: from third person narrative to a kind of lyric blessing addressed directly to Frances. The sapphic 'tag' to this poem, with its elements of prayer and conventional, even formulaic, tone, is unlike most of what we find in Horace himself, but typical of the mid-sixteenth-century use of sapphics in general (on which see Chapter 4). Drant's poem combines the standard metres of the mid-sixteenth century – elegiacs, hexameters and short moralizing sapphics – into a form which is flexible, easily recognizable but entirely unclassical.[34] This 'closural sapphic' was apparently quite widely adopted, and probably even taught at school – surviving manuscript examples, all but one of which date from the latter sixteenth century, include several which appear to be school exercises.[35]

Drant's unclassical combination of dactylic elements – here elegiacs followed by a single hexameter – is also typical. Willes claims to invent one particular version of this – stanzas formed of two hexameters followed by a single pentameter – a form found in several manuscripts dating from the late sixteenth or very early seventeenth century, and in fact also occasionally in medieval Latin verse.[36] Whether or not Willes was aware of the medieval precedent, his experimentation with new stanza forms

---

[34] Examples of poems with a 'closural sapphic' vary in length, and while most instances are elegiacs followed by sapphics, sometimes (as here) hexameters are also used. Nevertheless, the sapphic 'tag' makes the form easily recognizable.

[35] Examples include Somerset Heritage Centre, MS DD\WO/57/1/1 (late sixteenth century, two examples); Staffordshire County Record Office, MS D1287/19/6/50 (late sixteenth century, fifteen examples); CUL MS Add. 3873, containing act verses dating from 1575–84, includes a poem of six stanzas, each of which is made up of an elegiac couplet followed by a sapphic stanza. The latest instance of which I am aware is BL MS Harley 5110, a finely written manuscript by Sir Miles Hobart (1598/9–1632), dated 1613. Hobart matriculated at the Queen's College, Oxford in 1615, aged 16. This manuscript, made when he was around 14 years old, presumably represents school compositions. It has been wrongly described as a scribal production: in fact, Hobart indicates that he is both the scribe and the author of the work ('Milo Hobartus fecit et scripsit', fol. 19ʳ). His use of this relatively (by this point) old-fashioned verse form is perhaps attributable to his schoolmaster.

[36] Willes, *Poematum liber* (1573), 56 (poem 76, titled 'Mixtio noua Her. Vers.', 'A new mixture of heroic verse'). See also BL MS Cotton Faustina E. V, fol. 174ʳ (Camden papers, 1590–1605); Trinity College, Cambridge, MS R. 14. 18, fols. 74ʳ, 74ᵛ, 99ʳ, 107ʳ (before 1612). A medieval example is that of Godfrey of Viterbo, who uses the form in several poems (*Monumenta Germaniae Historica, Scriptores*, 22); see, very briefly, Norberg, *Medieval Latin Versification*, 63.

82 Metrical Variety

constructed from dactylic components was characteristic of the period more generally. Examples in manuscript sources include 'reverse' elegiac couplets (a dactylic pentameter followed by an hexameter); mixed hexameters and pentameters; and various types of dactylic stanza.[37]

This kind of innovation points the way towards more extended verse 'sequences'. Walter Haddon's *Lucubrationes*, published in 1567, is much less extravagantly varied than the Eton school collection of 1563 discussed above, and consists mostly of elegiacs and hexameters. It does however contain an interesting series of polymetric poems, including a metrical transition: in the pair of poems titled 'Uxor non est ducenda' ('Do not take a wife') and 'Uxor est ducenda' ('Do take a wife'), for instance, four lines of stichic lesser asclepiads act as a kind of coda to seven sapphic stanzas.[38] Although there are not a very large number of English examples of this kind of polymetric poem or verse 'sequence', there are a handful of parallels: Drayton's *Eclogues*, for instance, published in 1606, are characterized by various metrical transitions as well as inset songs, and George Herbert's English poem 'Good Friday' and his bilingual verse response to John Donne, 'In Sacram Anchoram Piscatoris', are both examples of poems with a metrical transition at around the mid-point. The quasi-dramatic potential of the polymetric poem or sequence became important in the seventeenth century and is discussed further in Chapter 5.

The development of the polymetric poetic sequence significantly expanded the possibilities of Latin lyric verse: by linking together a chain of lyric or mixed lyric and non-lyric metres, poets interested in formal innovation and metrical variety could embark upon larger-scale projects, such as polymetric devotional sequences or texts for performance. One early (mid-sixteenth-century) example, combining elegiacs and iambics with stanzas in sapphics and alcaics, is probably a text performed as part

---

[37] Reverse elegiacs in BL MSS Harley 5029, fol. 114^r (probably 1620s); Lansdowne 762, fol. 18^r (mid-sixteenth century); Add. 15227, fol. 90^v (early seventeenth century). Mixed hexameters and pentameters in Chetham's Library, MS Mun. A. 4.15, fol. 86^{r-v} (c.1600); CUL MS Mm. IV. 39, fol. 17^v (1564); BL MS Harley 3831 (late sixteenth century), multiple instances. Dactylic stanzas include three hexameters followed by three pentameters, found in both West Yorkshire Archive Service, MS WYL 115/F6/2, fols. 425 and 427 (mid-seventeenth century) and BL MS Add. 28644, fol. 77^{r-v} (late seventeenth century); six-line stanzas of one hexameter and five pentameters in Bod. MS Lat. Misc. e. 23 (c.1600), fol. 28^r; stanzas of four hexameters plus a single pentameter in Trinity College, Cambridge, MS R. 14. 18, fol. 80^v, 83^v and 124^v (early seventeenth century).

[38] Haddon, *Lucubrationes* (1567), 'Poemata', 70–1. Modern edition in Lees (ed.), *Poetry of Walter Haddon*, 139–41. I am grateful to Lucy Nicholas for discussion of this poem. Several of the Latin poems in *Lucubrationes* were translated by contemporaries, on which see Lees.

of a formal reception ceremony for the bishop of Winchester.[39] Similarly, a manuscript now in Cambridge contains a polymetric sequence composed by one Henry Holland to herald the arrival of Queen Elizabeth at Woodstock.[40] Holland's sequence moves from hexameters to elegiac couplets, the first pythiambic, sapphic stanzas and finally a long sequence of stichic adoneans. Such a combination is typical of the latter sixteenth century not only in its form – a polymetric verse sequence – but also in its choice of metres. It combines the hexameters, elegiacs and sapphics typical of mid-sixteenth-century Latin poetry with two metres – pythiambics and stichic adoneans – associated strongly (and in the latter case, almost exclusively) with the latter sixteenth century.

Fashionable Metres: The Adonean

An 'adonean' is the term given to the short five-syllable metrical phrase ($-\cup\cup--$) that forms the distinctive final line of the sapphic stanza, as in Buchanan, *Psalm* 5:

> O Potens rerum Deus, aure leni
> mitis exaudi mea Verba, mentis
> mente non dirae tetricúsque tristes
>   percipe questus.
>   (1–4)

> *O God who controls all, in your kindness*
> *hear my words with a gentle ear;*
> *heed the sad plaints of my mind with a mind neither stern*
>   *nor unforgiving.*

Or, as an English example, Mary Sidney's version of Psalm 125:

> As Zion standeth very firmly steadfast,
> Never once shaking: so on high Jehovah
> Who his hope buildeth, very firmly steadfast
>   Ever abideth.
>   (Psalm 125, 1–4)[41]

---

[39] BL MS Lansdowne 388, fol. 160ᵛ–1ʳ, referring to Robert Horne, bishop of Winchester between 1560 and 1579.
[40] CUL MS Kk. V. 14, fols. 40ʳ–5ʳ. If the sequence relates to a visit in the 1560s, this may be Henry Holland (1550–1625), who was at St John's College, Oxford between 1566 and 1569 before converting to Roman Catholicism and moving to France. The manuscript also contains (fols. 3ʳ–4ᵛ) a poem in Latin elegiacs by Christopher Jonson dated 1564.
[41] Mary Sidney's quantitative verse is discussed in Chapter 3; other examples of quantitative sapphics in English were composed by Thomas Campion and Francis Davison.

In Seneca and Boethius we find a few instances of the sapphic hendecasyllable (the longer first three lines of a sapphic stanza) used stichically, either without the adonean at all, or with the adonean appearing only infrequently.[42] This more flexible use of the sapphic hendecasyallable, though rare in classical poetry, is found fairly frequently in mid-sixteenth-century Latin verse, including, for instance, in Haddon's *Lucubrationes* (1567) and the 1563 Eton collection mentioned above (BL MS Royal 12 A XXX).[43] Such examples probably created a sense of the 'separability' of the adonean, leading in time to the appearance of poems written in adoneans alone, a practice for which the only ancient precedent is Boethius *Cons.* 1 met. 7, though there are also quite a number of medieval examples.[44] A poem in stichic adoneans appears in the 1563 Eton collection, but also in several other Latin verse collections of this period.[45]

In my database of English Latin verse found in manuscripts dating from between c.1550 and 1720, the majority (72 per cent) of stichic adoneans are in manuscripts dating from the latter half of the sixteenth century.[46] This form may have been taught at school by the 1580s: a Cambridge manuscript contains a moralizing poem in this metre dated 1586; composed by William Paget, then aged around 14, it is dedicated to his great-aunt (the collection also contains Latin verse for his grandmother's birthday). This charming poem thematizes its own artlessness, as in this extract:

> Amita chara
> Exiguum istud
> Munus amico
> Accipe vultu
> Sperne nec ista
> Carmina quamvis

---

[42] Stichic sapphic hendecasyllables are found at Seneca, *Phaedra* 274–324 and Boethius, *Cons.* 2. met. 6; Seneca, *Medea* 607–69 is mostly stichic with only occasional adoneans; Boethius, *Cons.* 4 met. 7 is stichic bar a single final adonean.

[43] Later examples are rare, though Somerset Heritage Centre, MS DD\SF/18/2/8, fol. 2ʳ, for instance, contains a poem from c.1668 by Edward Clarke on the death of his stepmother, consisting of fourteen sapphic hendecasyllables followed by a single adonean.

[44] For brief references see Norberg, *Medieval Latin Versification*, 72.

[45] E.g. CUL MS Kk. V. 14, fols. 44ʳ–5ʳ, part of the sequence described above; Bod. MS Lat. misc. e. 23 (c.1600) contains 195 poems, including examples of fashionable pythiambics, stichic adoneans, anacreontics and polymetric sequences.

[46] The examples in manuscripts of a later date may all be transcriptions of sixteenth-century verse. Durham Hunter MS 96 (early seventeenth century), for instance, includes two stichic adonean pieces by Nicolas Reusner (1545–1602), 179–89.

>   Ingenio li=
>   Mata nec arte
>   Minima magnos
>   Edere possunt
>   Semina fœtus.
>   Maxima quercus
>   Virga fuit &
>   Fluvius ingens
>   Exiguus fons
>   & vitulus quem
>   Horreo taurum
>   (11–27)[47]

> *My dear great-aunt*
> *This exiguous*
> *Gift accept*
> *With kindness –*
> *Reject not these*
> *Songs although*
> *They're finished neither*
> *With art nor skill:*
> *The smallest seeds*
> *May yet still*
> *Grow to be great.*
> *The mightiest oak*
> *Was once a shoot,*
> *A mighty river*
> *A tiny spring –*
> *And once a calf*
> *The bull I dread.*

The Boethian model probably accounts for the moralizing associations of this form, and it is obvious why schoolboys might have been drawn to it: in order to develop any facility in composing sapphic stanzas, each of which ends with an adonean, one has to have a ready store of phrases which fit this metrical pattern. Moreover, this metrical phrase is also a component part both of sapphic hendecasyllables and of the asclepiad metres which were particularly fashionable at this period (discussed further below).

---

[47] CUL MS Dd. V. 75, fol. 13ʳ. The poem to Paget's grandmother is accompanied by an English version but this piece addressed to his great aunt is not, implying that she had at least enough Latin to appreciate the gift.

Latin Verse in the Sidney Circle

Probably at almost the same time, and certainly before Sidney's death in 1586, Abraham Fraunce (1559?–1592/3?), well known as a friend of Sidney and a fellow-innovator of English quantitative poetry, dedicated a book of emblems to Sidney with a prefatory verse sequence which combines many typically late-sixteenth-century forms, such as an 'unclassical dactylic' (stanzas of three hexameters followed by three pentameters) and stichic adoneans, alongside sapphics and elegiacs.[48] The first very metrically varied verse collections by English authors to appear in print (rather than as presentation manuscripts) were, probably not coincidentally, commemorative collections on the death of Sidney: both of the Oxford publications (one from New College, the other from Oxford as a whole) are metrically very various, using many poems with short lines (such as anacreontics and stichic adoneans), and also creating lyric 'sequences' or longer poems with a series of metrical transitions.[49] Both volumes also include the kind of Latin 'figure poems' demonstrated by Willes and later made famous in their English form by George Herbert.[50] The New College volume also includes several poems in the first asclepiad and in stichic iambic dimeter, the latter an un-Horatian form found in late antique Christian hymns, which was used frequently by both Buchanan and Beza in their psalm paraphrases.[51]

While stichic sapphic hendecasyllables, adoneans, iambic dimeters and unusual combinations of dactylic lines are all found rarely if ever in classical Latin verse, other fashionable sixteenth-century metres – such as pythiambics and the various asclepiad metres – are found in Horace and late antique authors, but are much more frequently encountered in sixteenth-century Latin verse collections than a present-day classicist would expect. Of a total of 150 manuscript poems in asclepiad metres

---

[48] Bod. MS Rawl. D. 345. In the main work, each emblem representing an historical figure is also accompanied by a short Latin poem. The collection is described in the *ODNB* entry for Fraunce as a 'series of devices', without indicating the substantial role played by Latin verse – Barker, 'Fraunce [France], Abraham (1559?–1592/3?)'. As far as I am aware, it has never been published.

[49] Oxford University, *Peplus* (1587); Gager (ed.), *Exequiae* (New College, Oxford, 1587); Cambridge University, *Lachrymae* (1587). The Cambridge volume is formally more conservative, with all poems in hexameter or elegiacs apart from three short odes in asclepiads (1) and sapphics (2). The volume also contains several acronymic poems, as well as a handful in Greek and one in Hebrew.

[50] *Exequiae*, sig. G4ʳ, wings; *Peplus*, sig. A3ʳ, column (opening poem).

[51] Stichic iambic dimeters are found in Prudentius, Ambrose and Sedulius; 14 of Buchanan's psalm paraphrases and 11 of Beza's also use this metre. It was quite commonly used for songs, hymns or poems with hymn-like features in early modern Latin.

identified at the time of writing, 63 (42 per cent) date from the final third of the sixteenth century: in this period, uniquely, asclepiad metres are almost as common as sapphics (65 examples) and found much more frequently than alcaics (only 26).[52] Whether attributable to cause or effect, this preference for asclepiad metres is noticeable in the psalm paraphrase collections too: 20 of Buchanan's psalms are in asclepiads, and a further 4 in metres with asclepiad elements, compared to 10 in sapphic stanzas and 16 in alcaics; Beza's collection, though more metrically varied, follows a similar pattern – 12 of his psalms are in asclepiad metres, only 5 in sapphics and 3 in alcaics.

The Fashion for Asclepiad Metres

The asclepiad metres are based upon the choriamb (– ∪ ∪ –), a metrical phrase which also is also found in the sapphic hendecasyllable (– ∪ – x – ∪ ∪ – ∪ – –), the phalaecian hendecasyllable used frequently by Catullus (x x – ∪ ∪ – ∪ – ∪ – –), the adonean (– ∪ ∪ – –) and the first two lines of the alcaic stanza (x – ∪ – – – ∪ ∪ – ∪ –).[53] If you read or compose widely in hexameters and elegiacs, the ear is attuned to the dactylic measure (– ∪ ∪), while trochaic and iambic metres rely for recognition on the trochee (– ∪) or iamb (∪ –). Most English poetry has alternating stressed and unstressed syllables as its basic pattern, most frequently with the unstressed syllable leading (an iambic pattern, though in stressed rather than quantitative terms). Learning to hear and write in Latin lyric metres, however, relies upon recognizing (and producing) the distinctive musical motif of the choriamb (– ∪ ∪ –) which appears at least once in almost all lyric lines.

We can talk perhaps about a kind of 'choriambic pull' in the second half of the sixteenth century, a distinctive music of the Latin lyric of this period. It is hard to give a sense of what this revolution in the formal possibilities of Latin verse might have been like to experience as a reader, though perhaps an encounter with modernist poetry gives the best analogy: most readers will remember their first experiences of the aural landscape of, for instance, T. S. Eliot or Ezra Pound and how complex, various

---

[52] By contrast, only 11.4 per cent of the total corpus of verse is datable to this period. A further 19 poems in asclepiad metres (12.8 per cent) are datable to the mid-sixteenth century, a period to which only 6.5 per cent of the total corpus belongs. This preference for asclepiad metres disappears in the seventeenth century, while sapphics and alcaics become much more dominant. In Horace's *Odes*, 34 odes are in asclepiad metres, compared to 37 in alcaics and 25 in sapphics.

[53] These metrical descriptions follow the most common form of these lines in the Latin poets: the alcaic hendecasyllable, for instance, is in the form used by Horace rather than Alcaeus.

and newly beautiful it seemed in comparison to the poetry they already knew (even if, in practice, they initially found the parts of these poems written in the most aurally recognizable forms the most accessible).

Many choriambic lines require series of long syllables, as here in the glyconic (choriambic trimeter): – – – ∪ ∪ – ∪ – –. English has a much larger number of short, typically unstressed words – such as 'a', 'the', 'he', 'to' and 'with' – than Latin, in which these grammatical functions are performed largely by inflection. This feature of English means that it is hard to create repeated series of long and/or stressed syllables. Pound's 'The Return', first published in *Ripostes* (1912), is, as Donald Carne-Ross has demonstrated, a poem about the 'reconstitution' (the 'return') of the Sapphic stanza in English verse.[54] As such it contains repeated adoneans: 'These the keen-scented' (17); 'pallid the leash-men' (20, final line) as well as isolated choriambs ('Slow on the leash', 19), including the opening phrase of the poem ('See, they return', 1): what is returning in Pound's poem is the choriambic measures of Greek (and Latin) lyric. Several other modern English poets can also help us to 'hear' the choriamb. Hardy's poem 'In Front of the Landscape' (published 1914) similarly tests out English asclepiads and choriambs:

> Plunging and laboring on in a tide of visions,
>   Dolorous and dear,
> Forward I pushed my way as amid waste waters
>   Stretching around,
> Through whose eddies there glimmered the customed landscape
>   Yonder and near
>
> (1–6)[55]

Of all the modernist poets, the one most consistently drawn to choriambs – presumably due to his love of Horace – is Basil Bunting. His *Odes* 1.15, for instance, is about poetry ('man's craft'), and its distinctive measure is choriambic:

> Celebrate man's craft
> and the word spoken in shapeless night, the
> sharp tool paring away
> waste and the forms
> cut out of mystery
>
> (10–14)[56]

---

[54] Carne-Ross, 'New Metres for Old'. Text of Pound from *Poems and Translations*, 244.
[55] Hardy, *Collected Poems*, 275.   [56] Bunting, *Complete Poems*, 111.

The final three lines here scan quantitatively:

```
---UU-
-UU-
-UU-U-
```

Elsewhere, Bunting achieves some of the most effective asclepiad lines in English:

> Its ill-roped crates heavy with fruit sway
> (*Odes* 1.30.3)

```
-   -   -     -      -UU    -    -
```

Or alternatively, if scanning for stress rather than quantity (since 'its' is an unambiguously long syllable, but not naturally strongly stressed):

```
x /   /   /    / x x /   /
```

The metrical self-consciousness of Pound and Bunting – in which the 'form' that emerges from Bunting's 'paring' is the choriamb – has many sixteenth-century parallels. Thomas Drant's *A Medicinable Morall* (1566) is known primarily as an example of English verse satire (Drant translated Horace's hexameter verse). But the final portion of the volume, as we have already seen, contains a collection of innovative Latin verse, with a marked interest in the newfangled metrical experimentation. A poem on death described as 'Carmen gliconicum coriambicum' is in a very unusual metre, found just once in Prudentius, perhaps best described as a 'rising choriambic'. It consists of triplets of a choriambic trimeter (a 'glyconic'), tetrameter, and finally a pentameter (a 'greater asclepiad'):

> Mors, (ô) saeua, potens nimis,
> O mors, mors, quid ages? quoue feres pedem?
> Quantos saepe trahis, quanque bonos precipites viros?[57]

> *Death, o savage, o too potent*
> *O death, death, what will you do? Where will you next step?*
> *Why do you so often take such great men, and cast them down*
>   *even though they are good?*

There are no Horatian examples of three-line stanzas. Drant may have been aware of the example in Prudentius, but was more likely modelling

---

[57] Drant, *Medicinable Morall*, sigs. Liii^v–Liiii^r.

his poem on Buchanan, who used this metre for his version of Psalm 16.[58]

> O Rerum sator, & salus
> Humani generis certa periculis,
> Qui te respicis vnum, famulum instantibus eripe.
>
> (1–3)

> *O father of all, and the*
> *Sure salvation of human kind,*
> *Rescue your servant, who looks to you alone, from the dangers*
>   *that threaten him.*

Where educational material survives, it confirms the widespread teaching of asclepiad metres in the latter sixteenth century, especially the stichic choriambic tetrameter (also called the 'lesser' or 'first' asclepiad), the metre of Horace, *Odes* 1.1. This metre is found only three times in Horace, albeit at structurally important moments: the first (1.1) and last (3.30) odes of *Odes* 1–3, published together in 23 BC, and the central ode of the later fourth book (4.8). It is this form of the asclepiad, however, which is used most frequently by Buchanan and Beza, and Englished by Sidney, Stanyhurst and Campion among others:

> O sweet woods, the delight of solitariness,
> O, how much do I love your solitariness!
> Where man's mind hath a free consideration
> Of goodness to receive lovely direction.
>   (Sidney, *Old Arcadia*, 34, 1–4)

One of Thomas Campion's songs appended to Sidney's *Astrophel and Stella* (1591) is a particularly effective example of this form:

> What faire pompe have I spide of glittering Ladies,
> With locks sparckled abroad, and rosie Coronet
> On their yvorie browes, trackt to the daintie thies
> With roabs like *Amazons*, blew as Violet:
> With gold Aglets adornd, some in a changeable
> *Pale*, with spangs wavering, taught to be moveable.[59]
>
> (1–6)

The other lines which together form the standard asclepiad metres (the 'greater' asclepiad, glyconic and pherecratean) are all closely related to this tetrameter line, making it a practical starting point, and it is clear that

---

[58] For an early seventeenth-century Latin paraphrase of Psalm 16 in this metre, alluding explicitly to Buchanan, see Chapter 3.
[59] Sidney, *Astrophel and Stella* (1591), 77.

many schoolboys began their mastery of asclepiad metres by writing stichic choriambic tetrameters. BL MS Harley 6211, dating from 1594, is a presentation copy of sample compositions by boys at Ludlow grammar school. The poems, accompanied by metrical diagrams, are in a repeating cycle of forms described as 'Asclepiadea Μονόκωλα' (stichic choriambic tetrameter or 'first asclepiad'), 'Sapphica hendecasyllaba Δίκωλα' (sapphic stanzas), 'Choriambica Δίκωλα' (alternating glyconics and choriambic tetrameter, or 'fourth asclepiad' as in Horace, *Odes* 1.3) and 'elegiacs'.

This cycle of metres corresponds quite closely with those discussed in Book 1 of Johannes Despauterius' *Ars versificatoria*, the most influential single manual on the subject in the sixteenth century, which covers the hexameter, elegiac couplets, stichic ('first') asclepiad, sapphic stanzas and the phalaecian hendecasyllable.[60] Buchanan's own guide to Latin metre, *De prosodia libellus*, lays even greater emphasis upon asclepiad forms, teaching the lines required to compose all five of the Horatian asclepiad metres, as well as iambic trimeters and dimeters.[61] The evidence here for the widespread teaching of verse composition in asclepiad metres in the later sixteenth century fits with the high number of poems in asclepiad metres surviving from this period.

Pythiambics

Pythiambic metres (combinations of dactylic and iambic lines) are also found in Horace, but only in the *Epodes*: *Epodes* 14 and 15 are in the first pythiambic (an hexameter followed by an iambic dimeter); *Epodes* 16 in the second pythiambic (an hexameter followed by an iambic trimeter). Though not usually taught specifically in the kinds of school textbook described above, they appear surprisingly frequently in sixteenth-century Latin verse, including in advanced school compositions: once boys were confident in the composition of dactylic hexameters, pentameters and iambic metres, such composite forms were within their grasp. Once again, the popularity of these quite challenging forms – challenging both to write and to 'hear', because of the alternation between dactylic (– ∪ ∪) and iambic (∪ –) patterns – is probably related to the influence of psalm

---

[60] Johannes Despauterius (Jan de Spauter, d. 1520), *Ars versificatoria*, first published c.1511, with very frequent reissues. Despauterius describes the full range of possible metres in Book V, but Books I and II were probably considered particularly appropriate for school use. On Despauterius see Ford, 'Neo-Latin Prosody and Versification', 68–70.
[61] George Buchanan, *De prosodia libellus* (1621), originally published c.1595, on which see McFarlane, *Buchanan*, 442–4.

paraphrase: the second pythiambic is one of only 3 metres used more than 15 times by Buchanan, while Beza makes frequent use of both the first and second pythiambic, as well as several similar dactylo-iambic metres not found in Horace.[62] Horace, *Epodes* 16, the only Horatian poem in the second pythiambic (though the metre is also used by Prudentius, Boethius and Erasmus), is memorable both for its savage indictment of contemporary civil war, and for its political fantasy: the poet suggests that the Roman people should abandon their city in order to sail westward to seek out the Isles of the Blessed, a remnant of the Golden Age. This combination of intense reproach against the sinfulness of the people with equally intense hope for the future if God's favour is secured is indeed reminiscent of the tone of many of the psalms, from the second psalm onwards, and perhaps suggested the adoption of these metres. Here is an extract from Buchanan's version of Psalm 2:

> Quid trepidae gentes vano fremuere tumultu
>   minisque populi saeuiunt inanibus,
> et cum principibus magni coiere tyranni,
>   dominumque Christumque domini adversum truces?
> . . .
>   Deinde allocutus dominus est me: 'filius
> Tu meus es, genui te hodie; me posce, daboque
>   Omnes ut heres gentium fines regas,
> Qua circumfusis tellus se porrigit undis,
>   Regasque sceptro sempiternum ferreo;
> Cumque voles, tumidosque premas frangasque rebelles,
>   Ut ficta fragili vasa franguntur luto.'
>
>   (1–4; 14–20)

> *Why have the fearful nations exploded in vain uproar? And why do the peoples rage with empty threats? And why have great tyrants come together with princes, ferocious against the Lord and against the Lord's Christ?*
> . . .
> *Then the Lord addressed me, 'You are my son, today I have begotten you; ask me, and I will allow you as my heir to rule the lands of the nations, wherever the sea-girt earth extends, and to rule them for ever with an iron sceptre; and, whenever you wish, to overwhelm the proud and smash the rebellious, just as vessels of brittle earthenware are smashed.'*

---

[62] The first pythiambic is used once by Buchanan and 14 times by Beza; the second pythiambic 16 times by Buchanan and four times by Beza. Both poets also make use of related unclassical forms, such as an hexameter followed by a catalectic iambic dimeter (Beza, Psalm 119:Res), and stanzas of two hexameters followed by a single iambic trimeter (Beza, Psalm 87). Though not Horatian, such forms are recognizably 'pythiambic' in structure.

The second pythiambic, used here, is the third most common metre in Buchanan's psalter (after iambic distichs and alcaics, both much more common in Horace), and readers apparently came to associate Buchanan's psalms with pythiambics in particular: a Latin epigram in praise of Buchanan's psalter by the German poet Johannes Posthius (Johannes Posth, 1537–97) is written in the first pythiambic.

Trochaic Metres

William Ringler, in his edition of the poems of Philip Sidney, notes that Philip Sidney's 43 psalm paraphrases include 5 in trochaic metres, 'a metre new to the Elizabethans', which Sidney first mastered in the *Astrophel and Stella* songs of 1582.[63] The first of the Sidney psalms in trochaics is Psalm 16:

> Save me, Lord, for why thou art
> All the hope of all my heart:
> Witness though my soul with me,
> That to God, my God, I say:
> 'Thou, my Lord, thou art my stay,
> Though my works reach not to thee.'
> (1–6)[64]

Ringler suggests that Sidney may have been influenced in this regard by the Marot-Bèze French psalter, of which fifteen psalm translations are 'probably trochaic'.[65] Trochaic metres are unusual in classical Latin, and hardly found at all in poetry (as opposed to drama).[66] The use of trochaic metres for lyric was, however, one of the striking innovations of Buchanan's Latin psalter – which contains six psalms in trochaic metres – and much expanded by Beza, 19 of whose psalms are wholly or partly trochaic. Moreover, one simple trochaic form – stichic trochaic dimeter catalectic – is actually the fourth most common meter in Beza's psalter,

---

[63] Ringler, *Poems of Sir Philip Sidney*, 501. The eighth song of *Astrophel and Stella*, for instance, is trochaic.
[64] Text from Hamlin *et al.* (eds.), *Sidney Psalter*. [65] Ringler, *Poems of Sir Philip Sidney*, 507.
[66] Two Horatian odes (1.4 and 2.18) have trochaic elements, but in *Odes* 1.4 the trochaic element is found in only one half-line in each couplet, the other elements being iambic and dactylic; in *Odes* 2.18 the trochaic line is paired with an iambic one. Boethius *Cons.* 4 *met.* 2 also has a trochaic element. Prudentius uses the trochaic tetrameter, arranged in three-line stanzas, for *Cathemerinon* 9 and *Peristephanon* 1 and it is also the metre of Venantius Fortunatus' famous hymn *Pange lingua gloriosi*. It was apparently associated with triumph and celebration, hence Beza's use of the metre for psalms of praise and thanksgiving.

appearing 15 times.[67] Beza reused this memorable metre for his paraphrase of the *Song of Songs*, published in 1584.[68] Contemporary interest in trochaics is reflected, among other examples, in an anagram poem addressed by Melissus (in London) to Dousa in 1585, formed of couplets consisting of an hexameter followed by a trochaic pentameter.[69] Though none of the common introductory textbooks of the mid-late sixteenth century – such as those by Despauterius or Buchanan – includes trochaics, the metrical notes in a school manuscript dated 1605 include 'versus trochaicus' alongside the school staples of hexameters, pentameters, glyconics, asclepiads and pherecrateans, suggesting that the fashion had reached the schoolroom by the turn of the century.[70]

Both Dousa and Melissus published important volumes of Latin poetry in 1586: the second edition of Melissus' *Schediasmata poetica* and Dousa's *Odarum Britannicarum Liber*, dedicated to Elizabeth I. Both poets were well known in England and spent considerable time there, and there is evidence for the English circulation of both volumes. Dousa's collection, which includes a poem to Melissus as well as a series of major odes addressed to leading English nobles, was owned by Camden, who added a manuscript couplet to the end of Dousa's poem to Philip Sidney.[71] While Dousa's formal panegyric odes are all in sapphic stanzas, Melissus opens his volume with a sequence of 14 Latin odes in triadic Pindarics, beginning with a major Pindaric ode addressed to Queen Elizabeth. Latin Pindarics, discussed in detail in Chapter 5, are one of the few major formal innovations in Latin lyric verse in the latter sixteenth century which were *not* initially linked with the tradition of psalm paraphrase. Neither Buchanan nor Beza made use of this form, which was used largely for contemporary and political panegyric in the sixteenth century, though

---

[67] Following hexameter (22), iambic distichs (20) and the phalaecian hendecasyllable (17).
[68] Beza, *Canticum Canticorum* (1584). BL MS Add. 62138D is a manuscript copy of Beza's version in the hand of George Wyatt (1553–1624), wrongly described by the catalogue as Wyatt's own work. Wyatt, born in 1553, was old enough to have read Beza during the 1580s.
[69] BL MS Burney 370, fol. 67ʳ. The manuscript contains 59 Latin poems in 15 different metres, including several unusual combinations, such as Melissus' poem to 'Rosina' composed in four-line stanzas of an iambic tetrameter, scazon, trimeter and dimeter (fols. 53ʳ–5ʳ).
[70] Notebook of James Garnet (Nottingham University Library, MS 117, fol. 25ʳ).
[71] Westminster Abbey CB 7 (8), 54–5. This is a composite volume, almost entirely of Latin verse, of items owned by Camden and in several cases also annotated by him. Dates of publication range from 1580 to 1613, and the items include works by Andrew Melville, John Brownswerd, Robert Ashley's Latin translation of Du Bartas' *Urania*, and Ockland's *Anglorum Praelia*, as well as several multi-authored collections of commemorative Latin verse. Bound with these printed books is also Camden's scribal copy of John Johnston's Latin poems on British cities, with Camden's own annotations.

Hugo Grotius included a dithyrambic paraphrase of Psalm 104 (the second chorus of *Adamus Exul*) in his remarkable 1601 collection *Sacra*, published when he was only 18. From the mid-seventeenth century onwards, however, the traditions of the Pindaric panegyric ode and that of scriptural paraphrase were increasingly drawn together: this confluence is discussed further in Chapter 5.

For English readers, Latin poetry by 1590 had been transformed: whereas an enthusiastic reader of contemporary Latin verse in the 1550s would have encountered almost only elegiacs, hexameters and sapphic stanzas, unless he or she were reading a handful of difficult-to-obtain humanist authors, or widely in late antique and medieval Latin verse, by 1590 the same reader would quickly encounter modern examples of the full range of Horatian lyric forms; uncommon classical and late antique metres such as stichic sapphic hendecasyllables or the stanza forms of early Christian hymns; and also many new forms without classical precedent, such as grand odes in Latin Pindarics, and a host of new trochaic and iambo-lyric metres. Many metres used only once or twice in all of classical literature now had a wealth of recent examples, with concomitant literary and religious associations. If he or she had sons at school, they would be learning to compose, if not in all of these forms, at least in the building blocks for them. Latin poetry by the end of the sixteenth century *sounded* quite different from how it had fifty years before: it is no surprise that English lyric quickly did too.

CHAPTER 3

Buchanan, Beza and the Genre of the Sidney Psalter

The 'Sidney psalter' has received considerable attention – though not, perhaps, as much as it deserves – for the extraordinary metrical versatility displayed by Philip and (mostly) Mary Sidney in their composition of a complete set of psalm paraphrases in English verse.[1] The 150 translations incorporate 171 different forms, with only a single repetition of metre, and offer a treasury of English verse form of demonstrable importance for English lyric poets of the seventeenth century.[2] Though primarily stress-based, the collection includes an impressive and influential sequence in quantitative metres (Psalms 120–7) based upon those used for Latin poetry, reflecting contemporary interest in the possibilities of English quantitative verse. Neither this sequence, nor the work as a whole has, to my knowledge, been discussed in the context of the neo-Latin metrical usage and experiment of the latter sixteenth century described in Chapter 2, although the Sidney psalter precisely reproduces in English the literary achievement in Latin of the major Protestant psalm paraphrases by George Buchanan and Théodore de Bèze (Beza). Of great devotional and literary importance for Protestants throughout Europe, these two

---

[1] Philip Sidney completed translations of the first forty-three psalms before his death in 1586. Only two of the stanza forms used for these translations appear elsewhere in his work. The remaining 107 psalms were translated after his death by his sister, Mary Herbert (née Sidney), Countess of Pembroke. Scholarship on Mary refers to her variously as Mary Sidney, Mary Sidney Herbert, Mary Herbert, and the Countess of Pembroke. I have referred to her as Mary Sidney throughout. The precise date of the translations remains a matter for discussion: on which see Duncan-Jones (ed.), *Selected Poems*, xv (dating Philip Sidney's translations to c.1585); Rudenstine, *Sidney's Poetic Development*, 284–6 (arguing for an earlier date, c.1580–1); Brennan, 'Date of the Countess of Pembroke's Translations', 434–6. Work on the Sidney psalter has been much facilitated by the publication of the complete work by Oxford World's Classics (Hamlin *et al.* (eds.), *Sidney Psalter*). Ringler considers Philip Sidney's psalm paraphrases to be late compositions, perhaps as late as 1585, and points out that the use of the 1580 edition of Beza rules out a date before that year. As discussed below, Philip Sidney was also using Tremellius, also published in 1580. Gentili's failure, in the prefaces dedicated to Sidney in 1581 and 1584, to mention Sidney's own psalm paraphrases further suggests, though certainly does not confirm, a late date of composition.

[2] 'A School of English Versification' (Smith, 'English Metrical Psalms', 269).

collections were recognized immediately by contemporaries for their literary achievement, and Buchanan's, in particular, was routinely cited as a literary and metrical authority until well into the eighteenth century. The Buchanan psalter was an enormous publishing success, while Beza's version, though less successful internationally and with a shorter afterlife, was demonstrably important to the Sidneys and remained influential in England.[3] Taken together, they are crucial landmarks in the development of a Protestant Latin poetics, combining the literary achievements of humanism with a distinctively Protestant emphasis upon the original and literal meaning of the Hebrew Bible.

Existing scholarship, however, hardly mentions the existence of these Latin verse psalters, and very rarely acknowledges the great similarity between those literary projects and that of the Sidneys.[4] No existing scholarship describes the formal achievement or the literary quality, tone and flavour of these Latin psalters in relation either to each other or to contemporary poetry whether in Latin or the vernacular, even though these two collections would have been the obvious point of comparison for contemporary readers of a literary psalter.[5] The Latin psalm

---

[3] On the print history and lasting influence of Buchanan's psalms, see Green, *Poetic Paraphrase*, 88–97. The citing of Buchanan as a metrical authority in his own right is discussed further below. For Beza's fame in England, and the printing of his works there, see Prescott, 'English Writers'. FitzGeffrey, *Affaniae* (1601) includes a poem in praise of Beza, by then an old man (sig. K8ʳ⁻ᵛ), in a sequence which also includes verse in praise of Joseph Scaliger, Janus Dousa and Alberico and Scipio Gentili. The central section of Andrew Melville's *Anti-Tami-Cami-Categoria* is dedicated to the celebration of Beza, still alive at the time of its composition in 1604, and to his followers in the English Church. William Dillingham's collection of Latin verse, made in the late seventeenth century, includes two items by Beza, including the verse preface to his psalms (BL MS Sloane 1766, fol. 258ʳ).

[4] Greene, 'Sir Philip Sidney's Psalms', for instance, argues for the Sidney psalter as a landmark of fictional, secular poetics, not linked to liturgical use, but makes no mention at all of the Latin tradition of psalm paraphrase (which was, equally, not intended for liturgical use, and is intensely literary in its form, though hardly secular).

[5] William Ringler acknowledges the existence of Beza's and Buchanan's versions, but lists the Marot-Bèze French psalter as the 'artistic model' for the project (*Poems of Sir Philip Sidney*, 505, 507). Noel Kinnamon acknowledges in a footnote the importance of the Latin psalm paraphrase collections, especially that of Buchanan, as literary models for metrical variety and poetic ambition in a psalter, but does not expand on the point ('God's "Scholer"', 213–14, n3: 'certainly, Buchanan's version was well known as an aesthetic precedent for metrical paraphrase of the biblical texts'). Rivkah Zim alludes to the Sidneys' use of 'several scholarly translations and commentaries' (*English Metrical Psalms*, 152) but does not discuss the Latin psalters as models. Both the recent critical edition of Mary Sidney's works and Femke Molekamp's chapter on her psalms cite the Marot-Bèze French psalter, first published in Geneva in 1564, as the primary literary model for a polymetric psalm translation, without mentioning this feature of the Latin collections (Brennan *et al.* (eds.), *Collected Works of Mary Sidney Herbert*, vol. II, 4; Molekamp, *Women and the Bible*, 160). As discussed below, the influence of the Marot-Bèze collection, especially upon Mary Sidney, has probably been exaggerated.

paraphrases of Beza and Buchanan, and in a more minor way a host of earlier and later poets in the same tradition, are serious literary works, written not primarily as songs for communal liturgical use (as the Marot-Bèze or Sternhold and Hopkins psalters were), but – like the Sidney psalter and, later, Herbert's *Temple* – for private reading, devotion and literary as well as religious appreciation.[6] These works seek to deploy the full range of classical verse forms to create a version of the psalter which unites the biblical and classical lyric traditions, and sets out forcefully how great a *literary* achievement and storehouse of forms and voices are the psalms.[7] In doing so they activate a long-standing association between the classical lyric poets Horace and Pindar, and the psalmist David.[8] Jerome described the psalter as an anthology of classical metrical forms, claiming that it included iambics, alcaics and sapphics.[9] Philip Sidney himself points to this tradition in the *Defence of Poesie* (c.1579–80), describing the Psalms as

> a heavenly poesy, wherein almost [David] showeth himself a passionate lover of that unspeakable and everlasting beauty to be seen by the eyes of the mind, only cleared by faith ... and may I not presume a little further, to show the reasonableness of this word *vates*, and say that the holy David's Psalms are a divine poem? If I do, I shall not do it without the testimony of great learned men, both ancient and modern. But even the name of Psalms will speak for me, which being interpreted, is nothing but songs; then that it is fully written in metre, as all learned hebricians agree, although the rules be not yet fully found.[10]

Thomas Lodge makes similar remarks, as do many other contemporary critics and commentators.[11]

---

[6] Some were however set to music for subsequent school use, as in Nathan Chrytaeus' (1543–98) 1585 German edition of Buchanan with melodies (on which see Gaertner, 'Latin Verse Translations', 290). Several of Herbert's lyrics have similarly become hymns.

[7] Gaertner comments briefly on the association between Latin psalm paraphrase and formal or metrical experiment (Gaertner, 'Latin Verse Translations', 272–3). Buchanan and Beza are only two of a host of practitioners of this form, some of whose collections are equally if not even more formally varied; but as these two are by far the most influential England, they are the focus of discussion here.

[8] The psalm paraphrase and associated Latin lyric of the sixteenth century relies primarily upon Latin, rather than Greek models. The association between Pindar and the psalmist, however, became particularly important and fashionable in the seventeenth century (on which see further Chapter 5).

[9] Jerome, 'Preface to the Chronicle of Eusebius', 484. Josephus thought the psalms were in trimeters and pentameters; Origen that they were in trimeters and tetrameters (on which see Kugel, *Idea of Biblical Poetry*, 141, 147).

[10] Duncan-Jones and van Dorsten (eds.), *Miscellaneous Prose*, 77.

[11] Lily Campbell, for instance, quotes both Thomas Lodge and Thomas Churchyard on this point (*Divine Poetry*, 55), on which see also Barroway, 'Bible as Poetry' and 'Hebrew Hexameter'.

The Psalms in England before 1585

The Book of Common Prayer lays great emphasis upon the praying of the psalms: several (the exact number depending on the length of the psalms in question, but typically five a day in total) are set for recitation at Morning and Evening Prayer, forming a cycle that takes the worshipper through the entire Book of Psalms in each calendar month, twelve full cycles in the course of a year for someone saying Morning and Evening Prayer daily (as clergymen are expected to do); but even an ordinary churchgoer who hears one of these services only once or twice a week is quickly exposed to the full range of the psalms, and many pious laypeople used the Book of Common Prayer for family or private devotion at home.[12] In addition, several psalms or excerpts from the psalms (as well as other inset songs from the Bible, such as the Magnificat) are part of the routine liturgy, recited on every occasion. English metrical translations of the psalms, intended for singing, appeared from the mid-sixteenth century onwards, beginning with Robert Crowley, *The Psalter of David newely translated into Englysh Metre* (1549), and followed by collections by Archbishop Parker and, by far the most influential, the metrical psalms of Sternhold and Hopkins.[13] But the paraphrase of the psalms, in both English and Latin, was also an extremely common personal literary, educational and devotional exercise: hundreds of examples survive both in manuscript sources and in the work of poets who made it into print, from Thomas Wyatt's *Penitential Psalms* (1550) to Abraham Fraunce's *The Countesse of Pembrokes Emanuel* (1591). Surrey, Jonson, Donne, Herbert and Milton

---

[12] The Book of Common Prayer (BCP) reached its final form in the aftermath of the Restoration, in 1662. But the bulk of the text was composed by Thomas Cranmer and first published in 1549; and the text of the Psalms predates Cranmer, being the translations made by Miles Coverdale for his Bible, first published in 1535. For a very clear explanation of the details of the scriptural readings prescribed by the BCP, and the extent to which this differed from continental Protestant practice, see Ian Green, '"Hearing" and "Reading"'. On lay use of the BCP, see Maltby, *Prayer Book and People*. Hannibal Hamlin notes how well known were the psalms even in the twentieth century for anyone who had worshipped regularly with the Book of Common Prayer: much better known, indeed, than any other part of scripture (Hamlin, *Psalm Culture*, 253).

[13] For English psalms printed between 1530 and 1601, see the extremely useful appendix to Zim, *English Metrical Psalms*, 211–59. Lucía Martínez Valdivia points out that Sternhold and Hopkins outsold all other books in England for nearly 200 years from the late 1540s ('Psalms and Early Modern English Poetry', 287). The psalms were also sung in Latin in seventeenth-century England: several surviving Latin versions of the BCP include Latin 'metrical' (i.e. stress-based, rhyming) versions of the psalms, often in common measure (e.g. editions of 1614, 1660 and 1689, on which see Streatfeild, *Latin Versions of the Book of Common Prayer*). A 1594 edition of Haddon's Latin translation of the BCP, now in Westminster Abbey, is bound with a copy of Sternhold and Hopkins, suggesting a bilingual liturgy.

all produced psalm paraphrases in English, and Anne Lok's *Meditation of a Penitent Sinner* (1560), probably the first English sonnet sequence, is an extended paraphrase of Psalm 51. Early English examples in Latin include single paraphrases, or small collections, by Walter Haddon and Nikolaeus Mameranus.[14] Lloyd Jones notes that editions of the psalms are by far the most frequently printed piece of Hebrew scripture, suggesting that the psalter was commonly used in the teaching of Hebrew at school and university.[15] Buchanan's Latin psalms were in use in at least some English schools before his death in 1582.[16]

Reading the Psalms in England, 1571–1586

The study of the psalms, and their literary appropriation in England, is marked by a cluster of influential publications in the 1570s and early 1580s: this is the cultural and religious context in which Philip Sidney conceived his psalm paraphrase project. In 1571, Arthur Golding published his English translation of Calvin's Latin translation and commentary on the psalms; the Geneva Bible, with its useful explicatory notes, was first published in 1560 and printed in England for the first time in 1576.[17] Franciscus Junius (1545–1602) and Immanuel Tremellius' (1510–80) Protestant Latin translation and commentary on the psalms was printed in 1580: as Noel Kinnamon points out (though few critics have taken up), this is an important volume for the emphasis laid in the preface and notes on the rhetorical form and literary features of each psalm.[18] The translation is made directly from the Hebrew, and is frequently more literal than that of the Geneva Bible. Though most of these individual publications have attracted some scholarly attention, they have done so in very different contexts: the translation of Junius and Tremellius, for instance, has been much discussed in relation to the Protestant translation of the Bible and the knowledge of Hebrew, but rarely in terms of its literary influence. The following summary attempts to give some sense of the proximity,

---

[14] Haddon, *Oratio Iesu Christi* (1555) includes a verse paraphrase of Psalm 103 alongside various New Testament texts. Mameranus, *Psalmi Davidis quinque* (1557) are Latin hexameter translations, in the style of Hessus, of Psalms 1, 14, 36, 39 and 79.
[15] Given the relative difficulty of the Hebrew of the Psalms, this might seem surprising. But the intense familiarity of their standard English translations must have been a great help for learners. Lloyd Jones, *Discovery of Hebrew*, 259–60.
[16] Green, *Poetic Paraphrase*, 88.
[17] Golding, *Psalmes of David* (1571). On the influence of the Geneva Bible, see Molekamp, *Women and the Bible*, and Rienstra and Kinnamon, 'Revisioning the Sacred Text'.
[18] Tremellius and Junius, *Psalmi Davidis* (1580); Kinnamon, 'God's "Scholer"', 85.

interconnection and literary significance of the most important volumes in this crucial decade.

This was an equally important decade in terms of the literary (rather than liturgical) appropriation of the psalms in England. The Latin psalm paraphrases of Eobanus Hessus, written in the 1530s and 1540s, were published for the first time in England in 1575 (and again in 1581).[19] Each verse paraphrase is preceded by a prose argument and a brief verse summary, to aid understanding, and the volume opens with an alphabetical index of the first word of the standard Latin (Vulgate) translation of each psalm: these functioned as the titles by which individual psalms were known, and the index allowed readers to look up a psalm by its familiar opening phrase rather than its number. Hessus' psalms are composed entirely in Latin elegiacs, generally considered the most accessible of Latin metres, and the preface to the reader, emphasizing their enticing qualities of charming readability, suggests they are particularly suitable for adolescent readers. David (and, implicitly, Hessus himself) is compared to Orpheus, hinting at the literary seriousness of the project, and the volume was probably aimed at schools.

By far the most influential of the Protestant psalm paraphrases, however, were those of George Buchanan (1506–82). Though the complete set of Buchanan's Latin verse psalm paraphrases was widely available in continental editions from 1566 onwards, the first edition printed in England dates from 1580.[20] Buchanan's collection, like that of his most influential successors, is marked by metrical variety: he uses 29 different metres, 14 of them derived from Horace. The collected verse of Buchanan was one of the most widely owned volumes of poetry in late sixteenth- and seventeenth-century England, and the evidence for his influence in metrical terms has already been discussed in Chapter 2 (see also Chapter 6). He continued to be read well into the nineteenth century: one of my own editions was printed in London in 1686 but bears owners' signatures dated 1812 and 1843.

The Latin verse psalter of Théodore de Bèze (Beza) was published in the same year, 1580, and by the same publisher as the Buchanan edition; Anthonie Gilbie's partial English translation of Beza's work (without the literal translation or verse paraphrases) was also published in London in

---

[19] Hessus, *Psalterium Davidis* (1575 and 1581), also including a paraphrase of Ecclesiastes.

[20] Buchanan, *Paraphrasis Psalmorum* (1580). Further editions were published in London by Vautrollerius in 1583 and 1592; in Edinburgh in 1611, 1615 and 1621; and in London in 1620, 1640 and 1648. For a full account of the print history see Green, *Poetic Paraphrase*, 26–33, 83–97.

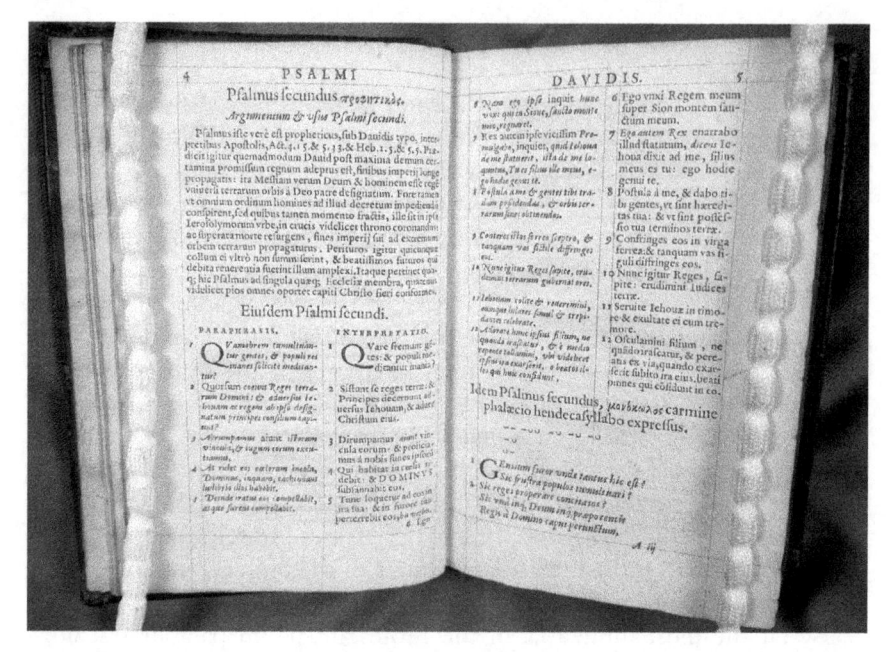

Figure 1 Theodorus Beza [Theodore de Bèze], *Psalmorum Davidis et aliorum prophetarum, libri quinque* (London: Thomae Vautroullerij & impensis Herculis Francisci, 1580), pp. 4–5 (Psalm 2)
By permission of the Master and Fellows of St John's College, Cambridge.

this year.[21] Beza's psalm paraphrases in Latin verse are preceded, for each psalm, by a prose summary, prose paraphrase (a kind of expanded translation, incorporating a degree of interpretation), and an 'interpretatio' (in fact a literal Latin prose translation) borrowed from the Hebrew scholar Heinrich Moller. Though discussions of Beza's work have tended to focus on the prose elements, and mention the verse *carmina*, if at all, as a kind of afterthought, Beza's Latin verse is set in a larger type than the prose material, suggesting to the reader that it represents the most significant element.

---

[21] Beza, *Psalmorum Davidis* (1580) and Gilbie, *Psalmes of David* (1580). The London edition of Beza was in fact a pirated version of the first complete edition, published in Geneva the previous year; a pirated version was also published in Antwerp in 1580. On the print history of Beza, see Thomson, 'Latin Psalm Paraphrases of Theodore de Bèze'. The enterprising publisher, Thomas Vautrollerius, was a Huguenot, who had probably met Buchanan (see Green, *Poetic Paraphrase*, 32). The publication of the complete Beza and Buchanan psalters in the same year may have been intended to encourage customers to buy both and bind them together – they were printed together in Morges in 1581 and Geneva in 1592.

Beza's versified psalms are unmistakeably heirs of Buchanan, and Buchanan himself praised Beza's poetry in high terms.[22] The projects are, however, significantly different: Beza's *carmina* are generally concise; they tend to follow the biblical text closely, without much significant expansion. Buchanan's paraphrases are freer, with a tendency to begin or end a stanza with directly biblical material, but to include also elements which expand upon the biblical text: in this respect, the Sidney psalter resembles Buchanan's psalm paraphrases more than those of Beza, though it is, as discussed below, demonstrably indebted to both. Stylistically, however, Buchanan 'classicises' much more than Beza, not only in terms of diction, style and metre, but also in content: at Psalm 96.11–12, for instance, in a well-known song of celebration, the biblical text describes the landscape itself rejoicing in the presence of the Lord:

> Let the heavens rejoice, and let the earth be glad: let the sea roar,   11
> and all that therein is.
> Let the field be joyful, and all that is in it: let all the trees of the   12
> wood then rejoice
>
> (Geneva Bible)

Buchanan interprets the 'rejoicing' of the fields and woods in terms of extraordinary fertility, a common classical trope:

> laetetur aether, gestiat
> tellus, fretum prae gaudio
> exsultet et quicquid freti
> salsas lacunas incolit.
>   campi virescant avii,
> se culta fruge vestiant,
> arrideantque floribus
> silvae et graventur fructibus.
> (41–8)
>
> *Let the sky rejoice, the earth dance, and the sea and everything in the sea's salt deeps exult for joy. Let the trackless plains burst into green, clothing themselves with cultivated crops, and let the forests be gay with flowers and laden with fruit.*[23]

---

[22] BL MS Lansdowne 15, fol. 49ᵛ, a letter from George Buchanan dated 6 August 1572. Gaertner considers Beza's psalms of inferior quality and other specialists of psalm paraphrase, most noticeably Roger Green, largely ignore them. Thomson's brief article ('Latin Psalm Paraphrases of Theodore de Bèze'), though focused on the complex print history, contains the only attempt at a literary appreciation of Beza's Latin psalms that I have been able to find, and suggests they may have been underrated. I have tried in this chapter to give some sense of the literary qualities and style of Beza's verse, which is significantly different from that of Buchanan but not in my view inferior.

[23] Text and translations of Buchanan's psalms are from Green, *Poetic Paraphrase*.

Mary Sidney frequently shows particular poetic interest in nature similes and metaphors; but here, where the metaphor of natural fertility is in Buchanan but not in the biblical text, she translates expansively but 'literally' – without interpreting the imagery of the Hebrew as Buchanan does:

> Starry roof, and earthy floor,
>   Sea and all thy wideness yieldeth:
> Now rejoice and leap and roar.
>   Leafy infants of the wood,
>   Fields and all that on you fieldeth,
>   Dance, oh dance, at such a good.[24]
>
>   (31–6)

In this, she follows Beza, whose version is obviously indebted to Buchanan's (and who, unusually, uses the same metre as Buchanan here) but who, like Sidney, avoids interpreting the biblical language with a different, and more classicizing, metaphor:

> Laetetur aether arduus,
> Tellus deorsum gestiat,
> Lateque fluctibus boans
> Testetur aequor gaudium.
>
> Quin arua & ipsa gaudeant,
> Aruisque messis insidens,
> Auraque percussum nemus,
> Suaui susurro sibilet.[25]
>
>   (41–8)

Let the steep heaven rejoice
Let the earth below dance
And, roaring with its waves far and wide,
The ocean testify its joy.

---

[24] The verb 'fieldeth' in this stanza is misinterpreted in Hamlin *et al.*, *Sidney Psalter*, in which the editors gloss it as 'obtains food in the field', noting that this significantly predates the first instance of such a use recorded by the *OED* (from Charles Darwin). But the phrase 'all that on you fieldeth' refers not to those who obtain food in fields, but to crops growing in the field. Buchanan's *culta fruge* points towards this, but Beza's *aruisque messis insidens* ('and the crops [literally, 'sitting'] in the fields') is clearer. The Hebrew is even simpler, being literally translated as 'the fields and whatever is in them'. Both the English of the Geneva Bible and Moller's literal Latin translation of the Hebrew offer close translations here.

[25] There is no modern edition of Beza's psalms. Quotations throughout are from the 1580 London edition, on the basis that this is the one the Sidneys are most likely to have owned. Translations are my own.

> *Let even the fields themselves exult*
> *And the crops in the fields,*
> *And the copse, beaten by the wind,*
> *Whisper with a sweet murmur.*

Protestant emphasis upon the literal (rather than allegorical or typological) meaning of the psalms is felt strongly in the Sidney psalter. Though both poets, and especially Mary, regularly expand and develop the imagery of the psalms, they do so within the framework of the 'literal' meaning as it was understood at the time and explained by the commentaries available to them. Neither Philip nor Mary introduce, for instance, typological interpretations referring to Christ, even when these were common in contemporary exegesis; similarly, where metaphors are introduced or expanded (as in Psalms 44 and 80, discussed below), those decisions are based upon available scriptural commentary. They do not, as Buchanan often does, recast scriptural imagery and metaphor in classical terms.

Beza's *carmina* may be closer to the scriptural text, and generally shorter than those of Buchanan, but they are even more metrically varied. Whereas Buchanan's collection includes 29 different metres, all but five with a classical model, Beza uses 47. Moreover, Beza, unlike Buchanan but in common with the Sidney psalter, also creates unclassical stanza groupings, and uses different stanzaic arrangements to further vary the structure of his poems: five of his 47 metres are found in more than one stanza form, leading to a further fifteen variations if counted separately.[26] The majority of Beza's metres are not found in Horace; though several of them can be traced to other ancient or late antique sources (such as the choruses of Seneca or the lyric verse of Prudentius), many others are either inventions of Beza's own, or are found only in other neo-Latin verse. In the 1580 London editions of both Beza and Buchanan, each Latin metrical form is identified and described, with diagrams supplied, allowing the reader to appreciate, and indeed drawing attention to, the metrical variety that they display: in other words, just as the Psalms themselves were understood as a treasury of Hebrew poetry equivalent to, or outdoing

---

[26] Phalaecian hendecasyllables are used stichically and in three- and four-line stanzas. Iambic trimeter is used stichically and in three- and seven-line stanzas. Iambic dimeter is used stichically and in three-, four-, five- and six-line stanzas. Trochaic dimeter catalectic is used stichically and in three-, four-, six-, seven, eight- and eleven-line stanzas. Anapaestic tetrameter acatalectic is used stichically and in four-line stanzas.

that of classical lyric, so these Latin versions of the psalms functioned as a kind of textbook of Latin metres as well as a resource for prayer or study.[27]

At this point, the practice of literary psalm paraphrase in classical metres began to be taken up in England: the following year, in 1581, Scipio Gentili (1563–1616) published a series of hexameter psalm paraphrases, including versions of 21 psalms, with a preface dedicating the work to Philip Sidney; a second volume, with a further 25 versions published in 1584, was once again dedicated to Sidney.[28] In 1582, Stephanus Parmenius' hexameter version of Psalm 104 was printed in London: like the psalm paraphrases of Hessus, Buchanan, Beza and Gentili, it was published by Thomas Vautrollerius, though Parmenius' poem has a personal and occasional force – he uses it to give thanks for having safely reached England from Hungary.[29] In the preface to his second volume, Gentili acknowledges by name the influence of Flaminio, Buchanan and Beza, and comments on the difficulty of following in their footsteps.[30] Gentili's collections are evidence of the particular interest in psalm paraphrase at this moment, and suggestive of Sidney's personal interest in the form.[31] Metrically, however, they are highly conservative: like Parmenius' version, all of Gentili's psalm paraphrases are in hexameters. This practice – though in this case into *English* hexameters – was followed also by

---

[27] This level of explicit metrical explanation and guidance is not typical of neo-Latin verse collections in this period, in which even metrical innovation usually goes unmarked. The exceptions are school grammars, textbooks and editions intended for school use: see for instance the detailed metrical guidance offered in an edition of Horace printed in London in 1592 (*Poemata. Nouis Scholijs & Argumentis illustrata*). Buchanan did not supply the metrical information himself, though it was widely added to editions of his psalms.

[28] Gentili, *Paraphrasis Aliquot Psalmorum Davidis* (1581) and *In XXV. Davidis Psalmos Epicae Paraphrases* (1584). Gentili also published Latin verse translations of Tasso.

[29] Parmenius, *Paean ... ad psalmum Davidis CIV* (1582), dedicated to Henry Unton.

[30] Gentili, *In XXV ... Paraphrases* (1584), sig. *3ʳ. In the first volume of 1581, Flaminio and Buchanan are alluded to but not named directly (Gentili had perhaps not yet read Beza at this point). Flaminio claimed to be the first to put the psalms into Latin lyric metres; though widely praised on the continent, his collection of 30 psalm paraphrases was apparently less popular and influential in England than those of Buchanan and Beza. Where he does appear in the English manuscript record, it is usually in strongly continentally influenced material: BL MS Harley 4935, fols. 1ʳ–3ᵛ, for instance, contains Flaminio's paraphrases of Psalms 23 and 25 (both in iambic distichs), in a miscellany containing many Dutch and Italian items.

[31] Both prefaces acknowledge Sidney's excellence as a poet, but neither mentions his writing of psalm paraphrases. Though Gentili may simply not have been aware of Sidney's own efforts in this direction, the repeated dedication of Latin psalms to Sidney suggests that Sidney's interest in the form was known, but that his own paraphrases belong to after this date, perhaps to the last year of his life (1585–6). As Ringler points out, if Gentili had known of Sidney's activity in this respect, it is likely he would have mentioned it (Ringler, *Poems of Sir Philip Sidney*, 501).

Abraham Fraunce, another member of the Sidney circle, in *The Countesse of Pembrokes Emanuel ... together with certaine Psalmes of David, All in English Hexameters* (1591).

Also in 1582, Richard Stanyhurst (1547–1618), an Irish Catholic who lived mostly on the continent, but who had links with the Sidney family, published *Thee First Foure Bookes of Virgil His Aeneis*.[32] Stanyhurst's translation attempts to render the quantitative metrics of the Latin hexameter in English, and has long been recognized as a landmark in English quantitative metrics.[33] For all its importance for the reception of Virgil, however, Stanyhurst's volume does not contain only the partial *Aeneid* translation: the final 25 pages are taken up with other compositions, beginning with four translations of the psalms into English versions of quantitative lyric metres. These poems have attracted some attention in relation to the wider interest in quantitative metrics, but they have mostly not been connected to the practice of Latin psalm paraphrase, of which they are a vernacular version.[34] As Stanyhurst himself puts it, introducing his translation of Psalm 1:

> As thee *Latinists* haue diuerse kindes of verses besydes the *Heroiacal*: so our *English* wyl easelye admyt theym, although in thee one language or oother they sowne not al so pleasinglie too the eare ... I haue made proof of the *Iambical* verse in thee translation of thee first *Psalme* of *Dauid*, making bold with thee curteous reader, too acquaynt hym there with.

THEE FIRST PSALME OF DAVID,
named in Latin, *Beatus vir*, translated in too English Iambical verse.

> That wight is happy and gratious,
> That tracks noe wicked coompanye;
> Nor stands in il mens segnorye;
> In chayre ne sits of pestilence.[35]
>
> (1–4)

---

[32] Though published at Leiden the book is obviously aimed at an English market, and gives the place of publication in English, not Dutch. A final list of errata is prefaced by a note from the printer, apologising for the errors: 'Thee noooueltye of imprinting English in theese partes, and thee absence of thee author from perusing soom proofes could not choose but breede errours' (110). Stanyhurst had been at school with Henry Sidney, the father of Philip and Mary.
[33] See e.g. Attridge, *Well-Weighed Syllables*, 166–72.
[34] Hamlin briefly compares the metres of Stanyhurst's *Psalms* 1–4 to those of Buchanan (Hamlin, *Psalm Culture*, 91).
[35] Stanyhurst, *First Foure Bookes of Virgil His Aeneis* (1582), 86.

In contrast to Hessus, Parmenius or Gentili, Stanyhurst follows the Latin practice of Buchanan and Beza, and anticipates that of the Sidney psalter, by translating the first four psalms in four different metres: iambic dimeter in four-line stanzas for the first psalm; elegiac couplets; stichic (or 'first') asclepiad; and finally sapphic stanzas. Though elegiac couplets, first asclepiad and sapphic stanzas are all very common metres at this particular period, the iambic dimeter is more unusual. Hannibal Hamlin, in his comments on this translation, wrongly assumes that all iambic metres have an invective association, which is not the case for stichic iambic dimeters. Stanyhurst's choice is probably influenced by Buchanan's very frequent use of iambic dimeters and, standing behind Buchanan, their use in early Christian religious poetry, such as Prudentius' *Cathemerinon* 1 and the hymns of Ambrose.[36] Indeed, iambic dimeters are the metre used by both Buchanan and Beza for their versions of Psalm 96, quoted above.

Stanyhurst's third psalm is in the first asclepiad, a choice which may have a programmatic force: the metre is used only three times in Horace – for *Odes* 1.1 and 3.30 (the first and last of the unitary first three books of *Odes*, published together in 23 BC), and again for *Odes* 4.8, the central ode in the fourth book, published ten years later. These are the only stichic odes in the entire collection, and the metre as a result often suggests the initiation (or completion) of a project. It is perhaps not coincidental that Buchanan also uses this metre only three times (Psalms 28, 40 and 80), though as noted in Chapter 2, it was widely taught. Overall, Stanyhurst's choice of metres, like those of Buchanan and Beza albeit across only four poems, suggests the generic range of the psalter and the wealth of literary history – ranging from Horace to Ambrose down to Buchanan – that it was understood to encompass.

The Sidney Psalter

This is the literary and scriptural context in which first Philip Sidney and then, following his death in 1586, his sister Mary, embarked upon

---

[36] Fourteen of Buchanan's psalms, including all of the final three (148–50) are in iambic dimeters. The hymns of Ambrose consist of eight stanzas each of four lines of iambic dimeter. Stanyhurst's paraphrase is also in four-line stanzas. Hamlin's discussion of Stanyhurst's English quantitative metres is muddled (Hamlin, *Psalm Culture*, 89–92). In addition to the confusion over iambics, the second psalm is identified as hexameter, though it is in fact in elegiac couplets; the third psalm is described as being in the same metre as Horace, *Odes* 1.5, but the first (stichic) asclepiad is the metre of *Odes* 1.1, not 1.5. Attridge identifies Stanyhurst's metres correctly (*Well-Weighed Syllables*, 169), though he does not distinguish between different forms of asclepiad. Philip Sidney's poem 'O sweet woods' (*Old Arcadia*, 34) is also in the first asclepiad (cf. Attridge, *Well-Weighed Syllables*, 186).

their paraphrase of the psalter: a project which, like the Latin verse psalters on which it was modelled, both exploited and significantly extended the range of formal and metrical possibilities of contemporary lyric verse.

Existing scholarship has acknowledged, and in several instances analysed in some detail the influence upon the Sidney psalter of a range of prose sources, including the Geneva Bible, the prose portions of Beza's psalm commentary (in his and Moller's Latin, and Gilbie's English), and the influential translation and commentary by Calvin (translated into English by Golding). Likely verse models have, however, been limited largely to the French Marot-Bèze psalms, of which Philip Sidney, in particular, probably did make considerable use, especially as a source of stanza forms, but which was never printed in England. There is much less evidence for Mary Sidney's use of the Marot-Bèze psalter and, though metrically creative, the French psalter was written for congregational singing, not as a showcase of literary lyric: in this important respect it is the Latin, not the French, psalters that are the model for the Sidney psalms.[37]

Surprisingly, there has been no serious discussion of the influence of George Buchanan's verse paraphrases of the psalms upon the Sidneys, even though the impact of Buchanan's psalms in England in general has been at least somewhat documented, and Buchanan was undoubtedly Beza's primary model. Moreover, there are several links between Buchanan and the Sidney circle; Sidney wrote to Buchanan in 1579 and mentioned his work in the *Apology for Poetry* (c.1580).[38] Existing scholarship has also made little reference to the important Latin translation and commentary on the Psalms produced by Junius and Tremellius, working directly from the

---

[37] For a detailed account of Philip Sidney's borrowing of line and stanza forms from the Marot-Bèze psalter see Ringler, *Poems of Sir Philip Sidney*, 507–8. The suggestions for parallels in wording or detail, however, are generally less convincing: Ringler's note on 2.8, for instance, implies that Sidney's 'yokes' in this line is derived from Marot ('le joug', 'the yoke'), because BCP and Geneva have 'cords'. But the note on this verse in the Geneva Bible offers 'yoke' as a gloss, and *iuga* (Latin for 'yokes', also in the plural as in Sidney but not in Marot) appears in Beza and Calvin. Richard Todd also argues that the influence of the Marot-Bèze psalter has been overestimated, though he suggests the Dutch *Souterliedekens* attributed to Jonkheer Willem van Zuylen van Nyevelt as another possible model (Todd, 'So Well Attyr'd Abroad'). Todd mentions Buchanan in passing, but is apparently unaware of Beza's Latin psalter, and does not acknowledge (or was unaware of) the great popularity of Buchanan in England. It is much more likely that the Sidneys were reliant upon Latin literary paraphrases published (repeatedly, in the case of Buchanan) in England, than on a Dutch collection. Todd is right, however, to emphasize that the liturgical, sung tradition of the Marot-Bèze psalter was, and was understood as, a quite different kind of poetry from that of the Sidney psalter.

[38] Phillips, 'Buchanan and the Sidney Circle'.

Hebrew.[39] Finally, though the scholarly influence of Beza's edition has been widely acknowledged, several critics conflate Beza's Latin edition of the psalms with the English translation by Gilbie published in the same year, though Gilbie translates only some of Beza's Latin material – crucially, neither the Latin verse nor Moller's literal translation – and his translations are not always close ones. Both Sidneys frequently derive material from elements of Beza's work which are not in Gilbie's English version, and Gilbie cannot be taken, as he often has been by scholars, as a proxy for Beza.[40] In general, Beza's Latin verse paraphrases have been neglected as a source for the Sidney psalter, despite their obvious potential as a model: no critic attempts to describe what these Latin poems are like, stylistically or metrically; how they compare to those of Buchanan; or why they might have been of interest to the Sidneys as a model.[41] My discussion demonstrates how Latin verse paraphrases of Buchanan and Beza

---

[39] Kinnamon (for Mary Sidney) and Ringler (for Philip Sidney) both state that there is no evidence for the Sidneys' use of either Tremellius-Junius or Buchanan. Kinnamon concedes, however, that 'While there is little, if any, verbal correspondence between the countess's Psalms and George Buchanan's Latin paraphrase or the text of the Tremellius-Junius Bible, her knowledge of both of them can hardly be doubted' ('God's "Scholer"', 214 n3). As discussed below, there is in fact strong, and in the case of Mary Sidney, plentiful, evidence for the direct influence of both Tremellius-Junius and Buchanan upon the Sidney psalter. See also Kaske, 'Another Echo of the Tremellius-Junius *Libri Poetici*'. Philip Sidney refers to Tremellius and Junius' categorization of the psalms, Song of Songs, Ecclesiastes, Proverbs, Job and the songs of Moses and Deborah as the 'poeticall part' of scripture – Sidney, *Defence of poesie* (1595), sig. C1^v–C2^r.

[40] Kinnamon's description of the difference between the Latin and English volumes ('God's "Scholer"', 214) is not entirely accurate: he states that Gilbie translates both Beza's *paraphrasis* and the *interpretatio* (borrowed from Moller). In fact, Gilbie translates only the *argumentum* (summary introduction) and the *paraphrasis*, not the briefer *interpretatio*. These Latin terms are themselves somewhat misleading. Heinrich Moller (1530–89) was Professor of Hebrew at Wittenberg, working directly from the Hebrew text, and the *interpretatio* is in fact a very literal translation, not an 'interpretation' in the modern sense. Explanatory material is added in the *paraphrasis*. Gilbie's volume therefore offers an expanded text and not at any point a literal translation. Kinnamon also does not mention that even where elements are ostensibly shared between the Latin and English texts, the actual contents, as discussed below, are sometimes significantly different.

[41] Kinnamon lists ten possible parallels with Beza's Latin verse in Mary Sidney's psalms, at 74.103–4 and 112–14; 83.25–6; 86.45–6; 89.1; 58.1–4; 89.13–14; 106.57; 110.13–16; 119I.15–16. He implies that this is a complete list, though, as demonstrated below, this is certainly not the case; in my discussion, I have focused on parallels not noted by Kinnamon. He also notes further parallels to the Latin prose of Beza's commentary. Ringler points out some parallels with Beza's Latin verse, but refers largely to the prose elements, and does not always make the distinction between prose and verse sources clear. Zim mentions the existence of Latin verse paraphrases of the psalms, but does not discuss any examples in detail; her use of Beza draws only upon his Latin prose paraphrases, usually with reference to Gilbie's translation (Zim, *English Metrical Psalms*, 189–98 and 299 n19). None of these critics discusses the stylistic or metrical features of Beza's Latin verse, or how it compares to that of Buchanan.

shaped the Sidney psalter generically, formally, metrically and in multiple instances of specific borrowing and allusion.

The neglect of the available Latin material has contributed to a tendency to overemphasize the 'originality' of the Sidney psalter, and the sense of a 'personal' or even 'autobiographical' lyric voice, especially in Mary Sidney's section. There are probably several elements at play in the critical desire to emphasize the personal, emotional and 'original' elements of her work: a modern preference for 'originality'; a failure to appreciate the cultural centrality – and literary dignity – of paraphrase in early modernity (which, as described in the Introduction, serves a different purpose from that generally conveyed by 'translation' in modern English); a desire to assimilate the Sidney psalter to a story about essentially Petrarchan vernacular lyric, rather than to one rooted in classical and biblical models of poethood; and perhaps also a lingering tendency to assume that the most effective lyric poetry, especially by women, is decodably 'personal'.[42] I consider the Sidney psalter to be the single best and most important work of English lyric of the second half of the sixteenth century: but it is also, in modern terms, both unoriginal and impersonal.

In practice, commentators have tended to describe as original interpolations any elements which are not in the Geneva Bible translation. Though the influence of the Geneva Bible is clear, it was in many instances not the most literal translation available to the Sidneys: the Latin translations by Tremellius and Junius, and that of Moller (included in Beza), are often closer to the Hebrew, and many supposedly 'non-biblical' elements of the Sidney psalter are in fact more faithful to the text of the Hebrew than is the Geneva Bible translation. Mary Sidney, in particular, made an apparently conscious effort to restore biblical metaphors flattened by the Geneva translation, such as in her consistently literal renderings of descriptions of God as the 'rock' of salvation or security.[43] Elements of the

---

[42] For examples of several of these tendencies, see for instance Greene, 'Sir Philip Sidney's Psalms', which reads the psalter as a landmark of fictional, secular poetics, understanding its non-liturgical nature as a rejection of the existing tradition. Greene does not acknowledge, or discuss, the Latin literary tradition of psalm paraphrase, though his sense of psalm paraphrase as a site of literary innovation in the latter sixteenth century is surely correct.

[43] Molekamp, *Women and the Bible*, 161, for instance, offers the phrase 'my rock, my safety's Treasury' in the earlier draft version of Psalm 62 preserved in MS *B*, as an example of a 'non-Biblical metaphor, which ... would seem inspired by Marot-Beza: "'Luy seul es mon roc esleué'", on the basis that there is no rock in the Geneva Bible translation. It appears, however, in the Hebrew text (צוּרִי); in Junius-Tremelleius ('rupes est & salus mea'); in Calvin (in both the Latin and in Golding's translation: 'But he is my rock, and my welfare') and in Moller's *interpretatio* printed in Beza ('ipse est petra mea & salus mea'). A very similar phrase, 'our safety's rock' (Psalm 95.4), is

Sidney psalter marked as obscure or original in the existing commentaries are frequently traceable to Moller, Tremellius, Beza or Buchanan, or a mixture of these. Psalm 28, for instance, has a colourful passage that appears to depart from the scriptural sources:

> Link not me in self-same chain,
> With the wicked-working folk:
> Who their spotted thoughts to cloak,
> Neighbours friendly entertain,
> When in hearts they malice mean.
>
> (11–15)

Ringler comments that '[Philip] Sidney's images of the "chain" and "spotted thoughts" are not in his sources.' Tremellius' note on his Latin translation for this verse reads:

> Ne trahas me] id est, ne inducas me in potestatem illorum, aut sinas **quasi mancipium ab illis rapi**, ut supra psal. 26.9 and 27.12
>
> *Do not draw me] that is, do not draw me into the power of those men, or allow me **as it were to be taken into slavery by them**, as above psal. 26.9 and 27.12.*

The Latin term *mancipium* can mean a purchase, property, the right of ownership, or slavery. This Latin gloss probably stands behind Sidney's 'chain'. Similarly, the 'spotted' thoughts derive probably from Buchanan's expansion of these lines:

> ne me connumera coetibus impiis,
> neu tanquam socium plecte nocentibus;
> quorum blanditiis illita mollibus
> lingua est, mens gelido **livida** toxico.
>
> (9–12)
>
> *Number me not with the companies of the unholy and punish me not as an accomplice of the guilty, whose tongue is smooth with sweet flatteries, whose mind is **livid** with cold poison.*

'Lividus' frequently means 'malicious' or 'wicked', and that is the meaning of the biblical text at this point; but the literal meaning of 'lividus' in Latin is 'black and blue', the variegated colour of bruising. This Latin word

---

noted in the critical edition of Mary Sidney's psalms (Brennan *et al.* (eds.), *Collected Works of Mary Sidney Herbert*, vol. II) as an expansion of the biblical text, because it does not appear in the Geneva Bible translation; but once again this phrase is a literal translation of the Hebrew, and is found closely translated in both Beza and Tremellius. On the question of Mary Sidney's knowledge of Hebrew, see note 59 below.

probably suggested Sidney's 'spotted' thoughts.[44] Similarly, Ringler notes that in the memorable lines 'And in thy fear, knees of my heart will fold / Towards the temple of thy holiness' (Psalm 5.19–20), Sidney's 'knees of my heart will fold' replaces 'worship' in the BCP and Geneva Bible. Ringler points out that the idea of bowing or folding the 'knees of my heart' was a common one, and cites a vernacular parallel from Wedderburn, *Spirituall Sangis* (1567).[45] The Hebrew verb here, however, does literally mean 'I shall bow myself down' or 'I shall bend myself'; and though often translated simply as 'worship', Tremellius offers the more literal 'incurvabo me versus templum sanctitatis tuae cum reverentia tui' ('I shall bend myself towards the temple of your holiness with fear of you'). This more literal translation also permits Sidney's more literal translation of the Hebrew phrase 'towards the temple of your holiness' (since you can't worship 'towards' in English, but can bend 'towards' something).

Both these examples are from Philip Sidney's portion of the psalter, but similar evidence for the careful consultation of Latin sources is if anything more available in the case of the psalms written by his sister. Mary Sidney's handling of one of the most difficult verses in the Hebrew Psalter, Psalm 68:13, also reflects the influence of Buchanan. This obscure verse appears to be assuring the addressee, dark with soot from the fireplace, that she shall shine as brightly as the dove, glittering with silver and gold. All the available translations and commentaries discuss and (attempt to) explain the imagery here, but only Buchanan, like Mary Sidney, has the idea of the addressee *outdoing* the dove in beauty:

> Though late the chimney made your beauties loathed,
> Now shine you shall, and **shine more gracefully,**
> Than lovely dove in clear gold-silver clothed,
> That glides with feathered oar through wavy sky.
>
> (29–32)

> vestra licet somno sternantur corpora nigrae
>   inter fuliginis ollas,
> **illa tamen vincent** nitidam candore columbam
>   rutilae cervicis honore,
> quae nunc argentum nitidum, nunc lumina blandum
>   radiantis provocat auri.
>
> (Buchanan, 68.39–44)

---

[44] This interpretation of *lividus* suggests that Philip Sidney was not, at least in this case, referring to the Hebrew, since the Hebrew term here means 'wicked' and has no visual connotation.

[45] Ringler, *Poems of Sir Philip Sidney*, 510.

Even if your bodies are prostrated in sleep among dark and sooty pots, **they will surpass** *the brightly glinting dove in the elegance of their shining necks, which rival glittering silver and the attractive glow of radiant gold.*

These kinds of small-scale points refine our understanding of the sources for the Sidney psalms, and the depth and complexity of the engagement between these English poems and their largely Latin models; but they don't give us much sense of the relationship between the poetic achievement of the Sidney psalter and that of the Latin poetic versions. Here it is Beza's verse that is of particular importance, though often, as we shall see, in conversation with that of Buchanan.

Mary Sidney Herbert and Beza

Psalms 120 to 127 in the Sidney psalter are in English versions of Latin quantitative metres. This portion is not chosen at random: it comprises the first half of the fifteen-psalm sequence traditionally known as the 'Songs of Ascents', understood since antiquity as a distinct group concerned with the return from exile, whether of the Israelites out of Babylon or the return of David from his wanderings. Philip Sidney was a pioneer in the vogue for English quantitative verse, and this sequence was probably intended by his sister as a homage to his enthusiasm; it has several times been discussed in relation to the quantitative verse movement, most authoritatively by Derek Attridge, but has otherwise attracted little critical attention.[46]

No existing discussion of the sequence explains what would have been obvious to contemporary readers, but is now obscure: namely, that the choice of metres is not primarily, or indeed much at all, classical. No ancient verse collection contains such disparate metrical forms – including hexameter, alcaics, iambic metres and lyric metres (on which see Chapter 2). Such a sequence is, rather, distinctly contemporary: an imitation in English verse of the extraordinary metrical versatility and experimentation of sixteenth-century Latin poetry.

Many common Latin metres are of course found in both Beza and Buchanan, and Mary Sidney could easily have used eight metres found in both poets – certainly any selection of the eight most 'obvious' Latin quantitative metres would likely have done so. Her sequence, however,

---

[46] Attridge, *Well-Weighed Syllables*, 203–6 identifies all but one of the metres, but does not relate the sequence to contemporary Latin verse practice. An interesting discussion of these psalms in Femke Molekamp's book is focused on the use of the Geneva Bible and does not discuss metrical choices (*Women and the Bible*, 152–78).

includes one metre (phalaecian hendecasyllables) used regularly by Beza but surprisingly not at all by Buchanan; another rare form (anapaestic tetrameter acatalectic, discussed below), used three times by Beza but not by Buchanan;[47] and also one metre ('anacreontic' iambic dimeter catalectic) used by both, but only once in each case.[48] In the choice of the latter, she was probably once again honouring her brother: Philip Sidney's *Old Arcadia* also includes a poem in this unusual metre.[49]

Buchanan's Latin psalm paraphrases use a total of 29 or 30 different metres (depending on the edition) for the 150 psalms; Beza a total of 47 for 171 (counting the 22 metrically distinct sections of Psalm 119 separately).[50] It is unlikely that Mary Sidney would, by chance, have chosen eight metres two of which are used only by Beza, and one of which appears only once in both. The quantitative sequence signals her significant indebtedness to both poets, with a slight emphasis upon Beza which reflects her practice as a whole.

Several other points make the metrical debt to Beza's Latin (rather than French) paraphrases especially clear: firstly, Mary Sidney follows Beza in translating each of the 22 eight-line sections of Psalm 119 in different metres, creating from this enormous poem a kind of lyric sequence or miniature anthology. Secondly, and most striking, is her handling of Psalm 126. Attridge commends her version of this psalm as particularly successful but adds that she has achieved this 'at the expense of metrical regularity: it is difficult to derive any consistent quantitative pattern from it'.[51] The poem begins:

---

[47] Though in practice the metre of Buchanan's Psalm 131, which is called 'anapaestic Pindaric dimeter acatalectic', is almost identical.

[48] Buchanan, Psalm 131; Beza, Psalm 61. The metrical terminology can be confusing here; Cowley, for instance, uses 'anacreontic' to refer to iambic dimeter acatalectic (eight syllables rather than seven); while Julius Caesar Scaliger's 'anacreontics' are irregular. Buchanan gives Boethius *Cons.* 3 *met.* 7 as his model for the form. Psalm 131 was included in the 1556 partial edition of Buchanan, and Stefan Tilg has identified it as the earliest example of Christian anacreontics. It may be the source for Estienne's influential Greek anacreontics (Tilg, 'Neo-Latin Anacreontic Poetry').

[49] Sidney, *Old Arcadia*, 32; Attridge notes that both Philip's and Mary's version of this metre make stress and quantity coincide (*Well-Weighed Syllables*, 203).

[50] I have been unable to find any existing scholarship on Beza's Latin metrical practice, despite its enormous and innovative variety. All metrical analyses are therefore my own. Readers wishing to follow up these matters should be aware that there are several typographical errors in the metrical diagrams and descriptions included in the 1580 London edition of Beza, which was a pirated version of the 1579 Geneva edition.

[51] Attridge, *Well-Weighed Syllables*, 204. The claim that this poem is not in a recognizable quantitative metre is reproduced in Hamlin *et al.* (eds.), *Sidney Psalter* and Brennan *et al.* (eds.), *Collected Works of Mary Sidney Herbert*, vol. II.

> When long absent from lovely Zion
> By the Lord's conduct home we returned,
> We our senses scarcely believing
> Thought mere visions moved our fancy.

This poem is certainly in an unusual metre but it is not unidentifiable: it is an English version of the unusual (and unclassical) metre Beza uses for his Latin version of this same psalm (126), a metre he describes as 'anapaestic tetrameter acatalectic'.

> Reduces subito patria regredi
> In sola quum nos Solymis exules
> Sinerent versi corda Tyranni
> Esse haec somnia mera credidimus.
>
> *When we, exiles from Jerusalem,*
> *Brought back suddenly to our native land,*
> *Found the tyrant's heart could be turned –*
> *We believed these things were mere dreams.*

This metre is hard to recognize because it is so flexible. According to the diagram printed above the poem in the 1580 London edition, each of the four metrical feet may contain either a spondee (two long syllables), a dactyl (a long followed by two short syllables) or an anapest (two short followed by a long syllable).[52] This is represented as follows:

$$\begin{array}{cccc} \cup - & \cup\cup - & \cup\cup - & \cup\cup - \\ -\cup\cup & -\cup\cup & -\cup\cup & -\cup\cup \\ - - & - - & - - & - - \end{array}$$

Mary Sidney's poem follows this pattern precisely, though making full use of the potential for variety it permits. The third line of the first stanza, for instance, is largely spondaic, with only nine syllables as a result:

$$- \ - \ - \ - \ - \ \cup\cup \ - \ -$$

We our senses scarcely believing

Whereas the first line of the second stanza uses many short syllables, extending as result to eleven:

$$- \ \cup \ \cup \ \cup \ \cup \ - \ - \ \cup \ \cup \ - \ -$$

Then in our merry mouths laughter abounded,

---

[52] Except for the first foot, in which an iamb is also permitted.

'Mere' in line 4 ('Thought mere visions moved our fancy') probably alludes to Beza's adjective *mera* (4): there is no adjective in the Hebrew text, nor in any of the other versions used regularly by Sidney. Conversely, the only version to attach an equally unscriptural adjective to Zion, as Sidney does here ('*lovely* Zion') is Buchanan ('Sionem / Dulcem', 'sweet Sion', 2). Other elements of metrical imitation are less obscure: Philip Sidney's choice of hexameter in rhyme royal for Psalm 18 ('Thee will I love, O Lord, with all my heart's delight'), for instance, may have been influenced by Buchanan, who also uses hexameter for Psalm 18, though the style of Sidney's translation, marked by emotive repetition, is closer to that of Beza.

Mary Sidney signals a particular debt to Beza from the start of the quantitative sequence. She begins her version of Psalm 120, the first of the fifteen 'Songs of Ascents', with four lines which, though based upon the biblical text, add to the original psalm the idea of calling repeatedly upon the Lord:

> As to th'Eternal often in anguishes
> Erst have I called, never unanswered,
> > Again I call, again I calling
> > Doubt not again to receive an answer.

The biblical text, by contrast, states simply: 'I called unto the Lord in my trouble, and he heard me' (Geneva Bible).

Buchanan also expands here, interpreting the generalized 'trouble' of the biblical verse as warfare and jealous assaults. But Mary Sidney's expansion, described as her original contribution in both available editions, in fact comes directly from Beza:

> Numen ô toties mihi vocatum,
> Expertum toties mihi vocanti,
> Tu me à criminibus calumniantum,
> Tu me à fraudibus hisce mentientum
> Linguarum obsecro vindicato iustus.

> *O Divine power so often called upon by me,*
> *That divine power I have so often tested by my calling* [or: *so often experienced in response to my call*],
> *Be just, I beseech you, when I have been vindicated*
> *From the accusations of those who defame me,*
> *And from the deceptions of lying tongues.*

Beza's Latin is here, as often, unclassical. Unclassical not in metre (this poem is in the same asclepiad metre as Horace, *Odes* 1.1), but in diction and sound. Despite the Horatian form, the poem sounds quite unlike Horace: much more so than anything in Buchanan. The repetition (*toties ... toties*; *mihi ... mihi*; *tu me a ... tu me a*), polyptoton (*vocatum ... vocanti*), alliteration (*criminibus calumniantum*) and rhyme (*calumniantum ... mentientum; criminibus ... fraudibus*) would all be unusual, even as isolated effects, in classical poetry. In such close proximity, the effect is quite unlike any classical verse, though all these features are found more frequently in late antique and medieval Latin poetry and are typical of Beza's Latin style. Mary Sidney's version responds directly to these rhetorical and stylistic features: the effectiveness of her stanza stems partly from its repetition (*called ... call ... calling*) as well as the repeated related vowel sounds. These effects, as well as the idea of the repeated calling, are inspired by Beza.

Indeed, the unclassical features of Beza's Latin verse – typical of much neo-Latin poetry of the sixteenth and seventeenth centuries, but still frequently denigrated or ignored by scholars – seem to have been particularly influential upon Mary Sidney. Her translation of Psalm 140, for instance, is written, as noted by Hannibal Hamlin, to a particularly sophisticated rhyme scheme, in which the end of each of the first four lines of every stanza rhymes with the middle of the following line, with the final two lines end-rhymed:

> Protect **me**, Lord, preserve **me**, set **me free**
> From men that **be** so vile, so viol**ent:**
> In whose int**ent** both force and fraud doth **lurk**
> My bane to **work;** whose tongues are sharper **things**
> Than adder's **stings;** whose rusty lips encl**ose**
> A poison's hoard, such as in aspic gr**ows**.
>
> (140.1–6)

Rhyme is not a classical feature, but, as we have already seen in the discussion of Psalm 120, Beza frequently uses some rhyme: this does not extend to what we would describe as a consistent 'rhyme scheme', but it is a distinctive feature of his style and distinguishes it sharply from that of Buchanan. The rhymes in Beza's version of the opening of Psalm 140 are not as consistently patterned as Mary Sidney's poem, but his repeated use of internal rhyme, followed by end rhymes in lines 5 and 6, creates a strikingly similar effect:

> Eripe me miserum scelerat**is**, erue saeu**is**
> Hostibus, inde dol**is**, hinc vi grassantibus ist**is**,
> Lethifer**um** quor**um** iaculatur lingua venen**um**,
> Quale vomunt saeu**is** metuendi dentibus angu**es**.
> Impia fac ne me rapiat manus: improba cont**ra**
> Istius immanis tu me molimine ser**ua**.[53]
>
> *Save me, wretched as I am, from wicked men, take me away*
>   *from ferocious men,*
> *The enemies who attack on all sides, with trickery on one side,*
>   *with violence on another,*
> *Those men whose tongues cast deadly venom,*
> *Such poison as fearful snakes spit from savage teeth:*
> *Let the hands of the wicked not seize me: protect me*
> *From the wicked devices of that wild man.*

Mary Sidney's psalms begin with number 44. The end of the first stanza of that psalm, the first of her poems, contains an expansion of a compressed and difficult portion of Hebrew verse. The expansion is, typically for her work, in keeping with the imagery of the psalms, and derived from suggestions in the commentaries, but conveys also structural and programmatic significance:

> Lord, our fathers' true relation
>   Often made, hath made us known
> How thy pow'r in each occasion
>   Thou of old for them didst show;
> How thy hand the pagan foe
>   Rooting hence [the pagan foe], thy folk implanting,
> Leafless made that branch [of the pagan foe] to grow,
>   This [of thy folk] to spring, no verdure wanting.
>   (44.1–8)

The final four lines here are hard to follow without reference to alternative translations or to a commentary. Zim suggests that Sidney's lines are 'over-ingenious' and obscure. But the obscurity of the passage – which is real – reflects an interpretative crux in the Hebrew. The Geneva Bible sets out the relevant verse with notes as follows:

---

[53] The final sound of 'angues' was pronounced in a similar way to that of '-is'. Leonine hexameters were a popular medieval form but are found surprisingly commonly also in early modern Latin verse. In this poem, the internal rhymes are most marked at the start, though the line end also rhymes with the middle in lines 9, 12, 13, 21 and 25.

> *How* thou hast driven out the [ª]heathen with thine hand, and planted [ᵇ]them: *how* thou hast destroyed the [ᶜ]people, and caused [ᵈ]them to grow.⁵⁴
>
> a. That is, the Canaanites.
> b. To wit, our fathers.
> c. Of Canaan.
> d. That is, our fathers.

The Hebrew text has four main verbs which are usually understood to have alternating objects: the 'other' nations in the case of the first and third verbs; the Jewish people in the case of the second and fourth. The Hebrew itself, however, admits of other interpretations, especially as the basic and usual meaning of the final verb is not 'cause to grow', but 'send' or 'send away'. This leads to Coverdale's version (the translation most familiar from liturgical use), in which the final verb also appears to refer to the displaced enemies:

> How thou has driven out the heathen with thy hand, and planted them in: how thou hast destroyed the nations, and **cast them out.**

The Geneva translation 'caused them to grow', and Mary Sidney's imagery of fertile growth, derive from the interpretation of this final verb in a special sense, to mean 'stretch out' or 'shoot forth [branches]'. Interestingly, this is a passage in which Beza's Latin prose paraphrase and Gilbie's English translation of it differ significantly: the imagery of a growing tree is in Beza's Latin (given below with a literal translation) but not in Gilbie's translation:

> Te videlicet tua ipsius manu populos, à quibus haec regio tenebatur expulisse, ut eos hic plantares, ac deinceps etiam, siqui ex illis gentibus supererant, attriuisse, ut longè latèque stirps illa maiorum nostrorum ramos diffunderet.⁵⁵
>
> *Indeed with your own hand you expelled the peoples by whom this region was formerly held, so that you might plant them* [the Jews] *here, and also thereafter, if any of those* [other] *peoples became powerful, you beat them* [the other peoples] *down, so that that stock of our ancestors might spread its branches far and wide.*

---

⁵⁴ Golding's translation of Calvin is very similar: 'Thou drivest out the heathen with thine own hand, and plantedst them: thou destroyedst the nation; and madest them to growe.'

⁵⁵ Beza, *Psalmorum Davidis*, 177.

Gilbie instead introduces the language of the 'flocke', suggesting animal rather than vegetable fertility: 'and moreover also that thou hast broken and consumed all that remayned of those Nations, that this flocke or linage of our elders should spread farre and wide'.[56]

Mary Sidney, in other words, follows the Geneva Bible in interpreting the final verb here as 'grow' (rather than 'cast out'); but she adds the image of the growth of a tree derived from Beza. She apparently also borrowed from Calvin's commentary the idea of God 'pluck[ing] up trees by the rootes' ('rooting hence'), in order to plant others in their stead.[57] Tremellius, too, uses the language of planting, and even of propagation: *Te manu tua gentes expulisse, & plantasse ipsos: malo affecisse nationes, & propagasse ipsos* ('that with your hand you have expelled the peoples, and planted these ones: afflicted the nations, and propagated these ones').[58]

The nuance of Sidney's translation, and the extent to which the compressed ambiguities of the final version reproduce the ambiguities of the Hebrew text – while deriving its interpretation from the commentaries – makes it probable that she either had herself some knowledge of Hebrew, or had the opportunity to discuss it in detail with those who did. She would surely in any case have been struck by the discrepancy between Coverdale's translation and that found in Calvin and Tremellius: such a discrepancy may have prompted her to consult the Hebrew even if this was not always her practice. Overall, her versions are consistently close to the Hebrew, more so than those of her brother, and I think it is very likely that she routinely referred to the Hebrew text directly.[59]

We know from the evidence of the Woodford manuscript that this was a psalm which Mary revised considerably: it is unsurprising that she should have taken particular care over the first of 'her' psalms. We can see here evidence for her sophisticated use of the commentaries available to her; from their cues she has developed the extended imagery of her version.

---

[56] Gilbie, *Psalmes of David*, 101.   [57] Golding, *Psalmes of David*, 171.
[58] Tremellius and Junius, *Psalmi Davidis*, 135.
[59] The introduction to the second volume of the critical edition notes that Mary may have had some knowledge of Hebrew learnt from Gervase Babington, the chaplain at Wilton in 1581–2 and a friend thereafter; adding that while there is no conclusive evidence for her knowledge of Hebrew, she tends, where sources differ, to follow the source which is closest to the Hebrew, and that there are several instances (not including this one) where her version suggests direct access to the Hebrew text (Brennan *et al.* (eds.), *Collected Works of Mary Sidney Herbert*, vol. II, 13, 16–17). My work tends to confirm this observation. On the (considerable) resources available for the study of Hebrew in the latter sixteenth century, see Lloyd Jones, *Discovery of Hebrew*. My own knowledge of biblical Hebrew is only modest, though I know the psalms in English well; with this combination as a starting point, the available late sixteenth-century reference works and commentaries are certainly sufficient to follow the detail of a textual crux of the kind discussed here.

The particular development of this image, however – which contrasts the leafless branch of the enemy with the 'verdure' of the Israelite's tree – adds even to the considerable detail of the commentaries, and links this psalm, the first in Mary's sequence, to the first psalm of all (of her brother and of the biblical book), in which the just man is compared to the tree planted by the waters, which flourishes and bears fruit and does not wither. But the *difficulty* of the English lines (in this case her revisions made the English more, not less, obscure) is not accidental: on the contrary, the difficulty we have in determining the subjects and objects of the final series of clauses in English reproduces very effectively the ambiguities of the Hebrew text. This combination of poetic imagination and commitment to scriptural 'literalism' is typical of Mary Sidney's work.

Moreoever, the commentary in Junius and Tremellius offers a useful cross-reference to a passage (in Psalm 80) which is also, not I think coincidentally, a site of significant expansion in the Sidney psalter. The note against verse 3 of Psalm 44 reads as follows:

> 3 Plantasse] vide Exod. 15.17. Propagasse ipsos] tum gentis incremento, tum amplificatione sedis: metaphora, ut Psal. 80.9.[60]
>
> *3 planted] see Exod. 15.17. Propagated them] [i.e.] both by the increase of the people, and by the broadening of their abode: a metaphor, as in Psalm 80.9.*

Psalm 80 compares God's care for the people of Israel to the nurture of a great vine. Coverdale has:

> 8. Thou hast brought a vine out of Egypt: thou hast cast out the heathen, and planted it.
> 9. Thou hast made room for it: and when it had taken root it filled the land.
> 10. The hills were covered with the shadow of it: and the boughs thereof were like the goodly cedar-trees.
> 11. She stretched out her branches unto the sea: and her boughs unto the river.
> 12. Why has thou then broken down her hedge: that all they that go by pluck off her grapes?
> 13. The wild boar out of the wood doth root it up: and the wild beasts of the field devour it.
> 14. Turn thee again, thou God of hosts, look down from heaven: behold, and visit this vine;
> 15. And the place of the vineyard that thy right hand hath planted: and the branch that thou madest so strong for thyself.

---

[60] Tremellius and Junius, *Psalmi Davidis*, 137.

The available commentaries all point out links here to the imagery used of Christ in the Gospels (Matthew 21:33, Mark 12:1 and Luke 20:9). It is typical of Mary Sidney's version, however, that her atmospheric expansion, though quite extensive, does not depart from the imagery of the Psalms themselves, and does not incorporate any explicitly Christian interpretation:

> A vine thou didst translate from Zoan plains,
>   And **weeding** them that held the place of old,
> Nor planting care didst slack, nor pruning pains,
>   To fix her roots, whom fields could not enfold.
> The hills were cloaked with her pleasing **cold**;
>   With cedar's state her **branches'** height contended:
> Scarce here the sea, the river there controlled
>   Her **arms**, her **hands**, so wide she both extended.
>
> Why hast thou now thyself dishedged this vine,
>   Carelessly left to passengers **in prey?**
> Unseemly rooted by the wood-bred swine,
>   **Wasted** by other beasts that wildly stray?
>   O God, return, and from thy **starry stay**
>   Review this vine, reflect thy looking hither;
>   This vineyard see, whose plot thy hand did lay,
>   This plant of choice, ordained not to wither.
>   (80.17–32)

If the addition of 'weeding' in line 18 reminds us of the expansion of Psalm 44 ('rooting hence'), the added phrase 'ordained not to wither' recalls once again her brother's translation of the first psalm ('Nor withered leaf shall make it fail to flourish', 10). Many of the details of the expansion here, described as characteristic of Mary Sidney's originality by the critical edition, can in fact be traced to Beza and Tremellius; the most significant model, however, is Buchanan. All of the elements printed in bold above correspond to or are suggested by words or phrases in Buchanan's version of the psalm which either do not appear in any of the other translations or commentaries typically used by Sidney, or which are expanded or emphasized by Buchanan as they are in Sidney's version:

> Traduxti Pharia **de scrobe** vineam,
> Prauarum expuleras semina gentium,
> Vt puro sereres purius hanc solo.
> Iam radix teneras fuderat vndique
>   Fibras: iam tremulo **frigore** texerat   25

>   Montes: aequa cedris **brachia** sparserat:
>   Tangebant **teretes** aequora **palmites**,
>   Euphraten teneri germina surculi,
>   Nudatam solitis cur modò sepibus
>   **In praedam** hospitibus deseris hanc vagis?   30
>   Cur hanc saeuus aper proterit? alites
>   Carpunt? omnigenae **depopulant** ferae?
>   O rex omnipotens, obsecro iam redi
>   Tandem, & **sidereo** prospice **de throno**:
>   Placatùsque tuam respice vineam,   35
>   Plantaras propria quam tibi dextera.
>   Hunc saltem placidus respice ramulum
>   Cui cultu assiduo conciliaueras
>   Robur, clara tui gloria nominis
>   Terrarum vt populis nota sit omnium.
>   (Psalm 80.21–40)
>
> *You transferred your vineyard from the Egyptian furrow; you expelled the seed of wicked races so that you might plant your vineyard more salubriously in healthy soil. Already the root had pushed up young shoots, everywhere; it had already covered mountains with its quivering shade* [literally: cold], *it had spread branches like those of cedars; the vine's smooth leaves were touching the sea, and the sprouting growths of the vine's tender twigs touched the Euphrates. Now it is stripped of its protective fences; why do you abandon it to these vagabond incomers for plunder? Why does the savage boar trample it, why do birds pluck at it and all kinds of beast devastate it? O king, all-powerful, return at least, I beg, and look out from your starry throne; be reconciled and consider your vineyard, which you planted for yourself with your own hand. At least look kindly on this small branch whose strength you built up with assiduous cultivation, so that the famous glory of your name could become known to peoples of all lands.*

Sidney's 'weeding' (18) (for the less vivid biblical 'brought') echoes Buchanan's expansion 'traduxti ... de scrobe' ('you have brought from the furrow (or hole) [in which it had been growing]', 21). The English 'pleasing cold' (21), for the biblical 'shadow', picks up Buchanan's use of 'frigore' ('cold', 25). Sidney's significant expansion of the personification here – by glossing the 'branches' (22), simply repeated in the scriptural text, as both 'her arms' and 'her hands' (24) – echoes Buchanan's very similar expansion ('brachia ... teretes ... palmites', 26–7). The difficult phrase 'passengers in prey' (26) is hard to understand: it means literally 'those passing by looking for prey to consume', quite a different phrase from the Geneva Bible's 'all they that go by pluck off her grapes'. Neither

Beza, Calvin, nor Junius-Tremellius introduces this idea of 'prey', which seems to come direct from Buchanan ('in praedam ... vagis', 30). Finally, only Buchanan interprets the scriptural 'look down from heaven' (v. 14) in terms of a throne: Buchanan's 'sidereo ... de throno' (34) has become Sidney's 'starry stay' (29).

The Sidney psalter was inconceivable generically without the literary precedent for metrical variety and literary ambition offered by Buchanan's and Beza's Latin psalm paraphrases: like Stanyhurst's four psalms, it belongs, in literary terms, to that primarily Latin tradition, not to that of Marot-Bèze or Sternhold and Hopkins. But the debt is not just a generic one. The Sidney psalter draws on both Buchanan and Beza in the handling of many individual psalms, with multiple specific borrowings; and Mary Sidney's portion has a marked metrical and stylistic debt to Beza in particular. Here, a fully bilingual study of the sources overlaps with the conclusions of Chapter 2: previous critics have shown little curiosity about the Latin psalm paraphrases as poetry, with almost none, for instance, acknowledging the basic point about how much Buchanan adds to his scriptural sources, and the ways in which he does so. Nor have any attempted to consider what influence Beza's distinctive and unclassical poetic style might have had upon the Sidneys. But as we saw in Chapter 2, Latin verse style underwent a revolution in the thirty years between 1550 and 1580: accordingly, Beza, though indebted to Buchanan, writes Latin verse quite differently from his predecessor. Mary Sidney, outliving her brother, had time to fully absorb that transition into her own astonishing collection.

Psalm Paraphrase after Sidney

The tradition of psalm paraphrase, first in Latin and then also in English, is of fundamental importance for understanding English poetic culture of the period. This is true both in terms of the tradition of psalm paraphrase itself – which endures as a foundational literary practice right through to the eighteenth century, where it merges with hymnody – but also in terms of the influence of psalm paraphrase upon the development of English lyric. This is certainly not confined to the (considerable) influence of the Sidney psalter alone. Modern anthologies and editions, even anthologies specifically of verse translation, rarely convey a sense of how ubiquitous psalm paraphrase was in early modern England, how closely it was associated with (and, very frequently, presented as equal to or pre-eminent over) classical translation, and to what extent it was involved in the development of English lyric as a whole.

The final poem of John Ashmore's important 1621 *Certain Selected Odes of Horace*, for instance, is, unlike the rest of the volume, neither a classical translation nor a version of a neo-Latin poem, but a paraphrase of Psalm 1.[61] Overall, Ashmore's printed collection closely resembles many surviving manuscripts from this period. Bod. Eng. poet. f. 17, for instance, though a particularly extensive example, is typical of the mixture of biblical, classical and original verse in seventeenth-century personal miscellanies. The Bodleian collection, which dates from the latter half of the seventeenth century, contains a few pieces of original verse, but is almost entirely taken up by verse translation, unified thematically by moralizing topics. The single largest component, by some margin, is psalm paraphrase, the first example of which is explicitly described as 'after Buchanan'.[62] In total, the manuscript contains 51 psalm paraphrases, just over a third of the total, alongside translations of Horace, Tibullus, Theocritus, Ausonius and contemporary poets, especially Buchanan, Sarbiewski and Milton.

Buchanan's enduring influence is evident not only in the many psalm paraphrases dependent upon his versions, but also in allusions to his metrical and literary authority. The large collection of Latin verse compositions made by Simonds D'Ewes (1602–50) in 1617–18 includes, for instance, a composition in a metre he describes in the margin as 'dactylic alcmanian'. He adds the comment: 'Hoc genere non scripsit Horatius, Buchananus tamen plurimas odes. De quo vid. pag. 146' (*'Horace did not write in this form, but Buchanan composed many odes* [in it]. *For which see pag. 146* [of an edition of Buchanan].)[63] John Dawson's 1639 collection of Latin verse paraphrases of scripture includes a metrical guide, with the reference texts for lyric metres given as Horace, Prudentius, Boethius and Buchanan.[64] Charles Hoole's grammar school teaching manual of 1661 specifically recommends the teaching of Buchanan from the fourth form upwards, commenting that '*Horace* and *Buchanan's Psalms* will sufficiently store [the pupil] with variety of Verses'.[65]

---

[61] Ashmore, *Certain Selected Odes of Horace* (1621), 95–6.
[62] A version of Psalm 137 on page 8, which follows Buchanan closely.
[63] BL Harley MS 121, fol. 79^r. This is the last of four volumes of D'Ewes' Latin verse exercises, beginning in 1615, when he was about 12 or 13. The first volume contains almost only poems in elegiacs, and the second and third a mixture of elegiacs and hexameters. This fourth volume contains 105 compositions in a large number of lyric, iambic and iambo-lyric metres as well as elegiacs and hexameters. His tutor at the time was Henry Reynolds (or Reginald), the father of the Latin poet Bathsua Makin (née Reynolds or Reginald, 1600–c.1675).
[64] Dawson, *Summa moralis theologiae* (1639), sig. H5^r–H6^r.
[65] Hoole, *New Discovery* (1661), 123.

Psalm Paraphrase after Sidney

In his preface to the 'Pindarique Odes', Abraham Cowley sets out his aspirations to write a 'divine poem' – a phrase which itself recalls Sidney, quoted above – and cites Buchanan as the most significant of his predecessors.[66] Sir Thomas Pope Blount's *Remarks on Poetry* includes Buchanan in a list of 11 recommended modern Latin poets.[67] Also in the late seventeenth century, the verse translations and compositions of one 'J. F.' are dominated by psalm paraphrase, and, as noted above, begin with a version of Psalm 137 'after Buchanan'.[68] Nearly a century after their first publication, John Kelsall (fl. 1683–1743), a Quaker schoolmaster in Wales, records in his notebook of verse compositions and translations a sequence of 'Several Psalms translated from Buchanan's Latin Version thereof', dated 1740.[69] The sequence is followed by a translation of Joseph Scaliger's Latin epitaph on Buchanan, pointing to the ongoing importance of Buchanan's Latin psalter even in the mid-eighteenth century.[70]

The Sidney psalter, though unpublished at the time, evidently circulated in manuscript since it is praised by several contemporaries or near-contemporaries, including Donne, Herbert and Samuel Daniel, and a relatively large number of manuscript copies of the whole or part of the collection survive.[71] It is the only well-known 'literary' psalter produced in this period (rather than a complete English psalter intended for liturgical use, such as that of Sternhold and Hopkins). But a very large number of poets, professional and amateur alike, produced paraphrases of individual psalms, and individuals frequently collected these for personal use. British

---

[66] 'And *Bucanan* himself (though much the best of them all [those who have imitated David], and indeed a great Person) comes in my opinion no less short of *David*, then his *Countrey* does of *Judaea*' (Cowley, *Poems*, sig. Aaa2ᵛ).

[67] Blount, *De re poetica* (1694), discussed by Williams, 'Canon before Canon'. Such lists of 'best authors' are common in manuscript sources, and Buchanan is very frequently included; compare for instance a similar commendation attributed to 'Mr Rosse' in Henry Oxinden's notebook (BL MS Add. 28010, fol. 66ʳ, probably mid-seventeenth century), in which Buchanan is one of only seven neo-Latin poets mentioned. 'Mr Rosse' is almost certainly Alexander Ross, himself a scriptural Latin poet. Ross's own *Rerum Iudaicarum memorabilorum* (1632), an epic verse paraphrase of scripture from the departure from Egypt to the destruction of Jerusalem, ends with a paraphrase of Psalm 104 introduced by Ross with a modest disavowal of any attempt to rival Buchanan (sig. D2ʳ).

[68] Bod. Eng. poet. f. 17, p. 8.

[69] Society of Friends Archive, MS Vol S 193/5, pp. 219–22. Psalms 93, 120 and 130 are translated. On Kelsall, see Allen, 'Kelsall, John (1683–1743)'.

[70] For further details, esp. on the educational use of Buchanan in Scotland into the nineteenth century, see Green, *Poetic Paraphrase*. Although not the subject of this chapter, Buchanan's non-scriptural Latin verse and his Latin drama were both also very widely excerpted, translated and commended.

[71] Ringler, *Poems of Sir Philip Sidney*, and Brennan et al. (eds.), *Collected Works of Mary Sidney Herbert*. See also, in Latin, Charles FitzGeffrey, *Affaniae* (1601), fol. G7ʳ⁻ᵛ, in praise of Mary Sidney as an embodiment of all nine Muses.

Library Add. MS 36529, for instance, includes psalm paraphrases (as well as verse paraphrases of Ecclesiastes) by Henry Howard, Earl of Surrey (d. 1547), Sir Thomas Wyatt (d. 1542), and others, apparently collected by Sir John Harington of Kelston (d. 1612), probably in the latter half of the sixteenth century.

Indeed, much of the evidence for Mary Sidney's revisions of her psalm paraphrases derives from a copy of her own manuscript made by Samuel Woodford in the second half of the seventeenth century, which carefully reproduces authorial revisions.[72] Woodford's particular interest in the Sidney psalms must be related to his own efforts in scriptural verse paraphrase, and in particular his paraphrase of the entire psalter into English Pindaric odes, published in 1667: the connection between the tradition of scriptural verse and Pindaric form in Cowley and his imitators, such as Woodford, is discussed further in Chapter 5.[73] Though none of Buchanan's or Beza's paraphrases is in Pindarics, the association they created between Latin lyric high style, metrical variety and experiment, and the translation of the Psalms, runs down into the seventeenth century and beyond.

Where individuals writing after 1600 sought to compose, or otherwise assemble, either a complete psalter or a relatively large collection of English literary psalm paraphrase, they showed a noticeable tendency towards metrical variety. Dating from the early 1650s, British Library Harley MS 6637 is a complete psalter translated into English verse, apparently unpublished and probably composed by the creator of the manuscript, complete with a detailed thematic index in the opening pages. The range of metrical forms is wide, and several psalms are paraphrased twice, in different forms (e.g. 121, 149).[74] Indeed, psalm paraphrases, sometimes in significant numbers, and very frequently distinguished by their metrical variety, are found in many of the landmark verse collections of the seventeenth century, in both Latin and English. David Hume's *Lusus Poetici* (1605) contains four moving and expansive Latin psalm paraphrases.[75] Phineas Fletcher's *Poeticall Miscellanies* (in *The Purple Island*, 1633) contains

---

[72] Bod. MS Rawl. poet. 25.
[73] Woodford, *Paraphrase upon the Psalms of David* (1667); followed by a paraphrase of the Song of Songs, *Paraphrase upon the Canticles* (1679). Woodford's English verse paraphrases were themselves translated into Latin in the latter seventeenth century; see for instance BL MS Add. 29241 (1690s).
[74] Though clearly dated 1651–2, the manuscript is anonymous, and I have been unable to find any clues to ownership or authorship. Some details of the translation suggest that Coverdale's version of the psalms may have been the main English source.
[75] Hume uses only hexameters and elegiacs, but transforms the scriptural texts into extended personal meditations. Compare also Stanley, *Poems and Translations* (1647).

translations of Boethius' verse as well as six poems which Fletcher describes as 'metaphrased' versions of the psalms. Published in the same year as Herbert's *Temple*, the metres of Fletcher's psalms are similarly varied and ambitious.[76]

Many poets, moreover, tackled the psalms in both Latin and English, testifying to an ongoing association between the Latin and English versions of the tradition. British Library Royal MS 12 A LXX contains a collection of psalm paraphrases in Latin verse by Christopher Windle (c.1560 to after 1625): though dating from 1618, Windle, a clergyman apparently imprisoned for debt at the time, had taken his BA in 1580 and was of the right generation to have been strongly influenced by the flurry of activity in psalm scholarship, commentary and paraphrase in the 1570s and 1580s. At the end of the first item in the manuscript, a Latin verse paraphrase of Psalm 16, he adds the following note: 'M. G. Buchananum carminis genere, stylo tamen et or[ati]one non hîc imitamur' (*I imitate here Buchanan in the type of poem, but not in the style or tone*). The opening of the poem demonstrates what he means:

In Psalmum decimum-sextum Windlei Carmen Choriambicum

> Conserv[e], peto, protege;
> Me defende, Pater, Mi Domine, et Deus.
> In Te namque meae pono Salutis modo spem optimam.[77]

> *Keep me safe, I pray, protect me;*
> *Defend me, Father, My Lord and God.*
> *For in you I place my greatest hope of salvation.*

This unclassical metre – none of the lyrics of Horace, Catullus or Statius is in three-line stanzas – is a kind of 'rising' choriambic: a choriambic trimeter, tetrameter and pentameter. Prudentius uses it in the Prologue of *Cathemerinon*; but, more importantly, it is the metre used also by Buchanan for his version of Psalm 16:

> O rerum sator, & salus
> Humani generis certa periculis,
> Qui te respicit unum, famulum instantibus eripe.
>   (1–3)

---

[76] See also the metrically varied psalm paraphrases in John Viccars, *England's Hallelu-jah* (1631). Viccars says he is paraphrasing 'according to French Forme and Metre' and probably has the Marot-Bèze psalter in mind; the final item in the collection is a text and translation of Beza's Latin poem celebrating the defeat of the Armada, which was circulated widely in England.

[77] BL MS Royal 12 A LXX, fol. 1ʳ. The end of the first word has been damaged, but almost certainly read 'conserve'.

> *O founder of the world, and sure salvation of the human race, rescue your servant, who looks to you alone, from the dangers threatening him.*

Both the direct borrowing from Buchanan, and the unusual choriambic metre probably gave it a slightly 'dated' feel by 1617 – as we saw in Chapter 2, Thomas Drant had used the same form for an original Latin poem published in 1566. In this respect, Windle is showing his age. In others, however, he anticipates the literary developments of the seventeenth century. The paraphrase of Psalm 16 functions as the preface to a collection which contains several examples of fairly conventional Latin panegyric verse, addressed to King James I among others. At the centre of the volume, however, is a pair of poetic sequences, first in English and then in Latin, which are not psalm paraphrases as such, but rather a response to or meditation on the psalms of David. Both are best characterized as 'sequences' because of their repeated metrical transitions: the first section of the English sequence ('Holie David his hearte. Or, The Psalmes Quintessence', fols. 17^r–21^v) is in common measure, the 'ballad metre' strongly associated with Sternhold and Hopkins. The second section, however, 'King Davids Harpe. Or, The Psalmes countenance', fols. 22^r–7^v) moves through a range of inventive measures, ranging from regular three- and four-line stanzas to much larger repeating strophes, which resemble Pindarics. It begins with two matching pages each of which forms a single large strophe of 38 lines.[78] The third section ('Davids harp with Davids hearte. Or, The Psalmes Influence', fols. 28^r–32^r) is written in six-line stanzas, but varying between four and six stresses a line. The verse is accompanied throughout by dense marginal references to scripture; particularly, though far from only, to the psalms.

The Latin version of the work echoes these structural divisions, replacing the common metre of the first section with hexameters (fols. 33^r–8^r). The second section, however, is highly inventive, with a large number of unusual or unique stanza forms. There are several points of contact with the tradition of Latin psalm paraphrase: like Beza and Buchanan, Windle makes significant use of various iambic metres, and uses a three-line stanza, of two iambic trimeters followed by an iambic dimeter, which is also used by Beza (Psalm 99); another iambic stanza (of two dimeters, a trimeter and a final dimeter) is similar to several of the iambic stanzas invented by Beza, though it is not precisely the same as any of them. Quite unlike anything

---

[78] The very unusual *mise-en-page* of these page-length stanzas is perhaps constructed so that the lengths of the lines suggest roughly the outline of Scotland, England and Wales, though if so both Wales and the West Country receive rather short shrift.

in Beza or Buchanan, however, is Windle's construction of units of verse which resemble large strophes: fol. 38^v, for instance, contains a section of eight iambic dimeters, two iambic septenarii, four trimeters, two iambic distichs, three dimeters and a final iambic dimeter catalectic. This entire 22-line pattern is repeated later in the sequence (fol. 39^r).

We can link Windle's Latin metrical practice to the metrical variety of the psalm paraphrase collections, and his frequent changes of metre within an overall sequence resemble the polymetric sequences typical of the latter sixteenth century (discussed in Chapter 2). But this kind of large-scale strophic composition looks towards the regular Pindarics composed both in Latin (as for instance by Melissus) and in the English experiments of Ben Jonson. These early regular Pindarics are not associated particularly with scriptural verse; but, as described in Chapter 5, Cowley's work of the 1650s established a strong connection between Pindaric form and scriptural content, here anticipated by the eccentric Windle.

The single most influential descendant of the Sidney psalter, however, is George Herbert's *Temple*, first published, posthumously, in 1633, and an immediate success. Herbert was himself an accomplished Latin poet, and his collection echoes Latin literary fashions of the previous century: the *Temple*'s well-known use of anagrams, figure poems and other visual devices is not a feature of psalm paraphrases in either Latin or English, though is, as we have seen, more generally typical of Latin verse collections of the latter sixteenth century.

Herbert's indebtedness to the psalter in general and to the Sidney psalter in particular has been frequently acknowledged.[79] *The Temple* includes, however, only one straightforward psalm paraphrase, that of Psalm 23:

> The God of love my shepherd is,
> And he that doth me feed:
> While he is mine, and I am his,
> What can I want or need?
>
> He leads me to the tender grasse,
> Where I both feed and rest;
> Then to the streams that gently passe:
> In both I have the best.

---

[79] 'The most important literary influence on Herbert's poetic forms was undoubtedly the translation of the *Psalms* by Mary Sidney and her brother Philip' (Wilcox (ed.), *English Poems of George Herbert*, xxviii). See also Lewalski, *Protestant Poetics*, 283–316 and Kinnamon, 'Notes on the Psalms'.

> Or if I stray, he doth convert
> And bring my mind in frame:
> And all this not for my desert,
> But for his holy name.
> ('The 23d Psalm', 1–12)

The metre here is the 'common measure' (sometimes known as 'ballad metre') in which much of Sternhold and Hopkins is written; Lucía Martínez Valdivia has argued convincingly that this metre was associated strongly with psalmody in early seventeenth-century England.[80] Herbert recalls Sternhold and Hopkins, the form in which the psalms were most widely known and sung, in his phrasing as well as his choice of metre – compare for instance lines 9–10 with the second of two versions in Sternhold and Hopkins, 'He did convert and glad my soule / And brought my minde in frame' (5–6). At the same time, the astonishing metrical variety of *The Temple* as a whole links it directly to the tradition of literary psalm paraphrase: the tradition of Buchanan, Beza and the Sidney psalter.

For all its artlessness, however, several elements of Herbert's translation are not derived directly from any of the standard available translations or versions of the Bible, such as Coverdale (included in the Book of Common Prayer) or the Geneva Bible, given below:

> 1. The Lord is my shepherd: therefore can I lack nothing.
> 2. He shall feed me in a green pasture: and lead me forth beside the waters of comfort.
> 3. He shall convert my soul: and bring me forth in the paths of righteousness, for his Name's sake.
>
> (Coverdale)

> 1. The Lord *is* my shepherd, I shall not want.
> 2. He maketh me to rest in green pasture, *and* leadeth me by the still waters.
> 3. He restoreth my soul, *and* leadeth me in the paths of righteousness for his Name's sake.
>
> (Geneva Bible)

Neither the biblical text nor either of the versions of the psalm in Sternhold and Hopkins emphasizes divine love as Herbert does, and Herbert's description of the speaker's 'mind' straying and then returning to the fold is an interpretation of the brief phrase 'he shall convert my soul' (Coverdale) or 'he restoreth my soul' (Geneva). Similarly, while some

---

[80] Valdivia, 'Psalms and Early Modern English Poetry'.

translations interpret verse 2 as 'feed' and others as 'make me to rest', Herbert combines the two ('Where I both feed and rest', 6). Buchanan's version of the poem similarly incorporates both these interpretations ('feed' and 'rest'), and also, like Herbert, adds the idea of the speaker's mind ('mens') straying into error or sin, only to be brought back to the path of righteousness.

> Per campi viridis mitia pabula,
> Quae veris teneri pingis amoenitas,
> Nunc pascor placidè, nunc saturum latus
>   Fessus molliter explico.
> purae rivus aquae leniter astrepens
> membris restituit robora languidis,
> et blando recreat fomite spiritus
>   solis sub face torrida.
> saltus cum peteret mens vaga devios,
> errorem teneras illecebras sequens,
> retraxit miserans denuo me bonus
>   pastor iustitiae in viam.
>   (Buchanan, Psalm 23:5–16)

Through the gentle pastures of the green plain, embroidered with the beauty of tender spring, now I feed quietly, now in weariness I softly lay down my well-fed body. A stream of pure water, gently babbling, restores strength to my tired limbs, and with its pleasing encouragement the wind refreshes me beneath the sun's roasting heat. Whenever my errant mind sought the pathless glens, following the tender inducements of error, the good shepherd, pitying me, brought me back at last to the way of justice.

Herbert was probably influenced by these elements of Buchanan's characteristically classicizing expansion of the biblical text. In its metrical simplicity, however, and emphasis upon God's love, Herbert's poem has more in common with Beza's very different version. Whereas Buchanan's psalm is in Horatian sapphics, and filled with classical echoes, Beza's is in stichic trochaic dimeter catalectic, an unclassical metre never used by Buchanan or Horace, which nevertheless becomes a kind of 'signature tune' for Beza, who uses it fifteen times in total, all for psalms of praise and thanksgiving, of which this is the first.[81]

---

[81] Also Beza 26, 27, 54, 75, 80, 98, 100, 118, 119:Daleth, 121, 125, 134, 139 and 147. The metrical line is found once in Horace, *Odes* 2.18, but as the first of a couplet, alternating with iambic trimeter catalectic. It is never used stichically in extant classical Latin poetry; in general there are very few classical Latin lyric (rather than dramatic) examples of trochaic verse. The emergence of trochaic metres in the later sixteenth century is discussed briefly in Chapter 2.

> Ipse me rerum parens
> Ecce pascit sedulus:
> Quae me egestas terreat?
> Ille me per florei
> Laeta prata graminis,
> Ille puros lassulum
> Ductitat per riuulos.
> Ille languens corculum
> Voce mulcet blandula.
> (1–9)
>
> *Look how he, the parent of all,*
> *Takes care to feed me;*
> *What lack could I fear?*
> *He leads me through the fertile meadows*
> *Of flowering grasses,*
> *When I am weary, he always leads me*
> *By the pure streams.*
> *Gentle he soothes me, his dear heart*
> *With a coaxing voice.*

The dominant tone of this poem is of loving care: the Lord of this version is a 'parens ... sedulus' ('attentive parent'), and the speaker is consistently described with unusual diminuitives ('lassulum', 'corculum') suggestive of a young child.[82] Herbert's apparently simple version of this psalm, in other words, bears evidence, like the Sidney psalter itself, that he has read and drawn upon the two quite distinct stylistic traditions represented by the Latin versions of Buchanan and of Beza.

Herbert's poem could *almost* belong to the Sidney psalter itself: almost, but not quite. The quasi-erotics of the third line ('While he is mine, and I am his') adds a detail which is not in the original text, and strikes a note that the Sidneys would have avoided, but which will come to characterize seventeenth-century religious lyric. The line echoes not the psalter itself, but the Song of Songs: 'My well-beloved is mine, and I am his: he feedeth among the lilies' (2.16).

The erotic poems of the Song of Songs are not explicitly religious at all, and make no mention of God. The book was traditionally interpreted as an allegorical text about the love of God for his people; then, by Christians, as an allegory for the love of Christ for the Church, or of each individual's

---

[82] 'lassulus' (wearied, dim. of 'lassus-a-um') is found, in classical literature, only at Catullus 63.35; 'corculum' ('little heart' or 'dear heart') is found in classical literature only in comedy, as a term of endearment.

soul. By alluding to this text in his paraphrase, Herbert further emphasizes the theme of divine love. In this, too, he appears to follow Beza, who went on to use the same (as we have seen, very unusual) metre for his verse paraphrase of the Song of Songs, published in 1584.[83] By folding into his poem a reference to the Song of Songs, Herbert follows Beza's metrical connection, and alludes to a tradition of allegorical and typological interpretation not only of the Song of Songs itself, but also of the Psalms and indeed all of scripture. Nearly a hundred years later, Isaac Watts borrows at several points from Herbert in his version of the same psalm:

> The Lord my shepherd is,
> I shall be well supplied;
> Since he is mine and I am his
> What can I want beside?
>
> He leads me to the place
> Where heavenly pasture grows,
> Where living waters gently pass
> And full salvation flows.
>
> If e'er I go astray
> He doth my soul reclaim,
> And guides me in his own right way
> For his most holy name.[84]

The importance of the paraphrase and imitation of the Song of Songs to the Latin and English religious poetry of the mid-seventeenth century is central to Chapter 6. Herbert stands on the cusp of that transition, and looks both ways.

---

[83] Beza, *Canticum Canticorum* (1584). Other links between the poems include specific vocabulary, such as 'ductitans', used by Beza in Psalm 23.7 (above) and also in his paraphrase of *Song of Songs* 2.16. Evidence for the readership of this work in England in the period of Herbert's adulthood is provided, among others, by BL MS Add. 62138D, a copy of Beza's version in the hand of George Wyatt, dating from before 1624.

[84] Text from Jackson (ed.), *Isaac Watts: Selected Poems*, 53; first published in Watts, *The Psalms of David Imitated* (1719).

CHAPTER 4

Formal Panegyric Lyric in England, 1550–1650

Chapter 1 outlined the importance of the broadly (though far from specifically) 'Horatian' tradition of the moralizing lyric in poetry between the mid-sixteenth and the early eighteenth centuries. Chapters 2 and 3 explored how the metrical variety of Horatian lyric, as it was imitated and extended by Seneca, Boethius and late antique lyric poets, stood behind the great explosion in metrical variety and experiment in both Latin and English poetry in the second half of the sixteenth century, associated in particular with the tradition of psalm paraphrase. This chapter turns to a third influential facet of the Horatian lyric tradition: namely, the development in English literary culture of the major political ode. Unlike moralizing lyric or psalm paraphrase, this form, of which the most famous early modern example is now Andrew Marvell's 1650 'Horatian Ode on Cromwell's Return from Ireland', made a relatively late appearance in English poetry, with only scattered and marginally canonical examples (such as those by Jonson, Drayton and Fanshawe) prior to Marvell.

This chapter therefore seeks to answer two related questions. What are the defining features of the political ode in early modern England, taking into account the full panoply of the Latin (and, for these purposes, primarily *neo*-Latin) tradition? And how different do the landmarks of English achievement in this form – including poems by Jonson and Drayton as well as Marvell and Cowley – seem if read within the Latin literary context from which they emerged? Inevitably, there are some areas of overlap here with related forms, especially the Pindaric ode, discussed in Chapter 5, and the moralizing lyric, in Chapter 1.

How Horatian Is Marvell's 'Horatian' Ode?

Marvell's 'Horatian Ode' has been widely admired for its formal originality; but such comment, while identifying various specific allusions, has tended to be vague both about the sources of the poem's form and (especially) about the cultural valency and familiarity of related forms at the time at which Marvell was writing.[1] Most importantly, discussions of the 'Horatianism' of the poem are focused almost exclusively upon Horace himself, typically relating the ode primarily to contemporary translations of the *Odes*.[2] The assumption that an 'Horatian' lyric form suggests or alludes directly if not only to Horace probably strikes most modern readers, if they think about it at all, as reasonable if not outright obvious. As we have seen, however, lyric verse in the 'Horatian' tradition was in the seventeenth century an enormously wide and varied category, comprising a range of classical, late antique and more recent authors – from Seneca or Prudentius, to Beza or Sarbiewski – writing poetry which was widely understood to be, in this general way, 'Horatian' both formally and thematically, but which was in many cases far removed politically, tonally or stylistically from anything that Horace himself wrote. Modern classics students are unlikely to encounter any Latin poem in, for instance, alcaics or asclepiads which is *not* by Horace; but any early modern reader did so routinely.

If we speak about the composition of an 'Horatian' ode, such as Marvell's, this should not therefore be taken – as it generally has been – to mean a poem modelled in formal terms only upon Horace. 'Horatian' is a generic and formal category as much, if not more, than an authorial one. Insisting that every instance of a Latin lyric in alcaics or asclepiads (let alone an English example) is related formally only to Horace is comparable to an assertion that every sonnet can, in formal terms, be understood only in relation to Petrarch (or Ronsard, or Shakespeare). This is not to deny the great importance of such poets for shaping the sonnet in a given language; but in the case of a form with as long and productive a history in vernacular poetry as the sonnet, any modern instance may derive its formal identity, characteristic style and tonal associations from a composite of many models far from confined to that of any single exemplar,

---

[1] Smith (ed.), *Poems of Andrew Marvell*, 270 summarizes assessments of the ode as 'one of the best, if not the best, English Horatian Ode'. Influential modern readings include Fowler, *Triumphal Forms*, 76–84; Norbrook, *Writing the English Republic*, 243–71; and Worden, 'Politics of Marvell's Horatian Ode'.

[2] Smith (ed.), *Poems of Andrew Marvell*, 268, for instance comments 'The compilation and translation of Horatian odes was in part a reaction to the experience of Civil War', citing Mildmay Fane's Horatian *parodia* (mentioned also in this context by both Smith and Norbrook). David Norbrook, in his chapter on the 'Horatian ode', refers to several pieces of contemporary Latin, including some lyric, though his discussion of Marvell's models is keyed to Horace rather than wider Horatianism (*Writing the English Republic*, 243–71). On Marvell's use of the stanza form developed by Fanshawe for his Horatian translations, see Simeone, 'Probable Antecedent'; Everett, 'Shooting of the Bears'; and Davidson (ed.), *Poems and Translations of Sir Richard Fanshawe*, vol. 1, 36–7.

however influential. Sonnets are also a good parallel for Latin lyric because of their recognized 'apprentice' role: most aspirant poets will have tried to write a sonnet at least once, and the composition of Latin verse in an Horatian lyric form was similarly a standard school exercise. While there is little evidence that English schoolboys were ever asked to compose Latin Pindarics until the latter part of the seventeenth century, there is ample evidence that boys in the upper forms of every grammar school in the country, from at least the final third of the sixteenth century onwards, learnt to compose in a wide range of Horatian lyric metres.[3]

The sheer frequency of this type of composition is clear from both the manuscript and print record. At the time of writing, my database of 27,854 post-medieval Latin poems in English manuscript sources dating from between c.1550 and 1720 records the location of 2,049 poems in lyric metres, of which 1,056 may be described as more strictly 'Horatian' lyric.[4] This does not include a similar total (1,149) of poems in iambic metres; the important iambic aspect of the Horatian legacy in English Latin verse is discussed in Chapter 8. To be clear: these figures for Latin lyric poems in the manuscript record exclude the thousands of classical, late antique and medieval Latin poems in such sources – in other words, none of these counted items are odes by Horace himself, or by Seneca, Boethius or Prudentius (to name only the most influential ancient models). Even allowing for a small number of popular poems appearing several times in the data, this represents a corpus of around 1,000 early modern Latin poems composed in an Horatian lyric form, and in a wide variety of contexts, ranging from professional presentation volumes to entirely private notebooks, and including popular and widely circulated translations of English poems into Latin lyric, as well as many school and university exercises. This is certainly not a complete list.[5]

Any full-scale analysis of Anglo-Latin poetry in print in this period would produce very similar results: if we look, for instance, just at the university anthologies produced between the death of Sidney in 1586 and

---

[3] On the teaching of Latin lyric metres, and the link between educational practice and changing literary fashions, see Chapter 2.

[4] This latter figure excludes rhyming poems and phalaecian hendecasyllables, a metre used by Catullus but not by Horace; but includes metres not used by Horace, but closely related to ones which are, such as the adaptations of Horatian metres found in Boethius and Prudentius, and modern innovations based upon them. For a fuller discussion see Chapter 2.

[5] The survey has not attempted to examine sources of English provenance now held elsewhere (such as Wales, Scotland, Ireland, France, the Netherlands or the United States). Nor is it a complete survey of English holdings, though it is large enough to be considered representative. I would estimate that the survey has recorded 50–70 per cent of relevant material in English holdings.

the Restoration in 1660, we find no examples that do not contain formal odes in Horatian lyric metres. In several collections, over 10 per cent of the Latin verse is in these forms. In the university collections, the highest proportion of odes is found in the first decade of the seventeenth century, and then again from the late 1630s to the 1650s: a rough, but reliable, index of the periods in which there was particular interest in poetry of this kind, especially in Latin but also in English: the experiments in lyric form of Jonson and Drayton, for instance, belong to the earlier period; those of Marvell and Cowley to the latter.[6]

From this point on, then, when referring to an 'Horatian' ode, I mean a Latin poem which by its metrical form recognizably belongs to this broad tradition with its roots in Horace: Latin odes written in sapphic, alcaic or asclepiad stanzas, and sometimes in more unusual Horatian lyric metres, such as pythiambics (on which see Chapter 2). While many of these poems are 'strongly' Horatian – containing, for instance, many allusions to or reworkings of passages from Horace – a great many are more 'weakly' so, tracing elements of their form, tone, content and structure to a wide range of post-Horatian sources.

The Panegyric Ode

The Horatian ode offered important models for several distinct (and in some cases overlapping) types of lyric poem in early modernity. In practice, one of the least imitable elements of Horace's style is how hard it is to define most of his *Odes* in typological terms: Horace's odes very rarely end where they begin, and the great majority of the poems usually described as, for instance, a love lyric, an invitation poem or a hymn contain other, and sometimes conflicting elements. Very few imitators of Horace have achieved such poised admixture, and indeed many were not aiming at it: most 'Horatian' poems are much more readily classifiable than Horace himself, and this is importantly true even of his earliest imitators, such as Seneca's moralizing choruses, Boethius' philosophical lyrics and the religious poetry of Prudentius.

Horace is best known today for his erotic and sympotic odes, evocative short lyrics suggestive of the pleasures both of sex and of (male)

---

[6] In Cambridge University, *Threno-thriambeuticon* (1603), for instance, 10 out of 89 Latin poems are in Horatian lyric metres; in Oxford University, *Bodleiomnema* (1613), 9 out of 73; Cambridge University, Συνῳδία (1637), 23 out of 155; Cambridge University, *Oliva Pacis* (1654), 11 out of 58, nearly 20 per cent. In the 1620s and 1630s we find a larger number of poems in iambic metres and phalaecian hendecasyllables.

companionship, and the fleeting nature of such pleasures. There are early modern examples of lyric poetry, both in Latin and in English, in this tradition – such as some of the poems of Herrick – and there are a relatively large number of Latin examples from the early eighteenth century, an interesting phenomenon which falls beyond the scope of this study.[7] But taken overall this aspect of Horatian lyric, the most recognizable today, is the least imitated in early modernity. By contrast, the most common types of Horatian lyric are moralizing poems, which moved early into English and are discussed in Chapter 1; religious and scriptural verse, discussed in Chapters 2, 3 and 6; and formal panegyric, the subject of this chapter.

The *Odes* of Horace contain many poems of formal praise of Octavian (who became Augustus) and of his associates and relations, such as Maecenas, Agrippa and Drusus Nero. Poems of this type are found throughout *Odes* 1–3 (published together in 23 BC) but are especially dominant in *Odes* 4 (published ten years later). *Odes* 4 is the book least taught and read today, but it was of particular importance in early modernity: *Odes* 4.4 has long been recognized as one of the models of Marvell's ode, along with *Odes* 1.2, 1.35 and 1.37, among others.[8] The *Carmen Saeculare*, the formal hymn written for performance at the secular games in 17 BC, is usually grouped with *Odes* 4 and is similarly out of fashion.[9] Modern appreciation of Horace, particularly subsequent to the rise of European totalitarian regimes in the mid-twentieth century, has been uncomfortable with formal political panegyric and has both sought out and focused on ambiguity: evidence for Horace's mixed feelings in relation to Augustus, and his interest in 'other perspectives'.

Many poets in early modernity, however, wanted and needed to produce effective panegyric verse addressed to monarchs, nobles and possible or actual patrons. Just as Claudian was the primary model for panegyric hexameter (discussed in Chapter 9), Horace was by far the most significant model for formal panegyric lyric. That is not to say that poets were not interested in incorporating elements of caution, warning, political ambiguity or alternative perspectives in such verse: Marvell's poem is famous for

---

[7] See Money, *English Horace*. The 'epistolary lyric', a verse letter in Horatian lyric form, is also a largely eighteenth-century phenomenon, on which see Hale, '"All Lingua's are to thee Vernaculus"' and 'John Beveridge'.
[8] Smith (ed.), *Poems of Andrew Marvell*, cites 1.2, 1.35 (the 'Fortuna' ode, anticipating the invasion of Britain), 1.37 (Cleopatra ode), 4.4, 4.5 (praising the Augustan peace), 4.14, 4.15 (praising the Augustan peace). See also Norbrook, *Writing the English Republic*, 254.
[9] Though see Putnam, *Horace's 'Carmen Saeculare'*.

the ambiguity of its depiction of both the strengths and virtues of Cromwell and the pathos of the regicide. But to focus *only* on such elements is to neglect the cultural, political and aesthetic importance of the formal lyric of political praise. The argument of this chapter is that the major instances of this form in English in the second half of the seventeenth century, including Marvell's 'Horatian Ode', belong recognizably to this essentially post-classical and primarily neo-Latin lyric tradition.

Horatian and Pindaric Panegyric

There has been relatively little recent scholarship on early modern English lyric of this formal panegyric type.[10] Most of the earlier examples are in Latin: as a genre, and despite some attempts around the turn of the seventeenth century (including poems by Drayton and Jonson), it moved into English at a late stage, while the great wealth of Latin examples have been very little read. Moreover, recent scholarship on formal panegyric in early modern England has been dominated by work on the reception of Pindar, especially a series of important contributions by Stella Revard.[11] In a sparsely populated field, these major studies have had a sometimes distorting effect: Revard has a tendency, for instance, to identify any panegyric trope as recalling Pindar specifically, even when discussing poems which in formal terms – such as metre or stanza structure – are much closer to Horace (or, indeed, to Claudian).[12] Her discussion of Marvell's 'Horatian Ode' approaches that poem (despite both the title and the form) in Pindaric terms, and neither her discussion of Fisher's *Irenodia Gratulatoria* nor of Marvell's 'First Anniversary' mentions Claudian, whose consular panegyrics are the generic model for both poems.[13]

All Renaissance readers understood that the imitation of Pindar was central to Horatian lyric; indeed editions of Pindar typically printed Horace's *Odes* 4.2 (on the imitation of Pindaric style) in their prefatory

---

[10] The best work is mostly older, such as Hardison, *Enduring Monument*; and Garrison, *Tradition of Panegyric*.
[11] Revard, *Pindar and the Renaissance Hymn-Ode* and *Politics, Poetics, and the Pindaric Ode*; see also Fitzgerald, *Agonistic Poetry*.
[12] Revard acknowledges the importance of Horace in the opening chapter of *Politics, Poetics, and the Pindaric Ode* (1–45) but this is not really borne out by the rest of the book, which tends to set obviously Horatian features (such as metre) aside to focus on thematic and stylistic elements perceived as Pindaric. For a very perceptive identification of this problem, see Maslov's review of Revard.
[13] Revard, *Politics, Poetics, and the Pindaric Ode*, 98–121. On both these poems, see Chapter 9.

material, and the comparison between Horace and Pindar was a standard set piece of literary criticism. Ronsard progressed from the explicit imitation of Horace to that of Pindar, and in England both Ben Jonson and Abraham Cowley drew on both poets as well as the area of overlap between them. Examples of the lyric *comparison* between Horace and Pindar – a tradition traceable directly to *Odes* 4.2 – are found frequently in early modernity: Ben Jonson alludes repeatedly to *Odes* 4.2, as does Thomas Bastard in the Latin poem discussed below; Cowley prints his version of the first 32 lines of *Odes* 4.2 (the comparison of Pindar and Horace) as the third item in the *Pindarique Odes*, complete with notes.[14] The link between Horace, Pindar and King David as inspired prophet-poets was a touchstone of early modern poetics; this association had particular valency in England, in which psalms played an unusually important liturgical role following the Reformation (see Chapter 3).

Such allusions point to the importance of both Horace and Pindar as models, but also a widespread perception of their differences. Although by the early seventeenth century there was a not insignificant tradition of 'Latin Pindarics', discussed mainly in Chapter 5, the tradition of the imitation of Horace was vastly larger and more various. The real cultural significance of Pindaric style in the period, and the areas of overlap in 'Horatian' and 'Pindaric' style and content, should not blind us to the basic differences between them, and the cultural primacy of Latin models over Greek.

Moralizing Elements in Political Panegyric

Stella Revard describes the inclusion of moral *sententiae* in Marvell's odes on Cromwell as a Pindaric feature, because 'gnomic' statements of this kind are more typical of Pindar's odes than they are of Horace's.[15] This is true if we think only of the text of Pindar versus the text of Horace: but it is not true if we think not of Horace's odes only, but of the wider sweep of 'Horatian' neo-Latin lyric – which is, as we have seen in Chapter 1, typically much more systematically moralizing than Horace himself.

---

[14] See Jonson, *Underwoods* 25, in Burrow (ed.) 'The Underwoods', and his 'Ode Allegorike'. The convention continues into modernity. Thom Gunn's poem 'Duncan', a tribute to the American poet Robert Duncan, implicitly compares Gunn's constrained, highly polished 'Horatian' style to Duncan's 'Pindaric' outpouring. Gunn may also have had in mind the marked contrast between the styles of Duncan and Yvor Winters, the two older poets to whom he was closest; see Moul, 'Robert Duncan and Pindar's Dance'.

[15] Revard, *Politics, Poetics, and the Pindaric Ode*, 105.

Andrew Melville's major Horatian ode on the Gunpowder plot of 1605, for instance (discussed further in Chapter 8), contains several highly excerptable gnomic comments, such as 'Tam potior dolus / Quam vera virtus' ('How much more powerful is treachery / Than true virtue', 66–7), as do William Gager's odes on the Parry plot of 1585, in which this kind of quotable expression ranges from the homely ('ardente vicini camino, / Vestra domus caueat fauillas', 'when your neighbour's chimney is ablaze, / Your house should beware of sparks', *Odes* 8.23–4) to the grandest Horatian register ('Coelo minatur, qui solio invidet; / Cognata regum est conditio Iovi', 'He who plots against a throne, threatens heaven: / The estate of kings is like to that of Jove', *Odes* 6.61–2). Moralizing or aphoristic content is, in other words, a traditional element of Latin panegyric lyric and is not, in an early modern context, primarily a Pindaric feature.

The association between Horatian lyric and moral aphorism could be exploited in rhetorically sophisticated ways. In a poem contributed to the 1603 Cambridge memorial volume for Queen Elizabeth, the author, one G. Smith of King's College, invokes the conventions of moralizing verse only to subvert them:

> Qui sibi fidit, tumidusque regni
> Iactat immoti stabiles habenas
> Esse, nec caecae metuenda sortis
>   Arma veretur;
> De suo motam sciat orbe Lunam,
> De polo lapsam sciat esse stellam,
> Et recordetur cecidisse summum
>   Numen, Elizam.[16]

> *He who has confidence in himself, and in arrogance boasts*
> *Of stable government of a kingdom that stands unshaken,*
> *And has no regard for the weapons of blind fate*
>   *Which deserve to be feared;*
> *Let him know that the moon has moved from his world*
> *That the star has fallen from his sky*
> *And let him be mindful that the greatest power, Eliza*
>   *Has fallen.*

The phrasing of the first stanza recalls especially the opening of Horace, *Odes* 3.3 (itself a model for Seneca's kingship chorus in *Thyestes*, as discussed in Chapter 1), on how the just man is unafraid of storms, tyrants

---

[16] Cambridge University, *Threno-thriambeuticon* (1603), 32.

or disasters. The trope of the virtuous man who remains calm regardless of circumstance is, as we have seen, extremely common. But the subject of Smith's poem, for all his fortitude and confidence in the realm, finds that *this* scenario – the loss of Elizabeth – has indeed upturned his world. The unexpected confounding of our expectations contributes to the effect of the lament: the collapse of generic and allusive convention suggests the disruption of the natural order.

The use of moralizing and aphoristic elements is a continuous feature of the tradition, traceable from late medieval examples through to Dryden and beyond. That is not to imply, however, that formal political panegyric lyric in England does not develop significantly between the mid-sixteenth and the mid-seventeenth centuries. In the course of the latter half of the sixteenth century, the typical panegyric Latin ode was transformed from an essentially hymnic form, almost always in sapphics, to a sophisticated vehicle of both political and poetic identity. Marvell's panegyric verse has been singled out by critics for its use of an external perspective (how the events described appear from abroad); its sense of speaking 'for the nation'; its tonal ambiguity, including considerable sympathy for the experience of the defeated; and finally for its laureate self-consciousness – the impression, though implicit in Marvell (as opposed to examples in Jonson, for instance), of the poet's power both to immortalize and to control the political message.[17] All four of these features can be seen evolving in the large quantities of Latin, and smaller numbers of English poems in this tradition composed between the mid-sixteenth and mid-seventeenth centuries. Each of these elements has parallels in Horace's *Odes*; but nevertheless the composite 'Horatian' ode that emerges is not in fact much like any of the odes composed by Horace.

The Elizabethan Sapphic I: Hymnic Sapphic

A peculiar feature of formal Anglo-Latin lyric in the mid-sixteenth century is its marked preference for odes composed in sapphic stanzas. In an analysis of Latin verse in lyric metres in manuscript sources datable to between 1534 and 1566, 50 per cent of the total are in sapphics, compared to just 4 per cent in alcaics. This is in sharp contrast to all later periods. Up until the 1580s, sapphics were the standard metre for major public odes in England. This sapphic dominance is, however, neither classical nor particularly

---

[17] See Patterson, *Marvell*, 32–57; Zwicker, *Lines of Authority*, 75–89; and Norbrook, *Writing the English Republic*, 243–71 and 337–57.

humanist. Although a couple of humanists preferred sapphics to other metres, and Pontano wrote all his odes in sapphics, the majority of fifteenth- and sixteenth-century poets, from Filelfo to Macrin, wrote in a range of Horatian lyric metres with a slight preference for alcaics for the grandest, stand-alone odes.[18] This is, by and large, the sort of pattern we would expect from Horace, whose four books of *Odes* (and *Carmen Saeculare*) include 37 poems in alcaics and 26 in sapphics, and almost all of whose most 'laureate' and public verse (such as the six 'Roman Odes', 3.1–6, or the 'Cleopatra ode', 1.37, on the victory at Actium) are in alcaics.

George Buchanan, in many respects the single most important literary model for English Latin poets of the latter sixteenth century, wrote only a handful of 'public' odes, divided equally between sapphics and alcaics, and in that sense typical of European humanist poets more widely.[19] Nor is the dominance of sapphics a feature of the influential psalm paraphrases, by Buchanan and others, discussed in Chapter 3: Buchanan uses alcaics (16 times) more often than sapphics (10 times) in his collection, and Beza has only five paraphrases in sapphics, three in alcaics. There is, therefore, no obvious explanation either in classical poetics or in wider neo-Latin literary trends for the preference for sapphics in the formal panegyric Latin odes of Elizabethan England, though that preference is very marked.

The fashion for poems of this type was probably shaped around mid-century by the natural link between hymnody addressed to the Virgin Mary and formal Latin verse addressed to Queen Mary I (1553–8) or to Mary, Queen of Scots (1542–67), and then extended and elaborated during the long reign of Queen Elizabeth I (1558–1603), coupled with the importance of the *Carmen Saeculare*, also written in sapphics, as a model for public praise in hymnic form. This may have been strengthened by a distant sense of the appropriateness of this stanza form, associated with an ancient female poet, for addressing a queen.[20] Such 'Elizabethan

---

[18] Pontano does not seem to have been particularly influential in England, though Maddison describes his sapphic epinicia as two of the earliest neo-Latin examples of the 'successful laureate ode' of the Horatian type (Maddison, *Apollo and the Nine*, 66). Macrin's 1530 collection contained 31 odes in alcaics, 34 in sapphics, alongside other Horatian metres; Marc Antoine de Muret's 1553 collection contained only alcaics and asclepiads.

[19] Buchanan's influential 1568 collection of Latin verse, *Franciscanus et fratres*, contains no sapphics at all. Thomas Schmitz's survey of the Latin ode in Renaissance France provides no overall evidence for a preference for sapphics; in his data, the two earliest described collections (dating from 1507 and 1516) use only sapphics, but after that date there is, as in Horace, a slight predominance of alcaics both for stand-alone formal odes and within lyric collections (Schmitz, 'L'Ode latine').

[20] Julie Crawford's thoughtful article on the use of English sapphics later in the century argues for the association between the form and Sappho herself; but the piece is seriously flawed by failing to

sapphics' are found not only in examples of accomplished adult verse but also frequently in school collections: an early example is BL MS Royal 12 A XXX, an astonishingly metrically varied Eton collection from 1563, written for the Queen's visit to Windsor: of the 73 numbered poems, 15 are in some form of sapphics.[21] Less remarkable though more typical is CUL MS Add. 8915, a collection of university verse presented to the Queen on her visit to Cambridge the following year, 1564: of 270 Latin poems, only 35 are in lyric or iambic metres (the rest being in the common elegiacs and hexameters); of those 35, 27 are sapphic odes.

Similarly, the surviving verse of the schoolmaster and clergyman Adrian Schoell contains Latin poetry composed regularly between the 1550s and the 1590s. Schoell is a product of his age: the great majority of his poetry is in elegiac couplets, with a handful of hexameters, and right through until the end of his life the only lyric metre he uses is sapphic stanzas.[22] A convinced Protestant, he celebrates the death in 1555 of the conservative bishop of Winchester, Stephen Gardiner, with great enthusiasm, including a long sapphic ode, comparable to Andrew Melville's use of sapphics for long polemical and satiric poems.[23] Indeed, a particularly late example of this type is Melville's *Anti-Tami-Cami-Categoria*, certainly composed in 1603 or 1604, though not printed until 1620.[24] Melville, born in 1545, was nearly 60 in 1603: in his response to the poem, written also in Latin

---

mention at any point either Horace or the ubiquity of the sapphic stanza in early modern Latin poetry (Crawford, 'Sidney's Sapphics'). To be clear: anyone at this period who knew even who Sappho was would have been very familiar with the Latin sapphic stanza and, at least in the case of men, would have composed in this metre as part of their education. What sapphics 'meant' to a reader of this period was, first and above all, the Latin form.

[21] Unusually, this collection includes poems in stichic sapphic hendecasyllables, some without adoneans (the brief fourth line) at all, some with only occasional or final adoneans; as well as poems with couplets formed of a sapphic hendecasyllable alternating with another lyric line (lesser asclepiad or phalaecian hendecasyllable). The collection has been edited and translated by David Money, in Goldring *et al.* (eds.), *Progresses and Public Processions*, 259–368; see also Money, 'Musarum Pueritia', and further discussion in Chapter 2.

[22] Schoell's verse collection is Corpus Christi College, Oxford, MS 324. A German Protestant émigré, he was mostly in London in the 1550s before becoming a schoolmaster in Childerditch, near Warley in Essex in the early 1560s, and then rector of Higham in Somerset around 1570. He is referred to in the clergy register as Shell or Shawe, both probably attempts to Anglicize his German name.

[23] Corpus Christi College, Oxford, MS 324, 41^(r–v). Schoell, born in 1530, was around fifteen years older than Melville.

[24] The poem responds directly to the Millenary Petition of 1603. A previously unnoted manuscript copy now in Lambeth Palace Library (MS 113, fols. 223^r–6^r) has significant differences from either of the published texts and probably represents an earlier version. There is good evidence for considerable English interest in Melville during the period in which he was imprisoned in the Tower of London (1606 to early 1611) and the Lambeth manuscript may well date from this period. The poem is discussed further in Chapter 8.

verse, George Herbert makes a point of mocking Melville's choice of metre, suggesting that it already appeared dated.[25]

The great majority of sixteenth-century instances of formal panegyric lyric are, therefore, in sapphics. The earliest examples comprise two main types. The first are brief, essentially hymnic poems, typically of only two to four sapphic stanzas; unlike later 'laureate' odes, which are distinguished by a sense of the poet's own voice and authority, lyrics of this kind are essentially impersonal. (In this respect, they are related to the 'moralizing lyrics' discussed in Chapter 1.) This sort of brief sapphic poem, typically syntactically simple, often repetitious and sometimes incorporating a refrain, is found widely in the mid to late sixteenth century. The origins of the association between sapphic ode and hymn are themselves classical: several of Horace's cletic (invocatory) hymns are in sapphics, and the first fragment in the Hellenistic edition of Sappho's poetry is an invocatory hymn to Aphrodite.[26] Nevertheless, this kind of brief, devotional or panegyric poem, with an impersonal, hymnic tone, simple structure and no ironic admixture, is not itself at all typical of Horace.

Indeed, this kind of brief, devotional Sapphic is indebted as much to medieval poetics as to the classical tradition. As Norberg points out, 'sapphic verse is as common in the Middle Ages as in antiquity', and most of the sixteenth-century examples of this kind of poem adhere to the formal conventions for the handling of the sapphic described by Norberg as typically medieval.[27] These conventions create an impression that each of the stanzas – which are generally end-stopped – is self-contained, and contribute overall to a 'level' tone. The adonean in poems of this kind is sometimes markedly 'separable', functioning as a kind of summary or refrain.

Many examples are described as prayers or hymns; where they are applied to a contemporary addressee, they tend to retain a prayer-like quality, describing the virtues of the addressee in the manner of a hymn. Cheke's 1551 anthology of Latin verse in honour of Martin Bucer, for instance, includes two examples of this form, one by Oswald Metcalf and a second by John Sheffeld:

---

[25] Herbert, *Musae Responsoriae* 5 ('In metri genus', 'On the metre').
[26] Sappho, fr. 1; see Horace, *Odes* 1.2, 2.10, 2.30, 2.32, 3.11, 3.18. Morgan, *Musa Pedestris*, 198.
[27] Namely, a long fourth syllable, a caesura always after the fifth syllable, an avoidance of monosyllables at the end of the verse (Norberg, *Medieval Latin Versification*, 71–2).

> Vita quae Christum sapit est beata :
> Vita sed Christum sapuit Buceri:
> Ergo ter felix fuit & beata
>   Vita Buceri.[28]

> *The life which knows Christ is a blessed one;*
> *But the life which has known the Christ of Bucer:*
> *Three times blessed was that life, and blessed*
>   *The life of Bucer himself.*

Poetry of this kind is found widely in both manuscript and print sources in the mid-sixteenth century: Walter Haddon's influential volume of *Lucubrationes* (1567) includes a version of the Lord's prayer in sapphic stanzas; in manuscript, Geoffrey Lewis' set of complimentary verses and address to the Queen, probably written for her visit to Oxford in 1566, makes similar invocatory use of the form, with only a single example (given below) of a stanza which is not end-stopped:

> Ecce foelices veniunt catervae
> Ecce regalis chorus, [ut] triumphat.
> Ecce diuinum nitidumque vultum
>   principis. ecce
> Fama reginae volitat per orbem:[29]

> *Behold the happy crowds are gathering*
> *Behold the royal chorus, [how] it exults.*
> *Behold the divine and shining face*
>   *Of the queen. Behold*
> *The Queen's fame flying throughout the world:*

This kind of prayer-like sapphic was not confined to England. The verse collection of Petrus Alites Carnutensis, for instance, published in Paris in 1561, concludes with an 'Authoris Oratio ad Christum' ('Prayer of the Author to Christ') in the form of a single sapphic stanza:

> Qui genus nostrum redimis cruore,
> Christe lux splendens miserere serui
> Alitis, dona nitidum precatur
>   Visere coelum.[30]

---

[28] Cheke, *De obitu ... Martini Buceri* (1551), sig. I.ii^v.

[29] BL MS Royal 12 A XXIII, fol. 1^r. A blot or stain obscures the middle of the second line. This manuscript has been digitized: www.bl.uk/manuscripts/FullDisplay.aspx?ref=Royal_MS_12_A_XXIII&index=137.

[30] Alites Carnutensis, *De Utroque Jesu Christi Adventu* (1561), sig. Oiii^r. A quotation from this volume appears in BL MS Add. 12067, a mid-seventeenth-century commonplace book of Sir James Turner, at fol. 87^v. Petrus Alites is probably the Latinized name of Pierre Loiseau.

> *You who redeem our people with your blood,*
> *Christ, splendid light, have mercy on*
> *Your 'winged' servant* [a pun on *Alites*], *grant his prayer to reach*
> *The gleaming heaven.*

Several surviving school collections include examples of this type of sapphic verse, suggesting that it was widely taught. A rather late example is Westminster Abbey MS 31, a presentation volume of verse by Westminster schoolboys as a New Year's gift to the Queen in 1587: the volume contains four poems in sapphics, of which only one is more than two stanzas long. The composition of short poems in sapphics stanzas, both as stand-alone prayers or invocations, and as lyric 'tags' in a hymnic style attached to the end of a (usually moralizing) poem in elegiacs or hexameter (discussed in Chapter 2), appears to have been a standard form in the latter half of the sixteenth century.

Modern Horatian scholarship has tended to consider Horace's sapphic verse as, by and large, less 'serious' than the more public-facing, formal and political verse in alcaics.[31] In the 'brief hymn' tradition of sapphics, however, early modern poets and teachers show themselves attuned to an aspect of Horace – the prevalence of hymns in his collection – which was no doubt magnified by the medieval tradition. Now very rarely discussed by classical critics, this tradition of Horace as a hymn-writer was of great importance to early modern readers, not least because it helped to associate the odes of Horace and the psalms of David.

Though composed in alcaics rather than sapphics, Phineas Fletcher's (1582–1650) Latin ode, composed for the Cambridge collection on the death of Elizabeth I, *Threno-thriambeuticon*, and written while a student at King's College, Cambridge, is an elegant demonstration of the use of the hymnic features of the Horatian ode to capture, we might say, 'officially' mixed feelings, appropriate to the death of one monarch and the succession of another:

> Quae, sicut rutilis Cynthia curribus,
> Lucebat solio splendida patrio,
> Sub laetho, (hei mihi laetho
> Fas tantum scelus est?) iacet.

---

[31] Llewelyn Morgan argues that even where Horace uses sapphics for markedly 'public' poems, he is consciously activating or playing upon its associations of constraint, intimacy, the domestic sphere and perhaps also the female poet, Sappho, herself (Morgan, *Musa Pedestris*, 181–270). I see no evidence of such an association in the sixteenth-century dominance of the form for public lyric, though there is a clear link between sapphic stanzas and hymns, and (perhaps) specifically with hymns addressed to women or female deities.

> Qui, sicut Clarius nube deus nigra,
> Occultus tenebris delituit suis:
> > Iam nuper Boreali
> > Sol nobis oritur plaga.
> Hanc si specto, nihil sum nisi lachrymae;
> Hunc si specto, nihil sum nisi gaudium;
> > Nil sum, si simul vno
> > Vtrunque intuitu noto.
> Sic navem retrahunt aestus, & aestui
> Robustè aura reflans; stat dubia, & nimis
> > Dum parebit utrique,
> > Neutri sedula paruit.
> Si, regina, tuo plausero funeri,
> Eheu parce precor; debita sunt meo,
> > Sunt & prima Iacobo
> > Plausus, quos fero, munera.
> Si sceptrum lachrymis sparsero, rex, novum,
> Eheu parce precor; debita sunt meae,
> > Heu sunt vltima Elizae
> > Fletus, quos fero, munera.[32]

She who, like Cynthia glowing in her chariot,
Shone radiantly in her father's throne,
> *Now lies (alas! is such*
> *An outrage possible?) in death.*
He who, like the Clarian god [= Apollo] in his black cloud,
Lay hidden in shadow:
> *Now rises as the sun*
> *For us on our Northern shore.*
If I think of her, I am nothing but tears;
If I think of him, I am nothing but joy.
> *I am at a loss, if I try to take*
> *Both these facts in view at the same time.*
So do the tides draw the ship back, and the breeze
Blows again boldly upon the waves; things stand in the balance, and
> *As long as one tries to behave appropriately to both,*
> *One cannot respond appropriately to either.*
If, queen, I shall have applauded your death,
Alas, spare me I pray; my James is owed
> *Certain gifts, the first of which*
> *Is applause, which I offer.*

---

[32] Cambridge University, *Threno-thriambeuticon*, 2–3. Fletcher also wrote an ode for a companion volume of English verse, *Sorrowes Ioy* (Cambridge, 1603), sig. D2^r–D3^v. His contribution, though quite different from the Latin poem, is one of the most ambitious and successful of the English poems.

> *If I sprinkle the sceptre with tears, o king, the new sceptre,*
> *Alas, forgive me, I pray; my mistress is owed*
> > *Certain gifts, and alas, to her, Elizabeth, I offer*
> > *My weeping, as my last gift of all.*

Here Cynthia (Diana) stands for the lost queen, and Clarius (Apollo) for the new king. Queen Elizabeth was of course frequently compared to Diana, but the combination here, and the balance of attention between the two, strongly recalls the repeated double invocation of Horace's *Carmen Saeculare*, the sapphic hymn composed by Horace for performance by 27 boys and 27 girls at the secular games celebrated in Rome in 17 BC, shortly after the death of Virgil. The *Carmen Saeculare* invokes Apollo and Diana together three times, at the start, middle and end of the hymn.

This tradition of a classicizing lyric in hymn form influenced English as well as Latin poetry; perhaps the most perfect example in English is Jonson's trochaic song from *Cynthia's Revels* (1600), in which Cynthia is both the moon and (by implication) Elizabeth:

> Queen and huntress, chaste and fair,
> Now the sun is laid to sleep,
> Seated in thy silver chair
> State in wonted manner keep:
> Hesperus entreats thy light,
> Goddess excellently bright.
>
> Earth, let not thy envious shade
> Dare itself to interpose;
> Cynthia's shining orb was made
> Heaven to clear when day did close:
> Bless us then with wished sight,
> Goddess excellently bright.
>
> Lay thy bow of pearl apart
> And thy crystal-shining quiver;
> Give unto the flying hart
> Space to breathe, how short soever:
> Thou that mak'st a day of night,
> Goddess excellently bright.

This poem in which Hesperus, the evening star, addresses Cynthia, the moon, is a kind of hymnic dramatization of the Horatian panegyric tag 'micat inter omnes / Iulium sidus, velut inter ignes / luna minores' ('[so does] the Julian star glitter among the others, like the moon among lesser fires [the stars]', *Odes* 1.12.46–8).[33] In Horace, the star of Julius Caesar – a comet which appeared during Octavian's victory games for Caesar in 44 BC, and which was interpreted as the apotheosis of Caesar himself – represents the divinely endorsed authority of Octavian/Augustus.

Elizabethan Sapphic II: The Long Sapphic Ode

Though clearly related to the hymnic sapphic, a second, more rhetorically sophisticated type of sapphic ode began to emerge around mid-century. Poems of this second sapphic type are longer – indeed, in some cases much longer than any example actually by Horace – and offer full-blown panegyric, with inset myths, similes and other apparatus of formal panegyric verse, while also retaining elements of hymn and prayer. In both cases, the stanzas are usually end-stopped, and the adonean, as in the simpler prayer-like sapphics, sometimes functions as a kind of summary or refrain.

Though characteristic of Elizabethan Latin verse, this kind of poem begins to appear before the accession of Elizabeth herself: several odes written to mark the accession of Mary I in 1553 are of this type, and Thomas Wilson's anthology of Latin verse in memory of the Brandon brothers, printed like the Bucer volume in 1551, includes examples of both kinds: two brief sapphic lyrics in the essentially hymnic tradition already described, but also three examples of longer panegyric odes in sapphic stanzas.[34]

The long Sapphic ode included in John Seton's volume for the accession of Mary I also belongs to this more ambitious category. Nineteen stanzas long, it blends the religious associations of the brief Sapphic hymn with the tradition of political panegyric and a 'national voice'. These are the final four stanzas:

---

[33] See also Walter Raleigh, 'Praisd be Dianas faire and harmless light', in *The Phoenix Nest* (1593), 69. On trochaic verse, see Chapter 2.

[34] Wilson (ed.), *Vita et obitus* (1551). Brief hymnic sapphics by Oswald Medcalf (sig. Biii^v) and Edward Earthley (sig. Ci^v); longer sapphic odes by Christopher Carleil (sig. Biii^r), Laurence Humphrey (sigs. Eii^v–Eiii^r) and John Mullyns (sigs. Hiii^v-Hiv^r), 7, 14 and 10 stanzas respectively. Carleil's ode, for instance, laments the loss of the Brandons by comparing them to a series of classical paragons of courage and wisdom (Achilles, Hector, Lycurgus, Paris, Solon, Nestor) followed by biblical parallels (Adam, Abraham, Lot, Job, Sampson), before a moralizing turn and a closing assurance of heaven. Oswald Medcalf, author of one of the brief hymnic lyrics in this volume, is also the subject of one of the two brief Sapphic pieces in the collection for Bucer (sig. Iii^r).

Elizabethan Sapphic II: The Long Sapphic Ode

> Quale spectaclum populo Britanno,
> Assidens uirgo solio supremo,
> Iura dans, regni retinens habenas
> > Ac moderamen ?
> Intuebuntur te oculo irretorto
> Quique mirantes muliebre pectus,
> Roboris tantum ingeniique habere, ut
> > Cuncta gubernes.
> Christe qui uerae es pietatis author,
> Qui tuis mandas sapere unitatem,
> Crescat inter nos fidei unitasque
> > Verus amorque.
> Quique Regum corda regis, guberna, &
> Principem serua Mariam Britannis,
> Vt diu laeti pariter sub illa
> > Pace fruamur.[35]
> > > (61–76)

> *What is this remarkable sight for the British people,*
> *A virgin seated on the supreme throne,*
> *Issuing laws, and holding the reins of the kingdom*
> > *And its balance?*
> *They shall look upon you, with an unbroken gaze,*
> *Each of them marveling that your womanly breast*
> *Holds so much strength and wisdom that*
> > *You govern all.*
> *Christ, the author of true piety,*
> *You who command your people to know unity*
> *May unity of faith grow among us,*
> > *And true love.*
> *And you who rule the hearts of kings, guide and*
> *Preserve Mary, Queen of the British people,*
> *So that just as happily we may long enjoy*
> > *Peace under her rule.*

Though retaining the associations of prayer and hymn, this is a much more sophisticated type of poem, poetically and rhetorically. It acknowledges the novelty of a female monarch ('quale spectaclum') and even perhaps hints at difficulty or reluctance in beholding her: the phrase 'oculo irretorto' ('without turning their gaze aside') is carefully chosen to hint at such difficulty while subsuming it within a framework of

---

[35] Seton, *Panegyrici in Victoriam*, sig. Biv^v. The volume contains four Latin poems: three long elegiac poems on Mary's victory, her coronation and the Real Presence of the Eucharist as well as this sapphic ode, which comes second.

conventional panegyric. The phrase is borrowed from Horace, *Odes* 2.2.23, where it describes the wise man who can gaze upon a heap of gold without being dazzled; as all the commentaries on Horace point out, the phrase recalls a proverbial expression about the eagle, who alone can look directly at the sun. This image is used as a comparison for the poet in the presence of the emperor by Claudian in the preface to *III Cons. Hons.*[36] In this way Seton's poem alludes to the panegyric trope of the king as the sun, dazzling in his glory, without using it directly. Seton also gestures towards the religious divisions in the country with his plea for unity in faith, and in the final two stanzas he transfers his address from Mary (both Mary I and, by association, the Virgin Mary seated in glory over a Catholic England) to Christ.

BL MS Cotton Titus A XXIV contains a sequence of Latin poems titled 'Anglia' ('England'), which refers to Mary I and her marriage to Philip in 1554. The sequence includes two sapphic odes, both of which allude self-consciously to Horace, *Odes* 1.2. The first of Horace's odes in sapphics, *Odes* 1.2 is a sharply political poem and a landmark in Roman political mythology: the first half reproaches the Roman people for the sin of civil war, and in early modernity the poem was often interpreted as referring specifically to the murder of Julius Caesar; the second half hails a divine deliverer in the form of Mercury, who is revealed at the end of the poem to be the 'new' Caesar – Octavian, the future Augustus.

The first of the odes in the Cotton Titus manuscript, at only four stanzas long, has many features of the 'hymnic sapphic', invoking Mary as a kind of tutelary deity for England, though it deploys – as is less typical of the purely hymnic form – specific Horatian allusions. The first line, 'Iam satis terrae sua ferit Angliae', alludes to the opening line of *Odes* 1.2 ('iam satis terris nivis atque dirae'), and the second stanza reworks in Mary's honour that passage of *Odes* 1.12, about the moon among the lesser stars, which is suggested by Jonson's hymn to Cynthia.[37] The second sapphic ode, which is longer and more sophisticated, adds an allusion to *Odes* 1.10, a prayer to Mercury also composed in sapphics. It introduces the figure of Mercury to celebrate the marriage of Mary and Philip in 1554 and hints at an association between Mercury (described, as in Horace, as 'filius Maiae',

---

[36] See also Lucan 9.902–6; the use of this image in Palingenian epic is discussed in Chapter 11.
[37] BL MS Cotton Titus A XXIV, fol. 92ʳ. 'In sinu crescit uelut herba terrae / Fama Mariae micat inter omnes / Mariae nomen uelut inter stellas / Luna uagantes', 5–8, reworks Horace, *Odes* 1.12.45–8, 'Crescit occulto velut arbor aevo / fama Marcelli; micat inter omnis / Iulium sidus, velut inter ignis / luna minores.'

'son of Maia') and Philip ('filius magni Caroli potentis', 'son of great powerful Charles', i.e. Charles V, Holy Roman Emperor). Mercury in *Odes* 1.10 has often been interpreted as a figure for Octavian/Augustus:

> Filius Maiae Jouis et deorum
> Nuntius, dulci celebrat Philippi
> Nuptias cantu: reliquique diui
>   Carmina cantant.
> Mars tegit corpus reprimens furorem
> Hostium dirum: sedet et Philippi
> Quae regit terram patulumque mundum
>   Pallas in ore.
> Cum piam natus tulit huc cateruam
> Vnus e multis Caroli Deorum:
> Ne roges cur sic canimus potiti
>   Hoc duce nostro.
> Nuper en senis fueras procellis
> Angle quassatus fuerat tuumque
> Nomen extinctum sed ouare debes
>   Quod renouetur.
> Fama nam uestra est celebrata toto
> Orbe, quod firmo Jou[a] misit almus
> Caelitus nobis Mariam et Philippum
>   Foedere iunctos
> Gaudeant omnes hilaresque sient
> Rustici, ciues, iuuenes senesque
> Et choros ducant, et ouent, canantque
>   Carmina laeti.
>   (13–36)[38]

> *Son of Maia and of Jove, and of divine powers*
> *The messenger, celebrate in sweet hymnody*
> *Philip's marriage feast: and the rest of the gods*
>   *Sing songs.*
> *Mars conceals his body, restraining*
> *The enemies' dreadful rage: even she who rules*
> *The earth and the spreading world, Pallas, sits*
>   *Upon Philip's brow.*
> *When one son out of the many of Charles' gods*
> *Brought hither a pious crowd:*
> *Don't ask why we are singing in this way, we who have claimed*
>   *This man as our leader.*

---

[38] BL MS Cotton Titus A XXIV, fols. 94ᵛ–5ʳ.

> Oh consider, England, how recently you had been
> Shaken by six storms, and how your name would have been
> Quite extinguished – but you ought to exult
> > Because your glory is renewed.
> For your fame is celebrated throughout the whole
> Globe, because – I confirm it – loving Jove has sent
> Mary and Philip to us from heaven, joined
> > In marriage
> Let everyone rejoice, and all be glad –
> The country people, the townspeople, old men and young;
> Let them lead dances, and celebrate and joyfully
> > Sing together in chorus.

This poem uses Horatian allusion to careful political effect, seeking to dilute the oddity of a female monarch by emphasizing the royal lineage of her husband, and indeed by transferring some imagery associated in Horace with Octavian/Augustus to Philip rather than Mary. The combination of marriage and a sapphic hymn is also intended, once again, to recall the *Carmen Saeculare*, in which Horace addresses Apollo (associated with Augustus) and Diana together, and imagines their enduring joint care for and protection of Rome. Whereas Fletcher in 1603 uses echoes of the *Carmen Saeculare* to suggest an essential continuity between Elizabeth and James I as paired tutelary deities, this poem uses it to suggest the unity and benevolence of the married royal pair.

Poems of this kind also survive addressed to Mary Queen of Scots (who reigned from 1542–67) and, following the accession of Elizabeth I, poets quickly transferred this increasingly sophisticated style of formal Latin lyric to the new English Queen.[39] Dating probably from 1566, early in Elizabeth's reign, Geoffrey Lewis marks the Queen's visit to Oxford with an ode in sapphics.[40] The poem is another good example of a fairly early stage in the emergence of the grander and more laureate Latin ode. Retaining several features of the hymnic or prayer-lyric – such as the

---

[39] For an example addressed to Mary Queen of Scots, see John Leslie, bishop of Ross's two sapphic odes of 1573, one a prayer to God to preserve the Queen in safety, and the first an interesting extended paraphrase, or meditation, on a single scriptural verse (Psalm 45.13, 'The king's daughter is all glorious within: her clothing is of wrought gold'), with an adonean refrain borrowed directly from the scriptural text (BL MS Add. 48180, fols. 1^{r-v} and 85^{r}–6^{r}, first and last items; printed with alterations in Leslie, *Piae Afflicti* (1574)). See also Lockie, 'Political Career of the Bishop of Ross'.

[40] BL MS Royal 12 A XXIII, a presentation volume. This manuscript has been digitized: www.bl.uk/manuscripts/Viewer.aspx?ref=royal_ms_12_a_xxiii_fs001r. Though some commemorative anthologies for non-royal figures, such as on the death of Bucer (1551), Sidney (1586), Hatton (1592) and Unton (1596), were printed, volumes with royal addressees were in manuscript in the sixteenth century.

incantatory repetition of key phrases ('ecce', lines 1–4; 'o dies', lines 13–15) – it is nevertheless longer, at seven stanzas, than earlier examples; and while it lacks a strong sense of authorial identity, it is 'laureate' in that it speaks explicitly for the people (in this case, probably, the fellows and students of Christ Church, Oxford) and alludes directly to Elizabeth's fostering of Latin and Greek learning both in herself and others. The presentation volume it opens includes material in both languages, and the poem links Elizabeth's support of scholarship to the flourishing of the Muses:

> Vidimus laeti decus, & [luc]ernam,
> Angliae matrem, patriae columnam.
> Artium cunctas veniens camaenas
>   Exhilarauit
>
> (9–12)

> *In joy we have seen her glory and her [brightness]*
> *The mother of England, the pillar of our native land,*
> *By her arrival she has caused all the Muses of the arts*
>   *To rejoice.*

The ode ends with a conventional prayer:

> Ac triumphanti tibi det salutem
> Corporis, mentis, Deus atque vitae.
> Affluas cunctis opibus superstes
>   Elizabetha.[41]
>
> (25–8)

> *May God grant you, in your triumph, health*
> *Of body, of mind and of life.*
> *And in your long life may you flow with every wealth*
>   *Elizabeth.*

Almost every example of the 'Elizabethan sapphic' incorporates – if it does not, as here, conclude with – Elizabeth's own name. Indeed, the metrical convenience of 'Elizabetha', which is an adonean, the closing aural tag of each Sapphic stanza, perhaps in part explains the intense and apparently distinctively English fashion for this metrical form in Elizabethan England.

The mini-tradition of the use of sapphic odes to address Queen Elizabeth culminates grandly in the lyric collection of Janus Dousa (1545–1604), a Dutch poet, whose *Odarum Britannicarum Liber* (*Book*

---

[41] BL MS Royal 12 A XXIII, fol. 1ʳ⁻ᵛ; stanzas 3 and 7 (of 7) quoted. A blot partly obscures the final word of the first line of stanza three.

of British Odes) was published in 1586 in Leiden, but dedicated to the Queen: William Camden's copy, complete with manuscript additions, is preserved as part of a composite volume, all of neo-Latin poetry, at Westminster Abbey (CB 7 (8)). Dousa's book of odes begins with seven major poems, all in sapphics, addressing first the Queen herself, then a series of contemporary luminaries including William Cecil and Philip Sidney.[42] Several of these are very long poems: the ode to the Queen has 39 stanzas (156 lines) and the ode to Cecil 51 stanzas (204 lines). Both of these are considerably longer than the longest lyric poem by Horace himself (*Odes* 3.4, 80 lines long).

The Mature Latin Political Ode in Late Elizabethan England

Bastard and the Sidney Collections

By the time of Dousa's collection, however, the almost exclusive use of sapphics for Anglo-Latin panegyric lyric was over. The death of Sir Philip Sidney following the Battle of Zutphen in October 1586 elicited an outpouring of commemorative verse both in England and elsewhere in Europe. The three collections printed in England – from Cambridge, Oxford and New College, Oxford – give a snapshot of the range of possibilities for public Latin lyric at this period.[43] They include examples of short sapphic poems with hymnic and invocatory elements alongside more ambitious narrative lyrics. These volumes – especially *Peplus* (1587), the New College collection – demonstrate the ongoing development of the self-consciously 'laureate' voice, speaking for the nation as a whole: a tone, derived from Horace and Pindar via Ronsard, which became so important to Jonson and is present too in Drayton.

The epigraph to *Peplus* is from Horace, *Odes* 4.8.28, 'Dignum laude virum Musa vetat mori' ('The Muse does not allow the man worthy of praise to die'), and in the first lyric poem in the collection, a sapphic ode

---

[42] The Dousa odes are discussed briefly by Revard, *Politics, Poetics, and the Pindaric Ode*, 74–6, who identifies Dousa's collection, alongside that of Paulus Melissus, *Oda Pindarica* (1582), as a key means by which 'Ronsardian odic poetics' were brought to England. Revard focuses on the Pindaric elements of this tradition and refers to Dousa's verse as 'strophic' odes, somewhat obscuring their Horatian metre. ('Strophe' is used more often in English of Pindaric forms.) She is surely right to point to the influence of these and similar collections upon English poets, but as we have seen, the 'laureate' Latin ode was already being written in England before this date (Revard, *Pindar and the Renaissance Hymn-Ode*, 2).

[43] Oxford University, *Peplus* (1587); Gager (ed.), *Exequiae* (New College, Oxford, 1587); Cambridge University, *Lachrymae* (1587, edited by Alexander Neville).

on page 10, the poet speaks of his own role in the first person and in language which evokes Horace, *Odes* 4.8 and 4.9, beginning:

> Non ego priscos celebrare versu
> Conor herôas, nec ego Philippi
> Aut Alexandri superantis, orno
>   Laude triumphos.
>
> Ast ego nostri celebro *PHILIPPUM*
> Temporis, clari sobolem parentis,
> Qui fuit nostrae columen decusqué
>   Nobile gentis.[44]
>
> *I am not attempting to celebrate ancient heroes*
> *in verse, nor do I deck with praise*
> *the enduring triumphs of Philip*
>   *or of Alexander.*
>
> *No – I am celebrating the PHILIP of our*
> *age, offspring of a famous parent,*
> *who was the noble column and*
>   *glory of our people.*

The poem is not particularly impressive or original, but the natural assumption of a personal laureate voice, beginning confidently by proclaiming whom 'I', the poet, shall immortalize in song, distinguishes even this rather routine example from the kind of panegyric exemplified by Seton, who speaks always collectively. Such verse stands behind the consummate achievement of Jonson's poem to Elizabeth, Countess of Rutland, in which Jonson refers explicitly to his personal poetic authority, identity and originality:

> Then all that have but done my Muse least grace,
> Shall thronging come, and boast the happy place
> They hold in my strange poems, which, as yet,
> Had not their form touch'd by an English wit.
>   (*Forest* 12, 79–82)

Jonson is the first poet to find a wholly successful tone and style in which to make such essentially Horatian statements of vatic authority in English. But he is far from the first to have worked out how to do so in relation to contemporary English subjects: the confidence and authority with which Jonson writes English lyric is audible in Anglo-Latin verse from the 1580s onwards.

---

[44] Oxford University, *Peplus*, sig. B1v.

Probably the best and most interesting Latin lyric poem in the Sidney collections is an ode in alcaics by Thomas Bastard (1565/6–1618), distinguished by its nuanced mode of public mythmaking, concerned as much with the *perception* of Sidney by the enemy as with the eulogizing of Sidney himself.[45] This interest in external perception – evident for instance in the Cleopatra ode, Horace, *Odes* 1.37, and also the speech of Hasdrubal in *Odes* 4.4 – is a particularly noticeable feature of Marvell's 'Horatian Ode'.[46]

Bastard's ode is a markedly good and interesting poem, and it is also a very restrained one: the praise of Sidney is conveyed almost entirely by a series of – in some cases, somewhat oblique – comparisons, describing the reaction of various groups to the sight of Sidney himself. Unlike Horace, *Odes* 4.9, to which it alludes, it does not proclaim its own immortalizing power, or overtly shift attention from the subject to the poet, but allows its allusive framework to speak for itself. I give the entire ode below:

>   Talem Britanni te modò viderant
>   *Sidnaee*, qualem viderat & Tagem
>   Thuscus colonus, non senili
>   Ore, sed ingenio senili.
>   Talem videbat te modò Belgica,   5
>   Qualem decoro vertice viderat
>   Inter nitentes eminentem
>   Militis Argolici phalanges

---

[45] Oxford University, *Peplus*, sig. E3[r–v]. Finkelpearl, 'Bastard, Thomas', describes him as an 'epigrammatist and clergyman'; Grosart (ed.), *Poems English and Latin of the Rev. Thomas Bastard*, viii–ix, prints the Latin text of this poem, without a translation. Bastard's literary reputation rests on the 285 English epigrams of *Chrestoleros* (1598; see Doelman, *Epigram in England*, esp. 241–3 and 292–5), and he had a formidable reputation, having lost his Oxford fellowship in 1591 as a result of a particularly notorious libel. Quite a lot of his Latin verse, however, is extant in the manuscript record: BL MS Lansdowne 104, item 78 (fols. 195[r]–214[r]), for instance, a volume of commemorative verse in memory of Ann, Countess of Oxford, who died in 1588, includes three contributions by Bastard. BL MS Royal 12 A XXXVI–XXXVII (1603) is a volume of complimentary poems by Bastard to James I, not mentioned by Finkelpearl. CUL MS Add. 8861/1, Miles Stapylton's notebook dating from between 1677 and 1684, includes a copy of one of Bastard's Latin epigrams, with an English translation (fol. 116[r]). Surviving translations of Bastard's English epigrams into Latin demonstrate the extent to which they were understood to belong to the Latin epigrammatic tradition (e.g. BL MS Sloane 1710, fol. 210[r], translation dated 1676). Bastard is not included in Dana Sutton's online anthology of British Latin verse, and I am not aware of any modern edition of his Latin verse other than that included in Grosart.

[46] Norbrook, *Writing the English Republic*, 245, points out that contemporary commentaries on Horace, *Odes* 4.4 draw attention to this motif as a panegyric trope, e.g. Spilimbergius, *Q. Horatii Flacci Carmina* (1584), fol. 143[v].

> Troianus altum rex Agamemnona:
> Qualemqué templo vidit, Apollinis   10
>   Pulchro virentem flore palmam
>   Et teneris folijs Vlysses.
> Sed qualis hosti visus Iberico es?
> Qualis per agros & sata proruit
>   Sternitqué torrens omne pratum,   15
>   Et pecora & stabula ipsa voluit.
> Qualisque Pallas Gorgone turbida,
> Armisqué cinctus Mars adamantinis
>   Versans cohortes, atque fusis
>   Hostibus ingeminans timorem.   20
> Impuné laeso quis fuit obuius ?
> Dextrae quis ictum sustinuit tuae,
>   Saeuam retorquentis securim
>   Et validam quatientis hastam ?
> Testatur hostis funeribus suis,   25
> Versisqué signis atque obitu ducum,
>   Virtus *Philippi* quanta, quantus,
>   Fulmineis fuit ipse in armis.

Not long ago the British people beheld you, Sidney, as the Tuscan farmer beheld Tages [an Etrurian divinity], not aged in his speech, neither aged in his sharpness of mind;

Recently Belgium was looking upon you, just as the Trojan king [Priam] looked upon tall Agamemnon, towering with his glorious head over the shining columns of the Greek army: and in the same way did Ulysses once behold the palm-tree in the temple of Apollo, flourishing with beautiful flowers and tender leaves.

But how did you appear to the Iberian enemy? Like a torrent that rushed forth through the fields and their crops, laid waste to all the meadows and overturned the cattle and their byres.

Such was Pallas when she terrified the Gorgon, and Mars girt with adamantine arms, routing the cohorts, and doubling the fear of the scattered enemy.

What harm went unpunished? Who sustained the blow of your right hand, as it bent back the savage axe and shook the mighty spear?

The enemy bears witness by their deaths, by their reversed standards and by the death of their commanders, how great was Philip's courage, and how great he was himself with his weapons of lightning.

For the British people, the sight of Sidney prompts the same wonder and joy as the sudden appearance of the Etruscan god Tages did for the Tuscan farmer: Tages, the grandson of Jupiter, is supposed to have sprung from the ploughed earth in the form of a boy. The comparison emphasizes Sidney's youth as well as his godlike prodigiousness, and also his 'homegrown' excellence. By contrast, the people of the Netherlands are awed by the Sidney of the battlefield, catching a glimpse of him as Priam inside Troy caught a glimpse of Agamemnon, towering over his troops: Agamemnon here suggests military prowess, the promise of future victory, and kingship. The Dutch perception of Sidney is compared, too, in the most enigmatic passage of the poem, to Ulysses' reaction to a beautiful palm-tree at Delos. This is taken from *Odyssey* 6, though in Homer it is part of a simile: Ulysses compares his wonder at the loveliness of Nausicaa to the young palm he remembers seeing in the temple of Apollo.[47] The Greek word, φοῖνιξ, meaning a date-palm, appears only here in Homer; but young warriors at the moment of their death are repeatedly compared to trees in the *Iliad*. Bastard's complex simile thereby suggests both Sidney's youthful beauty and the desire it may elicit, like that of Ulysses for Nausicaa; and also Homeric death on the battlefield (a polite evasion: Sidney in fact died, as Homeric warriors never do, of an infected injury nearly a month after being wounded in battle). The palm has biblical connotations too: palm-trees in the Bible represent both the flourishing of the just man (as in Psalm 92:12) and human beauty (as in Song of Songs 7:7). The unusual Greek word φοῖνιξ perhaps also recalls the phoenix, a common figure for Christ. To the Spanish enemy, by contrast, Sidney is like a terrifying river in spate; Pallas as she defeats the Gorgon; or Mars in all his armour.

Structurally, Bastard's poem demonstrates the new sophistication of Latin lyric in England of this period: it contains a precise sequence of tenses – pluperfect for the appearance of Sidney to the English, imperfect for the Dutch impressions of him, and perfect for his devastating power in the sight of the enemy – as well as working through a series of linked interrogatives and correlatives (*talis, qualis, quis, quantus*). Though most of the stanzas are end-stopped, lines 8–9 run over, and Bastard sustains relatively complex grammatical and syntactical structures within and sometimes across stanzas. Though linked by its Horatian metre, this poem sounds and reads entirely differently from the kind of hymnic sapphic we saw in the collections of the 1550s.

---

[47] Homer, *Odyssey*, 6.162–3. Apollo was born as Leto leant against a palm-tree. In Pindar, *Nemean Ode* 6, Apollo and Artemis are the palm-shoots of Leto.

Bastard's poem relies in various ways on a knowledge of the Horatian tradition for its full effect. The striking Greek accusative form 'Agamemnona' (9) recalls Horace, *Odes* 4.9.25 ('vixere fortes ante Agamemnona', 'many brave men lived before Agamemnon [but have been forgotten for lack of a poet]'), one of Horace's boldest statements of the immortalizing power of the poet himself and a poem of great importance to Ben Jonson.[48] Similarly, Bastard compares not himself, but Sidney, to the river in spate, bearing all before it (14–16), an allusion to the famous image of *Odes* 4.2 contrasting the style of Pindar (as a river) to that of Horace (the Matine bee).[49] Such decorous modesty on the part of the poet is particularly appropriate in a poem commemorating a man who was himself a poet and patron as well as an heroic soldier.

The second comparison, to Pallas Athene's defeat of the Gorgon, perhaps looks directly towards Pindar: the story of Athene's intervention in Perseus' battle with the Gorgon Medusa is told at some length in *Pythian* 12, which is also the only one of Pindar's victory odes to celebrate a musical rather than athletic victory.[50] Sidney was of course famous for his poetry as well as for his military valour, and *Pythian* 12 tells how Athene invented musical piping in imitation of the sound of the Gorgons as they lamented for Medusa, beheaded by Perseus.[51] Both these allusions suggest artistic mastery as well as military prowess. Moreover, the poem achieves a genuine solemnity of tone because this sequence of similes, the linked evocation of multiple remarkable sights, marks not a presence but a loss: a person who can no longer be seen.

William Gager and the Parry Plot Odes

Published in 1586, just before the Sidney commemorative collections, were William Gager's two books of odes on the Parry plot, *In Catalinarias Proditiones Odae 6* and, later the same year, *In Catalinarias Proditiones Odae 9*.[52] Leicester Bradner has remarked that Gager, 'almost

---

[48] See Moul, *Jonson, Horace*, 10–11, 13, 14–24, 72, 185.
[49] The appearance of the bee from *Odes* 4.2 at the end of Marvell's 'Garden' has a similar effect, directing us discreetly to a consideration of the author's own power and poetics.
[50] For Midas of Acragas, who won the pipe-playing contest in 490 BC.
[51] Pindar, *Pythian Ode* 12, 6–11 and 18–27. Compare the use of this myth by Jonson, also with reference to Pindar, in the highly self-conscious 'Ode' (*UW* 48), probably dating from around 1600 (see Moul, *Jonson, Horace*, 29–32).
[52] The *Odae* 9 volume reprints the six odes of *Odae* 6 and adds a further three at the end. Confusingly, none of these nine poems appeared in Gager's earlier collection, also on the Parry plot, *In Guil. Parry Proditorem* (1585).

alone among his contemporaries ... cultivated the forms of the alcaic and the sapphic odes and the Horatian style'.[53] Bradner is wrong to suggest that Gager was unusual in his use of Horatian lyric metres, though his sense of something new probably reflects the genuine development of Latin lyric style around this time – evident not only in Gager but also, for instance, in the work of Bastard, discussed above.

Gager's book of odes on the Parry plot is treated rather dismissively by Dana Sutton, who comments simply: 'Although they are fine specimens of odes of the Horatian type, there is something fundamentally unsatisfactory about Gager's ... cycle on the Babington episode.'[54] Sutton is perhaps right to feel that there is a mismatch between the gravity of the occasion and the ambition of the odes, but this is nevertheless an arresting sequence. In its development of an interlinked series of public odes, designed to explore different facets of a broadly Horatian response to public events, the sequence breaks new ground: in comparison, Drayton's not dissimilar attempt in his book of English odes, frequently hailed as innovative though published a full twenty years later, has an amateur feel.[55]

Only one of Gager's odes (Ode 3) is in sapphics, another indication of development. That poem pays homage to the 'Elizabethan sapphic', but develops it in a still more formal and vatic direction: the poem is filled with explicit reminiscences of Horace's *Carmen Saeculare*. This is the most self-conscious poem of the sequence, in which Gager compares himself directly to Catullus, Horace, Orpheus and Linus.

> Musa, dic cantus, age, seculares,
> Carmen in Festo mihi seculari
> Prome, quod longùm, Dea, seculari
>   Viuat honore.
>
> (5–8)
>
> Versibus non me superet Catullus,
> Nec lyrâ Flaccus, licet ille doctus,
> Hic licet praestet Lyricis, & astra
>   Uertice tangat.
>
> Quid moror? non me superabit Orpheús
> Thracius, quamuis pater hûic Apollo,
> Nec Linus, quamuis Dea mater illi
>   Calliopea.

---

[53] Bradner, *Musae Anglicanae*, 62.
[54] Sutton (ed.), *William Gager: The Complete Works*, introduction (www.philological.bham.ac.uk/gager/poetry/intro.html).
[55] Drayton, *Poemes Lyrick and Pastorall* (1606).

> Sospes exstructo (memorare dulce est
> Quod pati durum nimis ah fuisset)
> Sospes erepta est quasi fax Elisa
>   Nuper ab igne.
>   (25–36)
>
> Annuos laeto tamen ore cantus
> Funderem, ad remi modulantis ictum,
> Muneris tanti memor, exararem
>   Carmen arenâ.[56]
>   (45–8)

Come now, Muse, sing songs for the centuries, draw down for me a song for the Festival of a century, and long, goddess, may it live in the glory of the century . . .

Catullus will not surpass me in verse, nor Flaccus [Horace] on his lyre, although Catullus is learned, and Horace chief among the lyric poets, and touches the stars with the crown of his head.

Why do I delay? Thracian Orpheus will not outdo me, even though Apollo is his father; nor will Linus, although he has divine Calliope for his mother.

Unhurt now (it is sweet to recall, although the experience was exceedingly painful), unhurt is Elisa, like a brand snatched at the last minute from the mound of a fire . . .

[Even if I were an exile far away] *I would still pour forth annual songs with a joyful mouth, keeping time to the beat of my oar; always remembering how great a blessing we received* [of Elizabeth's salvation], *I would write my song even in the sand.*

Gager's sequence incorporates, while moving well beyond, the 'moralizing lyric' tradition discussed in Chapter 1. Several odes feature gnomic or proverbial elements, as here in the address to foreign princes in Ode 8:

> Unita sors est dominantium;
> Quemquam quod urit, quemque premat malum.
>   Ardente vicini camino,
>   Vestra domus caveat fauillas.
>   (21–4)

---

[56] Quotations of Gager's odes are taken from *In Catilinarias Proditiones, ac Proditores Domesticos, Odae 9* (1586), that is, the second volume of that year, which incorporates the earlier publication and adds three further poems. A digital edition of this text can be found on Dana Sutton's website, with hyperlinked translation, though there are several errors of transcription (www.philological.bham.ac.uk/gager/poetry/intro.html). A more reliable edition can be found in Tucker Brooke, 'Some Pre-Armada Propagandist Poetry'.

> *All those who rule are allotted alike: whatever evil burns one, may oppress any. If your neighbour's stove catches fire, your house should beware of sparks.*

The fourth ode combines proverbial wisdom ('walls have ears!') with a witty inversion of a moralizing trope: whereas the faithful have nothing to fear, the faithless must fear *everything*:

> Ne crede syluis, cùm scelus apparas,
> Aurita sylua est, ne domui tuae,
> Muris ocelli insunt, domusque
> Tota nefas videt, & recludet.
>
> Vt nemo prodat: ne tibi, ne tuae
> Confide menti: saepe tremens timor,
> Horrorque vultus, saepe pallor,
> Saepe stupor scelus occupauit.
> (33–40)

> *Do not trust the woods, when preparing a crime: the forest has ears. Nor your house: for there are eyes in the walls and your whole house sees and shall reveal your crime.*
>
> *Suppose nobody betrays you: trust not yourself, nor your own mind. Often a fearful trembling, an expression of dread, often pallor or paralysis have betrayed a crime in advance.*

Indeed, Gager's sequence showcases all of the features identified at the start of this chapter as typical of 'mature' panegyric lyric. His sequence speaks for, and to, the nation as a whole: the first ode, in particular, uses Horace, *Odes* 1.2 to evoke the sinfulness of the entire country. The specific crime of the Parry plot reflects a broader national corruption, just as the assassination of Julius Caesar does in Horace:

> Collecta, per tot secula, criminum
> In nos redundat sarcina, perdito
> Aeuo grauamur, quo malorum
> Omne genus, scelerumque regnat.
> (36–40)

> *A mass of guilt, gathered over so many centuries, surges against us; we are oppressed by this hopeless age in which every kind of evil and depravity reigns.*

Gager's sequence is self-conscious about the poet's own power and limitations, with a hint of stylized *recusatio*: he ends the second ode with a suggestion that the topic is inappropriate to lyric, and might be better served by tragedy or invective.[57] The seventh ode makes a memorable attempt to imagine the perspective of the traitors, and this kind of psychological imagination extends, in a remarkable passage, to the Queen herself, when in the sixth ode Gager imagines Elizabeth's emotions when she first heard of the plot:

> Ecquid timebas? ecquid et in genis
> Pallor sedebat? pectoris O fides:
>   Non tu timebas virgo multos,
>   Cerua canes, placida agna tygres.
>
> Illud gemebas, quòd fuerat tibi
> Stringendus ensis; quíd doleas tamen?
>   Effer secures, et nefandum
>   Poena comes scelus insequatur.
>   (9–16)

And were you afraid? Did a pallor settle on your cheeks? Oh, the confidence of your heart! You, though a maiden, had no fear of many men: the doe feared not the hounds, nor the gentle lamb the tigers.

This, though, you did lament: that your sword had to be drawn. But why should you regret it? Bring out the axes, let punishment follow close upon wickedness.

Elizabeth's courage and resolve are dramatically contrasted with the poet's own change of heart: in a kind of refrain, he first admits to feeling pity for the young executed conspirators, Tichborne and Salisbury (lines 17–20) before proclaiming that the Queen's example and the thought of his country have changed his mind:

> Tichburne (quaeso des ueniam Anglia,
> Et diua virgo) me miseret tui;
>   Dignaeque fato molliori
>   Salisberii miseret iuuentae.
>
>   . . .
>
> Sed charitates continet omnium
> In se una cunctas patria nobilis.
>   Tichburne, iam nec me tui, nec
>   Salsberii miseret iiuuentae.

---

[57] 'Quò tam impotenti Musa ruis pede? / Ah siste: res haec digna Philippicis, / Aut asperi diris Iambis / Archilochi, aut Senecae cothurno' (Ode 2, 36–40); 'My Muse, where are you rushing in such a powerless measure? / Oh stop there: this is matter worthy of Philippics, / Or of the terrible iambics of harsh / Archilochus, or of a Senecan buskin.'

> Tu me seuerum patria, tu facis,
> Regina, durum: me capitis tui
> Regina chari, me tuorum,
> Me patriae miseret, meique.
>
> (17–20, 29–36)

> *For your fate, though, Tichburne, I feel pity (I seek forgiveness from you, England – and from the divine virgin); and I feel pity for Salisbury in his youth, who was worthy of a better death ...*
>
> *But our noble nation contains within itself all types and conditions of charity. Tichborne, now I have no pity on your youth, nor that of Salisbury.*
>
> *You, my country – make me severe; my Queen, make me harsh. O Queen, I feel pity for your dear head, for your people, for our country, for myself.*

Moreover, the sequence addresses an international as well as a domestic audience. The eighth ode urges other Christian kings not to shelter the plotters, arguing that a traitor to one monarch is likely to be a traitor to another. Gager ends, however, by turning again to the English people, now with an explicit acknowledgement of their religious divisions (Ode 9):

> O Luce dulci Patria dulcior,
> Et chara Tellus, pars animae meae
> Non parva, ductricem Britannam
> Compositis odiis sequamur.
>
> Quaecunque nostras relligio imbuit
> Mentes, Elisam praeferat extero.
> Quaecunque discordes fatigat,
> In patriam pia nulla suadet.
>
> (1–8)

> *Oh Nation, sweeter than the sweet light, and our dear Land, no small part of my soul, let us follow our British queen, our enmities set aside.*
>
> *Whichever religion has filled our hearts, let it prefer Elisa to a foreigner. Whichever creates our wearying discord, no true and pious faith urges action against our nation.*

Thomas Goad (1576–1638) surely had Gager, above all, in mind when he produced his two collections of Horatian *parodia* to mark the thwarting of the Gunpowder Plot.[58] Like Gager, the second collection is slightly longer

---

[58] Goad, *Cithara Octochorda* (1605) and *Proditoris Proditor* (1606); see also BL MS Cotton Titus A XIII. Goad also published an hexameter poem on the same topic (*In homines nefarios*, 1605). His Latin verse appears to have circulated quite widely in manuscript; examples can be found in BL

than the first (expanded from eight to ten odes, though in Goad's case ten new poems), and like Gager his work is self-consciously laureate and Horatian. The *parodia* is a form, however, in which as many textual elements as possible are borrowed directly from a single text or (as here) author: to demonstrate his agility, each of Goad's odes is tagged in the margin with a dense series of numerical references to the relevant Horatian model. In the opening of the first ode of the 1606 collection, given below, I have supplied on the right-hand side the relevant Horatian quotation to which the marginal number refers:

Dira e remotis vrbibus audio.	2.19	[Bacchum in remotis carmina rupibus, 2.19.1]
Audistis? an me fallit inanitas	3.4	[Auditis? An me ludit amabilis
Rumusculorum? audite quicquid		insania? Audire et videor pios, 3.4.5–6]
Fama sonis vehit aestuosis.	2.7	[Unda fretis tulit aestuosis, 2.7.16]
Quám penè furuae regna Proserpinae	2.13	[Quam pene furvae regna Proserpinae,
Regina, Princeps, Rex, Proceres, Patres,		et iudicantem vidimus Aecum
Plebs fida viderunt, futuri		sedesque discretas piorum, 2.13.21–3]
Victima nil miserantis Orci?	2.3	[Victima nil miserantis Orci, 2.3.24]

I hear dreadful things from remote cities
Do you hear it too? Or does the emptiness
  Of trivial rumours deceive me? Listen to whatever
    Fame carries on her seething sounds,
How the Queen, the Prince, the King, the leading men, the Patres
And the faithful people all have almost set eyes upon
  The realm of dusky Proserpina, victims
    Of a future and unpitying Orcus.

Goad's work is intensely and at first sight rather deadeningly classicizing: we recognise the same reverence for classical texts that we find in, for instance, Jonson's formal panegyric of the period. The texture and tone of Goad's poems, though, are livelier and more contemporary than the insistent marginal references might suggest: the opening half-quotation of *Odes* 2.19, 'I hear dreadful things from remote cities', quite wittily transfers the distance from civilization associated with Bacchic worship to the rapid spread of political rumour, while also suggesting the poet's

---

MSS Sloane 1479, fol. 15ᵛ; Sloane 1766, fol. 43ʳ⁻ᵛ; Harley 6947, fol. 105ʳ; Bod. MS Rawl. poet. 246, fols. 44ʳ–5ʳ; and Leeds University Library, MS BC Lt 25, fol. 10ᵛ. This is certainly not a complete list. Bod. MS Malone 14 includes an English poem on p. 37 on 'Dr T. Goad & Dr H. King' (probably Henry King, 1592–1669, poet and bishop of Chichester) as divines and poets. I am not aware of any modern edition of Goad's Latin verse and his poetry is not included in Dana Sutton's online *Philological Museum*. There is however a brief *ODNB* entry (Allen, 'Goade [Goad], Thomas').

strength of feeling and authority: 2.19 is the most 'inspired' of all Horace's *Odes*. 'Rumusculorum' (3), though attested in Cicero, is a very rare word indeed and there is something both playful and ostentatious about fitting such an unusual word into such a restrictive metrical scheme. As the poem proceeds, there's an urgency and a relish to the description of the hellish plot that is recognizable from other contemporary Gunpowder Plot literature and does not really correspond to Horace at all (though is indebted to Claudian, on which see Chapter 9). There is even a hint of humour in applying Horace's tonally ambiguous poem on his own near-death experience, when he narrowly avoided being killed by a falling tree (*Odes* 2.13), to the narrow escape of the King and all his Parliament.

From the 1580s onwards, then, Anglo-Latin poetry is filled with examples of this 'mature' form of public political lyric in the Horatian tradition: indeed, there are many examples of odes of equivalent quality to those of Gager. In English, by contrast, we wait until Drayton's ode on the Virginia Company, published in 1606, before we find any serious English-language attempt at public lyric which combines laureate identity, allusive seriousness and a 'national' perspective:

> And in Regions farre
> such *Heroes* bring yee foorth
> as those from whome we came:
> and plant our name,
> under the starre
> not knowne unto our North.
>
> & where in plenty growes
> the lawrell every where,
> *Apollo's* sacred tree
> your dayes may see,
> A Poets Browes
> to Crowne, that may sing there.
>
> thy voyages attend
> Industrious *Hackluit*
> whose Reading shall inflame
> men to seek fame,
> and much commend
> to after times thy wit.[59]
>   (55–72, final lines)

---

[59] Drayton, *Poemes Lyrick and Pastorall* (1606), sig. C5ʳ.

The range and ambition of Drayton's book of odes are striking, but as poetry it is far less sophisticated and successful than many contemporary and indeed significantly earlier Latin examples: poets at this point were still working out how to import the form into English. Throughout the first half of the seventeenth century, formal vernacular odes of public panegyric or political celebration remained relatively rare: though Jonson wrote a great deal of Horatian verse in English, including major poems such as *Forest* 12 (to Elizabeth, Countess of Rutland), he did not address the monarch or, by association, the nation as a whole in poetry of this kind except in some of the songs in the court masques. His most successfully Horatian (and Pindaric) lyric remains, that is, at one remove from royalty.[60] Scattered examples of royal panegyric lyric in English include Fanshawe's 'Ode Upon the occasion of His Majesties Proclamation in the yeare 1630. Commanding the Gentry to reside upon their Estates in the Country', and some of the English poems included in largely Latin commemorative volumes, such as Cowley's English 'Ode upon the return of his Majestie' in the Cambridge anthology of 1641, discussed further below.[61] By contrast, Latin poems of this kind are routine: that 1641 anthology, for instance, contains 7 poems in English but 94 in Latin (and eight in Greek). Of those 94, 10 are in lyric metres used by Horace.[62]

Horatian Self-Consciousness

As we have seen, the major odes in this tradition are self-conscious, and in that sense 'laureate'; even at their most fully panegyric, they tend to include the poet himself, and some reflection upon his calling. Marvell's ode alludes to this tradition in its opening gambit:

---

[60] Examples include *Forest* 3 (for Sir Robert Wroth), 12 (to Elizabeth, Countess of Rutland), 13 (to Katherine, Lady Aubigny), 14 (to Sir William Sidney); *Underwoods* 25 (to James, Earl of Desmond), in Burrow (ed.), 'The Underwoods'.

[61] Fanshawe's ode was printed in *Il Pastor Fido* (1648), with manuscript copies in BL MS Add. 15228, fols. 32^r–4^v and Bod. MS Firth c. 1, fols. 82–6. See Davidson (ed), *Poems and Translations of Sir Richard Fanshawe*, 55–9. Cowley's ode appears in Cambridge University, *Irenodia Cantabrigiensis* (1641), sig. K1^{r-v}. Cowley also contributed a Latin poem to the volume (sig. B4^v). Fanshawe's odes have often been mentioned alongside Marvell's 'Ode', though Cowley's poem is in many respects a closer analogue.

[62] Not counting hendecasyllables (often considered a lyric metre, but not used by Horace) or iambic trimeter (used by Horace, but not usually considered a lyric metre).

> The forward youth that would appear
> Must now forsake his Muses dear,
>   Nor in the shadows sing
>   His numbers languishing.
>
> 'Tis time to leave the books in dust,
> And oil th' unused armour's rust,
>   Removing from the wall
>   The corslet of the hall.
>
> So restless Cromwell could not cease
> In the inglorious arts of peace,
>   But through advent'rous war
>   Urgèd his active star:
>
> (1–12)

This suggests a *recusatio*, in which the poet sets aside one type of poetry ('languishing' suggests love poetry or elegy) for another (we might assume epic, or panegyric). The ambitious young poet must graduate from one mode to another if he wishes to 'appear'; alternatively, perhaps, the ambitious young leader must graduate from poetry to action, or (like Sidney) some kind of combination of the two, if he is to be successful in public life. In time of civil war, the leaving of books and turning to armour sounds less metaphorical and more literal than it might in other contexts.

The ambiguity of these opening lines, which could refer either to the poet or to Cromwell, or both, blurs the distinction between poet and addressee in a way that goes back, via Horace, to Pindar – surely also much influenced by Jonson – and implicitly draws attention to the panegyric trope of the addressee's dependence upon his poet, and vice versa.[63] Even the 'So' of line 9 does not resolve the question. Does 'So restless Cromwell' amount to an identification of Cromwell with the 'forward youth' or (perhaps more likely and more natural) is it simply a comparison ('just so'; 'in the same way')? The pressure of events forces any 'forward youth' to abandon poetry; so too does that same pressure of events act upon Cromwell and drive him from the 'arts of peace' to active war.

---

[63] Moul, 'Horace', includes a section on Marvell's 'Horatian Ode'. I was originally asked not to discuss this poem, as it was due to be covered in another chapter. At a late stage, the editors required a discussion of Marvell's ode to be added to the completed chapter, but I was in hospital at the time and the additional section was written by Charles Martindale. It does not represent my views of the poem in either tone or detail, and I disagree with several aspects of the interpretation. As in Jonson's Cary-Morison ode (*UW* 70), 'And there he [Morison] lives with memory, and Ben. // Jonson, who sung this of him, ere he went / Himself to rest' (84–6).

Horatian Self-Consciousness 173

The conventional roots of this passage are demonstrated by the many parallels in contemporary or near-contemporary Latin verse. Marvell was perhaps particularly aware of the importance of marking the transition from peace to war as a virtuous (rather than sinful) move, in contrast with the standard characterization of civil war, in Roman and contemporary seventeenth-century poets alike, as particularly wicked. In 1641, Cambridge poets had marked the narrow (and, it turned out, short-lived) avoidance of war with *Irenodia Cantabrigiensis*, a collection of 94 Latin and 8 Greek poems, plus 4 in other languages (including Hebrew and Anglo-Saxon); the much shorter English section, consisting of only 7 poems, is typical of university volumes of the 1630s–1650s (before that period they tended to contain no English verse at all).[64] Ten of the poems are odes – eight in Latin, one Greek and one in English (the latter by a young Cowley). The opening of the longest Latin ode, by Peter Samways (1615–93), a fellow of Trinity, is a mirror image of the beginning of Marvell's poem.[65] Indeed, Marvell was still at Trinity in 1641.[66] It is very likely that he read the *Irenodia Cantabrigiensis*, and probable that he too had been obliged to compose a poem on the peace with Scotland which it commemorates.[67]

The *recusatio* with which Samways' poem begins is less subtle and much more conventional than Marvell's version:

>   Phoebus volentem praelia me loqui,
>   Victas & urbes, & fata languida,
>   Non falce sed stricti resecta
>   Praepropero gladii furore;

---

[64] Collections in the 1640s addressed specifically to the Queen rather than the King typically contain a larger proportion of English verse. Oxford University, *Flos Britannicus* (1637) unusually consists only of English poems.

[65] On Samways, see Vallance, 'Samwaies [Samways], Peter (1615–1693)'. Samways entered Trinity in 1635, took his BA in 1637 and his MA in 1641; he was a fellow of the college from 1640.

[66] Marvell was at Trinity from 1633 (aged only 12) until 1642; he took his BA in 1639 and contributed a Latin ode to an earlier volume of congratulatory verse on the birth of Princess Anne (Cambridge University, Συνῳδία, 1637), sigs. K4ʳ–L1ʳ.

[67] It is clear that students wrote Latin poems on the peace with Scotland which were not included in the *Irenodia Cantabrigiensis*: one example has been preserved in two separate manuscripts (Bod. MS Rawl. poet. 26, fol. 132ᵛ, and Kent History and Library Centre, MS U275/C1/12), the latter a letter from one William Johnson to Sir Edward Dering (1625–84), sent from America in October 1653. The letter refers to how they were both, as students in Cambridge in 1641, instructed to write Latin verses on the topic, and encloses an example, found also in the Bodleian manuscript, which he describes as unpublished (perhaps by Johnson himself). Dering was at Sidney Sussex, Cambridge, between 1640 and 1642. Dering's own poem on the theme appears in *Irenodia* (sig. B3ᵛ).

>   Non antè visa commonuit Dea,
>   Jussítque molli nectere carmine
>   Paci corollas, & superbos
>   Ducere laetitia triumphos.[68]
>
> *Apollo warned me, wanting to speak of war,*
> *And conquered cities, and the suffering in death,*
>   *Of those cut down not by a sickle, but the fury*
>   *Of a hastily drawn sword.*
> [He came along with] *the Goddess not seen before,*
> *And ordered me to weave garlands to peace*
>   *With soft song, and with joy to lead*
>   *Proud triumphs.*

Marvell's poem confronts the reversal of this happy scenario. The 'forward youth' of 1650 rather than 1641 must find a way to celebrate not peace, but war.

Abraham Cowley, like Marvell and Samways, was also at Trinity College, Cambridge in 1641. The English ode he contributed to the *Irenodia*, although not usually cited in relation to Marvell's poem, is a good comparison for it. Cowley's ode, like Marvell's, is explicitly Horatian, composed in four-line stanzas which visually recall Horatian metre (though Cowley alternates two different stanza forms), and its Horatianism echoes a feature of the collection as a whole. The main Latin portion of the volume opens with a sequence of poems depending strongly on allusions to Horace.[69] Moreover, Marvell's call to arms in 1650, urging the 'forward youth' to take down 'the corslet of the hall' perhaps knowingly reverses the movement of Cowley's poem of peace:

>   Welcome, Great Sir, with all the joy that's due,
>   To the return of Peace, and You.
>   Two greatest blessings which this age can know;
>   For that to Thee; for Thee to Heav'n we ow.
>
>   Others by warre their conquests gain,
>   You like a God your ends obtain:
>   Who, when rude Chaos for his help did call,
>   Did onely speak, and sweetly order'd all.
>
>   . . .

---

[68] Cambridge University, *Irenodia Cantabrigiensis* (1641), 'De rebus in Scotia per Augustissimum Clementissimúmque Regem non vi & armis sed lenitate compositis' (sig. I1ʳ).

[69] E.g. dialogue poem ('Pacificatio'), sig. ¶4ʳ, version of *Odes* 3.9; 'Ad Illustrissimam Reginam', sig. ¶4ᵛ, alluding to *Odes* 1.16.

> 'Twas onely Heav'n could work this wondrous thing,
>   And onely work't by such a King.
> Again the Northern hindes may sing and plow,
>   And fear no hurt but from the weather now.
>
> Again may Tradesmen love their pain,
>   By knowing now for whom they gain.
> Their Armour now may be hung up to sight,
>   And onely in their Halls the children fright.
>
>   (1–8; 17–24)[70]

Though there is, notoriously, no evidence that Marvell's ode was published or circulated during the 1650s, there are plenty of public odes in Latin from this period that were.[71] Indeed, the particular fashion for Horatian lyric form that is noticeable in the university volumes of the 1640s continues and if anything intensifies in the volumes produced for Cromwell in the 1650s: the Cambridge collection of 1654, *Oliva Pacis*, contains the highest proportion of Horatian lyric forms of all such volumes.[72] Marvell's transfer of verse forms associated with 1640s royalism to Cromwellian panegyric was in that sense part of a much wider trend: we find a similar marked continuity in the Claudianic hexameter panegyric of the 1650s (discussed in Chapter 9).

Of the many contemporary Latin examples, one of the most interesting comparisons with Marvell's poem is the formal Latin ode by Payne Fisher first published in 1652, and probably written at the end of 1651, 'Ad Illustrissimum Britanniarum Polimarchum, Oliverum Cromwellum'.[73] It shares many features with Marvell's ode, which dates almost certainly, at least in its initial form, from the summer of 1650. Like Marvell's poem, Fisher's ode is composed in four-line stanzas, and is of almost exactly the same length (116 lines to Marvell's 120). 'Horatian' odes on this scale are not themselves Horatian – the longest ode by Horace (*Odes* 3.4) is only 80 lines long. Such length links both poems rather with the neo-Latin Horatian tradition; as we have seen, early modern political odes of this type were frequently much longer than anything found in Horace – Melville's

---

[70] *Irenodia Cantabrigiensis*, sig. K1r.
[71] For a summary of the debate, see most recently Dzelzainis, 'Issues of Dating'.
[72] Of 58 Latin poems, 11 (19 per cent) are in Horatian lyric forms. The volume also includes two poems in Greek, though none in English.
[73] Fisher, *Irenodia Gratulatoria*, sigs. K1r–K3r. Fisher's poem includes a reference (69–84) to the death of Henry Ireton in November 1651. The poem also refers to Cromwell's campaigns in Ireland and Scotland, and looks forward to future foreign warfare. It is therefore likely that the poem was completed, if not composed in its entirety, in late 1651 or early 1652.

Gunpowder Plot poem is 108 lines long; the longest of Dousa's odes (to Cecil) is 204 lines; several of Sarbiewski's political odes are also very long, and the Cambridge verse collection marking the Restoration contains an ode in alcaics by Isaac Barrow that runs to 260 lines.[74] Fisher's Latin style is far removed from that of Horace, but the poem nevertheless contains multiple Horatian allusions, including to several of the same Latin poems which have frequently been identified as sources for Marvell's ode (such as *Odes* 1.34 and 4.4).

Fisher's celebration of Cromwell emphasizes his (Fisher's) personal change of heart, Cromwell's military accomplishments, the signs of God's favour, and his hopes for the future. There is no modern edition or translation of the poem and it has (to my knowledge) never been discussed at length in relation to Marvell's ode despite a striking degree of similarity.[75] Although Fisher tended to revise his work repeatedly on each republication, it is noticeable that he did not do so to any significant degree with this ode, perhaps suggesting that he was unusually satisfied with it.

The poem begins by confronting directly the question of the transfer of loyalties, going so far as to make Fisher's own change of heart the starting point of the panegyric – an interesting comparison to the scholarly debate around Marvell's political allegiances at this time.[76] Like Marvell's ode it situates itself in relation to Cromwell's military ventures. Whereas Marvell's poem belongs to the period in the summer of 1650 between the Irish and Scottish campaigns, Fisher's ode was clearly composed after both of those, to which it refers, had been concluded, and at a point at which Cromwell's attention was turning outwards to enemies abroad, probably either late in 1651 or early in 1652.

Fisher's ode is structured in four sections: the reasons for the poet's change of allegiance (1–36, stanzas 1–9); a celebration of Cromwell's achievements in war and religion (37–68, stanzas 10–17); an injunction to Cromwell not to grieve excessively for a beloved friend, identified in the

---

[74] Isaac Barrow, 'Augustissimo Regi suo reditum gratulatur Britannia', in Cambridge University, *Academiae Cantabrigiensis ΣΩΣΤΡΑ* (1660), sigs. G3ᵛ–H3ᵛ.

[75] Revard, *Politics, Poetics, and the Pindaric Ode*, 100–1, devotes a paragraph to Fisher's ode, acknowledging the general similarity to Marvell's, but without detailed discussion. Thomas Manley's translation of the poem, printed in *Veni; Vidi; Vici* (1652) is available on *EEBO* but is an unreliable guide to the form, meaning and allusive effect of the Latin poem. The final 61 lines of Manley's ode, discussed in Chapter 5, are entirely his own.

[76] Fisher's breakthrough success, *Marston-Moor* (1650), has its origins in a much shorter, and purely royalist, poem composed in the mid-late 1640s. Fisher had himself fought on the losing royalist side at the Battle of Marston Moor.

1654 edition as referring to Henry Ireton who died in November 1651 (69–84, stanzas 18–21); and finally, the future glory and achievements of both Cromwell and, by association, his poet (85–116, stanzas 22–8).

The first 20 lines of the poem form a single, impressive movement conveying all the various kinds of 'vis' ('force', 1) which have brought the poet to the point of supporting and praising Cromwell. Rhetorically this is a bold strategy: the emphasis upon Cromwell's power to compel support implies reluctance among many, including the poet, who are finally won over. Structurally, the single sentence running over twelve lines (9–20) recalls the Pindaric tour de force of the opening of Horace, *Odes* 4.4, in praise of Drusus Nero, also in terms of his military success. *Odes* 4.4 is, similarly, widely considered one of the main models of Marvell's 'Horatian Ode', and David Norbrook describes it as Marvell's 'closest model' in Horace.[77]

> Quae vis subegit, Suadave deviam
> Pellexit in mentem! unde volubiles
>   Sensus retrorsum in Institutum
>   Jam melius mihi fert voluntas?
>
> Me nempè (Flaccum ceu Cytharistrium)
> Causa merentem nuper in *irritâ*
>   T I B I *Hinc* clientem Nostra clades
>   Admovet, & tua *Clara* virtus.
>
> Vestroque Marti testis amicior
> N U M E N, nec actae fortuitò vices
>   *Rerum, Virorum*; sed Supremi
>   J U D I C I S ad trutinam reductae;
>
> Momenta Q U I dat Rebus, & abripit,
> Famamque mutat & precium viris,
>   (Biformis Actor) Magna parvis
>   Substituens, Apicesque Fundum
>
> Sternens ad imum; Authenticus Arbiter
> Figens, refigensque Omnia calculo,
>   Et Corda, Fines & viriles,
>   Funiculo facili, retorquens.[78]
>   (1–20)

---

[77] Norbrook, *Writing the English Republic*, 265.
[78] Text quoted from Fisher, *Irenodia Gratulatoria*, sig. K1ʳ–K3ʳ. The ode was reprinted in 1654 and 1656, but with only very minor typographical changes.

What force has overwhelmed [me], *or, with its persuasive power,*
Enticed [me] *to a change of heart! Why has*
  My will now borne
  My inconstant desires back to a firmer foundation?

To be sure I (or Horace who plays on the cithara)[79]
Was until recently a deserving follower in a vain cause:
  Our disaster has swayed me to You
  – Our disaster and your Famous virtue.

GOD is a kinder witness than your Mars;
The vagaries of history, and the changing fortunes of Men
  Are not driven by chance – but brought
  To the balance of the Supreme Judge.

He who gives impetus to things, and takes it away,
Switches men's glory and their value,
  (Bi-formed actor) substituting
  Great for small, casting the tops

To the very bottom; Original Arbiter
Fixing and refixing everything to your reckoning,
  Both the hearts and the ends of men,
  With a ready little rope, twisting them back.

Cromwell's 'force' is described initially in quasi-erotic terms, as in *pellexit* (2, 'enticed'), while *volubiles* ('turning', 'rolling'), an adjective usually used of water, is the final word of *Odes* 4.1, also a poem about a change of heart, in which Horace, longing for the boy Ligurinus, marks a late return to love poetry and recounts how even in dreams he constantly pursues Ligurinus, but can never catch him. As the start of Fisher's ode recalls the end of *Odes* 4.1, so his final stanza – which names Pindar, Archilochus and Virgil – recalls the beginning of *Odes* 4.2, on Pindaric style.

Fisher then analyses this distinctive 'force' first as the disastrous collapse of the poet's own cause (*Causa ... in irritâ ... Nostra clades*, 6–7); secondly in terms of Cromwell's courageous virtue (*tua Clara virtus*, 8), which is closely linked, thirdly, to the evidence of divine support for Cromwell's military campaigns (*Vestroque Marti testis amicior / Numen*, 9–10). This last observation is the starting point for the rest of this opening movement, a mounting vision of divine action that is built upon the classical imagery of *Fortuna* (especially as she appears in Horace, *Odes*

---

[79] 'Citharistrium' is unattested in the masculine in classical Latin; the feminine form, 'citharistria' ('she who plays upon the cithara'), is, however, used by Porphyry in his commentary on Horace, *Odes* 1.1.

1.34 and 1.35), but which emphasizes throughout (as Horace does not) the exercise of divine judgement. Fisher's poem is dependent upon Horace but rejects the Horatian perspective: lines 15–17, for instance, are a version of *Odes* 1.34.12–13 on the vagaries of fortune (*valet ima summis / mutare et insignem attenuat deus, / obscura promens*, 'the god has the power / to switch the lowest for the highest, to diminish glory / exalting the obscure'; see also *Odes* 1.35.1–4). Here, however, this motif is associated with God, the *Authenticus Arbiter*, rather than *Fortuna*, and recalls several scriptural texts with similar imagery, such as the Magnificat: 'He hath shewed strength with his arm: he hath scattered the proud in the imagination of their hearts. He hath put down the mighty from their seat: and hath exalted the humble and meek. He hath filled the hungry with good things: and the rich he hath sent empty away' (Luke 1:51–3). Marvell too notes that ''Tis madness to resist or blame / The force of angry Heaven's flame' (25–6).

The whole of this first movement of the poem is about the poet's change of heart: why he, who was fighting for the King, now supports Cromwell. The passage gives a rhetorical impression of honesty and of piety – honesty, because it admits the political reality of royalist defeat before describing the poet's change of allegiance; and piety, because God comes before Cromwell – before rising to a moment of real lyricism. The section ends with an image of God as the *Authenticus Arbiter* ('true judge') who:

> Figens, refigensque Omnia calculo,
>   Et Corda, Fines & viriles,
>   Funiculo facili, retorquens.
>   (18–20)
>
> *Fixing and refixing everything to your reckoning,*
>   *Both the hearts and the ends of men,*
>   *With a ready little rope, twisting them back.*

In classical terms, Fisher's *funiculus* (a slender rope, or cord) refers to the 'thread' spun by the Fates. But the repeated internal rhyme (*figens, refigens*; *omnia, corda*; *fines, viriles*), emphatic alliteration (*figens, refigens, fines, funiculo facili*) and the very unclassical touch by which the twisting of the threads extends to men's hearts (*Corda*) as well as their 'ends' (*fines*), moves the passage far from any classical poem. We think rather perhaps of Herbert:

> Yet through these labyrinths, not my groveling wit,
> But thy silk twist let down from heav'n to me:
> Did first conduct, and teach me, how by it
>   To climb to thee.
>   ('The Pearl (Matt. 13:45)', 37–40)

From this generalizing point about men's hearts and fates, the ode returns its focus to the poet's own trajectory, as he arrives *Ad vestra tandem Limina* ('at last at your threshold', 21). The middle section of the poem (lines 37–60, stanzas 10–15) describes Cromwell's achievement in war. Combined with the opening emphasis upon *Fortuna*, this links the poem to Horace, *Odes* 1.35 – a hymn to Fortune which celebrates Augustus' military victories, and is also considered to be one of Marvell's main models.[80] Fisher alludes to this ode as he turns from the general praise of Cromwell's defence of the kingdom to describing specific victories:

> TE Scotus asper; Gens vaga Hyberniae,
> Crepidinosae TE juga *Cambriae*,
>   Totusque passim *Noster Orbis*
>   Robore, Consilio & valentem
>
> Sensere pridem; sentiet *Exterus*,
> Quicunque damnis imminet Anglicis,
>   Axis, recentes seu ciebit,
>   Seu veteres refovebit iras.
>   (53–60)
>
> *You the harsh Scot, the wandering people of Ireland,*
> *You the ridges of rattling Cambria,*
>   *And all our world far and wide*
>   *Your strength in might and wisdom*
>
> *Long since have acknowledged; the foreigner shall experience*
> *Your power – any foreign region which threatens English losses,*
>   *Whether he shall rouse new*
>   *Or rekindle old angers.*

Line 53 recasts Horace, *Odes* 1.35.9 (*Te Dacus asper, te profugi Scythae*, 'the Dacian savage, the Scythian refugees ... entreat you'). As in Marvell, foreign powers (*Exterus*), just as much as the people of his own and adjacent countries (*Noster Orbis*, 55, here including Scotland and Ireland as well as England), are forced to acknowledge Cromwell's power and good judgement. Marvell describes the defeat of the Irish (73–4), predicts success against the Scots (105–12) and hints at future foreign campaigns in France and Italy (101–4). Like Fisher, Marvell also points out that the respect of one's enemies is particularly impressive:

---

[80] Smith (ed.), *Poems of Andrew Marvell*, 268.

> They can affirm his praises best,
> And have, though overcome, confest
> How good he is, how just,
> And fit for highest trust;
> ('Horatian Ode', 76–80)

There are also, however, significant differences in emphasis between the poems. The third movement of Fisher's poem (lines 69–84, stanzas 18–21), addressed to Cromwell directly, urges him not to grieve overmuch for the death of a friend, identified in later editions as Ireton (recalling Horace, *Odes* 1.27 to Virgil on the death of Quintilius): there is no hint of this kind of personal address in Marvell. Similarly, both Fisher and Marvell conclude their odes by urging Cromwell to continue to act justly, but Fisher (typically) adds to that exhortation an explicit reference to the immortalizing effects of poetry – that is, of course, of odes such as the one offered by Fisher himself – comparing himself to Pindar, Archilochus and Virgil.[81] There is nothing so blunt in Marvell, though the poem ends by acknowledging that power is maintained not only by 'force' (Fisher's *vis*) but also by 'arts'.

The considerable similarity of the two odes may suggest that Fisher had seen Marvell's poem (for which there is, however, no concrete evidence of contemporary circulation). Given the extent of the poetic relationship between Marvell and Fisher, which I have documented elsewhere, this seems not unlikely.[82] But we should be cautious on this point: the similarities of the two poems are much *more* certainly evidence of the extent to which Marvell's poem belongs within a well-established tradition of Horatian political and panegyric lyric, a tradition which has been obscured only because this was, as we have seen, almost entirely a neo-Latin tradition, not an English one. Marvell's 'Horatian Ode' appears strikingly fresh to a reader who comes to it from the 'cavalier' lyric of the 1630s and 1640s usually described as 'Horatian': set beside those poems it seems like a quite new version of Horatianism for its times. Fisher's Latin poem, by contrast – although a considerable achievement in its own right, and particularly memorable for its honest confrontation of changed allegiance – is not for an experienced reader of neo-Latin verse *formally* remarkable at all: merely another iteration of a form (the major panegyric ode) of which almost every serious neo-Latin author of the previous 150 years had produced at least one example, and for which the

---

[81] The end of Fisher's poem is discussed in Chapter 5.   [82] Moul, 'Marvell and Fisher'.

generic conventions – including laureate self-consciousness and a capacity to incorporate multiple perspectives – were well understood. In other words, these two poems are remarkably similar not necessarily or mainly because Fisher had read Marvell (though this remains possible), but more generally because they were *both* writing within a well-established generic tradition. Marvell's innovation was in his choice of language, not of form.

Marvell's 'Horatian Ode' is, of course, inconceivable without Horace. But its scope, tone and rhetorical strategies – the opening hint of *recusatio*; the sympathy for, and voice of the defeated (both the Irish and Charles I); its Latinate grammar and syntax; the 'outward-facing' emphasis upon how the English nation performs and is seen abroad; and the real patriotism of the poem – are all shaped as much by the neo-Latin lyric tradition as they are by Horace himself.

CHAPTER 5

Abraham Cowley and Formal Innovation
Verse Sequences, Inset Lyrics, Pindarics and Free Verse

Abraham Cowley's 1656 *Poems* is one of the landmark volumes of the seventeenth century. Less studied than Milton's 1645 *Poems*, it was markedly more influential: both the *Pindarique Odes* and the *Davideis* inaugurated or revived major literary trends. The *Davideis* is often considered a precursor for *Paradise Lost*, while the formal originality of the *Pindarique Odes* was quickly imitated. Anyone reading widely in fashionable lyric, especially religious and devotional lyric, of the later seventeenth and early eighteenth centuries is struck by the vogue for increasingly loose Pindarics, a trend routinely attributed directly to Cowley. This chapter argues that while the influence of the 1656 volume is undeniable, its formal originality has been overstated by critics who have taken Cowley's self-conscious remarks on this topic at face value, and, especially, have not considered the extent to which the volume successfully imported into English verse a range of formal features already well established in contemporary Latin poetry.

By placing Cowley's volume back into the bilingual literary context from which it emerged, we can reassess both Cowley's claims to formal innovation, and how those formal features were understood by his contemporaries.[1] Although the *Poems* contains only two items of Latin verse – the opening dedicatory poem and the Latin version of *Davideis* Book 1 – they stand first and last, framing the volume. Overall, the poetics of the 1656 *Poems* is indebted to the Latin as well as English elements of the wider literary culture, and both the extent of Cowley's innovation, and the cultural and political associations of *Poems* are better understood when read in relation to less well-known contemporary or near-contemporary material, such as the Latin verse produced by members of Oxford university during the 1640s and 1650s; Latin poetry

---

[1] An earlier version of parts of this chapter appeared as Moul, 'Abraham Cowley's 1656 *Poems* in Context'.

written and translated for Cromwell during the 1650s; widely read continental poets and critics such as J.-C. Scaliger, Maffeo Barberini and Emanuele Tesauro; and private manuscript verse collections of the 1640s and 1650s, in both Latin and English. Such a claim is not intended to undermine the importance of the volume but rather to resituate it. A fuller appreciation of the literary context helps us to understand better how and why it was read with such enthusiasm, and the extent to which it shaped contemporary understanding of Cowley as, above all, a scriptural and religious poet, whose work assimilated Pindar with the lyric and prophetic voices of the Old Testament.

Cowley's formal innovations in English poetry during the 1650s are linked to three distinct, though related, areas of significant formal innovation in late sixteenth- and seventeenth-century Latin verse: quasi-dramatic polymetric verse sequences; 'Pindaric' and 'dithyrambic' odes (in both the Jonsonian and the Cowleian iterations); and the appearance of Latin 'free verse' and 'literary inscription'. Only one of these – 'Pindaric' odes – became a major creative force in English poetry, and then only at the second attempt: Ben Jonson's regular Pindaric odes were little imitated in English. This chapter provides a literary history of these three related features. It tracks the development of the Pindaric ode to provide an instance of the influence of Latin verse fashion upon English poetry, and considers how the connotations of canonical English verse may change when read within the wider Latin literary context. The other two forms – quasi-dramatic polymetric sequences and the vogue for 'free verse' – are examples of historically important literary fashions which have remained almost invisible to scholarship because they were largely confined to Latin.[2]

Formal Self-Consciousness and the Politics of the 1656 *Poems*

To be entirely new is also to be – at least potentially – politically neutral, because without association; in the well-known preface to the 1656 *Poems*, Cowley lays claim to just such neutrality, insisting that he has made peace

---

[2] This chapter does not discuss a third form characteristic of the 1656 volume, Cowley's anacreontic verse, which is sometimes also described as innovative though is not flagged as such by Cowley in the same self-conscious way. There are many examples of anacreontics in both Latin and English in the seventeenth century: the best-known English examples are probably those of Robert Herrick, but there are many Latin examples, such as the popular Latin verse of the Jesuit Mario Bettini. Greek anacreontics were frequently translated into Latin, of which there are many examples in Farnaby, *Florilegium epigrammatum Graecorum* (1629). See also O'Brien, *Anacreon Redivivus*.

with the Protectorate. The title page to the volume draws particular attention to the *Davideis*, setting it in much larger type, with the full title ('*Davideis, or, a Sacred Poem of the Troubles of David*') taking up the central third of the page. The book is, as has often been noted, a peculiarly self-conscious volume, with marked use of paratext and authorial commentary, especially in the prefatory material and the authorial notes provided for *Pindarique Odes* and *Davideis*. In a much-cited passage of the preface, Cowley states that he has come to terms with the Cromwellian regime, and not only excluded from publication, but actually destroyed, his *Civil War*:

> I have cast away all such pieces as I wrote during the time of the late troubles, with any relation to the differences that caused them ... when the event of battel, and the unaccountable *Will* of *God* has determined the controversie, and that we have submitted to the conditions of the *Conqueror*, we must lay down our *Pens* as well as *Arms*, we must *march* out of our *Cause* it self, and *dismantle* that, as well as our *Towns* and *Castles*, of all the *Works* and *Fortifications* of *Wit* and *Reason* by which we defended it. *We* ought not sure, to begin our selves to revive the remembrance of those times and actions for which we have received a *General Amnestie*, as a *favor* from the *Victor*. The truth is, neither *We*, nor *They*, ought by the *Representation* of *Places* and *Images* to make a kind of *Artificial Memory* of those things wherein we are all bound to desire, like *Themistocles*, the *Art* of *Oblivion* ... And I would have it accounted no less unlawful to *rip up old wounds*, then to *give new ones*; which has made me not only abstain from printing any things of this kinde, but to burn the very copies, and inflict a severer punishment on them my self, then perhaps the most rigid Officer of *State* would have thought that they deserved.[3]

This preface is, however, preceded by a Latin poem dedicating the entire volume to the University of Cambridge (from which Cowley was ejected for his royalism in 1643), which has attracted much less attention. Despite Cowley's advocacy of the 'Art of Oblivion', the Latin elegy is marked by nostalgia and regret, and not only laments the loss of studious leisure but, more sharply, recalls the events of the civil war and regicide. In the prose preface, Cowley condemns the 'ripping up of old wounds' as no better than the giving of new ones. The final lines of the Latin poem, however, return insistently to imagery of wounding and blood:

---

[3] Cowley, *Poems*, sig. (a)4^{r-v}. Whether with Cowley's knowledge or not, copies of his *Civil War* survived. A short extract was printed in the later seventeenth century: Cowley, *Poem on the Late Civil War* (1679); the three books Cowley completed survive in two manuscripts in Hertford County Record Office (MSS Panshanger D/EP/F.48 and F.36), on which see Calhoun *et al.* (eds.), *Collected Works of Abraham Cowley*, 261–88.

> At nos exemplis *Fortuna* instruxit opimis,
>   Et documentorum satque supérque dedit.
> Cum *Capite* avulsum *Diadema*, infractáque *sceptra*,
>   Contusaque *Hominum Sorte* minante minas,
> *Parcorum ludos, & non tractabile Fatum*,[4]
>   Et versas fundo vidimus orbis opes.
> ...
>
> Ah quanquam iratum, pestem hanc avertere *Numen*,
>   Nec saltem *Bellis ista* licere, velit!
> Nos, tua progenies, pereamus; & ecce, perimus!
>   In nos jus habeat: Jus habet omne malum.
> Tu stabilis brevium genus immortale nepotum
>   Fundes; nec tibi *Mors* ipsa *superstes* erit.
> Semper plena manens uteri de fonte perenni
>   Formosas mittes *ad mare Mortis* aquas.
> Sic *Venus* humanâ quondam, *Dea* saucia dextrâ,
>   (Namque solent ipsis *Bella* nocere *Deis*)
> Imploravit opem superûm, questùsque cievit,
>   Tinxit adorandus candida membra cruor.
> Quid quereris? contemne *breves* secura dolores;
>   Nam tibi ferre *Necem vulnera* nulla valent.[5]

But Fortune has instructed us by excellent examples and given us more than enough proof [that human affairs are as nothing], *since we have seen a Crown torn from a Head, sceptres broken, the threats of Men crushed by threatening Chance, the games of the Fates, and Fate itself, which is not to be overcome, and all the wealth of the world turned upside down . . . Ah would that Divine power, although angered, should choose to avert this plague, or if Wars at least could be ruled out. Let us, your offspring, perish (and behold, perish we do), let every evil hold sway over us – as it does. Unmoved, you* [the University of Cambridge] *will pour forth an undying train of short-lived alumni, nor shall Death itself outlive you. Ever abiding, your womb full, from your constant fountain you shall send out beautiful waters towards the sea of Death. In the same way, the goddess Venus, when once wounded by human hand (for wars tend to hurt even the gods themselves) implored the other gods for help, and uttered her laments, and the sacred blood stained her white limbs. Why complain? You who are free from care can scorn short-lived pain, for no wounds can bring you death.*

---

[4] Cowley, *Poems*, here reads 'Factum', but all subsequent editions emend to 'Fatum', surely correctly.
[5] Cowley, *Poems*, sig. A2ʳ. Translations are my own. A complete text and translation of this poem by Dana Sutton can be found online (www.philological.bham.ac.uk/cowleypoems). The translation provided is not however entirely reliable.

The opening pages of the collection thereby set up a tension between Cowley's voice in English prose, and what is suggested by his own Latin poem, which stands first. This chapter takes its cue from the programmatic disjunction between the dedicatory poem and the prose preface, in examining how Cowley's repeated statements of formal originality in the 1656 *Poems* stand up to scrutiny within a wider (and specifically a Latin, as well as English) literary context.

Polymetric Verse and the Dramatic Sequence

Verse collections showcasing a large variety of metres are, as discussed in Chapters 2 and 3, particularly characteristic of the Latin poetry of the later sixteenth century: this is a pattern of composition which became common in English in the early seventeenth century, in collections such as Herbert's *Temple*. Cowley's precocious *Poetical Blossomes*, however, also published in 1633, when Cowley was only fifteen, points towards a related formal device which, though it also has its roots in the sixteenth century, became particularly characteristic of politically charged mid-seventeenth-century poetics: namely, the polymetric verse sequence, making use of changes of metre or inset lyrics within a single poem, often with distinct speaking voices resembling drama.[6] The two main items in *Poetical Blossomes*, 'Constantia and Philetus' and 'Pyramus and Thisbe', are both structured in this way. As has been pointed out, the formal experiments of *Poetical Blossomes* presage the similar interest in inset lyrics in both the *Davideis* of 1656 and, in fullest form, *Plantarum Libri Sex* (1668). Cowley himself was explicit about the boyhood influence of Spenser upon him, and the combination of lyric and narrative verse in *Poetical Blossomes* is plainly indebted to Spenser – there are inset lyrics in the *Shepherds' Calendar* – and perhaps also to later Elizabethan and early Jacobean works in this tradition, such as George Chapman's *Ovids Banquet of Sence* (1595) and Michael Drayton's *Eclogues*, published in 1606, both of which make similar use of inset songs.[7]

Such techniques, which have links to drama and liturgy, create the possibility of crafting long poems that are both formally and metrically varied and dramatically coherent. Frequently, the transition between metres is linked explicitly to a change of 'speakers' – as in Spenser's

---

[6] The collection may have been circulating for a couple of years by the time it was published, on which see Nethercot, 'Milton, Jonson, and the Young Cowley'.
[7] Maggie Kilgour discusses the influence of Spenser on Cowley, in 'Cowley's Epic Experiments'.

'April' Eclogue. Drama is properly beyond the scope of this study, but many examples of religious and allegorical verse, in particular, have strong dramatic features even where they are not (or probably not) intended as texts for performance.[8]

Indeed, a particular kind of a quasi-dramatic and highly emotional form of polymetric sequence appears to be characteristic of the seventeenth century.[9] At the start of the century, Thomas Goad's contribution to the Cambridge collection marking the death of Queen Elizabeth and accession of King James is a particularly lively example of a sequence of this kind.[10] Goad's poem begins in elegiac couplets before shifting into iambic trimeter followed by a concluding section in hexameter. The diction as well as the metre of these sections are distinct: the opening section is conversational and emotional; the second urgent, modelled tonally as well as metrically upon the political poems of Horace's *Epodes* and emphasizing the dangers to England of the Queen's death; while Goad raises his register towards epic in the final hexameter section, in markedly alliterative and celebratory verse, as he urges the fellows of his college to serve their country.

The sequence is also artistically self-conscious, marking its own generic and metrical transitions:

> Pompa alijs curae: tu faetum Elegeia pectus
>   Concute, quae lachrymis, carmine, laude vales.
> . . .
>
> Incipe: cùmque sacrum memorabis nomen Elisae,
>   Humectum lachrymis & graue carmen eat.
> Incipe. Stat, stupet, usque negat se posse, videntem
>   Orta tot ex vno vulnere damna, loqui.
> Hoc tantûm, quis nollet, ait, morientibus vnà
>   Pace, pijs, patria, relligione, mori?
> Siccine? ferales, infractum carmen, Iambi
>   Surgite: non elegis neruus, et ictus inest.

---

[8] Nottingham University Library, MS PwV 1456, for instance, preserves a text of 158 lines, dating probably from the mid-seventeenth century, which is a kind of composite paraphrase of the first two chapters of the biblical Song of Songs, consisting of five sections, each in a different metre. Two of these sections are in fact separate lyric paraphrases by Casimir Sarbiewski (*Odes* 2.25 and 4.21), who was well known for his versions of the Song of Songs in Horatian metres. The others may also be original or copied from elsewhere. In this instance, the alternating speakers of the scriptural text perhaps suggested dramatic variety of form and voice.

[9] For sixteenth century examples of polymetric sequences in Latin, such as those by Walter Haddon, see Chapter 2.

[10] *Threno-thriambeuticon* (1603), 63–6. This collection also includes verse by Phineas Fletcher, discussed in Chapter 4. William Camden owned a copy (Westminster Abbey CB 7 (1)). On Goad, see Chapter 4, note 58.

[switches into iambic trimeter]

The procession is the concern of others: you, Elegia, shake
  Your productive breast, you who prosper by tears, by song, by praise.
...

Begin: and when you recall the sacred name of Elisa [Elizabeth],
  Let a song proceed which is serious, and wet with tears.
Begin! [She] *stands, stupefied and repeatedly claims that, seeing*
  So many losses arisen from a single wound, [she] *cannot speak.*
Only this does she say: 'Who would not wish to die when others are dying
  For peace, for pious men, for one's land, for one's religion?
Is that how it is? Fierce Iambics, arouse, the broken song:
  There is no strength or impetus in elegiacs.

[switches into iambic trimeter]

There is a very similar quasi-dramatic sequence contributed by one G. Higges to the Merton College, Oxford commemorative volume on the death of Sir Thomas Bodley in 1613 (in this case, hexameter-elegiacs-trimeter).[11] As in the Goad piece, the changes of metre represent different voices. Both point to the dramatic possibilities of this kind of sequence.

Verse sequences of this sort seem to have become particularly fashionable in the period of great political upheaval in the mid-seventeenth century. A series of such Latin texts, several (though not all) of them markedly royalist, appeared during the 1640s – a period during which it was safer and easier to print or circulate overtly royalist material in Latin than it was in English. Many of these texts use extended allegory or scriptural paraphrase to comment upon contemporary events, and a substantial portion of them make use, like the *Davideis* (and, somewhat differently, Cowley's prosimetric 'Vision') of metrical transitions or inset lyrics to emotive effect.[12] Several also include examples of the other formal features flagged by Cowley in the 1656 *Poems* as original, including emotive half-lines and irregular Pindaric or dithyrambic verse.

---

[11] Oxford University, *Bodleiomnema* (1613), 54–8. Also owned by Camden (Westminster Abbey CB 7 (7)).

[12] There is a discernible subgenre at this time of political allegory in Latin verse; other examples without the formal features discussed here include Oxinden, *Religionis Funus* (1647); [Anon.], *Ex Spinosa Anonymi Sylva* (1649); Ball, *Europa Lachrymans* (1650); I. A., *Gigantomachia* (printed with Perrinchief, *Nuntius a mortuis* (1659), but dated 1645). Some of these are included in the discussion of scriptural and allegorical verse in Chapter 11.

The *Sors Caesarea*, for instance, a verse sequence lamenting the execution of Archbishop Laud under the guise of 'Polydorus', appears to have been produced by one or more students of St John's College, Oxford in 1645 or early 1646.[13] Indeed, it is possible that Cowley himself may have been at the college at the time it was composed: Cowley was attached to St John's in Oxford after being ejected from Cambridge in 1643 and was not certainly in France until early 1646.[14] It includes emotive half-lines, several changes of metre and two inset lyric songs (in sapphics and asclepiads). A popular satiric sequence on the visitation of Oxford, circulating widely in manuscript and printed in 1648, and probably by Adam Littleton (1627–94), is in hexameter with inset speeches in iambic trimeter.[15] These examples demonstrate the widespread formal experimentation of similar kinds to that found in Cowley's 1656 *Poems*, though chiefly in Latin, and associated in particular with royalist circles in Oxford in the 1640s.

On the religious and (probably) Parliamentarian side, Robert Hatcher's collections of Latin verse were published in 1645 (*Institutio, epithalamium, & militia viri*) and 1646 (*Paideutica*), with Cambridge (rather than Oxford) connections.[16] The preface to his 1645 volume has several points in common with Cowley's remarks in the preface of the 1656 *Poems*: Hatcher sets his work within the context of civil war and gives the horror of war as the reason for seeking consolation not in trivial, but in sacred verse.[17] Indeed, Hatcher's books contain several fashionable elements. His verse paraphrases of Proverbs and the Song of Songs (both in the 1645

---

[13] Bod. MS Tanner 306, fols. 149ʳ–62ᵛ. Edited and translated from this text by Dana Sutton and Martin Wiggins (www.philological.bham.ac.uk/sors). The work is dedicated to Richard Baylie, the President of St John's at the time. Laud, who was President of the college from 1611–21 and Chancellor of Oxford University from 1630 is never named, but Wiggins is surely correct to identify him with the 'Polydorus' of the sequence.

[14] Lindsay, 'Cowley, Abraham'.

[15] The poem was published (anonymously, and without place or printer) as *Tragi-Comoedia Oxoniensis* in 1648, but it was circulating in manuscript under the much more explicit title 'Lachrymae academicae fatum Caroli suumque deplorantes' ('University tears shed over the fates of Charles and of themselves'), see Bod. MSS Add. B. 109, fols. 124ᵛ–6ᵛ, and Wood D 19 (2), fols. 87ʳ–91ʳ. Littleton, to whom the work has been ascribed, went up to Christ Church, Oxford from Westminster School in 1644 and was ejected by the Parliamentary visitors in 1648 (Key, 'Littleton, Adam').

[16] Robert Hatcher is unidentified, though he was probably a relative of the Parliamentary officer and Lincolnshire MP Thomas Hatcher (c.1589–1677). The preface to the second volume dedicates the work to Henry Molle, university orator at Cambridge, and Hatcher is identified as 'Cantabrigiensem' ('of Cambridge') on the title page.

[17] Hatcher, *Institutio*, sig. A3ʳ. Hatcher's comments on his use of paraphrase (sig. A4ʳ) resemble those of Cowley in relation to his *Pindarique Odes*.

Polymetric Verse and the Dramatic Sequence 191

volume) are polymetric, using a different metre for each scriptural chapter, rather like the Nottingham MS paraphrase of Song of Songs chapters 1 and 2 described above (note 8). His collection the following year, however, attempts something different: 'Paideutica', a long poem in iambic trimeters on obtaining wisdom, is the main item in the volume of the same name. Divided into three books, the last includes an inset paraphrase of Job 28 in elegiac couplets, while an authorial note indicates that a paraphrase of Proverbs 9, though not included in the printed volume, was originally composed to end Book 2. Job 28 and Proverbs 9 are both biblical descriptions of true wisdom: by using Old Testament texts on moralizing themes, Hatcher offers a pious, improving and specifically Protestant version of the kind of formal experimentation typical of the more 'high church' Oxford compositions from the same period.[18]

Finally, and most strikingly, Peter du Moulin's 1649 allegorical *Ecclesiae Gemitus* is in iambic trimeters with two inset speeches. In Du Moulin's strange and memorable poem, which is discussed further in Chapter 11, a persecuted nymph represents the beleaguered Church of England. At the moment of greatest danger, collapsed at the foot of a tree and bleeding heavily, with soldiers – representing Parliamentarian forces and opponents of the established Church – now right upon her, the nymph cries out for rescue. By divine intervention, her wounds are healed by the blood and tears of Christ, and she is saved from death. As in the Latin version of the first book of Cowley's *Davideis*, the moment of salvation is marked by an inset ode in alcaics:

> ... quae vigil, & compos sui
> Admotáque coelo, magna, mira, illustria,
> Accepit oculis visa perspicacibus,
> Carnis tenebroso non videnda lumine.
>
>> Obsessa nullis lucida nubilis
>> Laetis refulsit aethra coloribus,
>> Risúsque diducti benigno
>> Sponte fores patuêre coeli.[19]

---

[18] Both Hatcher's poem and Du Moulin's *Ecclesiae Gemitus* are also discussed in Chapter 11.
[19] Du Moulin, *Ecclesiae Gemitus* (1649), 39–40. Though published anonymously (and pointedly dated 'in the first year of the era of the martyrdom of Charles I, King of Britain'), at least some readers were aware of its authorship: the Thomason Tracts copy has been annotated 'Du molin' on the title page. Du Moulin also wrote Latin verse invective against Milton, and he seems to have been chiefly responsible for a second anonymous tract against the regicide (and Milton himself) designed for European circulation, *Regii sanguinis clamor* (1652).

> ... *She who, watchful, and composed*
> *Accepted the great and marvelous visions come from Heaven,*
> *Which she watched with her perceptive and attentive gaze –*
> *Things that cannot be seen by the darksome light of the flesh.*
>
> *The bright heaven, unbeset by any clouds,*
> *Shone with glorious colours,*
> *And the gates of Heaven of their own accord*
> *Were laid open, split by the blessing of a smile.*

Cowley makes one of his several markedly self-conscious (and arguably disingenuous) claims to formal originality in relation to his use of inset lyrics in the *Davideis*: 'For this liberty of inserting an *Ode* into an *Heroick Poem*, I have no authority or example.'[20] He attaches this note to a rather expansive paraphrase of Psalm 114 included in the first book of the *Davideis*, at the point at which David averts Saul's anger against him by bursting into song:

> Thus *Davids Lyre* did *Sauls* wild rage controul,
> And tun'd the harsh disorders of his *Soul*.
>
> When *Isra'el* was from bondage led,
>   Led by th'*Almighties* hand
>   From out a foreign land,
> The great *Sea* beheld, and fled.
> As men pursu'ed, when that fear past they find,
> Stop on some higher ground to look behind,
>   So whilst through wondrous ways
>   The sacred *Army* went,
>   The *waves* afar stood up to gaze,
>   And their own *Rocks* did represent,
> Solid as *Waters* are above the *Firmament*.[21]

The point about salvation from danger is made twice over: Psalm 114, which here averts Saul's anger, is itself a celebration of the Israelites' escape from Egypt, and Cowley's version emphasizes this by adding references to the Israelite army passing safely through the sea which are not in the biblical text. In the English *Davideis*, quoted above, the inset lyric is in regular Pindarics of the kind written by Jonson (suggesting the strong traditional association between Pindar and David), whereas in Latin it is in alcaics: we find a similar pattern in the relationship between Fisher's Latin

---

[20] Cowley, *Poems*, 'Davideis', 37.   [21] Cowley, *Poems*, 'Davideis', 13–14.

ode to Cromwell and Manley's English translation of it (both 1652, discussed further below).

A narrative poem about David, traditionally the poet of the Psalms, is perhaps an obvious site for an inset lyric, given the strong tradition of psalm paraphrase in lyric form. Indeed, Robert Aylett, a prolific English verse paraphraser of scripture, had published a poem about David in 1638 which, just like the *Davideis*, incorporated an inset lyric paraphrase of a psalm – in this case Psalm 51, presented, according to the traditional superscription in the Hebrew Bible, as David's song of repentance when he realises the sinfulness of his actions in securing Bathsheba for himself (described in 2 Samuel 12:13):

> So it with *David* fares, whose heart relents,
> And shakes and trembles at Gods *menacements*,
> His sinne confessing, but his *Faith* holds fast,
> And sings this *Penitentiall Psalme* at last.

> Psal. 51.

> *Of thy great goodnesse, Lord, some pitty take*
>   *On me whom sinne*
>   *Doth now awake,*
> *If thou in loving kindnesse wilt begin,*
>   *All mine offences easely may,*
>   *Be by thy mercies done away.*[22]

It is possible that Cowley did not know Aylett's poem: *David's Troubles Remembred* was not among a selection of Aylett's work from the 1620s and 1630s that was republished in *Divine, and Moral Speculations in Metrical Numbers* (1653), and Cowley's interest in inset lyrics and related formal devices is evident from his adolescence; though on the other hand, it seems likely that Cowley would have taken an interest in earlier attempts to put David's story into English verse. In any case, Cowley's framing of the *Davideis* insists on the novelty of its genre (biblical epic) and form alike: he claims that both his use of 'heroic' verse with inset lyrics, and his use of half-lines in imitation of Virgil are formal innovations. Critics have tended to take these declarations of originality largely at face value.[23] By doing so,

---

[22] Aylett, *David's Troubles Remembred* (1638), 24ᵛ–5ʳ.
[23] On Cowley's use of half-lines, however, Henry Power has reached a similar sceptical conclusion: 'it is hard not to come to the conclusion that he was deliberately ignoring these precedents when he claimed to be the first English poet to have imitated this feature of the *Aeneid*' (Power, 'Teares Breake off My verse', 147); for further examples of the use of the emotive half-line especially in royalist poetry of the 1640s, see Moul, 'Abraham Cowley's 1656 *Poems* in Context'.

Cowley effectively distances his poem both from the tradition of scriptural verse paraphrase, such as that of Aylett, of which there were a particularly large number of examples produced in both English and Latin in the first half of the seventeenth century, and from the sort of quasi-dramatic polymetric material which, as we have seen, was particularly fashionable in the Latin poetry of the 1640s. (Indeed, there is an overlap between these categories, as several of the allegorical polymetric texts of the 1640s, like that of Hatcher, also have elements of scriptural paraphrase.) This is not to suggest that Cowley's claims for originality are entirely unfounded: none of the structurally similar texts offers exactly what Cowley does here, that is a Latin poem in hexameters with inset lyrics – but they are also much more similar than the notes to the *Davideis* imply.

Cowley's insistence that he is doing something quite new can be considered to be, as it were, 'decodably' misleading: university-educated contemporaries, especially (though not only) of royalist sympathies, would in fact have recognised many elements. In his major Restoration work, the *Plantarum Libri Sex*, published in its final form posthumously in 1668 and discussed at greater length in Chapter 11, Cowley would go on to explore the dramatic potential of the inset lyric to a much greater extent. The *Plantarum* is plainly a royalist work, but in a distinctively post-Restoration way, and it shares some of the tonal ambiguities of the 1656 *Poems*: in Books 3 and 4, for instance, set on the eve of the Restoration itself, Pomona, goddess of Spring, invites personified flowers to stand as candidates to rule their kingdom as a monarch. Each flower makes a speech, an electoral pitch for the monarchy, outlining their (primarily medicinal) utility to mankind, and these are the inset odes: but Pomona in the end decides against a monarch, and instead appoints a system of consuls and senators. At least in the first five books of the *Plantarum* – the last is more straightforwardly panegyric – the political impetus of the poem is repeatedly blurred, or defocused, by ambiguities of this kind. Overall, the didactic seriousness of the *Plantarum* is frequently prioritized over a clear political message, and the *Poems* of 1656 leaves a similar impression: the political associations of Cowley's formal innovations are, on the whole, royalist, but these affiliations are never allowed to overwhelm the scriptural and religious seriousnesss of his poetic undertaking.[24]

---

[24] On the use of Horace in the *Plantarum*, see Moul, 'Horatian Odes'; on the politics of the *Plantarum*, see Spearing, 'Fruits of Retirement'.

Pindaric Odes

These observations about the cultural and political associations of the formal features of the *Davideis* support Stella Revard's reading of the politics of the 1656 volume as essentially royalist, based upon its more famous component, the *Pindarique Odes*.[25] Though typically treated separately – there has been relatively little attention to the 1656 *Poems* as a whole, as there has for instance for Milton's *Poems* a decade earlier – the *Pindarique Odes* belong recognizably to the same shaping context of a bilingual poetic culture traumatized by civil war. In the preface, Cowley makes another self-conscious claim to formal originality, remarking that: '[Pindar's way and manner of speaking] has not been yet (that I know of) introduced into *English*, though it be the noblest and highest kind of writing in Verse'.[26] Several commentators, including Revard, have pointed out the oddity of this statement, given the high profile of Ben Jonson whose work includes multiple experiments in Pindaric form.[27] Such claims were in part conventional: in the preface from the printer to the reader attached to the 1623 edition of Maffeo Barberini's (Pope Urban VIII's) *Poemata*, the printer makes very similar claims for Barberini's innovations in Latin form, although Latin Pindarics were in fact well established by this period.[28] Claiming novelty for Pindaric form seems to have been almost a conventional element of the form itself. Nevertheless, Cowley's self-proclaimed originality, usually taken to refer specifically to the invention of *irregular* Pindarics, has largely been taken at face value by critics.[29]

As with the polymetric quasi-dramatic sequence, however, the roots of Cowley's formal innovation in the *Pindarique Odes* lie in the preceding century of largely Latin verse as much as they do in his encounter with

---

[25] Revard, 'Cowley's *Pindarique Odes*' and *Politics, Poetics, and the Pindaric Ode*. See also Potter, *Secret Rites and Secret Writing*, 143; Nevo, *Dial of Virtue*, 119–30.
[26] Cowley, *Poems*, sig. Aaa2ᵛ.   [27] Revard, *Politics, Poetics, and the Pindaric Ode*, 129n.
[28] Barberini, *Poemata*, sig. aiiʳ⁻ᵛ.
[29] See for example Nethercot, *Abraham Cowley*, 135; Wilson, 'Pindar', 160; Shankman, 'Pindaric Tradition', 229; Revard, *Politics, poetics, and the Pindaric Ode*, xii–xiii. The entry for 'Pindaric' in Baldick (ed.), *Oxford Dictionary of Literary Terms*, states plainly that Cowley's *Pindarique Odes* 'began this kind of [i.e. irregular] departure from strict Pindaric precedent'. Revard's extended discussion of Cowley's Pindarics focuses on their political connotations rather than their formal originality, remarking only that his failure to acknowledge Jonson as a model is 'puzzling' (Revard, *Politics, poetics, and the Pindaric Ode*, 125–52 (at 129). In *Pindar and the Renaissance Hymn-Ode*, 245, she acknowledges, building on Maddison, *Apollo and the Nine*, 351, 369–72, that Crashaw's experiments in irregular verse probably influenced Cowley. In fact, as discussed below, Crashaw was not the only possible model for metrically 'free' lyric available to Cowley in the early-mid 1650s, though given their personal friendship it remains likely that his influence was particularly important.

Pindar himself. Cowley's version of Pindaric form is built upon the two main traditions of Latin Pindarics – regular and irregular – familiar to a reader of contemporary Latin poetry in the mid-seventeenth century, and responds, also, to the particular interest in this period in 'free' and experimental Latin verse in general: a vogue which, as we shall see, extended beyond Pindarics as such, though was frequently associated with them. In his Pindarics, too, Cowley's apparent formal innovations were markedly 'of his moment'.

Types of Pindaric in the Seventeenth Century

Pindar's odes are, in early modern terms, composed in 'regular' Pindarics: each poem is made up of long stanzas (called 'strophes') of 8–16 lines, in a complex metrical pattern. In most Pindaric odes, these stanzas are arranged into tripartite patterns of repeating strophe-antistrophe-epode, in which each strophe-antistrophe pair, and each epode, has the same metrical scheme. It was this effect of complex structures repeated over relatively large distances but in a regular fashion that Jonson imitated in his English Pindaric poems. The best known of these, the late Cary-Morison ode (*UW* 70, commemorating the death of Henry Morison in 1629), is the only one in Pindaric triads of strophe, antistrophe and epode; but several of Jonson's other odes are in single-strophe Pindarics, such as the 'Ode to Himself' appended to *The New Inn* (1629), a poem itself frequently translated into Latin, and the impressive early ode to James, Earl of Desmond, almost certainly composed in about 1600:

> Where art thou, Genius? I should use
> Thy present aid. Arise, Invention,
> Wake, and put on the wings of Pindar's muse,
> To tow'r with my intention
> High as his mind, that doth advance
> Her upright head above the reach of chance.
> Or the time's envy.
> Cinthius, I apply
> My bolder numbers to thy golden lyre:
> Oh, then inspire
> Thy priest in this strange rapture; heat my brain
> With Delphic fire,
> That I may sing my thoughts in some unvulgar strain.[30]

---

[30] *UW* 25.1–13, discussed in Moul, *Jonson, Horace*, 32–40. The Cary-Morison ode has attracted considerable critical attention (see note 40 below); the earlier non-triadic Pindarics much less so.

Though Soowthern had attempted something similar in the latter part of the sixteenth century, Jonson was the first to import verse of this kind successfully into English. Pindaric forms of this sort did not, however, come into English solely or directly from Greek. Regular Pindarics, though never found in classical Latin, were an already well-established neo-Latin form when Jonson began experimenting with them in English.

Two landmarks of sixteenth-century poetics exemplify this point. The influential literary theorist, Julius Caesar Scaliger, whose *Poetices libri septem* (first published in 1561) became a standard reference work, published in 1574 a collection of his own Latin verse which, though not highly successful poetically, functioned as a kind of compendium of possible verse forms for poets of the period. Included in it is a nativity ode composed in triadic Latin Pindarics, clearly divided into strophes, antistrophes and epodes.[31]

Strophe

Vade taciti per amica caeli
Silentia silentia
Regina nox: cui latera stipat aurea
Immortale decus triplex.
Tibi militat omnia hora mundi
Aeternas accincta faces.
Tibi ridet hilarescens sinus aetheris,
Aligeros igneus ostentans animos
Patitur natura: suique
Nescia fati,
Mole noua premi stupet.
...

Epode

Vigil anime, vigil: O
Nocturni pastorum coetus
Peruigilum comes. qui me accentus
Animum ferit? mentem quatit?
Haurit cor? abit vigor. vt
Crebra ingruunt fulgura.
Puer vagit, & vagiens
Voce serenat florem caeli. O

---

[31] Scaliger, *Poemata* (1574), 'Natalia domini nostri Jesu Christi filii Dei viui', second section, 95–7. In the 1600 edition, Scaliger added a second Pindaric ode following this one, on the birth of the Virgin Mary. Scaliger also experimented with strophic choruses in his 1574 translation of Sophocles' *Ajax*.

> Secundis auspicia orsis. tener
> Splendet fletibus aether.
> Quis me rapit? quis me trahit?
> Quo sistes me ales o puer?

> *Go among the gentle*
> *Silences, the silences of the quietened heaven,*
> *Queen Night: for whom a triple immortal glory*
> *Crowds your golden flanks.*
> *Every hour of the world, armed with eternal torches,*
> *Fights for you.*
> *For you the lap of heaven, rejoicing, smiles,*
> *Fiery nature, displaying winged souls,*
> *Lies open; and unaware of her own fate*
> *Is astonished to be crushed by a new mass.*
> . . .
> *Wakefulness, soul, wakefulness: O*
> *Companion of the nocturnal gathering*
> *Of the ever-watchful shepherds. What blast or signal*
> *Strikes my heart? Shakes my mind?*
> *Drains my heart? My strength is gone. As if*
> *Repeated lightning-bolts are falling upon me.*
> *A child cries, and as he cries*
> *Calms with his voice the flower of heaven. O*
> *What signs of an auspicious beginning. The sky*
> *In tenderness glows with the weeping.*
> *Who is snatching me up? Who is dragging me along?*
> *Where, o boy, o bird, will you set me down?*

Scaliger combines distinctively Pindaric motifs ('Quis me rapit? quis me trahit?') with elements familiar from nativity odes in both Latin and the vernacular, such as the evocative nighttime setting, and the birth of a new order, including the defeat and dispersal of pagan powers.[32] Scaliger's style is, however, profoundly unclassical not only in form – Latin Pindarics were themselves a neo-Latin innovation – but also in sound: he makes use of multiple effects, such as repetition ('silentia, silentia', 2), polyptoton

---

[32] Compare also Milton's 'Nativity Ode' of 1629; the sources of Milton's poem have been discussed extensively, though with an emphasis upon vernacular rather than Latin elements. Milton's ode is not in Pindarics, though it is in two ambitious and original stanza forms. In one of the best single essays on Milton's poem, Broadbent, 'Nativity Ode', suggests that Milton's ode may be unique among nativity odes and hymns in its lack of interest in the imagery of motherhood; this, however, he shares with Scaliger's poem, in which Mary, strikingly, does not appear at all. Stella Revard discusses the specifically Pindaric elements of Scaliger's poem in relation to the nativity odes of Tasso and Milton (*Pindar and the Renaissance Hymn-Ode*, 225–8), though without quoting from the poem. On seventeenth-century nativity odes more generally, see Chapter 6.

('vagit, et vagiens') and quite frequent rhyme, both at the ends of lines ('coetus', 'accentus'; 'tener', 'aether', 'puer') and within lines ('ferit ... quatit ... haurit ... abit', 'cor ... vigor'), any of which would be unusual in isolation in classical verse, and are never found in such dense proximity.[33]

The interest in Latin Pindarics in the final quarter of the sixteenth century is clear also from manuscript sources, sometimes in surprising ways: an enigmatic late sixteenth-century translation of the song from Spenser's 'April' eclogue in the *Shepherds' Calendar* uses Latin Pindarics to create a repeating stanza form that loosely resembles Spenser's visually though is in fact metrically even more varied:

> Ye dayntye Nymphs, that in this blessed Brooke
>   Doe bathe your brest,
> Forsake your watry bowres, and hether looke,
>   At my request:
> And eke you Virgins, that on Parnasse dwell,
> Whence floweth Helicon the learned well,
>   Helpe me to blaze
>   Her worthy praise,
> Which in her sexe doth all excell.
>
>   (April, 37–45)
>
> Nymphae, candidulae Nymphae, sub flumine sancto
>   Colla quae lauitis comasque molles;
> Linquite caerula regna, meamque parumper amicè
>   Audite, quaeso, fistulam:
> Vos quoque, Parnassi colitis quae celsa, Camenae,
> Lucidus vnde Helicon fluit, alti carminis author,
>   Nunc opem, Diuae, date mî canenti,
>   Eius vt possim decorare nomen
>   Virginis, cunctas super vna celsum
>   Quae caput effert.[34]

Spenser's stanza consists of alternating iambic pentameters and iambic dimeters (1–4); two further iambic pentameters (5–6), two more dimeters

---

[33] Compare the discussion in Chapter 2 of Beza's Latin verse style in his psalm paraphrases. The stylistic differences between Beza's psalms, first published in 1579, and those of his model, Buchanan, pinpoint the stylistic revolution in Latin verse in the latter third of the sixteenth century reflected here also in Scaliger.

[34] BL MS Harley 532, fols. 1ʳ–4ʳ, titled (without mentioning Spenser) 'Hymnus Pastoralis in laudem serenissimae Reginae Elizabethae; ex Anglico sermone in Latinum traductus'. Monostrophic, 13 strophes. *CELM* SpE 27.3. See Bradner, 'Latin Translations of Spenser's *Shepheardes Calender*', 26n. Spenser's *Shepherds' Calender* was first published in 1579.

(7–8) and a final iambic tetrameter (9) – three different metrical lines in total. The Latin stanza replaces the iambic pentameters with dactylic hexameters (1, 3, 5–6), the first dimeter with a phalaecian hendecasyllable (2), the second with an iambic dimeter (4), and the final three lines of the English stanza with the four lines of a sapphic stanza (three sapphic hendecasyllables followed by an adonean).[35]

Indeed, multiple models for Latin Pindarics were available to English readers by the turn of the century. Of particularly sharp relevance in England, the German Latin poet Melissus (Paul Schede) opened his major collection of Latin verse, dedicated to Queen Elizabeth and published in 1586, with a grand Pindaric ode (itself previously published in 1578), which stands at the head of a sequence of 14 consecutive poems in this form.[36] Jonson owned a copy of Melissus' poetry, and nor was this the only example of triadic Latin Pindarics known to have been in his library: he also owned a 1619 volume of Latin verse by the Polish poet Szymon Szymonowicz, which opens with three major Latin triadic odes.[37] Maffeo Barberini (1568–1644), later Pope Urban VIII, whose skills as poet were acknowledged by George Herbert, opens his 1623 Latin verse collection with a sequence of three triadic Pindaric odes, on the King of France, Mary Magdalene and St Laurence.[38] In the transition from strophe to antistrophe in the first ode, Barberini shifts from the glory of Louis XIII to a self-conscious statement of his own laureate authority:

>   . . .
>   Ut inter omnes thure LUDOVICUS
>   Cultus & aris
>   Coelesti radiat vinctus diademate frontem!
>
>   Antistrophe I
>
>   Quas dudum mea parturit
>   Mens foeta laudes, Regis educ optimi
>   In lucis oras, Aonii lyra
>   Sonora cantus obstetrix.
>   An piae primum studium Parentis

---

[35] The use of the sapphic stanza as the final element is a common feature of polymetric verse in the final decades of the sixteenth century, as discussed in Chapter 2.
[36] Melissus, *Schediasmata poetica*. See Revard, 'Latin Ode'. For a metrical analysis of Melissus' Latin Pindarics, see Schultheiss, 'Zwischen philologischer Analyse und poetologischen Programm', 126–30.
[37] Simonidae, *Poematia Aurea* (1619).
[38] Barberini's Latin and Italian Pindarics are discussed briefly in relation to those of his friend and contemporary Gabriello Chiabrera (in Italian) by Revard (*Pindar and the Renaissance Hymn-Ode*, 263–9), though with an emphasis upon Chiabrera, whom Revard considers more innovative.

> Formandi puerum moribus integris,
> Doctaeque raris Palladis artibus;
> An celsae decus indolis
> Dircaeis celebrem modis?
> En blanda prodis Comitas, Pudórque,
> Lenis & oris
> Majestas, ac forma, decens & Gratia linguae.[39]
>
> *As LOUIS, worshipped with incense and altars,*
> *shines among all,*
> *his forehead bound with a heavenly crown!*

Antistrophe

> *These praises which my fertile mind*
> *Long since poured forth, bring out upon the shores of light*
> *Of the best of Kings, resounding lyre, the midwife*
> *Of Aonian song.*
> *Is it the early care of a pious Mother*
> *In forming her son in accordance with correct morals,*
> *And by the rare arts of learned Pallas;*
> *Or is it the glory of an inborn lofty nature*
> *That I should celebrate in Dircaean measures?*
> *Look how you step out, kind Courtesy, and Modesty,*
> *And, with gentle expression,*
> *Majesty, and beauty, refinement and Grace of speech.*

This is fully developed high panegyric in the Pindaric tradition, used by Barberini for praise of the extraordinary achievement of both king and saints. In true Pindaric fashion, he draws attention to the importance of the poet himself for conferring praise ('my fertile mind ... that I should celebrate'). Jonson's Pindarics are highly self-conscious in much the same way, most memorably in the positioning of his own name across the antistrophe-epode transition in the Cary-Morison Ode of 1629:

> *The Counterturn*
>
> Call, noble Lucius, then for wine,
> And let thy looks with gladness shine;
> Accept this garland, plant it on thy head,
> And think, nay know, thy Morison's not dead.
> He leaped the present age,
> Possessed with holy rage

---

[39] Barberini, *Poemata*, 1–9 (quotation from p. 2). The stanzas are labelled 'Strophe I', 'Antistrophe I', 'Epode I', and so on. This ode has five complete triads, 165 lines altogether.

> To see that bright eternal day;
> Of which we priests and poets say
> Such truths as we expect for happy men,
> And there he lives with memory, and Ben
>
> *The Stand*
>
> Jonson! Who sung thus of him, ere he went
> Himself to rest,
> Or taste a part of that full joy he meant
> To have expressed
> In this bright asterism;
> Where it were friendship's schism
> (Were not his Lucius long with us to tarry)
> To separate these twi-
> Lights, the Dioscuri,
> And keep the one half from his Harry.
> But fate doth so alternate the design,
> Whilst that in heaven, this light on earth must shine.
> (*UW* 70, 75–96)[40]

Although most analysis of his Pindarism has focused on this late ode, Jonson was demonstrably experimenting with monostrophic Pindaric form from around 1600, the date of the Desmond ode, and many of the songs from the masques are also indebted to Pindaric form and features.[41] As is often the case, Jonson's technical innovation consisted in importing to English a form already well-established in contemporary Latin poetry.

Latin Pindarics continued to be frequently composed in seventeenth-century England. One widely circulating example in England in the 1630s was in fact Thomas Randolph's translation of Jonson's own 'Ode to Himself' into Latin, which implicitly acknowledges the neo-Latin roots of Jonson's vernacular innovations.[42] Both manuscript and print sources demonstrate that 'regular' Pindarics continued to be composed in England well beyond the point at which Cowleian 'free' Pindarics had become fashionable: Samuel Woodford's influential translation of the complete psalter into English lyric of the Cowleian type, first published in 1667 and

---

[40] On the Cary-Morison ode, see Moul, *Jonson, Horace*, 48–53; Revard, 'Pindar and Jonson's Cary-Morison Ode'; Woods, 'Ben Jonson's Cary-Morison Ode'; Fry, *Poet's Calling*, 17–26; Donaldson, 'Jonson's Ode'; Oates, 'Jonson's "Ode Pindarick"'.
[41] On Pindaric style in the masques, see Moul, '*Mirror for Noble Deeds*'. Jonson's use of Pindaric forms in his earlier poetry is discussed in Moul, *Jonson, Horace*, 13–48.
[42] Randolph's poem is found in Bod. MS Rawl. poet. 209, fols. 22ʳ–3ʳ; Bod. MS Rawl. poet. 62, fols. 40ᵛ–1ᵛ; CUL MS Add. 79, fols. 28ᵛ–31ᵛ. There are also several Latin translations of this poem in Horatian metres (see Moul, *Jonson, Horace*, 202–6).

reprinted several times, uses a mixture of regular and irregular Pindarics, with in fact a preponderance of the former. Woodford's English psalms were themselves translated frequently into Latin.[43]

The history of 'regular' Pindarics in both English and Latin is crucial to our understanding of Cowley for several reasons. A single example in Cowley's own *Pindarique Odes*, 'The Exstasie', is in regular rather than irregular Pindarics: the source and significance of this important poem, and why he might have marked it out in this way from the other odes in the volume, are discussed in Chapter 6 on religious and devotional lyric. More generally, scholarly discussion has often related the 'freedom' of English Pindarics to the idea that contemporary readers did not understand Pindaric metre, and that this lack of understanding in some sense licensed free strophic forms. In a mid-seventeenth-century context, however, this is an exaggeration: the (by this point) already long-standing tradition of regular Pindaric odes in both English and (mostly) Latin demonstrates that poets and readers understood the basic principles of Pindaric strophic structure – that each strophe and antistrophe correspond with each other, and the epodes share a different pattern – even where they might use different terminology from that of a modern scholar in the metrical analysis of a given passage. It is important for our understanding of the aesthetic and emotional effect of 'free' Pindarics, in both Latin and English, that regular Latin Pindarics continued to be produced frequently throughout the seventeenth and into the eighteenth century.

Nevertheless, there is a clear distinction between the 'regular' Pindarics of Scaliger, Melissus, Jonson or Barberini and the kind of 'irregular' Pindaric popularized rapidly in English by Cowley's *Pindarique Odes*. Typically, these free or 'irregular' Pindarics of the Cowleian type are divided into strophes, and sometimes into strophes, antistrophes and epodes, but the strophes themselves are of varying lengths and metrical structure. The impact of Cowley's collection is felt very quickly in English verse: Bod. MS Sancroft 53, for instance, preserves Thomas Sprat's Pindaric Ode on the death of Cromwell in 1658, written in 16 irregular Pindaric stanzas of the Cowleian type. Like Cowley, Sprat connects Pindaric form and Old Testament prophecy and poetics, here comparing Cromwell to Moses:

---

[43] For translations of Woodford into Latin, see BL MS Add. 29241, fols. 68^r–66^v (rev.) and 74^r–73^v (rev.), probably from Peterhouse College, Cambridge, c.1670; possibly university exercises. The manuscript also includes Latin translations of Cowley and Dryden.

> Nor didst thou only for thy Age provide,
>   But for the years to come beside,
>   Our after-times, and late posterity
>   Shall pay unto thy Fame, as much as we;
>   They too, are made by thee.
> When Fate did call thee to a higher Throne,
>   And when thy Mortal work was done,
> When Heaven did say it, and thou must be gon:
>   Thou him to bear thy burthen chose,
> Who might (if any could) make us forget thy loss:
>   Nor hadst thou him design'd,
>   Had he not been
>   Not only to thy Blood, but Vertue Kin;
>   Not only Heir unto thy Throne, but Mind.
> 'Tis He shall perfect all thy Cures
> And, with as fine a Thread, weave out thy Loom.
> So, One did bring the Chosen people from
>   Their Slavery and Fears,
> Led them through their Pathless Road,
>   Guided himself by God,
> He brought them to the Borders: but a Second hand
> Did settle and Secure them, in the Promis'd Land.[44]

Sprat's praise of Cromwell – 'Nor didst thou only for thy Age provide' – echoes Jonson on Shakespeare ('He was not of an age but for all time!', 'To the Memory of My Beloved the Author, Mr William Shakespeare', 43), forging a link between inspired poetry and (quasi-)kingship which is both a traditional element of Pindaric panegyric, and also biblical, since King David exemplifies both. The quality and coherence of Cowley's *Pindarique Odes* united these elements, already strongly present in the culture, with unsurpassed authority, and Cowley's point about Pindarics as uniquely suited to scriptural verse had a great impact upon the poets of the subsequent generation.

Latin Dithyrambics, Lapidary Verse and the Origins of Cowley's Irregular Pindarics

John Milton's Latin Pindaric ode, 'Ad Joannem Rousium', written in 1647, represents a mid-point between the regular and irregular Pindaric form in Latin: although written in strophes and antistrophes, with a single

---

[44] 'To the happy Memorie of the most renowned prince, Oliver, Ld Protector &c. A Pindaric Ode', Bod. MS Sancroft 53, pp. 14–26 (16th and final stanza quoted here).

final epode, the metrical patterns of the strophes and antistrophes are similar but not identical.[45] Queen's College, Oxford, MS 284 preserves an ode in Latin Pindarics by one William Nicholson on the Journey of the Magi, which, like Milton's poem, consists of strophes that resemble one another visually and metrically without being identical.[46] This kind of 'loosely regular' Latin Pindaric probably contributed to Cowley's development of his English form.

Such poems are, however, far from the only possible models. Though it has not been reflected in criticism, Cowley's experiments with 'irregular' Pindarics in the 1650s, like Jonson's earlier experiments with a regular version, represent an importation into English verse of an established form found prior to this point mostly (though, as discussed below, not exclusively) in Latin. The case here has been somewhat obscured by terminology: prior to Cowley, most examples of Latin poems which combine a variety of classically metrical lines in different patterns, but without grouping them in repeating strophes, were termed not Pindaric but 'dithyrambic'.[47] Scaliger's comments on this form emphasize its metrical variety, unusual diction and 'inspired' quality:

> Erat stilus tumidus, atque, ut ille ait, plenus deo, plenus numerorum, plenus compositarum vocum: quas ampullas & sesquipedalia Satyri nostri appellarunt. Horatius iccirco Dithyrambos audaces vocat ... Exultans igitur, & inconstans, tumidum: atque vt vno verbo absoluam, totus Bacchus.[48]

> *It was an elated, high-flown style, and, so to speak, filled by the god, full of different measures, full of compound words: the sort of thing that our Satirists have called 'bombastic and excessively long'.[49] Horace for that reason calls Dithyrambs 'audacious' ... Therefore the style is exultant, almost riotous, constantly changing, high-flown: and, to sum it up in a single word, pure Bacchus.*

---

[45] For the metres of the Rouse ode (1647) see MacKellar, *Latin Poems of John Milton*, 358–60; Bradner, *Musae Anglicanae*, 107; Oberhelman and Mulryan, 'Milton's Use of Classical Meters'.
[46] Queen's College, Oxford, MS 284, fol. 31ʳ, 'In Magos Christum quaerentes'. The reverse is dated 1670 but it is not clear whether or not this refers to the poem.
[47] This term is not, for instance, in the index of either of Revard's books on the imitation of Pindar in Renaissance poetry (*Pindar and the Renaissance Hymn-Ode*; *Politics, Poetics, and the Pindaric Ode*).
[48] Scaliger, *Poetices* (1617), 111–13. Scaliger also discusses the related form of 'Hyporchemata', which he describes as similar, but 'laxius hoc, atque remissius: gestuosum tamen, affectuum plenum' ('even looser and more free: but full of movement, and emotion').
[49] A reference to Horace, *Ars poetica* 97, describing an affected and indulgent style (*ampullas et sesquipedalia verba*). An *ampulla* is a vessel with a rounded middle, so an 'inflated' style; *sesquipedalia* means literally 'foot-and-half-foot' – i.e. over-extended; pretentious. On this word in Jonson and Donne, see Moul, 'Donne's Horatian Means'.

In his translation of the first part of Horace, *Odes* 4.2, which is included in the *Pindarique Odes* just as the Latin original was routinely printed in the prefatory material to editions of Pindar, Cowley alludes to the Pindaric associations of the dithyramb: 'So *Pindar* does new *Words* and *Figures* roul / Down his impetuous *Dithyrambique Tide*' (12–13).[50] His note here, however, points out that Pindar's dithyrambs were, strictly speaking, a separate genre from the victory odes, none of which has survived: 'There are none of *Pindars Dithyrambiques* extant. *Dithyrambiques* were *Hymns* made in honor of *Bacchus* … It was a bold, free, *enthusiastical* kind of Poetry, as of men inspired by *Bacchus*, that is, *Half-Drunk*.' Cowley's remarks here are close to those of Scaliger and probably derive directly from him. It is typical of Cowley's evasive practice in the 1656 *Poems* that he goes on to refer to what he takes to be Horatian imitations of dithyrambic style, in *Odes* 2.19 and 3.25, but does not mention the distinct tradition of the neo-Latin 'dithyramb', even though his 'free' Pindarics in practice combine the tradition of 'regular' Pindarics (in repeating stanzas) and that of 'dithyrambics' (irregular, and not usually stanzaic).

Hugo Grotius used dithyrambic for the second chorus of his biblical play *Adamus Exul* (1601), an expansive paraphrase of Psalm 104, one of the psalms of praise.[51] Described in the original publication as 'Ex vario Carminum genere' ('of various types of lyric'), the chorus is very long (147 lines), strikingly metrically irregular and, though not formally separated into stanzas, visually structured in a way that suggests stanzas of uneven length. Grotius emphasizes the elements of the psalm's imagery which overlap with Pindaric style (such as God walking upon the 'wings of the wind'), and his choice of form is surely influenced by Scaliger's definition of the dithyrambic as 'plenus Deo'. Compiling a personal anthology of largely religious verse, in both Latin and English, in the mid-seventeenth century, William Sancroft (1617–93), later archbishop of Canterbury, included this chorus in a sequence containing multiple examples of Pindaric poems of various kinds: regular and irregular, Latin and English, including Milton's 'Nativity Ode' and several of Cowley's Pindarics.[52]

---

[50] Cowley freely incorporates the most 'Pindaric' parts of Horace in his translations of Pindar, as at the opening of *Olympian* 2 (sig. Bbb3ᵛ), note 2: '*Horace* translates this beginning, *Lib.* 1. *Ode* 12. *Quem virum aut Heroa Lyrâ vel acri Tibiâ sumes celebrare Clio. Quem Deum cujus resonet* jocosa *Nomen Imago?* The latter part of which I have added to Pindar.'

[51] Grotius, *Sacra* (1601), 27–32.

[52] Bod. MS Tanner 466, fols. 29ᵛ–31ᵛ. Sancroft also identifies Grotius' scriptural source, as the original publication did not.

Grotius' chorus is a very early example of this kind of irregular Pindaric or dithyrambic: it is telling that Sancroft includes it in his collection of otherwise much more recent poems, the majority of which date from the 1630s–1650s. In English sources, this kind of Latin poem begins to appear from the 1620s onwards. In printed English sources, two of the earliest examples are found in Oxford commemorative volumes of 1623 and 1633, in both cases marking the King's return from Scotland.[53] The 1639 Oxford collection, *Musarum Oxoniensium charisteria*, marking the birth and immediate death of Princess Catherine on 20 January of that year, contains three poems in this form, suggesting that dithyrambic, associated with strong emotion, could be appropriate for both celebration and lament – or, as here, a combination of the two.[54]

By the 1640s and 1650s examples of Latin dithyrambics are found quite widely, both in print and manuscript. Mildmay Fane's 1648 collection, *Otia Sacra*, for instance, includes an interesting example of a political poem in this form, 'My Newyears-gift to the Times', lamenting the horror of civil war in which 'pro Purpureo victore, / Quisque nunc tingitur Fratris Cruore' ('for the sake of the purple of victory, / Each man is now stained by his brother's blood').[55] At the head of a manuscript poem in irregular verse dated in the same year, 1 October 1648, Christopher Wase (1627–90), then at Cambridge, helpfully explains his choice of form: 'Varietas carminis et delectationem inducit et majestatem concinnat, et versum a pigrâ necessitate expletivarum exemptum dat' ('The [metrical] variety of the poem evokes pleasure and contributes to a majestic effect, and also grants the verse an exemption from the tiresome necessity of filling out the lines').[56] The poem itself, titled 'Hypotyposis est Resurrectionis' ('A Description of the Resurrection'), is rather extraordinary, and begins with a comparison to a bee which recalls Horace's characterization of his own style in relation to that of Pindar in *Odes* 4.2:

---

[53] William Axon, dithyrambic poem, *Carolus redux* (1623), sigs G4^v–H1^r; Edward Marow, dithyrambic poem, *Solis Britannici Perigaeum* (1633), sig. DE3^v–DE4^r. Both were members of New College.

[54] Oxford University, *Musarum Oxoniensium charisteria* (1639), dithyrambic verse on sig. C1^{r-v} (also by Edward Marow of New College), sig. DD2^v–DD3^r (R. West of Christ Church) and sig. DD4^{r-v} (M. Lewellin of Christ Church, the poet Martin Llewlyn, 1616–82).

[55] Fane, *Otia Sacra* (1648), 130–1.

[56] Bod. MS Add. B. 5, fols. 63^r–62^v (rev.), a collection of Latin letters and verse by Christopher Wase, probably in the hand of his friend Henry Some. Wase went up to King's College, Cambridge from Eton in 1645 and took his BA in 1649. He was ejected for royalism in 1650. He published various classical translations and his treatise on the iambic senarius appeared in 1687.

> Aura venit terram rimata
> Et molli cinerem pretiosum subvehit alâ
> Qualis apis rores et mella reportat.
> Iam passim omnibus aruis
> Humanam videas flauescere messem
> Sic latebris pecudes paullatim erepere
>
> *A breeze has come and split the earth*
> *And lifts on soft wings the precious ash*
> *As a bee carries dew and honey back to the hive.*
> *Now everywhere over the fields*
> *You would see the human crop ripening*
> *Like cattle gradually creeping out from the coverts*

At much the same time, the 1647 edition of Sarbiewski's verse includes a commendatory dithyramb at the end of the volume.[57] By the late 1640s English enthusiasm for Sarbiewski's verse – discussed in Chapter 6 – was at its height.

Oxford publications continued to be particularly likely to include dithyrambic verse in the 1650s: the dedicatory verse to John Ailmer's paraphrases of Jonah, Jeremiah and Daniel into Greek verse includes two examples (by Robert Matthew and Hugo Willis, both, like Ailmer himself, of New College).[58] The volume of verse compiled by Oxford in 1654 to commemorate the Cromwellian peace between Britain and the Netherlands also contains two dithyrambs.[59] One of these was chosen by Richard Enock when he selected six of the poems from this print collection for transcription into his personal notebook in 1677.[60] Although several of these commemorative collections include sections of English verse after the Latin, there are no English poems in similar irregular forms.

The peculiar blend of celebration (for the Queen's survival) and lament (for the baby's death) found in the 1639 Oxford collection is shared by a striking manuscript sequence, also dating almost certainly to the 1650s. Bod. MS Rawl. poet. 65 contains a series of six dithyrambic Latin poems, all ascribed to 'T. E.'. The catalogue describes the manuscript as containing verse collected in the 1680s by a member of St John's College, Oxford.

---

[57] 'Nicolai Kmicii è Societate Iesu Dithyrambus' in Sarbiewski, *Lyricorum Libri V* (1647), 370–8.
[58] Ailmer, *Musae Sacrae* (1652), sigs. A1ʳ–A2ᵛ, A4ᵛ–A5ʳ. The volume also includes a Greek version of the lament of David over Saul and Jonathan, though it is not listed on the title page, possibly because of the political connotations of David poems at the time.
[59] Oxford University, *Musarum Oxoniensium Ἐλαιοφορία* (1654), Richard Paige of St John's College, 26; Dan. Danvers of Trinity College, 28–9.
[60] BL MS Sloane 1458, fols. 19ʳ–21ᵛ. Enock, like Danvers whose poem he copies, was at Trinity College, Oxford.

Though this may be true, the poems in the initial sequence were almost certainly written under the Protectorate: the opening pages include an epitaph for John Selden (who died in 1654), and a series of epigrams on a rivalry between John Harmar and John Hulett. Harmar (c.1593–1670) was a figure of fun in Oxford in the 1650s following his appointment as Regius professor of Greek in 1650. He was deprived of his chair at the Restoration in 1660, after which he retired to Hampshire. Hulett, who taught at Oxford from the late 1630s, died in 1663. As discussed below, the political content of this part of the manuscript also suggests a date in the early-mid 1650s.[61]

The first four of the dithryambs in the manuscript are devotional: 'In Christi Natalitia', 'In Passionem domini', 'In Resurrectionem domini' and 'In Ascensionem domini'.[62] These are poems broadly within the tradition of Scaliger's Pindaric nativity ode, and point to the established religious connotations of the form on which Cowley also drew. The following three items, however, are political, beginning with a dithyrambic poem on the Gunpowder Plot, and followed by two referring explicitly to events of the civil war, of which 'In tertium Septembris' is the first:

In tertium Septembris.

Eheu Monarchiae hic dies cinerum,
   Solis Britanici Tropicus:
   Non tantùm mundi (parum illud)
Sed ipsius Caroli Climactericus.
    Fiat Anathema posteris
      Phoebíque radijs
   In aeternum sequestretur.
      Jovem hodie
   È Caelo suo fugarunt
      Terrae filii.
Sporadésque catervatim plaustrum Carolin[um]
   Orbe exspulserant britannico.
Proh dolor! abortionem patitur Caesaris fid[es]
Deque militanti eclesiâ triumphat mund[us]
    At hoc interim juvat
   Carolum nostrum fato evasisse
    Sic de eâ re, nec moramur nos

---

[61] 'T. E.' is possibly Thomas Edwardes (1633–98), who entered Merchant Taylors' School in 1647 and matriculated at St John's in November 1650, taking his BA in 1654 and MA in 1657, before going on to be a clergyman.
[62] Bod. MS Rawl. poet. 65, fols. 2^v–3^v.

Festum hunc diémque ponere gratiarum
    Et quasi secunda ejus natalitia,
      In sempiternum celebrare
    Fas non est de fortunâ }
    Conqueri salvo Caesare} Sen: ad Polib
                            T. E.[63]

Against the third of September.

Oh! This day of ashes for the Monarchy,
  Tropic of the British sun:
And of not only the world (that's by the by)
But of Charles himself the Climacteric.
  Let it be an Anathema to our descendants
    And from the rays of the sun
  Let it be sequestered for all time.
    Today the sons of the earth
  Have put to flight Jove
    From his own heaven.
And in troops the Sporades have expelled Charles' wain
  From the British realm.
For shame! Loyalty to Caesar is miscarried
And the world triumphs over the church militant [with a punning suggestion of 'because the church is fighting itself']
    But meanwhile we are pleased that
  Our Charles has escaped death
    In this situation, and let us not delay
This celebration and [let us not delay to] *set down a day of thanksgiving*
    To celebrate for evermore
  Even as it were his second birth.

    "It is not right to complain of ill fortune when Caesar has been saved."
    Sen: ad Polib. [Seneca, *Ad Polybius*]

The title of the poem, 'Against the third of September', refers to the Battle of Worcester on 3 September 1651, the final royalist defeat in the English civil war, after which the future King Charles II famously escaped by hiding in an oak tree in Boscobel Wood. The poem laments the defeat, while celebrating Charles' survival and suggesting that the day should remain a day of celebration. The use of the unusual Latin word 'climactericus' ('climacteric') is very close to that of Andrew Marvell, describing Cromwell ('And to all states not free, / Shall climacteric be', 'Horatian

---

[63] Bod. MS Rawl. poet. 65, fol. 4ᵛ. A second copy appears to be in Rosenbach Museum and Library, MS 232/14, p. 60. I have not seen this manuscript myself.

Ode', 103–4), dating almost certainly from the summer of 1650.[64] Like the examples from 1639, this poem exhorts both intense lament (for the royalist defeat) and genuine celebration (for the King's survival).

The 'Third of September' poem is followed in the Bodleian MS by a longer item titled 'Cippus', which is explicitly anti-Cromwellian, referring to the 'Oliva putris, perfidus Cromwellius' ('corrupted olive, treacherous Cromwell').[65] A *cippus* is a small standing stone, such as a tombstone or boundary stone. This equally interesting poem is transcribed continuously, but falls into two halves: 22 lines of dithyrambic Latin verse, followed by 43 lines of iambic trimeter. In other words, it combines in a single work two varieties of formal experimentation typical of the period – the polymetric sequence, discussed above, and the dithyrambic ode.

The title 'Cippus' suggests that the poem can be understood as an inscription: not a transcription of an actual inscription, but a kind of 'literary inscription'. In this respect, the anonymous 'T. E.' brings together the neo-Latin dithyrambic tradition of emotive free verse on religious or political topics with the related tradition of 'lapidary' verse or 'literary inscription': a highly fashionable form at this period across Europe.[66] Works of this kind, marked by extravagant rhetoric and often sharply contrasting expressions, can be poised ambiguously between verse and prose: many *carmina lapidaria* are centred, like an inscription, and have few if any metrically identifiable lines.[67] In England, the most influential model was the *Caesares* collection of literary inscriptions on Roman emperors and figures of the early Church made by the Italian poet and ex-Jesuit Emanuele Tesauro (1592–1675).[68] First published in 1619,

---

[64] The overlap might be evidence for the circulation of Marvell's ode, though Nigel Smith points to some English parallels in formal commemorative verse of the 1630s and 1640s. The term may have been more, rather than less, common in Latin.

[65] Bod. MS Rawl. poet. 65, fols. 7ʳ⁻ᵛ.

[66] The relation between dithyrambic and 'lapidary' verse is a complex one, discussed further below. On the latter see Kajanto, 'On Lapidary Style'.

[67] Kelliher describes *carmina lapidaria* as lying 'midway between poetry and oratory' ('John Dryden: A New Work', 351). Bradner, however, considers them free verse, on the grounds that they sometimes include metrically definable lines (*Musae Anglicanae*, 109). A large number of *carmina lapidaria* can be found in collections of the 1660s and 1670s, as for instance Trinity College, Cambridge, MS O. 6. 1, many of which seem closer to highly rhetorical prose than poetry; but the examples discussed in this chapter, typically marked by self-consciously Pindaric elements and often a parallel English poem in a conventional form, were clearly understood as verse. For an excellent discussion of the Latin free verse phenomenon, based on German Latin sources but in relation also to modernist free verse, see Tilg, 'Die "argute" Inschrift'. See also Jantz, 'Baroque Free Verse'; and John Sparrow, *Visible Words*, esp. the final chapter, 'The Inscription as a Literary Form'.

[68] Tesauro left the Jesuit order in 1634 and was thereafter a secular priest. Comparable earlier collections which were probably more influential on the continent than in England include Reusner, *Icones* (1587) and Sweertius, *Selectae Christiani orbis deliciae* (1608).

Tesauro's collection was printed in England in Oxford in 1637, and again in London in 1651.[69] Originally undertaken to celebrate the election of Ferdinand II as Holy Roman Emperor in 1619, the collection importantly offers models for negative or condemnatory as well as panegyric 'literary inscriptions', such as that for Nero. Tesauro later produced an influential analysis and guide to the form. His description encapsulates the rhythmic characteristics of these pieces, somewhere between poetry and prose, describing them as 'marked by a certain rhythm, which is less noticeable than poetical rhythm, but still surpasses that of oratory'.[70]

The two editions of *Caesares* printed in England suggest its popularity, and perhaps also the potential for political interpretation – in the 1650s much royalist material was published under the guise of scholarship or translation, especially in Latin.[71] Although the tone of Tesauro's work is serious, his model probably also stands behind a mid-late seventeenth-century vogue for Latin free verse satire, ranging from 'mock-epitaphs' on famous public figures, such as Cardinal Mazarin, Louis XIV or Bishop Burnet, to more local examples, such as a free verse satire on an Oxford fellow expelled by the visitation of 1648.[72] Several of these examples of satiric free verse are among the most widely circulating Latin verse items of the latter seventeenth century: this fashion is discussed further in Chapter 8.

One of the earliest examples of the merging of Tesauro's 'literary inscriptions' with the Pindaric associations of the dithyramb is Robert Waring's poem on the death of Ben Jonson, first printed in Brian Duppa's commemorative volume *Jonsonus Virbius* of 1638, and dating from immediately after the first printing of Tesauro's work in England.[73] Waring, like Jonson, had been at Westminster, and went up to Christ Church, Oxford in 1630. The poem is titled simply *Vatum Principi, Ben Jonsono Sacrum* ('Sacred to Ben Jonson, Prince of Poets') in *Jonsonus Virbius*, but in later

---

[69] Tesauro, *Caesares* (1637); Tesauro, *Poemata* (1651).
[70] Tesauro, *Il Cannocchiale* (1655; translated into Latin in 1698), quotation from the fifth edition (1670), 595; see Kajanto, 'On Lapidary Style', 155.
[71] On translation, see for example the political force of John Ogilby's 1650s translations of Aesop and Virgil (Patterson, *Fables of Power*, 85–109; Calvert, 'Slanted Histories'). On political allegory in Latin verse at this period, see Chapter 11.
[72] Corpus Christi College, Oxford, MS 317, fols. 312^r–13^v, titled 'Dr Winnard expelled for the neglect of a Ceremonie – Jul. 1. 1648', accompanied by a rhyming English version.
[73] Duppa, *Jonsonus Virbius* (1638), 66–70; Waring's poem is also found in contemporary manuscript sources, e.g. Bod. MS Rawl. poet. 171, fols. 6^r–7^r. It was reprinted in the third and subsequent editions of Waring's *Amoris effigies* (1664, 1668, 1671, 1682). For another early example in English, see Quarles, *Memorials upon the Death of Sir Robert Quarles* (1639), a poem of 253 lines divided into fourteen *elogia* each occupying a single page.

editions it bears the title *carmen lapidarium*. Waring repeatedly describes Jonson's vatic inspiration, echoing Jonson's own use of this language.[74] The sense of 'Pindaric' inspiration is not strictly a feature of lapidary poems, but it came to be characteristic of this merged Pindaric-dithyrambic tradition of free verse.[75]

Waring here honours Jonson's reputation for Pindaric imitation with a fashionable new version of Pindarism. In the 1640s and 1650s, the use of dithyrambics for panegyric in the university collections addressed to royalty may have given the form a more specific political connotation: the final poem of Henry Birkhead's anonymously published *Poematia* of 1645, a strongly royalist collection, is a Latin dithyramb commemorating the death of Archbishop Laud;[76] Henry Oxinden's sharply political scriptural paraphrase, *Iobus triumphans* (1651), is preceded by a dedicatory poem by William Nethersole of the Inner Temple which is also in dithyrambic form.[77]

It is certainly not the case, however, that the 1650s examples of this form were only by royalists. Payne Fisher's collected poems, *Piscatoris Poemata*, published like Cowley's *Poems* in 1656, includes a poem commemorating Henry Ireton, who had died in November 1651, which is in Latin free verse with a parallel English version: as in many examples of this form, the English version is metrically more conventional, and demonstrates that the Latin text was also understood as poetry:

> Divinam sensit indolem *CROMWELLUS*,
>   Cùm sibi Generum adscivit;
>   Dumbiúmque
>   An tali *Socero* Gener,
>   An tali *Genero* Socer
>   Felicior evaserit:
>
>   (stanza 3, 9–14)

---

[74] Waring uses terms such as 'vates' ('inspired prophet or poet'), 'numen' ('godhead, divinity'), 'entheatus' ('filled with the divine'). On Jonson's use of vatic imagery, see Moul, *Jonson, Horace*, esp. 13–53.

[75] As an example of the increasing blurring of these terms, Sir Peter Pett's (1630–99) 1672 poem addressed to the political economist Sir William Petty (1623–87) contains many of the features of 'lapidary' verse – it is a long poem, a humorous mock-epitaph with no strophe divisions or regular metrical structure, and it is centred throughout – but it has been endorsed by William himself as 'Sir Peter Pett's Pindaric on the Politicall Arithmetick'.

[76] [Birkhead], *Poematia* (1645), 12–14. In the 1656 edition of the *Poematia*, which identifies Birkhead as the author of the preface, though not on the title page, the ode is reprinted but tactfully retitled to refer to Cranmer (70–4). See Bradner, *Musae Anglicanae*, 359–60.

[77] Oxinden, *Iobus triumphans*, A2ʳ–A3ʳ. Latin dithyrambic commendatory poems by Thomas Price are also prefaced to Elys, *Dia poemata* (1655), sig. A5ʳ⁻ᵛ and *Miscellanea* (1662), sig. B2ᵛ.

> Sure 'twas by Divine instinct,
> And Piety was with Policy linkt
> When provident *CROMWEL* did designe
> His *Daughter* unto *IRETON'S* Line;
> And 'twas a doubt which was most happy rather,
> Sire in a *Son,* or Son in such a *Father.*[78]

Other examples of this form from the same period include one of the earliest of John Dryden's attested works and his only known Latin poem, a *carmen lapidarium* for the Cambridge Platonist John Smith, who died in 1652.[79] The Cambridge University anthology marking the Restoration includes two poems in this form.[80]

Latin dithyrambics (without stanza divisions) and 'irregular' Pindarics (with stanza divisions, but without repeating stanza structures) continued to be written throughout the later seventeenth century. A manuscript poem on the death of the painter and Cowleian poet Thomas Flatman (1635–88), dated 1690, demonstrates the convergence of the various elements. The poem is titled 'Carmen Lapidarium' and, like Tesauro's literary inscriptions, is centred and has no stanza breaks. Unlike the 'literary inscription' tradition, however, it invokes Pindar directly: 'Hic non Pindaricos haustus expalluit: / Hic Pindarum [T]utò studet aemulari, / Non Ponto, sed toti Terrarum orbi / Perenne Nomen relicturus' ('This man [Flatman] did not pale at Pindaric draughts; / He can safely seek to emulate Pindar [contradicting the cautionary note of Horace Odes 4.2], / He shall leave an enduring name / Not for a sea [like Icarus], but for the whole globe of the earth.'[81]

Irregular Lyric Verse in English before Cowley

The most original feature of Cowley's experiments with 'free' Pindarics in the *Pindarique Odes* was, therefore, not the form itself, but his choice

---

[78] This section of Fisher's *Piscatoris Poemata* (1656) is unfoliated and without pagination, but it comes between *Marston-Moor* and the *Irenodia Gratulatoria*.
[79] Preserved only in CUL MS Mm. I. 36, fol. 406^r. Printed (with translation) in Hammond (ed.), *Poems of John Dryden*, vol. 1, 11–13; see Kelliher, 'John Dryden: A New Work'. Dryden, born in 1631, had gone up to Trinity College, Cambridge from Westminster School in 1650, and graduated BA in 1654.
[80] Cambridge University, *ΣΩΣΤΡΑ* (1660), 'Inscriptio libera' ('Free inscription'), sig. C2^v–C3^r by H. Paman and (without title) D4^{r-v} by Thomas Gale.
[81] BL MS Add. 29241, fols. 78^v–77^r (rev.). The title refers to 'John' rather than Thomas Flatman, but this is presumably a mistake. Flatman's *Poems and Songs* was published in 1674, with three further editions over the following twelve years.

of English. Even here, though, he was not quite alone. First published in 1652, and probably written at the end of 1651, Payne Fisher's Latin ode 'Ad Illustrissimum Britanniarum Polimarchum, Oliverum Cromwellum' shares many features with Marvell's famous 'Horatian Ode', presumed to date from the summer of 1650. Fisher's celebration of Cromwell, discussed at greater length in Chapter 4, emphasizes his (Fisher's) personal change of heart, Cromwell's military accomplishments, the signs of God's favour, and his hopes for the future. Relevant to Cowley's formal innovations in the *Pindarique Odes*, though, is not Fisher's Latin ode but Thomas Manley's 'translation' of it, published in his 1652 English version of the *Irenodia*.[82] Fisher's ode is in Latin alcaics, a standard Horatian form of four-line stanzas strongly associated with formal panegyric. For his translation, Manley chose not a close English equivalent – such as the four-line stanzas used by Fanshawe and Marvell for Horatian-style English verse – but 'regular' monostrophic Pindarics: that is, stanzas formed of lines of various lengths and scansion, but where the sequence of lines is repeated in each strophe, as in most of Jonson's English Pindaric odes.

Manley's translation is a fairly loose one throughout, and not on the whole a reliable guide to the Latin. The final 61 lines of Manley's poem are not, however, based on Fisher at all, but are his own rather sprawling addition to the poem. At the point of the transition from translation to original material, Manley also changes form: from 'regular' to 'irregular' Pindarics, of a type strikingly similar to that of Cowley's 'Pindarique Odes' published four years later. Here we see the transition:

> Thus do you sit exalted high
> Applauded by the joyfull Cry
> Of the pleas'd City; those who are
> Truly religious send a prair
>   To heaven for thee;
>   (Poor Poets) so do we.
> Now on a *Dytherambicke* Lyre
> Anon in a *Pindarick* Quire,
> Or else like *Virgil* we thy deeds rehearse,
> And joy'd return in an heroike verse.
> [*this is the end of the translation*]

---

[82] Manley, *Veni; Vidi; Vici* (1652), sigs. H6ʳ–I3ᵛ.

>   Reader (if ought)
>   Come and be taught,
>   Why do you so
>   Look on a *picture*, or *dumbe show*?
> Would you unconquer'd *Cromwell* know? alas!
>   View not then a carved face,
>   But mark his vertues manifold,
> Then Brass more lasting, more desir'd then gold.
>   Attentive be;
>   *This, This* is He,
>   Who, for the *Publike* born, doth *Live*
>   To that, for which Nature did Give
>   Him life; whose sharper wit
>   For all great counsels fit[83]

Manley's change of form signals both the departure from translation, but also a kind of one-upmanship. English free Pindarics in 1652 were, in literary terms, the cutting edge: much more fashionable than the 'regular' Pindaric associated with Jonson and the previous generation. Manley 'outdoes' Fisher by recontextualizing Fisher's own reference to dithyrambics, 'Now on a *Dytherambicke* Lyre', as a kind of cue to introduce his own original contribution in this more fashionable dithyrambic form. But the effect is political too. The end of Fisher's ode draws attention as much to Fisher himself as to his addressee, comparing the poet fortunate enough to have Cromwell as a subject to Pindar, Archilochus and Virgil (Manley's version suppresses the mention of Archilochus, probably to raise the register of the passage overall):

>   Sic *Pindarus* (Dux) ecstaticis furens
>   Te Dithyrambis *Archilochus* suis
>   Redux Iambis te *Maronis*
>   Atque Epicum celebrabit oestrum.
>
>   *Thus* Pindar *(the Leader) raging with his ecstatic*
>   Dithyrambs *shall celebrate you;* [so too] Archilochus
>   Reborn *with his iambs shall celebrate you;* [so too] *even*
>   The epic inspiration of Virgil *shall celebrate you.*

The interdependence of the panegyric poet and the object of his praise is a standard feature of Pindaric poetry, found not only in Pindar himself but also, for instance, at the end of Horace's most famous 'Pindaric' ode (*Odes* 4.2); in Jonson's imitations of this style; and also in Casimir Sarbiewski,

---

[83] Manley, *Veni; Vidi; Vici*, sig. I1ᵛ–I2ʳ.

probably the single most influential model for Horatian-Pindaric style at this period. As so often, Cowley spells out the point in one of his notes: 'And the *Reader* must not be chocqued to hear him [the author] speak so often of his own *Muse*; for that is a *Liberty* which this kind of *Poetry* can hardly live without.'[84]

Manley, however, avoids ending, as Fisher does, with the poet. By restarting the poem, in a new and more fashionable mode, he returns attention to Cromwell, and continues with a string of panegyric motifs which were conventional at the time: Cromwell is the '*fort* and *Patron* of [England's] Liberty'; '*Brittaines Alcides* [= Hercules]' who is 'Keeping upright, what would precipitate'; '*Englands* new leading *Ioshuah*'; 'A Deadly scourge of Tyranny' who has brought peace to the land. The extra material is unoriginal (except in its form) but significantly shifts the balance in the poem overall towards Cromwell and his celebration, and away from Fisher's own journey from royalism to Cromwellianism, or the power of poetry to exalt the new ruler. Manley's free version of Fisher is not a particularly good poem: it is certainly much less successful than the original Latin ode; it is also plausible that Cowley had not read it. Manley's poem is important though as evidence for the wider literary moment in which Cowley was writing, in which experimentation with English free Pindarics was 'in the air'.

Cowley may not have read Manley, but he certainly did read the poetry of his own good friend Richard Crashaw. Cowley and Crashaw knew each other from Cambridge and are believed to have spent time together in Paris: Cowley's ode on Hope, and Crashaw's response to it, stand at the end of Crashaw's *Steps to the Temple*. Crashaw experimented widely with irregular and mixed metres in both Latin and English in the 1630s and 1640s, and several of his Latin poems, such as an impressive paraphrase of the first psalm, incorporate multiple changes of metre.[85] As Crashaw's editor Martin has pointed out, some of Crashaw's English poems, in print

---

[84] Cowley, *Poems*, sig. Bbb1ʳ. Prefatory note to the translation of Pindar, *Olympian* 2.
[85] Printed in Martin (ed.), *Poems of Richard Crashaw*, 353, a polymetric sequence of phalaecian hendecasyllables, a sapphic stanza, iambic trimeters, and an alcaic stanza. It is included in Sancroft's collection of Crashaw's verse (Bod. MS Tanner 465, dating probably from the late 1630s) as well as in Sancroft's personal collection of religious verse (Bod. MS Tanner 466, discussed further below). Crashaw's practice points to the association between metrical variety and the paraphrase of the psalms discussed in Chapter 3. The formally experimental Latin hymns of Peter du Moulin, though not published until 1671, probably also date in part from the 1650s and may have been influenced directly by Crashaw (Du Moulin, Πάρεργα, 1671). Hymns 8–13 are polymetric and the ninth hymn (42–5), incorporates even more metrical transitions than Crashaw's first psalm. As noted above, the structural similarities between the *Davideis* and Du Moulin's *Ecclesiae Gemitus* of 1649 also suggest a link between Cowley and Du Moulin.

a nearly a decade before Cowley's *Pindarique Odes*, anticipate them in their irregular metrics.[86] Those of Crashaw's poems which most closely resemble Cowley's irregular Pindarics are all religious pieces, several of them on similar devotional and meditative themes to the series of religious dithyrambs in Bod. MS Rawl. poet. 65 (described above).

Indeed, Crashaw's revisions to one of the most impressive of these poems, 'On the Assumption', track literary developments of the period. On its first publication, in *Steps to the Temple* (1646), the piece resembles the kind of quasi-dramatic sequence with which this chapter began, printed to indicate a clear distinction between the main narrative and two 'inset lyrics', which are centred. The poem uses a version of the Song of Songs – a highly fashionable text in that decade – to dramatize the Roman Catholic belief in the Assumption of Mary:

> Rise up my faire, my spotlesse one,
> The Winter's past, the raine is gone:
> The Spring is come, the Flowers appeare,
> No sweets since thou art wanting here.
>
> Come away my Love,
> Come away my Dove
>   cast off delay:
> The Court of Heav'n is come,
> To wait upon thee home;
>   Come away, come away.
>
> Shee's called againe, and will shee goe;
> When heaven bids come, who can say no?
>   (9–20)[87]

In the revised version of the poem published in Paris six years later, the text is not significantly expanded (69 versus 64 lines) but the structure has been broken up, losing the impression of a clear distinction between narrative and inset lyric, and moving instead towards the metrically free odes of the type composed by Cowley.[88]

---

[86] Martin (ed.), *Poems of Richard Crashaw*, xxxiv. Martin mentions Crashaw's 'On the Assumption'. Other major odes in irregular form in the 1648 edition of *Steps to the Temple* include 'Upon our B. Saviour's Passion', 'On the name of Jesus', 'A Hymne for the Epiphanie', 'An ode which was prefixed to a Prayerbooke given to a young Gentle-woman', 'The same partie Councell concerning her choice' and 'Charitas nimia, or the deare bargaine'.

[87] On the imitation of the Song of Songs, a trend derived primarily from Jesuit poets and intensely fashionable in England the 1630s and 1640s, see Chapter 6. For a fine discussion of the working out of this same imagery to markedly different theological purposes in the work of Crashaw and John Saltmarsh, see McDowell, 'Beauty of Holiness'.

[88] Crashaw, *Carmen Deo Nostro* (1652), 81–3.

Cowley's *Pindarique Odes* are certainly a major achievement, and their influence upon 'Pindaric' form in English verse in the latter seventeenth century is undeniable. Nathaniel Stogdill, building on comments by Nigel Smith, claims that the formal features of the *Pindarique Odes* are a 'poetic complement for a culture that had lost the stable sources through which it recognized and reproduced social meaning'.[89] Both critics are surely correct to point to the links between the formal innovations of mid-seventeenth-century poetry and the social and political upheaval of the period. But close attention to the precursors of Cowley's innovative features, especially in Latin as well as English poetry, suggests that they are less purely 'innovative', and more, we might say, 'fashionable', than Cowley himself indicates: that's not to say that there is nothing new about Cowley's practice in the 1650s, but to acknowledge that none of his innovations is without recognizable sources in broader literary culture. It may have been in Cowley's interest to pretend to a degree of innovation which concealed the somewhat Laudian and royalist associations of his techniques.

Contemporary Reception

The forms and techniques of Cowley's 1656 *Poems* may be less original, and more politically and poetically legible, than criticism has acknowledged. But that does not alter the reality of their impact: it is clear that Cowley's collection very quickly exerted significant influence upon his contemporaries, and that this impact lasted, especially in the fashion for religious verse and scriptural paraphrase in increasingly loose Pindarics, well into the eighteenth century.[90]

Cowley's Pindarics are Pindar as sung by King David (via Horace and Sarbiewski): in this sense the formal innovation that is so characteristic of seventeenth-century Latin verse in English – verse sequences, polymetric poetry, Latin Pindarics, dithryambics and other kinds of free verse – is continuous with, and a new version of, the intense interest in metrical variety and diversity typical of the latter sixteenth century. Cowley's Pindarics maintain a connection between formal innovation and scriptural verse that was established by the sixteenth-century collections of psalm paraphrases discussed especially in Chapters 2 and 3: although Cowley's odes have in recent years been discussed largely in terms of their politics, or

---

[89] Stogdill, 'Cowley's "Pindaric Way"', 489 citing Nigel Smith, *Literature and Revolution*, 4–5.
[90] On the eighteenth-century fashion, see Wilson, 'Pindar'.

in relation to classical reception, both the book of *Pindarique Odes* and the larger volume of verse in which it sits (containing also the *Davideis*) stake Cowley's claim as a scriptural poet in the Davidian tradition.

The religious content, inspiration and orientation of Cowley's most innovative lyric has typically not been the main focus of critical attention: but his imitators were dominated by religious poets. BL MS Add. 29241, for instance, dating from the later seventeenth century, includes translations into Latin of the beginning of the second book of the *Davideis* (fols. 72ʳ–70ᵛ, reversed) and of the poem 'Love Given Over' from *The Mistresse* (fols. 76ʳ–75ᵛ).[91] The Latin translation of the *Davideis* imitates Cowley's own practice, much more marked in the Latin version, of using half-lines for dramatic or emotive effect, and the same technique is used in a religious poem in hexameters, 'In Resurrectionem Christi'.[92] The collection as a whole also includes two poems in Latin Pindarics, translations of Samuel Woodford's English scriptural paraphrases into Latin, and ends with a Latin verse paraphrase of Psalm 137.[93] Overall, this manuscript suggests that both the *Davideis* (including its inset lyrics) and the *Pindarique Odes* were influential on Latin literary practice in the later seventeenth century, and that those two traditions were perceived as belonging together within the wider tradition of scriptural verse.

Robert South's manuscript notebook, now BL MS Lansdowne 695, dating probably from the 1660s, offers similar evidence: it includes a neat transcription of his very popular Latin verse sequence, *Musica Incantans*, which was published in 1655 but also circulated widely in contemporary manuscript collections, and which is transcribed here after a short series of other Latin and English poems. That series includes an irregular English ode – described as a 'Pindaric' – very much in the style of Cowley though, unlike the *Pindarique Odes*, it is a love poem. South is apparently self-conscious about this departure from Cowleian precedent, as the copy of this English poem is followed by a defensive Latin note, beginning

---

[91] Nottingham University Library, MS PwV 1345, though undated, probably belongs to a similar period and contains Latin verse translations from Cowley, Waller and Camden. This kind of translation of well-known English poetry into Latin is found more frequently in the latter seventeenth and early eighteenth centuries than in earlier periods, though the bilingual circulation of topical and popular verse (such as epigrams, satirical songs and so on) is more typical of the earlier seventeenth century. These patterns are discussed in more detail in Chapter 7.

[92] BL MS Add. 29241, fols. 53ᵛ, 71ᵛ–72ʳ.

[93] Drawn from Woodford, *Paraphrase upon the Canticles* (1679), 61–4. Woodford's scriptural hymns are formally indebted to those of Cowley, Crashaw and Du Moulin, with examples of both irregular Pindarics and polymetric sequences.

'Levitatem subjecti, Vir laudiss: spem alo Te praeteriturum' ('I hope, most praiseworthy sir, that you will pass over the lightness of the subject').[94] The English Pindaric is followed immediately by a Latin 'literary inscription' or free verse poem, in commemoration of John Wilton, chaplain of Merton College, Oxford, who died in 1665.[95]

The strong association between Cowley and scriptural verse continues to be evident in both printed and manuscript sources to the end of the century and beyond: a Cambridge University Library manuscript, dating probably from the latter seventeenth century, which contains several Pindaric poems in both Latin and English, has a note at the bottom of a very long (44 stanzas) scriptural paraphrase in irregular Pindarics: 'After the Pindaric way; recommended to all the lovers of religious poetry by a Divine of the Church of England'.[96] Woodford's very popular *Paraphrase upon the Psalms of David* (1667) translated the entire psalter into a mixture of regular and irregular Pindaric odes, making explicit the link between sections three and four of Cowley's *Poems*, the Pindarics and the *Davideis*. This work, the single largest printed collection of English Pindaric verse, went through several editions in the 1660s and 1670s; extracts are found frequently in manuscript sources, and the poems themselves sometimes translated into Latin.

At the very end of the century, in 1697, Daniel Baker, rector of Fincham St Michael's in Norfolk, published a collection of verse including a poem in regular Pindarics 'On Mr. Abraham Cowley's Works' (first published in 1668). One whole section of the collection is headed 'Pindarique Odes', and includes a poem in Pindarics on Herbert's *Temple* (first published 1623), which compares Herbert, in Cowleian style, to the psalmist David, as well as a large number of scriptural paraphrases, and paraphrases of Horace, *Odes* 2.14 and even *Eclogue* 4 (often associated with the prophecies of Isaiah), all also in irregular Pindarics.[97] The early

---

[94] BL MS Lansdowne 695, fol. 5ʳ.
[95] The British Library catalogue describes this manuscript as dating to South's period as a student at Christ Church (matric. 1651; BA 1655; MA 1657). He certainly wrote *Musica Incantans* during that period, but this particular manuscript apparently dates from the 1660s.
[96] CUL MS Dd. V. 77, item 3. This is an English verse paraphrase of the 'Song of the Three Children', a passage which appears after Daniel 3:23 in some biblical traditions. It is included in the Septuagint but omitted from most Protestant Bibles. The text is considered non-canonical by the Church of England but its second half (known as the *Benedicite* after its first word in Latin), which is itself a kind of expanded paraphrase of Psalm 148, is used in the service of Morning Prayer in the Book of Common Prayer. Presumably for this reason, it was a fairly popular text for verse paraphrase in England in the seventeenth century.
[97] Baker, *Poems upon Several Occasions* (1697). BL MS Add. 11723 is a manuscript collection of his verse, made by his nephew after his death in 1723.

work of Isaac Watts, the first of the great English hymn-writers, includes several examples of irregular Pindaric poetry (on the Cowleian model) in both Latin and English, as well as Latin verse in a range of forms, influenced above all by Sarbiewski. Such models are a surprising foundation for a poet whose mature style is famous for its metrical regularity and simplicity of diction: Watts, and the roots of eighteenth-century hymnody in devotional verse of the seventeenth century, are discussed further in Chapter 6.[98]

Conclusion

Cowley's 1656 *Poems*, and especially the *Pindarique Odes*, had a major impact upon subsequent poetry in both English and Latin. In formal terms, however, the collection was as much, if not more, fashionable as it was innovative: for all Cowley's implication that his *Pindarique Odes* might prove incomprehensible to most readers, they were, on the contrary, immediately and enthusiastically imitated. The volume appeared at a moment in which Latin Pindaric, dithyrambic and increasingly 'free' verse, such as that found in *carmina lapidaria*, were all highly popular, and in which many poets, both Parliamentarian and royalist, turned to explicitly scriptural, especially Old Testament, verse both as a marker of piety and as a response to the horror of civil war. Moreover, Cowley's achievement was largely understood, by his readers and imitators in the latter seventeenth century, in 'Davidic' terms: as having introduced a form and style of verse particularly appropriate for the paraphrase of the Old Testament, and for religious and devotional poetry more widely.

---

[98] On Watts and Pindar, see also Wilson, 'Pindar'.

CHAPTER 6

Religious and Devotional Epigram and Lyric

Seventeenth-century English poetry is renowned for its religious lyric, especially that of Herbert, Donne, Crashaw, Vaughan and Traherne, poets often grouped together as 'metaphysical' despite significant differences in style. In Chapters 2 and 3 we saw how the interest in metrical and formal variety, which is such a marked feature of Herbert's *Temple* (1633), can be traced back to the Latin poetic experiments and innovations of the latter sixteenth century, and specifically to the technical and tonal variety of the most influential of the psalm paraphrase collections. This chapter deals in large part with another of the influences upon Herbert's distinctive style – namely the largely (though not exclusively) Jesuit poetics of Latin devotional verse, which combined with the tradition of formal variety, scriptural paraphrase and religious epigram to revolutionary effect in seventeenth-century England.

Religious poetry is everywhere in early modern England, in Latin no less than in English, ranging from psalm paraphrases to Herbert's *Temple*, Milton's *Paradise Lost* and the hymns of Isaac Watts and Charles Wesley. 'Religious poetry', however, describes the subject of verse, not its form or genre. Religious poetry is found in all forms and across genres: not only in the most obvious categories, such as lyric or hymn, but also, for instance, in panegyric epic – which in the seventeenth century frequently incorporated passages of scriptural paraphrase – and in epigram. Religious poetry deals with various distinct though related and sometimes combined subjects – including specific verses or passages of scripture; religious rituals (such as baptism); feasts (such as Christmas); devotional objects (such as a religious painting or a particular church) or emotions and experiences (such as penitence, hope of heaven, receiving communion); and points of religious controversy, debate or allegiance (such as infant baptism, the Papacy, or Quakers). Many of these topics and questions, which were of the utmost importance and part of the common currency at the time, are now matters of scholarly reference for most readers. This can make it particularly hard to appreciate the emotional or aesthetic effect of verse which depended for its impact upon the striking or surprising presentation of material that was assumed to be highly familiar.

Since many of the political controversies of the period had a theological or confessional dimension, forms such as panegyric and commendatory verse, satire and invective were also frequently used to tackle questions of religious practice or allegiance: Daniel Baker's collection of verse compositions, for instance, includes a long hexameter poem in praise of Thomas Burnet's *Telluris Theoria Sacra, or Sacred Theory of the Earth* (first published in 1681).[1] Similarly, there are hundreds of extant poems, in both Latin and English, on churchmanship and liturgy: George Herbert's first verse collection, *Musae Responsoriae*, is a response to a single long poem by Andrew Melville on questions such as the baptism of infants, the use of the sign of the cross and the role of church music.[2] This kind of polemical poetry is not the focus of the chapter, though some examples are discussed in Chapters 7 (on epigram) and 8 (on satire and invective).

The fashionable styles and forms for religious verse in both Latin and English are a useful index of changing poetic tastes: while some subjects had a strong association with confessional identity, many trends in religious verse crossed confessional divides; equally poets with very similar religious convictions and identities, and even writing in closely related forms, might write quite differently as literary fashion evolved. Beza and Buchanan were both convinced Protestants who produced complete Latin verse paraphrases of the Psalter within about 30 years of each other. As discussed in Chapter 3, the significant differences in style between the two – though reflecting to some degree an increased concern with the original meaning of the text and a greater understanding of Hebrew – are also an index of much wider changes, and one of the first signs, around 1580, of what has variously been described as 'mannerist', 'baroque', 'prebaroque' or (in England) 'metaphysical' verse.[3] In some instances, the long productive writing life of a single poet demonstrates such changes in

---

[1] The first part of Burnet's work, a speculative cosmogony attempting to explain how the earth was created and how geological features arose, appeared in Latin in 1681 and in English in 1684; the second part in 1689 and 1690. Newton admired Burnet's work and corresponded with him. Baker's poem is in BL MS Add. 11723, fols. 30^r–1^r.

[2] Herbert, *Musae Responsoriae*, not published until 1662, but probably completed around 1620. Andrew Melville, *Anti-Tami-Cami-Categoria*, first published in 1620, but written and almost certainly circulated in manuscript in response to the Millenary Petition of 1603. See Cummings, 'Andrew Melville'.

[3] On this terminology see, among others, de Mourgues, *Metaphysical, Baroque and Précieux Poetry*; Warnke, *European Metaphysical Poetry*, 1–86; Davidson, *Universal Baroque*, esp. 1–24.

action: in the 1737 edition of his *Horae Lyricae* (first published in 1706), the hugely popular religious poet Isaac Watts prefaces his sequence of 22 poems on divine love with a memorable *caveat lector*, evidently conscious of how old-fashioned (and, implicitly, 'Catholic') his early poetry, strongly influenced by the Jesuit poet Sarbiewski, seemed to readers by the 1730s:

> Different Ages have their different Airs and Fashions of Writing. It was much more the Fashion of the Age, when these Poems were written, to treat of Divine Subjects in the Style of SOLOMON'S SONG than it is at this Day, which will afford some Apology for the Writer, in his youngest years.[4]

How to Write a Nativity Poem in Early Modern England

Any survey of poems on a common religious subject accordingly finds patterns of composition reflecting changing literary fashions. Poems on the Nativity of Christ were unsurprisingly a very popular topic for poets in both Latin and English throughout the seventeenth century; examples include such famous English poems as Milton's 'Nativity Ode' and Southwell's 'Burning Babe'. The essential subject – and many of the constituent elements – are held in common, but the form of these poems tracks wider literary changes. In the early seventeenth century, a period in which epigrams are at their most intensely fashionable, we find many examples of Christmas epigrams, such as this one on the symbolism of celebrating mass three times at Christmas, which ends:

> Nocte prior, sub luce sequens, in luce suprema
>   Sub Noe, sub templo, sub cruce sacra notant
> Sub Noe, sub Dauid, sub Christo sacra fuere
>   Nox, aurora, dies, vmbra, figura, deus.[5]
>
> *The first at night, the next at dawn, the last in the daylight*
>   *They mark rites under Noah, under the temple, under the cross*
> *Under Noah, under David, under Christ were sacred*
>   *Night, dawn, day, shade, shape, god.*

The very popular *Epigrammata* of the Jesuit poet Bernhard Bauhusius, first published in 1616, treats the topic entirely differently. Bauhusius writes in

---

[4] Watts, *Horae Lyricae* (1737), 107. On Watts and Sarbiewski see Money, 'Aspects of the Reception of Sarbiewski'; and below; on Watts as a lyric poet, Davie, *Gathered Church*, 19–36, 'Edward Taylor and Isaac Watts', and the preface to *Augustan Lyric*, 1–29.
[5] Bod. MS Barlow 10, fol. 38ᵛ, 'De tribus missis in natali Domini'.

a highly emotive and imaginative mode, as if the poet were present at the manger, singing to the baby, and reminding Mary to shut the stable door.

> Lectule, lectule mi, dulcissime lectule, salue;
>   Lectule liliolis, lectule strate rosis.
> Ah nec strate rosis, nec liliolis formosis;
>   Verum & liliolis, & benè digne rosis.
> ...
>
> Claude MARIA fores, en algida, nuda tremensque
>   Prae foribus stat hyems; claude MARIA fores.[6]
>
> *Crib, my crib, my sweetest crib, greetings;*
>   *Crib spread with tiny lilies, spread with roses.*
> *Ah not spread with roses, nor with beautiful tiny lilies;*
>   *But truly worthy of tiny lilies, and well worthy of roses.*
> ...
>
> *Mary, shut the doors, look how icy, naked and trembling*
>   *Stands winter at the doors; Mary, shut the doors.*

This placing of oneself at the biblical scene derives from Jesuit meditative practice, but was quickly influential upon poets who were not themselves Jesuits or even Roman Catholics, including George Herbert, who, along with George Buchanan and Casimir Sarbiewski, was among the most influential religious poets of the period in England.[7]

In a manuscript from 1630s Oxford, we find the same topic handled in iambic trimeter.[8] Iambic metres, used in classical literature primarily for drama and invective, became highly fashionable in the first half of the seventeenth century, and were used for many types of verse. Milton's 'Nativity Ode' of 1629, on the other hand, belongs formally to a Pindaric tradition of grand religious lyric traceable to the Italian humanists and fashionable in the late sixteenth and early seventeenth centuries: both Julius Caesar Scaliger and Maffeo Barberini, later Pope Urban VIII, composed devotional odes in Latin Pindarics. An anonymous poet in the 1650s begins a manuscript collection with two nativity poems, one in hexameter and the second in dithyrambics, a highly irregular verse form

---

[6] Bauhusius, *Epigrammata* (1616), sig. A5r, 'In lectulum dulcissimi Infantis Iesu recens nati'.
[7] The influence of Buchanan is discussed especially in Chapters 2 and 3; for Herbert and Sarbiewski see below.
[8] Bod. MS Lat. misc. e. 32, fols. 3v–4r; the same poem is also in Bod. MS Add. B. 109, fol. 105r–v (c.1650–4).

linked to Pindar which became intensely fashionable around this time (see Chapter 5).[9]

Some modes were enduringly popular. The similarity in imagery between Virgil's *Eclogue* 4 and the biblical Book of Isaiah led to a long tradition of understanding *Eclogue* 4 as itself 'messianic': prophesying the birth of Jesus.[10] Many imitations of and allusions to this eclogue incorporate this element, and the role of the shepherds – the singers of classical pastoral – in the nativity story tended to reinforce the association. 'Nativity eclogues' are found throughout the period: Scipio Gentili published one, 'Alcon', in a collection containing mostly psalm paraphrases dedicated to Philip Sidney in 1581; over a hundred years later, a student at St John's College, Oxford, in 1693 composed a Latin Christmas eclogue, probably as a university exercise.[11]

Well into the eighteenth century, the young Thomas Birch, probably in conscious imitation of Milton, whose 'Nativity Ode' was dated Christmas morning 1629 (when Milton was 21), notes that his Nativity ode was composed on Christmas Day, 1723, aged 17.[12] Birch's ode, in alcaic stanzas, is also however a translation *into* Latin, apparently from the English of J. Hughes. This, too, is typical of wider patterns: by the early eighteenth century, Latin lyric verse written in England was almost exclusively in alcaics and sapphics, and this is the period in which the translation of English verse into Latin was at its most popular.[13]

When Ben Jonson, as Drummond reported, reacted with surprise and admiration to Southwell's 'Burning Babe', supposedly saying that 'had [he] written that piece of [Southwell's] ... he would have been content to destroy many of his [own poems]', he was recognising something new, and quite different from the tradition of religious verse represented by the Sidney psalter.[14] This chapter focuses on the transformation of religious

---

[9] Bod. MS Rawl. Poet. 65, fol. 2^{r-v}, ascribed to one Thomas Bickly; BL MS Lansdowne 846, dating probably from the 1680s, contains an example of Latin free verse on the nativity (fol. 75^v).

[10] On the reception of *Eclogue* 4 see Houghton, *Virgil's Fourth Eclogue*.

[11] Gentili, *Paraphrasis Aliquot Psalmorum Davidis* (1581), 'Alcon, seu, De Natali Iesu Christi. Ecloga', sig. Eii^r–Eiv^v. Bod. MS Rawl. D. 237, 'In Christum Nascentem, Ecloga', fol. 3^{r-v}. Eclogues are one verse form the production of which, at least in Latin, is stable throughout the period of this study. In the manuscript poetry data, the distribution of recorded 'eclogues' maps almost exactly the distribution pattern of the corpus as a whole.

[12] BL MS Add. 4456, fols. 20^r–1^v.

[13] The early eighteenth century lies largely beyond the scope of this study, though Latin verse continued to be read and composed in this period in large quantities. For the trend of translating English verse into Latin, see Chapter 7.

[14] Jonson, 'Informations' to William Drummond of Hawthornden', 369.

verse in the earlier part of the seventeenth century, and on the working out between the early seventeenth and early eighteenth century of the influence of the new kind of devotional poetry that Jonson recognized in Southwell. In this period, a primarily Protestant tradition of scriptural paraphrase, especially of the Old Testament; the particularly English devotion to the psalms as a source of and model for poetry; and the sensuality, intimacy and imagination of primarily Jesuit poetics combined to astonishing effect to create a golden age of religious lyric which runs from the Sidney psalter, via Herbert, Crashaw, Vaughan and Dryden through to Watts and – beyond him and beyond the scope of this book – Wesley, Smart and Cowper.

Herbert and the Emergence of Personal Devotional Verse in England

For modern English readers, the best known of these poets is Herbert, whose collection *The Temple* was published posthumously in 1633 and remains probably the single best-loved collection of English devotional verse. At the time of his death, however, Herbert was known as a Latin poet, several of whose Latin epigrams had been circulating at least since 1618, and who had gained a reputation for his Latin verse while university orator at Cambridge between 1620 and 1627.[15] At his death, one complete Latin verse collection had appeared in print, the remarkable *Memoriae Matris Sacrum* written in memory of his mother in the aftermath of her death in 1627. Three other complete Latin verse collections, however, survive: the *Musae Responsoriae*, a collection composed in response to Andrew Melville's long Latin poem the *Anti-Tami-Cami-Categoria*, and probably completed around 1620, possibly with elements dating back to Herbert's schooldays at Westminster; *Lucus*, a miscellaneous collection of religious and moralizing epigrams; and *Passio Discerpta*, a meditative sequence of epigrams on the Crucifixion which follows the order of scriptural events.

All three of these unpublished Latin verse collections are, essentially, collections of epigrams; set alongside *The Temple*, to which they correspond in multiple ways, they form a bilingual body of work in religious epigram and lyric respectively, with – as is typical of the period – some areas of overlap: *Lucus* 35, for instance, 'Ad Dominum' ('To the Lord'), has the paradoxical quality characteristic of Latin epigram, but in tone,

---

[15] A copy of 'Roma' in BL MS Harley 6038, fol. 15ᵛ is dated 1618.

register and position reflects the hymn or lyric prayer typically found at the close of collections (such as Jonson's *Forest* 15, 'To Heaven'). Similarly, several of the lyrics of *The Temple* have specific scriptural references in their titles, aligning them to the tradition of scriptural epigram.[16] Taken as a whole, Herbert's body of religious verse resembles the work of several influential early seventeenth-century authors of devotional verse in Latin, especially Jesuit poets such as Bernhard Bauhusius, Jacob Bidermann and Casimir Sarbiewksi, as well as non-Jesuits such as Maffeo Barberini (Pope Urban VIII from 1623). Each of them produced religious verse, like Herbert, in two main forms: epigram and lyric.[17] Although this chapter discusses the traditions of religious epigram and religious lyric largely separately, for poets and readers of the period they belonged closely together, were read and copied alongside one another, and were frequently associated too with other related forms, especially psalm paraphrase: Herbert included a single English psalm paraphrase (of Psalm 23) in *The Temple*, though another seven, perhaps evidence of an attempt at a complete psalter, are attributed to Herbert in a publication of 1671.[18]

In the late sixteenth century, there were limited available models in English for religious verse with a strong personal voice. The main examples were either instances of scriptural paraphrase – especially of the psalms or the Song of Songs – or they were by Catholic, and often Jesuit, poets, such as Robert Southwell (1561–95) whose poem 'The Burning Babe' so impressed Ben Jonson. Southwell's poem is marked by its first-person voice, dramatic immediacy, the combination of sensory realism ('stood shivering in the snow') with visionary detail, and the incorporation of Christ as a speaking character:

> As I in hoary winter's night stood shivering in the snow,
> Surpris'd I was with sudden heat which made my heart to glow;
> And lifting up a fearful eye to view what fire was near,
> A pretty Babe all burning bright did in the air appear;
> Who, scorched with excessive heat, such floods of tears did shed

---

[16] 'Coloss. 3:3', for instance, in its brevity, wordplay and specific scriptural reference recalls many of Herbert's Latin epigrams.

[17] Bauhusius' *Epigrammata* contains (despite the title) poems in a range of forms, including lyric. Maffeo Barberini's 1623 *Poemata* collection also includes some scriptural paraphrase, and a sacred eclogue. Sarbiewski wrote epodes as well as odes and epigrams, though his epodes are very similar in tone and content to the odes. Bidermann's epigrams are all fairly short, though metrically varied.

[18] Psalms 1–7, attributed to Herbert in Playford, *Psalms & Hymns* (1671). There are no extant examples of more extended scriptural paraphrase by Herbert, though both 'The Sacrifice' (in *The Temple*) and the entire sequence *Passio Discerpta* track the scriptural account of the Crucifixion and have elements of this tradition.

> As though his floods should quench his flames which with his tears were fed.
> "Alas!" quoth he, "but newly born, in fiery heats I fry,
> Yet none approach to warm their hearts or feel my fire but I!
> My faultless breast the furnace is, the fuel wounding thorns,
> Love is the fire, and sighs the smoke, the ashes shame and scorns;
> The fuel Justice layeth on, and Mercy blows the coals,
> The metal in this furnace wrought are men's defiled souls,
> For which, as now on fire I am to work them to their good,
>   So will I melt into a bath to wash them in my blood."
>   With this he vanish'd out of sight and swiftly shrunk away,
>   And straight I called unto mind that it was Christmas day.[19]

The first part of Herbert's 'Christmas' (from *The Temple*) has some of the same features, including a transition from realism to a kind of vision:

> After all pleasures as I rid one day,
> My horse and I, both tir'd, bodie and minde,
> With full crie of affections, quite astray;
> I took up in the next inne I could finde.
>
> There when I came, whom found I but my deare,
> My dearest Lord, expecting till the grief
> Of pleasures brought me to him, ready there
> To be all passengers' most sweet relief?
>
> Oh Thou, whose glorious, yet contracted light,
> Wrapt in night's mantle, stole into a manger;
> Since my dark soul and brutish is thy right,
> To man of all beasts be not thou a stranger:
>
> Furnish & deck my soul, that thou mayst have
> A better lodging, then a rack, or grave.

Herbert's poem is divided between narrative and direct address to God; in this example, God does not reply, although God or Christ speaks directly in many of Herbert's poems, usually at the end.[20]

The lack of available models for 'personal' devotional and religious lyric in the late sixteenth century is not a purely vernacular phenomemon: if we think of the most popular religious poets of this period writing in Latin we find a similar pattern. George Buchanan, whose *Poemata* was one of the most widely owned volumes of contemporary Latin poetry, produced a full set of psalm paraphrases, which was often printed first in collected editions

---

[19] Text from Davidson and Sweeney (eds.), *Collected Poems of Southwell*.
[20] On the conversational and dramatic features of Herbert's English verse, see Jennings, *Every Changing Shape*, 72–8.

of his verse; he also wrote a morning hymn, a paraphrase of the Song of Simeon (Luke 2) and a large number of epigrams relating to points of religious controversy, alongside examples of love elegy, satire, panegyric, occasional poetry, commendatory verse, invective, Latin drama and even didactic poetry. Buchanan provided Protestant poets of the later sixteenth century with a model for almost every kind of Latin verse – but his poetry includes almost no devotional verse that is not closely scriptural. We find the same kind of range in the verse of Andrew Melville, a very prolific Latin poet whose literary achievement has been underacknowledged because much of his verse circulated only in manuscript: Melville produced large quantities of Latin epigram on doctrinal and liturgical questions as well as extended scriptural paraphrase but, again, no devotional poetry of a personal kind.[21]

This basic pattern of late sixteenth-century Protestant poetics, in which religious verse is confined almost exclusively to scriptural paraphrase or polemical epigram, can still be seen in, for instance, the accomplished Anglo-Latin verse collections of the turn of the century, such as William Vaughan's *Erotopaignion Pium* (1597): Vaughan's book consists of a series of scriptural verse paraphrases, and includes only two verse prayers which are not keyed directly to scripture. Even later in the seventeenth century, a work like that of the French Protestant Paul Thomas (1565–1636), whose 1627 *Poemata* was owned by Ben Jonson, follows this older pattern. Thomas' poetry, which went through several editions, includes a volume of sacred verse, *Silva sacra*, which is almost entirely composed of scriptural verse paraphrase.[22]

Robert Southwell was a Catholic who had been educated in France since adolescence: several of his Latin poems from the period of his education and formation have survived in manuscript.[23] Such a Catholic tradition of devotional or meditative Latin verse has left traces also in the English manuscript record: BL MS Harley 3258, for instance, is a large collection of Latin verse dating apparently from the late sixteenth century, and clearly written by a Roman Catholic.[24] Like comparable Protestant collections, it contains poems on contemporary events, panegyric and commendatory verse, and polemical epigram, including poems in praise of Edmund

---

[21] For Melville's polemical epigram, see Chapter 7.
[22] Editions of Thomas' verse were published in 1617, 1627, 1633 and 1640. Jonson owned the 1627 edition of his *Poemata* (McPherson, 'Ben Jonson's Library', no. 189).
[23] Stonyhurst College, Lancashire, MS A. v. 4; see Davidson and Sweeney (eds.), *Collected Poems of Southwell*, 147–50.
[24] One of the final items in the manuscript is dated 1597 (fol. 83ᵛ).

Campion, Thomas More and John Feckenham, last abbot of Westminster, as well as satirical attacks on Luther, Zwingli, Calvin and Queen Elizabeth, the 'papess of the English'.[25] Unlike typical Protestant compositions of this period, however, it also contains a series of devotional poems which, though they follow the life of Christ, and are carefully annotated with marginal scriptural references, are not themselves scriptural paraphrase.

There is a sharp contrast between the religious verse we associate with the seventeenth century – with its personal tone, direct expression, strong emotion, sensuous imagery and baroque compression – and poetry on religious topics typical of the later sixteenth century. If we are reading chronologically in English, Herbert's verse feels quite new in its speaking immediacy, the combination of realism and a kind of domesticated mysticism, the nearness of God, and the impression of a fully digested scriptural foundation which is nevertheless not narrowly scriptural. Formally, Herbert's concise lyrics are both metrically various and inventive – heirs to the tradition of psalm paraphrase described in Chapters 2 and 3 – and also characterised by the kind of condensed wit or rhetorical 'turn' typical of epigram. What Herbert is doing in fact fits into a larger story that comprises both his own literary bilingualism and the much broader current of Latin religious verse in the latter sixteenth and early seventeenth centuries, and which combines the primarily Protestant form of scriptural epigram with the, initially largely Catholic, tradition of devotional verse.

Scriptural Epigram

The writing of scriptural epigrams in Latin was a very common school or university exercise in the seventeenth century. Equivalent exercises in the latter sixteenth century seem more often to have been on generalizing moralizing rather than specifically scriptural themes, though the verse exercises prescribed by archdeacon Thomas Watts for the scholars at Pembroke College, Cambridge in 1570 are an early example of a specifically scriptural requirement:

> And also that euery of the said six schollers shall for euery of the feast Dayes here vnder named . . . cawse to be sett vp vpon the skrene, in the hall of the said College Immediately before dynner, vpon euery of the sayd dayes, fower hexameter & pentameter verses in latyn, and as manye of the same matter In greke wrytten with their owne handes. And also shall make, and

---

[25] BL MS Harley 3258, fol. 80ʳ.

in lyke manner sett vp for and vpon euery sondaye and euery other holy daye in the yere, two hexametre & pentametre verses in latyn, and as many of the same matter in greke, takyng alwayes thargument of the said verses, out of som parte of the scriptures red vpon such dayes in the service of the Churche for the which verses so made and sett vp.[26]

In some institutions, a particular student had a responsibility for this kind of composition: Richard Crashaw's (1613?–49) collection of Latin scriptural epigrams, published as *Epigrammatum sacrorum liber* (1634), has its origin in school compositions.[27] As a Foundation Scholar at Charterhouse in the late 1620s and early 1630s, it was his duty to write and display epigrams in Latin and Greek on the day's scriptural readings, and as a Watts scholar afterwards at Pembroke, he was likewise obliged to produce epigrams each Sunday, just as Lancelot Andrewes had done sixty years before.[28] Several other collections published in adulthood had similar schoolboy origins, including James Duport's (1606–79) *Epigrammata Sacra*, published in 1662 but drawing on work composed originally at Westminster in the 1610s, and John Suckling on the days of the Christmas season.[29]

Crashaw's sacred epigrams are 'scriptural epigrams' in the strictest sense, in that each corresponds to a specific verse of scripture – not just a more general chapter, theme or episode. Scriptural epigrams in this narrow sense are a primarily Protestant phenomenon, though the treatment of scripture could be imaginative: a Bodleian manuscript, for instance, contains a poem in the tradition of the *Heroides*, but in the person of Hagar, the mother of Ishmael who was rejected by Abraham after Sarah gave birth to Isaac.[30] Extant collections by Roman Catholic students tend to be less strictly scriptural, even where the forms and metres used are identical. Bod. MS Rawl. Poet. 215, for instance, is a collection of largely religious Latin verse exercises made by Catholic students in the mid-seventeenth century, and

---

[26] Indenture of Thomas Watts, Pembroke College Archives, College Box L.4. Lancelot Andrewes was one of the first of these scholars, elected in 1571. I am grateful to Peter McCullough for this reference.
[27] Crashaw, *Epigrammatum sacrorum liber* (1634); see Larsen, 'Crashaw's *Epigrammata Sacra*'.
[28] See Healy, 'Richard Crashaw'; Doelman, *Epigram in England*, 74.
[29] Duport, *Epigrammata Sacra* (1662), published with Duport's *Canticum Solomonis* (a Latin verse paraphrase of the Song of Songs), John Vivian's *Ecclesiastes Solomonis* (a Latin verse paraphrase of Ecclesiates), George Herbert's epigram sequence *Musae Responsoriae* and Andrew Melville's *Anti-Tami-Cami-Categoria* (to which Herbert's sequence responded). Duport's own preface acknowledges the youthful origin of his epigrams (sig. ¶6ʳ). On Suckling, see Doelman, *Epigram in England*, 75.
[30] Bod. MS Malone 15, fol. 1ʳ (early seventeenth century).

divided into *Elegiae*, *Epigrammata* and drama.[31] Rather than being keyed to specific passages of scripture, the religious poems commemorate religious feasts, such as the Assumption or Purification, and include several addressed to, or speaking in the voice of, well-known saints. Others comment on the Roman Catholic cause on the world stage: India lamenting that she is not Catholic; a poem in the voice of St Aloysius Gonzaga addressing his brother; and a poem in praise of Fr Henry More, an English Jesuit of the early part of the seventeenth century.

Scriptural epigram, in both Latin and English, has been associated in scholarship primarily with the first half of the seventeenth century.[32] Walter Haddon's prolific, innovative and influential Latin verse of the mid-sixteenth century, by contrast, includes many examples of scriptural verse paraphrase, but none of epigrammatic length, although he wrote many epigrams on other topics. This impression of a distinctively seventeenth-century phenomenon may, however, be in part an accident of scholarly attention rather than an accurate reflection of early modern practice. Though no sixteenth-century examples of the work of the Watts scholars at Pembroke have apparently survived, other examples include, for instance, the 160 epigrams on the New Testament, each a single elegiac couplet, by John Shepreve (c.1509–42), preserved in a later sixteenth-century manuscript in Corpus Christi, Oxford, and incorporated several times in later publications.[33]

Another unpublished and indeed hitherto undescribed collection of manuscript verse also at Corpus was kept apparently throughout his adult life by Adrian Schoell, a German Protestant émigré. The volume contains an interesting sequence dated 1565, including seven scriptural epigrams based on verses from Job, Psalm 39 and Psalm 90; these are immediately preceded by four single-couplet epigrams defending Protestant religious practice.[34] Later rector of Higham in Somerset, Schoell was at this point

---

[31] The catalogue dates the manuscript to c.1600, but this is certainly wrong. It is probably a manuscript from the Jesuit school for English boys at St Omer, dating from the 1650s. I am grateful to Alison Shell for assistance on this point.

[32] Doelman gives the mid-1630s as the 'high-water mark' of English religious epigram, in which he includes both scriptural and more general devotional epigrams (*Epigram in England*, 345); see also Doelman, 'Religious Epigram in Early Stuart England'.

[33] Corpus Christi College, Oxford, MS 266; see Introduction, note 51.

[34] Corpus Christi College, Oxford, MS 324, fols. 130^r–1^r. He appears in the clergy register as Adrian Shell (1570) and Adrian Shawe (1590), probably both attempts to Anglicize the name, which is clearly Schoell in the manuscript. He was born near Leipzig in 1530 and had spent several years in Italy and Spain before traveling to England around 1554. He married in 1561. His manuscript includes a handful of compositions in Greek, but no English or German verse of his own composition.

a schoolmaster (and probably also already a clergyman) in Childerditch, near Warley in Essex: the majority of his Latin verse, perhaps composed on request, marks births, marriages and deaths among his friends and local dignitaries, occasional royal visits to the area, and wider events of particular interest to Protestants, such as the death of Gardiner in 1555 and that of Mary Queen of Scots in 1587. One of the longest poems in the collection, composed in 1555 under Mary I, defends the translation of scripture into the vernacular. Many other poems record events in Schoell's own life, and there is no evidence that any of his poetry was published. The presence of scriptural epigrams as well as epigrams on religious practice in the personal verse of a provincial schoolmaster at this period suggests that such forms were already well-established in educated Protestant circles. Although a prolific and frequently personal Latin poet, Schoell composed very few if any poems which could be described as purely devotional (one late example is a prayer for his own health, dated 1592, fol. 182^r): in this, his work conforms to the patterns of sixteenth-century composition described above.

It is possible that scriptural epigram was simply less likely to be printed in the sixteenth century than in the seventeenth. Abraham Hartwell's interesting 1565 volume marking the visit of Queen Elizabeth to Cambridge is a highly fashionable production: in addition to the main long poem in elegiacs, a kind of masque of welcome for the Queen, it includes a figure poem (in the shape of an hourglass, sig. Fiiii^r), and a poem in which the first letter of each line spells out 'Elisabeta' while the last (or nearly last) letter spells out her name in reverse ('Atebasile', sig. Fv^r).[35] This is the kind of experimental Latin verse found also in the work of Walter Haddon, and well represented in Richard Willes' *Poematum Liber* of 1573 (see further Chapter 2). In Hartwell's volume, the Elizabeth poem is followed by a series of 19 scriptural epigrams, each a single elegiac couplet, titled with a reference to a chapter of scripture relating in some way to kingship. These 'Disticha de Rege ex variis sacrae scripturae locis' ('Distichs on the King from various places in sacred scripture'), which are given in biblical order, are suprisingly keen-edged. They emphasize the link between the king and his people, the subordination of the king to God, and the inevitable failure and defeat of all kings who are not obedient servants of

---

[35] Hartwell, *Regina Literata* (1565).

Christ.[36] The only 'queen' of the sequence is borrowed from Luke 11 and Mark 12 and makes much the same point:

> Ex Austro Regina aderit decus illa suorum,
>   At circumcisis dedecus illa graue.
>
> *From the South shall come a Queen, the glory of her people,*
>   *But a grave reproach upon the circumcised* [i.e. the Jews as opposed to Christians].

Such a sequence celebrates the glory of the monarch, while insistently reminding her of the possibility of failure and the primacy of religion. In this way apparently bland examples of what we might call 'scriptural literature', easily passed over by modern readers, may have political or polemical force. In his seminal study of Latin psalm paraphrase, Johannes Gaertner noted that such authors exercised a surprising level of freedom in their response to scripture.[37] We find a similar political application of apparently narrowly scriptural verse in the large quantity of extended scriptural verse paraphrase produced in the politically turbulent period of the 1640s and 1650s, some of which is discussed in Chapter 11.

Many of the early examples of scriptural epigram have, like Hartwell's sequence, a didactic rather than devotional edge: Henry Dethick's *Feriae Sacrae* (1577) consists of eight books of Latin verse amounting to a kind of versification of the Bible, starting from the creation of the world as described in Genesis and ending with the earliest Christian martyrs, and including a sequence of epigrams at the end of Book 6 on classical poets (Ovid, Lucan, Horace, Statius, Juvenal and Virgil). Binns points out that one of the important models for this kind of verse was the *Dittochaeon* or *Scenes from History* of the late antique poet Prudentius: rarely read today, it consists of 49 hexameter quatrains each referring to a separate biblical incident from the Old or New Testament.[38] Other important early Christian models for scriptural epigram include Gregory of Nazianzus: James Duport compared Herbert's religious verse explicitly to that of Nazianzus, and Thomas Drant's *Epigrams and sentences spirituall* (1568) consists entirely of verse translations of Gregory's epigrams and some

---

[36] E.g. 4 Kings 19, on how an impious people choose a corrupt king; Job 30 on how the robber fears the judgement of the king, the king the judgement of God; Jeremiah 22 on how the king of Judah will fall and the kingdom of David, interpreted as the glory of Christ's kingdom, will endure for ever.

[37] 'We ... sometimes wonder that ecclesiastical authorities grew not more excited about these poetical exercises' (Gaertner, 'Latin Verse Translations', 281).

[38] See Binns, *Intellectual Culture*, 104–8. On the importance of Prudentius as a metrical authority, see Chapter 2.

longer poems.[39] The particular popularity of scriptural epigram in the first half of the seventeenth century was certainly related to the intense fashion for epigrams in general: although John Owen composed only a few specifically scriptural epigrams, his enormous popularity, not only in England, surely stands behind the vogue for the shorter and pithier type of epigram, including examples on scriptural and devotional topics.[40]

Of the many collections of epigrams, in both Latin and English, published in the first half of the seventeenth century in England, several dedicate an entire book to religious verse, and the same is true of examples elsewhere in Europe: John Pyne's 1626 *Epigrammata*, for instance, are divided into three books, the first of which are 'religiosa'; of Thomas Bancroft's *Two Bookes of Epigrammes* (1639), the first is secular and the second moralizing, scriptural and religious. In England, such collections, like Herbert's own *Passio Discerpta*, frequently follow a scriptural sequence: John Saltmarsh's 1636 collection of *Poemata Sacra* combines Latin epigrams and English meditations, and at least initially follows a roughly biblical order.[41] Francis Quarles' *Divine Fancies* (1632) is also arranged in a way that corresponds loosely to the Bible, treating the Old Testament in Book 2 and the New Testament in Book 3.[42] Even Robert Herrick's *Hesperides* (1648) contains a set of sacred epigrams, *His Noble Numbers*, printed at the end of the volume with its own title page and dated the previous year. Closely related to scriptural epigram are the collections of *Emblemata*, symbolic images accompanied by brief poems, whether in Latin or the vernacular. Francis Quarles – who had already published a sequence of long-form scriptural paraphrases in English verse – had a major success in the 1630s with his *Emblemata*, a self-consciously Protestant version of the Jesuit Herman Hugo's popular *Pia Desideria*

---

[39] See Prancie, 'Ora pro me, sancte Herberte'. Gregory of Nazianzus was also translated into Latin verse: a translation by Christopher Manley is included in Wright, *Delitiae delitiarum* (1637).

[40] Owen's two main sequences of religious epigrams are 3:15–24 and 3:40–64, on topics such as 'God', 'The spirit and the flesh', 'The Apocalypse of St John' and 'The weeping of Mary Magdalene'. In the early 1606 edition, two of these have marginal scriptural references (no. 51 to Psalm 51; no. 53, line 4 to Genesis 3.6, linking the weeping of Mary Magdalene with the weeping of Eve after the Fall). But many of Owen's epigrams which are not explicitly religious draw on scriptural references, as for instance 3.141 ('Roma') which links Romulus and Remus to Cain and Abel. Stradling, *Epigrammatum libri quatuor* (1607) is, like Owen's collection, mostly secular, but also includes a sequence of 35 religious and largely biblical epigrams in Book 3 (pp. 106–14). It is likely that Stradling is in this respect imitating Owen directly.

[41] On Saltmarsh, see Doelman, *Epigram in England*, 351; Killeen, 'My Exquisite Copies for Action'.

[42] See Liston (ed.), *Divine Fancies*; and Doelman, *Epigram in England*, 350.

(first edition 1624).[43] Epigrams from emblem collections are frequently found in manuscript without their accompanying images.

There was an audience for the best examples of this kind of scriptural epigram beyond their author and immediate circle. Crashaw's epigrams, for instance, circulated in manuscript as well as – and probably before – being printed.[44] Individual epigrams, or short linked sequences, were frequently copied separately into commonplace books and miscellanies, whether from other manuscripts or printed books. Crashaw's epigram on Acts 8:18, for instance, appears in an undated (apparently seventeenth-century) Chetham's Library manuscript on a page filled largely by Quarles' English epigrams from *Divine Fancies* (1632).[45] It is one of only a handful of Latin verse items in the manuscript, all of them epigrams on religious topics, though the rest are topical rather than scriptural, taking aim at Catholics and Puritans alike.

Collections and sequences of scriptural epigrams appear frequently in the manuscript record, in a range of contexts. Bod. MS Rawl. poet. 57, for instance, is an apparently presentation manuscript of a set of scriptural epigrams, each titled with reference to a specific biblical verse, dedicated to Sir Orlando Bridgeman (1606–74) and signed 'Andreas Silvius, Rector Thermocomiensis'. This must be Andrew Wood, rector of Warmingham, appointed to that position in February 1623 and certainly rector there until 1641. Warmingham is in the diocese of Chester, and John Bridgeman, Sir Orlando's father, was bishop of Chester between 1619 and 1652. The volume therefore probably dates from between 1623 and the 1640s, and may represent an appeal for particular patronage or favour. Wood was a fellow of St John's College, Cambridge, as well as rector of Warmingham, and Cooper's *Memorials of Cambridge*, noting his death in 1680, describes him as an 'able Latin poet'.[46]

Wood's sequence of scriptural epigrams is preceded by a dedicatory poem, and the final two pieces also address Bridgeman directly, creating a kind of liminary frame typical of presentation collections addressed to a specific dedicatee.[47] The epigrams are keyed largely, though not exclusively, to verses from the New Testament; five have Old Testament references, and several are titled without reference to any specific portion

---

[43] Quarles, *Emblemes* (1635) and *Divine Fancies* (1632). On emblemata, see Enenkel and Visser (eds.), *Mundus Emblematicus*.
[44] Doelman, *Epigram in England*, 352. [45] Chetham's Library, MS Mun. A. 2.91, fol. 17ᵛ.
[46] Cooper, *Memorials of Cambridge*, 117. Bod. MS Ashmole 36/37 contains copies of some poems by Wood, who was a friend of Ashmole.
[47] I am grateful to Raffaella Colombo for this point.

of scripture. There is a loose sense of chronological structure – the first of the epigrams refers to Genesis 1.3 – but Old Testament sources are mixed with New Testament ones throughout, and the sequence includes epigrams on points of religious practice, such as infant baptism and kneeling to pray, in addition to strictly scriptural poems. In this way the sequence, like Herbert's *Musae Responsoriae*, gives an indication of churchmanship.[48] By contrast, we also find sequences – usually shorter sequences – of scriptural epigrams in personal miscellanies and commonplace books, such as Bod. MS Rawl. poet. 246, a mid-seventeenth-century collection, mostly of verse, made by someone in Cambridge who had been at Eton. The manuscript includes many of the fashionable poems of the time, with Latin verse by Alexander Gill, Thomas Goad, Albertus Morton, George Herbert and Raphael Thorius. A sequence of eight scriptural epigrams, all on a single page, are attributed to an unidentified 'R. S.'.[49]

The choices made by Abraham Wright in compiling his 1637 anthology of Latin epigrams *Delitiae delitiarum*, suggest the evolution of literary taste in England by this date: the two largest sections are those containing poems by Bernhard Bauhusius (1575–1619, 52 epigrams, poetry first published in 1616) and Hugo Grotius (1583–1645, 75 epigrams, poetry first published in 1601), though Grotius' epigrams are moralizing rather than religious.[50] These two poets, Bauhusius and Grotius, neatly represent the broadly Jesuit versus Protestant traditions of religious epigram. Other authors who contribute significant quantities of religious verse to Wright's anthology include Mario Bettini (1582–1657, 46 poems; poetry first published in 1632), Jacob Bidermann (1577–1639, 39 poems; poetry first published in 1620) and Casimir Sarbiewski (1595–1640, 11 poems; poetry first published in 1625), all three still alive at the time of publication.[51]

---

[48] Another of Wood's presentation manuscripts has also survived, CUL MS Dd. III. 78, a litany in Latin verse dedicated to Henry, Lord Holland, Chancellor of the University, written probably in 1629; Wood also contributed several poems to university anthologies.

[49] Bod. MS Rawl. poet. 246, fol. 62r.

[50] Wright's *Delitiae* contains poems by 122 authors, the great majority of whom (98) are represented by fewer than 10 poems; it is a collection of epigrams in the broad sense, including some lyric poems and some poems of medium length. Doelman wrongly describes it as a 'collection of religious epigrams' (*Epigram in England*, 354): although many of the poems are religious, it includes verse on a wide range of topics. The collection includes, for instance, the epigram by Girolamo Amaltei (1507–74), 'De horologio pulvereo', which is the source of Jonson's popular poem 'Do but consider this small dust' (*UW* 8). Some omissions are also striking – Herman Hugo's epigrams, the model for Quarles' very popular *Emblemes* (1635), are not represented, perhaps because of the need to reproduce images.

[51] Bauhusius, *Epigrammata* (1616); Bidermann, *Epigrammatum Libri Tres* (1620), quickly followed by subsequent editions; Bettini, *Florilegium* (1633); Sarbiewski, *Lyricorum libri tres* (1625; multiple

Bauhusius, Bettini, Bidermann and Sarbiewksi, though from four different countries (the Netherlands, Italy, Austria and Poland) were all Jesuit poets. Wright's *Delitiae*, though it includes poets born from the latter half of the fifteenth century onwards, and writing in a wide array of Latin verse styles, has overall a fashionable, baroque feel because of the weight of Jesuit verse. It offers a vivid glimpse of the appetite and enthusiasm in England for verse in this style by the 1630s, and several surviving English manuscript miscellanies include selections of epigrams deriving directly from Wright's anthology.[52]

Reading George Herbert within a Latin Context

Herbert's composition of scriptural and devotional epigrams as well as devotional lyric is typical of the period: both Sarbiewksi and Bauhusius, for instance, wrote both epigram and lyric. But Herbert's religious poetry also shares many stylistic features with the Jesuit Latin verse of the early seventeenth century. One of the most distinctive features of Herbert's style is the abrupt beginnings to many of his poems, and the liberal use of direct speech, including the speech of God or of Christ himself. Both these features are found, too, in his Latin religious verse. In a few cases, a Latin and English passage seem to 'belong' together. In 'The Sacrifice' for instance, Christ speaks, both through scripture (the italicized line is a quotation of Lamentations 1:12) and as himself:

> *O all ye who passe by, behold and see;*
> Man stole the fruit, but I must climbe the tree;
> The tree of life to all, but onely me:
>   Was ever grief like mine!
>   ('The Sacrifice', 201–4)[53]

Herbert uses the same expression of 'climbing the tree' to describe the Crucifixion in *Passio Discerpta* 12, 'In Christum crucem ascensurum':

---

further editions). Bauhusius and Bidermann had already been published together in volumes of verse printed in 1620 and 1623.

[52] BL Add. MS 61744, for instance, a mid-seventeenth-century collection of poems and translations by Sir Reginald Forster made between 1643 and 1653, includes 49 neo-Latin epigrams with English translations, most of which are found in Wright's *Delitiae*.

[53] Lamentations 1:12, 'Is it nothing to you, all ye that pass by? behold, and see if there be any sorrow like unto my sorrow, which is done unto me, wherewith the LORD hath afflicted me in the day of his fierce anger.'

> Zacchaeus, ut Te cernat, arborem scandit:
> Nunc ipse scandis, ut labore mutato
> Nobis facilitas cedat & tibi sudor.
> Sic omnibus videris ad modum visûs.
> Fides gigantem sola, vel facit nanum.
>
> *Zacchaeus, in order to see you, climbed a tree:*
> *Now you've exchanged tasks – it's you who climb,*
> *To bring ease for us and sweat for you.*
> *Each man sees you from his own perspective:*
> *Faith alone makes a giant, or a dwarf.*[54]

These passages are connected in other ways: Christ and Zacchaeus switch places in the Latin epigram, Christ and Man in the English stanza. The English lines urge passers by to watch what is happening – a motif which links both Zacchaeus and the penultimate line of the Latin epigram ('Each man sees you from his own perspective').

There has been much less scholarship on Herbert's Latin than on his English verse, and what does exist has mostly not thought directly about the relationship between the Latin and English poetry. The small amount of commentary which has addressed this question has pointed out the extent to which the themes and techniques of *The Temple* can be seen emerging in the earlier Latin verse, but also that the Latin work contains some typically 'baroque' features which are avoided or muted in *The Temple*.[55] Both bodies of work, for instance, show a marked interest in liquid imagery, associated by Miller with Salesian meditation; in the Latin verse, however, we find this motif playing out in moments such as this poem, *Lucus* 34, addressed to John as he leans on the breast of Christ:

> Ah nunc, helluo, fac, ut ipse sugam:
> Num totum tibi pectus imputabis?
> Fontem intercipis omnibus patentem?
> Quin pro me quoque sanguinem profudit,
> Et ius pectoris inde consecutus
> Lac cum sanguine posco devolutum;
> Ut, si gratia tanta copuletur
> Peccati veniae mei, vel ipsos
> Occumbens humero Thronos lacessam.

---

[54] Based on Luke 19.2–6. Zacchaeus was a small man, which is why he climbed the tree for a better view. The end of the epigram claims that true 'stature' is a function of faith, not physical size. Quotations of Herbert's Latin verse are from Drury and Moul (eds.), *Complete Poems*.

[55] Discussions include Whitlock, 'Baroque Characteristics'; Miller, 'Herbert's Baroque'; Wickenheiser, 'Epigrammatic Tradition'.

> *Ah now, you glutton, come on, let me suck too:*
> *Surely you won't claim the whole breast for yourself?*
> *Do you snatch away that spring that lies open to all?*
> *For he shed his blood for me as well,*
> *And I too have a claim upon the breast:*
> *I demand the milk mingled with blood.*
> *If enough grace comes with it*
> *To cleanse my sin, then I'll strike with my shoulder*
> *Even those thrones as I fall and die.*[56]

This striking or even shocking imagery of feeding like a nursing baby on the blood from Christ's side has parallels in other neo-Latin poetry. We might think in particular of Richard Crashaw's Latin epigram on Luke 11:27, in which he imagines Mary drinking from her son's side as he had drunk from her, as well as his notorious English epigram 'On the Infant Martyrs' ('To see both blended in one flood, / The mothers' milk, the children's blood', 1–2). *Lucus* 34 also recalls many other examples of liquid imagery – of flowing water, tears, blood, ink and even saliva – in Herbert's poetry, as well as a similarly shocking poem written after the death of his mother in which he imagines himself gaping, open-mouthed, longing to feed from the breast offered by her ghost.[57] There is nothing quite so baroque in *The Temple*, but nevertheless several similar passages, and an equally consistent use of liquid imagery:

> Who knows not Love, let him assay
> And taste that juice, which on the crosse a pike
> Did set again abroach; then let him say
> If ever he did taste the like.
> Love is that liqour sweet and most divine,
> Which my God feels as bloud; but I, as wine.
>   ('The Agonie', 13–18)

Multiple elements of Herbert's mature style of religious lyric have parallels in the largely continental, and mostly Catholic, Latin verse of the early part of the seventeenth century. Of many possible links, there are a particularly large number of overlaps with the work of Bernhard Bauhusius (1576–1619), a Dutch Jesuit whose *Epigrammata* were first published in Antwerp in 1616.[58] Bauhusius' verse is personal, emotive and highly religious without being narrowly scriptural. Like Herbert, he makes extensive use of direct speech and, again like Herbert, begins many poems with striking immediacy, as if arriving in the middle of a conversation.

---

[56] Based on John 21:20 describing the disciple John 'who leaned upon [Christ's] breast at supper'.
[57] Herbert, *Memoriae Matris Sacrum* (1627), poem 7.   [58] Further publications in 1617 and 1634.

Compare for instance Bauhusius' handling of the Song of Simeon (Luke 2.29–32) with that of George Buchanan. Buchanan's paraphrase of the Canticle was often printed with a handful of other Latin verse prayers at the end of his collection of psalms. His version adds an initial few lines glossing the significance of the text, but is otherwise an elegant but fairly literal version of what was for English readers one of the single most familiar pieces of scripture, recited in every service of Evening Prayer.

> Eia nunc patribus, Deus,
> Adiungis placide me famulum tuum
>   Ut vox pollicita est tua.
> His namque, his oculis ille Salutifer
>   Humani generis tuus
> Est visus mihi ...
>   ('Canticum Simeonis', 1–5)

> *Oh now, God, you are kindly joining me,*
> *Your servant, with my forefathers*
>   *As your voice has promised.*
> *For with these – with these my eyes he, your own bringer of Salvation*
>   *For the human race*
> *Has been seen by me ...*

Bauhusius, by contrast, ventriloquizes St Simeon much more dramatically:

> Ten' video? caeci-lux optatissima mundi!
>   Ten' teneo? ô veterum clamor amorque Patrum!
> Ten' teneo & video? teneo te dulcis IESV!
>   Te video IESV! te teneo & video!
> ...
> Ah, ah, pande mihi clausos, Puer auree, ocellos,
>   Occludam gaudens tunc ego, CHRISTE, meos.[59]

> *Do I really see you? O most longed for light of this blind world!*
>   *Do I really hold you? O the love and acclamation of the ancient Fathers!*
> *Do I truly hold and see you? I hold you, sweet Jesus!*
>   *I see you Jesus! I hold you and I see you!*
> ...
> *Oh, oh, open my locked eyes, golden Boy,*
>   *In joy then shall I shut them* [i.e. in death], *O Christ.*

One of the early poems in Bauhusius' *Epigrammata*, 'Ecce Homo', has several points of contact with the opening poem of Herbert's *Lucus*:

---

[59] Bauhusius, *Epigrammata* (1616), sig. A5ᵛ.

1. Homo, Statua.

Sum, quis nescit, Imago Dei, sed saxea certè:
  Hanc mihi duritiem contulit improbitas.
Durescunt proprijs euulsa corallia fundis,
  Haud secud ingenitis dotibus orbus Adam.
Tu, qui cuncta creans docuisti marmora flere,
  Haud mihi cor saxo durius esse sinas.

1. Man, a Statue

I am – in case you didn't realize – the Image of God; but one made of stone, that's for sure:
  It was sin that brought this hardness upon me.
Coral flowers torn from their proper bases grow hard;
  So too Adam, once deprived of his natural inheritance.
You who, creating all things, taught marble to weep,
  Do not allow my heart to be harder than stone.

This unusual poem replaces several conventional opening gambits – such as the address to a Muse, a patron or dedicatee – with a prayer to God, requesting not inspiration but some softening of the heart which is reimagined as a partial reversal or at least limitation of the effect of the Fall. The emotional tone is complex: in a manner typical of Herbert's English poetry, it suggests both intense dependence on and devotion to God alongside a hint of frustration and resentment, as one might feel towards a recalcitrant lover. Bauhusius' 'Ecce Homo' ('Behold the man'), begins:

> Si mihi flet Libycum lapidoso in pectore marmor,
>   Et scissum è medio sit mihi cor Sipylo,
> Nunc tamen vnda fluat, nunc se mea pectora scindant,
>   Nunc in aquas mea se marmora dissolûant
> Ecce meus IESUS pro me, liuorque, cruorque,
>   Et tabum, & sanies! ECCE HOMO, nullus homo!
> . . .
>   O pie CHRISTE, quis est, quem tu adamas? Adamas.[60]

> *If only the Libyan marble could weep in my stony breast,*
>   *And my heart could be torn from the midst of Sipylus,*[61]
> *Now let the water flow, let my heart tear itself apart,*
>   *Now let my marble dissolve into water*

---

[60] Bauhusius, *Epigrammata* (1616), sig. A2ᵛ–A3ʳ.
[61] Sipylus is a mountain on the boundary of Lydia and Phrygia, on which Niobe was changed into stone.

> – *See how my Jesus is, for my sake, bruising, and blood,*
>   *Foul gore and bleeding! Behold a man, who is no man!*
> ...
>
> *O saintly Christ, who is it whom you truly love? Adamant.* [i.e. the man of stone, with play on 'Adam']

Though Herbert's epigram is more concise and emotionally more constrained, the two poems make very similar use of the imagery of flesh as stone and water, and both contain a play upon the Hebrew meaning of the name 'Adam' ('of the earth'), which resembles the Latin noun 'adamas' ('adamant', a very hard stone).

Herbert's very popular epigram on 'Roma' also has several similarities to Bauhusius' poem on the same topic (a link discussed further in Chapter 7, on epigram). Richard Crashaw, probably the most influential religious poet of the following generation and a friend of Cowley, apparently knew Bauhusius' work well: his remarkable poem 'Bulla' ('Bubble'), though significantly longer, is similar in content, style and overall structure, to Bauhusius' 'Homo Bulla' ('Man a Bubble').[62] Combined with the significant representation of Bauhusius in Wright's anthology, there is overall good evidence for the reading of Bauhusius, and of Jesuit devotional verse more widely, in England in the 1620s and 1630s.

After the publication of his 1633 English collection, *The Temple*, Herbert himself quickly became famous and widely imitated.[63] His influence on subsequent devotional lyric, in terms of form, style and tone, has been well documented: landmark collections by Richard Crashaw (*Steps to the Temple*, 1646), Henry Vaughan (*Silex Scintillans*, 1650 and *Olor Iscanus*, 1651), and, later, Thomas Traherne demonstrate Herbert's impact. These are familiar names, but a host of minor and amateur poets were similarly struck by *The Temple*. One of the earliest extant responses is that of John Polwhele, a clergyman whose poetry is dominated by classical translation and influenced stylistically more by Jonson than by Herbert, but whose rapturous response to his reading of 'The Church', dating apparently from soon after Herbert's death in 1633, describes it as a 'devine poeme'.[64] Other

---

[62] Crashaw's poem was first published in Heinsius, *Crepundia Siliana* (1646), printed without pagination after the index; Bauhusius' poem in *Epigrammata* (1616), sig. C1^v–C2^r. Crashaw's 'Bulla' has been acclaimed for its originality, and the similarity to Bauhusius' piece has not to my knowledge been previously noticed.

[63] On which see Ray, 'Herbert Allusion Book'. Ray details correspondences in Vaughan, Crashaw, Traherne and prints a transcription of Polwhele's poem (10).

[64] Bod. MS Eng. poet. f. 16, fol. 11^r. Polwhele was born in 1606 and entered Lincoln's Inn in 1623; a poem in the manuscript indicates that he was at school in Tavistock, Devon. This poem is quoted and briefly discussed by Wilcox, 'Puritans, George Herbert'.

mid-seventeenth-century examples include Sir Humphrey Wanley, whose *Scintullae Sacrae*, surviving in a series of manuscripts, is heavily indebted to Herbert, and Ralph Knevet's *A Gallery to the Temple*.[65] A Durham manuscript preserves a series of translations of Herbert into Latin, the first of which is dated 1634.[66]

Herbert's *Temple*, as we have seen, drew upon an already rich tradition of English scriptural and devotional verse, with a particular reverence for the Sidney psalter, and blended this tradition with the emotional immediacy, realism and visionary detail learnt from contemporary Jesuit poetics; in its turn it became part of a specifically English tradition of religious poetry. William Sancroft, later archbishop of Canterbury, compiled a collection of verse probably in the 1650s which includes poems and scriptural paraphrases by Donne, Wotton and Herbert as well as more immediate contemporaries, such as Cowley.[67] Bod. MS Rawl. C. 580, a miscellany of religious verse made apparently by a woman in the 1670s, includes a copy of Herbert's poem 'The Bag' ('Away despair! my gracious Lord doth heare'), transcribed from George Swinnock's pastoral work *The Christian-Man's Calling*, published several times from 1662.[68] The poems of the Rev. Daniel Baker (1654–1722), rector of Fincham St Michael's in Norfolk, some of which were printed in 1697, demonstrate the influence of Herbert's *Temple* extending to the end of the century and beyond. Baker's poetic tastes are demonstrably post-Cowleian, and his original verse, paraphrases and translations include several Pindaric odes, in both regular and irregular (Cowleian) forms. Although his style is far removed from that of Herbert, his reverence for him is clear: the English odes in free Pindarics include a paraphrase of Psalm 128, a version of *Eclogue* 4 (the Messianic eclogue) and also a poem on Herbert's *Temple* in which Herbert is compared to David.[69]

The religious verse of George Herbert, alongside that of George Buchanan and of the Polish Latin poet Casimir Sarbiewski, whose

---

[65] On Wanley, see West, 'Nathaniel Wanley and George Herbert' and Martin (ed.), *Poems of Humphrey Wanley*. Surviving manuscripts are BL MSS Add. 22472 and 70492; Harley 6922; and William Clark Memorial Library, MS W2485M3. Ralph Knevet's verse is preserved in BL MS Add. 27447; see also Charles (ed.), *Shorter Poems of Ralph Knevet*; Charles, 'Touching David's harp'; El-Gabalawy, 'Two Obscure Disciples of George Herbert'; Merchant, 'Ralph Knevet of Norfolk'.

[66] Durham Cathedral Library, MS Hunter 27, fols. 192^r–203^v. See Gibson, 'James Leeke, George Herbert'.

[67] Bod. MS Tanner 466, discussed further below.

[68] A quarto miscellany dating from between c.1668 and 1678, inscribed on the cover 'This book was wrot by my grandmother Moye; keep it always in the family, for in it lies *summum bonum*, tho deep yet clear. 1678'. The Herbert poem is on p. 314.

[69] BL MS Add. 11723.

influence in England largely post-dates *The Temple*, shaped the religious poetry of subsequent generations across divides of churchmanship. Though Herbert is strongly associated today with traditional 'Anglicanism', and his work defends Church practices such as infant baptism, the use of vestments and church music, his poetry was widely admired by readers belonging to quite different traditions: famously, *The Temple* was a favourite of both Charles I and Cromwell.[70] The religious poetry of Buchanan, an early Protestant convert, and of Casimir Sarbiewski, a Polish Jesuit, perhaps surprisingly had a similar reach.

Sarbiewski and the Song of Songs in England, 1630–1700

The English enthusiasm for, and response to, Jesuit devotional verse preceded the specific craze for Casimir Sarbiewski, which seems to be datable largely to the 1630s onwards: as we have seen, Herbert's poetic style, in both Latin and English, strongly suggests the influence of continental Catholic and especially Jesuit Latin poetry printed in the first third of the century. Wright's *Delitiae delitiarum* (1637), a useful snapshot of the English appreciation of this material in the mid-late 1630s, includes only 11 of Sarbiewski's poems compared to 52 by Bauhusius, 75 by Grotius (a Protestant poet) and more than 30 of seven other poets, of whom three were Jesuits.

Nevertheless, scholars have several times noted the peculiar English enthusiasm for Sarbiewski – an enthusiasm lasting right through to Coleridge, who planned a complete translation – and the editors of an anthology on the topic suggest that Sarbiewki was more popular and widely read in England than anywhere else outside Poland.[71] Sarbiewski combined a Jesuit sensuality and imagination in religious verse, demonstrably already popular in England, with a strong scriptural foundation: Røstvig describes Sarbiewski's verse as 'a conscious effort to apply the allegorical techniques of *Canticles* [Song of Songs; Song of Solomon] to the classical *beatus ille*-themes'.[72] Though he also wrote effective political panegyric, his main influence upon English poets was in this blend of

---

[70] On evidence for the reading and appreciation of Herbert, see Patrides (ed.), *George Herbert*; and Ray, 'Herbert Allusion Book'. On 'Puritan' readers of Herbert, see Hutchinson (ed.), *Works of George Herbert*, xliii–xliv.

[71] Fordoński and Urbański (eds.), *Casimir Britannicus*, 21. For the popularity and importance of Sarbiewski in the 1640s and 1650s, see also Davidson, *Universal Baroque*, 31–2; Gömöri, 'Polish Swan Triumphant'; Money, 'Aspects of the Reception of Sarbiewski'; Moul, 'Horace, Seneca'.

[72] Røstvig, 'Introduction', ii.

Horatian form, scriptural content, an intensely emotional tone and religious allegory. Unlike that of many other Jesuit poets, Sarbiewski's verse is not very strongly Marian, and nor is there a large number of poems dedicated to Catholic saints: the scriptural basis, including in the Old Testament, combined with the focus on Jesus (rather than Mary), probably made him particularly appealing, readable and imitable in a largely Protestant English context. His preference for Horatian metres also perhaps contributed to his popularity: as discussed in Chapter 3, England by the early seventeenth century had a rich and well-developed tradition of formal Horatian lyric in Latin.

Like Herbert himself – and, as we have seen, many other contemporaries – Sarbiewski published both lyric and epigrammatic devotional verse. The selected 1646 English edition by G. Hils, with a parallel text translation, was evidently produced in response to considerable demand, and selects from both the lyric and the epigrammatic corpus (29 of 130 odes and epodes; 6 of 145 epigrams), with a strong preference for odes from Sarbiewski's fourth book. The epigrams chosen by Hils appear continuous with the lyric: two are also paraphrases of, or responses to, verses from the Song of Songs (Epig. 4 and 37).

Nevertheless, Sarbiewski was, and was understood to be, a lyric poet above all, and his influence was greatest upon religious lyric written from the 1630s onwards. Though he wrote only in Horatian lyric metres, his influence extended to poets, such as Cowley and Watts, writing in the Pindaric and free verse forms fashionable in the latter half of the century. The enormous impact of Sarbiewski's style and content is easily demonstrated, and has been acknowledged by several scholars working on specific authors or forms, but it has not been fully connected to the evolution of English religious verse: Noam Flinker's monograph, for instance, provides a very helpful survey of poetry in English responding to the Song of Songs but mentions neither William Vaughan's *Erotopaignion* (discussed further below), nor the versions of the Song of Songs produced by Beza or Sarbiewski, both demonstrably influential in England.[73] Similarly, Nicholas McDowell, in an excellent chapter, demonstrates the shared roots of the religious imagery of authors as theologically distant as John Saltmarsh and Richard Crashaw in the fashionable poetics of Cambridge in the 1630s.[74] He rightly describes this poetics, with its particular preoccupation with the erotic imagery of the Song of Songs, as Jesuit, but only in relation to Jesuit rhetorical manuals and patristic commentary: his chapter does not

---

[73] Flinker, *Song of Songs*. [74] McDowell, 'Beauty of Holiness'.

mention Jesuit *poetry* such as that of Sarbiewski, Bauhusius or Bettini, the most significant factor in the development of a Jesuit-inflected Anglo-Latin poetics among English poets of the 1630s and 1640s.

That is not to suggest that the tradition of the verse paraphrase of the Song of Songs began with Sarbiewski, or indeed Beza. The length, poetic form, alternating speakers and controversial erotic content of this unusual biblical book – the only book of the canonical Old Testament without a single explicit reference to God, or to the people of Israel – had made it a popular choice for verse paraphrase from an early stage. The Christian allegorical interpretation in which the Bride and Bridegroom of the poem represent the Church and Christ goes back to Origen, though the Church Fathers were themselves building upon a traditional Jewish understanding of the poem as referring to the relationship between God and the individual soul, or the soul and the body. Early English examples of verse paraphrase include Baldwin (1549), and a series of such publications in both English and Latin appeared in the latter sixteenth century, often in association with paraphrases of other verse portions of the Bible.[75] Edmund Spenser made a version, which is lost. William Vaughan's *Erotopaignion* (1597), which contains multiple scriptural verse paraphrases, opens with a version of the Song of Songs in which the speakers are clearly divided between 'Ecclesia' (the Church), 'Christus' and (in chapters 5 and 6), 'Turba Israelit.' ('a crowd of Israelites').

The popularity of this text accelerated in the second quarter of the seventeenth century: Chamberlin lists 17 English print translations or paraphrases of this work between 1620 and 1660, including translations by George Wither (1621), Robert Aylett (1621), Francis Quarles (1625) and John Cotton (1642) as well as a paraphrase by George Sandys (1641).[76] In the same year as Herbert's *Temple*, Arthur Johnstoun published a Latin paraphrase of the Song of Songs in London.[77] This biblical book was often paraphrased alongside other parts of the Old Testament, as in John Dawson, *Summa moralis theologiae* (1639), containing paraphrases of Ecclesiastes, Proverbs and the Song of Songs, and in the 1640s James Duport (1606–79), a fellow in Cambridge, paraphrased the same three biblical books in Greek verse (Σολομῶν Ἔμμετρος, 1646). Duport also produced a Latin verse paraphrase of the Song of Songs, which, like many psalm paraphrases, uses a different, mostly lyric, metre for each chapter of

---

[75] Smith, *A Misticall Deuise* (1575); Fenner, *Song of Songs* (1587); Markham, *Poem of Poems* (1596); Drayton, *Harmonie of the Church* (1591); Bellehachius, *Sacrosancta bucolica* (1583); Vaughan, *Erotopaignion pium* (1597) and *Erotopaignion pium, pars secunda* (1598).
[76] Chamberlin, *Catalogue of English Bible Translations*, 404–5.
[77] Arthur Johnstoun, *Canticum Salomonis* (1633).

the biblical text. Though not published until 1662, Duport indicates in the preface that the paraphrase (like the epigrams with which it was published) was a work of his youth: as he was born in 1606, this probably refers to his time at Westminster before 1622 or at Trinity College, Cambridge, thereafter. The Song of Songs also attracted dedicated commentaries at this period, such as that of Jacob Durfeld (1633).

In Hils' 1646 selected and parallel text edition of Sarbiewski, six of the poems are titled with direct reference to the Song of Songs, and almost every poem makes marked use of related imagery, in which the language of sexual desire, courtship and physical beauty is transferred to a divine object, or to the longing for the divine. The almost complete critical neglect of Latin scriptural lyric of this kind, as it was enthusiastically received in England especially in the second and third quarter of the seventeenth century, risks distorting our interpretation of vernacular examples. Elizabeth Clarke, for instance, in her monograph on the Song of Songs in seventeenth-century England, argues that the Song of Songs is an 'oppositional' text associated with the Independents in the decade leading up to the outbreak of civil war.[78] 'Opposition' could of course come from multiple directions – McDowell points out that both Crashaw and Saltmarsh were adrift of the religious mainstream in the 1640s, albeit in roughly opposite directions.[79] But it would be wrong to suggest that an intense engagement with the Song of Songs in markedly political poetry is associated only with Independents in the 1640s or 1650s, or only with ejected Nonconformists in the 1670s: on the contrary it was, as we shall see, just as often appropriated by royalists in this period.[80]

The particular prominence of versions of or responses to the Song of Songs in the poetry of the 1630s and 1640s, however, is certainly related to the reading of Jesuit verse such as that of Sarbiewski; both Herman Hugo's *Pia desideria* (1624), and its English imitation, Quarles' *Emblemes* (1635), also include many pieces based on the Song of Songs.[81] Five Latin poems

---

[78] Clarke, *Politics, Religion and the Song of Songs*, 2. There is no index entry for Sarbiewski.
[79] McDowell, 'Beauty of Holiness'.
[80] There is sometimes still an assumption that royalists or those of a 'high church' persuasion were less interested in the Bible. As Kevin Killeen crisply puts it: 'Royalist writers deemed themselves not a whit less biblical and were equally comfortable with the notion that the scriptural past could be transposed onto the present. Indeed, it [biblical literacy] is not infrequently the source of a misdiagnosis of a writer as 'Puritan', when in other respects they are nothing of the sort' (Killeen, *Political Bible*, 6).
[81] Elizabeth Clarke describes Quarles' work as 'the most popular treatment of the Song of Songs in the 1630s' (*Politics, Religion and the Song of Songs*, 84). This may be true if we think only in terms of verse in English, but it seriously underestimates the impact of the many Latin verse versions of and responses to the Song of Songs in this period, of which Sarbiewski's was only one.

preserved in the Portland Collection, for instance, forming together a sequential paraphrase of chapters 1 and 2 of the Song of Songs, are all unattributed: of these, the third and fourth items, in an asclepiad and archilochian metre respectively, are in fact transcriptions of Sarbiewski (*Odes* 2.25 and 4.21), though the other portions are not.[82] A large folio commonplace book, dating probably from the 1630s, records almost in 'real time' one reader's encounter with the 'Polish Horace': the first layer of entries, at the top of each thematically headed page, is confined largely to classical texts, especially Horace, Seneca and Boethius. At this point, however, the compiler of the manuscript apparently began to read Sarbiewski and has enthusiastically added a very large number of citations and cross-references to Sarbiewksi's Latin verse. The Sarbiewski references here extend well beyond the limited selection of Hils' 1646 volume, and in any case the book almost certainly predates that publication.[83]

The vogue for versions of the Song of Songs could be combined with other fashionable features. Joseph Beaumont's poem on Jesus sleeping between Mary's breasts ('Jesus inter Ubera Mariae'), for instance, echoes the breastfeeding imagery we find in Herbert and several Jesuit poets; its subtitle ('Cantel. 6.') draws attention to the repeated borrowings from the Song of Songs:

> In the coolnesse of the day
>   The old Worlds Even, *God* all undrest went downe
>   Without His Roab, without His Crowne,
> Into His private garden, there to lay
>   On spicey Bed
>   His Sweeter Head.
>
> There He found two Beds of Spice,
> A double Mount of Lillies, in whose Top
>   Two milkie Fountaines bubled up.
> He soon resolv'd: & well I like, He cries,
>   My table spread
>   Upon my Bed.[84]
>
>   (1–12)

---

[82] Nottingham University Library, MS PwV 1456. Both poems were included in Hils' 1646 volume of selected poems with parallel translations. I have not yet been able to trace the source of the other elements.

[83] CUL MS Dd. IX. 59. Datable excerpts include many from Burton's *Anatomy of Melancholy*, first published in 1621, and Farnaby's *Florilegium epigrammatum Graecorum*, first published in 1629. The volume also includes quotations from Donne and Shakespeare which are not recorded in the *CELM*. The compiler drew upon a cluster of works printed in the early 1630s, but none after 1634. It is very likely that the volume therefore dates from the mid-1630s.

[84] As printed in Robinson (ed.), *Minor Poems of Joseph Beaumont*, 16–17, based on an autograph MS which is no longer available. The poem is also found in Bod. MS Rawl. Poet. 62, fol. 18^{r-v}.

A copy of Beaumont's poem appears in Bod. MS Rawl. poet. 62, a miscellany of verse compiled in Cambridge between 1627 and 1643; Beaumont was in Cambridge between 1631 and 1644 and this poem probably belongs to the 1630s. The conversational tone here has much in common with Herbert, while the imagery is influenced above all by fashionable Jesuit verse: compare for instance Bettini's poem 'Jesus lactens' and its companion piece, with the Song of Songs imagery even more overt, 'Jesus lactens. Qui pascitur inter Lilia &c' ('Jesus at the breast. He who feeds among the Lilies &c'):

> Pupule virginei
> Sinus inter lilia
> Instar agni pasceris.
> Idem es virgineae
> Suave vallis lilium.
> Vivum nempe lilium
> Viva pascunt lilia.[85]
>
> *Little boy among the lilies*
> *Of the virgin breast*
> *Like a lamb you graze.*
> *You are, too, the sweet*
> *Lily of the virgin's valley.*
> *Living lilies, then,*
> *Feed a living lily.*

Bettini makes frequent use of anacreontics and other metres with very short lines, like a song. The metre here is stichic trochaic dimeter catalectic, a very simple (and unclassical) form which suggests childish simplicity, but which is in fact carefully chosen: it is the metre used by Beza for his Latin version of the Song of Songs, to which this brief lyric alludes. Overall, Bettini's style is quite different to Sarbiewski's larger-scale Horatianism, though it has many points of contact with the poetry of, for instance, Herrick's *Hesperides* (1648) and the 'Anacreontiques' included in Abraham Cowley's 1656 *Poems*.

Similarly, a Latin verse paraphrase of the Song of Songs, presented in 1647 by Matthew Robinson (1628–94) to his tutor Zachary Cowdrey (1618–84), is plainly strongly influenced by Sarbiewski, although written entirely in elegiac couplets. Unlike Sarbiewski, who cites only a few words of the Latin scriptural text at the head of each poem, this manuscript presents the full biblical text, in Latin, on the left-hand page with the very

---

[85] As it appears in Wright, *Delitiae delitiarum* (1637), 77.

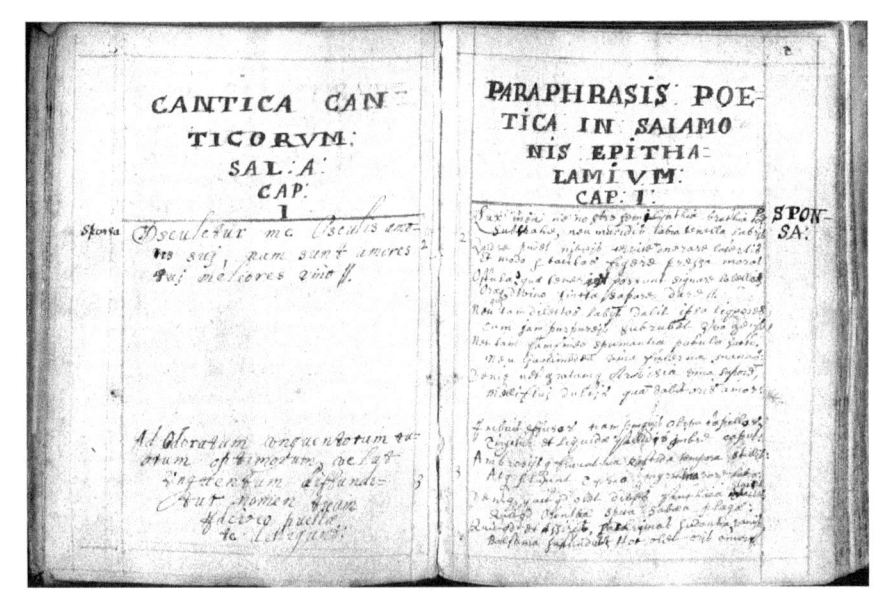

Figure 2 St John's College, Cambridge, MS O.65, pp. 1–2.
By permission of the Master and Fellows of St John's College, Cambridge.

expansive verse paraphrase on the right-hand side (Figure 2).[86] Both the choice of text and the dedicatory poem emphasize the piety of the gift and its dependence upon Cowdrey's teaching, but also employ rather erotic and familial language: Robinson describes himself as a nestling recently fallen from his mother's nest, casts Cowdrey as his father, and describes the warmth of their relationship with imagery of kissing and fondling.[87]

While the element of scriptural paraphrase in Sarbiewski was particularly appealing to Protestant poets, it is unsurprising that English Catholic poets were also influenced by his style. Bod. MS Tanner 330, for instance, preserves a collection of 39 Latin poems, by John Aston, apparently a member of the Catholic and royalist Aston family, dated 1648.[88] The

---

[86] St John's College, Cambridge, MS O.65. See also Queen's College, Oxford MS 347, containing a Latin verse paraphrase of the Song of Songs, followed by religious epigrams, by Francis Vaux, dated 1658.
[87] St John's College, Cambridge, MS O.65. The prefatory pages are unpaginated.
[88] I have not been able to determine exactly how this John Aston fits in to the family, but Sir Arthur Aston (c.1590–1649) was a royalist army officer and a Catholic; Herbert Aston (1614–88/9) was a poet whose 1630s miscellany is Beinecke Library, MS Osborn b. 4. Herbert's sister Constance Fowler also compiled a manuscript miscellany (Huntington Library, MS HM 904) of poetry to and by her circle of largely Catholic family and friends, including the poet Richard Fanshawe.

collection is neatly presented, with a separate title page, and looks like material prepared for publication. (I have not however been able to trace any record of its printing.) It is unmistakably influenced by the style of Sarbiewski and other Jesuit poets: the 39 poems are mostly odes on scriptural and devotional topics, including one based explicitly on the Song of Songs (fols. 15ᵛ–16ᵛ), though with overall a much greater emphasis on Marian devotion than in Sarbiewksi himself.

Richard Crashaw, a friend of Cowley, who became a Catholic in France before his early death in 1649, employs an unmistakably Sarbievian mode to describe, not an allegory of the Church, or of the body and the soul, but the Assumption of Mary, a specifically Roman Catholic doctrine:

> Harke shee is called, the parting houre is come,
> Take thy farewel poore world, heaven must go home.
> A peece of heavenly Light purer and brighter
> Then the chast stars, whose choice Lamps come to light her.
> While through the christall orbs clearer then they
> Shee climbes, and makes a farre more milky way;
> Shee's call'd againe, harke how th'immortall Dove
> Sighs to his silver mate: rise up my Love,
> Rise up my faire, my spotlesse one,
> The Winter's past, the raine is gone:
> The Spring is come, the Flowers appeare,
> No sweets since thou art wanting here.
>
> (1–12)[89]

The doctrine of the Assumption of the Virgin Mary has no specific scriptural basis; instead, this poem depends primarily upon the Song of Songs: the Bridegroom's address to the Bride is recast as the Holy Spirit (or perhaps Christ) calling to Mary. Lines 9–12 are a version of Song of Songs 2.10–12:

> My beloved spake, and said unto me, Rise up, my love, my fair
>   one, and come away.
> For, lo, the winter is past, the rain is over and gone;
> The flowers appear on the earth; the time of the singing of birds
>   is come, and the voice of the turtle is heard in our land . . .

The bride of the Song of Songs is twice described as a dove (2.14 and 5.2), though the detail of a *silver* dove (line 8) alludes probably to an enigmatic portion of Psalm 68 ('Though ye have lien among the pots, yet shall ye be as the wings of a dove covered with silver, and her feathers with yellow

---

[89] *Steps to the Temple* (1646), 90. On the formal differences between this version of the poem and that published in 1652, see Chapter 5.

gold', verse 13).⁹⁰ The opening movement of the poem, however, recalls Sarbiewski, *Odes* 2.5, his best-known poem of spiritual ascent, as much as any specific piece of scripture. The first 12 lines of Sarbiewksi's poem are given here with Hils' translation:

> Humana linquo : tollite praepetem
> Nubesque ventique. Ut mihi devii
>   Montes resedere ! ut volanti
>   Regna procul populosque vastus
> Subegit aër ! Iam radiantia
> Delubra divûm, iam mihi regiae
>   Turres recessere, et relictae in
>   Exiguum tenuantur urbes :
> Totasque, qua se cumque ferunt vagae,
> Despecto gentes. O lacrimabilis
>   Incerta fortunae! O fluentum
>   Principia interitusque rerum!
>   (1–12)

> *Lift me up quickly on your wings,*
>   *Ye Clouds, and Winds; I leave all earthly things.*
> *How Devious Hills give way to mee!*
>   *And the vast ayre brings under, as I fly,*
> *Kingdomes and populous states! see how*
>   *The Glyst'ring Temples of the Gods doe bow;*
> *The glorious Tow'rs of Princes, and*
>   *Forsaken townes, shrunke into nothing, stand:*
> *And as I downward looke, I spy*
>   *Whole Nations every where all scattred lye.*
> *Oh the sad change that Fortune brings!*
>   *The rise and fall of transitory things!*

Sarbiewski's ode produced an entire tradition of imitations, but also belongs itself to a recognizable tradition. Book IV of Bauhusius' *Epigrammata* (1616) begins with a poem titled 'Aspirat ad caelestem patriam' ('He aspires to his heavenly native land'):

> Siderei colles, Diuûm fulgentia templa,
> . . .
> O, ego te quando! quando mea patria cernam!
> . . .
> O amor! ô desiderium! mea fax! mens ignis!
>   Cur me sic uris? cur? quia tam procul es.
>   (1, 5, 19–20)

---

⁹⁰ Mary Sidney's translation of this psalm is discussed in Chapter 3.

O starry hills, gleaming temples of the Gods
...
O when shall I, when shall I ever see you, my native land!
...
O love! o longing! my torch! my fire!
   Why do you burn me like this? Why? Because you are so far away.

Abraham Cowley, Crashaw's close friend, makes use of the same piece of Sarbiewski in a poem, 'The Ecstasie', discussed further below. But one of the most striking features of the impact of Sarbiewski in England is not that this Jesuit poet was popular with fellow Roman Catholics, or with poets within the Church of England whose devotional practice had Catholic elements, but that this style of devotional poetry was almost equally influential upon poets with no such associations. Hils' edition of a selection of Sarbiewski's poetry was published in London in 1646, a year after Robert Hatcher published *Institutio, epithalamium, & militia viri*, printed at his own expense. In the preface, Hatcher uses the political context of civil war in all its horror to explain his attempt to seek consolation not in trivial, but in sacred poetry. The volume is intensely 'Sarbievian': it contains a whole book of odes as well as verse paraphrases of Job 28–31, Proverbs 1–9 and of the Song of Songs, both of the latter works in polymetric form, with different metres employed for each scriptural chapter. The volume also includes an allegorical poem, 'Funus corporis et animae conjugium' ('The death of the body and the marriage of the soul'), with links to the traditional allegorical interpretation of the Song of Songs, and a series of *Emblemata* at the end, with space left for adding images. Hatcher, however, was a Parliamentarian – his collection *Paideutica*, dedicated to the Cambridge university orator and published in 1646, includes material praising Fairfax and Cromwell.[91] He was probably a relative of the Parliamentarian officer and Lincolnshire MP Thomas Hatcher (c.1589–1677).[92]

If Hatcher was a student in Cambridge in the mid-1640s, then he was of a similar age to Andrew Marvell (1621–78), whose poetry of the 1640s and 1650s also shows the marked influence of Sarbiewski. It has often been recognized that the sensuousness of Marvell's 'Garden', which dates probably from the 1650s, derives in part from the biblical tradition of the *hortus*

---

[91] The title poem of this volume, 'Paideutica', is discussed in Chapter 11.
[92] Though not apparently his son, who was called John.

conclusus, especially as it is depicted in the Song of Songs.[93] The combination of erotic content in the Song of Songs with a *non*-erotic interpretative tradition fits well the ambiguities of both 'The Garden' and its Latin companion poem 'Hortus': although handled differently, in both poems plants themselves take on an erotic character.[94] Contemporary commentary on the biblical text is not, however, confined to the Christian allegory of Christ and his Church. Jacob Durfeld's 1633 commentary on the Song of Songs, for instance, glosses the 'hortus' of verse 4:12 ('Hortus conclusus, soror mea sponsa, hortus clausus, fons obsignatus'; 'A garden inclosed is my sister, my spouse; a spring shut up, a fountain sealed') under three allegorical headings: as a natural allegory (that is, a comparison to the beauties, pleasures and implied fertility of an actual garden), a political allegory (representing a flourishing and well-governed kingdom) and finally 'metaphorically, standing for the Church'.[95] Marvell's poem is far removed from a formal commentary; but this kind of juxtaposition of natural, political and religious allegory, typical of biblical and classical commentary of the period, captures something of the polyvalency of imagery in Marvell's garden.

One portion of Andrew Marvell's 'Garden' has already been linked to Sarbiewski by commentators. Sarbiewski's *Odes* 4.21, 'Ex sacro Salomonis Epithalamio', one of the poems included in Hils' volume (and one of many responding directly to the Song of Songs), has been identified as a likely source for one of the most striking passages in 'The Garden':

> What wond'rous life in this I lead!
> Ripe apples drop about my head;
> The luscious clusters of the vine
> Upon my mouth do crush their wine;
> The nectarine and curious peach
> Into my hands themselves do reach;
> Stumbling on melons as I pass,
> Ensnar'd with flow'rs, I fall on grass.
>
> (33–40)

---

[93] Although some scholarship in the last 30 years has suggested a post-Restoration date for the 'Garden' and 'Hortus', I consider this unconvincing. See Moul, 'Date of Marvell's *Hortus*'; and Dzelzainis, 'Issues of Dating'.

[94] This conceit is dealt with at greater length in the Latin poem, in which the poet compares traditionally attractive elements of the female body with their plant equivalents (the colours of flowers, leaves, branches, the whispering noise made by the leaves) and declares the latter superior ('Hortus', 20–4). The poem returns to the motif of preferring plants to women in its latter half, which offers a substantially expanded version of the conceit of the gods now in love not with women themselves, but the trees or plants to which they might be metamorphosed (40–8, compare lines 27–32 of 'The Garden'). For further discussion of this poem, see Moul, 'Date of Marvell's *Hortus*'.

[95] Durfeld, *Commentarius*, 527–9.

This corresponds to Sarbiewski's Latin lines (followed by Hils' translation):

> Cetera non desunt, pronis vindemia pendes
>   Officiosa botris,[96]
> Hîc etiam vulgò violas, albentia vulgò
>   Ungue ligustra leges:
> Ipsa tibi, leti succos oblita priores,
>   Mitia poma cadent ...
>
>   (37–42)
>
> *No want appeares; th'officious Vine doth stand*
>   *With bending clusters to our hand.*
> *Here, thou shalt pick sweet Violets, and there*
>   *Fresh Lillyes all the yeare:*
> *The Apple ripe drops from its stalke to thee,*
>   *From tast of death made free.*

The vine clusters offering themselves to Marvell and the apples falling about him are borrowed from Sarbiewski, but both poems also acknowledge the Fall: whereas Sarbiewski's sweet apples 'leti succos oblita priores' ('have forgotten their former taste of death'), an allusion to the apple eaten by Adam and Eve, Marvell's speaker stumbles on melons, and falls, but only upon grass.[97] Both poems include a kind of pun on the idea of falling without sin: 'I fall on grass'; 'Mitia poma **cadent**'.

This passage of 'The Garden' has no close equivalent in 'Hortus', but Marvell also drew on Sarbiewski for a passage which is present only in the Latin poem. Hils' selection also included Sarbiewski's fourth epigram, 'Veniat delectus meus in hortum suum. *Cant.* 5', which I quote below in its entirety, followed by Hils' translation:

> Pulcher Amor sumpsit rudis instrumenta coloni,
>   Et sua deposuit tela suasque faces:
> Et manibus stivam rapuit; castique laboris
>   Ad sua ruricolas junxit aratra boves.
> Ilicet, ut facili subvertit vomere corda,
>   Castaque virginibus Gratia crevit agris;
> Flos, ait, unus abest: sunt cetera millia florum;
>   Ut nullus possit, *Christe*, deesse, Veni.

---

[96] Botrus, i, (f), *the grape*. Unattested with this meaning in classical Latin, this transliteration of the Greek βότρυς appears in the Vulgate (Micah 7:1). It is also found in the form 'botrys' in Pliny, meaning the plant artemisia or mugwort; but 'grapes' are clearly what are meant here.

[97] Neither Smith (ed.), *Poems of Andrew Marvell*, nor Haan, *Latin Poetry* note this additional parallel between Marvell's English poem and Sarbiewski.

Love takes the tooles of a rude Country clowne,
  His owne Artill'ry, and his torch layes downe;
With staffe in's hand, Oxen to th'Plow he set
  For tillage, and such honest labour fit;
Straight, as he turn'd up hearts with easie share,
  And grace i'th'virgin-furrowes did appeare,
'Mongst thousand others, one flower, quoth he, is mist:
  That none may wanting be, come thou, O Christ.

This epigram resembles closely the passage in 'Hortus' in which Love retreats to a garden which both is and is not presented in erotic terms:

> Hic Amor, exutis crepidatus inambulat alis,
> Enerves arcus & stridula tela reponens,
> Invertitque faces, nec se cupit usque timeri;
> Aut exporrectus jacet, indormitque pharetrae
> Non auditurus quanquam Cytherea vocarit;
> Nequitias referunt nec somnia vana priores.
>   Laetantur Superi, defervescente tyranno ...
>   (*Hortus*, 32–8)

Here Love, stripped of his wings, walks around in sandals,
Setting aside his unstrung bows and his whistling weapons,
And turns his torches upside down, not wishing to be always feared;
Or he lies outstretched, and falls asleep upon his quiver
So that he won't hear even though Venus calls him;
And his empty dreams tell nothing of his earlier crimes.
  The Gods above rejoice, now that the tyrant is calming down ...

There are several parallels here which suggest a direct influence: compare in particular Sarbiewski's 'sua deposuit **tela** suasque **faces**' (2) and Marvell's '**tela** reponens, / Invertitque **faces**' (33–4).[98] Possible further links include Marvell's 'invertit' (34) and Sarbiewski 'subvertit' (5, though there referring to the metaphorical 'ploughing' of hearts), and the lines '**Virgineae** quem non suspendit **Gratia** formae?' ('Hortus', 20, 'whom does the Grace of a girl's beauty not capture?') and 'Castaque **virginibus Gratia** crevit agris' (*Ep.* 4.6, 'Chaste Grace grew in virgin fields'). 'Gratia' in Marvell must mean (primarily) 'beauty' whereas in Sarbiewksi it is functioning as a kind of pun – 'virginibus Gratia' does not in fact refer

---

[98] Haan, *Latin Poetry*, 81 suggests that the details of Cupid's weaponry at 'Hortus', 32–5 might be indebted to the description of the Rose as bearing Cupid's weapons, in Hawkins, *Partheneia Sacra* (1633). The parallels with Sarbiewski are however closer than to Hawkins, both in their context and details.

to the beauty of virgins, but to the 'grace' that grows in the previously untilled 'fields'. Love's new kind of labour cultivates grace in hearts not previously 'worked' by the plough. Sarbiewski's poem is about the difference between Amor as Cupid, concerned with youthful beauty; and Amor as divine Love, concerned only for men's hearts.

It is noticeable that Marvell's two poems employ language which is suggestive of religious metaphor without quite making it explicit; this sense of 'latent' religious feeling is derived in part from the religious content of his models. Sarbiewksi's combination in *Ep.* 4 of the Song of Songs with the language of Latin love elegy echoes aspects of both 'The Garden' and 'Hortus': the biblical elements are more marked in the former and the classical parallels in the latter. Moreover, a reader who encountered Sarbiewski's epigram in its original context, did so as part of a sequence: the whole epigram book is subtitled 'sua de Diuino Amore Epigrammata' ('his epigrams on Divine Love') and 26 of the first 40 epigrams, as well as several later ones, concern either Love ('Amor'), or the Beloved of the Song of Songs, and often both. Though some recent critics have denied a significant religious element to 'The Garden', recognizing the Sarbievian elements in Marvell's paired poems supports a religious interpretation.

The Garden-State

Marvell's Love retreats into the garden only to find that the plants within it can rival any human beauty. This motif of an enclosed world which harbours superior versions of or alternatives to all that is beyond it can be turned to powerful political effect. In the only explicitly 'garden' poem of Mildmay Fane's *Otia sacra* (1648), the secluded and self-sufficient garden of sensory delight is also – as in Shakespeare's *Richard II* (II.1 and III.4) – the 'Anglia Hortus', the garden of England herself.[99] If the royalists in defeat were tempted to imagine themselves as a state within a state, so too, after the Restoration, were those who remained separate from the established Church, including the first great English hymn-writer, the dissenter poet Issac Watts:

---

[99] Fane, *Otia Sacra*, 133. Leishman notes that lines 1–5 of Fane's poem are echoed directly by Marvell in 'Upon Appleton House', 321–4 (Leishman, *Art of Marvell's Poetry*, 283–4).

The Church the Garden of Christ
Sol. Song 4.12, 14, 15. and 5.1

We are a Garden wall'd around,
Chosen and made peculiar Ground;
A little Spot inclos'd by Grace
Out of the World's wide Wilderness.

Like Trees of Myrrh and Spice we stand,
Planted by God the Father's Hand;
And all his Springs in Sion flow,
To make the young Plantation grow ...[100]

Watts is writing long after the Restoration, but this fine hymn, based also upon the Song of Songs, draws some element of its separatist power from the royalist poetry of the 1640s and 1650s: in the latter part of the seventeenth century, dissenters, like the royalists of an earlier generation, found themselves politically isolated and in retreat. Indeed, there is clear evidence of Watts turning in his youth precisely to the poetry of the mid-century. The 1715 edition of his collection *Horae Lyricae* includes 'Meditation in a Grove', a poem which, like Marvell's 'Garden', offers an erotic description of an explicitly non-erotic landscape, and works its own variant upon Marvell's inscribed trees:

Sweet Muse, descend and bless the Shade,
 And bless the Evening Grove;
Business and Noise and Day are fled,
 And every Care but Love.

But hence, ye wanton Young and Fair,
 Mine is a purer Flame;
No *Phillis* shall infect the Air,
 With her unhallowed Name.

...

His [Jesus'] Charms shall make my Numbers flow,
 And hold the falling Floods,
While Silence sits on every Bough,
 And bends the list'ning Woods.

 I'll carve our Passion on the Bark,
  And every wounded Tree

---

[100] First published in *Hymns and Spiritual Songs* (1707), and probably composed in the late 1690s. Text from Bishop, *Hymns and Spiritual Songs*. The garden (the Church) goes on to invite the Beloved (Christ) to enter (17–18).

>   Shall drop and bear some mystic Mark
>   That *Jesus* dy'd for me.
>
>   The Swains shall wonder when they read
>   Inscrib'd on all the Grove,
>   That Heaven itself came down, and bled
>   To win a Mortal's Love.
>   (1–8, 17–28)[101]

The erotic poetics of the Song of Songs, especially as it was recast as Christian devotional verse by Sarbiewski and others, is of enormous importance for understanding English religious poetry in the seventeenth century. Models of this kind provided a poetic style and emotional register that take us from George Herbert to Isaac Watts. If Horace and the Song of Songs are the foundational texts for Sarbiewski, Horace and Sarbiewski played the same role, by his own account, for the young dissenter poet:

> The Inscriptions to particular Friends are warranted and defended by the Practise of the two best *Lyric* Writers *Horace* and *Casimire* [Sarbiewski]: And tho' the Authority of the first be more Venerable, yet if in some Instances I prefer the latter, I pray the Criticks to forgive me; and I hope my Friends will excuse the Freedom of the Address.[102]

Watts begins his version of Psalm 23 – the only psalm paraphrased in Herbert's *Temple* – as follows:

>   The Lord my shepherd is
>   I shall be well supplied;
>   Since he is mine and I am his
>   What can I want beside?[103]

In this version, the third line is unscriptural, but canonical in another sense, since it is quoted almost directly from Herbert (who has 'While he is mine and I am his'). Herbert's Psalm 23, one of the least regarded poems in *The Temple* by modern scholars, was popular during the seventeenth century.[104] Herbert's line, borrowed by Watts, is derived not from the Psalm itself, but from the Song of Songs: by including it in his psalm translation, Herbert points towards the tradition of interpreting the Song of Songs as referring to the relationship between God and the individual

---

[101] Watts, *Horae Lyricae* (1715), 115–17. This poem not included in the first two editions of 1706 and 1707.
[102] Watts, *Horae Lyricae* (1706), sig. A6ᵛ.
[103] First printed in Watts, *Psalms of David Imitated* (1719).
[104] Ray, 'Herbert Allusion Book', 178.

soul. By alluding to Herbert, Watts in turn endorses that interpretative tradition and also indicates the importance both of Herbert and of the Song of Songs for his own devotional poetry.

Cowley to Watts

The preface to Watt's *Horae Lyricae* (1706) resembles in several respects the preface to Cowley's *Poems*, published fifty years earlier: like Cowley, Watts champions divine poetry, and biblical over classical themes, and like Cowley, he stresses the relative limitations of classical myth as a poetic subject compared to biblical stories and the teachings of Christianity (though here Watts emphasizes the New Testament over the Old). Like Cowley, Watts draws attention to the role of 'Pindariques' in his collection (though unlike Cowley, they are not printed in a distinct 'book', but scattered throughout *Horae Lyricae*). Finally, Watts' description of his imitation of Sarbiewski is close to Cowley's explanation of how he has imitated Pindar:

> The Imitations of that Noblest *Latin* Poet of Modern Ages *Casimire Sarbiewski* of *Poland* would need no Excuse, did they but arise to the Beauty of the Original. I have often taken the Freedom to add ten or twenty Lines, or to leave out as many, that I might suit my Song more to my own Design, or because I found it Impossible to present the Force, the Fineness, and the Fire of his Expression in our Language. I wish some *English* Pen would import some of the Treasures of that rich Genius and bless our Nation.[105]

Cowley's comments on his imitation of Pindar are very similar:

> Upon this ground [the deficiencies of all close translations], I have in these two *Odes* of *Pindar* taken, left out, and added what I please; nor make it so much my aim to let the Reader know precisely what he spoke, as what was his *way* and *manner* of speaking; which has not been yet (that I know of) introduced into *English*, though it be the noblest and highest kind of writing in Verse.[106]

Indeed, though not acknowledged by Cowley, Sarbiewski represents a further link between the two collections. Cowley's poem 'The Exstasie' is in fact a kind of blended paraphrase of Sarbiewski, *Odes* 2.5 and the assumption of Elijah, in 2 Kings 2.[107] Cowley gives no indication of his

---

[105] Watts, *Horae Lyricae* (1706), sig. A6^{r-v}. [106] Cowley, *Poems* (1656), sig. Aaa2^v.
[107] Numbered *Odes* 2.5 in Hils' 1646 edition of selected odes from Sarbiewski with facing translation (Hils, *Odes of Casimire*, 16–25); in other editions, however, it is number 5.9, e.g. Sarbiewski,

models, either in Sarbiewski or in the Bible, though his first line ('I leave *Mortality*, and things below') is a close translation of Sarbiewski's opening phrase ('Humana linquo').

> 1.
> I Leave *Mortality*, and things below;
> I have no time in *Complements* to waste,
>   *Farewel* to'ye all in haste,
>   For I am *call'd* to go.
> A *Whirlwind* bears up my dull Feet,
> Th'officious *Clouds* beneath them meet.
>   And (Lo!) I *mount*, and (Lo!)
> How small the biggest Parts of *Earths* proud *Tittle* show!
>
> 2.
> Where shall I find the noble *Brittish* Land?
> Lo, I at last a *Northern Spec* espie,
>   Which in the *Sea* does lie,
>   And seems a *Grain* o'th' *Sand*!
>   For this will any *sin*, or *Bleed*?
>   Of *Civil Wars* is this the *Meed*?
>   And is it this, alas, which we
> (Oh *Irony* of *Words*!) do call *Great Britainie*?

Odes 2.5 was at this time one of the most widely quoted, excerpted and translated of Sarbiewski's odes, and was certainly widely known.[108] Strikingly, this is the only one of the *Pindarique Odes* to which Cowley provides no notes, and it is also the only ode composed in regular (that is, precisely repeating) stanzas. Despite Cowley's fondness for self-conscious self-annotation, he does not draw attention to this point.

Before switching to material derived primarily from the biblical ascent of Elijah, Cowley returns to Sarbiewski. The sixth stanza corresponds to the final eight lines of the Latin poem (both given below), though Cowley modestly makes less of himself than Sarbiewski does and adds a reference to St Paul:

> Where am I now? *Angels* and *God* is here;
> An unexhausted *Ocean* of *delight*
>   Swallows my *senses* quite,
>   And drowns all *What*, or *How*, or *Where*.

Lyricorum Libri V (1647), 294–7. The imitations by both Cowley and Watts are discussed in Hardie, *Celestial Aspirations*. I am grateful to Philip Hardie for sharing this work with me in advance of publication.

[108] For other imitations of this poem, see Fordoński and Urbański (eds.), *Casimir Britannicus*.

> Not *Paul*, who first did thither pass,
> And this great *Worlds Columbus* was,
> 　　The *tyrannous pleasure* could express.
> Oh 'tis *too much* for *Man*! but let it nere be *less*.
> 　　　　　　　　(41–8)

> Suoque semper terra minor globo
> Iamiamque cerni difficilis suum
> 　　Vanescit in punctum? ô refusum
> 　　　　Numinis Oeanum! Ô carentem
>
> Mortalitatis portubus insulam!
> O clausa nullis marginibus freta!
> 　　Haurite anhelantem, & perenni
> 　　　　*Sarbivium* glomerate fluctu.
> 　　　　　　(81–8, final lines)

> *The earth which alwayes lesse hath beene*
> *Then's Globe, and now, just now can scarce be seene,*
> *　Into it's point doth vanish, see!*
> *Oh the brim'd Ocean of the Deitie!*
> *　Oh Glorious Island richly free*
> *From the cold Harbours of mortality!*
> *　Yee boundlesse seas, with endlesse flouds of rest*
> *Girt round* Sarbivius *your panting Priest.*

Though composed in alcaics, both the sublimity and the self-referentialiy of Sarbiewski's poem recall Pindar; it is unsurprising that Cowley, actively engaged in the imitation of Pindar himself, should have been attracted by the poem. Watts' early poem, 'God Incomprehensible', written in irregular Pindarics of the Cowleian kind, suggests in turn the influence of both Sarbiewski and Cowley, as well as Crashaw and Milton:

> 　　　　　　I
> 　Far in the Heav'ns my God retires,
> 　　My God, the point of my Desires,
> 　　And hides his Lovely Face;
> 　When he descends within my View
> 　He charms my Reason to pursue,
> But leaves it tir'd and fainting in th'unequal Chase.
>
> 　　　　　　II
> 　Or if I reach unusual height,
> 　　Till near his Presence brought;
> There Floods of Glory check my Flight,
> Cramp the bold Pinions of my Wit
> 　　And all untune my Thought;

> Plung'd in a Sea of Light I roll,
> Where Wisdom, Justice, Mercy Shines;
> Infinite Rays in Crossing Lines
> Beat thick Confusion on my Sight, and overwhelm my Soul.[109]

Watts' devout version invokes the sublimity of Pindaric flight and imagines it modestly constrained by the vastly greater glory of God. Watts pursues God with Reason, though Reason is inevitably defeated by such an 'unequal Chase' (6), in lines which point towards the end of Crashaw's 'Answer for Hope', itself a reply to Cowley: 'True Hope's a glorious huntress, and her chase, – / The God of nature in the field of grace!' (47–8). Formally, the long final lines at the end of each stanza recall Milton's 'Nativity Ode'. As in Sarbiewski, the poet imagines himself 'Plung'd in a Sea of Light' (12) and ends the poem drowned in the 'trackless Seas of Light' (28) of the divine.[110]

Such extravagant Pindaric verse, however, is not the poetry on which Watts' reputation has rested. If his name is known at all today, it is for his hymns; in the eighteenth and nineteenth centuries he was also famous as a writer for children.[111] In both cases, he is associated with a masterful ability to distil religious teaching into simple, elegant verse which is easy to sing and to recite: indeed, many of his hymns are still sung today. Nevertheless, there is a traceable line from his earliest work, inspired by the baroque stylistics of Cowley and Sarbiewski, to his mature style. The early poem 'Breathing towards the Heavenly Country' for instance, is based, as the headnote in the 1706 edition of *Horae Lyricae* makes clear, on Sarbiewski, *Odes* 1.19. Sarbiewski's ode is in an asclepiad metre, but Watts' poem, in the fashion of the time, is a kind of dithyrambic or irregular Pindaric without stanza divisions:

> The Beauty of my Native Land
> Immortal Love inspires;
> I burn, I burn with strong Desires,
> And sigh and wait the high Command.
> There glides the Moon her shining Way,
> And shoots my Heart thro' with a Silver Ray;
> Upward my Heart aspires:

---

[109] Watts, *Horae Lyricae* (1706), 16.
[110] In general, Watts' Pindarism is shaped by both Sarbiewski and Cowley. Other poems by Watts modelled upon Sarbiewski include 'False Greatness' (see Sarbiewski, *Odes* 4.34), ''Tis Dangerous to Follow the Multitude' (*Odes* 4.10) and 'The Kingdom of the Wise Man' (*Odes* 4.3).
[111] Lewis Carroll's poem 'How doth the little crocodile' is a parody of Watts' 'How doth the little bumblebee'.

> A thousand Lamps of Golden Light
> Hung high in vaulted Azure charm my Sight,
> And wink and becken with their Amorous Fires.[112]

Like Cowley's ode, Watts' poem combines a Christian hope of heaven with an Old Testament motif, of Moses' longing for the Promised Land; he later reworked the theme as the hymn 'The Prospect of Heaven makes Death easy':

> There is a land of pure delight
> Where saints immortal reign;
> Infinite day excludes the night,
> And pleasures banish pain.
>
> There everlasting spring abides
> And never withering flowers:
> Death, like a narrow sea, divides
> This heav'nly land from ours ...
>
> Could we but climb where Moses stood
> And view the landscape o'er
> Not Jordan's streams nor death's cold flood
> Should fright us from this shore.

As Cowley was stimulated by the extravagant imagery of Crashaw and Sarbiewski to experiment with Pindaric form, here we find movement in the reverse direction: in his mature poetry, Watts distils the religious passion of Crashaw, Cowley and Sarbiewski back into a disciplined and impersonal form, suitable for congregational singing, which is both formally closer to the stanzaic structures of Horace (and Sarbiewski, whose lyric is entirely in Horatian metres) and recalls the simplicity of diction associated with Herbert.[113] In its impersonality, hymnody draws upon the long tradition of moralizing verse which, as we saw in Chapter 1, also has roots in Horatian lyric and its imitation.

Religious Poetry in Practice: Mixture

For organizational reasons, this book discusses various kinds of religious verse – including scriptural paraphrase, epigram and devotional lyric – separately, despite the many areas of overlap between them. These are not invalid distinctions: many landmark collections of verse were organized

---

[112] Watts, *Horae Lyricae* (1706), 108.
[113] See Fordoński, 'Sarbiewski and English Dissenting Poets'.

generically, and certain poets and periods are associated only with a specific type. In practice, however, readers, and many poets too, mingled these modes, and well into the eighteenth century continued to produce poems in forms – such as psalm paraphrase or moralizing lyric – which in this book have been discussed primarily in relation to sixteenth- rather than seventeenth-century poetics. It is not that the kind of imaginative devotional poem typical of Sarbiewski and inspired by the sensuality of the Song of Songs *replaced* the tradition of psalm paraphrase: the two are frequently, if not typically, found together, though the style in which psalms were paraphrased was also influenced by changing fashions. This brief final section gives some examples of how religious verse of all kinds was, in practice, collected and read.

Peter du Moulin's volume of *Sylva Variorum* published in his *Poematum Libelli Tres* (1671) but including poetry dating from considerably earlier, contains a range of Latin verse typical of the mid-seventeenth century, all dependent upon scriptural sources, albeit at various removes. It includes three psalm paraphrases (Psalms 137, 44 and 98), and three poems obviously dependent upon the Song of Songs: 'Sponsae lapsus & poenitentia, Cant. 5.2', 'Sponsa mittit ad Sponsum' and 'Sponsus mittit ad Sponsam'.[114] In addition, one Latin poem titled 'Beatus ille' suggests both the first psalm (which begins in Latin 'Beatus vir qui ...') and Horace, *Epodes* 2 ('Beatus ille qui ...'). In fact, Du Moulin's 'Beatus ille' poem is neither a scriptural paraphrase nor a direct response to *Epodes* 2, but a more generalizing moral poem, in the tradition discussed in Chapter 1. The following poem, 'Arx mea Deus' ('God my refuge'), also contains echoes of the first psalm.

The poems in this sequence have an emotional intensity familiar from many of the examples discussed in this chapter: in addition to the distinctive Song of Songs imagery, many of Du Moulin's hymns are marked by Sarbievian tropes of exaltation, inspiration and the removal of agency.[115] In a sequence of hymns which follow the statements of the creed, the third, 'And [I believe] in Jesus Christ his only son our Lord', begins in the Sarbievian high-style, with no immediate point of contact with the statement of the title:

---

[114] Du Moulin, Πάρεργα (1671); BL MS Add. 10446 appears to be the manuscript copy of this edition prepared for the printer.
[115] For a full discussion of the 'exaltation' motif, though without reference to Du Moulin, see Hardie, *Celestial Aspirations*.

> Quò me tumentem, Christe rapis tui?
> Quid palpitanti pectore fervidum
> Exultat? Ohe jam micantes
> Est animus super ire zonas.
>
> $(1-4)^{116}$

> *Where are you taking me, Christ, filled with you as I am?*
> *What feverish excitement is leaping*
> *In my trembling breast? O now it is my will and delight*
> *To go beyond the glittering zones.*

The poem continues with an extended vision of heaven. It has much in common with Sarbiewski's *Odes* 2.5 and the tradition of poems deriving from it.[117] Both the ninth and the eleventh hymns, titled also from the creed ('Thence he shall come to judge the living and the dead' and '([I believe in the] Holy Catholic Church, the Communion of Saints'), similarly begin with the imagery of the Song of Songs:

> Qualis absentis cupiens mariti,
> Heu procul longùm peregre morantis,
> Nupta cui castum generosa pulsat
> > Flamma pudorem
> > (Hymn 9.1–4)[118]

> *Like a bride who longs for her absent husband*
> *Who alas is long delayed far away from home,*
> *A bride in whom a noble flame drives*
> > *Her modest chastity.*

> Conjugio Nymphê Christi dignata superbo,
> Te canimus summi Nata Nurúsque Dei.
> > (Hymn 11.1–2)[119]

> *Nymph [i.e. the Church], worthy of the wonderful marriage of Christ,*
> > *We sing of you: Daughter and Bride of the greatness of God.*

But the most vivid demonstrations of the ways in which people wrote and read religious verse, juxtaposing now-traditional forms alongside new and fashionable ones, are found in manuscript collections. Bod. MS Tanner 466, for instance, a probably 1650s collection made by William Sancroft (1617–93), later archbishop of Canterbury, is an enormously rich and

---

[116] Du Moulin, Πάρεργα, 14.
[117] Though writing primarily of eighteenth-century verse in English, Penelope Wilson has acknowledged the influence of Sarbiewski 2.5 upon the whole genre of what she describes as 'ecstasy narratives' ('Pindar', 164).
[118] Du Moulin, Πάρεργα, 42.   [119] Du Moulin, Πάρεργα, 50.

varied selection of religious verse in both Latin and English, including, for instance, a series of Nativity poems by Milton, William Cartwright and Martin Llewelyn (fols. 32^r–6^v), hymns by Donne, Wotton, Cartwright and Milton, and a very large quantity of scriptural verse paraphrase, including psalm paraphrases by Henry Wotton, Donne, Crashaw, Herbert, Milton, Thomas Mead, Hugo Grotius and Cowley, as well as scriptural poems by Joannes Tollenarius (Ecclesiastes 12:1–7), Clement Paman (Judges 11, in quasi-dramatic form) and three of Cowley's Pindaric odes with scriptural elements ('Isaiah 34', 'The Plagues of Egypt' and 'The Exstasie'). It also includes twelve extracts from Cowley's *Davideis*, five in Latin and seven in English, including Cowley's Latin paraphrase of Psalm 114 which is part of *Davideis* 1.[120] In his formal tastes, Sancroft is influenced by the fashions of the time – many poems are in Pindarics or related forms, including Crashaw's polymetric paraphrase of Psalm 1 and the dithyrambic chorus to Hugo Grotius' play *Adamus Exul* (1601), itself a free paraphrase of Psalm 104, which is discussed briefly in Chapter 5. Sancroft's annotations supply scriptural sources for several works – such as the Grotius chorus and Cowley's 'The Exstasie' (based partly on 2 Kings 2) – which are not indicated in the published versions. Overall, such a sequence demonstrates the range of contemporary poetry, in both Latin and English, which could 'belong' together in a devotional context, and also suggests how a poet like Cowley could be read and understood in primarily scriptural terms as a 'Davidic' poet. By the mid-eighteenth century Watts himself had been absorbed into this tradition.[121]

If anything, readers' tastes appear more open in their selection and assembly of religious verse than for poetry of other kinds, and less constrained by contemporary trends. Devout readers of one denomination apparently had little difficulty in appreciating poetry associated with another, and strongly scriptural verse in particular, even when composed in forms that must by then have seemed old-fashioned, had considerable longevity, presumably because readers' familiarity with the scriptural text itself remained unchanged. By the 1730s Watts was embarrassed enough by his erotically inflected religious verse, so redolent of the mid-late seventeenth century, that he felt the need to add an explanatory note – but he did not remove it.[122]

---

[120] The latest datable source for Sancroft's selection is Cowley's *Poems* of 1656.
[121] See e.g. Society of Friends Archive, MS Vol S 193/5, a Quaker manuscript described in Chapter 1, in which Watts' hymns are paraphrased alongside translations of Buchanan's psalms.
[122] This note appears first in the 1736 edition.

CHAPTER 7

Epigram Culture and Literary Bilingualism in Early Modern England

The rise of the epigram, that most distinctively early modern genre, emerged from the confluence of several elements of literary culture, including an admiration for humanist Latin epigrams; a distinct though related tradition of moralizing and didactic distichs and other short poems; the role of verse composition in schools and universities; and the increasingly important role of translation and bilingual circulation. This chapter outlines the relationship between Latin and English epigram in England between the mid-sixteenth and the later seventeenth century: in doing so, it builds upon previous work which has concentrated on the English-language tradition, and extends the chronological range of the existing studies, none of which ranges beyond 1640.[1] By focusing in particular upon the ways in which epigrams circulated in the manuscript record, it considers epigram culture as a bilingual literary phenomenon, the bilingualism of which evolved over the course of the later sixteenth and seventeenth centuries, and demonstrates how the typical 'witty', topical and frequently satiric epigram, which most critical work has prioritized, sits within a broader and on average more serious and more generalizing literary phenomenon.

The ubiquity of epigram in early modern England is a basic point about the literary culture of the period but it requires emphasis if only because epigrams are not a particularly familiar feature of poetic culture, insofar as it survives, today. Perhaps for this reason, early modern epigram has attracted relatively little critical attention in relation to its cultural dominance. The poems or songs that modern English speakers are most likely to know or be able to call to mind tend to be, broadly speaking, lyric in their

---

[1] Doelman, *Epigram in England* (covering 1590–1640); also Whipple, *Martial and the English Epigram* (up to 1616) and Hudson's unfinished *Epigram in the English Renaissance* (until c.1600). Two specific subtypes of English epigram have attracted attention over a wider chronological span, namely epitaph (e.g. Scodel, *English Poetic Epitaph*, and Newstok, *Quoting Death*) and verse libel (e.g. Bellany, 'Railing Rhymes Revisited', and Bellany and McRae (eds.), *Early Stuart Libels*).

structure and effect. That is not to say there are no modern examples of effective epigram. Two relatively familiar twentieth-century epigrams are, for instance, the following poems by A. E. Housman and Robert Graves:

> Here dead lie we because we did not choose
> To live and shame the land from which we sprung.
> Life, to be sure, is nothing much to lose;
> But young men think it is, and we were young.
> A. E. Housman (1859–1936)

> Love without hope, as when the young bird-catcher
> Swept off his tall hat to the Squire's own daughter,
> So let the imprisoned larks escape and fly
> Singing about her head, as she rode by.
> Robert Graves (1895–1985)

Even so, both of these examples are rather closer to brief lyric than are most epigrams of the early seventeenth century, the period of most intense epigrammatic activity: neither depends on wordplay or lexical ambiguity; both have a message, but neither is straightforwardly or conventionally moralizing; and the Graves piece would be closer to the typical early modern epigram if it had kept back the 'point' of the poem – the slogan 'love without hope' – until the end rather than placing it in the title and first line.

Latin Epigram in the Manuscript Record

It is hard to overstate the prominence of epigram in the manuscript record. At the time of writing, of 22,282 post-medieval Latin poems assigned to a generic form as part of the *NLPEM* project, 13,415 (60.2 per cent) have been classified as epigrams, and of those 860 (6.4 per cent) have so far been identified as being by the Welsh Latin epigrammatist John Owen alone.[2] Such a statistic requires some contextualization: not all Latin poems in this dataset have been assigned a generic category (about 6,000 remain unassigned), and work is ongoing. The project has also adopted an intentionally broad definition of epigram: any short poem (of 10 lines or fewer) on a specific, usually topical, satiric or moralizing subject has been included, as well as a handful of slightly longer items which are explicitly described as epigrams or belong to a sequence of epigrammatic exchange. This includes

---

[2] Data correct at 18 May 2021. The *NLPEM* project has gathered data specifically on post-medieval Latin verse in early modern English manuscripts, excluding classical, late antique and medieval texts, as well as items demonstrably or probably composed before 1550 or after 1720.

religious and scriptural epigrams as well as many other possible categories (emblems; chronograms; commemorative and satiric epigrams and so on); but also mnemonic epigrams; supposedly extempore epigrammatic exchanges; large collections of distichs and monostichs, typical especially of the sixteenth century; as well as some items which are actually quotations from longer works (such as Mantuan), but are functioning within a given manuscript as a self-contained epigram summarizing a particular point or perspective. The numbers of epigram would of course be vastly further increased if English or earlier Latin examples were included.[3]

This habit of extracting epigram-like units from longer works in order to memorize them creates a grey area of items not originally composed as stand-alone poems but sometimes functioning as such: what one mid-seventeenth-century collection describes as 'Sentences Epigrammelike'.[4] The style of many popular school texts, such as Mantuan's *Adulescentia* and Palingenius' *Zodiacus Vitae*, makes them much more readily excerptable than most long classical poems, and the tendency to include pithy and quotable summaries of a given point is characteristic also of much late antique poetry. Such manufactured 'epigrams' may be created for the first time by the compiler of a given manuscript, but they may also be copied from another source. The compiler of one large print collection, *Fasciculus Florum: or, a nosegay of flowers* (1636), for instance, cites Farnaby, Owen and Martial in the preface, and clearly conceives of the work as a collection of epigrams, but in practice includes many items which are 'epigrammatized' extracts from longer works.[5] Moreover, none of the items is attributed, though English translations are (unusually for the date) provided for all of them. Such a collection differs quite markedly from the print anthologies of neo-Latin epigrams, widely used as sources for manuscript miscellanies, which present epigrams grouped by named (well-known, and mostly humanist) authors and without translations.[6] The circulation of individual epigrams was also influenced, especially from the mid-seventeenth century onwards, by some widely read prose works, such as Robert Burton's *Anatomy of Melancholy* (first published 1621), which quotes many Latin epigrams. In summary, the 'epigram' discussed in this

---

[3] *CELM* records, for instance, substantial numbers of English epigrams by Sir John Harington, Sir John Davies and Ben Jonson. The most important Latin epigrammatists, including indeed John Owen himself, do not have a *CELM* entry.
[4] Leeds University Library, MS BC Lt q 18 (c.1650), fol. 6ᵛ.
[5] The editor is named as 'Lerimos Uthalmus': presumably a pseudonym, and probably an anagram. This anthology is described briefly by Doelman, *Epigram in England*, 355.
[6] E.g. Wright, *Delitiae delitiarum* (1637) and Johnston, *Delitiae Poetarum Scotorum* (1637).

chapter is not confined solely to the witty, usually satiric, version of the form associated above all with Martial.[7]

Epigrams are particularly suited to manuscript transcription and circulation, being brief to copy and easily memorized. Of the most frequently found authors of Latin verse in the manuscript corpus, most are represented wholly or largely by epigrams. John Owen, who wrote only Latin epigrams, is by far the most frequently found neo-Latin poet (of any genre, nation or period) in English manuscripts, but other notably popular poets represented largely by epigrams in the manuscript record include George Buchanan, Andrea Alciato, Thomas More, Theodore de Bèze, William Alabaster, Jacopo Sannazaro, George Herbert, Andrew Melville and Hugo Grotius. In many cases, we would not now associate these authors primarily with epigram, and in some cases perhaps not with poetry at all.[8]

In practice, those collecting and translating Latin verse drew upon the full range of Latin epigram from Catullus to the present day. Whereas large organized collections of epigrams often divided material into 'ancient' and 'modern' sections, individuals compiling a personal miscellany, notebook or commonplace book typically drew freely on a wide range of sources and juxtaposed texts of very different periods. Similarly, it is common to find a mixture of types of epigram, and various modes of bilingualism, in a single manuscript. This chapter, unlike existing studies of early modern epigrams, aims to consider how epigrams were created (both by composition and excerpting), read and circulated in early modern England as a whole: that is, across the full range of the period, and taking account of the copying, translation and circulation of classical, medieval and earlier neo-Latin poems as well as contemporary or near-contemporary works.

Epigrams and other related types of brief poem or extract are frequently encountered in bilingual presentation of various kinds, but the patterns of bilingualism associated with epigram culture shift over the course of the second half of the sixteenth and into the seventeenth century. In the mid to late sixteenth century, bi- or multilingual sequences of epigrams are

---

[7] On the critical tendency to dismiss non-satiric epigram as not 'really' epigram, see Crane, '*Intret Cato*'.

[8] On the influence of Beza's epigrams, translations of which are included in Tottel's miscellany, see Prescott, 'English Writers'. Despite the very extensive evidence for the wide reading of Buchanan's Latin psalms, including multiple allusions, cross-references and translations in manuscript, transcriptions of Buchanan's Latin verse are mostly of his epigrams. This is probably in part because the Latin psalms were so frequently owned as a printed book.

typically thematically related, but less likely than in later periods to be recognizably composed of translations or versions of the 'same' poem: many collections from this period, in which epigram was a primarily Latin rather than vernacular form, are in Latin with only a handful of English items. In the late sixteenth and early seventeenth century, the period in which the English epigram came into fashion alongside an intense vogue also for the Latin form, we find a particularly large quantity of epigrammatic 'exchanges' between poets, carried out in one language or both, but typically without many examples of strictly bilingual 'pairs' of poem and translation. From the second third of the seventeenth century onward the 'translating pair', a strictly bilingual epigram, becomes increasingly characteristic: most often, such pairs are composed of Latin text accompanied by English translation; not infrequently, however, we find pairs working the other way round, and the translation of epigrams *into* Latin is increasingly a feature of manuscript material in the late seventeenth and early eighteenth centuries. In the 1590s poets writing English epigrams were conscious that they were importing into English a form which, up to that point, was almost exclusively in Latin; by 1700 the linguistic associations of the 'epigram' were much more equally balanced, and at least for some readers and authors, probably associated *more* strongly with contemporary English satire than with the Latin tradition.

As discussed in Chapter 1, the juxtaposition and relationship between texts in a miscellany is one of the features least well captured by existing catalogues, databases and first-line indices (which, in any case, generally omit Latin material). The *NLPEM* project has experimented with ways to present and analyse these features more systematically: by tagging epigrams accompanied by translations as a distinct category of 'bilingual epigram', for example. The data so far suggests that around 1 in 10 post-medieval Latin epigrams in early modern English miscellanies and commonplace books (excluding large dedicated collections) appears in bilingual presentation: this figure drops if we include very large collections of epigrams (which are more likely to be monolingual), but rises markedly if we look only at collections dated from the mid-seventeenth century onwards.[9] Most scholarship on the English epigram has focused on the early

---

[9] At the time of writing, the *NLPEM* data includes 25 manuscript collections that contain 100–200 Latin epigrams, 3 over 200, 3 over 400, 1 over 700 and 1 with over 1,000. Overall, of 13,415 epigrams, 7,331 (54.6 per cent) are in these large manuscript collections (containing 100 or more epigrams), leaving 6,084 (45.4 per cent) across 551 manuscripts containing between 1 and 99 epigrams each. Of the 7,331 epigrams in large collections, only 293 (4.0 per cent) are bilingual epigrams; 558 (9.2 per cent) of the 6,084 in smaller collections are bilingual.

seventeenth century, and the largest number of surviving Latin epigrams are also from this period; the mid to late seventeenth century, however, is the peak period for the circulation of epigrams in a bilingual format.[10]

Epigram before 1590

Epigrams in English date mainly from after 1590; as a result, there has been relatively little consideration of the largely Latin 'epigram culture' in England before this point.[11] Surviving manuscripts, however, are full of Latin epigram of all periods, and it is clear that the compilers of these manuscripts occasionally – though much less frequently than in later periods – ventured their own English translations, and also that they regularly composed Latin epigrams of the humanist kind themselves. There are two main types of epigrammatic poem at this time: epigrams or 'manufactured' epigrams (created by excerpting larger texts) on moral themes; and epigrams on contemporary or near-contemporary events, often with a marked political or religious agenda (such as poems celebrating the Protestant martyrs of the 1550s, or satirizing the papacy).[12] In this period, there are strikingly *few* epigrams or other short poems of a devotional type (a form which becomes very common in the seventeenth century), and epigrams tend to be grouped thematically rather than by author: indeed, the great majority of epigrams at this period circulate anonymously, drawing no distinction between classical, medieval, earlier humanist and contemporary material. Accompanying translations are infrequent.

Egerton 2642, for instance, is a large manuscript compiled mainly during the reign of Elizabeth by Robert Commaundre (d.1613), rector

---

[10] Neo-Latin epigrams are found most frequently by far in manuscripts dating from the first third of the seventeenth century (of 13,415 items identified as epigrams, 4,068 (30.3 per cent) are datable to this period alone, the single largest chronological category by a considerable margin); of 851 items identified as 'bilingual epigrams', however, 581 (68.2 per cent) are in manuscripts dating from the middle or final third of the seventeenth century, while only 112 (13.2 per cent) are dated to the first third.

[11] Exceptions include Crane, '*Intret Cato*', and Whipple, *Martial and the English Epigram*, 300–26, which acknowledges the importance of neo-Latin epigram as a model for poets in English.

[12] In the mid-sixteenth century in particular, 'epigram' was often used for a wide variety of short, medium and sometimes even quite long poems: one of the contributions made by the schoolboy Giles Fletcher to an Eton manuscript for Queen Elizabeth in 1563, for instance, is titled 'Epigramma 59' though it runs to over 300 lines (BL MS Royal 12 A XXX, fols. 37ʳ–49ᵛ); similarly, humanist printed collections of epigrams sometimes included long poems (a feature imitated by Jonson, whose *Epigram* 133, 'On the Famous Voyage', is 196 lines long). This chapter, however, deals only with short poems.

of Tarporley, co. Chester, and chaplain to Sir Henry Sidney. The volume contains a substantial section of around 60 leaves consisting largely of verse, with some prose, in both English and (mostly) Latin and arranged loosely according to theme. Out of 185 items of neo-Latin verse (not counting many classical and medieval extracts), 152 have been classified as epigrams, the others being various types of longer Latin poem. Of these 152 epigrams only 20 are accompanied by English translations: a low proportion typical for a miscellany of this date. Although very few poems are attributed, identifiable authors include Mantuan, Borbonius (Nicholas Bourbon, 1503–50), Sannazaro, Haddon, Gower and Stephen Gardiner, bishop of Winchester (1483–1555), with items grouped thematically and not by author: the first section, 'De Morte et Vita' ('On Life and Death', fols. 210^r–11^r), for instance, contains eight epigrams on the brevity of human life, one of which is accompanied by an English translation, alongside a series of quotations from scripture on the same theme (all but one also in Latin).[13] The collection also includes (fol. 246^r) a copy of Surrey's translation of Martial 10.47, one of the most popular of Martial's epigrams throughout early modernity, and (not coincidentally) one of the very few that is straightforwardly moralizing.[14]

In common with several similar collections from this period, the many epigrams in BL MS Egerton 2642 are divided roughly equally between moralizing poems and (broadly speaking) political or topical items, such as a series of epigrams on the death of Lady Jane Grey, executed in 1554 (including two items, given in both Latin and English, attributed to Lady Grey herself); a sequence commemorating Protestant martyrs of the 1550s, including Thomas Cranmer (fol. 218^v, burnt 1556), Nicholas Ridley and Hugh Latimer (fol. 219^r, burnt 1555), John Bradford (fol. 219^r, burnt 1555) and 'Hoper' (i.e. John Hooper, burnt 1555, fol. 219^v); and a sequence of 17 Latin poems, both epigrams and longer satiric pieces, attacking the papacy and the Catholic Church (fols. 228^r–9^v), incorporating popular items such as extracts from Mantuan and two of Sannazaro's anti-papal epigrams, alongside several other less well-known pieces. Again, only two of these have a translation attached, including one epigram, titled 'Verses against Pope Alexander':

---

[13] This manuscript has been refoliated at some point after the compilation of the catalogue; the updated foliation (used here) therefore does not match the catalogue foliation.
[14] This copy of Surrey's translation is not recorded in *CELM*.

> Vendit Alexander Cruces, Altaria, Christum
> Vendere Jure potest, Emerat ille prius.
>
> Alexander oure holy Father the Pope of Rome
> Selleth for mony boeth right and dome
> And all kynde of hollynes, the holly father doothe not sticke
> To Sell, to Sell, readye mony for to gett
> And eke Christe hymselff hee dares bee bold
> To chopp and chaunge for Sylver and Golde
> And why should eny thincke this to bee sore,
> For what doeth hee sell, but that hee bought before.[15]

The Latin here is a couplet from a widely circulated verse libel on the death of Pope Alexander VI in 1503; the English appears to be unique and is probably Robert Commaundre's own work. Such anti-papal verse – especially the tradition of 'pasquils' or 'pasquinades', publicly displayed satiric epigrams – had obvious appeal to sixteenth-century Protestants, especially when composed by Catholics themselves.[16] The other translations in the volume are similarly awkward attempts at English verse, very far from the concision of the Latin.

In Commaundre's miscellany, few if any of the Latin items appear to be his own work (whereas the relatively small number of accompanying English translations probably mostly are). In comparable collections of original compositions, however, we find similar patterns in theme and subject. Corpus Christi College, Oxford, MS 324 is a particularly fascinating collection almost exclusively of Latin verse dating from between 1555 and 1597, kept by one Adrian Schoell, a German émigré resident first in London and then as a clergyman and schoolmaster in Essex and Somerset.[17] Though some of these 461 Latin poems are translations, from Greek or Schoell's native German, only a handful are attributed to anyone other than Schoell himself.[18] Schoell's poetry tracks contemporary fashions. He is fond of chronograms and *aenigmata* (riddle poems), and writes many poems commemorating events in his life and those of his patron,

---

[15] BL MS Egerton 2642, fol. 229ʳ.
[16] Pasquils or pasquinades were verse libels, typically attacking senior Church officials, displayed at a statue in Rome from the late fifteenth century onwards. They were frequently collected and circulated; a particularly important collection was published in Basel in 1544 (Curio (ed.), *Pasquillorum tomi duo*). There was also an Edinburgh edition in 1565 (*Pasquillorum versus aliquot*), on which see Crane, '*Intret Cato*', and Doelman, *Epigram in England*, 101–5. For the tendency of English compilers to select anti-Papal poems by Italian authors, see Facchini, 'Reception of Italian Neo-Latin Poetry'.
[17] Corpus Christi College, Oxford, MS 324. I am not aware of any previous scholarship on this manuscript, but I am preparing a fuller study.
[18] Such as a poem by Thomas Blake recorded along with Schoell's response, dated 1562 (fol. 128ʳ⁻ᵛ), and some items attributed to his pupils.

friends and neighbours – marking births, marriages and deaths, but also giving striking glimpses of domesticity. One poem tells how his wife was frightened by finding a dormouse in the henhouse (fol. 129^v, dated 1563); another is on snowfall in April (fols. 143^r–4^r, dated 1570). Many epigrams mark events in public life, such as the death of Mary Queen of Scots in 1589 (two epigrams, fol. 173^r) and of Christopher Hatton in 1591 (seven epigrams, fol. 179^v).

Although Schoell's volume, unlike Commaundre's, appears to be almost exclusively his own work, the types of epigram he writes strongly resemble those selected by Commaundre, dividing almost entirely into either moralizing or topical poems. Schoell was clearly a convinced Protestant – one very long early poem defends the translation of scripture, and he celebrates the death in 1555 of the conservative bishop of Winchester, Stephen Gardiner, with great enthusiasm. As is typical of the Latin verse of Protestant poets of this period, however, the few religious (rather than polemical) poems included are almost exclusively paraphrases of scripture, especially of the psalms, with the scriptural reference given first in English:

> Lorde let me knowe myne ende and the number of my dayes; that I maye be certified howe longe I have to live.

> Sic
>
> Nosse mihi detur finem numerumque dierum:
> vt, vitae reliquum quod manet, inde sciam.
>
> Vel
>
> Scire, deus, finem cupis seriemque dierum:
> certior ut reddar, quae stata meta manet.[19]

The only three pieces of non-scriptural, devotional verse are all versified prayers in sapphic stanzas. As we saw in Chapter 4, this use of sapphics is typical of the mid-sixteenth century.

The centrality of Latin epigram to Renaissance literary culture, and in particular to humanist self-fashioning, has been well described by scholars of neo-Latin literature.[20] Karl Enenkel has even suggested, without too much exaggeration, that the definition of a humanist might be 'a person

---

[19] Corpus Christi College, Oxford, MS 324, fols. 130^v–1^r. Psalm 39:5. The English text is that of Coverdale, as incorporated into the Book of Common Prayer.

[20] De Beer *et al.* (eds.), *Neo-Latin Epigram*; Cardini and Coppini (eds.), *Rinnovamento umanistico*; Cummings, 'Epigram'; Schnur, *Galle und Honig*; Laurens, *L'Abeille dans l'ambre*; Gaisser, *Catullus and his Renaissance Readers*; Hutton, *Greek Anthology in Italy* and *Greek Anthology in France*.

who composes Neo-Latin epigrams'.[21] Most work on European humanist epigram has focused, however, upon the carefully assembled printed collections (rather than manuscript circulation) of leading professional poets in France, Italy and the Netherlands, and has tended to emphasize classical models at the expense of non-classical ones.[22] Clearly, individuals like Commaundre and Schoell were reading these sorts of authors – Commaundre's collection includes poems by Nicholas Bourbon and Jacopo Sannazaro – but the ways in which they read and wrote Latin epigrams seem nevertheless quite far removed from the kind of sophisticated literary self-fashioning which has been the focus of scholarship. In particular, Commaundre's and Schoell's manuscripts – unlike many of the large seventeenth-century epigram collections – contain relatively few classical epigrams and no or very few Latin poems translated from the Greek Anthology; fashionable humanist epigrams, where they do appear (in Commaundre's collection), are generally unattributed; and any individual epigram is valued, apparently, for its relationship to a given theme or topic, and frequently for its pithy conventionality, rather than for being the work of a specific author or for its classical qualities.

Epigram after 1590

The epigram in English, in the primarily satiric and collection-based form in which it is usually studied and against which Jonson reacted in his *Epigrams*, emerged quite suddenly in the 1590s, with a string of influential collections by Everard Guilpin, Thomas Bastard, Sir John Harington, Sir John Davies and others, in some cases circulating in manuscript in advance of print publication. English epigram of this kind, though never critically fashionable, has been the subject of several important studies, especially those of Whipple, Hudson and, most recent and comprehensive, James Doelman's *The Epigram in England, 1590–1640*.[23] Critical assessments

---

[21] Enenkel, 'Neo-Latin Epigram', 1–2.
[22] The chapter on epigram in *Brill's Encyclopaedia of the Neo-Latin World*, for instance, is titled 'Epigrams – The Classical Tradition', claiming: 'The Neo-Latin idea of an epigram was founded ... on Roman authors, and really on just two of them, each making a distinct contribution: Catullus, and Martial' (Nisbet, 'Epigrams', 380). Robert Cummings' essay (Cummings, 'Epigram') is wider ranging and more subtle but similarly emphasizes the 'pointed', witty, satiric and often obscene form of epigram derived from Martial. Cardini and Coppini focus on the imitation of Martial, Catullus and the *Greek Anthology* (*Rinnovamento umanistico*). On Anglo-Latin epigram, see Binns, *Intellectual Culture*, chaps. 4, 5 and 10.
[23] Hudson, *Epigram in the English Renaissance*; Sullivan, 'Martial and English Poetry'; Whipple, *Martial and the English Epigram*; Young, 'Jonson, Crashaw'; Sullivan, *Martial*, 253–312.

have tended to characterize the genre as satiric and disruptive, composed in self-conscious imitation of Martial, and linked to the wider interest in classical satire during the 1590s: Sir John Davies' epigrams, among the first of this new wave to be printed, was probably one of the volumes targeted by the 1599 'Bishops' Ban' on the printing of 'Satyres or Epigramms'.[24] Much recent work has focused on the subversive potential of the verse libel, especially in manuscript circulation.[25] Doelman's book, which is commendably wide-ranging and acknowledges the role of Latin epigram, is nevertheless also strongest on topical and satiric verse.

All of the authors who came to prominence for their English epigrams in the period between 1590 and 1610 produced entire books of epigrams. This move to the production of book collections marks out the English-language epigrammatists of the 1590s from the kind of topical English epigram composed before this date: there are certainly many widely circulating epigrams in English before 1590, such as the poem on the extravagant size of Sir Christopher Hatton's tomb, erected after his death in 1586, and discussed in Chapter 8, or the sort of topical epigram composed by Adrian Schoell. Single-authored books of English epigrams, however, are largely new.[26] At first, the move towards the epigram 'book' seems to imitate the practice of the humanists, whose Latin verse usually includes at least one volume of *epigrammata*. Humanist epigram collections, however, typically have a larger proportion of poems of praise and commendation than we find in the 1590s English examples, and also tend to be less miscellaneous. The characteristically aggressive, explicit, satiric or invective collections of the late 1590s, such as Thomas Bastard's *Chrestoleros*, Everard Guilpin's *Skialethia* and Robert Joyner's *Itys* (all entered on the Stationers' Register in 1598), are by contrast (and in imitation of Martial) markedly miscellaneous. Whereas work on the humanist epigram, reflecting classical scholarship, has emphasized erudition, wit, intellectual display and international circulation in the form of carefully curated and organized print collections, work on the English epigrammatists of the late sixteenth century has tended to emphasize satire, invective, political subversion, free speech and miscellaneity.

---

[24] Issued by John Whitgift, archbishop of Canterbury, and Richard Bancroft, bishop of London, on which see McCabe, 'Elizabethan Satire'.
[25] E.g. Bellany, 'Railing Rhymes Revisited'; Eckhardt, *Manuscript Verse Collectors*; Swann, 'Copying Epigrams'.
[26] The most obvious exception is Heywood, *An hundred epigrammes* (1550), based on proverbs, and still quoted in the seventeenth century. See also Crowley, *One and Thyrtye Epigrammes* (1550) and Turberville, *Epitaphes, Epigrams, Songs and Sonets* (1567).

Jonson, Cato, Owen and the Moral Seriousness of Latin Epigram

It is this aggressive, invective and somewhat chaotic type of English epigram book that Jonson rejects in the opening sequence of his own *Epigrams* (1616):

> It will be looked for, book, when some but see
>   Thy title, 'Epigrams', and named of me,
> Thou shouldst be bold, licentious, full of gall,
>   Wormwood, and sulphur; sharp, and toothed withal;
> Become a petulant thing, hurl ink and wit
>   As madmen stones, not caring whom they hit.[27]
>   (*Epigrammes* 2.1–6)

Jonson signals the moral seriousness of his enterprise in the preface, in a passage which both alludes to and distances himself from Martial:

> For such [critics of his work, who prefer not to consider 'truth or virtue'] I would rather know them by their vizards, still, than they should publish their faces at their peril in my theatre, where Cato, if he lived, might enter without scandal.

As critics have noted, this reverses the preface to Martial's first book: 'non intret Cato theatrum meum, aut si intrauerit, spectet' ('let Cato keep out of my theatre; or, if he comes in, let him stay to watch', Prologue, prose) and 'cur in theatrum, Cato seuere, uenisti? / an ideo tantum ueneras, ut exires?' ('Why, severe Cato, have you entered the theatre? / Or rather, did you enter only so that you could make a point of leaving?' Prologue, verse, lines 3–4). But at this period any mention of 'Cato' in relation to epigram immediately suggests *Cato's Distichs*, frequently referred to simply as 'Cato'.[28] This was the first collection of Latin epigrams read by boys at school, and a prominent element of many large sixteenth-century epigram collections. Indeed, one of those owned by Jonson himself, Léger Duchesne's popular *Flores Epigrammatum* (1555–60), consists mostly of epigrams selected from humanist rather than ancient authors, and includes no Martial at all, but prints all four books of *Cato's Distichs* – by some

---

[27] Text from Burrow (ed.), 'Epigrams'.
[28] Cato the Elder (234–149 BC) had a reputation as a stern moralist, hence the traditional attribution, though the text in fact dates from late antiquity, probably the late third century AD. J. C. Scaliger considered it to be a classical work, though not by Cato. Some other early modern editors continued to consider the attribution to Cato plausible.

margin the largest element from any single author.²⁹ By welcoming Cato into the 'theatre' of his epigrams, Jonson is indicating not just that his collection is morally serious in a way that Martial's is not, but specifically that it could be read alongside and within the wider tradition of improving and didactic epigram to which Cato's distichs belong, rather than the narrower vernacular invective tradition of the previous decades.

'Cato' was very widely taught in the early years of grammar school and must have been often memorized as a result; extracts and imitations are found very frequently indeed in manuscript material, though the work has attracted almost no critical attention, being relegated to a footnote or passing reference in almost every study of epigram.³⁰ Moreover, *Cato's Distichs* are themselves just one particularly influential and widely read example of the moralizing, didactic or mnemonic Latin epigram that was – as we saw in Commaundre's notebook – particularly characteristic of the sixteenth century but remained also an underestimated feature of seventeenth-century literary culture. Several very large manuscript collections of 'monosticha, disticha et polisticha' (monostichs, distichs and polystichs) survive, usually arranged alphabetically and often running to hundreds of individual items.³¹

Jonson was memorably rude about the Welsh epigrammatist John Owen (1563/4–1622?), probably at least partly out of professional jealousy.³² But Owen's books of Latin epigrams, which began to appear in 1606, anticipated a very similar turn to that generally attributed to Jonson himself. Mary Crane has described how 'the development of the epigram in England in the course of the sixteenth century involved a struggle between … the epigram in the tradition of Martial as a witty, youthful "trifle," and the epigram in the tradition of several classical and nonclassical sources as a serious didactic kind'.³³ The popularity of Owen's *Epigrams*

---

[29] A Quercu [Duchesne], *Flores Epigrammatum* (1555–60); McPherson, 'Ben Jonson's Library', no. 149. Cato's distichs are printed on fols. 196ᵛ–204ᵛ.

[30] The main exception is Crane, '*Intret Cato*', whose essay, more often cited than absorbed, remains the best introduction to the distichs themselves. There were at least 24 editions of *Cato's Distichs* with Erasmus' notes published in England between 1553 and 1657, not including editions printed after that date; in other countries (including Scotland); or which are no longer extant. See also, more generally, Manley, 'Proverbs, Epigrams, and Urbanity'.

[31] Examples include Bod. MS Tanner 406, dated 1555; Surrey History Centre, MS LM/1327/41, undated (probably latter sixteenth century); BL MS Lansdowne 722, fols. 94ʳ–9ᵛ (undated); Corpus Christi College, Oxford, MS 258, fols. 2ʳ–64ᵛ (mid-sixteenth century).

[32] 'Owen is a pure pedantic schoolmaster, sweeping his living from the posteriors of little children, and hath nothing good in him, his epigrams being bare narrations' – Donaldson (ed.), 'Informations to Drummond', 166–8.

[33] Crane, '*Intret Cato*', 159.

arises from their dextrous combination of these two previously largely distinct literary modes: fashionable humanist wit and wordplay combined with the tradition of pithy, didactic and frequently moralizing Latin epigram of the kind found in *Cato*. Jonson's achievement, too, rests on his combination of the Martialian features of concision, wit, miscellaneity and a satiric edge, with an un-Martial-like moral seriousness and focus upon the improvement of the general reader (rather than simply the humiliation of the victim). Other elements of Jonson's collection, such as the variety in verse form and length, the balance of praise and blame, and the collection's careful organization, point to the tradition of the humanist epigram book, many examples of which Jonson owned.[34]

Owen's ten books of Latin epigrams were published in stages between 1606 and 1612, and were immediately popular: the first was reprinted twice in 1607. Later editions included as an eleventh book a collection of moralizing distichs in fact by the Italian author Michele Verino (d.1487), pointing to the contemporary understanding of Owen's verse as part of a moralizing tradition.[35] His work was an almost immediate success across Protestant Europe. In a letter to William Camden in 1612 the Antwerp historian François Sweerts (1567–1629) adds an urgent postscript to a piece of scholarly correspondence: 'Optarem mitti Poëmata omnia OWENI, pretium reponam. Incredibile quanto sint in Sonore & aestimatione apud omnes Poëtas' ('I would like to be sent the complete poems of OWEN, I'll reimburse you. It's amazing how highly he is rated and how much he is being spoken about by all poets').[36] Though the phenomenon of Owen's great popularity has been noted, mainly by neo-Latinists and book historians, it has been very little studied from a literary perspective.[37] The cultural significance of the craze for Owen has also been barely

---

[34] On praise and blame in Jonson's epigrams, see esp. Partridge, 'Jonson's *Epigrammes*'. Jonson owned copies of the following collections (among many others) containing significant numbers of Latin epigrams: A Quercu, *Flores Epigrammatum* (1555–60); Marullus, *Poetae Tres Elegantissimi* (1582); Pithou, *Epigrammata et Poematia vetera* (1590); Veen, *Amorum Emblemata* (1608); La Faye, *Emblemata et Epigrammata Miscellanea* (1610); Thomas, *Poemata* (1627). Despite our unparalleled knowledge of Jonson's library, the great majority of which was in Latin, his reading of contemporary Latin has been little pursued by scholars.

[35] A further twelfth book of epigrams attributed to Owen was also included in later editions; see Enck, 'Owen's *Epigrammata*'.

[36] BL MS Cotton Julius C. V., fol. 139ʳ. For the international popularity of Owen, see Poole-Wilson, 'Best-Seller Abroad', and Shaaber, *Check-list*, nos. 82–94. For Owen's influence in other countries, see Laurens, *L'Abeille dans l'ambre*; Urban, *Owenus und die deutschen Epigrammatiker*.

[37] Bradner, *Musae Anglicanae*, 86–90, remains one of the best summaries of Owen's style and achievement. See also Jones, 'John Owen, Cambro-Britannus' and 'John Owen, the epigrammatist'; Martyn, 'John Owen and Tudor patronage'; Davies, *Latin Writers*, 46–58; Sacré, 'Übersehenes Epigramm'; Enck, 'John Owen's *Epigrammata*'; Leach, *History of Warwick School*,

acknowledged by those working on directly adjacent vernacular works, such as Jonson's *Epigrams* (1616).[38] Astonishingly, given that Owen was almost certainly the most widely read British author in the whole of Protestant Europe, there is still no available edition of Owen's verse with a modern English translation.[39]

Owen's epigrams are short, pithy, memorable, often funny and highly quotable. Many are only two lines long, and the great majority are of either two or four lines. All but four are in elegiac couplets.[40] This metrical consistency must have lent them a distinctive flavour and feel at a moment which was close to the peak of metrical variety at least in British Latin verse (on which see Chapter 2): what might seem monotonous today probably struck readers at the time as a fresh kind of discipline. His almost exclusive use of the elegiac couplet marks – and may indeed partly have helped to effect – the transition from hexameter to elegiacs for short moralizing verse of this type: in the sixteenth century, in imitation of *Cato's Distichs* and many medieval texts, such verse is usually in hexameter, a very unclassical feature (hexameter is almost never used for short poems in classical Latin).

Owen avoids very topical, highly political, scurrilous or otherwise obscene subjects, and though many of his epigrams contain scriptural allusions, only in Book 3 is there a significant number of explicitly religious poems.[41] While his poems of praise, commendation and dedication are addressed to specific named individuals – such as Lady Mary Neville, to whom the first book is dedicated; Sir Robert Cotton (4.32); and Owen's publisher, Simon Waterson (4.12) – and some humorous epigrams tease friends by name (such as 3.95 and 4.36, to John Suckling,

---

124–33; Schneditz-Bolfras, 'John Owen'; Durand (ed.), *John Owen*; Harries, 'John Owen the Epigrammatist'; Jansen, 'Microcosmos of the Baroque Epigram'.

[38] I have been guilty of this myself: Moul, *Jonson, Horace*, 54–70 identifies an element of moral seriousness in Jonson's *Epigrams* largely alien to Martial, but does not associate it as I now would with the larger tradition of moralizing Latin epigram.

[39] Owen would probably be overtaken by John Barclay if Catholic Europe were included. Martyn (ed.), *Joannis Audoeni epigrammatum* prints only the Latin. There is a good modern French edition with a very substantial commentary, Durand (ed.), *John Owen*. Dana Sutton's online edition includes an English translation, but, except for Book 12, it is a seventeenth-century one which can be hard to follow (www.philological.bham.ac.uk/owen).

[40] The rest are hexameters: one (8.50) of four lines and three hexameter monostichs (4.256, 5.56 and 5.75). A handful of others do not scan conventionally (e.g. 1.34 and 1.171 which are partly made up of musical notation). Both text and numeration of Owen's epigrams are taken from Durand (ed.), *John Owen*.

[41] Book 3 contains two religious sequences (3.15–34 and 3.40–64). Martyn considers 247 out of 1,492 epigrams broadly 'religious' in topic, including satirical attacks on the Catholic Church. Doelman describes Owen's epigrams as 'largely secular' (*Epigram in England*, 353); this is, however, misleading. Although there are few devotional epigrams, as Bradner rightly notes Owen 'was very fond of Biblical subjects and of the commonplaces of religious teaching' (*Musae Anglicanae*, 88).

1569–1627), the satiric pieces are all addressed to individuals named by type ('In quondam ineptum scriptorem', 'On a certain foolish writer', 8.47) or with a classical pseudonym ('In Quintum immisericordem', 'On unmerciful Quintus', 8.45; 'Ad Faustinum', 'To Faustinus', 8.57). This is the same practice followed by Jonson.

Although Jonson's use of Martial as a model has been the main focus of critical attention, his epigrams have many parallels with those of Owen: Jonson's poem on the union of England and Scotland as a marriage, over which the king presides as a priest, echoes Owen's series of epigrams on the same subject, most of which also employ the image of a marriage, and one of which is given below.[42]

> On the Union
> When was there contract better driven by Fate?
>   Or celebrated with more truth of state?
> The world the temple was, the priest a king,
>   The spousèd pair two realms, the sea the ring.
>   (Jonson, *Epigrams* 5)

> Unio. Ad Britannos Coniuges
> Servat ab interitu Deus unus, et unio mundum.
>   Coniugium in terris unio prima fuit.
>   (Owen, 4.164)

> *Union. To the British marriage-pair*
> *God, who is one, preserves the world from death, and so too does union.*
> *The union of marriage was the first union on earth.*

At the opening of Parliament in March 1603, James I compared the Union of England and Scotland to the marriage of husband and wife, though in slightly different terms: 'I am the husband, and all the whole isle is my lawful wife.'[43] Jonson, like Owen, makes the two nations into the 'spousèd pair' (in Latin, *coniuges*), and Jonson's setting of the marriage within the wider context of the 'world' perhaps also echoes Owen's *mundum* ('world').[44]

Although rarely polemical, Owen's epigrams are clearly Protestant in sympathy and include several direct attacks upon Roman Catholic

---

[42] Owen's other epigrams on this topic are 3.39, 3.204, 4.4, 5.22 and 5.24.
[43] McIlwain (ed.), *James I: Political Works*, 271–2. James also compared the union to that of Lancaster and York, a motif picked up in two of Owen's other epigrams on the topic (3.39, 5.22).
[44] Owen's epigram relies also on 'unio' as 'oneness', linked to the 'oneness' of God. Owen 4.4 plays upon an alternative technical meaning of 'unio', as a pearl. There is something slightly passé about Jonson's poem: by 1616, 13 years after the accession of James I, enthusiasm had waned. There is some evidence that a version of Jonson's epigrams may have been printed in 1612, though if so, that version is now lost (Burrow (ed.), 'Epigrams', 103 and 115).

practice; as a result, Owen's work was placed on the 'Index librorum prohibitorum', a point which probably only enhanced his popularity in Protestant countries. On the whole, though, Owen's satiric mode is generalizing. His avoidance both of obscenity (excepting a handful of poems) and of strongly topical, local or polemical subjects no doubt contributed to his popularity, rendering his epigrams both readable throughout Europe and also highly teachable. Poole-Wilson has identified 45 continental editions of Owen printed before 1800, and his epigrams were included in printed school anthologies at least by the mid-seventeenth century.[45]

Reading Owen in England

Dana Sutton has suggested that despite his popularity abroad, 'Owen was not taken very seriously in his own country.'[46] This is not borne out by the evidence. English manuscript sources contain hundreds if not thousands of copies of Owen's epigrams, and his verse is found many times more frequently in English manuscript sources than that of any other single neo-Latin poet, of any period or country.[47] Many manuscripts contain just a handful of his poems, but, unlike any other Latin epigrammatist of this period, there are also a relatively large number containing many: this is perhaps surprising given how often these works were printed, and how widely they must have been owned in print form, but it suggests how individual compilers were interested in making their own personal selections of his work.[48]

Emmanuel College, Cambridge, MS 105, for instance, Archbishop William Sancroft's (1617–93) commonplace book dating from the latter

---

[45] Poole-Wilson, 'Best-Seller Abroad'. Despite official prohibition, his work was also well known in Catholic countries. Charles Hoole's *A New Discovery of the Old Art of Teaching Schoole* (1661), 158, recommends the use of Owen in the fourth form, and Owen's epigrams are included in the frequently reprinted school anthology *Epigrammatum Delectus* (1683 onwards).

[46] Sutton, Introduction to Leech, www.philological.bham.ac.uk/leech/intro.html.

[47] At the time of writing, I am aware of 860 copies of epigrams by (or attributed to) Owen in 27 manuscripts dating from the early seventeenth to the early eighteenth century, but this is certainly a significant underestimate. (By contrast, the next most popular author, George Buchanan, has 145 items.) A great deal of work remains to be done: Owen's epigrams were particularly likely to circulate anonymously, which has no doubt contributed to the underestimate of his popularity and importance.

[48] Examples of very large collections of Owen's epigrams include BL MSS Harley 5365 (100 epigrams, dated 1610) and Sloane 1867 (105, before c.1622); Trinity College, Cambridge, MS R. 7. 23 (105, dated 1610); Emmanuel College, Cambridge, MS 105 (220, discussed below); Durham Cathedral Library, MS Hunter 96 (217, discussed below).

seventeenth century, contains 428 Latin epigrams. David Money slightly exaggerates when he says that two thirds of these are by Owen – the figure is in fact just over half, 220 out of 428.[49] The volume also includes, however, John Bowman's epigram in praise of Owen, and the spirit of Owen's *Epigrammata* pervades the selection. Durham Cathedral Library, MS Hunter 96, of a similar size though from the early part of the century, contains 421 Latin epigrams of which 217 are from Owen or attributed to him. This collection has a more 'British' feel than the Emmanuel manuscript, with significant sections of Latin epigrams by Fitzgeoffrey (51), More (38), Buchanan (18) and Stradling (10) instead of large numbers by continental Latin authors. Like many similar collections, it has a substantial section of classical epigrams by Catullus, Martial and Ausonius; more unusually, it also includes a sizeable collection of Thomas Bastard's English epigrams.

A particular testament to Owen's influence is the relatively large number of poems about him or responding directly to his work, such as the Bowman epigram included by Sancroft. BL MS Harley 1823, dating probably from around 1620 and in the hand of John Burrus, includes a note and two poems, both themselves Latin epigrams, titled 'To Mr Peter Jackson upon the front of Owen the Welshmans epigrams wch I sent him'.[50] BL MS Harley 3910, probably also dating from the early 1620s, contains two Latin epigrams marking the death of Owen, one of which is by John Hoskyns (to whom Owen had addressed three of his own poems, 1.3, 1.96 and 4.152).[51] Owen's epigrams were still being quoted and translated well into the eighteenth century: John Whaley quotes Owen in a letter to Horace Walpole dated 1736.[52]

Just as vernacular authors of epigram were quickly influenced by Owen's popularity and success, so too were Latin poets. A huge collection of 712 Latin epigrams in six books, composed by John Russell (d.1687) in 1625–6 while an undergraduate at Magdalene College, Cambridge, is plainly inspired by Owen. The great majority of Russell's poems are, like Owen's, in elegiac couplets, and the range of topics and overall tone are very similar. Two epigrams in the first book (1.93 and 1.116) address Owen directly; and in 1.116, the final epigram, Russell directly

---

[49] Money, 'Owen, John'. Other authors well-represented in this collection include Bernhard Bauhusius (63 epigrams), a poet discussed in Chapter 6.
[50] BL MS Harley 1823, fol. 9^r.   [51] BL MS Harley 3910, fol. 57^r.
[52] BL MS Add. 71125, fol. 10^r.

acknowledges Owen's fame and apparent inimitability.[53] Around a decade later, one Thomas Ventris dedicated a collection of 68 epigrams to his tutor, in a collection which includes multiple references to Owen as well as Martial.[54]

The currency and familiarity of Owen's epigrams are suggested also by their frequent imitation, adaptation and updating. A Latin epigram from the 1620s updates one of Owen's epigrams on the union of England and Scotland in 1603 (Owen, 3.204) to apply it to the politics of the day:

> Ad Carolum Principem.
> Gallia visa mihi galea est, et Scotia scutum
> Anglia jam tutò bella movere potes.[55]

> *To Prince Charles.*
> *France seems to me like a helmet, and Scotland like a shield.*
> *England, now you can safely start a war.*

Epigram and Convention in Sir John Gibson's Collection

Owen's epigrams were quickly absorbed into the broader currents of highly quotable Latin verse. While imprisoned in Durham castle during the 1650s, Sir John Gibson (1606–65) kept a notebook of quotations, extracts and meditations. Dedicated to his son, and with a clear thematic focus upon exile, suffering and endurance, Gibson's use of Latin verse is both typical of the period – in its sources and overall variety of material – and highly personal. The effect of Gibson's quotations, conventional as they are, is far from dry: there is no suggestion here of erudition for its own sake; rather, every piece of Latin verse that

---

[53] BL MS Add. 73542, fol. 15ᵛ. The manuscript is an autograph fair copy, with some corrections and revisions, containing a total of 712 Latin poems arranged in 6 books of epigrams of 110–20 poems each, plus an opening sequence of 9 prefatory, dedicatory and commendatory epigrams; it is discussed briefly by Doelman, *Epigram in England*, 83–4, 311, 336. The latest datable events to which the poems refer took place in the summer of 1625; Russell matriculated as a pensioner in Easter Term of that year.

[54] Bod. MS Rawl. poet. 62, fols. 1ᵛ–6ʳ; of which 63 are in elegiacs, 5 in iambic trimeter.

[55] BL MS Add. 15227, fol. 77ʳ. Adapting Owen, 3.204, 3–4: 'Wallia cui vallum contingit, Scotia scutum, / Anglia, securam iam licet esse tibi' ('The county who has Wales for its rampart, Scotland for its shield, /As you do, England, can stand secure'). I am grateful to Edward Taylor for the transcription and identification of the allusion here.

Gibson cites speaks directly to the political and religious situation in which he finds himself.[56]

Near the start of the collection we find a series of extracts from Cato's Distichs (fol. 3ᵛ):

Catonis Distica

Rumores fuge, ne inicipias novus autor haberi:
Nam nulli tacuisse nocet; nocet esse locutum.

Shun rumors, least thou beest as th'Author nam'd;
Silence hurts none, but some for words are blamed.

Cum rectè vivas, ne cures verba malorum
Arbitrij nostri non est quid quisque loquatur.

When thou livest well, mind not what lewd folks say:
It is not in our power their tongues to sway.

Dilige non aegrâ charos pietate parentes,
Nec matrem offendas, dum vis bonus esse parenti.

Thy parents love, the one as well as th'other;
To please thy father, doe not crosse thy mother.

Tranquillis rebus quae sunt adversa caveto:
Rursus in adversis melius sperare memento.

When things goe well adversitie beware;
Againe, when things goe ill, doe not dispaire.

Although unnumbered, these are distichs 1.12, 3.2, 3.24 and 4.26 – that is, although none of them are sequential in the original work, they are arranged in the order in which they are found in a complete edition.[57]

Almost every extract of Latin verse in Gibson's notebook is accompanied by a translation; in most cases, the translations are unattested and are

---

[56] BL MS Add. 37719, including also English verse translations of Ovid and the Song of Songs; extracts from *Eikon Basilike*; a timeline of the English revolution; Laud's speech from the scaffold in 1644; and a drawing of Gibson's prison cell. Smyth, 'Textual Transmission', uses Gibson's notebook as the starting point for a discussion of the challenges of editing early modern manuscript material. Microfilm images are available online: www.ampltd.co.uk/digital_guides/renaissance_commonplace_books_british_library/publishers-note.aspx.

[57] There are some differences in numbering between modern and early modern editions. In the editions available to Gibson, these are distichs number 1.12, 3.1, 3.23 and 4.26. 3.1 and 3.23 are the first and last distichs of the third book. The text of 4.26 differs from that found in modern editions, which read 'rebus semper adversa timeto' in the first line.

probably by Gibson himself.[58] The Latin verse in the volume is typical in several respects: chronological range (classical to contemporary, with late antique material well represented); the inclusion of many extracts from familiar school authors (Cato, Mantuan, Owen); a fashionable interest in inscriptions; and in terms of classical tastes: Gibson has a marked preference for Ovid's exile poetry. The *Tristia* and *Ex Ponto* were common school texts in early modernity, but for Gibson the theme of exile has a personal application, as it did for many royalists in actual or internal exile during the 1650s.[59]

In several cases, Gibson adapts and personalizes familiar passages to create 'epigrams'. The following couplet, for instance, is from the opening of Ovid, *Tristia* 1, in which Ovid imagines his book travelling without him to Rome (from which he is banished). Gibson has replaced 'in urbem' ('into the city') with 'ad Welburne' ('to Welburne').

> Parve (nec invideo) sine me Liber ibis ad Welburne
> Hei mihi, quod domino non licet ire tuo.
>
> *Poore litle Booke, thou must to Welburne goe,*
> *O that thy captive Master could doe soe.*[60]

Two of Gibson's verse aphorisms are apparently derived from or related to epigrams by Owen: 'Raro placent aliis, qui placuere sibi' ('Rarely do they please others, who have pleased themselves', fol. 4[r], the last line of Owen 10.89, not translated by Gibson); and another single hexameter line, 'Foelix quem faciunt aliena pericula cautum' ('Lucky is he whom the dangers of others make cautious', fol. 212[r]), is very similar to the first line of Owen 1.147 ('Felix, quem faciunt aliorum cornua cautum').[61]

Gibson's use of Cato, Ovid and Owen suggests the pain of his personal circumstances. Similarly, he copies the Latin motto from the end of *Eikon Basilike*, followed by an English couplet which does not translate the Latin, but comments upon it:

---

[58] The translations of Cato, however, are probably by Charles Hoole. Hoole's 1651 textbook *An easie Entrance to the Latine Tongue* contains a selection from Cato (376–81), which includes 1.12 with the translation given here (though not the other three, which are found only in subsequent editions printed after the Restoration). Hoole, however, published a very large number of textbooks throughout the 1650s, and it is not unlikely that an earlier edition containing the other three translations has not survived. Though schoolbooks were often printed in large quantities, they tended to be used until they fell apart.

[59] Compare for instance the role of such translations in Vaughan, *Olor Iscanus* (1651).

[60] Ovid, *Tristia*, 1.1.1–2; text and translation as in BL MS Add. 37719, fol. 113[v]. Gibson's father bought an estate in Welburn, North Yorkshire, in the late sixteenth century.

[61] In Owen, this line is presented as direct speech. The sentiment is a conventional one.

> C. R. [= Carolus Rex]
> Vota dabunt, quae bella negarunt.
>
> It was my Master's; and a Martyr's phraise,
> Let him the Glory, let him haue the Bayes.[62]

He also adapts a well-known and probably medieval example of fatally ambiguous Latin, quoted among others by Sir John Harington in his epigrams.[63] Gibson reimagines it applied to God and to Parliament, and adds as a rider, a quotation from Ovid, *Met.* 7.20–1, which he attributes to John Bradshaw:

> Deus. Carolum occidere noli, timere bonum est
> Pa[r]lia: Carolum occidere noli timere, bonum est.
> Bradshaw iudex: ——— Video meliora, proboque
>   Deteriora sequar.[64]
>
> God: 'Do not kill Charles; it is good to be fearful'
> Parliament: 'Do not be afraid to kill Charles, it is good'
> Bradshaw the judge: 'I see the better path, but I approve
>   And follow the worse one.'

Owen's epigrams include several poems based upon grammatical ambiguities of this sort.[65] But whereas Harington and Owen employ syntactical ambiguity for amusement, Gibson returns the anecdote, originally about the death of King Edward, to the realm of contemporary political tragedy. There is something peculiarly powerful about this utilization of highly familiar, quasi-proverbial material in the extraordinary and specific circumstances of the regicide.

Although he freely adapts existing texts, a good example of what Arthur Marotti has termed the 'social textuality' of epigram culture, Gibson does not appear to have composed Latin epigrams himself.[66] The handful of original compositions are in English, and the Latin sources on which he draws are mostly (like Owen) from the previous generation, where they are not classical or medieval. Moralizing or didactic epigrams continued to be

---

[62] BL MS Add. 37719, fol. 173ʳ.
[63] Harington, in the note prefixed to his epigram 1.64, writes: 'It is said that king Edward of Carnaruan lying at Berkly Castle Prisoner, a Cardinall wrate to his keeper. *Edouardum occidere noli, timere, bonum est* ['Do not kill Edward; it is good to be fearful'], which being read with the point at *timere* ['Do not be afraid to kill Edward; it is good'], yt cost the king his life' (Kilroy (ed.), *Epigrams of Sir John Harington*, 116).
[64] BL MS Add. 37719, fol. 198ʳ.
[65] Owen's 'grammatical' epigrams include 1.29 and 1.34. On grammatical verse, see Moul, 'Grammar in Verse'.
[66] Marotti, *Manuscript, Print*, 135–208.

composed, however, throughout this period: routinely, of course, as school exercises, but also in other contexts. David Wedderburn's *Meditationum Campestrium, Seu Epigrammatum Moralium, Centuria Tertia* was published in Aberdeen in 1644. This collection of 300 Latin epigrams makes few concessions to fashion: a single 'aenigma' is tacked on to the end, but the poems are otherwise highly traditional meditations on standard moralizing themes given a topical edge by their wartime context. *Campestria* ('of the camp') refers to a military encampment: these are conceived as poems of use for men at war.

As well as classical, late antique and neo-Latin examples, early modern manuscript collections also commonly included medieval material. Gibson's, for instance, has copied a couplet by Peter Abelard; Harley MS 6038 (c.1620), discussed further below, includes an 'epigrammatized' extract, with translation, from a medieval didactic work by Alan of Lille.[67] Such medieval material could be recontextualized in the same way as Ovid or Owen. BL MS Harley 6383, dating from the late 1630s or early 1640s, includes a copy of a medieval verse prophecy, here titled 'Carmina Latina de Scotorum dominatione in Anglia' ('Latin verses on the domination of the Scots in England', fol. 62ᵛ) and plainly included for its contemporary resonance.[68] (The volume also includes a poem attacking the Scottish rebellion against Charles I in 1638 and commending the invasion of Scotland in the Bishops' Wars of 1639 and 1640.) Works such as Camden's *Remaines* ensured continued or renewed circulation of many pieces of medieval Latin verse.[69]

Printed anthologies for school use reflect what we find in manuscript sources in their tendency to draw on late antique and neo-Latin sources as well as the obvious classical authorities: *Epigrammatum delectus* (*Choice of Epigrams*), for instance, an anthology printed multiple times in the latter seventeenth century, contains five books of epigrams selected from Martial, followed by a sixth book of short poems and extracts from various ancient and late antique authors (Catullus, Virgil, Seneca, Claudian, Ausonius, Pope Sixtus, Ennodius, Boethius and some Latin translations from the Greek anthology).[70] Book Seven progresses to 'recent' poets,

---

[67] BL MS Add. 37719, fol. 192ᵛ; BL MS Harley 6038, fol. 43ᵛ (Latin derived from Alan of Lille, *De arte praedicatoria* 3.117A).
[68] Essentially the same medieval text is also found in BL MS Harley 913, fol. 53ᵛ.
[69] Durham Cathedral Library, MS Hunter 96, for instance, a large collection of Latin epigrams dating from the first decade or two of the seventeenth century, contains 20 Latin poems titled 'Choyce Epigrammes out of Camdens remaines' (pp. 139–46).
[70] [Anon.], *Epigrammatum Delectus* (1683, with several subsequent editions).

beginning with Italian neo-Latin authors, of which Sannazaro, particularly popular in the seventeenth century in England, stands first.[71] Epigrams by John Owen occupy numbers 15–39 in this book, the largest contribution by any single author, though others who are well represented include ten poems by Buchanan and ten by Grotius. The volume is rounded out with a book of 'Sententiae' and then, with a new title page, a further volume of selected epigrams from the most recent poets, with an emphasis upon British authors. This includes an extract from Abraham Cowley's *Plantarum Libri Sex* (1668) as well as pieces by René Rapin (1621–87) and Peter du Moulin (1601–84). Volumes of this sort continued to be used for many decades: this anthology is probably the work to which a note in Thomas Birch's school timetable for January 1720 refers.[72] Birch wrote many Latin epigrams himself, including one on the works of John Owen, dated 1723; in his notes on modern poets, made in the early eighteenth century, both Cowley and Rapin appear in the list of noted recent authors.[73]

Readership, Authorship and Comprehension

Overall, existing scholarship, with its focus on sophisticated, ambitious and self-consciously literary print collections of Latin epigrams by well-known humanists on the one hand, and the slightly chaotic satiric impetus of the English collections of the 1590s on the other, has tended to make Latin and English epigram cultures look more distinct than they were. There were, of course, real differences in potential readership, though perhaps fewer than we tend to assume. As the anonymous author of the 1616 collection *Time's Whistle* put it, 'Scribimus indocti doctique epigrammata passim' ('we all write epigrams everywhere, learned and unlearned alike').[74] The wordplay associated with epigram can lead us to assume that it is a 'difficult' genre; scholarship emphasizing the intellectual display of humanist collections has reinforced this impression.[75] But

---

[71] On Sannazaro in English manuscripts, see Facchini, 'Sannazaro's Latin epigrams'.
[72] The note 'Epigram: Delectus' appears under Tuesday afternoon and Friday morning (BL MS Add. 4457, fol. 201ʳ). Birch (1705–66) was educated at Quaker schools in Hemel Hempstead and Clerkenwell.
[73] Latin epigrams in BL MS Add. 4456 and 4457. The complete list of modern Latin authors noted by Birch are Buchanan, Cowley, Fracastoro, Grotius, Giraldus, Heinsius, Milton, Petrarch, Rapin, Sannazaro and Vida (BL MS Add. 4456, fols. 107ʳ–8ᵛ). Only Cowley and Milton appear in both Latin and English lists.
[74] Quoted by Doelman, *Epigram in England*, 3.
[75] See for example many of the contributions to de Beer et al. (eds.), *Neo-Latin Epigram*.

difficulty or obscurity were not apparently the dominant associations of epigram at the time.

Joseph Mead, writing regularly from Cambridge to his friend Sir Martin Stuteville in the country in the early 1620s, frequently includes Latin epigrams commenting on contemporary affairs in his charmingly chatty letters. Typically he does not translate them. The only example for which he does provide the translation is indeed unusually obscure. Describing the visit of King James I to Cambridge in February 1623, he writes:

> Dr Richardson brought before the King a paper of 4 verses in manner of a Epigram which B. Neale read & others. A freind of mine ouer the Bishops shoulder gott two of them by heart which were
>
> > Dum petit Infantem[α] princeps, Grantamque[β] Jacobus,
> >   Cuiusnam major sit dubitatur amor[e]
>
> α Infanta
> β Cambridg.
>
> The other 2 which resolue the doubt [i.e. solve the riddle] he could not tell me perhaps I shall send you them hereafter.[76]

A week later he follows up, as promised, and adds a complete translation:

> Howsoeuer I will giue you the Epigramme whole which our orator made, & Dr Richard[son] brought to be read before the King at dinner when he was here, the halfe of which I sent you before
>
> > Dum petit [etc . . .]
> > Vicit more suo noster ; nam millibus Infans
> >   Non tot abest, quot nos Regis ab Ingenio
>
> > The king descended more miles to visit
> > us at Cambridge then the Prince is gone
> > to see the Infanta. Ergo the Kings loue is
> > the greater. Rex amore vincit principem.[77]

The 'orator' in question, and the author of the epigram, was George Herbert, university orator at Cambridge between 1620 and 1628. Mead's anecdote offers a vivid glimpse of the kinds of conditions under

---

[76] BL MS Harley 389, 298ᵛ, dated 15 March 1622/3.
[77] BL MS Harley 389, 300ʳ, dated 22 March 1622/3. The poem was first published in Cambridge University, *True Copies of all the Latine Orations* (1623). Other manuscript copies include CUL MS Gg. I. 29, fol. 21ʳ; Houghton Library, MS Eng. 1544 (Lobby X.1.1.), p. 61; Harvard *EC.H4157. W670w2; Nottingham University Library, CI LM 59/1.

which this sort of occasional piece was produced by one person, read out by another – Herbert does not appear to have been present – and memorized or partly memorized on the spot by various others.

Herbert's epigram is an *aenigma*, a fashionable verse riddle, posing a question in the first couplet which is resolved in the second. The answer, however, is somewhat strained and obscure, far from the best of Herbert's Latin epigrams, and it is this difficulty which explains the translation. Mead, who does not usually provide translations for the Latin pieces he sends to Stuteville, senses that this one requires some explanation. Epigrams could certainly be obscure, but on the whole they were not intended to be.

Indeed, epigram culture arose in a period during which pedagogical practices and tools linked brief Latin verse with the earliest stages of education: from the mnemonic verse tags in Lily's grammar to the versified 'morals' attached to Aesop's fables or read in *Cato's Distichs*, boys (and educated girls) would have encountered this type of 'epigram' from the beginning of a Latin education. Several of Owen's epigrams pastiche the kind of 'grammar in verse' found in most elementary textbooks, and brief epigrammatic summaries of a topic, in elegiac couplets, were also the first kind of verse children were expected to produce themselves.

A manuscript in the Essex Record Office contains a series of 68 highly conventional Latin epigrams in elegiacs apparently written by a young woman, Ann Loftus, whose name is faintly visible on the inside cover of the manuscript. Ann (born c.1626), an heiress, married Richard Barrett, to whose family collection the manuscript belongs, at a relatively late age, probably due to a wrangle over the wealth she brought with her; once she did marry, aged about 27 in around 1653, she had four babies in six years and died of the last of them.[78] It is unlikely that she had much leisure for writing Latin verse in this period. But alongside the standard 'school exercise' style epigrams in this notebook on subjects such as 'Spring', 'Aeneas' and 'Virtue', are several which refer explicitly to events of the English Civil War, including the relief of Newark in 1644:

> Oppidulum, immortali famâ emeritum atque
> Perge; licet cinctum es hostibus inumeris[79]
>
> *Little town, and deserving of immortal fame*
> *Carry on – even though you are surrounded by countless enemies.*

---

[78] Barrett-Lennard, *Account of the families of Lennard and Barrett*, 412.
[79] Essex Record Office, MS D/DL F106, fol. 13ᵛ.

Ann's Latin is rather uncertain: 'immortali' has been corrected from 'immortale'; 'inumeris' (for 'innumeris') is misspelt, 'atque' is very oddly positioned and there are problems with the scansion of the hexameter. But the subject makes the notebook highly datable: clearly royalist in sentiment, there is however no explicit mention of the regicide (only of the horror of civil war), and they almost certainly date from before 1649. It is not likely that Ann put her (maiden) name in a blank notebook which was then used later by her sons: an epigram of this kind seems an improbable subject for a boy in the 1660s or early 1670s. The epigrams, then, are almost certainly hers. Her relatively late marriage apparently gave Ann time and leisure in her late teens or early twenties to attempt the kind of beginners' exercises in verse composition that were typical of the period.[80]

Latin epigram was of course accessible only to those who had some Latin. But for those who did, it was one of the modes of Latin literature which most readily invited participation and response. The relatively weak sense of authorship attached to the genre contributed to this: as we saw in the case of Gibson, individuals could and did freely amend epigrams as well as respond to them. This – alongside the sheer practical brevity of most examples – perhaps explains the intensely 'conversational' literary practices associated with this form, both within Latin and between Latin and English.

Conversation, Response and Exchange

Thomas Bastard is well known to have lost his Oxford fellowship in the early 1590s for writing an invective epigram in English, and indeed his later reputation probably rested on his notoriety. But epigram writing was not only politically dangerous for those writing in the vernacular. Latin epigrams could also get their authors into significant, if not even greater trouble: the Protestant divine Andrew Melville was imprisoned in the Tower of London in 1606 for four years, despite being over 60 at the time, for writing an epigram (discussed further below) that mocked the Catholic elements in the King's style of worship. Melville, apparently uncowed by imprisonment, appears to have spent most of his time in the Tower writing and exchanging further, largely satiric or invective, epigrams: I have recently identified an overlooked manuscript which appears

---

[80] Reversed, the volume also includes a section of mostly classical extracts, including quotations from Martial and Virgil.

to date from these years and contains a large number of Latin poems by Melville that were not previously known.[81]

Throughout the period under consideration, epigram culture is characterized by conversation and response: one epigram responds to, answers, reinforces or challenges another, forming chains and clusters of poems sometimes orchestrated by the authors themselves but very often created by compilers of manuscript miscellanies or (less often) printed volumes. The most typical characteristics of such interactions, however, change over the course of the period. In the earlier phase, epigrammatic conversation and response is primarily monolingual. For the epigrammatists of the early seventeenth century, educated in Elizabethan England, Latin and English epigrams seem on the whole to have been understood as related but distinct phenomena. Fitzgeoffrey, Stradling and Owen wrote only in Latin; Bastard, though an able Latin poet whose Latin verse is discussed in Chapter 4, composed his epigrams only in English (though some were later translated into Latin). Campion has several related poems in Latin and English, but they are formally distinct: Latin epigrams corresponding to English songs or sonnets. The circulation of Owen's epigrams is largely monolingual until the mid-seventeenth century, and epigrammatic exchange and response in this earlier part of the period are mostly held 'within' one language or the other.

One enduringly popular type barely represented in print collections is the recording of supposedly 'extempore' epigrammatic compositions or exchanges. One of the most famous and widely circulated of these was supposedly between Queen Elizabeth I and Philip II of Spain, in which Philip's four lines of hexameter are capped by Elizabeth's single verse.[82] In one manuscript the same exchange is attributed instead (though rather improbably) to Elizabeth and the Pope (the order of lines in the four-line epigram also differs from most versions):

> Papa ad reginam Elizabetham
>
> Quas Pater evertit, jubeo te condere cellas
> Quas Dracus eripuit, gazae reddantur oportet
> Relligio Papae fac restituatur ad unguem
> Te veto ne pergas armis defendere Belgos.

---

[81] Bod. MS Cherry 37, discussed further below.
[82] Copies, among others, in Bod. MS Rawl. poet. 148, fol. 3^v; Bod. MS Douce 280, fols. 199^v–200^r; BL MS Harley 3831, fol. 18^r; BL MS Add. 23723, fol. 25^v and BL MS Add. 18044, fols. 83^v–4^r. The exchange is discussed by Booth, *Body Politic to Govern*, 141–2. Edited text in Marcus et al (eds.), *Queen Elizabeth I: Collected Works*, 409–10.

The monasteries which your father destroyed, I order you to rebuild them;
The treasure which Drake stole must be returned;
The religion of the Pope must be restored in every particular:
I forbid you to continue defending the Belgians with your weaponry.

To which Elizabeth apparently replied:

Resp: Elizab:

Ad Graecas isthaec fient mandata calendas.[83]

On the Greek calends these things shall be done.

The point is that the Greeks, unlike the Romans, did not measure time according to the calendar; 'on the Greek calends' is a proverbial expression for 'never'.

Well over a century later, another Elizabeth, Elizabeth (or Elisa) Carter, is credited with a witty and supposedly extempore Latin verse exchange with Alexander Pope:

Ad Elizam in Popi Horto Lauros carpentem

Elysios Popi dum ludit læta per Hortos,
   En! avidâ Lauros carpit *Eliza* manu.
Nil opus est furto; Lauros tibi, dulcis *Eliza*,
   Si neget optatas, Popus, Apollo dabit.

To Eliza picking laurel in Pope's garden

While she was playing happily in Pope's Elysian gardens,
   Look how Eliza *plucked some laurel with a covetous hand.*
There was no need to steal. If, sweet Eliza, Pope
   Denies you the laurels you long for, Apollo shall grant them instead.

Answers to the Epigram.

En! marcet Laurus, nec quiquam juvit *Elizam*
   Furtim sacrilegâ diripuisse manu:
Illa petit sedem magis aptam, tempora *Popi*;
   Et florere negat pauperiore solo.
              Eliza.

The following translation of Carter's poem is probably by Thomas Birch, a friend of hers, whose papers preserve two copies of this exchange:

---

[83] BL MS Add. 15227, fol. 81ᵛ. This very interesting manuscript, dating from around 1630, also includes epigrams by many of the most popular poets of the period, including Alabaster, Ayton, Beza, Buchanan, Melville, Randolph and six by John Owen, as well an otherwise unpublished poem attributed to George Herbert, on the death of Edward Gale, an apothecary, in 1630.

> *In vain* Eliza's *daring hand*
> *Usurpd the Laurel Bough:*
> *Remov'd from* Pope's, *the Wreath must fade*
> *On ev'ry meaner Brow.*
>
> *Thus gay Exotics, when transferr'd*
> *To climates not their own,*
> *Lose all their lively bloom, & droop*
> *Beneath a paler Sun.*
>
> *Eliza*[84]

Dozens of similar examples are found in personal notebooks and miscellanies, typically attributed to a fellow student or colleague, or supposedly recording the compiler's own quick-thinking.[85] A few of the cleverest achieved wider circulation and are found in several manuscripts. Owen's *Epigrammata* include several supposedly extempore compositions of this type and many of his epigrams show an awareness of the proximity of the form to conversation and oral performance (e.g. 3.208, 'De viva voce et scriptis').

Herbert's first epigram collection, *Musae Responsoriae* (dating from around 1620 but probably begun earlier) is itself a response to a polemical Latin poem by the elderly Andrew Melville. A large manuscript, Bod. MS Cherry 37, consisting almost entirely of Latin epigrams, probably represents work completed by Melville in the Tower of London, where he was imprisoned between 1606 and 1610.[86] This collection of Melville's work, titled 'Epigrammata et alia Andreae Meluini carmina' ('Epigrams and other poems of Andrew Melville'), is prefaced with an indignant note, which records what Melville states to be the complete and original version of the epigram on the king's preferred style of worship which – in, he claims, a

---

[84] Latin texts and this translation from BL MS Add. 4457, the second volume of the Birch papers, fols. 73ʳ and 123ᵛ. Latin letters by Elisa Carter are preserved in BL MS Add. 4456, fol. 59 (dated 1738) and BL MS Add. 4457, fol. 112 (dated 1739).

[85] Examples include BL MS Harley 6054, fol. 19ʳ, an 'extempore verse' attributed to a 'boy at Winton' (i.e. Winchester College); Bod. MS Malone 19, p. 137 (also attributed to a Winchester pupil); BL MS Sloane 2764, fol. 40ʳ (attributed to Daniel Heinsius), fol. 68ᵛ (on the execution of the Duc de Guise in 1588) and fol. 155ʳ (again Heinsius); Essex Record Office, MS D/DW Z3 (unnumbered item, probably eighteenth century, attributed to a University of Dublin student 'spoken extempore'). The many large collections of Westminster 'election' verses, effectively an oral competition for scholarships at Christ Church, Oxford, and Trinity College, Cambridge, also record extempore or near extempore compositions.

[86] This manuscript, though clearly docketed as Melville's work ('Melvinus' is the standard Latin form of his name), has been overlooked by Melville scholars. It contains perhaps as many as 70 previously unknown poems (identifying the exact number of 'new' poems is complicated by many pieces which are variant versions of known epigrams). I plan to publish a more detailed analysis of this complex manuscript in due course.

corrupted form – got him into so much trouble.[87] The poem Melville gives here is 14 lines long; the generally circulated version consists of only the first six lines:

> Cur stant clausi Anglis libri duo Regia in ara,
>   Lumina caeca duo, pollubra sicca duo?
> Num sensum cultumque Dei tenet Anglia clausum,
>   Lumine caeca suo, sorde sepulta sua?
> Romano aut ritu dum regalem instruit aram
>   Purpuream pingit relligiosa lupam?

> *Why do two books stand closed to the English on the royal altar,*
>   *Two blind eyes; two dry basins?*
> *Surely England is not holding the presence and worship of God closed –*
>   *Deprived of its light, entombed in filth?*
> *Or, as she adorns the royal altar in a Romish style,*
>   *Does religious England depict a purple she-wolf* [i.e. the whore of Babylon]?

In fact, a significant proportion of the epigrams in the Cherry manuscript are not poems by Melville himself, but answers to him – epigrammatic exchanges with a range of contemporaries, especially John Barclay, another Scot who spent time in France though, unlike Melville, a Catholic. Many of these exchanges relate to the original 'Cur stant clausi' poem. Barclay's first reply is as follows:

> J. Barclaius pro ara regia
>
> Quid mirum est sacram Miluinis vnguibus aram
>   Tentari? est auium non magis vlla rapax;
> Harpyae volucres olim foedissima monstra
>   Sic mensae instructas diripuere dapes
> Atque his virgineus fuerat decor oris, at vncis
>   Vnguibus armatae terribilesque manus.
> O nimium impuri facies quibus illita fuco est,
>   Dum reliquis puros se magis esse putant.

---

[87] Bod. MS Cherry 37, fol. 21ᵛ. Melville describes it as 'The true version of the poem which in a muddled and ... curtailed form, was brought as a charge against me in the Royal Council last November, 1606, and yet again on April 26, 1607'. The manuscript also includes a 6-line version which is close to (but not identical with) the one generally circulated, as well as an 'explanatio plenior' of 14 lines, different again from either. It is not clear whether the Cherry manuscript is autograph. A manuscript poem by Melville in the same hand has previously been described as Melville's autograph (Bod. MS Cherry 5, fol. 188ʳ–9ᵛ); but this hand appears quite different from other known examples, so this is uncertain. Nevertheless, the 'voice' of Cherry 37 is a strongly personal one, with many comments in the first person: if the hand is not Melville's own, it must be that of a scribe or secretary working closely with him.

>   Aedes quisque suas ornabit diuite censu
>   Ornatamque Dei non licet esse domum?
>   Scilicet institui non aram, sed cupis haram
>   Porcorum stabulam quo venerere Deum.[88]

> *Why be surprised that the sacred altar has been attacked*
>   *By the kite's* [Melville's] *claws? No other bird is more rapacious;*
> *The Harpy birds, those foulest of monsters, once*
>   *Snatched the food laid out on a table in this way*
> *And their faces had a virginal beauty, but their hands*
>   *Were terrible, armed with hooked claws.*
> *O how foul are the faces of those, smeared with make-up* [or 'pretence, deceit'],
>   *Who think themselves more pure than the rest.*
> *Each one shall dress their temple with their own rich gifts –*
>   *Can a house which has been adorned not be a house of God?*
> *But of course you don't want an altar to be set up; you prefer a goose-pen*
>   *Or a pig sty – that's where you'd worship God.*

This reply, like several others, Latinizes Melville's name not as 'Melvinus' but as 'Milvus', the Latin name for a kite, and links the bird of prey to the monstrous Harpies who snatch the food laid out by Aeneas and his followers in *Aeneid* 3. This is followed by seven responses from Melville, another by Barclay, and an eighth by Melville; the printed collection *Melvini Musae* (1620) also prints an exchange of epigrams between Melville and Barclay, only two of which however are part of the manuscript sequence.[89]

The epigram on the king's altar is often found circulating together with another written during his time in the Tower, referring to the imprisonment, also in the Tower, of Sir William Seymour for his secret marriage to Arabella Stuart in 1610:

>   Communis tecum mihi causa est carceris, Ara-
>   bella tibi causa est; Araque sacra mihi.

> *You and I share the same cause for our imprisonment: a beautiful*
>   *altar* [i.e. 'Ara – bella'] *is why you are here; and a sacred altar is why I am.*

Many manuscripts – like Harley MS 6038, discussed above – contain only these two. They are also quite frequently found in miscellanies

---

[88] Bod. MS Cherry 37, fol. 24[r–v].
[89] Melville, *Melvini Musae* (1620), 24–7. M'Crie, *Life of Andrew Melville*, vol. II, 243, suggests that response poems of this kind attributed to others are in fact by Melville himself: but as we have seen, such exchanges were a very common feature of literary culture and the fact that the Cherry MS also attributes these epigrams to Barclay and others strongly suggests they are genuine. See also Doelman, *King James I*, 63–8.

accompanied by verse responses. Corpus Christi College, Oxford, MS 294, a mid-seventeenth-century collection, contains copies of three of Melville's Latin epigrams (including these two) followed by four epigrammatic responses to Melville by William Swaddon.[90] Another Corpus Christi manuscript (MS 311) includes epigrams which are part of a complex chain of defence and attack, carried out in both Latin and English, verse and prose, between William Alabaster, who had converted to Catholicism in 1597/8, and Bishop William Bedell (1571–1642). Such epigrammatic exchange continued well into the eighteenth century, and not only in the most elite literary circles of the kind around Pope: the Quaker John Kelsall records in his notebook 'The Following [Latin] Disticks, on my Verses upon the hard Frost' which 'were wrote & sent me by Math: Graves Schoolmaster & Curate, of John's in Chester'. Kelsall's poem and the response it elicited date from 1740.[91]

This kind of 'conversational' exchange of epigrams could take place at considerable geographical distance. George Herbert's anagram epigram, 'Roma' ('Rome'), is found in three different settings: circulating individually in manuscript miscellanies from around 1618, with or without an English version; as part of the *Musae Responsoriae* sequence in Herbert's own autograph manuscript dating from about 1620; and then incorporated in *Lucus*, an epigram sequence probably put together in its final form in or shortly after 1623.[92] This poem's 'dual' career, both as a stand-alone epigram and as part of a sequence – indeed in this instance within two different sequences – is typical of neo-Latin epigram as a whole:

> Roma. Anagram: *Oram. Maro. Ramo. Armo. Mora. Amor.*
>
> ROMA, tuum nomen quam non pertransiit ORAM,
>   Cum Latium ferrent secula prisca iugum?
> Non deerat vel fama tibi, vel carmina famae,
>   Unde MARO laudes duxit ad astra tuas.
> At nunc exucco similis tua gloria RAMO
>   A veteri trunco et nobilitate cadit.
> Laus antiqua et honor periit: quasi scilicet ARMO
>   Te deiecissent tempora longa suo.

---

[90] Corpus Christi College, Oxford, MS 294, pp. 128–9. The same sequence is also in Corpus Christi College, Oxford, MS 309 (fols. 11ᵛ–12ʳ), a late seventeenth-century collection of notes and extracts on recent poets by made by William Fulman (1632–88).
[91] Society of Friends Archive, MS Vol S 193/5, p. 234.
[92] *Musae Responsoriae* (43 poems) may have its origins in compositions made when Herbert was at Westminster School (1605–9).

> Quin tibi tam desperatae MORA nulla medetur,
>   Qua Fabio quondam sub duce nata salus.
> Hinc te olim gentes miratae odere vicissim;
>   Et cum sublata laude recedit AMOR.

Rome. Anagram: *Frontier. Maro* [= Virgil]. *Branch. Shoulder. Delay. Love.*

> *ROME, what FRONTIER has your name not crossed,*
>   *Since the ancient times bore the yoke of Latium?*
> *You did not lack fame, or the songs of fame,*
>   *By which MARO bore your praises to the stars.*
> *And now your glory, like a withered BRANCH*
>   *Falls from an aged trunk and from nobility.*
> *Ancient praise and honour have perished: as if from their SHOULDER*
>   *Distant times had cast you down.*
> *Indeed no DELAY can cure you in your despair,*
>   *Although once, when Fabius[93] ruled, delay brought salvation.*
> *Hence the nations who once admired you now hate you in their turn;*
>   *And when praise has subsided, LOVE withdraws.*

The relatively brief length, wordplay and 'pointed' focus upon clever or unexpected observations relating to a single familiar word or idea all identify the poem as a humanist epigram, albeit a relatively long and complex example of that form. More specifically, this is a sophisticated instance of the fashionable 'anagram epigram', playing in this case upon six Latin words made of the same letters as the title and subject, 'Roma' (Rome): 'Oram' (frontier), 'Maro' (Virgil), 'Ramo' (branch), 'Armo' (shoulder), 'Mora' (delay) and 'Amor' (love).[94]

Unsurprisingly, Rome was a popular subject for epigrams among both Catholic and Protestant authors, and surviving manuscript and print collections both include hundreds of examples.[95] Nor was Herbert the first to write an anagram poem on this popular topic. The poem is probably related in particular to Owen 2.119, 'Anagramma Romae. Ad

---

[93] Quintus Fabius Maximus, appointed dictator by the Romans to deal with Hannibal's invasion of Italy, pursued a policy of delay.

[94] For an English example see Herbert, 'Anagram of the Virgin Marie' (in *The Temple*); on the vogue for this form, see Hallyn, 'Light-Weight Artifice', and Doelman, 'Herbert's *Lucus*'. John Ashmore's *Certain Selected Odes of Horace* (1621) contains a fashionably large number of anagram epigrams.

[95] Examples include Durham Cathedral Library, MS Hunter 96, p. 100b (two consecutive pages with this pagination), 'In Romam', c.1620 (anti-Catholic); East Sussex Record Office, MS FRE/599, p. 539, 'Mihi iam non regia Roma' (notebook of Archbishop Frewen, d.1660, on setting aside ambition in old age, and not being Catholic); BL MS Harley 4484, fol. 46ʳ, 'De Roma' (Catholic, probably French, late seventeenth century).

Carthaginienses', which uses the same play upon 'Roma' and 'mora', and makes the same connection to the Punic wars:

> Annibal in paucas fortunam distulit horas,
>   Non bene Romanas praemeditatus opes.
> ...
> Servata est minima maxima *Roma mora.*
>
> *Hannibal postponed fate for a few hours,*
> *Because he had not accurately foreseen Roman military strength.*
> ...
> *The greatness of* Rome *was saved by the smallest of* delays.

For a Protestant epigrammatist of around 1600, by far the most obvious point to make in an epigram on 'Rome' would be a polemical one about the superiority of Protestantism, and the corruption of the papacy. Owen, however, avoids the polemical associations of his topic and confines the 'point' of the epigram to ancient history.

Alongside its performative cleverness, Herbert's poem has a clear argument: that 'Rome' was enormously powerful and deserving of respect, both in terms of its military prowess and cultural capital ('Maro' means Virgil); but that Rome is also past her peak, now discarded and set down. In that sense it is – unlike Owen's epigram – a specifically *Protestant* poem. Indeed, Herbert probably intended that it should recall and as it were reply to Catholic versions of the same theme, perhaps in particular the following poem by the popular Dutch Jesuit poet Bernhard Bauhusius which was first published in 1616:

> Anagrammata,
> Roma, Amor, Maro
>
> Utcumque Romam verteris,
> Reges in illâ inueneris:
> Namque ipsa ROMA regibus,
> MARO dominator vatibus;
> Rex ille cordis, omnibus,
> Rex ille quem vocant AMOR.[96]
>
> *However you jumble 'Rome'*
> *You'll find kings in her:*
> *For as ROMA herself rules over monarchs,*

---

[96] Bauhusius, *Epigrammata* (1616), 20 (penultimate poem in Book 1). Bauhusius was widely read in early modern England and is well represented in English anthologies. On his influence on English writers including Herbert, see Chapter 6.

> *So MARO rules over poets;*
> *He who is the king of every man's heart,*
> *That king is the one they call LOVE.*

'Roma' is, grammatically speaking, a feminine singular word in Latin and Herbert makes use of this feature in the delicate personification of the end of his poem: Rome is like a woman who, no longer widely admired, begins to be rejected. Here he goes beyond anything suggested by Bauhusius. There's a hint of a kind of routine misogyny here, and also a relatively nuanced brand of anti-Catholicism: that Catholicism is about beauty and display, not inner piety.

As English anti-Catholicism goes this is restrained; but to what extent this seems like a specifically anti-Catholic or even anti-Jesuit poem depends on the context in which we encounter it. In BL MS Harley 6038 (and also the related manuscript Harley MS 1221), Herbert's 'Roma' is accompanied by a facing English poem, described in the catalogue as a translation, but really something more like a response or even rejection of Herbert's moderation. The English poem, which is much longer than the Latin, includes only the single anagram pair Rome/More, beginning:

> Rome, thou that calst' thy-selfe a Queene, a Whore
> Thou art, and yet thy anagram is More,
> For wth the wine of thy adulterous Lust
> The Kings & dwellers of the Earth thou do'st
> Make drunke, that More with them thou maist, & More
> Act the behavior of a shamelesse Whore.[97]

The poem is not a translation at all, but something closer to a riposte to Herbert, and takes the understated personification of the end of Herbert's poem as the starting point for a virulently (if rather unoriginally) anti-Catholic piece: Rome as the whore of Babylon.

But Herbert's own successive placement of his poem within two distinct epigram sequences also influences our reading of it. In *Musae Responsoriae*, a sequence addressed to (and rejecting the position of) Andrew Melville, by then an old man, it is preceded and introduced by a poem in which Herbert mocks Melville for his hysterical fear of the 'Vatican she-wolf' and adds 'We have learnt to steer with equal care / Around that Charybdis, and your [i.e. Melville's] Scylla, armed with stakes against both: / The British

---

[97] BL MS Harley 6038, fols. 15[v]–16[r], in which the Latin poem is attributed to 'G. H.' and dated 1618; also at BL MS Harley 1221, fol. 102 [r–v].

Fox, and the Roman Wolf. / I shall demonstrate the truth of this with an Anagram'.[98] The anonymous translator/responder of Herbert in the Harley manuscripts seems to be aware of this context of conscious moderation, and to be rejecting it.

When Herbert reused this poem for the second time in an epigram sequence, in *Lucus*, he placed it ahead of a sequence of poems about the election of Pope Urban VIII, born Maffeo Barberini, in 1623. Urban was well known as a Latin poet, and in this sequence 'Roma' is followed by a response attributed to Barberini himself:

> Cum Romam nequeas, quod aves, **evertere**, nomen
>   **Inverteris**, mores carpis & obloqueris:
> Te Germana tamen pubes, te Graecus & Anglus
>   Arguit, exceptos quos pia Roma fouet:
> Hostibus haec etiam parcens imitatur Iesum.
>   **Invertis** nomen. Quid tibi dicit? AMOR.
>   (*Lucus* 26)

> *Since you cannot do what you crave and overturn Rome, you jumble*
> *Her name instead, and you attack and abuse her customs;*
> *The youth of Germany, of Greece and of England all*
> *Censure you, all of whom Rome has dutifully welcomed and cherishes:*
> *In sparing her enemies she imitates Jesus.*
> *You jumble her name. But what does it tell you? LOVE.*

In two further poems, Herbert replies to Barberini (*Lucus* 27 and 28). The scholarly assumption for several years was that Herbert had also written the epigram in the voice of the Pope, and Hutchinson even suggested that Herbert respectfully allows the pope to 'have the better' of the exchange.[99] In fact, as James Doelman has pointed out, all the evidence is that this epigram really *was* written by the future pope, since it is included (without Herbert's original) in Barberini's 1623 volume of *Poemata*.[100] Barberini was not himself a Jesuit, but he was educated by them and responsible for the canonization of Ignatius of Loyola: as a keen Latin poet, it is certainly likely that he had a good knowledge of contemporary Jesuit verse. Indeed, in his response to Herbert, he seems to allude to Bauhusius' epigram on the same theme (quoted above), with the repeated play 'evertere / inverteris / invertis'. Herbert then apparently

---

[98] *Musae Responsoriae*, 30.3–7.   [99] Hutchinson (ed.), *Works of George Herbert*, 592.
[100] Barberini, *Poemata* (1623), 60–1. Doelman, 'Herbert's *Lucus*'. This article is difficult to access in the UK. I am very grateful to the author for sending me a hard copy.

incorporated Barberini's riposte in *Lucus* in the same way as Bod. MS Cherry 37 incorporates responses to Melville alongside the original epigrams. When Herbert's *Musae Responsoriae* was published in 1662, that volume similarly reprinted Melville's *Anti-Tami-Cami-Categoria* (to which Herbert was responding), so that readers could appreciate the relationship between these works.[101]

Here we see how the culture of epigram exchange functioned in multiple ways: Herbert's 'Roma', probably initially composed as a stand-alone instance of the fashionable anagram epigram on a conventional topic, first circulated individually; was then incorporated into an epigram sequence (*Musae Responsoriae*) which was itself part of a versified debate (with the aged Andrew Melville, representing a more austere form of Protestantism than Herbert himself); at some point it was seen by Maffeo Barberini, who responded to it with a witty epigram of his own; as Pope Urban VIII, he included his reply in his collected verse; Herbert responds (rather graciously) to the Pope's riposte, and incorporates the entire sequence into a new book of epigrams, *Lucus*. Finally, the anonymous (but somewhat hostile) compiler of Harley MS 6038, perhaps aware of the relatively gracious tone of the exchange between Herbert and the Pope, or of Herbert's advocation of moderation in *Musae Responsoriae*, responds to the epigram with an aggressively anti-Catholic English 'version' of Herbert's poem. Herbert's 'Roma' alludes to the Latin verse of his contemporaries and is part of a conversation not, primarily, with the ancient world, but rather with the Calvinist divine Andrew Melville, the Jesuit Bernhard Bauhusius and the poetry of the newly elected pope, Barberini – contemporary poets from Scotland, the Netherlands and Italy. It is in that sense part of a public or at least partly public conversation about the most important religious questions of the day, as well as personal and national religious and political identity.

All these features are typical of Latin epigram culture as a whole; but 'Roma' is also distinctively *Herbertian* in its blend of assured and ambitious address (first to the aged Melville, then to the newly elected Pope) with real generosity and modesty: this peculiar combination is typical of Herbert and is particularly clear in his Latin work, partly because it is the Latin poetry that belongs to the 'public facing' and more conventionally ambitious phase of his life as a fellow and then university orator at Cambridge.

---

[101] Vivian *et al.*, *Ecclesiastes Solomonis*.

BL MS Harley 6038: Classical and Contemporary, Translation and Response

Harley MS 6038, dating probably from around 1620, is representative of a collection dating from a moment of cultural transition: the compiler of this manuscript, which contains mostly English verse and only a relatively small proportion of Latin poetry (including, as we have seen, Herbert's 'Roma'), is particularly interested in translating and responding to Latin poems in English. This is a fairly early example of a feature which was to become typical of the mid-seventeenth century, when large quantities of epigrams begin to appear in bilingual presentation in manuscripts. The compiler's taste in Latin epigram is also typical in several respects.

The following sequence, for instance, is found in Harley MS 6038 as well as two other related miscellanies:[102]

> Qui Laqueum collo nectabat repperit aurum
>   Thesariique loco deposuit Laqueum.
> At qui condiderat, postquam non repperit aurum
>   Aptavit collo quem reperit Laqueum./

> A poore man, with a rope, having in mind
> To hang him-selfe, a purse of gold did find;
> And where he gladly did the gold receaue
> The rope as gladly did behind him leaue.
> But he that closely ~~there~~ ^had^ the gold there hid
> When that he mist his money, sadly did
> His former resolucion also alter
> And fitted for his necke the new-found halter.
>   R.H:/[103]

> Hâc jacet in cartâ nocturno Tempore partâ
> Mitis ad austerum responsio Cadwaladerum.
>   J: D:/

---

[102] BL MS Harley 6038, fol. 17ʳ. These four items are part of a longer sequence which appears in the same order in a related manuscript, BL MS Harley 1221, fol. 103ʳ, though without initials attributing authorship. BL MS Harley 7316, dating from the early eighteenth century, does not reproduce the longer sequence, but does contain the same four items given here (fol. 3ᵛ), without initials. It was presumably copied from BL MS Harley 1221 or another related manuscript which does not survive.

[103] These initials are hard to read, as the letters overlap, but appear to be a kind of bespoke monograph of an overlapping R. and H. This is probably why Richard Harley is denoted in this manuscript by Ri: H. (rather than just R. H.), to avoid ambiguity.

/
Opprest with greife & sicknesse here I lie
Stopt in my middle course & soone made dead.
Grudge not at god young man though soone thou die
But know he trembles favor on thy head.
　Who for thy mornings worke equals thy pay
　W^th those that haue endur'd the heat of day./
                                                  W: B:

This sequence of four items, two Latin and two English, juxtaposes a late antique poem (by the fourth-century poet Ausonius) and a single hexameter couplet which appears to be contemporary (beginning 'Hâc jacet'). Attribution is uneven and obscure: the first item, in fact by Ausonius, is not attributed, presumably because it is considered highly recognizable.[104] The other items are attributed only by initials, and none of these has been traced securely, though initialled attributions elsewhere in the manuscript appear to be largely accurate.[105] Several translations in the manuscript are, like the translation of Ausonius here, attributed to an 'R. H.', and 'R. H.' (perhaps Sir Robert Harley, 1579–1656) may also be the compiler. The Latin couplet attributed to 'J. D.' is not one of the known epigrams of John Davies of Hereford (c.1565–1618), a noted Latin epigrammatist. As discussed below, this couplet dates probably to the 1580s or 1590s. It is just possible that J. D. may stand for John Donne, whose Latin epigrams are lost, though it does not correspond obviously to any of the English translations of Donne's epigrams published by Jasper Mayne in 1652.[106]

Thirdly, the sequence is intensely bilingual although, on close examination, it is bilingual in more than one way. The first pair of poems consist of a Latin text (Ausonius) accompanied by a somewhat expansive, but otherwise fairly straightforward, translation into R. H.'s characteristically rather mediocre English verse. The second pair, however, which at first sight seem similar, are not in fact original and translation. The English poem beginning 'Opprest with greife and sicknesse' is not a translation of the Latin couplet, which means: 'On this piece of paper, born of the night,

---

[104] Ausonius was much more widely read in early modernity than today, and his epigrams were routinely included in epigram collections as well as anthologies of classical Latin verse.
[105] The copy of Herbert's epigram 'Roma' discussed above is (accurately) attributed to 'G. H.' and dated 1618, one of the earliest attestations for the circulation of this popular poem. Another English epigram known only from this manuscript, 'Here Lye two Bodyes happy in their kinds', is also attributed to 'G. H.' and the attribution to Herbert, though found only here, has been accepted by *CELM* (HrG 290.5, 290.6 and 290.8), on which see Whitlock, 'Authorship,' and Doelman, 'Herbert's couplet'.
[106] Donne, *Paradoxes, Problemes, Essayes, Characters* (1652).

lies / A gentle response to the harsh Cadwalader', playing upon the conventional 'hic iacet' ('here lies') formula of memorial inscriptions. Indeed, this piece is probably not, strictly speaking, a self-contained epigram at all, despite appearances: it seems to be an introductory couplet intended to stand before a further item, whether poetry or prose. As it appears here – and also in the related manuscripts Harley 1221 and 7316 which contain the same four items in the same order though without attributions – it is most naturally taken as introducing the piece of English verse which follows it. Understood as such, the Latin couplet contextualizes and introduces the English poem. A final layer is added by the obvious scriptural resonance of the English poem, which alludes to the parable of the workers in the vineyard (Matthew 20:1–16).

Even in this period in which the bilingual presentation of epigrams becomes increasingly popular, miscellanies often include translations or responses for some epigrams and not for others: Harley MS 6038, for instance, includes 13 Latin epigrams overall, 7 of which are accompanied either by translations or by responses in English. In one case (fol. 66ʳ), R. H.'s English version is given before the Latin epigram to which it corresponds (attributed to Ri: H., Richard Harley, Robert Harley's uncle, and dating probably from the 1580s). On the same page, the translation of a very widely circulating epigram on the Jesuit house at Dole in France is also ascribed to R. H.[107] It is noticeable that the majority of the Latin pieces recorded without English translations or responses are topical epigrams of, as it were, the previous generation: one on the insignia of Queen Elizabeth (fol. 66ᵛ), one on the Parry plot of 1585 (fol. 30ʳ), as well as (yet again) Andrew Melville's two most famous epigrams, on the King's altar and on Arabella Stuart (fol. 66ᵛ).[108] Indeed, the enigmatic Latin couplet referring to 'Cadwalader' probably also dates from the 1580s or 1590s: the line probably refers to Cadwallader Owen (c.1562–1617), who had a great reputation as a debater in Oxford in the 1580s and 1590s, and who was tutor to Robert Harley during his years at Oriel College in the late 1590s. Harley's mother died while he was young, and he was instructed in part by his uncle, Richard Harley, probably the Ri: Harl: to whom several of the earlier Latin pieces in the manuscript are ascribed.

---

[107] This epigram appears in many manuscripts of the 1620s and is also quoted, with an English translation, in Howel, *Epistolae Ho-Elianae* (1645), 55 (letter dated 1621).

[108] The epigram on Parry is also ascribed to Ri: H. It is also found in Bod. MS Rawl. poet. 85, fol. 65ʳ, headed 'Verses made upon Dr Parrye the Traytor' and ascribed 'R. H.'. William Parry was executed for a plot against the Queen in March 1585. Several other epigrams in Harley MS 6038 are also ascribed to Ri: H., including another Latin epigram without translation (fol. 66ʳ).

The anonymous compiler of Harley MS 6038 – most likely Robert Harley himself – offers an insight into the role of Latin and English epigram around a quarter of the way into the seventeenth century. An educated man, with an appreciation for Latin verse but not apparently actively engaged in writing it himself, he is attracted by epigrams from antiquity to the present, most of which either comment upon political and religious matters of the last fifty years, or offer pithy summaries of conventional moralizing tropes. Several are unattributed, and where there are attributions (as in the case of Herbert ('G. H.'), 'J. D.' and 'Ri: H.'), comparison with the related seventeenth-century manuscript Harley 1221, which is without attribution, suggests that the compiler has added these himself from his own knowledge or supposition. He is interested in translation, and is probably (if he is indeed 'R. H.') a keen, though not particularly talented, translator himself; but most of the translations are his own, and several of the older topical epigrams go untranslated: in other words, he is not writing at a period when most epigrams circulate bilingually, or in which there is a large store of English translations on which to draw.

The Mid-Late Seventeenth Century and the 'Bilingual Epigram'

We have seen how the earliest collections are dominated by Latin epigrams, arranged thematically; and how the epigram culture of the early seventeenth century tended to run in 'parallel', with intense epigrammatic exchange and response between and within languages, but relatively little direct translation and bilingual circulation of individual poems. The shift towards the kind of bilingual circulation of epigrams that is so marked a feature of mid-late seventeenth-century notebooks and miscellanies is noticeable too in large dedicated collections. Among the largest manuscript epigram collections, those with the greatest proportion of bilingual epigrams all date from the mid-seventeenth century or later.

A particularly revealing example of this tendency is Leeds Brotherton Collection MS Lt q 18, a substantial collection of 120 epigrams compiled around 1650 and presented in parallel text format throughout. The collection is divided into four parts: an opening section from Martial; a second section consisting of around 50 mostly neo-Latin but some classical pieces; a third section of 'Epigrammes or Sentences Epigrammelike' from a wide range of classical authors; and finally a section of 71 poems titled 'Epigrammes by mee long since made in Latin and of late Englished'. Two things are striking here: the basic format of the collection – beginning with a section dedicated to Martial, then continuing with mixed neo-Latin and classical epigrams – reflects many similar collections from the early part of the seventeenth century. The compiler only occasionally indicates authors, a feature which places him mid-way between broadly sixteenth- and broadly seventeenth-century tendencies. Of those poems which are identified, Owen unsurprisingly is the best represented single modern poet, with four epigrams, and in general the selection of neo-Latin poems is very typical of the period, including Sannazaro's epigram on Venice; Alabaster on the brothers who switched religion; one of Beza's early epigrams; and two from Hugo Grotius. The only unusual feature is the systematic translation. Moreover, the compiler himself indicates that, in the case of the large final section of epigrams of his own composition, the Latin poems were written 'long since' (perhaps, we imagine, at school or university) while the translations are new ('of late Englished'). For this individual, apparently composing epigrams over many years, the switch towards large-scale translation is a recent phenomenon.

This shift is reflected also in print anthologies and the ways in which they are mined by the compilers of manuscript miscellanies. John Ashmore's 1621 collection, usually (though rather misleadingly) referred to as *Certain Selected Odes of Horace*, is poised on the cusp of this tradition. Sections 1, 3 and 4 consist primarily of scriptural and classical translations (and some from recent Latin); while section 2 is insistently bilingual in its jumble of Latin and English epigrams, including Ashmore's own four versions of the very widely circulating epigram on Buckingham (beginning 'Buckinghamus Iö maris est praefectus'), variously attributed to Sir John Ayton and to King James himself.[109] In manuscript, BL MS Add. 61744 provides similar evidence for the mid-century vogue for bilingual presentation: it contains a long sequence of epigrams most of which were apparently copied between 1643 and 1653 from Abraham Wright's popular monolingual Latin epigram collection, *Delitiae delitiarum* (1637).[110] Here, however, they are all accompanied by English translations. The print anthology by 'Lerimos Uthalmus', *Fasciculus Florum: or, a nosegay of flowers*, published in London in 1636, which unusually provides English translations for every epigram, is an early indication of the changing fashion.

---

[109] Ashmore, *Certain Selected Odes of Horace* (1621). The translations of the Buckingham epigram, marking his appointment as Lord Admiral in January 1619, are at 41–2. Strikingly, Ashmore does not give the Latin poem, but simply titles his English versions 'ex Latino', assuming that all his readers were familiar with such a famous poem.

[110] Wright's collection is discussed further in Chapter 6.

In many manuscript collections of the mid-late seventeenth century, then, we find an increased proportion of near-contemporary and topical epigrams accompanied by English translations, though it remains common for older items to circulate monolingually. In Harley MS 6054, for instance, most of the Latin epigrams relating to the events and figures of the late seventeenth century have translations, while older pieces – such as epigrams by Thomas More (fol. 28ᵛ), George Buchanan (fol. 28ᵛ) and John Owen (1.217, fol. 25ᵛ) as well as items by Ausonius and Martial – appear only in Latin.

A volume now in the Society of Friends (Quaker) archive, MS Vol S 80, titled *Rhapsodia*, preserves a collection of verse by Thomas Ellwood (1639–1714). Almost all the Latin verse included in the volume is in the form of brief epigrammatic items, and of 30 pieces, 25 are accompanied by English translations. A series of 22 English couplets (pp. 117–23) are all translations of single lines of Latin verse of this kind:

> Beauty adorns, yet boast not: tis a flow'r
> Both Age & Sicknes have it in their pow'r.
>
> Res fragilis Forma est: Praestant aeterna caducis.
>
> Fear of the Lord preserves the heart from sin:
> But fear of Man lets troops of Evils in.
>
> Quid Hominem timeas? solus Deus est metuendus.[111]

Towards the end of the volume a single Latin epigram in praise of the village of Beaconsfield is followed by 10 separate English epigrams on the same theme.

In collections of this sort we see how conservative epigram culture, broadly understood, could be: Ellwood's collection of moralizing Latin hexameter monostichs accompanied by English distich translations belongs clearly to the tradition of *Cato's Distichs* and the many (typically Latin-only) large collections of such verse found in sixteenth-century manuscripts. The chief difference from the sixteenth-century examples is not in theme, style or metre but in the systematic use of accompanying English versions which in many instances, like those given above, precede the Latin.

The most popular epigrams of the late sixteenth and early seventeenth centuries had a long life: Bod. MS Tanner 306, a late seventeenth- and early eighteenth-century collection, gathers many poems dating from the

---

[111] Society of Friends Archive, MS Vol S 80, pp. 118–19.

1630s and several from well before that, including popular epigrams by Beza and Alabaster. In both cases, however, the copies of these poems include unusual vernacular versions typical of the later seventeenth century: the page containing six of Beza's epigrams is accompanied 'cum versione Scottica', a translation into Scots; while Alabaster's famous epigram on the brothers who changed religions is recorded alongside three different translations: one by Alabaster himself, one by William Sancroft and one by Francis Mundie.[112]

In this later period, the most topical epigrams increasingly appear in different collections accompanied by the same or very similar translations: evidence of their circulation as a 'translated pair'. Marvell's bilingual epigram, 'Bludius et Corona' is one widely circulating example. *CELM* records 28 copies of the English version, 14 of them accompanied by Marvell's Latin, though this list excludes at least one example of the Latin epigram circulating alone.[113] The poem commemorates the attempt by Thomas Blood, an unhappy Cromwellian who had lost lands at the Restoration, to steal the crown jewels from the Tower of London on 9 May 1671. The poem is striking in its sympathy for Blood, whom Marvell may have known, though the two versions have some significant differences.[114] (Indeed, there is no certainty that both Latin and English are by Marvell, though they are both attributed to him in several contemporary sources.)

> Bludius, ut ruris damnum repararet aviti,
>   Addicit fisco dum diadema suo:
> Egregium sacro facinus velavit amictu:
>   (Larva solet reges fallere nulla magis).
> Excidit ast ausis tactus pietate prophana,
>   Custodem ut servet, maluit ipse capi.
> Si modo saevitiam texisset pontificalem,
>   Veste sacerdotis, rapta corona foret.
>
> *When daring Blood his rent to have regained*
> *Upon the English diadem distrained,*
> *He chose the cassock, surcingle and gown,*
> *The fittest mask for one that robs a crown.*

---

[112] Bod. MS Tanner 306, fol. 138ʳ–9ᵛ (Alabaster); fol. 145ʳ (Beza).
[113] One is accompanied by a different translation. Bod. MS Eng. poet. f. 13 (fol. 147ʳ) contains an additional copy of the Latin epigram only, unknown to *CELM*. It is likely that further Latin-only copies will be identified with further research.
[114] For links between Marvell and Blood, see Smith (ed.), *Poems of Andrew Marvell*, 413–14, and Smith, *Andrew Marvell*, 240–1.

> *But his lay pity underneath prevailed,*
> *And while he spared the keeper's life he failed.*
> *With the priest's vestments had he but put on*
> *A bishop's cruelty, the crown had gone.*[115]

Overall the Latin epigram is more successful, and was almost certainly written first. Lines 5–6, in particular, are much more effective in Latin. In Latin, the real *pietas* – that resonant Virgilian word associated above all with Aeneas – belongs to Blood. His virtue is real even if it is *prophana* ('profane') – that is, both not-priestly and also 'willing to profane' (the dignity of the crown). Marvell translates *pietas* as 'pity' (to which it is etymologically related), but Latin *pietas* has a different range of reference, incorporating both religious 'piety' as we would understand it, and also the strong sense of duty towards one's ancestors, parents, family and country that typifies Aeneas. Blood has real *pietas* because he knows it would be wrong to kill the innocent guard; this implies that the desire to seize the crown in the first place is *not* impious in this sense. The oxymoronic Latin phrase 'pietate prophana' is sharply memorable, while 'lay pity' is rather obscure; that 'lay' means 'not ordained' here is only really clear by comparison with the Latin, and 'underneath prevailed' is similarly hard to follow. The Latin is more vivid, and hard to translate concisely. Indeed, it is hard to imagine anyone writing the line 'And his lay pity underneath prevailed' except under the pressure of translation. Similarly, 'while he spared the keeper's life, he failed' is weaker than the Latin equivalent, which emphasizes Blood's conscious decision to preserve the guard's life at his own expense. The Latin means 'in order to save the guard, he preferred to be caught himself'.

The Latin poem is also particularly effective because it activates a series of largely Latin-based set scenes and associations: the loss of ancestral land recalls the land confiscations following the Roman Civil War that are the dramatic setting for Virgil's *Eclogues*. This association links Blood's Cromwellian and Parliamentarian sympathies to the losing side in the Roman Civil War: several prominent figures in Augustan Rome, including Horace, were veterans of the losing side, and Virgil is traditionally believed to have lost land in the confiscations.

Furthermore, the motif in which a wicked deed is undertaken in clerical disguise recalls a long-standing trope of anti-clerical and anti-monastic satire: in Milton's *In Quintum Novembris*, the devil disguises himself as a monk in order to inspire the Pope to wickedness, and Marvell's Latin

---

[115] These lines also form lines 192–9 of Marvell's poem 'The Loyal Scot'.

phrase 'saevitiam ... pontificalem' can be translated either as the savagery of 'bishops' or specifically of the Pope. Corrupt clergy and bishops are routinely described in terms of predation and disguise in popular early modern Latin texts, including both Mantuan and Palingenius: the related motifs in Spenser's *Shepherds' Calendar* and Milton's *Lycidas* ('Blind mouths! That scarce themselves know how to hold / A sheephook', 119–20) are derived from these very frequently excerpted passages.[116] Marvell's Latin epigram draws in this way upon a long lineage of Protestant and proto-Protestant anti-clerical, anti-monastic, anti-episcopal and anti-papal imagery in order to imply that Blood's daring attempt at a heist belongs to this essentially noble tradition.

Translation into Latin

In the later part of the seventeenth century we find increasing numbers of epigrams translated from English into Latin: this is one element of a broader phenomenon, in which the translation of English poetry into Latin became increasingly common, though it may also reflect a sense of the 'maturity' of the English genre of epigram and, perhaps, a reduced production of original epigrams in Latin. BL MS Harley 6054, for instance, includes a particularly large number of epigrams translated into Latin, including seven consecutive translations by 'Mr Redman' of an epigram on Cleveland.[117] A collection made by William Parry, a fellow of Jesus College, Oxford, between 1713 and 1728 contains several such translations, including this amusing Latin version of a 1590s epigram by John Davies of Hereford (1565–1618):[118]

> A true Copy of a Certificate given to a New Married Couple in Carmarthenshire, Southwales.
>
>> Under this Hedge, in rainy Weather,
>> I join'd this Rogue & Whore together;
>> And none, but He that rules the Thunder,
>> Can put this Rogue & Whore asunder.
>>   John Davies of the County of Carmathen-

---

[116] Mantuan and Palingenius were writing, of course, before the Reformation, but their poems were widely interpreted as being proto-Protestant in sympathy. On this trope, see also Chapter 11.
[117] BL MS Harley 6054, fol. 24ʳ. The manuscript also includes translations into Latin of poems which are not epigrams, such as an extract from Denham's 'Cooper's Hill' (fol. 24ᵛ).
[118] This refers not to Sir John Davies (1569–1626) who published English epigrams in the 1590s, but John Davies of Hereford, whose work is not included in *CELM*. The English poem is attributed to Jonathan Swift in several printed works of the eighteenth century.

Thus Translated-

> Sente sub hoc viridi Nebulonem hunc & Meretricem
>   Conjunxi multâ dum ruit Imber aquâ:
> Jam qui disjungat Nebulonem hunc & Meretricem,
>   Quos ego conjunxi, Jupiter unus erit.
>   T. Holland[119]

This large collection, containing 351 items altogether, includes 85 of Junius' *aenigmata* (riddle poems), and a selection of the most popular individual epigrams of the seventeenth century, such as Sannazaro's poem on Venice, Alabaster on the brothers who changed religion and Marvell's 'Bludius et Corona' (without translation, and hence missed by previous scholarship). It also records a very large number (224) of Oxford 'quaestio' verses, giving a sense of how this kind of epigram, which students were required to produce as part of their studies, was read and circulated alongside the sort of topical epigram we are more likely to consider of literary interest.

As we saw in the case of earlier manuscript collections, this kind of translation into Latin can involve excerpting (and then translating) in such a way as to 'create' epigrams from longer works. BL MS Harley 6054 also includes, for instance, a translation of an extract from Samuel Butler's *Hudibras* into four lines of hexameter, effectively a 'manufactured' epigram of the same kind as we saw generated (without translation) from Mantuan or Palingenius; other poets frequently excerpted and translated into Latin in this way include John Denham, Abraham Cowley and John Milton. In a Bodleian manuscript dated 1688 we find three couplets excerpted from George Herbert's poem 'Charms & Knots' presented as stand-alone epigrams of the moralizing type, accompanied by translations into Latin:

> Who goes to Bed, & doth not pray,
> Maketh 2 Nights from eury Day. Herb.
> Siquis eat cubitum, nec pulset ad Ostia Caeli,
> Duplicat Sic Noctem, & peioribus aggravat Umbris.
>
> Who reads a Chapter ere they rise,
> Shall n'er be troubled wth ill Eyes. Herb.
> Glaucoma ab Oculis ut quis avertat suis,
>   Possitque acutum cernere:
> Is manè multo surgat, Lecto recens
>   Sacram & revoluat paginam.

---

[119] Bod. MS Eng. poet. f. 13, fol. 193ᵛ.

> When th'Haire is sweet thro pride, or Lust,
> The powder doth forget ye Dust. <u>Herb:</u>
> Opplens odoro puluere insultum Caput
> Se pulverem obliviscitur.[120]

George Herbert began his career with a sequence of polemical epigrams, the *Musae Responsoriae*, which themselves respond to a famous author of polemical epigrams, the elderly Andrew Melville. As university orator, he was called upon to compose the sort of extempore or highly topical epigram of the kind reported by Joseph Mead to his friend Martin Stuteville. But Herbert also composed poetry in that moralizing tradition which represents a very significant, albeit generally neglected, aspect of early modern epigram culture: as well as 'Charms and Knots', his long poem which opens *The Temple*, 'The Church Porch', is essentially a series of versified moral precepts of the kind familiar from *Cato's Distichs*. Though usually passed over by critics today, it was the most frequently quoted of all Herbert's poems in the seventeenth century.[121]

Conclusion

The epigram culture of early modern England drew upon several distinct though related habits typical of the sixteenth century: the humanist epigram, courtly or satiric but highly literary and almost exclusively in Latin; the moralizing, didactic or proverbial distichs and other short poems typical of educational material and personal miscellanies in the later sixteenth century; and an emerging culture of epigrammatic exchange, both satiric and panegyric, a practice rooted in the changed educational practices of the post-Reformation schoolroom. The most significant changes in epigram culture between the mid-sixteenth and early eighteenth centuries were not ones of form, style or content, but of language, as a genre which was already mature in Latin in the mid-sixteenth century emerged and developed in English. As epigrammatic concision became stylistically and tonally possible in English, epigram developed into a fully bilingual phenomenon, with translation and response travelling in both directions.

---

[120] Bod. MS Sancroft 28, p. 139. These extracts do not follow the order of the original: the first couplet is lines 7–8, the second lines 1–2 and the third lines 13–14; the Latin versions are in hexameters (in the first case), followed by two iambic distichs.

[121] Ray, 'Herbert Allusion Book', v and 176.

CHAPTER 8

Satire, Invective and Humorous Verse

The final chapter of this section deals not with a single form or genre, but with the satiric, invective or humorous use of several.[1] As it happens, the patterns of previous scholarship have proved particularly distorting in relation to Anglo-Latin satiric verse. Most scholars with neo-Latin interests and expertise have a background in the classics, and studies of Renaissance and early modern Latin literature have largely been organized by (classical) genre.[2] For this reason, we have the beginnings of a guide to how the classical Roman genre of formal hexameter verse satire, as written by Lucilius, Horace, Juvenal and Persius, was imitated and imported by early modern Latin poets. Certain key collections – such as those of Francesco Filelfo (1398–1481), Thomas Naogeorg (1508–63), Jakob Balde (1604–68) and Lodovico Sergardi ('Sectanus', 1660–1726) – have emerged as landmarks in the field, frequently interpreted in terms of 'Horatian' vs. 'Juvenalian' (less often Persian) style.[3] Nevertheless, there has been almost no work on early modern Latin satiric and invective poetry more generally: that is, attempting to survey the various ways in which Latin verse of various genres might function as satire or invective, without conforming to the patterns of 'hexameter satire'; and, not unrelatedly, there has been very little work indeed on satirical Latin verse of any kind in England.[4]

---

[1] This chapter is an expanded version of a shorter survey (Moul, 'Anglo-Latin Satiric Verse in the Long Seventeenth Century'). On satire as 'mode' rather than genre see, for instance, Fowler, *Kinds of Literature*, 106–29; Marshall, *Practice of Satire*, 5–8.
[2] Ijsewijn, *Companion to Neo-Latin Studies, Part I*; Ijsewijn and Sacré, *Companion to Neo-Latin Studies, Part II*; Knight and Tilg (eds.), *Oxford Handbook of Neo-Latin*; Moul (ed.), *Guide to Neo-Latin Literature*. An interesting exception is Korenjak, *Geschichte der Neulateinischen Literatur*.
[3] On neo-Latin hexameter satire, see Ijsewijn, 'Neo-Latin Satire'; Hintzen (ed.), *Norm und Poesie*; Haye and Schnoor (eds.), *Epochen der Satire*; Coronel Ramos, *La sátira latina*, 157–94.
[4] Ingrid de Smet comments briefly that 'the British Isles, for instance, were not short of [Latin] satirists, but verse satire adhered less closely to the classical canon [of hexameter satire]' ('Satire', 204). Even John Owen (1564–c.1628), a Latin epigrammatist read enthusiastically across Europe,

Given the significant but generally understudied role played by the production and consumption of neo-Latin poetry in early modern England, what kind of satiric verse do we find in Latin in this period and what is the relationship between Latin and English satiric poetry? This seems like a basic question of literary history, but it is one that has gone largely unasked, let alone answered. Manuscript circulation is a particularly important mode of dissemination for topical, satiric, comic, scabrous or potentially libellous verse, and one of the major obstacles to assessing the role of neo-Latin poetry in English literary culture is its almost complete invisibility to scholars even at the level of manuscript catalogues and first-line indexes. This chapter therefore draws frequently upon the findings of my ongoing research project devoted specifically to surveying manuscript verse, though clues are also to be found elsewhere: Harold Love's *English Clandestine Satire*, for instance, includes at the back a first-line index which contains a much larger number of Latin first lines than you might expect from the minimal discussion of Latin texts in the main body of the book. Love himself returned to the question of the role of Latin verse for satirical and comic purposes at the end of his life.[5]

Several distinct periods are associated particularly strongly with formal verse satire in English – that is, broadly speaking, with verse satire as a 'genre', on the model of Horace and Juvenal. The great age of 'Augustan' satire of this type is the early eighteenth century, with important precursors in the proliferation of verse satire during the Restoration period, such as those by Marvell and Dryden. Behind them, the brief but vigorous vogue for formal verse satire in the 1590s, to which both John Donne and Ben Jonson contributed, was also modelled directly upon the classics. In all three of these periods we find clusters of medium to long English poems which imitate in form, tone and often also in content the hexameter verse satire of Horace, Persius and Juvenal; many of the satiric poets also translated or paraphrased these classical works into English verse, such as Jonson's *Poetaster* (partly a dramatization of Horace's *Satires*) and Pope's *Imitations of Horace*.

---

has attracted little attention from British scholars, though there is now a good critical edition in French, Durand (ed.), *John Owen*.

[5] Love, 'Sir William Petty'. Bellany and McRae (eds.), 'Early Stuart Libels' does not include Latin but does sometimes indicate where a poem is a translation of a Latin epigram. May and Bryson, *Verse Libel*, contains little discussion of Latin but usefully emphasizes the formal creativity of verse libel.

The Missing Genre: The Absence of Hexameter Verse Satire in Anglo-Latin Poetry before c.1700

Several chapters of this book trace a pattern of generic and formal similarities between Latin literary culture (both local and international) and English vernacular poetry: we see this at work in the fashion for metrical variety in the latter sixteenth century; in the rise of both regular and irregular Pindaric verse first in Latin and then in English; in the vogues for epigram, mythological epyllia and biblical paraphrase; and in the appearance in English of formal panegyric odes and 'panegyric epic' of the Claudianic type. In many of these instances, a verse form which had become conventional – sometimes to the point of being widely taught – eventually moves from Latin into the vernacular. In a few other instances, I have described fashionable and influential Latin forms for which there were no or few obvious vernacular analogues, such as the 'free verse' and 'literary inscriptions' of the latter half of the seventeenth century, or the fashion in the first half of the seventeenth century for quasi-dramatic verse sequences incorporating several changes of metre. Equally, though not the focus of this book, there are several examples of ubiquitous vernacular forms for which there are no straightforward Latin equivalents. The most obvious example here is that of the sonnet: where sonnets were translated into Latin, as they quite frequently were, the metres and forms chosen are various. For early modern poets there was no obvious single way to 'write a sonnet' in Latin, and this remained true throughout the period under discussion in this book.[6]

In the case of hexameter verse satire, however, we have an unusual example of a form which, at least for poets writing in England, appears to develop roughly contemporaneously in English and Latin, with the English vogue perhaps slightly precedent. Given the intense imitation of Horace, Persius and Juvenal, all of whom wrote in hexameters, in late seventeenth- and early eighteenth-century English satire, it is unsurprising that we find similarly classicizing examples of Latin satire in hexameter at this period. A highly selective list might include, for instance, the anonymous 1702 *Satyra in poetastros O——C——enses*, an attack on the university anthologies marking the accession of Queen Anne; Thomas Hill's hugely popular *Nundinae Sturbrigienses*, a good-humoured satirical depiction of Stourbridge Fair, outside Cambridge, which was both printed by Tonson

---

[6] Francis Thorius, for instance, used six different Latin metres in translating Ronsard's sonnets into Latin verse in the latter sixteenth century (BL MS Sloane 1768, discussed in Chapter 2).

and pirated by Curll in 1709; Edward Holdsworth's *Muscipula* (1709), a mock-epic parody of Virgil at the expense of the Welsh, in which Taffy invents a mouse-trap; the *Commercium ad mare australe* of 1720, a very good satire on the bursting of the South Sea Bubble, perhaps by Herbert Randolph of Christ Church; the Juvenalian *Poemata* of 1729, composed by a dissenting clergyman in Kent; and William King's successful verse satires and epistles of the late 1730s.[7] All these works are verse satire of the sort that a classicist or a reader of Pope would recognize. What is more surprising, however, is that we find almost no examples of hexameter verse satire in this classical mode before the early eighteenth century. Although, as noted above, there are some important continental models – such as the satires of Naogeorg, Balde and Sergardi – there appear to have been few if any attempts by British authors to write in this form.

When Anglo-Latin poets turned to formal hexameter satire in the early eighteenth century, moreover, they did not do so in a purely classicizing way: these works seek to insert themselves within a national as well as a classical tradition of satiric verse, and by so doing offer some useful indications of the contemporary understanding of that tradition. The 1702 pamphlet, *Satyra in poetastros O———C———enses*, for instance, an anonymous attack upon the fawning verse anthologies produced by Oxford and Cambridge to commemorate the accession of Queen Anne, alludes in its title to Andrew Melville's polemic against Oxford and Cambridge, the *Anti-Tami-Cami-Categoria*. Melville's work was part of a debate about churchmanship at the time of the accession of James I in 1603: in the Millenary Petition of that year, Puritan ministers lobbied James to outlaw various Church practices, such as making the sign of the cross, which they considered too Catholic. In response, Oxford and Cambridge produced a joint riposte defending these practices and their role in the English Church. Melville's poem excoriates the position of the universities (*Tami-* refers to the Thames which runs through Oxford, *Cami-* to the river Cam) and defends the original Millenary Petition. It was almost certainly both written and circulated in manuscript in 1603 or 1604, though it was not published for the first time until 1620, and was brought back into political valency by being reprinted as late as 1662 alongside George Herbert's youthful response to it, his *Musae Responsoriae*.[8]

---

[7] [Anon.], *Umbritii Cantiani poemata* (1729); King, *Miltonis Epistola ad Pollionem* (1738) and *Sermo pedestris* (1739).

[8] On Melville's poem, see Cummings, 'Andrew Melville'. Cummings states that there is no evidence of circulation in England in manuscript before 1620; he was unaware, however, of a copy of Melville's poem now in Lambeth Palace Library (MS 113, fols. 223^r–6^r). This manuscript version

The term 'poetastros', which is not classical, probably recalls Ben Jonson's 1601 play *Poetaster*, which dramatized portions of several of Horace's *Satires*, and included Horace himself as a character.[9] In these two respects, this anonymous work of the early eighteenth century recalls literature associated with a similar moment of national transition a century before.

Melville's *Anti-Tami-Cami-Categoria* is a long poem, of 204 lines, but, surprisingly (for a modern classicist) it is not in hexameters but in sapphic stanzas: as we saw in Chapter 4, the use of sapphics for long, public odes is strongly associated with the latter half of the sixteenth century, and Melville, who was nearing 60 in 1603, here shows his age. He certainly does not mince his words:

> Turbida illimi crucis in lavacro
> Signa consignem? magico rotatu
> Verba devolvam? sacra vox sacratâ im-
>   Murmuret unda
>
> Strigis in morem? Rationis usu ad-
> Fabor infantem vacuum? canoras
> Ingeram nugas minus audienti
>   Dicta puello?[10]
>
>   (29–36)

> *Should I make muddy marks*
> *Of a grimy cross in the tub, should I roll out*
> *Words with a magical whirling? Should the holy voice*
>   *Mumble from within sanctified water*
>
> *In the style of a screech-owl? By the use of reason shall I really*
> *Address an empty infant? Shall I force sing-song*
> *Trifles upon a child, who is barely capable of hearing*
>   *What is spoken to him?*

Cummings points out that the poem as a whole may be best understood as polemic rather than satire: its central movement is dedicated to the praise and celebration of Beza and his followers in England (65–128).[11] Nevertheless, substantial sections are undeniably satiric, and the 1620

---

    differs significantly from either of the printed versions (1620 and 1623), including two additional stanzas early in the poem in praise of King James, and is probably significantly earlier. Melville's poem was reprinted alongside Herbert's response in Vivian *et al.*, *Ecclesiastes Solomonis* (1662).

[9] See Moul, *Jonson, Horace*, 135–72.
[10] Quoted from the first print edition: Calderwood, *Parasynagma Perthense* (1620), 41–2.
[11] Cummings, 'Andrew Melville'.

collection of Melville's verse published in Amsterdam presents him primarily as a poet of satire and invective.[12] Several features of Melville's style suggest specific adaptations of sapphics for polemic. As well as the insistent series of rhetorical questions, Melville twice in these 13 lines splits a word between the third and fourth line, something Horace does only very rarely.[13] Elements of his vocabulary, moreover, recall the Horace not of the *Odes* but of the *Epodes*: the screech-owl *(strigis,* 5), for instance, comes from the *Epodes*, and Melville describes liturgy of which he disapproves (such as making the sign of the cross) with terminology (as, in this passage, 'magical whirling', 2) borrowed from classical descriptions of magic such as that ascribed to the witch Canidia in *Epodes* 17.[14] Politically, this is astute: Canidia's black magic acts against individuals, but is associated structurally in the *Epodes* with other forces of disempowerment and disruption, chief among which is civil war itself.

Melville, whose widely circulating satiric epigrams were discussed in Chapter 7, seems also to have had a particular interest in the satiric deployment of long lyric forms. Perhaps the most impressive of these is his poem on the Gunpowder Plot. Shorter than the *Anti-Tami-Cami-Categoria*, at 108 lines in 27 alcaic stanzas, the poem is dramatically sophisticated, filled with direct speech and rhetorical questions.[15] Strikingly, it does not recount or even allude to the foiling of the plot, or the prosecution and execution of those held responsible for it. All the triumphalism of the poem is that of the (failed) plotters.

Melville has a flair for memorable invective; here are the Jesuits setting out for England:

> Urbem relinquunt protenus: Alpium
> Fastigia alte ninguida transuolant,
>   Cursuque transmittunt Britannum
>   Oceanum, penetrantque Regnum.
> Devota sacris pectora caedibus
> Instructa technis agmina bellicis,
>   Spinturnices inauspicatae
>   Spintriae, & ignivomi & salaces:
> In tecta repunt Nobilium artibus

---

[12] Melvillve, *Melvini Musae* (1620), on which see see Reid, 'Melville's Anti-Episcopal Poetry', 137.
[13] On three occasions only, *Odes* 1.2.19–20, 1.25.11–12 and 2.16.7–8.
[14] *Strigis* is found at *Epodes* 5.20. The witch Canidia has a magical 'top' which rotates (*Epodes* 17.7). The *Epodes* were a popular source for depictions of classical witchcraft and pagan magic; Jonson drew on them extensively in the *Masque of Blackness*.
[15] Melville, *Melvini Musae* (1620), 15–18.

> Freti dolosis, vellere & aureo:
> Sed veste mutata togisque
> Compositis sagulorum in usum.
> Ceu militaris copia Martiis
> Horrens maniplis, tecta adamantino
> Thorace, torquens bubalinum
> Tergus, & exuvias Leonis ...
>
> (21–36)

Thence they leave the city: they fly high across the snowy gables of the Alps, and in their course they cross the British ocean, and penetrate the kingdom.

Breasts vowed to sacred slaughter, ranks prepared with techniques of war, unsightly birds, prostitutes of ill omen, fire-breathing and salacious: trusting in the deceitful arts and in a golden fleece, they creep into the houses of the Nobility: but first they change their clothing and rearrange their togas [probably here denoting clerical robes] *into soldiers' short cloaks.*

Like a military force, bristling in armed companies, covered by a breastplate of iron, wielding the skin of an African gazelle, and the hide of a Lion ...

This is quite alien to anything Horace wrote in alcaics, though elements of the tone are (once again) comparable to parts of the *Epodes*. Melville here draws as much upon late antique and near-contemporary Latin verse as upon classical models. *Ninguidus* ('snowy') is found only in late antique authors, such as Ausonius and Prudentius; the juxtaposition of the rare (and, in the latter case, obscene) words *spinturnices* and *spintriae* suggests a kind of false etymology linking the obscure 'foul bird of ill-omen' (*spinturnix*) as it flies across the Alps with the anal sphincter (*spintria*, or *sphinthria*) which comes to mean a male prostitute.[16] The detail of *tecta Nobilium* (the houses of the nobility) presumably alludes to the role of the recusant aristocracy in sheltering priests. Meanwhile the details of the priests' disguise – clerical robes repurposed as *saguli* (a kind of short military cloak) – recalls several contemporary versions of this trope in other Gunpowder Plot poems.[17] Melville's Latin verse was well known

---

[16] *Spinturnix* (spintharis, Gk) Poët. ap. Fest. p. 330 sq. Müll.; Plin. 10, 13, 17, § 36; *sphinthria* or *spintria*, ae, m. from σφιγκτήρ, the contractile muscle of the anus, I *a male prostitute*, Tac. A. 6, 1; Suet. Tib. 43; id. Calig. 16; id. Vit. 3 *fin.*; cf. Aus. Epigr. 119 (Lewis and Short, *Latin Dictionary*).

[17] In both Francis Herring's *Pietas Pontificia* (1606) and Michael Wallace's *In Serenissimi Regis Iacobi Liberationem* (1606) the devil or a demon disguises himself as a Jesuit. Best known is Milton's description, in his later example of the genre (*In Quintum Novembris*, c.1626) of the devil disguising himself as a Franciscan in order to visit the Pope (80–5), a passage which is itself indebted to George Buchanan's satiric portrait of St Francis and Franciscan friars in his Latin verse satire *Franciscanus*.

and widely read in England in the early part of the seventeenth century and poets continued to engage with his Latin verse polemics until mid-century at least.[18]

Melville's work points to a tradition of formal Latin satire and invective composed not in hexameter but in lyric metres, combining the forms of Horace's *Odes* with diction, allusions and invective force associated with the *Epodes*. George Herbert's response to Melville, however, though also in Latin verse and probably dating in its earliest form to the first decade of the seventeenth century, is not a single poem at all, but a sequence of 40 epigrams (*Musae Responsoriae*), dealing individually with Melville's objections, and incorporating 11 different metres. Neither of these forms – a single long lyric poem or a polymetric sequence – is an obvious choice for political or theological polemic from a classical Latin perspective. But both poets were in fact being faithful, in their choice of form, to their age and formation: Melville, as noted above, to the fashions of the mid-sixteenth century, while Herbert's choice of form reflects the late sixteenth- and early seventeenth-century vogues for epigram and for metrical variety.[19]

Here already we see a clear distinction in formal terms between the early seventeenth- and early eighteenth-century versions of Anglo-Latin verse satire: the anonymous *Satyra* of 1702 inserts itself in a specifically *British* tradition which takes in Jonson, Melville and Herbert, and concisely associates controversy around the accession of Queen Anne with similar debate arising from the succession of King James I a century earlier. But the natural *form* of that satirical comment has changed. If, in other words, we wish to understand the role of Latin poetry in early modern English satire, we need to look beyond the apparent absence of hexameter verse satire, and look instead for the satiric deployment of other poetic forms.

The last of the eighteenth-century hexameter satires mentioned at the start of this chapter are those of William King (1685–1763), whose poems of 1638 and 1639 both quickly went into second editions. King was principal of St Mary Hall in Oxford between 1719 and 1763, and a leader

---

All three of these scenes are discussed by Haan, 'Milton's *In Quintum Novembris*' (two parts). See also Hale, 'Milton and the Gunpowder Plot'.

[18] William Fulman's (1632–88) notebooks, for instance, demonstrate that Melville retained a literary reputation for both epigram and extended polemic in the latter half of the seventeenth century (Corpus Christi College, Oxford, MSS 294 and 309).

[19] On metrical variety, see Chapters 2 and 3. Epigrams are the main subject of Chapter 7, though with some discussion also in this chapter and (for scriptural epigram) in Chapter 6.

of the Jacobite party.[20] The first of his poems, like the anonymous verse satire of 1702, also looks back self-consciously to the seventeenth century, though to a different moment – and perhaps an unexpected one for a leading Jacobite. The full title page of the poem, which is dedicated to Alexander Pope, reads: 'Miltonis Epistola ad Pollionem. Edidit & Notis illustravit F. S. Cantabrigiensis' ('Letter of Milton to Pollio. Edited with notes by F. S. of Cambridge').

The poem is presented as a recently discovered Latin verse satire by John Milton, excoriating the tyranny, flattery and insincerity of the royal court, which King pretends to be transcribing and editing for the first time. This is a satire of the age of Bentley and of the *Dunciad*: the poem is accompanied by dense and learned notes speculating on the identification of various classically named figures in the poem. A note attached to line 16, for instance, comments on the introduction of the main target of the satire, the imperial favourite Pallas:

> Infanda en, iterum PALLAS sua dona paravit,
> Solicitans pretio cives, & *nobile* vulgus,
> Pollicitus quod quisque petat! Captantur avari,
> Et quos praecipites luxus rapit.
>
> (16–19)

Look, yet again PALLAS *has prepared his unspeakable gifts,*
Soliciting with cash the citizenry, and the 'noble' crowd,
He has promised whatever anyone asks for! Greedy types are captivated,
And luxury seizes those who fall for it.

v.16. PALLAS] Libertus fuit Claudii Caesaris, qui summo Imperatoris favore imbutus, summum fastigium tenuit, plebem, patres, consules, Augustam, Augustum, Augustos Lares pro arbitrio suo gubernans. Ditissimus erat Romanorum, vel Crasso ditior vicies & quinquies centenis millibus. Exinde natum proverbium,

> *Ego possideo plus*
> Pallante.   Juvenal. *Sat.* 1.

De hujusce viri insolentiâ, senatûs humilitate, Caesaris patientiâ, *vide* Plin. *Ep.* 6. *Lib.* 8. & Tacit. *Annal.* 12.

Sunt qui GEORGIUM VILLIERS *Buckingamiae ducem*, qui praefectus erat regni regnante Jacobo I. & Carolo I. hoc nomine designari volunt. Verùm

---

[20] Sharp, 'King, William (1686–1763)'; Greenwood, *William King*. King's first published English poem, *The Toast* (Dublin, 1732 and London, 1736) was dedicated to Jonathan Swift in its final form.

nescio, an astute conjecturam faciunt de GEORGIO isto, quum nobis parum certum sit de anno, quo scripta esset haec epistola.

v.16 PALLAS] A freedman of Claudius Caesar, who having the utmost favour of the Emperor, obtained the highest rank, thus governing the people, the senators, the consuls, even the Empress and Emperor and the Augustan Lares at his whim. He was the richest of the Romans, even 250,000 times richer than Crassus. Hence he gave rise to the following proverb:

> I possess more even
> Than Pallas.   *Juvenal. Sat. 1* [108–9]

Of this man's insolence, his humiliation of the senate, and the suffering of Caesar, see Pliny Epistle 6 Book 8, and Tacitus Annals 12.

There are those who like to say that George Villiers, Duke of Buckingham, who was Lord Admiral of the kingdom under James I and Charles I, is referred to by this name. But I do not know whether they are right to make such a conjecture about that George, since we are not sufficiently certain of the year in which this letter was written.

King reports with mock-objectivity that some consider Pallas to refer to George Villiers, first Duke of Buckingham, the controversial royal favourite murdered in 1628; but that he himself has doubts, given the uncertainty over the date of the epistle. (Milton, as he does not say, was only 20 in 1628.) 'Pallas' is in fact meant to represent Robert Walpole, the long-standing prime minister and the chief object of King's satire, as would have been obvious to all contemporary readers. King, a strongly Tory and Jacobite poet, here deploys Milton as a mouthpiece of *libertas* against Whig dominance.[21]

Milton did not write hexameter satire but he was famous for his satirical and invective Latin prose during the 1650s, as well as being an outstandingly good Latin poet. King's knowing hoax cleverly collapses several elements originating in different moments of the seventeenth century – Milton's reputation for satiric attack belongs to the latter 1640s and 1650s; most of his Latin poetry to the two decades before 1645; whereas George Villiers, Duke of Buckingham, *was* indeed the locus of a great deal of satiric verse, both Latin and English, but in the 1610s, during his rise to power, and in the run-up to his murder in 1628. By supplying Milton with an example of a genre he never actually produced, King implicitly acknowledges the point with which this chapter began: despite the

---

[21] A later Latin poem by King, *Templum libertatis* (*The Temple of Liberty*, 1742–3) was an unfinished allegorical epic inspired by *Paradise Lost* and celebrating the resilience of British liberty even under threat.

apparent 'obviousness' of hexameter as the metre for extended verse satire on the classical model, hexameter satire was in fact *not* an established genre for English Latin poets before the eighteenth century.

Where we do find examples of satiric verse in hexameter during the seventeenth century, they are in most cases rather far removed from the classical tradition of *sermones* (verse satires or epistles) as written by Horace, Juvenal or Persius. In 1643, Peter Smart, a convinced Calvinist by then aged 76, who had been repeatedly imprisoned for opposing Arminianism in general and latterly Laud in particular, published a pamphlet of Latin prose followed by verse in five short hexameter 'Partes', entitled *Cantus epithalamicus*.[22] A vituperative attack upon Arminius, Arminianism and High Church practices, the allegorical 'marriage' of the poem sees the Bride (the Church of England) married off to Antichrist (Catholicism) in an extravagantly corrupt version of the 'true' marriage between Christ and his Church, a union restored only at the end of the work. The pamphlet, presumably intended as part of the campaign against Laud, is a striking demonstration of the ways in which the fashion for allegorical Latin verse and the devotional vogue for texts based upon the Song of Songs could be exploited by Puritans as they were by Laudians and royalists.[23] For all the interest of Smart's poem, and its obvious satiric force, it is far removed in structure, conception or tone from the verse satires of Horace, Juvenal, Persius, or their imitators. Similarly, William Hogg's (c.1655–c.1702) *Satyra sacra vanitatem mundi et rerum humanarum* (1685), mentioned by de Smet in her survey of neo-Latin satire, is, like Smart's poem, based primarily upon scriptural paraphrase rather than classical satire.[24]

One other rare example of hexameter verse that can be understood as satire, also from the late 1640s, points in a different direction. Robert King's *Satyra Aethiopica, sive Speculum Britannicum* purports, like William King's poem nearly a century later, to be presenting another's text for the first time.[25] The brief introduction explains that the work is a translation into Latin hexameters of a work in Aethiopian by 'Presbyter Johannes', the mythical 'Prester John', a Christian king in Africa. In this version of the story, Prester John, on receiving merchants from London, launches into a

---

[22] Smart, *Septuagenarii senis itinerantis* (1643), signed and dated 'Petrus Smartus Febru. 16, 1643, aetatis 76' on sig. A2ᵛ.
[23] For further discussion of this poem, and related royalist works of political allegory, see Chapter 11. The imitation of the Song of Songs is also discussed in Chapter 6.
[24] De Smet, 'Satire', 205.
[25] Printed in King, *Catena* (1647). I have not been able to identify this Robert King.

consideration of whether it is better to be a king or a priest, given the vagaries of civil disobedience and disrespect to which a king may be subject. The whole piece is a comment, just as surely as the spurious Milton poem, on the political situation in England at the time of its composition, as the subtitle *sive Speculum Britannicum* ('or a Mirror of Britain') makes clear.

Iambic Satire and Invective: The Legacy of Horace's *Epodes*

Despite the fictional ploy of an African monarch, King's work denounces the sinful violence of civil war directly; and in this, although a hexameter poem, it is indebted to the related satiric and invective tradition of Horace's *Epodes*, a work completed very shortly after the end of the Roman civil war, and which confronts it directly. We have already seen that the diction and tone of Melville's invective, though lyric in form, also draw on the *Epodes*. Around 1620 a young Oxford student or recent graduate of St John's College, one Thomas Atkinson, responding probably to the first print publication of Melville's *Anti-Tami-Cami-Categoria* in that year, argued against it in Latin verse, just as Herbert had done, and presented a neat copy of the finished piece as a gift to the President (Master) of his college, William Laud. Laud was well known for his High churchmanship and natural hostility to Melville's position, which opposed practices such as infant baptism, the use of church music or making the sign of the cross.[26]

Atkinson's poem presents itself as a satire: it is titled *Melvinus Delirans, Sive Satyra Edentula Contra Ejusdem Anti-Tami-Cami-Categoriam* (*Crazy Melville, Or a Toothless Satire against his Anti-Tami-Cami-Categoria*). Like Melville's work, it is a single long poem (444 lines), but written neither in hexameter nor a lyric metre, but in iambic trimeter.[27] In fact, iambic trimeters are also the second most frequently used metre – after elegiac

---

[26] BL MS Harley 3496. Laud (1573–1645) was President of St John's between 1616 and 1621, when he became bishop of St David's. He went on to be a controversial archbishop of Canterbury (1633–40) and was executed in 1645. Thomas Atkinson, the author of the poem, was born in 1599 and went up to St John's from Merchant Taylors' school in 1615, aged 16, graduating in 1619. This manuscript must date from before 1622, as it addresses Laud as President, not bishop. A note at the foot of the title page identifies the volume as part of Laud's library. Another manuscript presented to Laud, an allegorical Latin tragedy *Homo*, is probably also by Atkinson (BL MS Harley 6925).

[27] Not in hendecasyllables, as Cummings says ('Andrew Melville', 166), a rare mistake in an otherwise excellent chapter.

couplets – in Herbert's response to Melville, the *Musae Responsoriae*.[28] This association between iambics and contentious, invective or satiric verse is also derived from Horace's *Epodes*.

The *Epodes* is a collection of 17 relatively short poems in both iambic and iambo-lyric metres, most (but not all) of which consist of satire or invective against various targets, including the witch Canidia; the people of Rome, for becoming embroiled in civil war; and even Maecenas, the poet's friend and patron. The book was modelled on the works of the Greek invective poet Archilochus and the *Iamboi* of Callimachus, and may include Horace's earliest work. With a dramatic setting in the period immediately before the decisive Battle of Actium in September 31 BC, the latest 'datable' poem (*Epodes* 9) deals with Actium itself, and the collection returns repeatedly to the experience of civil war.[29] Horace had himself fought with Brutus, on the losing side, at the Battle of Philippi in 42 BC, though like many of his generation he came to terms with Octavian and became ultimately, after the death of Virgil, the poet laureate of the Augustan regime. We have already seen, in Chapter 2, that many iambic and iambo-lyric metres derived from the *Epodes* were adopted by early Christian poets, and then by neo-Latin poets, especially in the search for metrical variety characteristic of the later sixteenth century.

For modern scholars, even of Horace, and certainly of Roman satire as a form, the *Epodes* are marginal at best: most introductions to Roman verse satire do not include them. But iambic and iambo-lyric Latin poetry is – unlike hexameter verse satire – a strikingly fruitful form in Anglo-Latin verse of the sixteenth and seventeenth centuries: iambic metres were widely used for a large number of medium-length satiric poems, though certainly not exclusively for satiric or invective purposes. George Buchanan's enormously influential collected verse, for instance, regularly reissued across Europe in the later sixteenth and seventeenth centuries, includes only a single hexameter verse satire, 'Franciscanus et fratres', but a whole book of iambics.[30] This pattern was typical: many of the most influential Latin

---

[28] The 40 poems of *Musae Responsoriae* contain 6 in iambic trimeter, and a further 3 in other iambic forms.

[29] Horace himself probably referred to the collection as *Iambi*, and many early modern iambic collections were titled in this way, rather than as *Epodes*. The poems were probably composed between 42 and 30 BC. On the *Epodes*, see Bather and Stocks, *Horace's Epodes*.

[30] Another hexameter verse satire by Buchanan, 'Satyra in Carolum Lotharingum, cardinalem', was not included in collected editions of his verse until 1715, when this form had become fashionable (on which see Ford, 'George Buchanan and the *Satyra in Carolum Lotharingum Cardinalem*'; and Courtial, 'George Buchanan'). A manuscript copy of it is in Bod. MS Tanner 306 (fols. 63ʳ–5ʳ), a collection made by William Sancroft (1617–93) probably in the late seventeenth century.

poets, including Julius Caesar Scaliger (1484–1558) in the sixteenth century, and Casimir Sarbiewski (1595–1640) in the seventeenth, produced entire books of iambics or epodes.

Atkinson makes the literary lineage of his work clear in the opening lines:

> Huc huc Iambus, qualis Archilochum sapit,
> Scribenda Satyra est rigida, acetosa, horrida:
> Sed nostra Musa reptilis, et infans adhuc,
> Dentata nondum est. Ampla materiae seges
> Vitioque justa (justa si quando ultio)
> Prodire mandant:
> ...
> Atqui debeo vel infans loqui.

> *Come here, here, Iambus, the kind that tastes of Archilochus,*
> *Satires must be written in harsh, bitter, bristling form:*
> *But our Muse creeps along, still a child,*
> *She has not yet grown teeth. The great crop of material*
> *Deserving of reproach (if ever vengeance is deserved)*
> *Orders us to make a sally:*
> ...
> *And I must speak out, even though I am a child.*

Atkinson's poem, like the *Epodes*, invokes the iambic tradition derived from Archilochus. The first line summons the 'iambus' with a phrase ('huc huc') recalling Horace's definition of the *Epodes* as 'free-speaking anger': 'ut ora vertat huc et huc euntium / liberrima indignatio?' (*Epodes* 4.9–10, '[do you see how] my free-speaking anger / turns here, and here again, the faces of those who pass by?').[31]

Atkinson calls his poem a 'toothless satire' and explains in the opening lines that it is 'toothless' because he, the author, is so young; nevertheless, the horror of the impiety around him forces him to produce satirical verse. This imagery of toothed or toothless satire is derived from the *Epodes*, which return repeatedly to images of animal attack and human impotence, although it was already well-rooted in English literature: it is found frequently, for instance, in the English satiric verse of the 1590s.[32] In

---

[31] Perhaps also recalling the opening of one of Poliziano's epodes, 'In Anum', beginning 'huc, huc, iambi, arripite mi iam mordicus'.

[32] Hall, *Virgidemiarum* (1597–1602) contains three books of 'Tooth-lesse Satyrs' and three of 'byting Satyres'. On Jonson's use of the *Epodes*, see Moul, *Jonson, Horace*, 99–134. William Scott's *The model of Poesie* (1599) distinguishes between 'some more mild and toothless' satirists and those who are 'more curst and bitter' – Alexander (ed.), *Model of Poesy*, 25. I am grateful to Javiera Raty for this reference.

Horace, critical attention has focused upon the sexualized descriptions of impotence, of the poet and others, though weakness and vulnerability are also evoked in terms of childhood. In a particularly unpleasant poem, the witch Canidia starves a boy to death, buried up to his neck in sight of food, in order to create a love philtre from his organs (*Epodes* 5). Atkinson adapts these tropes of youthful impotence, describing himself as too young to have any effect – especially in contrast to Melville, who was 75 in 1620.[33]

The word 'edentula' ('toothless') is not found in extant classical Latin, though it does appear in both pre-classical texts (including Plautus, widely read at this period) and post-classical ones (including Prudentius and Tertullian). In fact, Herbert uses the same term for his poetic attack upon Melville, referring to his 'edentula Musa' ('toothless Muse') in the only poem of the *Musae Responsoriae* sequence that addresses Melville directly (*Musae Responsoriae* 37.12). Herbert was elected as University Orator at Cambridge in 1620; though only six years older than Atkinson he had been at Trinity College since 1609, and a fellow since 1614. The coincidence of terminology in poems to the same addressee, responding to the same publication and making essentially the same polemical point, suggests strongly that one of these texts is imitating the other. Although there is no evidence for the circulation of this particular poem of Herbert's, other examples of his Latin verse were certainly in circulation before 1620.[34] The balance of likelihood is that the young Atkinson is here alluding to Herbert rather than vice versa.

In purely metrical terms, Atkinson's choice of continuous iambics is typical of the moment: his is just one of hundreds of examples of Latin verse in iambics dating from the early to mid-seventeenth century. In the surviving manuscript record, iambic verse makes up a much larger proportion of the total corpus in the early and mid-seventeenth century than at any other time.[35] Not all of these are satiric, invective or humorous, but

---

[33] 'Melvine, nam Te provoco, Juvenis Senem / Infans adultum provoco' ('Melville, for I a young man, am goading you, an old one / As a small child provokes a grown-up', 17–18). Herbert's sequence also makes a version of this point, though less insistently and more tactfully.

[34] There is a tradition that Herbert begain the *Musae Responsoriae* sequence while at Westminster School, before 1609. His epigram 'Roma' is dated 1618 in BL MS Harley 6038, fol. 15^v.

[35] About 7 per cent of the total corpus, and 53 per cent of the total of lyric and iambic verse combined in poetry datable to between 1601 and 1633; about 5 per cent of the total corpus, and 37 per cent of the total of lyric and iambic verse combined in poetry datable to between 1634 and 1666. In this data, pythiambic verse has been treated as lyric, not iambic. Comparable statistics in adjacent periods range between 1.5 per cent and 3 per cent of the total corpus, and 14–25 per cent of the lyric and iambic total combined. These statistics exclude Latin drama, which was regularly composed in iambic 'senarii', a form of iambic trimeter; many poets would have had considerable experience of speaking iambics in school and university drama.

many are. Here, then, the exploration of Anglo-Latin satire begins to diverge significantly from what we would naturally expect, or guess, based on a knowledge of English poetry: although there are a few scattered hints of the importance of epodes at the time – both Ben Jonson and Richard Lovelace, for instance, make occasional use of the term 'Epode' in the title of a poem – this statistically very distinctive feature of the Latin poetry of the period does not correspond directly to anything in English.[36]

Iambic Verse in the Mid-Seventeenth Century

We can see from the Atkinson example that a tradition of iambic composition in Latin was already well-established by the early seventeenth century – that is, it was a natural form for a student such as Atkinson to use for satiric or invective Latin verse. Given the political context and content of Horace's *Epodes*, it is unsurprising that such poems were particularly popular during the period of the English Civil War. In the immediate aftermath of the execution of Charles I in 1649, we find a particularly large number of examples of invective political verse, often printed anonymously, using the tradition of Horatian iambics to excoriate those responsible for recent events.

Peter du Moulin's (1601–84) long-form *Ecclesiae Gemitus* (1649), discussed in Chapter 11, is in iambic trimeter with inset lyric, and is allegorical rather than straightforwardly invective, imagining the suffering of the English Church at the hands of Cromwell and his allies in the form of a beleaguered nymph. Dating also from the early 1650s, Du Moulin's poem attacking Milton for his defence of the regicide is, however, a straightforward example of Horatian invective.[37]

In impurissimum Nebulonem Joannem Miltonum, Parricidarum & Parricidii Advocatum

    Quò quò citato ruitis injussi pede
    Acres Iambi? Nempe properè calcibus
    Tritum Gigantum ignobilem nepotulum,

---

[36] Lovelace's use probably reflects that of Sarbiewski and other Jesuit poets, in which books of 'Epodes' are metrically distinct but tonally little different from books of 'Odes'.

[37] There is no evidence that it was printed at the time though it may well have circulated. Autograph manuscript copies at BL MS Add. 10418, fols. 19ʳ–57ʳ (with corrections) and 10446 (very neat, probably the printer's copy of Πάρεργα, 1671). Du Moulin was almost certainly the author of *Regii sanguinis clamor* (1652), a royalist tract attacking Milton.

> Regnum Patronum dente rodentem fero,
> Ipsósque Reges. Méne virus hoc malum
> Hoc carcinoma tangere? Ah piget, pudet.
>
> *Where, where are you rushing, uncommanded, on swift feet,*
> *Harsh iambics? Of course I'm rushing to tread*
> *Beneath my feet that base grandchild of Giants,*
> *Who is gnawing with his teeth upon the kingdom who defends him*
> *And upon even kings themselves. Can I bring myself to touch this*
> *   this dreadful poison,*
> *This tumour? Ah it is disgusting and shameful to do so.*

Line 4 alludes to 'biting' satire, though transfers the image to the damage done to the kingdom and the monarchy by Cromwell (the 'Gigantum ignobilem nepotulum'). The clearest allusion here is to the opening of *Epodes* 7, usually considered to date from around 38 BC, in which Horace attacks the entire Roman people for the sin of their descent into civil conflict.

> quo, quo scelesti ruitis? aut cur dexteris
>   aptantur enses conditi?
>   (1–2)
>
> *Where, where are you rushing, wicked people? Why do your hands*
> *   Wield swords which had been sheathed?*

Belonging clearly to the same literary tradition is an anonymous pamphlet published in 1649, titled *Ex Spinosa Anonymi Sylva, Folia quaedam; Sibyllinis licet veriora, Procellosis forte tamen ludibria hîc evolant ventis jactanda* ('From the thorny wood of Mr. Anonymous, certain leaves; although more true than those of the Sibyl, they have drifted here to be tossed as mere playthings of the storm-winds'). Printed almost certainly in Edinburgh, it has neither author nor place of publication. The pamphlet contains three pieces: two long poems in iambic trimeters followed by a shorter commemorative poem for David, second son of David, Earl of Wemyss (1632–c.1649), who seems to function as a kind of proxy for the dead king. The first of the trimeter poems is dated 1 January 1649 (that is, just before the execution of Charles I) and like Epodes 7 and 16, it is addressed not to an individual but to the rulers of the Scottish people.

Like Du Moulin's *Ecclesiae Gemitus*, the poem is a political allegory, here of the ship of state at risk of shipwreck – an ubiquitous political image itself derived primarily from one of Horace's *Odes* (1.14), though also found several times in Claudian and other ancient authors. The image was used very widely in the seventeenth century.[38] John Polwhele, a royalist clergyman, makes the same connections: his volume of manuscript verse, containing many heavily corrected translations from the late 1640s and 1650s, includes two versions of *Odes* 1.14 as well as versions of *Epodes* 7 and 16.[39] We find a similar set of Horatian texts, including both *Epodes*, in Fanshawe's *Selected Parts of Horace* (1652).

The second poem in the Scottish pamphlet, dated Feburary 1649 (immediately after the regicide) is titled 'Iamborum ensis, ab *Archilocho* veridico in *nostri tempori* Gigantas, Regicîdas & Sacricîdas, destrictus' ('The sword of iambics, drawn by a truth-telling Archilochus against the Giants, Regicides and Killers of what is holy in our time'). It is a version of the story of the Giants (or Titans) threatening Olympus – both Du Moulin's poem and also Abraham Cowley's prose pamphlet on Cromwell, unpublished until after the Restoration, use this story as a political allegory. Its popularity in political verse is probably derived primarily from the cultural valency of Claudian, who repeatedly uses the Gigantomachy to evoke political threat, especially internal threats by Roman rivals rather than external enemies, and their defeat by Theodosius, Honorius and Stilicho.[40] We tend to think of Claudian as a poet of political panegyric, but satire and invective aimed at the rivals or enemies of the *laudandus* are natural counterparts to panegyric: two of Claudian's works, *In Rufinum* and *In Eutropium*, are dominated by invective, whereas many of his consular panegyrics include passages intended to demonize the enemy. Recent work has demonstrated the consistency of imagery across Claudian's corpus, a point which must have been obvious to many early modern readers, both because they were much more likely to know Claudian well, and also because of the early modern habit of excerpting and gathering similar passages under topical headings.[41]

These printed examples of political satire and invective in iambics are matched by many similar poems in manuscript. Bod. MS Rawl. poet. 246, made in the mid-seventeenth century, for instance, contains many

---

[38] Examples in verse anthologies include Oxford University, *Academiae Oxoniensis Pietas* (1603), 163; Cambridge University, *Anthologia in Regis Exanthemata* (1633), 31. On the particularly intense use of this image during the Civil War, see Moul, 'Marvell and Fisher'.

[39] Bod. MS Eng. poet. f. 16. See Moul, *Jonson, Horace*, 198–202 and Gillespie, 'John Polwhele's Horatian Translations'.

[40] See Coombe, *Claudian the Poet*, 93–122.

[41] Both *Ruf.* and *Eutr.* are well represented in seventeenth-century miscellanies and commonplace books. See also Gillespie, 'Two Seventeenth-Century Translations'.

examples.[42] Two poems in iambic trimeters demonstrate the strong association of the epodic tradition with political and sexual themes. The first, 'Rebellis Scotus' ('The Rebel Scot', fols. 7ʳ–9ʳ), is dated 1650. A furious invective against the Scots, the poem survives in both Latin and English forms: the English certainly by John Cleveland (1613–58), the Latin, apparently a translation, probably by Thomas Gawen (c.1610–83).[43] The opening of the Latin poem as it appears in Bod. MS Rawl. poet. 246 is given below followed by the corresponding section of Cleveland's English:

> Curæ Deo sumus ista si cedant Scoto?
> Variata splenijs Domina est Psyche suis:
> Aut stellionatus rea. ὕστερον πρότερον
> Campanulæ omnes: Totus Ucalegon suo,
> Coriaceæ cuj millies mille hydriæ
> Suburbicanis pensiles parœcijs
> Non sint refrigerio. Poëticus furor
> Camerante non minus, vel ore flammeo
> Commune despuente fatum stellulâ
> Dirum ominatur.
>
> (1–10)

> *How, Providence? and yet a Scottish crew?*
> *Then Madame Nature wears black patches too!*
> *What shall our nation be in bondage thus*
> *Unto a land that truckles under us?*
> *Ring the bells backward! I am all on fire.*
> *Not all the buckets in a country quire*
> *Shall quench my rage. A poet should be feared,*
> *When angry, like a comet's flaming beard.*

The poem was written originally in 1644, after the Scottish Covenanters invaded England on the Parliamentarian side. By 1650, however, the Scots were opposed to Cromwell and allied with the exiled king, Charles II. This

---

[42] The compiler appears to have been at Eton and Cambridge, and the manuscript is possibly in the hand of one Henry Some. It contains several fashionable and widely circulating poems, such as Melville's 'Tower' epigrams from the first decade of the century (discussed in Chapter 7), a sequence on Francis Bacon's *Instauratio Magna* (1620), including several of George Herbert's Latin poems; and other typical genres such as scriptural epigrams and Latin commemorative verse.

[43] The Latin poem is attributed to Thomas Gawen of New College, Oxford, in this manuscript, and described as a translation; an earlier copy of the Latin (Bod. MS Rawl. poet. 142, fols. 35ᵛ–6ᵛ) names Cleveland as the author, but the attribution of the Latin version to Gawen, which is also found elsewhere, is probably correct. A note in Rawl. poet. 246 made in a different hand indicates that the Latin poem was printed in 1658. I am grateful to Edward Taylor for the transcription of this poem and for information on Thomas Gawen.

1650 copy suggests how the same poem could be redeployed from different political perspectives in changed circumstances.

Horace's *Epodes* are a markedly varied collection, and early modern iambics were certainly not confined to political verse. Despite his reputation as a devout religious reformer, George Buchanan's book of *Iambi*, for instance, includes attacks on the physical repulsiveness of aged prostitutes modelled on Horace's notorious *Epodes* 8 and 12 (poems still expurgated in the edition of Horace prescribed when I was an undergraduate). A second poem in Bod. MS Rawl. poet. 246 (fols. 43^v–4^r), by Alexander Gill (the younger, 1597–1642), reflects this aspect of the iambic tradition; it is titled 'In Casabundum Colonellum cui mos est servulos suos masturbare' ('Against Colonel Casabund, whose habit it is to masturbate his serving boys').

Iambics could also, however, be quite gently humorous, just as Horace's collection includes poems such as *Epodes* 2, a subtly satiric poem which is ironized only by its concluding lines, and *Epodes* 3, a mildly rude but essentially affectionate piece reproaching Maecenas for 'poisoning' him with excess garlic at a banquet. Arising broadly from this tradition are works such as the *Pia Hilaria* of the French Jesuit Angelin Gazet (1568–1653), the first part of which was published in 1618; the first London edition was not printed until 1657 but by then the work had gone through multiple editions elsewhere in Europe, including a French translation in 1647.[44] The *pia hilaria* ('pious amusing things') of the title are a series of amusing religious stories, all in iambic metres.

The widespread use of iambic metres in the first half of the seventeenth century, especially (though far from only) for satiric and invective verse, suggests an entire area of 'classical reception' that has gone unremarked in existing scholarship. To my knowledge no study of the reception of Horace has mentioned, even in passing, the vast quantities of iambic Latin verse produced in early modernity, or the adoption of metres from the *Epodes*, via late antique poetry, for Latin lyric verse of various kinds (as described in Chapter 2). In this case, attention to Latin poetry changes our sense of the scope and associations of 'Horatianism' in early modern England, and the apparent 'absence' of hexameter verse satire begins to make sense. In the early or mid-seventeenth century, the 'obvious' form for political satire or invective in Latin was not hexameter, but iambic.

---

[44] There are many surviving copies of the London edition. Earlier editions were printed in various countries in 1618, 1619, 1623, 1625, 1629 and 1631. The work was still being printed in the 1680s.

Satire and Bilingualism in Epigram and Lyric

The routine use of iambic verse for satiric and invective material is a good example of a literary phenomenon which 'disappears' if we treat early modern English poetic culture as monolingual. But this is not to suggest that satiric or humorous verse functioned entirely differently in English and in Latin. On the contrary, many types of verse satire – which include many of the most widely circulating poems of the period – were markedly bilingual. Cleveland's poem on the 'Rebel Scot', as we have seen, was written and circulated in both Latin and English versions. Indeed, most satiric and humorous poems written in English are either epigrams or longer rhyming lyrics, often in ballad metres – topical songs and catches of all types. Latin examples of both these forms are frequently found, and in many cases the manuscript circulation of the most popular poems is interestingly bilingual. The final section of this chapter looks at satiric epigram – supplementing the more general study of epigram in Chapter 7 – and popular satiric lyric.

Satiric epigram is the most common kind of verse satire throughout the early modern period. Thousands of these epigrams were produced and circulated, many only in manuscript, and often in a dizzying array of different versions and accompanied by multiple translations. Though some effort has been made to catalogue the English aspect of this phenomenon, the Latin dimension – and therefore also the overall bilingualism – has attracted much less attention.[45] A single double-page spread from a miscellany dating from the 1590s, for instance, contains a mixture of Latin and English epigrams and longer poems, including two items presented bilingually. In both cases, a Latin epigram is followed by an English translation:

> Epitaphs. of Sr Fra: Wal: & S^r Ph: Sid:
>
> Nullus Francisco tumulus nullusque Philipo,
>   Christoforo mons est, ac tumulus cumulus.
>
> *Philipe and Fra[ncis] haue noe Tombe,*
>   *for Christopher hath all the roome.*

---

[45] Doelman's recent monograph, *Epigram in England*, however, offers an excellent overview. Doelman is particularly strong on satiric epigram and, unusually, also takes neo-Latin epigram into consideration.

> Hic Catharina jacet, jacet, vrsula, barbara, tres hae,
> Frater et Andreas qui lapidauit eas.
>
> *Kate, Ursley, Barbara that's 3. Virgins lye here,*
> *And frier Andrew, whom those 3. did beare.*[46]

These epigrams are typical of the kinds of satiric material we find in early modern England, the first referring to contemporary events (the death of Sir Christopher Hatton in 1591), the second apparently a version of an evergreen anti-monastic joke. Sir Francis Walsingham (the father-in-law of Philip Sidney, who had died in 1590), Philip Sidney himself (d. 1586) and Hatton, the Lord Chancellor, all had tombs in St Paul's, but Hatton's enormous monument towered over the altar, obscuring the view of the other two. Using only Christian names, this highly topical poem relies (in both Latin and English) upon readers recognizing to whom they refer, though in this manuscript a title has been added which goes some way to explaining the joke.

The second poem, again using only Christian names, has no such heading and seems to be a general, rather than specific piece of anti-monastic satire, implying that monks and nuns, supposedly vowed to chastity, in fact routinely sleep with one another. Barbara, Ursula and Catherine (irreverently abbreviated to 'Kate') are all saints' names, and perhaps suggest in particular St Ursula and the 11,000 British virgins, her travel companions, supposedly massacred in Germany for defending their chastity. The English version sharpens the point by adding 'Virgins' to the first line. Whereas topical pieces like the Hatton poem naturally tended not to circulate for long, except in cases where they were successively reapplied to fresh scandals, epigrams of this rather general kind had an enduring popularity. Indeed, this poem may well be much older than the 1590s, and it was certainly still circulating over a hundred years later. In a British Library manuscript dating from around 1700, we find what is recognizably a version of the same poem:

> An Epitaph upon a Scotch monarch;
>
> Vertitur in cineres, flos fratrum, flent moniales
> Hic Jacet Andrea, qui lapidavit eas.[47]

---

[46] CUL MS Add. 4138, fols. 47ᵛ and 48ʳ.
[47] BL MS Stowe 305, fol. 217ʳ; the poem is also found in Nottingham University Library, MS PwV 929, probably from around the same date, and accompanied by a very similar, though single, translation ('That bicker'd att their bumm's').

This time it is followed by four attempts at translation, apparently by the same person, titled 'Translated thus by an unlucky fellow:'

> *This flowr of fryars, is turned to Asse*
> *Therefore ye nuns doe weepe*
> *ffor Andrews head lyes fast in presse*
> *That made ye Buttocks dreepe.*
>
> *The flowr of fryars is turned to Asse*
> *Therefore lament yee nuns*
> *ffor Andrews head lyes fast in presse*
> *That Bickered at your bumbs.*
>
> *The flowr of fryars, is turned to Asse*
> *Lament ye nuns therefore*
> *Ffor Andrews head lyes fast in presse*
> *That wombled at your Bore.*
>
> *Here lies Andrew the father o'the nuns*
> *Who when he lived beliguered all their Bumbs.*

The second line of both Latin texts is very similar, and both associate friar Andrew with women who are supposedly celibate (*moniales* is a medieval word for nuns). In the British Library manuscript, the first three translations are almost identical, and in all four cases the main difference is in the translation of the Latin term *lapidavit*, the third-person singular perfect tense of *lapido*, a verb meaning 'to stone', as in 'to stone someone to death'. No dictionary of which I am aware records it being used to mean 'to beat or whip' (which seems to be, broadly speaking, the meaning of all these translations) or to mean 'have sex with' which is the implication of the earliest translation ('whom those three did bear'). *Lapis* however can mean 'testicle' which probably suggested the sexual meaning. In both manuscripts, however, our sense of what *lapido* actually means is derived almost entirely from the accompanying English, and in the later manuscript the ambiguity of this word seems to have prompted the translator to particular lexical ingenuity: although their essential meaning is made clear by the repetition, 'dreepe', 'bickered' and 'wombled' are all very unusual words.[48] These two manuscripts are distanced by about a century, but in

---

[48] *OED* 'dreep / drepe, *v*.', Scots dialect form of 'drip', meaning either 'drip' or 'droop', fig. 'lose courage, grow faint'. *OED* 'bicker, *v*.', 1.a. 'To skirmish, exchange blows' and 2. 'To attack with repeated strokes'. 'Womble' as a verb does not appear in the *OED* but is perhaps a version of 'wamble, *v*.', II. 2. 'To turn and twist the body about, roll or wriggle about, roll over and over' and 4. *transitive* 'To twist or turn (something) over and over'. The 'Monarch' of the title seems to mean 'monk', perhaps with a pun. 'Monk' is derived from the Latin 'monachus'. 'Asse' is a Scottish variant for 'ash'.

Rhyming Verse 343

both cases the Latin and English versions seem intended to be appreciated together, not as alternatives.[49]

Rhyming Verse

Although metrically conventional (all single elegiac couplets), none of the three Latin epigrams discussed above is very classical in style. Most marked is the use of strong alliteration (*Francisco ... Philipo ... Christoforo*; *flos fratrum, flent*), repetition (*nullus ... tumulus nullusque ... tumulus*; *jacet, jacet*) and internal rhyme (*nullus ... tumulus nullusque ... tumulus cumulus*; *Andreas ... eas*; *cineres ... moniales*). All these elements bring the Latin style closer to that of the vernacular. Rhyming Latin verse is generally considered, where it is discussed at all, to be a primarily medieval phenomenon, with ongoing composition into early modernity confined to Catholic hymns and anthems.[50] Many early modern English manuscripts demonstrate the ongoing circulation of rhyming medieval Latin, and a few collections contain contemporary rhyming hymns alongside late antique or medieval examples.[51] But one surprising finding of the survey of Latin verse in English manuscript sources is the relatively large number of rhyming poems that appear to be post-medieval – contemporary or near-contemporary compositions, not just copies of late antique or medieval Latin texts – most of which are not religious.[52] 'Rhyming' here covers a variety of forms, including what we might call 'fully' rhyming Latin poems, written in a stress-metre – often 'ballad' or 'common' metre – with a regular pattern of end-rhymes of the sort one might encounter in vernacular as well as medieval poetry; but also examples of poems which

---

[49] On the changing patterns of bilingualism in the composition and circulation of epigrams, see Chapter 7.
[50] Ijsewijn and Sacré (*Companion to Neo-Latin Studies, Part II*, 10–14 and 99) stress the rarity of rhyming neo-Latin verse in the sixteenth and seventeenth centuries, noting however that 'after the seventeenth century medieval forms got a clear revival in Germany and English, especially in students' songs and church hymns' (12). The English manuscript evidence would suggest that this was already true at an earlier period.
[51] Of medieval material, extracts from the *Schola salernitatis* and various alchemical works are particularly widespread, especially in the latter sixteenth century. Medieval rhyming satires in circulation include for instance the anti-monastic poem beginning 'O Monachi vestri stomachi', quoted by George Puttenham in the *Art of English Poesy*, chap. 7, and found in BL MS Harley 6914, fol. 65ʳ (late seventeenth or early eighteenth century) among others. Bod. MS Rawl. poet. 72 is an example of a seventeenth-century collection of Latin hymns, several in rhyming metres, by both ancient (Prudentius, Ambrose), medieval (Bede, Aquinas) and more modern authors (such as George Fabricius, 1516–71, and George Buchanan, 1506–82).
[52] At the time of writing, the *NLPEM* project has identified 484 rhyming Latin poems which appear to be of post-medieval origin (plus a further 95 in leonine hexameters).

scan both quantitatively and by stress (as is common in medieval Latin verse), with an element of rhyme. In these cases the rhyme is internal, as in the 'leonine' hexameter and pentameter of *moniales ... cineres; Andreas ... eas*. Also found are poems in free verse or 'literary inscription' form which make some use of rhyme as a structural device.

Not all examples of such rhyming verse are comic or satiric.[53] Nevertheless, rhyming Latin does seem to have been particularly associated with humorous rather than serious poetry, and in the manuscript record it is found most frequently in the final third of the seventeenth century, which is also the period to which the largest proportion of satiric, invective and humorous verse belongs.[54] Many of these rhyming Latin poems were clearly intended to be sung at a given event, often in an institutional context (such as a college banquet, or the end of term), and they are sometimes accompanied by music or an indication of the tune.[55]

In the earlier period in particular, rhyming Latin verse is often described as a 'carmen rithmicum'. Richard Willes' 1573 volume of exemplary Latin verse compositions includes an example of a poem in leonine hexameters, titled simply 'Rithmus' and with the marginal explanation: 'Monachorum & fraterculorum versus ad augendam memoriam fere sunt huiusmodi' ('The poetry of monks and friars was of this type, in order to make it easier to remember').[56]

---

[53] Examples of apparently 'serious' panegyric odes in rhyming Latin verse include (in print) two poems in Fisher, *Oratio Secunda Anniversaria* (1657), 'Ode Gratulatoria' (sig. B3[r–v]) and 'Paean Votivus' (sig. G3[v]–G4[r]), both in praise of Cromwell; and (in manuscript) BL MS Add. 72899, fols. 39–42, two rhyming Latin poems attributed to a Donald Brennan, of county Kerry in Ireland, and dated 1675. They both appear to be poems in praise of William Petty, who owned land in the area, thanking him for reducing land taxes. I am grateful to Edward Taylor for his research on this point.

[54] 158 (32.6 per cent) of rhyming Latin poems have been dated to the final third of the seventeenth century (1667–1700); these figures do not include an additional 95 examples of leonine hexameter (with internal but no end-rhymes), a strongly medieval form most commonly found in the earliest period. A total of 361 poems have so far been identified as satiric (234), invective (41) or humorous (86). This work is ongoing, but at the time of writing all three of these categories are found most frequently in the final third of the seventeenth century; this is in contrast to the corpus as a whole: of the corpus as a whole, the largest proportion by some margin (31 per cent) have been dated to the first third of the seventeenth century, only 16 per cent to the final third.

[55] Manchester John Rylands Library, MS Eng. 410, for instance, includes a Latin drinking song 'in laudem vini' (fol. 20[v]), a mock-hymn in four-line stanzas of alternating trochaic dimeter and trochaic dimeter catalectic (that is, lines of alternating eight and seven syllables), with each second and fourth line rhyming. CUL MS Dd. III. 73 preserves a Latin comedy by Matthew Johnson performed in February 1638. Two songs, in acts IV and V, are in rhyming Latin verse accompanied by music.

[56] Willes, *Poematum Liber* (1573), 63 and 'Scholia', sig. Dv[r].

Rhyming Verse

A Cambridge University Library manuscript preserves a poem in rhyming Latin verse on Mary Queen of Scots, dating probably from the 1570s – a popular subject for both invective and panegyric Latin poems, depending on political allegiance:[57]

> In Mariam Scotiae Reginam adulteram, veneficam et viricidam Dutani Patricii Knocfargensis Rithmus satyricus
>
>> Maria Scota meretrix O vndique nota
>> impura illota veneri deditiss[ima] tota,
>> quae stimulis mota mersos trahis ad tua vota,
>> vinoque perpota futuis vt rancida gota.[58]

On Mary Queen of Scots, adulteress, poisoner and murderer; rhyming satire of Patrick Dutan of Knockfargensis

> *O Scottish Mary, a whore everywhere notorious,*
> *Wholly impure, filthy, entirely given over to sex,*
> *You who, goaded by lust, force drowned men to follow your wishes,*
> *Constantly drunk with wine, you fuck like a rancid goat.*

More than half a century later, an interesting piece of rhyming Latin verse marks the outbreak of civil war in 1642. It is accompanied by an English version, given here:

> De Bello Intestino.
> 1642.
>
>> Invidia quondam Europæorum,
>> Iam despecta Gens Anglorum,
>> Discerpta manibus tuorum
>> Obmutesce et stupesce,
>> Et non potens fari,
>> Disce silentio miserias admirari.

---

[57] CUL MS Dd. V. 75, fol. 43ʳ. See May, *Henry Stanford's Anthology*, 21–2 and 70–1, with brief notes though no translation, and some errors of transcription. The poem is also found in BL MS Harley 7371, fol. 132ᵛ, apparently a later copy. May collates the Harley version.

[58] I have not been able to find 'gota, -ae' for a female goat attested in any Latin dictionary. Given the traditional association between goats, sexual appetite and smell ('rancid'), however, this is surely what it means. There are several oddities in the Latin of this poem, though the meaning is clear. I have been unable to identify the Patrick Dutan to whom the poem is apparently attributed. The adjective 'Knockfargiensis' perhaps refers to Knockfarrel (Gaelic 'Cnoc Fearghalaigh') in the Scottish Highlands.

Of the Civil Warre.

> *England, once Europes Envy, now its scorn*
> *Ambitious to be forlorn,*
> *Self by self torn:*
>   *Stand amazd, thy woes are blazd*
>   *With silence best:*
> *And wanting words, wonder out the rest.*[59]

Given its popular and often occasional nature, rhyming Latin verse of this period was printed less frequently than more formal modes, and this is probably also why previous scholarship has tended to underestimate its prevalence. Where such items did make it into print, however, they were often a commercial success, such as Richard Braithwait's (c.1588–1673) very popular *Barnabae Itinerarium* (1636), and George Ruggle's partly macaronic Latin play *Ignoramus* (1615), which includes several rhyming Latin songs. Those songs are frequently found excerpted in manuscript collections of the early- to mid-seventeenth century and sometimes beyond – Nottingham MS PwV 1343 preserves one early eighteenth-century copy, as well as an adapted version of one of the speeches, probably for a performance of the play at Westminster School.[60]

Satiric rhyming verse in Latin is very frequently, like *Ignoramus*, macaronic – that is, employing a mixture of languages. Thomas Randolph's (1605–35) comic poem addressed to the graduating students at Oxford in 1632 belongs to this tradition and circulated widely. Preserved in a large number of manuscripts around this time, it is in leonine hexameters which scan both quantitatively and by stress, and with both internal and end-rhymes. The poem makes liberal use of English words and contemporary cultural references, beginning:

> Iam sileat Jack Drum, taceant miracula Tom Thumb;
> Nec se Gigantem jactet Garagantua tantum.

> *Now let Jack Drum be silent, Tom Thumb should not recount miracles;*
> *Nor should Gargantua boast that he's such a great giant.*[61]

---

[59] Corpus Christi College, Oxford, MS 317, fol. 303ʳ. I am grateful to Edward Taylor who transcribed the poem. The Latin text is signed 'H. P.' and the English 'T. [or F.] F.'. Neither of these has yet been identified.

[60] A copy of the 1731 edition of *Ignoramus*, with an ownership signature 'W. Sancroft', is bound into Bod. MS Tanner 306. Manuscript copies of parts of *Barnabae Itinerarium* are found, for example, in BL MS Harley 6396, fols. 2ʳ–8ʳ.

[61] BL MS Add. 44963, fol. 26ʳ. Found also at Bod. MS Rawl. poet. 62, fol. 1ʳ, among others.

Jack Drum refers probably to John Marston's play *Jack Drum's Entertainment* (c.1599); Tom Thumb is a character in English folklore, and *The History of Tom Thumbe, the Little* (1621) has been called the first fairy tale printed in English. Gargantua (here spelt Garagantua) appears in Rabelais *La vie de Gargantua et de Pantagruel*, published in five volumes between c.1532 and 1564. To similar effect, a popular macaronic poem in (roughly) elegiac couplets on the unfortunate physical effects of smoking tobacco, requires, I think, no translation:

> Gorgon per stomachon vomitos facit et cacothumpon
> Fartera brich-bottom out belchizerando cogit.[62]

Such humorous bilingualism surely reflects the realities of everyday experience in educational and professional institutions, such as schools, university and the Inns of Court, in which spoken Latin remained in ordinary use.

John Allibond's (1597–1658) very popular satire on the visitation of the Parliamentary committee to Oxford in 1648 – which was in effect a purge of royalist loyalists in Oxford – was published as both a broadsheet and a pamphlet, and also circulated in manuscript.[63] Allibond's Latin lyrics, a rather sophisticated example of rhyming Latin satire, are laid out to resemble Horatian stanzas, but are in fact rhyming verse:

> Rumore nuper est delatum,
> Dum agebamus rari,
> Oxonium, iri Reformatum
> Ab his qui dicti Puri.
>
> *Recently a rumour has spread,*
> *While we few have gone on as before,*
> *That Oxford is going to be Reformed*
> *By those who are called Pure.*

This kind of 'fake formality' is perhaps part of the satiric point: the Parliamentary reformers are aping authority without really inhabiting it.

---

[62] First two lines of a poem found also in BL MS Harley 791, fol. 59ᵛ among others. Compare the nonsense language spoken by tobacco in Tomkis, *Lingua* (1607), 4.4 (sig. H5ᵛ).

[63] Allibond, *Rustica academiae oxoniensis* (1648), in both quarto and broadside. Described by the *ESTC* as a 'celebrated and clever Latin ballad, partly macaronic, on the desolate condition of Oxford as newly reformed by the Parliamentary visitors'. Manuscript copies at BL MS Add. 23904, fol. 1ʳ; Bod. MS Lat. misc. e. 38, pp. 160–58 (rev.); Corpus Christi College, Oxford, MS 317, fols. 314ʳ–15ʳ, with probably many others extant and unidentified. The work was printed with an English translation in 1717 by Ned Ward; it also appears in *The Gentleman's Magazine* 74 (1793), 1095–7, with some explanatory notes.

Something not dissimilar is central to the satiric effect of formal *parodia*. Early modern *parodia* – a form in which a canonical text is rewritten with as few changes as possible, but in order to produce a quite different meaning – are not necessarily satiric, nor does the form imply any sort of mockery of the original, as the modern term 'parody' does. Many early modern examples are sacred parodia, in which a pagan text is rewritten to convey a Christian message. Some examples, however, are certainly intended as satire. Dating probably from the late 1640s, Mildmay Fane's version of Horace, *Odes* 1.37, for instance, is a sharply effective example. The original Latin poem, the 'Cleoptra' ode celebrating the defeat of Antony and Cleopatra at the Battle of Actium in 23 BC, begins with the well-known tag 'Nunc est bibendum' ('Now is the time to drink [in celebration])'. Fane's bitter version of the poem starts instead 'Nunc est lugendum' ('now is the time to grieve').[64] Metrically, too, Fane's *parodia* assumes the controlled beauty of Horace's lyric only to abandon the metre after a few lines, giving a very powerful effect of disintegration.

Free Verse and Literary Inscription

This sense of metrical disintegration was put to satiric use in the many humorous or satiric examples of Latin free verse or 'literary inscription'. As we have seen in Chapter 5, this kind of poetry has links to Latin Pindarics and dithyrambics, forms composed since the sixteenth century, as well as the 'literary inscriptions' popularized by Emanuele Tesauro (1592–1675). While the earliest examples are almost exclusively panegyric, satiric and invective versions became increasingly popular in England in the mid to late seventeenth century.

One satiric poem on Gilbert Burnet (1643–1715), bishop of Salisbury, for instance, is preserved in at least 12 manuscripts, most of which appear to date from shortly after Burnet's consecration as bishop of Salisbury in 1689. It may have been written by Thomas (or Tom) Brown (1651–1704), a popular satiric poet in both Latin and English, although it was only attributed to him posthumously.[65] The poem refers to Burnet's self-imposed exile on the continent during the reign of James II (1685–88), as well as to his Scottish origins. Burnet was a close personal

---

[64] Houghton Library, MS Eng. 645, p. 64. Thanks are due to Jill Woodberry to whose transcription of the manuscript I have referred.

[65] For further discussion see Moul, 'Satire on the Bishop of Salisbury'. I have become aware of further copies since the publication of that edition. Such a large number of extant examples suggests wide circulation, and it is very likely that more copies remain to be identified.

friend and advisor of King William III, who deposed James II in 1688. The poem is plainly satirical or even invective in tone, excoriating Burnet for his disloyalty to James II (who was a Roman Catholic), in contrast to his earlier vigorous defence of the royal authority of his brother Charles II:

In Episcopum Quendam

E Scotia Presbyter Profugus
In Angliam ad bene mentiendum
Reipublicae causa aliquando venit
Ibi primum Dominum suum
    Deinde Regem
Tandem patriam et Ecclesiam prodidit.
Egregius mehercule simulator,
...

Rogandus est, ut inter alias novas
  Quas meditatur formulas
Hanc precatiunculam secundum usum Sarum
    Interseri curaret:
'Hic in Templo negociator.
Da mihi fallere, da Justum Sanctumque
videri noctem peccatis et fraudibus objice nubem.'
Vivit nobis, Vae nobis in Anglia
  vivit Mazarinus,
Alterum vidimus triumphare fugitivum
  Et regnare exulem.[66]
        (1–7 and 43–53)

Against a certain Bishop

A fugitive priest from Scotland
Once came to England to do some good lying
In the cause of the Republic
There he betrayed first his own Lord [John Maitland, second Earl of Lauderdale]
Then the King
And at last his country and the Church.

---

[66] Text based on Bod. MS Rawl. D. 383, fol. 136ʳ, probably one of the earliest versions, with a few readings adopted from other manuscripts. Additional manuscript copies in, among others: Leeds University Library, MS BC Lt q 38, pp. 97–9 (1690s); BL MS Egerton 3880 fols. 277ᵛ–8ʳ (probably 1690s); Nottingham University Library, MSS PwV 1347 (late seventeenth century), Portland PwV 47/31/1, fols. 46ᵛ–7ᵛ (1688–91), and Portland PwV 48/31, fol. 54ʳ⁻ᵛ (1688–90); BL MS Lansdowne 852, fol. 38ʳ⁻ᵛ (probably 1690s); BL MS Stowe 305, fol. 188ʳ (probably 1690s); BL MS Harley 7315, fols. 203ʳ–4ʳ (late seventeenth century); Durham PG Library, MS P 29, fol. 33ʳ (early eighteenth century). This is certainly not a complete list.

Goodness me, what an extraordinary dissimulator!
...

We must ask him, how it is that, among the other
Novel forms he has in mind,
He is so particularly keen to see inserted
This little prayer
According to the Sarum Rite:
'Here in the Temple grant me, as your chief agent,
The right to cheat, the right to seem Just and Holy;
And cast the darkness of night around my sins, and a cloud
*   of obscurity around my deceptions.'*
He lives for us; alas, for us in England
Mazarinus lives,
A second Mazarin, whom we have seen triumph as a fugitive
And reign as an exile.

The poem ends by comparing Burnet explicitly to Cardinal Mazarin (1602–61), and the use of satirical free verse probably alludes to a slightly earlier, and also very popular mock-epitaph for Mazarin himself, beginning:

Hic iacet Julius Mazarinus
Galliae rex, Italus
Ecclesiae Praesul Laicus
Europae praedo purpuratus,
Fortunam omnem ambiit, omnem corrumpit,
Aerarium administravit, et exhausit;
Civile bellum compressit, sed commovit;
Regni iura tuitus est, et invasit;
Beneficia possedit, et vendidit;
Parem dedit aliquando, sed distulit,
Hostes cladibus, cives oneribus affligit,
Arrisit paucis, irrisit plurimos,
      Omnibus nocuit.

Here lies Jules Mazarin
King of France, though an Italian,
Prelate of the Church, though a lay-man,
Plunderer of Europe, though clad in purple,
He strove for every kind of good fortune, and corrupted every one of them;
Put in charge of the treasury, he drained it dry;
He put down civil war, but also incited it;
Made guardian of the laws of the kingdom, he invaded it;
Having gained various privileges, he sold them;
Sometimes he acted fairly, but was then unjust;
On the enemy he inflicted disaster, but burdened too his own people,

He smiled kindly upon few, though he mocked many –
In short, he was a danger to everyone.

In one manuscript, now in Leeds, this poem is (improbably) attributed to John Milton, linking this example of free verse satire to the very different kind of formal hexameter *satyra* composed by William King (but attributed to Milton) more than 70 years later.[67]

Conclusion

Although largely ignored by literary scholarship, there was a lively tradition of satiric, invective and humorous Latin verse in early modern England. Several features of that literary culture track the English-language tradition with which we are more familiar: the importance of manuscript transmission and circulation; the late sixteenth-century distinction between the 'toothed' and 'toothless' satire; the rise of the satiric epigram in the early seventeenth century; and the fresh interest in formal hexameter verse satire and mock-epic in the early eighteenth century all correspond to contemporary features of vernacular literary culture, though offer interesting new perspectives upon it.

Other elements of what we find, however, have no clear parallel in the vernacular literary tradition. These are the features of the Latin verse satire of the period that we probably would not have predicted based solely on a knowledge of English literature or of the existing scholarship on classical reception. Of these I think it is worth highlighting three areas in particular: firstly, the enormous importance of iambic verse, especially for political invective which could be aimed at, or appreciated by, audiences well beyond England. Secondly, the enduring evidence of an essentially

---

[67] Leeds University Library, MS BC Lt 71, fol. 38^v. The Mazarin poem was also printed in [Anon.], *Poems on Affairs of State* (1702–7). Other manuscript copies include Bod. MSS Lat. misc. c. 19, pp. 204–5 (probably 1660s); Lat. misc. e. 19, fols. 80^r–2^r (c.1680–1); Ashmole 826, fol. 45^{r-v} (with an English translation, probably 1660s); Durham PG Library, MS P 29, fol. 70^r (early eighteenth century); Bod. MS Rawl. poet. 171, fols. 238^r (c.1674); Society of Antiquaries (London), MS SAL 330, fol. 71^v (c.1672). Love's first-line index (*English Clandestine Satire*, 341) records four manuscript copies, the Society of Antiquaries copy noted above, and three at Yale (Beinecke Library MSS Osborn b. 52, fols. 26 and 44, and Osborn b. 136, fol. 12), which I have not examined myself. He does not discuss the poem in the body of the book. There is a further possible copy in the Biblioteca Nacional, Madrid, MS 23888, fol. 84, which I have not examined. I have been unable to find any discussion of this poem, or of the attribution to Milton, in existing scholarship. An edition of Milton's Latin letters for Cromwell, including nine to Mazarin, was published in 1676. As the manuscript which attributes the poem to Milton appears to date from the 1690s, it may be influenced by knowledge of the letters, or more generally by the association of Milton in the latter seventeenth century with the Whig cause.

medieval tradition of rhyming Latin verse satire, an extremely persistent feature of what we find especially in the manuscript record, though occasionally breaking through, as in *Barnaby's Journey*, into popular print. Thirdly, the satiric possibilities both of extreme closeness to a canonical model – as in the classical *parodia*, where the satiric effect is produced by small but telling changes – but also of unclassical freedom, as in the breaking down of metrical structure in Fane's Horatian *parodia*, and in satirical and invective uses of fashionable Latin free verse.

PART II

Longer Verse

CHAPTER 9

Panegyric Epic in Early Modern England

Several of the most remarkable political poems of the mid-seventeenth century, including Marvell's 'First Anniversary' (1655) and Dryden's *Astraea Redux* (1660), belong to a genre which has not been clearly defined in English literature. These substantial poems, each of several hundred lines, derive elements from a range of panegyric forms, including the tradition of the political ode discussed in Chapter 4; but the main generic model for poetry of this sort, which is little represented in English before Marvell's 'First Anniversary', is the panegyric epic of the late antique poet Claudian: a genre, new to Latin when Claudian began writing, which combined the techniques of prose panegyric with contemporary (rather than mythological) epic. This chapter seeks to set the major seventeenth-century English examples of this form – as well as a handful of English-language precursors – within the wider context of a Latin genre which, though now obscure, was both widely understood and frequently composed.[1]

Previously addressed almost exclusively to royalty, the political turmoil of the mid-seventeenth century saw innovative developments in formal panegyric epic: Marvell's adaptation of the form for the praise of Cromwell, the Lord Protector, derives many of its elements not just from the Latin genre as a whole, but specifically from the work of Payne Fisher, the Latin poet laureate of the Cromwellian Protectorate.[2] Fisher's verse, which is markedly un-Virgilian in style, draws upon a very wide range of classical and late antique models, including Lucan, Statius, Silius Italicus, Valerius Flaccus and Prudentius, as well as earlier neo-Latin poets such as George Buchanan (1506–82) and Mantuan (Baptista Spagnuoli, 1447–1516), and even works (by John Milton, Caspar Barlaeus and

---

[1] Portions of this chapter expand upon an argument made initially in Moul, 'England's Stilicho'.
[2] On Fisher, see Moul, 'Revising the Siege of York', 'Marvell and Fisher', and 'Date of Marvell's *Hortus*'.

Charles I) published within the previous decade.[3] By far the most frequent source, however, and the model for the form of Fisher's poems as well as the source of many specific quotations, is the political poetry of Claudian. Fisher systematically transfers the panegyric imagery applied to Stilicho (c.359–408 AD), regent for the underage emperor Honorius, to Cromwell: a figure who, like Stilicho, was in power though explicitly not on the throne. Fisher's work, though now almost completely forgotten, represents a sustained engagement with the Claudianic genre of panegyric epic at a time of great political change, and draws on many contemporary or near-contemporary poets working in the same form (such as Barlaeus, Alabaster and Milton) as well as upon classical models; in addition, Fisher's work appears to have been a key conduit for the formal appropriation of Claudianic panegyric in English, and was demonstrably influential upon Protectorate and Restoration poetics. For all these reasons, his work is a focus of the central section of this chapter.

Claudian and Claudianic Genres

Since Claudian is only rarely read today even by classicists, at least in the Anglophone world, it may be helpful to set out briefly the scope of his work, and what is most distinctive about his style. Claudian (Claudius Claudianus), a man probably of Alexandrian origin, was the most successful court poet of the late Roman empire: active between 395 and 404 AD, he composed in both Latin and Greek, though the great majority of his extant poetry is in Latin. Although recent classical scholarship has begun to take the literary achievement of late antique poets including Claudian seriously, he has traditionally been read largely as an historical source: his works comprise 11 major poems in hexameter composed in celebration of the consulships of Probinus and Olybrius (in 395), the emperor Honorius (in 396, 398 and 404), Fl. Manlius Theodorus (in 399) and Stilicho (in 400); specific military victories (against the Berber general Gildo in 398, and in the Gothic War of 402–3); and the defeat or death of two Roman rivals of Stilicho, Rufinus, Praetorian Prefect of the East who was

---

[3] Fisher's *Marston-Moor* (1650) borrows twice from Milton's *In Quintum Novembris*, published in the *Poems* (1645) and discussed below; *Irenodia Gratulatoria* (1652) applies to Cromwell an image famously used of Charles I in the *Eikon Basilike* (a work purportedly by Charles I himself, published in 1649); *Inauguratio Olivariana* (1654) alludes at least twice to the work of Caspar Barlaeus, in one instance to a poem (*Panegyris de laudibus ... Richelii Ducis*) published only in 1641. See Moul, 'Revising the siege of York', for more detailed discussion of the allusive range of *Marston-Moor*.

murdered in 398, and his successor, Eutropius, who died in 399.[4] In addition, Claudian's long hexameter poems include an *Epithalamium* (*Epith.*) for the marriage of the young emperor Honorius and Stilicho's teenage daughter Maria in 398, and a fragmentary mythological epic, *De Raptu Proserpinae* (*Rapt.*), which shares many stylistic and thematic elements with the other long verse, though without any explicit contemporary application.[5]

In addition, there are 52 *Carmina Minora* (*CM*, shorter poems) in modern editions, not counting the *Fescennine Verses* (a series of four short pieces written for the marriage of Honorius and Maria), and several Greek poems, including a portion of Greek mythological epic, the *Gigantomachy*. A handful of Claudian's shorter poems are found very frequently in both Latin and English translation in early modern English commonplace books and miscellanies: two of the most frequently quoted, imitated or translated are 'The Phoenix' (*CM* 27) and 'The Old Man of Verona' (*CM* 20). The latter, a poem about the superiority of the unsophisticated rural life to that of the city, was particularly popular in the mid-seventeenth century and was translated by Thomas Randolph (1638), Mildmay Fane (1648), Abraham Cowley (1668) and Henry Vaughan (1678) among many others.[6] It is discussed briefly in Chapter 1, as an influential example of moralizing verse.

Although modern scholarship is doubtful on this point, Claudian was understood in early modernity as a Christian poet, on the basis of a handful of explicitly Christian poems attributed to him at the time.[7] This is important to his reception history: even though Claudian's panegyric epic contains almost no traces of Christian belief or practice, and indeed makes extensive use of the conventional pagan divinities, his

---

[4] This chapter uses the following conventional abbreviations for these works: *III Cons* (Panegyric on the third consulate of Honorius Augustus); *IV Cons.* (Panegyric on the fourth consulate of Honorius Augustus); *VI Cons.* (Panegyric on the sixth consulate of Honorius Augustus); *Epith.* (Epithalamium on the marriage of Honorius Augustus); *Eut.* 1 and 2 (Against Eutropius, Books 1 and 2); *Get.* (on the Getic War); *Gild.* (on the Gildonic war); *P&O* (Panegyric for the consuls Probinus and Olybrius); *Rapt* 1, 2 and 3 (On the Rape of Proserpina, Books 1, 2 and 3); *Ruf.* 1 and 2 (Against Rufinus, Books 1 and 2); *Stil.* 1, 2 and 3 (On the consulate of Stilicho, Books 1, 2 and 3); *Theod.* (Panegyric for the consul Mallius Theodorus).

[5] The poem has sometimes been read as a political allegory, see e.g. Duc, *Le 'De Raptu Proserpinae'*; and Kellner, *Die Göttergestalten in Claudians 'De Raptu Proserpinae'*.

[6] Gillespie, 'Claudian's *Old Man of Verona*', assembles translations dating from between 1629 and 1992. On the Restoration translations of Claudian made by Thomas Ross, see Bond, 'The Phoenix and the Prince'.

[7] Only one of these (*CM* 32, 'De Salvatore') is now generally considered to be by Claudian, with the rest attributed to other late antique authors.

Christianity lent him an authority distinct from that of the unarguably pagan poets such as Virgil or Lucan. The commonplace book of classical extracts compiled by the future Charles I for his father, for instance (discussed further below), includes the whole of *Miracula Christi* as the only item under the heading 'De Christo' and a quotation from *In Rufinum* is the first entry under 'De Deo'.[8] The prominence of Claudian, chronologically the latest of the Latin poets in Charles' collection, testifies both to his importance as a political poet, and to his unique status as a poet considered to belong both to the classical canon and to the ranks of Christian poets.

Recognising Claudianic Style and Influence

Despite its importance in early modernity, Claudianic panegyric epic is a good example of a specifically Latin genre, originating in the ancient world, which is nevertheless not (at least for most Anglophone readers) recognizably 'classical': although Claudian was indebted both to earlier Latin epic poets, especially Virgil, Lucan and Statius, and to Statius' panegyric and occasional verse in the *Silvae*, his landmark genre – long hexameter poems which are nevertheless not of epic length, and which blend epic and formal panegyric elements to describe contemporary or near-contemporary events – was innovative in many respects.[9] Since many modern classicists do not know Claudian well, the cultural significance of this entire genre in early modernity has been largely missed: if you have read Claudian, it is immediately obvious that the style, form and tone of hundreds of early modern examples of verse panegyric are modelled upon his panegyric epic; but if you have not read Claudian, as even many trained classicists in the UK and America have not, the genre of these poems is elusive. This illegibility has led to critical distortion: there are relatively few examples of full-scale Latin epics in early modernity (and even fewer that were finished), but they have attracted considerable attention from classically trained neo-Latinists used to privileging the work of Homer or Virgil.

---

[8] *Miracula Christi* is one of the Christian poems no longer considered to be by Claudian. It was included however in early modern editions. An eighteenth-century Amsterdam edition, for instance, with notes by Heinsius and Burmann, prints *Miracula Christi*, *Laus Christi* and the *Carmen Paschale* in a final section of possible attributions, and also prints Lactantius' *De Phoenice*, previously attributed to Claudian – Heinsius *et al.* (eds.), *Claudii Claudiani Opera* (1760).

[9] On Claudianic genre, see Hofmann, 'Überlegungen'; Coombe, *Claudian the Poet*, 18–22; Perrelli, *I proemi Claudian*; Felgentreu, *Claudians Prefationes*; Schindler, *Per Carmina Laudes*, 1–14. Ware, *Claudian and the Roman Epic Tradition*, argues that the poems are best understood as epic.

Recognizing Claudianic Style and Influence 359

On the other hand, there are hundreds of shorter (but still long) hexameter poems which conform to the generic outlines of panegyric epic in the style of Claudian, but no existing surveys of neo-Latin literature identify this as a distinct genre.

Indeed, although Claudian's poetry has attracted increased scholarly attention in recent years, there has been almost no dedicated work on the reception of Claudian in early modern England.[10] Cheney and Hardie's recent *Oxford History of Classical Reception in English Literature*, volume II: *1558–1660*, for instance, has no chapter on Claudian or on panegyric epic, though Claudian is mentioned in passing in the 'epic' chapter. Enterline's chapter on 'Elizabethan Minor Epic' (or 'epyllion') in the same volume makes no mention of Claudian at all, understanding this form – of which only English examples are discussed – solely in terms of Virgil and Ovid, although the only ancient mythological epyllion regularly read in early modern schools was Claudian's (fragmentary) *De Raptu Proserpinae*; as discussed in Chapter 10, the style of Elizabethan epyllion, in both Latin and English, is much more like that of Claudian than of either Virgil or Ovid. Peter Davidson, in a typically acute aside, notes the significance of Claudian as a model for 'baroque Latin', though this important stylistic point has not been taken up.[11] The fullest treatment of the reception of Claudian's political poetry in English literature remains Garrison's 1975 monograph *Dryden and the Tradition of Panegyric*, which, despite the title, devotes a significant proportion of the book to panegyric verse before Dryden. The importance of Garrison's argument for understanding formal panegyric verse in early modernity has however gone largely unacknowledged in subsequent literary criticism.[12] This chapter accordingly offers a survey of the place of Claudian (especially, but not only, his political verse) and of the Claudianic genres in the literary culture of the later sixteenth and seventeenth centuries, drawing on both print and manuscript sources, before turning to the specific use of Claudian by

---

[10] Scholarship dealing with Claudian's reception in Renaissance literature more broadly includes Braden, 'Claudian and His Influence'; Döpp, 'Claudian und die lateinische Epik'; Fuhrmann, 'Claudian in der Neuzeit'; and Felgentreu, 'Claudian'. Keith Sidwell's recent editions of O'Meara's *Ormonius* and the anonymous *Poema de Hibernia*, however, both point out many allusions to Claudian – Sidwell and Edwards (eds.), *Tipperary Hero*; Lenihan and Sidwell (eds.), *Poema de Hibernia*.
[11] Davidson, *Universal Baroque*, 47.
[12] Probably because until recently Claudian was read largely as an historical source, historians have been slightly more likely to acknowledge his importance as a model (e.g. Miller, *Roman Triumphs*, 36–7).

Fisher, Marvell and subsequently Dryden in the latter half of the seventeenth century.

Recent scholarship has recognized that Claudian's poems celebrating the consulships of Honorius, Stilicho and others; his works celebrating victory in battle over Gildo and the Goths; and his invective poems focusing upon the downfall and death of Stilicho's Roman political opponents in the East, Rufinus and Eutropius, all belong to essentially the same genre, and that the other long hexameter poems – the *Epithalamium* and the mythological epic, *De Raptu Proserpinae* – have many thematic and stylistic similarities.[13] This insight has important implications for the reading of early modern poetry: it suggests, in particular, that hexameter panegyric verse of medium to long (but not epic) length on the accession or return of a monarch (such as Jonson's *Panegyre* or the many Restoration examples); on a great victory against a foreign enemy (such as Barlaeus, Campion or the pseudonymous 'Eleutherius' on the Armada, or Fisher on the Battle of Marston Moor); on the defeat and humiliation of internal traitors (such as the many Gunpowder Plot poems), or even on a royal wedding (such as Chapman's *Andromeda Liberata*) all belong, in Claudianic terms, to essentially the same form; and that they may have strong links to more purely mythological poems – such as Campion's *Umbra* or even, perhaps, Shakespeare's *Venus and Adonis* – of a similar length. (The particular links between Elizabethan erotic epyllion and Claudianic poetry is the subject of Chapter 10.)

Claudian's verse offered early modern readers a unique combination: an author hallowed by centuries on the school curriculum, who was understood to have been a Christian, and whose work offered examples not only of epigram and attractive mythological narrative, but who was also the only 'classical' Latin poet to provide models for a broad range of the kind of courtly panegyric (and corresponding invective) that was so central a feature of early modern literary culture.[14] Several of his formal innovations – such as his use of short prefatory poems in elegiacs attached to each book of the longer hexameter works, and the polymetric sequence of short songs, including one rhyming poem, in the *Fescennine Verses* – were influential upon many medieval and early modern Latin poets.

None of this, however, suggests the appeal of Claudian's verse for the reader. Though routinely derided by classicists who compare him

---

[13] See Coombe, *Claudian the Poet*, 5–6.
[14] As discussed in Chapter 4, Horace and Pindar were the chief models for panegyric lyric; Statius is also important for the development of formal epithalamia, as discussed in Chapter 10.

unfavorably to Virgil, Claudian's style is both highly readable and, frequently, ravishing – even if somewhat repetitive if read in bulk. His extraordinary talent for poetic description is fully exploited in the rich larding of his political panegyric with an unusually large number of similes: he uses more similes than any of the earlier classical epic poets, and frequently runs a string of brief similes together.[15] He makes repeated use of certain 'set-piece' comparisons, such as of the emperor or other *laudandus* to the steersman of a ship or to the returning sun; and – conversely – enemy forces, whether contemporary enemies or their mythological counterparts, are linked to storms, darkness and elemental chaos. The consistency of Claudian's imagery across poems is one of the most striking features of his work, and enhances its political force: the actions of, for instance, Stilicho, Honorius and Theodosius are drawn together in a shared web of imagery; and we find the same imagery associated with a range of benevolent or glorious entities, such as Nature or the Phoenix.[16] This makes for highly effective political poetry: the strength of the associations around specific images allows even poems without any explicit contemporary or political content to function in a political way.

This technique was widely imitated by early modern poets, and indeed shared between them: verse anthologies, such as those marking the accession of a monarch, often contain poems by many individual poets with shared clusters of imagery. Similarly, a single poet could, like Claudian himself, develop the associations of particular images in multiple poems addressed to the same or related addressees: Fisher's construction of a non-kingly (but quasi-royal) poetics for the celebration of the Protectorate, discussed further below, depended heavily on the borrowing of Claudianic motifs, and more generally upon the development of linked images associated primarily with Cromwell, but applied also to the Earl of Manchester, John Bradshaw (President of the Council of State), General Monck, various foreign allies and even to the poet himself.

---

[15] According to Müllner, Claudian contains 145 similes in 8,468 lines of the major poems compared to 105 in the 9,898 lines of the *Aeneid* (Müllner, *De imaginibus*). Christiansen, *Use of Images*, however, counts 354 'images' (a broader category than similes strictly understood), comprising 1,402 lines out of a total of 9,884 lines of poetry (including, as Müllner does not, the minor as well as the major poems). Among his predecessors, Claudian's practice is closest to that of Statius, who like Claudian makes fairly frequent use of double or even triple similes – Dominik *et al.* (eds.), *Companion to Statius*, 266–8. Claudian's similes also tend to be longer than those of his predecessors (Cameron, *Claudian*, 297–8).

[16] The single most useful work on Claudian's imagery as a whole remains Christiansen, *Use of Images*, though frustratingly without indices. Coombe, *Claudian the Poet*, insists like Christiansen on the coherence of Claudian's scheme of imagery; and though less thorough, it is more user-friendly.

Above all, Claudian's style is instantly recognizable. As such, it was widely imitated and indeed taught. Faminiano Strada's (1572–1649) extremely popular Latin poem, 'The Nightingale' (*Prolusiones* 2.6), is a good example.[17] The amusing narrative – in which a musician and a nightingale attempt to outdo one another in the beauty of their music, until the nightingale perishes from the effort and falls dead at the musician's feet – is a poetic mnemonic for the distinctive features of Claudianic style:

> Iam sol à medio pronus deflexerat orbe
> Mitius è radiis vibrans crinalibus ignem
> Cum fidicen propter Tiberina fluenta, sonanti
> Lenibat plectro curas, aestumque levabat
> Ilice deffensus nigrâ, scenaque virenti.
> Audiit hunc hospes sylvae Philomela propinquae,
> Musa loci, nemoris Siren, innoxia Siren,
> Et prope succedens stetit abdita frondibus, alte
> Accipiens sonitum, secumque remurmurat, & quos
> Ille modos variat digitis, haec gutture reddit.
>
> (1–10)

> *Now the declining sun 'gan downwards bend*
> *From higher heavens, and from his locks did send*
> *A milder flame, when near to Tiber's flow*
> *A lutinist allay'd his careful woe*
> *With sounding charms, and in a greeny seat*
> *Of shady oake took shelter from the heat.*
> *A Nightingale oreheard him, that did use*
> *To sojourn in the neighbour groves, the muse*
> *That fill'd the place, the Syren of the wood;*
> *Poore harmless Syren, stealing neare she stood*
> *Close lurking in the leaves attentively*
> *Recording that unwonted melody:*
> *Shee cons it to herselfe and every strayne*
> *His finger playes her throat return'd again.*

Strada's poem was widely translated and imitated in early modern England, from around the 1620s onwards – it stands behind the first

---

[17] Strada, an Italian Jesuit, published *Prolusiones*, aimed at advanced students and teachers of Latin, in Cologne in 1617. Its many editions included one in Oxford in 1631, and it was certainly recommended to university students in England by the 1630s (on which see Gillespie, 'After Strada'). The various 'prolusiones' demonstrate different Latin styles, but this is one of the most frequently excerpted, and in the latter part of the seventeenth century it began to be regularly included in school anthologies of Latin verse, e.g. [Anon.], *Epigrammatum Delectus* (1683), 405–7.

scene of John Ford's play *The Lover's Melancholy*, printed in 1629, and William Strode's (c.1601–45) translation (given above) was probably made in the 1620s and circulated very widely. Richard Crashaw's 1646 *Music's Duel* is also an (expansive) version of the same poem.

Robert South's (1634–1716) very popular poem, *Musica Incantans*, in which a young man is driven mad, and finally drowns himself, not for romantic love, but for love of music, belongs to the same literary family, and indeed South uses the same Latin word for the musician, *fidicen*, as in Strada's poem.[18] There is something both seductive and ultimately worrying about such consummate and powerful style, especially if one feels or suspects that it lacks serious content: indeed, the singer who inspired the young man in South's poem ends up prosecuted for (though ultimately acquitted of) his murder. In short, poets and readers in sixteenth- and seventeenth-century England, if they had any Latin education at all, would have read Claudian, been aware of the range of models his work offered especially for public-facing verse, and would have readily recognized imitations of his very distinctive style.

Reading Claudian in Early Modern England

In the final pages of his magisterial monograph, Alan Cameron discusses in some detail the evidence for the medieval readership of Claudian and stresses the particular importance in England of Theodosius' speech on true kingship in *IV. Cons.* 214–352. His examples, however, are drawn largely from texts dating from the twelfth to fifteenth centuries, and his brief discussion of the seventeenth century is focused mainly on prose.[19] Given the lack of existing scholarly overviews, we need to turn to manuscripts and archives for a sense of the cultural role of Claudianic verse in early modern England.

Ben Jonson's own working copy of Claudian has survived, and bears out the point made by Cameron: the single most underlined text is *IV Cons.* But the volume as a whole is heavily marked: all the political poems as well

---

[18] South wrote the poem, which was published in 1655 but circulated also in manuscript, as an undergraduate at Oxford in the early-mid 1650s. Strada's *Nightingale* was certainly well known by this point, although South's poem probably also has a political or religious connotation, perhaps related to the Puritan restrictions on Church music in place under the Protectorate. South illegally attended Church of England services while at Oxford (Griggs, 'South, Robert').

[19] Cameron, *Claudian*, 419–33. He also discusses the cluster of seventeenth-century translations of Claudian's 'Old Man of Verona' (*CM* 20), on which see Gillespie, 'Claudian's *Old Man of Verona*'.

as *Rapt.* have many underlinings.[20] Indeed, Jonson uses a paraphrase of the same three lines (*Stil.* 3.113–15) both in the text for his celebratory pageant for the entry of James I to London (*The King's Entertainment*, 1604) and in his almost exactly contemporaneous exploration of corrupt kingship in *Sejanus* (1603): 'Men are deceived who think there can be thrall / Beneath a virtuous prince. Wished liberty / Ne'er lovelier looks than under such a crown' (*Sejanus* 1.407–9).[21] Jonson's engagement with Claudian at this period is discussed further below, and briefly again in Chapter 10.

Jonson, Drayton and Daniel all produced formal English panegyric for the accession of James I. Though this attempt to make such verse a standard English (rather than purely Latin) genre did not catch on in the first decade of the seventeenth century, their interest in Claudian is far from unique. Surviving manuscripts and archives offer plentiful evidence for the very widespread reading of Claudian in early modern England, dominated not by the shorter *Carmina Minora* (on which minimal existing scholarship on Claudian's English reception has focused), but by the political poetry.

The best-known printed commonplace book in the early seventeenth century was Octavius Mirandula's *Illustrium Poetarum Flores*, first published in 1507, and containing extracts from 24 different Latin authors. The volume includes late antique and Christian poets as well as pagans, and contains many extracts from Claudian: two out of five under 'De Ambitione', for instance, three out of nine under 'De Christo', and eight out of ten under 'De Clementia'.[22] Among many manuscript examples, the large collection of classical Latin verse extracts prepared by the future Charles I as a gift for his father is particularly interesting.[23] Claudian is the

---

[20] By contrast, the various marriage poems, the poem on Serena, Stilicho's wife, and most of the *Carmina Minora* are only lightly marked, if at all; the exceptions are 'De sene Veronensi' (*CM* 20) and three epigrams (*CM* 13, 14 and 15). The volume is a copy of the Pulman edition, printed in Antwerp in 1585; Bodleian 80 c 90 Art. Sel.

[21] Compare *The King's Entertainment*, in which Jonson explains the image of Liberty trampling Servitude accompanied by the phrase 'NEC UNQUAM GRATIOR', as 'alluding to that other of Claudian, *Nunquam libertas gratior extat, / Quam sub rege pio*, and intimated that liberty could never appear more graceful and lovely than now, under so good a prince' (Bevington *et al.*, *Works of Ben Jonson*, vol. II, 449). Peterson suggests allusions to Claudian in Jonson's *Epigrams* 14 and 76 (*Imitation and Praise*, 44–5, 68–9, 88).

[22] The first extant English edition dates from 1598, though as works of this kind were often used in schools until they fell apart, there may have been earlier London printings which have not survived. See Moss, *Printed Commonplace-Books*, 95–8, 182, 189–90, 215–17.

[23] BL MS Royal 12 D VIII, dating from before 1625. Elyot, *The boke named the Gouernour* (1531), particularly recommends Claudian for the education of princes (Book 2, chap. 1), and James I also quotes from Claudian in *Basilikon Doron* (1599), urging Prince Henry to follow the teaching on kingship in *IV Cons. Hons.* 214–352 – Craigie (ed.), *Basilikon Doron of King James VI*, 1.53.

fourth most cited author (after Ovid, Seneca and Horace), with more quotations (44) than Virgil (41) or any other epic poet. Quotations from Claudian are particularly prominent under headings that might be of particular relevance to a future king, including 'De regno' ('On ruling', two extracts from *IV Cons.*), 'De Principibus' ('On Princes', again two from *IV Cons.*) and 'De potentia' ('On power', one from *III Cons.* and one from *De sepulcro speciosae*, a poem no longer attributed to Claudian).

Although Prince Charles' collection includes extracts from Claudian's invective verse and shorter poems, the great majority are from the works of political panegyric, and by far the largest number of citations from a single work (16) are from *IV Cons.* This is typical of the citation of Claudian in manuscript material at this period, and accords with Cameron's observations of the importance of this text in English culture of an earlier period. Given Charles' personal enthusiasm for Claudian, he must have been particularly flattered by a clever piece included in a volume of 31 Latin poems presented to Charles by boys at Westminster School on the occasion of his coronation in 1626:

> Claudiani umbra. querula }
> Hos ego versiculos feci}
> De laud: Stil: l. 3. de 6° cons: Hon:
>
> Agnosco (vates maxime) agnosco tuos
> Aegyptiace, verosque versiculos simul
> Rerum potito, Musa, Stiliconi, tua
> Honorioque saepè blandita est nimis:
> Stiliconis ac Honorii nomen, stylo
> Poeta rade, pone Stewardum, et sape,
> Historia vera sic erit, et encomium.[24]
>
> The shade of Claudian. Lament }
> I have made this little poem}
> De laud. Stil. Book 3; VI. Cons. Hons.
>
> *I know your work well (great poet) I know well,*
> *Egyptian, the truth of your poems;*
> *But when Stilicho was in power, your Muse*
> *Too often flattered him excessively, as she did Honorius:*
> *With your pen, poet, scratch out the names of Stilicho and of Honorius,*
> *Put instead 'Stewart', and be wise:*
> *That way you'll have a true history, and a real encomium.*

---

[24] BL MS Royal 12 A LVII, fol. 10ʳ.

This poem is in iambic trimeters (or the 'iambic septenarius'), a popular Latin metre at this period which was also standardly used in Latin drama: in other words, it is *about* Claudian but does not itself imitate his form or style. Framed as an address to the 'ghost of Claudian', it is probably intended to recall the conventional appearance of a ghost or deity in a Latin play. The speaker of the poem suggests to the ghostly Claudian that the last of the poems in praise of Stilicho and Honorius (*Stil.* 3 and *VI Cons.*) were a step too far, and that the house of Stuart would be a juster recipient for such lavish adulation.

Many other manuscripts attest to familiarity with Claudian, and an assumption of familiarity in those addressed. By and large, the pattern of references accords with that noted above: *IV Cons.*, most often Theodosius' speech to Honorius on true kingship (214–352), is the single most cited text, especially (for obvious reasons) in a royal context. An early example is CUL MS Mm. IV. 39, which preserves various poems and speeches composed for the visit of Queen Elizabeth to Cambridge in 1564: the speech on fol. 32^v cites Claudian *IV Cons.* Similar examples can be found from manuscripts dating from throughout the seventeenth century.[25] In general, we find more references to the political poetry (both panegyric and satiric) than to the non-political verse, though *'The Old Man of Verona'* (*CM* 20) is not the only one of Claudian's shorter poems that was popular, especially in the latter seventeenth century.[26]

The standing in which Claudian was held as a Latin stylist is also demonstrated by contemporary criticism; in a letter dated 1 February 1640, the Dutch Latin poet and critic Caspar Barlaeus, at that point Professor of Philosophy at Amsterdam, writes 'Virgilium, Lucanum,

---

[25] Trinity College, Cambridge, MS R. 3. 60 (c.1600), fol. 12^v, quotes *IV Cons.* 222–5; Leeds University Library, MS BC Lt 13 (1680), fols. 23^r and 57^r, quotes both *IV Cons.* and *Ruf.* 1; Leeds University Library, MS BC Lt q 18 (mid-seventeenth century) includes eight extracts attributed to Claudian in a section titled 'Epigrammes or Sentences Epigrammelike' (fols. 6^v–8^v). Of these, three are in fact quotations from Juvenal, Propertius and Lucan; the remaining five are from *IV Cons.* (2), *Stil.* (1), *Theod.* (1) and *Ruf.* (1). The confusion between Juvenal's *Satires* and Claudian's satiric verse is quite common, suggesting Claudian's strong association with political satire. English translations in manuscript include Leeds University Library, MS BC Lt 40, fol. 59^r (Sir Philip Wodehouse) and Bod. MSS Rawl. poet. 114, pp. 114–16 (John Morrice, part of *Ruf.* 1, dated 1707); Rawl. poet. 154, 'Claudian his Panegyrick upon the Fourth Consulship of Honorius', dated 1665 (fol. 49^v), and 'A translation of Claudian's first book against Eutropius', dated 1664 (fols. 27^r and 38^v).

[26] Bod. MS Rawl. poet. 166 (c.1625–30), p. 64, includes a translation of 'In sphaeram Archimedes' (*CM* 51). In a late example, Charles Caesar quotes a poem then attributed to Claudian, the 'Carmen de Christo', in his commonplace book of 1705 (BL MS Add. 43410, fol. 174^v). Quotations or translations from the 'Phoenix' (*CM* 27) are also common, e.g. Bod. MS Sancroft 26 (1691), p. 17.

Claudianum imitandos censeam in Epico carmine' ('I would recommend for imitation in Epic verse, Virgil, Lucan and Claudian', fol. 11ᵛ); the letter goes on to include two quotations from Claudian, both (typically enough) from the kingship speech in *IV Cons*. (lines 269 and 294).[27] Barlaeus' own panegyric verse (discussed further below) is strongly indebted to Claudian, and his 'Elogia aliquot Poetarum Latinorum', a series of couplets on each of the classical Latin poets, ends with Claudian:

> Te sequimur Phario vates celebrate Canopo:
>   Solaque laus nostri carminis, umbra tui est.[28]

> *We follow you, celebrated* vates *from Pharian Canopus* [i.e. Egypt]:
>   *And the only praise of our verse, is* [that it is] *the shadow of yours.*

Claudian's satiric verse was also being critically appraised at this time: a mid-seventeenth-century manuscript collection of letters from famous authors includes a letter by Nicolaas Heinsius (1620–81) on Claudian's *In Eutropium*, dated 1645.[29]

Imitation of Claudian in Early Modern England

Given this wealth of evidence that Claudian's poetry was very widely read, quoted and discussed, why do we find this so little reflected in English literature of the period, and the scholarly guides to that literature? There is I believe a clear answer to this: namely, that until the mid-1650s, and perhaps specifically until Marvell's 'First Anniversary', Claudianic panegyric-epic was – bar the occasional exception such as Jonson's experimental *Panegyre* – an almost exclusively Latin genre in England as elsewhere in Europe. Not only that, but many of the Latin poems composed in this tradition, especially in the sixteenth century, were prepared and presented in manuscript rather than print. These two features of the genre – often in manuscript, and almost exclusively written in Latin – has meant that a form which was, in practice, standard, has become almost invisible to critics and historians. Recent scholarly consensus, for instance, has been that Marvell's 'First Anniversary' belongs to 'no recognizable ancient genre'.[30]

---

[27] BL MS Add. 23719, fols. 5–12.   [28] Barlaeus, *Poematum* (1631), 476.
[29] BL MS Harley 4933, fol. 21ʳ. See Gillespie, 'Two Seventeenth-Century Translations'.
[30] Smith (ed.), *Poems of Andrew Marvell*, 285. Anthony Miller, however, correctly identifies the genre: 'The generic models of Marvell's *First Anniversary* are the consular panegyrics of Claudian' (*Roman Triumphs*, 177). Garrison implicitly makes the same point when he stresses the 'traditional' features

In practice, there are a large number of surviving examples of British Latin short panegyric-epic, dating mostly from the latter sixteenth and first half of the seventeenth centuries, and found in both manuscript and print sources. Influential early examples include Erasmus' *Gratulatorium Carmen* (1504, printed with his prose treatise on the topic) and Thomas More, *Carmen Gratulatorium* (1509, on the coronation of Henry VIII).[31] As noted above, Latin verse of this type was frequently presented in manuscript before around 1600, though examples by famous authors, such as More and Buchanan, were often printed later in collected volumes; most of the print rather than manuscript examples date therefore from the seventeenth century.[32] The great majority of full-length panegyric poems are addressed either to the monarch, his or her representative, or to a prominent member of the royal family, though the interesting work of John Sictor, a Bohemian exile writing in London in the 1630s, includes a panegyric poem of this type addressed to Richard Fenn, the Mayor of London.[33]

Surviving manuscript examples are often presentation volumes, a particularly large number of which can be found in the Royal Collection of the British Library.[34] A Westminster School presentation manuscript from 1587, a New Year's gift for Queen Elizabeth, demonstrates the extent to

---

of the poem (*Tradition of Panegyric*, 134) but his work has not been much acknowledged in recent scholarship.

[31] Both discussed in Garrison, *Tradition of Panegyric*, passim.

[32] Examples include Allen, *Carmen encomiasticum* (1571); Echlin, *De regno panegyricon* (1603); King, *In Iacobum sextum* (1603); Herring, *In foelicissimum* (1603); Dempster, *Panegyricus* (1615); Kell, *Carmen gratulatorium* (1617); Gohaeus, *Carmen Panegyrikon* (1621), commemorating the visit of Honoré d'Albert, Duc de Chaulnes, representing the French King Louis XIII; Du Moulin, *Carmen heroicum* (1625); Sictor, *Panegyricon* (1626); Boyd, *Ad augustissimum monarcham Carolum* (1633), unusually followed by an English verse paraphrase; Gill, *Gratulatoria* (1641).

[33] Sictor, *Panegyricon inaugurale*, published both in London (by Thomas Harper) and Cambridge (by Roger Daniels) in 1638. The London edition also includes a panegyric Latin poem by Edward Benlowes, who later paid for publication of Fisher's *Marston-Moor* (1650). Sictor contributed a commendatory poem on *Marston-Moor* to Fisher's collected works (*Piscatoris Poemata*, 1656, sig. M2^{r-v}). Sictor's work in the 1630s prefigures Fisher's use of the form not only for Cromwell, but also for Bradshaw, Whitelocke and foreign dignitaries including Mazarin (*Epinicion, vel elogium*, 1658) and the Marquis de Lede (*Apobaterion*, 1655). On Sictor, see Poole, 'Down and Out in Leiden and London'.

[34] BL MSS Royal 12 A LXI (1604, anonymous, to James I), 12 A VII (Nicolas Denisot, c.1547, on the accession of Edward VI; largely lifted from earlier neo-Latin authors, on which see Vredeveld, 'Nicolas Denisot and the Seymour Sisters'), 12 A XXXVI–XXXVII (Thomas Bastard, 1603, for James I); 12 A XLIII (George Carleton, c.1597, to Queen Elizabeth), and 12 A LVI (also Carleton, after 1603, to James I). Examples from other collections include Trinity College, Cambridge, MS O. 6. 1, pp. 46–8; National Archives, MS SP 78/94/56, fol. 170^{r-v} (1633, addressed to King Louis XIII of France); Bod. MS Douce 387, fols. 75–80^v (1594–5, to Ernest, Archduke of Austria). This is by no means a complete list.

which the composition of panegyric verse in Claudianic form was a standard exercise: of the 16 sets of contributions by individual pupils, all but 4 begin with a 'carmen gratulatorium', a long hexameter poem in Claudianic style. In each case, this is the longest contributed poem, as well as standing first.[35]

Shorter instances of Claudianic-style panegyric were often included within multi-authored collections of commemorative or panegyric verse, or printed alone as broadsheets.[36] The anonymous poem *In illustrissimi comitis Leicestrensis Oxoniensis* (1585), on the return of the Earl of Leicester, is only 36 lines long but incorporates multiple features typical of Claudianic panegyric. The Earl is compared to Apollo, and to the returning sun; in the opening lines, all the citizens rush into the streets to greet him:

> Quis stupor hic oculos, quaeue admiratio mentes
> Detinet attonitas? mediarum in strata viarum
> Cur pueri, matres, ac tota effusa scholarum
> Agmina? cur vacuas conferti liquimus aedes?
>
> (1–4)
>
> *What astonishment, what admiration is seizing here*
> *Their eyes and minds? Why have boys, mothers, and all the*
> *Ranks of the schools flooded out into the middle of the streets?*
> *Why have they all gathered together and left the buildings empty?*

This recalls the people's excitement at the return of Honorius in *III Cons.* 126–30:

> Quanti tum iuvenes, quantae sprevere pudorem
> spectandi studio matres, puerisque severi
> certavere senes, cum tu genitoris amico
> exceptus gremio mediam veherere per urbem
> velaretque pios communis laurea currus!
>
> (126–30)
>
> *How many young men, how many mothers cast their modesty aside in their eagerness to look upon you! Severe old men jostled with boys, to find a place from which to watch how you, in your father's gentle embrace, were carried through the city and a single shared branch of laurel shaded the dutiful chariot!*

---

[35] This manuscript is now Westminster Abbey Muniments Room, MS 31. The boys named almost all matriculated at Oxford or Cambridge between 1588 and 1590 and were therefore in their last few years at school at the time of composition.

[36] Examples in commemorative anthologies include Oxford University, *Academiae Oxoniensis pietas* (1603), 63–8 and 184–7.

Jonson incorporates a version of the same motif in his *Panegyre* heralding the accession of James I in 1603:

> No age nor sex so weak, or strongly dull,
> That did not bear a part in this concent
> Of hearts and voices. All the air was rent,
> As with the murmur of a moving wood;
> The ground beneath did seem a moving flood:
> Walls, windows, roofs, towers, steeples, all were set
> With several eyes, that in this object met.
> Old men were glad their fates till now did last;
> And infants, that the hours had made such haste
> To bring them forth; whilst riper aged, and apt
> To understand the more, the more were rapt.
>
> (58–68)

Jonson's language is vivid compared to the rather pedestrian descriptive Latin of the Leicester piece; Jonson has learnt from Claudian's use of metaphor in particular. There are several Claudianic versions of this scene – including *III Cons.* 126–30 cited above – but Jonson seems to have *VI Cons.* 543–51 particularly in mind:

> Omne Palatino quod pons a colle recedit
> Mulvius et quantum licuit consurgere tectis
> Una replet turbae facies: undare videres
> Ima viris, altas effulgere matribus aedes.
> Exultant iuvenes aequaevi principis annis;
> temnunt Prisca senes et in hunc sibi prospera fati
> gratantur durasse diem
>
> (543–9)

> *One huge crowd filled all the slope between the Palatine Hill and the Mulvian bridge and as far up as it was possible to go on the roofs: you could see the lowest depths seething* [literally, 'undulating'] *with men, and the tall buildings were aglow with mothers. The young men rejoice in a prince the same age as themselves; the old reject the past and consider themselves lucky to have lived to see such a day.*

Jonson's line 'The ground beneath did seem a moving flood' picks up Claudian's striking 'undare videres / ima viris', 'You would have seen the depths waving [literally 'being waves', 'undulating'] with men'. In Jonson's poem Themis, the personification of justice, goes on to instruct the King 'How he may triumph in his subjects' breasts / With better pomp' (76–7). Her instructions are an artful paraphrase of Theodosius' advice to Honorius (*IV Cons.* 269–75), one of the best-known and most widely quoted passages of Claudian at this period, with elements which tactfully recall James' own reflections on this theme in *Basilikon Doron* (1599), a treatise on kingship addressed to his son, Prince Henry.[37] Jonson flatters the king by echoing the association, already implicit in *Basilikon Doron*, between King James and Theodosius and between Prince Henry and Honorius. But he also recasts it: in Jonson's poem, the didactic role of Theodosius is taken by the allegorical figure of Themis – who speaks, if for anyone, for the poet himself – casting James at least temporarily as the youthful Honorius. The complex dynamic in Claudian between the authority of Theodosius, of the regent Stilicho, and of the (glorious but largely powerless) child-emperor Honorius was a rich source of political subtlety for poets throughout early modernity.

Jonson's innovations in English verse repeatedly attempted to import into the vernacular forms typical of contemporary neo-Latin poetry: this is true, for instance, of his development of the regular Pindaric ode around 1600 (discussed in Chapter 5), and his self-conscious imitation of the characteristically neo-Latin *sylva* collection in English (*The Forest*; *Underwoods*). Alongside Samuel Daniel and Michael Drayton, Jonson made a similar attempt to 'English' formal hexameter panegyric in his compositions marking the accession of James I in 1603, including in his *Paneyre* (1604).[38] This impressive poem has been largely overlooked by critics: James D. Garrison's 1975 discussion, as background to Dryden's achievement, remains the best informed. Garrison deserves much more credit than he has received for his acknowledgement of the Claudianic roots of the tradition in which Jonson was writing, and for pointing out that this was a living Latin poetic form in the sixteenth century, though he makes little use of neo-Latin panegyric other than that of More and Erasmus.[39]

Jonson's engagement with Claudian at this period is apparent in a series of early Jacobean texts. The detailed notes he attached to *The King's*

---

[37] See Bevington *et al.* (eds.), *Works of Ben Jonson*, vol. II, 478–9. A later passage, *Panegyre* 125–7, has the same double relation to Theodosius on kingship (*IV Cons.* 299–301) and King James to Prince Henry (Craigie, *Basilicon Doron of King James VI*, I.53). James himself cites Claudian in the latter instance.

[38] Garrison, *Tradition of Panegyric*, 85–91 discusses Jonson's *Panegyre* (1603) in relation to Samuel Daniel's panegyric of the same year.

[39] Garrison, *Tradition of Panegyric*, 84–99. Subsequent scholarship, including the 2012 Cambridge edition, has tended to cite the parallels with More and Erasmus suggested by Garrison without further comment or exploration.

Entertainment include repeated citations of Claudian – as many as of Virgil – but the verse of the *Entertainment* includes paraphrases of at least three further well-known passages of Claudian that Jonson does not explicitly mark as such in the notes.[40] Taken as a whole, the work is more Claudianic than it is Virgilian or Ovidian (the other most commonly cited authorities), though Claudian's panegyrics are themselves of course indebted to both Virgil and Ovid.

Panegyric Epic in a European Context

Latin verse panegyric was a highly international form; practising poets read others' work from across Europe and commonly addressed works to foreign monarchs: examples on English themes written elsewhere in Europe include the German collection *Triumphalia de victoriis Elizabethae regina Angliae* (1588), commemorating the Armada; Adolpho van Dans, *Eliza* (1619?); and several works by Dutch authors, such as Caspar Barlaeus' *Britannia Triumphans* (1626) and Grotius, *Inauguratio Regis Britanniarum* (on James I), which were certainly read in England.[41] As discussed below, Fisher's Claudianic panegyric borrows significantly from both Grotius and Barlaeus.

Caspar Barlaeus, from 1631 the Professor of Philosophy and Rhetoric at the Amsterdam Athenaeum, was a leading intellectual of the age and his *Britannia Triumphans*, first published in 1626 but frequently reprinted, is a particularly clear example of self-conscious Claudianic style. A pointed opening passage, in which the poet asks for forbearance for his work on the basis of literary precedent, makes concise reference to most of Claudian's extant political panegyric:

---

[40] Martin Butler notes three passages which amount to translations: *King's Entertainment* 295 (*VI Cons.* 610); 507–13 (*IV Cons.* 493–9) and 650–5 (*Stil.* 2.111–15) (Bevington *et al.* (eds.), *Works of Ben Jonson*, vol. II). Other parallels not noted by Butler include the personification of London as a woman adorning herself as for a husband (220–5) indebted to Claudian *VI Cons.* 529–31 – an imitation further expanded in *Panegyre* (50–6) and discussed below. The slightly earlier *Entertainment at Althorp* also has Claudianic elements.

[41] The *Triumphalia* volume is attributed to 'N. Eleutherius', presumably a pseudonym. It is a mixed collection of verse, but includes two long poems in the Claudianic panegyric tradition – 3–22 (anonymous), and 32–41 (by Julius Riparius, unknown) – as well as lyric and elegiac verse. It is discussed in Miller, *Roman Triumphs*, 72–6. Grotius' *Inauguratio* was printed in his *Poemata collecta* (Leiden, 1637), 72–98.

> Non abnuit amnes
> Calliope, cum docta canunt commenta Serenam,
> Et Pelusiacae turgent Stilicone Camoenae,
> Et Latii cantatur apex, aut templa futuro
> Assurgunt Tiberina Duci: seu Mallius annum
> Consul init, Geticisque insignis Honorius armis
> Grandiloquo praecone tumet; vel laetior aether
> Adspicit Arcadium, vel magni fata Probini,
> Et decantati trabeas miratur Olybri.[42]
>
> *You did not reject the rivers,*
> *Calliope, when learned rhetoric sang of Serena,*
> *And the Pelusiacan [i.e. Egyptian] Muses were swollen with Stilico,*
> *And the peak of Latium was the subject of song, or the temples of the Tiber*
> *Rose for a future Lord: if Mallius began the year*
> *As consul, or Honorius, honoured by the capture of Getic weapons,*
> *Was vaunted by a boastful herald; or heaven looked gladly*
> *Upon Arcadius, or the fate of great Probinus,*
> *And wondered at the consulate of Olybrius, the subject of lengthy song.*

Serena was the wife of Stilicho; the poem in her praise (*CM* 30), though considered part of *Carmina Minora* (*Shorter Poems*), is 236 lines long; Felgentreu treats it as part of the political poetry.[43] 'Commenta' here means 'rhetorical figures'. 'Mallius' is Manlius Theodorus, consul in 399 and subject of *Theod.* Arcadius was Eastern Roman Emperor from 395–408, and eldest son of Theodosius. Probinus and Olybrius, the addressees of Claudian's *P&O*, were brothers and consuls together in 395.

Not all claims to be heir to the tradition of Claudian are as overt: some features were familiar enough to be recognizable even in the absence of specific references or marked stylistic imitation. The scene in Clemens' *Gustavis*, for instance, where Relligio, accompanied by Piety and Faith, appear in a bedraggled and desperate state to plead with Jupiter for the salvation of Germany, is a version of the memorable scene in *De Bello Gildonico*, in which first Rome, starving and forlorn, and then Africa, plead (successfully) with the Olympian gods for mercy.[44] We find the same

---

[42] Barlaeus, *Britannia Triumphans* (1626), 2–3.   [43] Felgentreu, 'Claudian'.
[44] Helander does not offer any specific parallels to Claudian in his discussion of this passage, but does comment 'It is quite clear that Clemens owes much to Claudian too. It is my firm opinion that Claudian's spirit moves upon the face of the whole work' (Helander, '*Gustavis*').

motif applied to England or the English Church in royalist verse describing the suffering of the country under the Protectorate.[45]

Both *Rapt.* and Claudian's Greek poem on the Gigantomachy begin with an enigmatic allegorical prefatory poem on a sea voyage, which has traditionally been taken to refer to the poet himself, launching upon a new poetic project:

> Inventa secuit primus qui nave profundum,
>   et rudibus remis sollicitavit aquas,
> qui dubiis ausus committere flatibus alnum,
>   quas natura negat, praebuit arte vias.
> tranquillis primum trepidus se credidit undis,
>   litora securo tramite summa legens:
> mox longos temptare sinus et linquere terras
>   et leni coepit pandere vela Noto.
> ast ubi paulatim praeceps audacia crevit
>   cordaque languentem dedidicere metum,
> iam vagus irrumpit pelagus caelumque secutus
>   Aegaeas hiemes Ioniumque domat.[46]

> *He who first made a ship and split the deep, who troubled the waters with rough-hewn oars, who first dared to trust his alderwood vessel to the uncertain winds, and who by his skill demonstrated routes which nature forbids – fearfully at first he ventured upon the smooth waves, skirting the shore in a cautious route. But soon he began to attempt wide bays, to leave the land behind and spread his sails to the gentle south wind; and when, little by little, his courage increased and his heart forgot the fear that held him back; now travelling freely he burst out into the ocean, followed the sky and tames the storms of Aegean and the Ionian sea.*

Both Payne Fisher and William Alabaster, in his unfinished *Elisaeis*, make use of a similar opening device:

> Multa quoque et regno passa est furialibus ausis
> Pontificum: dum Romuleis erepta ruinis
> Fragmina: uictura pietatis condidit arce.
>   Quis mihi tentantem tumidi maris aequora nauem
> Ducet? et aequatis lentabit carbasa ventis?
> Quis deus inuidiae caecis in fluctibus aras
> Despuat infames? caligantesque serenet
> Luce oculos?

---

[45] As for instance in the Cambridge Restoration anthology, *Academiae Cantabrigiensis* ΣΩΣΤΡΑ (1660), sig. B4ᵛ (the opening of a poem by M. Barlow, fellow of King's College). For other parallels in early modern Anglo-Latin poetry, see Chapter 11.

[46] *Rapt.* 1. *Pref.* For the same image applied to the poet, see also *Gig. Gr.* 1–15. On the depiction of the poet in Claudian's verse, see Guipponi-Gineste, *Claudien*, 281–331.

> *Much also did she* [Elizabeth] *suffer in her rule from the frenzied attempts of popes, until she established on the conquering citadel of piety the fragments saved from the ruins of Rome.*
>
> *Who will pilot my ship as it ventures on the expanse of rising seas, and who will spread my sails to the steady winds? What god can shun those notorious shoals in the dark seas of hostile envy and enlighten men's mist-enshrouded eyes?*[47]

Here it is the 'poet as pilot' motif which is most obviously Claudianic. But Alabaster's striking phrase 'Romuleis erepta ruinis / Fragmina' ('fragments snatched from the Romulean [i.e. Roman] ruins', 12–13) is equally, though more subtly, derived from Claudian: Claudian uses forms of the noun *ruina* 18 times, all but once as the final word in an hexameter line; and in one case also, as in Alabaster, referring specifically to the ruins of Rome:

> Numina Romanis necdum satiata ruinis,
> si iuvat imperium penitus de stirpe revelli,
> uno si placuit deleri saecula lapsu,
> si piget humani generis, prorumpat in arva
> libertas effrena maris vel limite iusto
> devius errantes Phaethon confundat habenas.
> (*Ruf.* 2.206–11)
>
> *O Gods not yet sated by the ruin of Rome, if it is your will that our empire be entirely uprooted, if it is your pleasure to destroy centuries of history in a single collapse, if you are weary of humankind, then let the sea be let loose to crash in freedom over the fields, or let Phaethon, straying from his proper course, drive his wandering team in confusion.*

In his *Paean Triumphalis* of 1657, a poem celebrating Cromwell and dedicated to Cardinal Mazarin, Fisher hails the salvation of England, repeatedly rescued from ruin:

> *Anglia* sed primùm tantos mirabitur actus
> Vulneribus defensa Tuis; Salva *Anglia* Tete
> Vindice, & à rapidis toties erepta ruinis.[48]
>
> *But England,* defended by your wounds, *shall first wonder at such great deeds;* England *saved by you, her avenger, and snatched so many times from toppling ruin.*

---

[47] Alabaster, *Elisaeis*, 11–18. Text and translation from O'Connell (ed.), '*Elisaeis* of William Alabaster'. Alabaster's language here also recalls Palingenius, *Zodiacus Vitae*, 2.458–60, a highly influential text discussed further in Chapter 11. Compare the poet as pilot in Fisher at *Marston-Moor* 1–3 and *Irenodia Gratulatoria* sig. B3ʳ.
[48] Fisher, *Paean Triumphalis* (1657), sig. B2ʳ.

Here the phrase 'erepta ruinis', borrowed from Alabaster (and sounding generally Claudianic), implicitly links Cromwell's military successes of the 1650s to the defeat of the Armada nearly 70 years earlier.

Similarly, the opening of Claudian's *Ruf.* 1, an attack upon Stilicho's powerful enemy Rufinus and a celebration of his defeat, contains a much-imitated scene (25–122) in which the forces of darkness – led in Claudian by Allecto – gather and decide upon a wicked scheme (the 'Council in Hell'), ending with the dispatch of an agent of the underworld (in Claudian, the fury Megaera) to enact the plan. *Ruf.* 1 stages a further debate between the fury Megaera and Iustitia (Justice, 354–87) and *Ruf.* 2 ends with Minos, the judge of the underworld, consigning Rufinus to the deepest part of Tartarus forever (496–527).

The famous version of the 'Council in Hell' scene in *Paradise Lost* has been associated in existing scholarship mainly with English 'Gunpowder Plot' poems, though it is more properly a standard feature of the characterization of the enemy in Latin poems in the Claudianic tradition.[49] English examples of this motif dating, for clarity, from before 1605, include Alabaster's *Elisaeis* (c.1591, lines 132–52) and George Carleton's *Ad serenissimam Elizabetham* (1592).[50] In many English poems, it is Catholic Rome, or specifically the pope, who is depicted in these hellish terms.

Similar scenes are a feature of several influential Latin poems by earlier Italian poets, including Jacopo Sannazaro (*De partu virginis*), Marco Girolamo Vida (*Christias*) and Torquato Tasso (*Gerusalemme liberata*).[51] Scipio Gentili chose Tasso's version of this scene for the first instalment of his Latin verse translations of *Gerusalemme liberata* (*Plutonis concilium*, 'The council of Pluto', 1584).[52] Later examples include, as well as the many Plot poems, the fifth book of Venceslaus Clemens, *Gustavis* (1632)

---

[49] Hammond, '"Concilia Deorum" from Homer through Milton'; and Burrzone, 'Il "concilium deorum"'. On the rather different Underworld setting of the opening of the *De Raptu Proserpinae*, see Wheeler, 'Underworld Opening'.

[50] BL MS Royal 12 A XLIII. Printed edition in Goldring *et al.* (eds.), *Progresses and Public Processions*, 657–74.

[51] See Moore, 'Infernal Council'; Hammond, '"Concilia Deorum" from Homer through Milton'. For discussion of Milton's *In Quintum Novembris* and other English Gunpowder Plot poems, including those by Campion, Herring, Fletcher and Pareus, see Haan, 'Milton's *In Quintum Novembris*'; and Hale, 'Milton and the Gunpowder Plot'. Neither Haan nor Hale mentions Claudian as a model. Binns gives a list of Gunpowder Plot poems (*Intellectual Culture*, 457 n31), but there remain a large number of unstudied examples in manuscript, especially from the mid to later seventeenth century. Fisher's own Gunpowder plot poem, for instance, survives only in manuscript (see note 35 above).

[52] Followed by *Solymeidos libri duo* (1584), Cantos 1–2 and *Solymeidos liber primus* (1584), Canto 1.

Panegyric Epic in a European Context

and, indeed, Fisher's *Marston-Moor* (1650, pages 3–7), discussed below.[53] There is even a hint of it in Jonson's *Panegyre* of 1603. The poem opens with the rising sun of James I, whose 'searching beams' pry even into men's private sins, described by Jonson, with a relish typical of Claudianic style, in hellish terms:

> But these his searching beams are cast to pry
> Into those dark and deep concealed vaults
> Where men commit black incest with their faults,
> And snore supinely in the stall of sin;
> Where Murder, Rapine, Lust do sit within
> Carousing human blood in iron bowls,
> And make their den the slaughter-house of souls;
> From whose foul reeking caverns first arise
> Those damps that so offend all good men's eyes,
> And would, if not dispersed, infect the crown,
> And in their vapour her bright metal drown.
> (8–18)[54]

The personifications of line 12 probably derive from a similar description of 'Avaritia' (Greed) and 'Ambitus' (Ambition) bound and lamenting in the underworld in *III Cons*. 185–8, but the more general strategy of contrasting the king's goodness and majesty with the forces of evil conspiring in hell is indebted in particular to *Ruf*. Jonson's employment of this motif even in so straightforwardly panegyric a work – the poem does not mark or anticipate the defeat of any enemy, and is if anything rather pro-Catholic – suggests how strongly it was associated with Claudianic panegyric in general at this period.[55]

Although the English versions of formal Claudianic panegyric produced around the accession of James I were not widely imitated, and the genre did not 'catch on' as an English form, many Latin examples continued to

---

[53] The motif is found in other genres too. Robert Southwell's Latin poem on the Assumption of Mary, for instance, includes a 'Council of Death' scene. For Southwell's poem, see Davidson and Sweeney (eds.), *Collected Poems of Southwell*. On Clemens, see Helander, '*Gustavis*'; and Poole, 'Down and Out in Leiden and London'.

[54] As Garrison points out, William Drummond's 1617 poem celebrating King James' visit to Scotland alludes to this passage, echoing Claudian via Jonson: 'That Murder, Rapine, Lust, are fled to Hell, / And in their Roomes with us the Graces dwell' – *Forth Feasting*, 255–6 in Kastner (ed.), *Poetical Works of Drummond*, vol. I, 149; Garrison, *Tradition of Panegyric*, 95–6.

[55] Themis' speech to James I which, as we have seen, recalls Theodosius' speech to Honorius, ends with a warning to avoid imitating Henry VIII, and specifically condemns the dissolution of the monasteries (99–106). Jonson was a Roman Catholic between 1598 and 1610, when he reverted to Protestantism.

be produced. Nearly 40 years after Jonson's poem, Alexander Gill praised Charles I for his (as it turned out, short-lived) avoidance of civil war:

> Utque soles posito, *Neptune,* tricuspide telo,
> Cùm grave spirantes et ëunt in praelia venti,
> Et nigram glomerant hyemem, dispellere nubes,
> Et prohibere *Euros,* clarumque reducere solem:
> Haud secùs insolitos aestus, populique tumultus,
> Arma, minas, iras, Rex dissipat omnia solus,
> Quo nihil in terris animosius aspicit aether.[56]

> *Just as you, Neptune, when ominously blowing winds are rushing into battle and gathering a black storm, set your trident aside and scatter the clouds, ban the storm-winds, and lead back the bright sun: so too is the King alone able to scatter all troubles – the unusual unrest and tumult of the people, weapons, threats and fury – for heaven looks upon nothing on earth with greater pride than he.*

Claudianic Panegyric in the 1640s and 1650s

The specifically royal associations of Claudianic panegyric were sharpened for writers in the context of the English Civil War: this is clear, for instance, from Henry Birkhead's choice of a pointed epigraph from Claudian for his anonymously published *Poematia* of 1645.[57] The epigraph, 'Carmen amat, quisquis, carmina digna gerit' ('whoever achieves deeds worthy of a poem, loves poetry'), is a quotation from *Stil.* 3.6. Birkhead's collection is strongly royalist, with an opening poem addressed to James, Duke of York, epigrams on themes such as 'De Proditoribus' ('On Traitors') and a final dithyrambic ode commemorating Archbishop Laud. In this context, praise of Stilicho is meant to suggest the glory and honour of fighting on behalf of the king. Indeed, William Alabaster had used the same line as the epigraph to the first (and, it turned out, only) book of his poem in praise of Elizabeth I, the *Elisaeis*.[58] This is the cultural setting in which Payne Fisher began to write Latin verse in imitation of Claudian in the mid-late 1640s: a milieu

---

[56] Gill, *Gratulatoria* (1641), sig. A2ᵛ.
[57] [Birkhead], *Poematia* (1645). Birkhead was a fellow of All Souls, though the volume was published anonymously, probably in Oxford. The Bodleian copy digitised by *EEBO* has been annotated on the title page to identify the author: 'Scripsit Henricus Berket è Coll. Omn. Anim. Oxon'. Cameron notes a similarly royalist deployment of Claudian as an epigraph to Sir Robert Filmer's *Anarchy of a limited or mixed Monarchy* (1648) and *Patriarcha, or the Natural Power of Kings* (c.1640; pub. 1680) as well as in several political tracts from the mid-seventeenth century (Cameron, *Claudian,* 435–7).
[58] O'Connell (ed.), '*Elisaeis* of William Alabaster'.

in which the specifically Claudianic Latin verse genres of panegyric epic, invective, short mythological epic and formal epithalamia were well established and frequently composed by authors both in England and elsewhere in Europe. It was a form with strong traditional associations with royalty, and indeed Fisher himself was imprisoned after fighting at the Battle of Marston Moor in the summer of 1644, on the losing royalist side.

The earliest examples of Fisher's experiments with Claudianic hexameter verse are found in two copies of (almost) the same verse collection, both manuscript presentation volumes now in the British Library dating from 1647/8.[59] These collections, which contain both Latin and English verse in a variety of forms, were no doubt designed to show off his poetic range; both include two strongly Claudianic items: an hexameter poem on the Gunpowder Plot (*On the Gunpowder-treason*) and the first version of the poem (here titled *De obsidione Praelioque Eborocensi vulgo Marstonmoore appellato*, 'On the siege and battle at York, called in the common language Marstonmoore') which would later be greatly expanded as *Marston-Moor*. There is also an English version of the Siege of York poem (*An abstract of yorke: seige and fight*, interestingly in blank verse), though not of the Plot poem. As discussed above, the Gunpowder Plot poem was an intrinsically Claudianic genre, and this is especially true of Fisher's fragment, which, rather like Milton's *In Quintum Novembris*, and indeed probably directly influenced by that poem, is almost entirely taken up by the evocation of the underworld and the horror of the subject itself:

> Quae serpentifero noua monstra eduxit hiatu
> Prodigiale Chaos! noua quae Portenta Barathrum
> Euomuit, nostrisque audax immiscuit Oris?
> Eloquar an sileam! tam formidabile pandam
> Flagitium? primisue pauens conatibus obstem!
> Quis furor horrificis incendit pectora flammis
> Perfidiosa cohors? Quae vos stimulauit Erynnis?
> Siccine sulphureis saeuire per omnia telis
> Mens erat, attonitis et voluere Regna tenebris!
> Nullane vos Patriae Pietas! reuerentia nulla!
> Tam formidandis poterant deflectere coeptis?[60]

---

[59] BL MSS Add. 19863 and Harley 6932. These manuscripts are described in more detail in Moul, 'Revising the Siege of York'.
[60] BL MS Add. 19863, fol. 31ʳ.

> *What new monsters has dread Chaos drawn out of its serpent-clad maw?*
> *What portents has the pit of the underworld vomited up, and*
> *Boldly sent to penetrate our shores?*
> *Should I speak, or should I be silent? Can I set out so dreadful*
> *A disgrace? Or should I stumble, trembling, on my first attempts?*
> *What fury has fired your hearts with dreadful flames,*
> *You treacherous army? What Erynnis has goaded you into action?*
> *Was it such a mind that raged with weapons of Sulphur over everything*
> *And spun our Realm into sudden darkness?*
> *Do you have no loyalty to your native land – no sense of respect –*
> *That could have deflected you from such a dreadful endeavour?*

The vivid noun 'hiatus' ('gaping') appears 12 times in Claudian, all but once in the final position in the line, as in the first line here; in 10 of those instances, it is, as in these lines, preceded by a finite verb, and once (*CM* 29.6) also with a part of 'duco'.[61] Fisher was perhaps remembering in particular *Ruf.* 1.66, 'mugiit et totos serpentum erexit hiatus', describing Allecto: 'so she spoke with a dreadful roar and raised up all of her gaping serpent-mouths'. The final word of his second line, 'Barathrum', also imitates Claudian's diction.[62]

More original is Fisher's use of Claudian in the 275 lines of *De obsidione:* this is a straightforwardly royalist poem, which turns to Claudian, and especially *Ruf.*, in order to demonize Cromwell. This is Cromwell's first appearance in the poem. In the extract below, words in bold indicate borrowings from Claudian:

> Vix iam somniferis elata cubilibus alto
> Impulerat coelo gelidas Aurora tenebras,
> Rorantes excussa comas; rutilantibus armis
> Agmina quam *Adversis* campo fulsere Maniplis.
> Stat cuneis defixa *Acies*; et fulgida ferro   5
> Ingeminat splendore solum, coelumq*ue* corusco
> Primus honoratis *Ductor Mancest're* cateruis
> Anteuolas aciem: validoque hortamine pulsans
> Pectora moliris primae fundamina pugnae.
> Tùm formidando *Coromell* cui fulgur in ore   10
> Et *Bellum Ciuile* sedet sub **fronte minaci**
> Proximus ingreditur; Thorace et Casside **tectus**:
> **Ferrea Compago laterum**; totosque per artus
> **Ferrea** clauigeris surgebat **lamina** nodis.

---

[61] *CM* 29.6 'ducat hiatus'.
[62] The word is used four times by Claudian, three of them in final position as here, e.g. *Rapt.* 1.37, 'iam quaecumque latent ferali monstra barathro'.

>   Nec minùs **horribiles ferro** micuere cohortes: 15
>   Dissiluisse nouo penitus Telluris hiatu
>   Cyclopum Portenta putes; **simulachra mouere**
>   **Credideres**, viuoque **viros spirare Metallo**.
>   Hinc **ferro** stipata acies, longo ordine Belli
>   Constitit, *Aduersis* et se ostentauerat armis.[63]   20

Scarcely had Aurora, just now arisen from her chambers of sleep, driven the cold shades from the height of the heaven, and shaken out her dewy locks, than the ranks began to shine on the plain, their weaponry glowing red, visible to the enemy companies.

The battle-rank stands arranged in wedge-formations; the shine from the armour makes the ground and the heaven seem double with the glistening splendour of iron.

You, Earl of Manchester, with your honoured companies, were the first to fly before the battle line: and rousing their hearts with powerful encouragement, you set in motion the first stirrings of battle. Next came Cromwell, the lightning bolt on his dreadful face, and Civil War sitting on his menacing forehead; covered by a breast-plate and a helmet; his sides covered in a network of iron; and iron plates joined by bolts were rising over all his limbs. No less did the cohorts flash with iron, a horrible sight: you would think that strange horrors of the Cyclopes had leapt forth from a sudden gaping of the Earth; you would believe that images were moving, and that men were breathing in living metal. So in dense ranks of iron did the battle-line draw up, in the long ranks of war, and displayed itself to the opposing army.

There is a complex series of allusions at work in this passage: the italicized *Bellum Ciuile* resting upon Cromwell's forehead suggests Lucan's poem of that title, but much of the rest is structured around borrowings from Statius' epic *Thebaid*.[64] Cromwell's notorious 'ironsides' armour, however – a soubriquet supposedly coined by Prince Rupert in the immediate aftermath of the Battle of Marston Moor – is sketched in a pair of lines (13–14) which combine an allusion to Statius' description of the House of Mars (*Theb.* 7.43–4) with a passage in Claudian (*Ruf.* 357–62) on the awe inspired by troops in full armour:

---

[63] BL MS Add. 19863, fol. 12^{r-v}; I have quoted this MS rather than the text as it appears in BL MS Harley 6932 as the minor differences between the manuscripts suggest that the Add. MS version is fractionally earlier.

[64] Lines 1–3 are indebted to *Theb.* 2.134–6; lines 13–14 to *Theb.* 7.43–4; line 16 is borrowed from *Theb.* 8.19, in which Amphiaraus arrives in the Underworld; the phrase 'totosque per artus' (13) may recall the description of another warrior, Tydeus, at *Theb.* 1.416.

> conjuncta per artem
> Flexilis inductis animatur **lamina** membris,
> **Horribilis** visu. **Credas simulacra moveri**
> **Ferrea**, cognatoque **viros spirare metallo**.
> Par vestitus equis. Ferrata **fronte minantur**,
> Ferratosque levant securi vulneris armos
>
> *Ruf.* 2.357–62

> *the limbs within give life to the armour's pliant scales so artfully conjoined, and strike terror into the beholder. You would believe that iron statues moved and men breathed who are cast from that same metal. The horses are armed in the same way; heads are encased in threatening iron, their forequarters move beneath steel plates protecting them from wounds.*[65]

Fisher's vignette, which verges on allegory, carries ominous allusive associations: Cromwell is a version of the House of Mars (that is, the physical manifestation of personified War) and the scene reminds the poet of Amphiaraus in the underworld, as well as a moment of particular menace in Claudian. In *Ruf.* 2, the ominous beauty of the imperial forces drawn up outside Constantinople in full armour immediately precedes the moment when those same soldiers tear Rufinus apart. The allusive atmosphere conveys above all the overwhelming sensory experience of a great war, by turns beautiful and horrific.

The printed version of *Marston-Moor* that appeared in 1650, published by Benlowes, was massively expanded from the manuscript poems, now running to 1,367 lines in five metra (short 'books'). Though Fisher removed almost nothing from his first attempts (apart from the description of Cromwell discussed above), and effectively preserved the poem's core of royalist lament, its description of the Parliamentarians' victory was such a success that it secured Fisher a paid position as the official poet of the Council of State and then of the Protectorate for the rest of the 1650s.[66]

Marston-Moor makes extensive allusive use of Claudian, whose works are drawn upon more than any other poet.[67] Fisher began by adding an

---

[65] Text and translations of Claudian from Platnauer (ed.), *Claudian*, with some adaptations.
[66] For Fisher's career as a whole, see Peacey, 'Fisher, Payne'. There are many inconsistencies between sources, however, and Fisher probably concealed details of his parentage and immediate family for political reasons. He may also have been older than he claimed. See also Moul, 'Revising the Siege of York' and 'Marvell and Fisher'.
[67] At least 16 unambiguous allusions to or borrowings from Claudian, balanced in this work, more than in later ones, by a significant dependence also upon Statius' *Thebaid* (12 identified allusions). I have identified allusions also to Lucan (3), Silius Italicus (4), Valerius Flaccus (1), and Prudentius (2), and this is certainly not a complete list. Modern sources include the Latin poetry of Milton

extended set piece of the 'Council in Hell' (pages 4–7) an element which (as noted above) was a standard feature of patriotic panegyric-epic, not an element confined to the 'Gunpowder Plot' poems with which it has mostly been associated.[68] Fisher's lavish version of the scene borrows both structural elements and specific lines from Claudian's *Ruf.* Mars summons personifications of evil (p. 4) just as Allecto does in Claudian (*Ruf.* 1.28–44); Mars is compared to Jupiter unleashing the winds (p. 7), as Rufinus is compared to Aeolus (*Ruf.* 2.22–6).[69] The opening of the scene is a particularly vivid example of Fisher's allusive technique and the extent of the borrowing from Claudian:

> His ubi **Conventis Stipata est *Curia* Monstris**,
> Extemplo ominuit rapido Diademate *Mavors*
> Imbutam quatiens *Titanum* Caedibus Hastam.
> Torva quidem Facies, et non adeunda Senectus:
> Terribiles Horrore Jubae; conóque Corusco   5
> Scintillâre Faces; fremuítque **adamantinus Ordo
> Dentis, ut *Armorum Fragor*, ictáque cuspide cuspis**.
> Postquam jussa quies, suasítque silentia terror,
> IPSE (Catervatim Comitum Cingente Coronâ)
> Horrendas **quatiens galeato in vertice Cristas**   10
> Talibus excussam patescit vocibus Iram:
> Surgite Concordes Socii, coeptísque favete:
> Ulteriùs pigeat, pigeat latuisse pudendo
> Pulvere, & Ignotis animas traxisse tenebris.
> **Siccine** securos semper spectabimus *Anglos*?[70]   15

> *When the Council was packed with the gathered monsters,*
> *Mars suddenly towered over them with a swift Diadem*
> *Shaking a Spear dyed with Titan gore.*
> *His grim face, and his Old age made him fearful to approach:*
> *His crests were terrible with horror, and the torches*
> *Glittered on the Flashing peak of his helmet; and the adamantine Row*
> *Of his teeth clashed, like the Crash of Armour, like spear struck upon spear.*

(discussed below) and George Buchanan. Fisher noticeably avoids alluding to Virgil, though many of the passages he borrows from later authors are themselves indebted to Virgil.

[68] Dana Sutton's introduction to Milton's *IQN*, the most studied of the 'Plot' poems, for instance, sets out clearly how Milton's hell fits into a broader tradition of what he calls 'historical epic', but does not mention Claudian at all (http://philological.bham.ac.uk/milton/intro.html). See also Haan, 'Milton's *In Quintum Novembris*'; and Hale, 'Milton and the Gunpowder Plot'.

[69] As there is no modern edition of the poem, and neither the 1650 nor 1656 editions are lineated, I have lineated longer passages. Page numbers refer to the 1650 edition unless otherwise noted. I am preparing an edition of *Marston-Moor*, with translation and notes, to be published by Bloomsbury probably in 2023.

[70] Fisher, *Marston-Moor*, 4–5.

After he had ordered calm, and terror had persuaded them to silence,
HE HIMSELF (with a crown of companions wreathing him in their companies)
Shaking dreadful crests on his helmeted peak
He laid bare his Anger, shaken out with these words:
'Rise up Allies of the same heart, and bless what we have undertaken:
It would be more shameful, more shameful to have lain low in shaming
Dust, and to have dragged our souls amidst the shades of the unknown.
Are we always to look upon the English, safe as they now are and free from care?'

In this 15-line extract, lines 1, 13–14 and 15 are all direct borrowings from Claudian, taken from corresponding points in the Council in Hell scene in *Ruf.* (1.40, 58–9 and 45). These borrowings range from almost direct quotation ('His ubi convent**is stipata est *Curia* Monstris**', 1; 'torvaque collect**is stipatur curia monstris**', *Ruf.* 1.40); to a comparable construction with only the opening word in common ('**Siccine** securos semper spectabimus *Anglos*?', 15; '**Siccine** tranquillo produci saecula cursu, / sic fortunatas patiemur vivere gentes?', 'Shall we allow centuries to roll on calmly like this, and people to live in such good fortune?', *Ruf.* 1.45–6); to a parallel with no specific echoes, but making the same rhetorical point ('Ulteriùs pigeat, pigeat latuisse pudendo / Pulvere', 13; 'at nos indecores longo torpebimus aevo / omnibus eiectae regnis!', 'Shall we, expelled from every kingdom, lie for a long age in shameful torpor?', *Ruf.* 1.58–9).

Typically for Fisher, the Claudianic structure of the scene is spliced with a further borrowing, this time from the early Christian poet Prudentius, whose allegorical poem *Psychomachia* was widely read, and to which Fisher alludes on several occasions. Line 10, describing Mars, is derived from Prudentius' description of 'Ira' (personified Rage).

> hanc procul Ira tumens, spumanti fervida rictu,
> sanguinea intorquens subfuso lumina felle,
> ut belli exsortem teloque et voce lacessit,
> impatiensque morae conto petit, increpat ore,
> hirsutas **quatiens galeato in vertice cristas**.
> (*Psychomachia*, 113–17)

> *On her from a distance swelling Wrath, showing her teeth with rage and foaming at the mouth, darts her eyes, all shot with blood and gall, and challenges her with weapon and with speech for taking no part in the fight; irked by her handing back, she hurls a pike at her and assails her with abuse, tossing the shaggy crests on her helmeted head.*

Finally, the passage pays tribute to one of the most recent versions of the genre by incorporating an allusion to Milton's *In Quintum Novembris*. Lines 6–7 ('adamantinus ... cuspis') are taken, without alteration, from

IQN 39–40, where they describe Satan himself.[71] This is not the only borrowing from *IQN* in *Marston-Moor*.[72] Fisher thus indicates that his poem and Milton's belong to the same Claudianic genre. The second of these borrowings dates back to the early manuscripts: Fisher must therefore have read Milton's 1645 *Poems* very soon after publication, and his lively and inventive scene deserves to be set alongside the various Gunpowder poems as a possible intermediate source for Milton's further development of the idea in *Paradise Lost*.

There is an intrinsic and unexpected ambiguity to Fisher's depiction of hell. Both in Claudian and in the many previous neo-Latin examples, scenes of this type are politically unambiguous: the forces of evil plot trouble (military attack, or terrorism) to be launched by a minion of hell (typically, in Protestant versions, the Pope or an agent of the Pope; in Claudian, Rufinus) against the virtuous nation. But the poem introduced here is in fact strikingly even-handed: though successful in its praise of Cromwell – and increasingly focused on Cromwell in the later 1656 revision – it has its roots in an entirely royalist poem which, as we have seen, was unhesitating in linking Cromwell with Mars, an agent of evil. Fisher was perhaps exploiting here an irony intrinsic to the Protestant appropriation of Claudianic panegyric: whereas in Claudian it is Rome that is threatened, in Protestant versions Rome herself is usually the source of the threat. The most famous version of this type of scene in English, in Books 1 and 2 of *Paradise Lost*, must as a result have had a markedly political connotation to its early readers.

Indeed, the pattern of Fisher's use of Claudian in the poem reveals its underlying royalism: this is one facet of the complex allusive politics of the poem that helps to make it such a startling read. Much more than in his later poems, Fisher in *Marston-Moor* draws predominantly upon Claudian's negative rather than positive portrayals: near the end of the poem, the confusion of the royalist army in defeat is like a whale without a pilot-fish (*MM* 64), alluding to *Eutr.* 2.423–31; mid-battle, Alexander Lesley, Earl of Leven and Lord General of the Scottish Army of the Solemn League and Covenant, as he vainly attempts to rally his troops and bring them to order, is compared to a shepherd trying to recall bees

---

[71] Milton's lines themselves incorporate phrases from Lucan (1.569) and Statius (the memorable 'cuspide cuspis' is from *Theb.* 8.399). Cowley has a similar description at *Davideis* 1.129–30.

[72] 'Persequitur trepidam nemorosa per Avia Praedam / Nocte sub Illuni, & somno Nictantibus astris' ('He pursues his fearful prey through the trackless groves / in a moonless night, and in night with glittering stars', p. 21) is only slightly adapted from *IQN*, 21–2, again describing Lucifer.

with a gong, an image used of Alaric (the enemy of Stilicho) as his army deserts him in *VI Cons.* 259–64:

> Sic ubi Ruricolus *Pastor*, **revocare fugaces**
> ***Tinnitu*** meditatur ***apes*, quae sponte relict**os
> Destituêre ***favos***, nunc servens lignea pulsat
> Vascula, susceptúmque manu contundit *ahenum*,
> Rauca repercussis miscens crepitacula Sylvis.
> Incoeptum nec sistis Iter, per Saxa, per amnes,
> Per Juga consequitur, donec defessus **inani**
> Spe, revocat gressus, & *Cerea Castra* revisans,
> **Perfida** conquiritur **vacuis *Examina*** Cellis.[73]

> *Like a country Shepherd, attempting to recall*
> *His fleeing bees with a ringing noise – bees who of*
>   *their own accord*
> *Have abandoned their combs; he fervently beats*
> *The wooden beehives, and pounds a bronze vessel*
>   *he holds up with his hand,*
> *Mingling the loud rattling with the echoing woods.*
> *Once begun, he does not stop, but follows on*
> *Over the rocks, the rivers, the ridges, until*
> *Exhausted, and all hope spent, he retraces his path*
> *And returns to the waxen camps, complaining*
> *Of his treacherous swarm to the empty cells.*

>   qualis Cybeleia quassans
> Hyblaeus procul aera senex **revocare fugaces**
> **Tinnitu** conatur **apes, quae sponte relict**is
> Descivere **favis**, sonituque exhaustus **inani**
> Raptas mellis opes solitaque oblita latebrae
> **Perfida** deplorat **vacuis examina** ceris.
>   (Claudian, *VI Cons.* 259–64)

> *As an old bee-keeper of Hybla, beating Cybele's gong, tries, by the ringing, to recall his scattered bees, who have abandoned their combs and fled from the hive; until, exhausted by the useless clamour, he weeps for the loss of his store of honey, and curses the faithless swarm that has forgotten its usual home and left the cells empty.*

The equation of the Scots and Alaric is a sophisticated comparison: in 1644, at the time of the battle, the Scots were allies of Parliament – and indeed their contribution was key to the Parliamentarian victory – whereas

---

[73] Fisher, *Marston-Moor*, 51–2 (italics original). The italicized phrase 'cerea ... castra' is found in Virgil, *Aen.* 12.589 and Claudian, *Rapt.* 2.124–8.

by the time of the publication of *Marston-Moor*, in 1650, they were enemies of Cromwell. Stilicho had likewise fought in alliance with Alaric earlier in his career, before Alaric changed sides and became his enemy. In this way, the simile borrowed from Claudian to describe Alaric alludes to the changing relationship of the Scots to Cromwell.

Indeed, the only extended straightforwardly panegyric or celebratory adaptation of Claudian in *Marston-Moor* describes not the eventual Parliamentarian victory but rather a moment of (albeit short-lived) hope and celebration for the royalists. When Prince Rupert raises the siege and relieves York, the city's celebration is described in a memorable personifying simile adapted from Claudian, *VI Cons.* 523–9, in which Rome, adorning itself to welcome Honorius like a girl being dressed for the arrival of her suitor, has become the city of York welcoming Rupert.[74] Insofar as the arrival of Prince Rupert suggests a marriage, however, it was a doomed one for the royalists. York was relieved on 1 July 1644, and the battle, ending in disaster for the King's armies, took place just outside the city the following day.

In short, even in the published version of *Marston-Moor* (1650), which was so successful with Cromwell, the almost exclusively *negative* use of Claudian preserves the core of lament inherited from the original royalist poem. Although Fisher removes the near-demonization of Cromwell found in the earliest versions, there is no adulation of him either, and the only celebratory borrowing from Claudian is reserved for a moment of royalist hope. Though Fisher adapted his poem to reflect and honour the victorious Cromwell, its allusive patterns remained conservative: preserving the traditional association between formal Latin panegyric and a royal addressee.

Cromwell Becomes Stilicho

In Fisher's poems for Cromwell in the following years, however, and especially with the start of the personal Protectorate in 1653, he increasingly turned to Claudian for positive rather than negative images. In particular, Fisher developed a sophisticated literary equivalence between Cromwell and Stilicho, with obvious political utility: like Cromwell, Stilicho was a de facto ruler who was explicitly *not* a monarch.[75] The

---

[74] Fisher, *Marston-Moor*, 37; Claudian, *VI Cons.* 523–31.
[75] There is an intervening transitional period, noticeable especially in *Irenodia Gratulatoria* (1652) and corresponding to the politically transitional phase between 1649 and 1653, during which stock tropes of Claudianic panegyric associated with Stilicho, such as preventing disaster by holding up

388 Panegyric Epic in Early Modern England

gradually intensifying association is worked out both allusively and directly. In Fisher's *Anniversarium*, extant only in the *Piscatoris Poemata* (1656), but presumably written for the anniversary of the Protectorate in December 1654, Fisher makes the relationship between Cromwell and Stilicho (and himself and Claudian) quite plain:

> Tunc faciles in coepta *novem* fluxere sorores,
> Et Musis patuere adytus, cum Carmine **Praeco Grandiloquus,** *Stylico* vestras super aethera laudes
> Tollebat. *Geticis* cum **Consul Honorius** armis,
> ***Mallius*** aut Reducem Pompis solennibus annum
> Induerant; quis *Vate* prior fulgentia Rostra
> Clarius intravit? paribusve furoribus actus
> Annua sceptriferi cantavit Festa ***Probini,***
> Bisque triumphati **trabeas** celebravit ***Olybri?***
> Haec veteres cecinere Patres: sed nostra *Thalia*
> Majus opus meliusque movet; de Cardine Mundi
> Nempe alio, mihi ***Consul*** adest; mihi ***Mallius*** alter;
> **Alter adest** ***Stylico***[76]

> *Then the nine sisters flowed readily into new topics, and the shrines were laid open to the Muses, when a herald, eloquent in song, was raising your praises, Stilicho, above the heavens. When Consul Honorius, with captured Getic weapons, or when Mallius were adorning the year on its return with solemn processions; who entered the gleaming stage with more renown than a Poet? or, driven by equal furies of inspiration, sang the annual rites of sceptre-bearing Probinus, and celebrated the consulship of Olybrius, who had twice triumphed? These things were the subjects of song for the ancestors: but our Thalia [a Muse] is embarking upon a greater and a better work; about a different hinge of the World, a Consul for me today; for me another Mallius; he is a second Stilicho.*

The passage is both generally and specifically reminiscent of the example of the passage in Barlaeus' *Britannia Triumphans*, quoted above: the phrase 'Praeco Grandiloquus' and the term 'trabeas' (used here as in Barlaeus in a sense specific to Claudian, indicating a consulship) are both apparently borrowed directly from Barlaeus' poem.[77] Although Fisher cites a range of Claudian's panegyric – for Honorius, Mallius and Probinus and Olybrius – it starts and ends with Stilicho. By the opening passage of

---

the world, or steering the ship of state, are applied to Bradshaw (President of the Council of State, and officially the dedicatee of the poem) as well as Cromwell.

[76] Fisher, *Piscatoris Poemata*, sig. B1ᵛ–B2ʳ.
[77] For 'trabea' meaning 'consulship' (rather than a robe of office), see *Ruf.* 1.249; *Eutr.* 2. prologue 10; and *Stil.* 2.3.

Apobaterion, a poem written to mark the arrival of Marquès de Lede, Ambassador Extraordinary of Archduke Leopold Wilhelm of Austria, governor of the Spanish Netherlands, in the spring of 1655, the equivalence is well enough established that Fisher can declare: 'Cedite maiores. Priscaeque silescite chartae; / Non mihi iam *Stylico* tanti' ('Ancestors give way. Be silent, ancient works; / Stilicho means less to me now *[because Cromwell has outdone him]*').[78]

The most striking instance of this equivalence is the engraving in the *Irenodia Gratulatoria* of 1652 (Figure 3). Alongside the portrait of Cromwell on the battlefield is a quotation, 'Similem *Quae protulit Aetas / Consilio vel Marte* VIRUM' ('What age has produced his equal either in wisdom or in war?'), with a pointer indicating the source: 'Claud: lib. de laud. Stil.'[79] In his 1656 collected works (*Piscatoris Poemata*), Fisher revised *Marston-Moor* to add a description of Cromwell as 'a man even greater than Mars', echoing several descriptions of Stilicho in these terms (e.g. *Stil*. 2.367–70; *Goth*. 468) as well as the 1652 engraving.

Alongside direct references of this kind, Fisher increasingly attributed to Cromwell features associated particularly with Stilicho in Claudian: in the *Inauguratio Olivariana* of 1654, Fisher compares Cromwell to Titan and Hercules, and describes him as holding up the people singlehanded.[80] At the end of *Irenodia Gratulatoria* (1652), Cromwell is 'vigilantior *Ipse*' ('even more watchful', sig. H3ᵛ) although at this point withdrawn from active combat, just as Claudian describes Stilicho as a kind of divine guardian, ever alert (*VI Cons*. 233–4). This is markedly similar imagery to that used by Marvell in the first of his Claudianic poems, 'The First Anniversary': 'Some lusty mate, who with more carefull eye' (273).[81]

As Christiansen has shown, Claudian frequently attributes similes of support and strength to Stilicho (and sometimes Theodosius), though not to Honorius, the actual (though ineffectual) emperor.[82] The clemency and piety Claudian attributed to Stilicho (e.g. *Theod*. 166–71) are made a recurring feature of the praise of Cromwell (e.g. *Inauguratio Olivariana*, 1654, sig. B1ᵛ), and a passage on Stilicho's ingenuity (*Gild*. 1.318–20) stands behind the praise of Cromwell's *virtus* in Fisher's *Anniversarium*

---

[78] Fisher, *Apobaterion*, sig. b1ʳ.   [79] The quotation is in fact from *Theod*. 162–3.
[80] Fisher, *Inauguratio Olivariana* (1654), sig. A2ʳ, echoing *Stil*. 1.142–3; see also *Ruf*. 1.273–4, and (of Theodosius) *IV. Cons*. 55–62.
[81] See also 'those wakeful eyes', Marvell, 'A Poem upon the Death of O. C.', 248. 'Vigilans' means both 'watchful', 'carefull' and (literally) 'staying awake'.
[82] Christiansen, *Use of Images*, esp. 16–26.

Figure 3 Payne Fisher, *Irenodia Gratulatoria* (London: T. Newcomb, 1652), frontispiece engraving
By permission of The Warden and Fellows of All Souls College, Oxford.

(1656, sig. F2ʳ). Claudian's descriptions of Stilicho as a star to sailors (e.g. *Eutr.* 2.507–8; *Ruf.* 1.275–7) and a steersman (e.g. *Stil.* 1.286–90) find multiple parallels in Fisher, discussed further below.

From time to time, Fisher makes use of other examples in Claudian of non-royal addressees. One passage in *Inauguratio Oliviariana* (1654, sig. B4ᵛ), for instance, compares Cromwell to the bright peak of Olympus, never obscured by cloud, in lines borrowed in large part from *Theod.* 205–13. In a particularly sophisticated passage from the same poem, Fisher uses a combination of Claudian and (again) the contemporary Dutch poet Caspar Barlaeus to tackle the sensitive question of Cromwell's refusal to accept the crown. After a series of panegyric comparisons, to the stars and to the Phoenix (recalling Claudian's poem on the Phoenix, *CM* 27), the section concludes:

> moderatior at *Tu* [Cromwell]
> Aerios **plausus**, vacui crepitacula **vulgi**,
> **Despicis**, & **dignos** Tibi **quos** concessit **Honores**
> *Anglia*, concelas, **dum vis Privatus haberi**
> Qui **cunctos praestans**, meritis virtutibus anteis,
> **Solis ad exemplum, qui fusis lumina Terris**
> **Dividit, oblitúsque sui, communia curat**
> **Commoda, nec sibi sed** mundo splendescere gestit.[83]

> *But with greater moderation you* [Cromwell]
> *Look down upon airy applause, the rattle of the vacuous crowd,*
> *And you conceal the Honours England has granted you,*
>   *deserved as they are,*
> *As you, who excel all others, who exceed everyone in virtue,*
> *Prefer to be considered a Private citizen,*
> *In the manner of the Sun who spreads and shares its light*
> *Upon the earth, and forgetful of itself, cares only*
> *For the common good, and seeks to make resplendent,*
>   *not himself, but the world.*

This is a careful blending of two passages. The first two lines have several points in common with the much-quoted opening passage of *Theod.* on Virtue as its own reward:

> Ipsa quidem Virtus pretium sibi, solaque late
> Fortunae secura nitet nec fascibus ullis
> erigitur **plausuve** petit clarescere **vulgi**.
>   (Claudian, *Theod.* 1–3)

---

[83] Fisher, *Inauguratio*, sig. A3ᵛ.

> *Virtue is its own reward; alone with its far-flung splendour it mocks Fortune; no honours raise it higher nor does it seek glory from the applause of the mob.*

This is combined with a larger number of more readily recognizable borrowings from a poem by Barlaeus, praising – significantly – not the French King, but his second-in-command, Cardinal Richelieu, published only in 1641:

> **quos** donat **honores**
> Regia, dissimulas. tibi **vis privatus haberi,**
> **Dum cunctis,** Armande, **praes** ...
> **Solis ad exemplum,** cunctis qui **lumina terris**
> **Dividit, oblitusque sui communia curat**
> **Commoda, nec sibi, sed** nobis mortalibus ardet.[84]

> *those honours which the court gives you,*
> *You conceal. You prefer to be considered a private citizen,*
> *While in fact, Armand, you excel all ...*
> *In the manner of the Sun who divides his light between all the lands*
> *And forgetful of itself, cares only*
> *For the common good, and blazes not for himself, but for us mortal men.*

To describe how Cromwell remains a private citizen, Fisher borrows a phrase from Barlaeus; but Barlaeus himself is here building upon Claudian, who praises Manlius Theodorus on the grounds that 'frons privata manet nec se meruisse fatetur, / quae crevisse putat' ('Your appearance remains that of a private citizen, and does not acknowledge that it has in fact earnt, / What it thinks has grown by itself', *Theod.* 245–6). It is a trope found repeatedly in Cromwellian panegyric, both in Marvell ('Who from his private gardens where / He liv'd reserved and austere', 'Horatian Ode', 29–30) and Dryden ('He, private, marked the faults of others' sway / And set as sea-marks for himself to shun', 'Heroic Stanzas', 33–4).

Like Claudian, Fisher reused images, specific similes, or even entire lines for a new addressee. At *Eutr.* 1.163–6 Claudian compares Eutropius' ruthless treatment of those who had brought him to power to Phalaris, the Sicilian tyrant who had Perillos, the designer of his brazen bull, put to death in the device he had designed; Fisher uses versions of these lines to describe first the defeated Scots and then the Dutch.[85] Such techniques are most obvious in *Piscatoris Poemata* (1656), which reprints all Fisher's previous major poems (*Marston-Moor, Irenodia Gratulatoria* and

---

[84] Barlaeus, *Panegyris* (1641), 138.
[85] Fisher, *Irenodia Gratulatoria*, sig. B3ᵛ; *Inauguratio*, sig. Dd4ʳ.

Inauguratio Olivariana), as well as several shorter ones. The overall impression of *Piscatoris Poemata* is that of a 'Claudianic' career: Fisher even includes in the volume an early exercise in Claudianic epithalamium, a poem on the marriage of Col. Thomas Tomkins and Lucy Neale in 1643, which borrows significantly from Claudian's *Epith.* (this poem is discussed briefly in Chapter 10). In this way Fisher demonstrates his mastery of a range of Claudianic genres.

By the mid-1650s Fisher had succeeded in adapting Claudianic panegyric, traditionally addressed to monarchs, to the praise of Cromwell, a man who refused to be king, and whose power derived principally from his military achievements. Edmund Waller's 'Panegyric', entered on the Stationers' Register in May 1655 alongside Marvell's 'First Anniversary', was published, like most of Fisher's official poetry of the period, by Thomas Newcomb. Waller's poem prints as an epigraph on its title page the same two lines from Claudian used by Alabaster in the early 1590s and by Birkhead in 1645.[86] Those lines, a byword for ardent royalism for Birkhead, were by 1655 straightforwardly applicable to Cromwell, and indicate the genre to which Waller's poem belongs.

Claudian, Fisher and Marvell's 'First Anniversary'

Marvell's 'First Anniversary' is one of the most impressive, as well as one of the earliest attempts to transfer Claudianic panegyric into English, and it is demonstrably influenced by Fisher. As I have shown elsewhere, both Fisher's general political evolution from royalist to Cromwellian, and details of his acquaintances mirror those of Marvell: both men were linked to figures such as John Hall, Marchamont Nedham, Bulstrode Whitlocke and Edmund Waller.[87]

---

[86] 'Gaudet enim virtus testes sibi jungere Musas, / Carmen amat quisquis Carmine digna gerit', pr. 5–6. Waller's poem was also published in the same year by Richard Lowndes, in a less polished edition, in four-line stanzas and without an epigraph, both features which tend to obscure its generic identity. It circulated widely in manuscript (29 copies noted in *CELM*) and is sometimes accompanied in manuscript by the Claudian quotation (as in BL MS Burney 390, fol. 22^r). Holberton, *Poetry and the Cromwellian Protectorate*, 90–1, comments briefly on Waller's relationship to Claudian.

[87] For Marvell and Hall, see McDowell, *Poetry and Allegiance*, 2; for Marvell's and Milton's work alongside Marchamont Nedham in the 1650s, see Worden, *Literature and Politics*; on Marvell and Whitlocke's embassy to Sweden, see Holberton, *Poetry and the Cromwellian Protectorate*, esp. pages 26–36; on Marvell and Waller, see Holberton, *Poetry and the Cromwellian Protectorate*, 87–118. For further details of the many connections between these figures, and a longer discussion of Marvell's 'First Anniversary', see Moul, 'Marvell and Fisher'.

The two most extended (and implicitly related) similes for Cromwell in the poem compare him to a star or the sun (101–4 and 325–46) and, most famously, to the steersman of the ship of state (265–78):

> So have I seen at sea, when whirling winds,
> Hurry the bark, but more the seamen's minds,
> Who with mistaken course salute the sand,
> And threat'ning rocks misapprehend for land;
> While baleful Tritons to the shipwreck guide,
> And corposants along the tacklings slide.
> The passengers all wearied out before,
> Giddy, and wishing for the fatal shore;
> Some lusty mate, who with more careful eye
> Counted the hours, and every star did spy,
> The helm does from the artless steersman strain,
> And doubles back into the safer main.
>
> (265–76)

Both of these images are used repeatedly by Claudian. Here for instance Stilicho is compared to a sailor who takes responsibility in a storm when no-one else will do so:

> ceu flamine molli
> tranquillisque fretis clavum sibi quisque regendum
> vindicat; incumbat si turbidus Auster et unda
> pulset utrumque latus, posito certamine nautae
> contenti meliore manu seseque pavere
> confessi (finem studiis fecere procellae):
> haud aliter Stilicho, fremuit cum Thracia belli
> tempestas, cunctis pariter cedentibus unus
> eligitur ductor
>
> (Claudian, *CM* 30.201–9)
>
> *As when on a calm sea*
> *Every sailor claims his right to take the tiller,*
> *But if the blustering south wind bears down upon them, and*
> *They are buffeted by the waves on either side, then the vying for*
>   *control ceases and the sailors*
> *Admitting their fear accept a more skilful hand (for the storm sets*
>   *a limit on their enthusiasm);*
> *Just so was Stilicho, when the storm of war raged in Thrace,*
> *Selected as commander, with all rivals ceding to him.*

Elsewhere, Stilicho is like a steersman ('arbiter alni') in a storm, guiding the empire away from disaster (*Stil.* 1.286–90); like a star in a storm at sea (*Ruf.* 1.275–7); and his hair shines like a star heralding salvation for besieged Rome (*Get.* 457–60). Manlius Theodorus is also like a skilled steersman (*Theod.* 42–50), while Honorius is compared to the topmost star (*VI Cons.* 18–24). Marvell compares Cromwell's recovery from his coaching accident to the experience of the first men who, after the first ever night, see the sun returning (325–46); Honorius is compared at length to the outburst of light amid an unnatural darkness at *IV Cons.* 172–91. Such imagery is of course highly conventional in Claudianic panegyric.

Marvell's application of the steersman image to Cromwell is almost certainly influenced by its repeated, almost obsessive, use by Fisher in his panegyric poetry published between 1650 and 1654. In its first appearance, however, the image refers not to Cromwell but to the courage of the royalist Sir Thomas Glemham as he attempted to defend York against the Scottish and Parliamentarian besiegers in 1644 (*Marston-Moor*, 30–1) – this is typical of *Marston-Moor*, in which, as noted above, allusions to Claudian tend to reveal an underlying royalism. Two years later, however, Fisher made the image effectively the leitmotif of the *Irenodia Gratulatoria* (1652): around 1,300 lines long, that poem contains nine separate versions of the motif of the ship in a storm, two of them referring directly to Cromwell as a salvific steersman, and a third to Bradshaw.[88] By using versions of the same image to evoke the destruction and distress of political chaos and military defeat in the body of the poem, as well as the gratitude due to those who 'take the tiller' in such a storm, Fisher unifies multiple perspectives.

Fisher reworked the simile of the 'ship of state' yet again, on only the second page of *Inauguratio Olivariana* (1654), in a version of the motif which combines a modesty topos (Cromwell is Palinurus, not Aeneas) with quasi-divine imagery (Cromwell is also a constellation shining from Olympus):

>   Propria cum sponte *Senatus*
>   Obstreperus surgens, *Navim* Rectoris egentem
>   Liquerat, ambiguis & caligantibus undis,
>   *Ille* insperato *Cynosura* eluxit olympo,
>   *Ille* idem *Palinurus* erat; *Navarchaque* gnarus
>   Admisit vidui, clemens moderamina, clavi.

---

[88] Cromwell as steersman through storm (sig. B1ᵛ); poet as steersman through storm, risking wreck (sig. B3ʳ); Scottish casualties at Dunbar like a wrecked ship (sig. C4ᵛ); Scots as a whole like a storm-tossed sailor, with no star to steer by (sig. E3ᵛ–E4ʳ); the city of Worcester, like a pirate ship now itself plundered [Claudian on Alaric] (sig. F3ʳ); Battle of Worcester compared to a storm at sea, ships tossed this way and that (sig. F4ᵛ); Cromwell has saved us from shipwreck, struck only Scots with lightning (sig. H1ᵛ); Grey of Groby at Battle of Worcester like an anchor in a storm (sig. H2ʳ); Bradshaw as a faithful Palinurus (sig. I3ᵛ).

> *When the nation's own Parliament, rising up noisily and of its own accord, had abandoned the ship of state without a steersman, amid dark and unpredictable waves – then that man, like the constellation Ursa Minor, shone forth unexpectedly from Olympus, that man was a second Palinurus. Like a skilled ship captain, he gently took up the controls of the abandoned rudder.*[89]

When Fisher, on the first page of his poem on the anniversary of the Protectorate, claims that Cromwell 'fidâque levavit / Naufragium commune manu, totiesque *Rogatus,* / *Invitus,* vidui subiit moderamina Clavi' ('has with a loyal hand relieved the common shipwreck, and, though unwilling every time he was asked, taken over the steerage of the abandoned tiller'), he is alluding to his own mythologizing of Cromwell as much as he is to any prior source.[90]

Whereas Palinurus in the *Aeneid* is determined to keep his eyes on the stars and not to fall asleep (*Aeneid* 5.851–2), but cannot resist the will of the gods, Cromwell at the beginning of the *Inauguratio* is both the steersman and the stars by which he steers.[91] Marvell's poem makes the same move, since Cromwell is also described as a star earlier in 'The First Anniversary':

> And in his sev'ral aspects, like a star,
> Here shines in peace, and thither shoots in war.
> While by his beams observing princes steer,
> And wisely court the influence they fear.
>
> (101–4)

Marvell's poem is known for its emphasis upon the foreign perception of Cromwell (both in the lines above and, especially, in the speech of the 'princes', 349–94). This is another feature shared with Fisher, whose *Anniversarium* likewise emphasizes, towards the end of the poem, both the successes of the English navy and the perception of Cromwell by the rulers and people of other nations.[92] These structural similarities extend to Fisher's treatment of the coaching accident, which, although commemorated by him in a separate work, *Pro recuperata valetudine*, adopts the same strategy as the corresponding section in Marvell's 'First Anniversary': both works describe first the grief-stricken response to Cromwell's death ('First Anniversary',

---

[89] Knoppers, *Constructing Cromwell*, 89–90, comments on the negative portrayal of Parliament here, though mistranslates *liquerat*.
[90] *Anniversarium* (1654) in *Piscatoris Poemata* (1656), sig. B1^{r-v}.
[91] In the final lines of *Irenodia Gratulatoria* (1652), it is Bradshaw, President of the Council of State and nominally the addressee of the poem, who is Palinurus.
[92] Fisher, *Anniversarium*, in *Piscatoris Poemata*, sigs. F2^v–G1^r.

201–14; *Piscatoris Poemata*, sig. H1ʳ), and then his departure for heaven ('First Anniversary', 215–38; *Piscatoris Poemata*, sigs. H2ʳ–I1ʳ).[93]

It was Marvell's achievement to bring Claudianic panegyric so successfully – and, it turned out, enduringly – into English. Whereas the experiments in English formal verse panegyric composed by Jonson, Daniel and Drayton for the coronation of James I in 1603 did not mark the emergence of a true English genre to stand alongside the Latin, from the mid-1650s onwards we do find an increasingly mature English form: Waller's 'Panegyric' and Marvell's 'First Anniversary' were followed by, among others, Dryden's 'Heroic Stanzas' (on the death of Cromwell in 1658) as well as Marvell's poem on the same occasion ('A Poem upon the Death of his Late Highness the Lord Protector') and Waller's 'Of a War with Spain, and Fight at Sea' (1658). Fisher himself perhaps recognized the significance of the transition into English which he had helped to initiate. The final item in *Piscatoris Poemata* (1656) is a poem of lavish praise for Waller's 'Panegyric', pointing out, in particular, its achievement in the vernacular.

Restoration Panegyric

At the Restoration, we find a wealth of formal verse panegyric in both Latin and English. Claudian was the principal classical source for the coronation celebrations for Charles II in 1661, and many short examples are included in the two university collections published in 1660, Oxford's *Britannia Rediviva* and the *Academiae Cantabrigiensis ΣΩΣΤΡΑ*.[94] Major poems on the theme published separately that year include Dryden's *Astraea Redux* and (in Latin) Christopher Wase's *In mirabilem Caroli II ... Restitutionem Carmen Gratulatorium*.[95] Discussion of this Restoration panegyric has focused almost exclusively upon poems in English, though many of the motifs are shared by examples in both languages. Poets turned, unsurprisingly, to imagery associated with the return of a king or emperor, such as the passage on Rome's joyful reception of Honorius in *III Cons.* already discussed briefly above: the return of the King is like the return of the sun after night or eclipse; the settling of a

---

[93] Patterson, *Marvell*, 44–6, usefully relates Marvell's poem to the conventions of *soteria* (commemorating recovery) but does not consider contemporary Latin examples; Fisher's *Piscatoris Poemata* (1656) also includes a poem for Edmund Ludlow described as a *soteria* (sigs. Ii4ʳ–Kk1ᵛ).
[94] Knowles (ed.), *Entertainment*, 50.
[95] See Swedenberg, 'England's Joy'; and Garrison, *Tradition of Panegyric*, 155–64.

storm; the rebirth of the Phoenix, and so on.[96] Such imagery is conventional, though some features distinguish it from the Claudianic tradition as a whole: like the formal panegyric of the 1650s, Restoration panegyric continued to make greater use of biblical themes, stories and allusions than poetry of this kind had done before that time. In addition, in Restoration panegyric we find, unsurprisingly, an admixture of elements which are particularly resonant for Charles II, such as an emphasis upon the experience of political exile and return; the martyrdom of Charles I; and the story of the Boscobel Oak – a highly popular and artistically productive episode in part because it echoed well-established imagery, both in classical panegyric and in the Bible, linking strong leadership with mighty trees.

For all Claudian's praise of Honorius, however, the poet's real allegiance was to Stilicho: as critics have pointed out, the young Honorius is praised in terms of glory and brightness, but not with the imagery of strength, support and heroism that are applied to Stilicho (and the dead Theodosius).[97] The most sophisticated of the Restoration poems are alert to this pattern, and employ the conventional motifs of Claudianic panegyric to suggestive effect. Dryden's *Astraea Redux* is a particularly impressive example. Dryden uses the story of the Gigantomachy, a favourite of Claudian's, to dispel any shame attached to the original deposition and execution of Charles I, and to associate the demand for 'liberty' with rebellion against the divine:

> Thus when the bold Typhoeus scaled the sky,
> And forced great Jove from his own Heaven to fly,
> (What king, what crown from treason's reach is free,
> If Jove and Heaven can violated be?)
> The lesser gods, that shared his prosperous state,
> All suffer'd in the exiled Thunderer's fate.
> The rabble now such freedom did enjoy,
> As winds at sea, that use it to destroy:
> Blind as the Cyclops, and as wild as he,
> They own'd a lawless, savage liberty;
> Like that our painted ancestors so prized,
> Ere empire's arts their breasts had civilized.
> (*Astraea Redux*, 37–48)

---

[96] The King is the returning sun, for instance, at the opening of Wase, *In mirabilem Caroli*, and in multiple poems in the university collections (Cambridge University, *Academiae Cantabrigiensis ΣΩΣΤΡΑ*, sigs. E1^r–E2^r, E4^{r-v}, F4^{r-v}, H4^{r-v}; Oxford University, *Britannia Rediviva*, sigs. a1^r, B2^r, Ee2^v), including one in English by the young John Locke, then at Christ Church (*Britannia Rediviva*, sig. Ff2^v-Ff3^v).

[97] Christiansen, *Use of Images*, esp. 16–26 (Stilicho), 28–34 (Honorius).

As Clare Coombe has demonstrated, the motif of the Gigantomachy is one of the most important structuring myths in Claudian.[98] It is also a noticeable feature of the anthology produced by Cambridge University to mark the Restoration: the poem 'Ad Serenissimum Magnae Britanniae Regem Carolum II, De Triumphata Tyrannide, Barbarie, & Exilio, Gratulatio' ('To the most Serene King of Great Britain, Charles II, a Celebration of Triumph over Tyranny, Barbarity and Exile'), for instance, is structured as a Gigantomachy. After the people weary of the fire, slaughter and 'Chaos' (that very Claudianic word) of the rule of the Giants, they plead for the return of the exiled gods, and Charles II is their Jupiter, first exiled and then restored. Their joy at his return is linked closely to their memory of the darkness and disorder of the Interregnum:

> Haud equidem credo, populi maiore triumpho,
> Exulem & extinctum per tot Quinquennia solem
> Exciperent reducem, memores caliginis atrae
> Atque decennalis noctis, quàm lucis alumnum
> Et coeli Carolum, laetum in sua regna reversum.
> Nec furit hic populus: quid enim felicius illo,
> Naufragio elapsum gremio comprêndere Regem,
> Atque in Rege suo totum comprêndere Mundum?[99]
>
> *Indeed I do not believe that the people would receive with greater triumph*
> *Even the sun itself, exiled and extinguished for so many years,*
> *On his return, remembering the dark mist*
> *And the decade-long night – than the return of that foster-child of light*
> *And son of heaven, Charles, joyful to come back into his kingdom.*
> *Nor are they wrong to react in this way: for what could be more wonderful,*
> *Than to embrace one's King, rescued from shipwreck,*
> *And in one's King, to contain the whole world?*

The distinctively panegyric reuse of stock images, even across such stark political divisions as between Charles I and Cromwell, and between Cromwell and Charles II, can sometimes seem absurd. At its most nuanced, however, such repeated imagery can tacitly acknowledge and absorb the difficulty of historical transitions within the generic frame. In *Astraea Redux*, for instance, Dryden describes England as a lion who lashes itself with its own tail, before turning round to attack the enemy:

---

[98] Coombe, *Claudian the Poet*, 93–122.
[99] Cambridge University, *Academiae Cantabrigiensis ΣΩΣΤΡΑ*, sig. F2^{r-v}, poem ascribed to 'T. B.', a fellow of Corpus Christi.

> Tremble, ye nations, which, secure before,
> Laugh'd at those arms that 'gainst ourselves we bore;
> Roused by the lash of his own stubborn tail,
> Our lion now will foreign foes assail.
> (*Astraea Redux*, 115–18)

Dryden here echoes Waller:

> A lion so with self-provoking smart,
> (His rebel tail scourging his noble part)
> Calls up his courage; then begins to roar
> And charge his foes, who thought him mad before
> ('To My Lord of Falkland', 37–40)

Images of lions are used dozens of times in Claudian, in comparisons which themselves build upon models in Homer, Virgil and Lucan; both Dryden and Waller are here borrowing in particular from Lucan, who compares Caesar, rousing himself to battle, to a lion provoking his own anger by beating himself with his tail.[100] Dryden's version of the image adds several elements to Waller's heroizing adaptation: by making the lion the nation, rather than an individual ruler, he links the self-inflicted violence to that of civil war, and he adds also the incredulity of the neighbouring rulers, who think England, so maddened, can no longer be a danger to them.

Moreover, Dryden's motif of self-injury seems conscious of the literary and political history of the image. In Claudian, it is Stilicho who is most often compared to a lion, and Cromwell in turn was repeatedly described as a lion, both by Fisher and by Dryden himself in the 'Heroic Stanzas':

> He made us freemen of the continent
> Whom nature did like captives treat before,
> To nobler preys the English lion sent,
> And taught him first in Belgian walks to roar.
> (113–16)[101]

Dryden's lion simile in *Astraea Redux*, in which the lion first injures himself and then performs his proper function as heroic predator, alludes not only to the historical fact of the Civil War (a kind of self-inflicted

---

[100] Lucan 1.205–12. There are around 32 instances of lion imagery or comparison in Claudian. See also Homer, *Iliad* 11.548–55 and 17.657–64, and Virgil, *Aen.* 9.791–8 (of Turnus; adapted by Dryden, *Annus Mirabilis* 381–8, for Monck).

[101] Stilicho as a lion at *Get.* 323–9, *Ruf.* 2.252–6, *Stil.* 2.20–2, among others. Manchester/Cromwell as a lion in Fisher, *Marston-Moor*, 21 (the image refers to Manchester in the 1650 edition, Cromwell in the 1656 revision); Cromwell in *Irenodia Gratulatoria*, sig. D2ʳ.

injury), but also to the literary history of the previous decade: to the maddened lion that was Cromwell.

We find similar nuance in the treatment of the term 'freedom' in Restoration verse. The Protectorate panegyric of the 1650s associates Cromwell with the struggle for, and reassertion of, national freedom: '*Libertas* medio emersit Rediviva sepulchro' ('Revived *Freedom* has emerged from the midst of the tomb'), with an obvious suggestion of the Resurrection.[102] With freedom so recently defined as freedom *from* monarchical rule, the poets of the Restoration sought ways to redefine it, and here too they turned to imagery derived from Claudian. Both Claudian's own much-quoted aphorism on the 'true freedom' enjoyed under a virtuous prince, discussed above, and the typically Claudianic association of excess freedom or licence with chaos, division and destruction were frequently employed to characterize, respectively, the 'real' freedom of the Restoration and the 'false' freedom of the Protectorate:

> The rabble now such freedom did enjoy,
> As winds at sea that use it to destroy:
> (*Astraea Redux*, 43–4)

> 'Twas Monck whom Providence designed to loose
> Those real bonds false freedom did impose.
> (*Astraea Redux*, 152–3)

Or, more plainly:

> Free-men we cannot; Slaves we will not be:
> Subjects we are. That's all the liberty,
> That we desire, or can contain. What's more,
> Doth but oppress us with impertinent Store.[103]

Just as Claudian extols the glory and majesty of the young Honorius, but attributes to Stilicho (not Honorius) the power to conquer the enemy and protect Rome, so *Astraea Redux* distinguishes between the returning King, repeatedly described as suffering passively if virtuously, and the active forces first of disorder (Typhoeus/Cromwell) and then of the Restoration (Booth's abortive but 'fair' attempt and then Monck's successful action, 151–78). Paradoxically, Charles belongs to a 'too, too active age' (111), but is never depicted as himself acting. In perhaps the most remarkable passage, the long-awaited moment of the Restoration is figured in terms

---

[102] Fisher, *Irenodia Gratulatoria*, in *Piscatoris Poemata* (1656), sig. Hh1ʳ.
[103] Edward Littleton in Oxford University, *Britannia Rediviva*, sig. Aa4ʳ-Bb1ʳ.

that recall the Gigantomachy, and suggest too both the Incarnation, and divine rape:

> The Prince of peace would like himself confer
> A gift unhoped, without the price of war:
> Yet, as he knew his blessing's worth, took care,
> That we should know it by repeated prayer;
> Which storm'd the skies, and ravish'd Charles from thence,
> As heaven itself is took by violence.[104]
>
> (*Astraea Redux*, 139–44)

The commentaries here note a scriptural parallel (Matthew 11:12, 'the kingdom of heaven suffereth violence') but the combination of 'ravished' and 'heaven itself is *took* by violence' suggests something starker than the Gospel verse: the rape of Proserpina and of Ganymede (who is taken to rather than from heaven) and the (in Claudian, poetically linked) storming of heaven by the Giants.

When the moment is ripe, it is not Charles, but General Monck who acts. He does so cautiously and carefully, without undue haste:

> Twas not the hasty product of a day,
> But the well ripened Fruit of wise delay.
> He like a patient Angler e're he stroak,
> Would let them play a while upon the hook.
> Our healthful food the Stomach labours thus,
> At first embracing what it strait doth crush.
> Wise leeches will not vain receipts obtrude,
> While growing Pains pronounce the Humors crude;
> Deaf to complaints they wait upon the Ill,
> Till some safe *Crisis* authorize their Skill.
>
> (*Astraea Redux*, 169–78)

The simile of the fisherman here has its roots in a passage in Silius Italicus. Here Hannibal – a famously brilliant tactician, albeit an enemy of Rome – pretends to retreat in order to tempt Minucius into a pitched battle:

> **ut parvo mariora ad proelia damno**
> **eliceret, dabat interdum simulantia terga.**
> **non aliter, quam qui sparsa** per stagna profundi
> **evocat e** liquidis **piscem penetralibus esca,**
> cumque levem summa vidit iam nare sub unda,
> **ducit sinuato captivum ad litora lino**.
>
> (Silius Italicus, *Punica* 7.498–503)

---

[104] See also 'By that same mildness, which your father's crown / Before did ravish, shall secure your own' (258–9).

Restoration Panegyric

> *Now and then he pretended to retreat, using minor losses to tempt* [the Romans] *to battle. Just as a fisherman scatters bait on a pool to lure a fish from the depths and then, when he sees his agile prey just beneath the surface, he draws him in, a captive, on his line to the shore.*

The simile in Silius is memorable, not least because there are few such domestic similes in the *Punica*; but it is not very close to the situation described by Dryden. In Silius, the pretence at retreat is like the bait that tempts the fish; whereas in Dryden, the focus is on the idea of allowing the fish to 'play' on the hook, without realizing it has been captured. This detail Dryden seems to have borrowed from an expansion of Silius' simile in Fisher's *Marston-Moor*:

> Nec levior *Ductoris* erat vigilantia, multa
> Dum virtute suà miscet Stratagemata, fraudes
> Et versipellis vario sub Imagine versat.
> Et nunc **ut parvo graviora in damna periclo**,
> **Eliceret, dabat interdum simultantia Terga**
> Obliquànsque suas ficta in simulachra Cohortes,
> Saepe lacessitos spe *sublactaverat* Hostes.
> Nulla vacant Incoepta dolis; versatilis arte
> Nunc premit instantes turmas, nunc Castra relinquit
> Callidus, ut totos invitet Prodigus Hostes.   10
> **Non aliter quàm qui** *Thamesis* per flumina **sparsâ**
> **Evocat è** vitreis **Piscem Penetralibus escâ**,
> Jam rapit; inde vagum sollers exporrigit hamum;
> Donec inescatum liquido sub Marmore cernens
> Pisciculum, virgam retrahit, **sinuatá**que volvit
> Serica, **captivo ducens ad littora lino**.[105]

> *No lighter was the General's vigilance, as he combined*
> *Courage with many strategems, and cunningly pondered*
> *Deceptions in various guises.*
> *And then, in order to incite the enemy to more serious losses*
> *With only a small danger to himself, he would feign retreat*
> *And steer his men to the side in pretence.*
> *Often in this way he duped the enemy forces, who were led on by hope.*
> *Nothing he undertook was without guile; crafty in his skill*
> *At one moment he urges on the squadrons in their attack, the next*
> *He abandons the camp, a generous invitation to all the enemy.*
> *Just like a man who, scattering food on the surface of the river Thames,*
> *Summons up a fish from the glassy depths –*
> *Who then pounces upon it; he then skillfully lets his hook wander out;*

---

[105] Fisher, *Marston-Moor*, 21–2.

Until, catching sight of a little fish who has taken the bait
Beneath the liquid marble, draws back his rod, and twisting the silk,
Draws it back to shore on a captive line.

In the 1650 edition of *Marston-Moor* (quoted above) this simile describes the tactical cunning of the Earl of Manchester, besieging York in 1644 and awaiting the right moment to attack. In the 1656 revised version of the poem, however, the simile is attributed not to Manchester, but to Cromwell.[106] Dryden's comparison of Monck to skilful doctors ('wise leeches') also has a double echo, in both Claudian and, again, in Fisher.[107]

In general, Dryden transfers the characteristically 1650s Cromwellian motifs of activity, urgency, military courage but also patience, good judgement and watchfulness – which are themselves derived from Claudian's depiction of Stilicho (rather than Honorius) – to Monck (rather than Charles II).[108] In doing so, his Restoration verse, which returns the panegyric tradition to its traditional royal addressees, demonstrates what he has learnt from the Claudianic poems of the 1650s.

Fisher's appropriation of Claudianic panegyric-epic in his poems for Cromwell in the 1650s is of fascinating complexity and political sophistication. His work offers a rare instance in which we have fairly complete evidence for the development of a poetic style, including revision and republication of existing works, in direct response to events. His resilient creativity in the face of a rapidly changing political context is comparable to similar shifts during this period in the work and orientation of Marvell, Cowley and Dryden. But we cannot begin to assess the originality of what any of these poets were doing without understanding the generic context in which they were working, and the framework offered by the lively and, by the 1650s, already long tradition of Renaissance and early modern Latin panegyric-epic in the style and tradition of Claudian. This chapter has aimed to fill in at least the key features of that tradition, as well as offer an analysis of Fisher's particular contribution to it, demonstrating the sophistication with which Fisher uses Claudian; the extent to which his verse draws upon contemporary poets – such as Milton and Barlaeus – whose work he recognised as belonging to the same Claudianic tradition as his

---

[106] Fisher, *Piscatoris Poemata*, sig. T1^(r–v). Marvell famously compares Cromwell to Hannibal in the 'Horatian Ode' of 1650 ('A Caesar he ere long to Gaul, / To Italy an Hannibal', 101–2); Fisher also compares Cromwell to Hannibal in *Irenodia Gratulatoria* (1652).
[107] Stilicho is a careful surgeon (*Get.* 120–3) and a doctor treating a wound (*Stil.* 2.204–5); Cromwell as a careful surgeon (*Irenodia Gratulatoria* in *Piscatoris Poemata* (1656), sig. Ee2^v, a simile not in the earlier 1652 edition).
[108] On watchfulness in Claudian, Fisher and Marvell, see Moul, 'Marvell and Fisher'.

own; and the ways in which Marvell and Dryden, in transferring this tradition into the vernacular, learnt from Fisher and from the wider Latin tradition.

An understanding of the early modern imitation of Claudian is essential to any appreciation of what a poet like Fisher, Marvell or Dryden is doing, but not only for that: a knowledge of the Claudianic genres and style helps us to read the great wealth of British Latin panegyric verse dating from both before and after this period (including, for instance, the 'Gunpowder plot' poems which have typically been studied in isolation); it helps immeasurably in the reading of so-called Renaissance 'short epic' or 'epyllion' as a whole, especially though not only in Latin; it also demonstrates the international currency of this form, in which poets routinely learnt from and imitated one another across national boundaries, and frequently both expected and intended to be read by addressees of other nations. Finally, it illuminates the style and sources, and demarcates the originality, of a wide range of English verse, especially of the later seventeenth century, which most readers now find hard to access or appreciate. Claudian was not so much a possible, as the *obvious* model for formal panegyric verse in early modern Europe, and any reading of such poetry, whether in Latin or the vernacular, must take that as a starting point.

CHAPTER 10

Latin Style and Late Elizabethan Poetry
Rethinking Epyllia

Critics have long recognized that a group of English narrative poems, dealing largely with mythological love affairs and including Shakespeare's *Venus and Adonis*, and which appeared in the last 11 years of the sixteenth century, form a coherent generic cluster and testify to an intense albeit apparently rather short-lived literary vogue.[1] Lynn Enterline describes the Elizabethan epyllia as a 'series of Elizabethan narrative poems that responded to one another through the mediation of mythological material drawn largely from Ovid's *Metamorphoses* and *Heroides*'.[2] The most influential recent critics writing on Elizabethan minor epic, or the 'erotic epyllion' as it is sometimes called, have stressed the link to pedagogical practices in general and to the reading of Ovid in particular, with several scholars seeing in this combination a form of resistance to the educational, social and political expectations of the period.[3]

---

[1] Georgia Brown describes epyllia as 'one of the most characteristic forms of the 1590s' (*Redefining Elizabethan Literature*, 102). The core texts are usually taken to include Thomas Lodge, *Scillaes Metamorphosis* (1589; sometimes called *Glaucus and Scylla*); Marlowe's *Hero and Leander* (before 1592), with Chapman's completion (1598); Shakespeare, *Venus and Adonis* (1593); Thomas Edwards, *Cephalus and Procris* (1593); John Weever, *Faunus and Melliflora* (1600); and Francis Beaumont, *Salmacis and Hermaphroditus* (1602). Miller, 'Elizabethan Minor Epic', considers Shakespeare's *Rape of Lucrece* (1594), Michael Drayton's *Endimion and Phoebe* (1595), Thomas Heywood's *Oenone and Paris* (1594) and Chapman's *Ovids Banquet of Sence* (1595) to be marginal cases due to an admixture of the core genre with complaint, pastoral or the neo-Platonic philosophical poem. Clark Hulse, *Metamorphic Verse*, includes also Spenser's *Muiopotmos* (1591) as well as Drayton's historical poems *Complaint of Rosamond* (1592) and *Peirs Gaveston* (1593). Belated seventeenth-century examples include Phineas Fletcher, *Venus and Anchises: Brittain's Ida* (1628) and James Shirley, *Narcissus or The Self-Lover* (1646, though possibly published initially in 1618). The category remains, however, rather imprecisely determined.
[2] Enterline, 'Elizabethan Minor Epic', 253–4.
[3] The use of the term 'epyllion' is contentious in classical studies; it was not used as a critical category in either antiquity or early modernity. Appropriated in the nineteenth century by classicists to describe a rather heterogeneous set of texts which include inset narratives within larger poems, such as the Orpheus and Eurydice episode in *Georgics* 4, as well as the stand-alone Catullus 64, it was taken up in the twentieth century by English literary scholars and applied to the (in fact rather more coherent) group of late Elizabethan erotic-mythological poems. The most complete survey of the

Although the Elizabethan grammar school was focused on producing boys adept at composition and oratory in Latin (rather than English), there has been almost no discussion of how the style of these poems compares to that of their supposed Latin models. Many Elizabethan epyllia include a closural metamorphosis, a device obviously derived from Ovid. It is also true that several borrow their stories from Ovid's *Metamorphoses*, either substantially or in part: the final 300 lines of Francis Beaumont's *Salmacis and Hermaphroditus*, for instance, follows Ovid, *Met.* 4.285–388 fairly closely; the story of Scylla and Glaucus is told in Ovid (*Met.* 13.898–14.74), though quite differently from Lodge's version in *Scillaes Metamorphosis*; while others, including some of the best known, such as *Hero and Leander*, deal with stories not told in Ovid at all. All the standard recent studies identify these poems as 'Ovidian'; but none distinguishes clearly between 'plot' and style.[4]

For the reader, however, what is most memorable about these poems is their distinctive style, characterized by a sensuous pleasure in description for its own sake. Here for instance is the arrival of Venus in Thomas Lodge's *Scillaes Metamorphosis*, generally accepted as the first example of the genre:

> No sooner from her reverent lips were past
> Those latter lines, but mounting in the East,
> Faire Venus in her ivorie coatch did hast,
> And toward those pencive dames, her course addrest;
> Her doves so plied their waving wings with flight,
> That straight the sacred Goddesse came in sight.
>
> Upon her head she bare that gorgeous Crowne,
> Wherein the poore Amyntas is a starre;
> Her lovely lockes, her bosome hang adowne
> (Those netts that first insnar'd the God of warre:)
> Delicious lovely shine her prettie eies,
> And one her cheekes carnation cloudes arise,

---

history of the term is Tilg, 'Origins of "epyllion"'; see also Bär, 'Elizabethan Epyllion'. Classical practice has influenced that of neo-Latinists who have tended to use the term for inset mythological episodes within humanist didactic epic, such as those in Fracastoro's *Syphilis* and Vida's *De bombyce*, as well as for stand-alone works (as for instance in Korenjak, 'Short Mythological Epic'). Influential recent studies of the Elizabethan 'epyllion' include Donno (ed.), *Elizabethan Minor Epics*; Keach, *Elizabethan Erotic Narratives*; Ellis, *Sexuality and Citizenship*; Weaver, *Untutored Lines*; Brown, *Redefining Elizabethan Literature*, chap. 3; Enterline (ed.), *Elizabethan Narrative Poems*.

[4] As well as Enterline, quoted above, Hulse says epyllia 'characteristically follow Ovid's *Metamorphoses* as a model' (*Metamorphic Verse*, 17); Ellis describes them as 'a group of poems based on stories from Ovid' and also identifies their tone as Ovidian (*Sexuality and Citizenship*, 5).

> The stately roab she ware upon her back
> Was lillie white, wherein with cullored silke;
> Her Nimphes had blaz'd the yong Adonis wrack,
> And Laedas rape by Swan as white as milke,
> And on her lap her lovely Sonne was plaste,
> Whose beautie all his mothers pompe defaste.
>
> A wreath of roses hem'd his Temples in,
> His tresse was curlde and cleere as beaten gold;
> Haught were his lookes, and lovely was his skin,
> Each part as pure as Heavens eternall mold,
> And on his eies a milkewhite wreath was spred,
> Which longst his backe, with prettie pleits did shed.
>   (stanzas 83–6)[5]

The lingering sensuality of this verse, and its constant resort to extended description, is not Ovidian. Though there are famously erotic passages in Ovid (such as the description of Corinna in the afternoon half-light in *Amores* 1.5), Ovid does not sustain this kind of tone at length and it is not typical at all of the style and tone of the *Metamorphoses*, usually cited as the main source of the Elizabethan genre. Similarly, the English poems are characterized by lengthy descriptive diversions from the plot (such as it is), a technique which tropes delayed sexual gratification: as Lynn Enterline has put it, writing of *Hero and Leander*, 'ekphrasis derails the poem's erotic plot so early and often that Judith Haber suspects Marlowe of developing "an aesthetic of pure pointlessness"'.[6] Though the *Metamorphoses* are memorable for their artfully nested stories, extensive ecphrasis – rather than the single telling phrase – is not typical of the work. Ovid's fast-paced, witty, sidelong Latin has little in common with the lush and lingering erotics of most of these English poems. Indeed all of the English epyllia are vastly longer than any single episode in the *Metamorphoses*, and whereas the great majority of the stories of sexual pursuit in the *Metamorphoses* describe rape, attempted rape or, at best, seduction achieved by the deception of (mostly) women and girls by men or male divinities, several of the Elizabethan epyllia are focused upon essentially consensual, if frequently doomed, partnerships.

Overall, the determination to understand these poems as, primarily, Ovidian has tended to conceal one set of significant models and

---

[5] Text of Lodge from Donno (ed.), *Elizabethan Minor Epics*. *Scillaes Metamorphosis* is considered the first example of the form by, among others, Kahn, 'Venus and Adonis', 19.
[6] Enterline, 'Elizabethan Minor Epic', 259; referring to Haber, *Desire and Dramatic Form*, 39–43.

over-emphasize another. Most of the standard introductions to the English 'epyllion' begin by citing a series of English translations of Ovid made in the 1560s, without attempting to explain the chronological gap of 20 to 30 years between those publications and the appearance of the English form, or the marked discontinuities of style: none of the erotic 'epyllia' of the 1580s and 1590s are, stylistically, anything like Golding's *Metamorphoses*. Other elements of the early modern 'epyllion' also do not derive from or correspond to Ovid: these are stand-alone poems of medium to long length, not a form in which Ovid composed.

No experienced reader of Latin, then, would immediately associate the lush extended description typical of these poems primarily with Ovid, even where the names of the characters are derived from stories told, or alluded to, in the *Metamorphoses*, and nor is their form particularly Ovidian. As Tania Demetriou has recently pointed out, the length, form and subjects of these English poems more closely resemble Hellenistic and later Greek mini-epic such as Callimachus' *Hecale*, Musaeus' *Hero and Leander*, Moschus' *Europa* and Colluthus' *Raptus Helenae* – though the style of these poems, too, is not much like the Elizabethan examples.[7] George Chapman himself pointed out that the 'character' of Marlowe's *Hero and Leander* is far removed from that of Musaeus.[8] Some of the earliest scholarship on the genre acknowledged this essential un-Ovidianism: Paul Miller, for instance, lists the prominence of lengthy descriptions, strained figures, very long speeches and sometimes contrived imagery as unclassical features, derived neither from Ovid nor from Hellenistic short epics. Ovid's style seems, he comments, 'restrained' in comparison to the style of these English poems, though he does not propose any alternative model.[9] More recent scholarship, however, has tended to elide any distinction between Ovidian mythological elements and non-Ovidian style.[10]

---

[7] Demetriou, 'Non-Ovidian Elizabethan Epyllion'.
[8] Chapman describes Marlowe's and Musaeus' poems as 'in nothing alike; a different Character being held through, both the Stile, Matter, & invention' (Chapman, *The Divine Poem of Musaeus*, sig. A8ʳ). I am grateful to Javiera Raty for this reference.
[9] Miller, 'Elizabethan Minor Epic', 32–3.
[10] Burrow and Martindale, for instance, identify many possible classical allusions in Clapham's *Narcissus*, almost all to Virgil and Ovid, but do not comment on the overall style of the poem (Burrow and Martindale, 'Clapham's *Narcissus*'). This is a similar phenomenon to that found in the discussion of the satire of the 1590s, in which the Juvenalian *tone* of these works has been taken as a basis for their general description, although the harsh, densely metaphorical, frequently elliptic *style* of 1590s satire is typically not much like Juvenal. On the style/tone distinction in Elizabethan verse satire, see Selden, 'Roughness in Satire'.

Stepping Back: English and Latin, Epyllia and Epithalamia

This chapter steps back from the assumption that these poems are unambiguously 'Ovidian', and instead attempts to locate them within the bilingual literary context from which they emerged. It considers these poems as part of a wider category of medium-length mythological narrative poems, all of the Latin examples in hexameter, and unified by a distinctive sensuous and ecphrastic style as well as several shared features, including recurring stock characters (such as Venus, Proserpina and Glaucus) and set pieces (such as versions of the 'Garden of Venus' motif). Latin examples of this type precede the first English instances, and, where studied at all, have been variously described as epyllia and epithalamia, but have almost never been discussed in relation to the English genre.[11]

Crucial to the analysis is a serious attention to the style of these poems, in both Latin and English, and to models for this style which point, in Latin terms, not to Ovid but rather to Catullus 64 and (especially) Claudian. I will end with a brief discussion of a remarkable application of this distinctive mode, harnessing its sexual associations and mythological force in the service of medical didactic: David Kinloch's 1596 *De hominis procreatione*. The didactic use of generic conventions depends upon their familiarity: Kinloch's extraordinary poem points to a widespread familiarity with this kind of verse among the readers he envisaged for his work.

Catullus 64, widely cited by classicists as the main Latin model for the epyllion, is a marriage poem, an example of formal narrative epithalamia. The tradition of erotic epyllia has not, to my knowledge, been discussed in relation to epithalamia of this longer narrative kind, but the two forms have much in common. Both are (in Latin metrical terms) hexameter poems of medium to long length; both typically make extensive use of mythological material. Both are concerned primarily with the expectation, hope for, deferment or frustration of sexual consummation. Both are characterized, stylistically, by a lingering eroticism in which the poem both suggests and continuously postpones the act to which it points. The ways in which most of the English poems of the 1590s tease their

---

[11] A recent exception is Garrison, 'Campion's *Umbra* and Shakespeare's *Venus and Adonis*', though his discussion treats Campion's poem in isolation, and does not discuss Latin style more generally; see also Burrow and Martindale, 'Clapham's *Narcissus*'. Sutton describes Campion's *Umbra* (1595) as 'a standard epyllion of the Ovidian erotic-psychological kind' (www.philological.bham.ac.uk/campion/introduction.html), though goes on to admit that the story of Iole and Melampus is apparently Campion's own invention, and is not found in Ovid.

readers with the evocation, but never quite consummation, of sexual desire has been well described by multiple critics.[12] But this motif is a stock feature also of marriage poems, especially of the longer narrative type of epithalamium. Formal Latin epithalamia were a standard poetic genre in early modern Europe, frequently produced and circulated both in print and as presentation manuscript volumes. Composed routinely in England until the 1580s, they largely disappear, presumably for political reasons, in the final 15 years of Queen Elizabeth's reign: that is, exactly the period in which we find the intense but short-lived flowering of the late Elizabethan erotic epyllion.[13]

The career of George Chapman suggests the generic affiliations in this period between epyllion and epithalamium: Chapman wrote one particularly lavish and complex epyllion of his own, *Ovids Banquet of Sence* (1595), and completed Marlowe's famous example of the genre (*Hero and Leander Completed*, 1598), including within it a lyric epithalamium as an inset song; but he also published two formal epithalamia, for the marriage of Princess Elizabeth and Frederick, Elector Palatine, in 1613 (*A Hymne to Hymen for the Most Time-Fitted Nuptialls*, an 84-line marriage song in the tradition of Catullus 61 and 62) and the longer *Andromeda Liberata* (1614, 643 lines) for the marriage of the Earl of Somerset and the Countess of Essex. Although not to my knowledge included in any lists of epyllia, *Andromeda Liberata* fits well the standard definition: the poem is a self-contained mythological mini-epic, rich in description and rhetoric, which incorporates within it the song of the fates at the marriage of Perseus and Andromeda, and in typical epyllion fashion, condenses the metamorphosis of the pair into the final four lines of the main poem, a concise afterthought much like the transformation of Adonis at the very end of Shakespeare's poem.[14] Finally, in 1616 Chapman published his own translation of Musaeus' *Hero and Leander*, the model for Marlowe's poem (*The Divine Poem of Musaeus: Hero and Leander*). These works – epyllia, epithalamia and translation – have, in critical terms, been treated

---

[12] Haber calls it the 'disruption of end-directed sexuality' (*Desire and Dramatic Form*, 43); see also Bromley, 'Let it Suffise'.

[13] I am not aware of any examples of formal Latin epithalamia in manuscript dating certainly from between 1580 and 1600, versus 28 from between 1550 and 1580 and around 65 from between 1600 and 1720. Spenser's two English marriage poems, discussed further below, are an interesting exception.

[14] Tufte describes this work as 'one of the strangest and most interesting works in the epithalamic tradition' (*Poetry of Marriage*, 201).

separately, though formally and stylistically they belong together and offer a revealing glimpse of how poets at the time understood these forms.

Narrative Epithalamia

Formal epithalamia, or marriage poems, to which I argue the epyllia are closely related, were a largely though not exclusively Latin form in the sixteenth century (Spenser's *Epithalamion*, 1595, and *Prothalamion*, 1596, being the most well-known English examples in this period). Properly speaking, there are two main kinds of epithalamia. The first type are songs for performance (or imagined as written for performance) at the actual ceremony, further subdivided according to the moment at which they are performed; these songs are modelled primarily on Catullus 61 and 62 and Claudian's *Fescennine Verses* for the marriage of Honorius and Maria. The second kind of epithalamium, on which this chapter is focused, are extended narrative poems, in hexameter in Latin versions, typically containing extensive mythological and sometimes allegorical material. These poems are modelled primarily on Catullus 64, Statius' *Epithalamium in Stellam et Violentillam* (*Silvae* 1.2), Claudian's *Epithalamium* for Honorius and Maria (341 lines) and his shorter hexameter epithalamium for Palladius and Celerina (*Carmina Minora* 25, 145 lines).[15] Although Claudian's development of the genre depends heavily upon Statius' example, it is Catullus and Claudian, rather than Statius, who were the most influential models in early modernity. Scaliger, for instance, includes several quotations from Claudian, though none from Statius, in his remarks on epithalamia.[16] In early modernity, the biblical marriage poem, the Song of Songs (Song of Solomon; Canticles), well known for its erotic content as well as a tradition of allegorical interpretation (discussed in Chapters 6 and 11), was also an important model.

Catullus 61 and 62, Spenser's *Epithalamion* (1595, unusually composed for his own marriage), Chapman's 1613 *Hymne to Hymen*, as well as the inset song in his *Hero and Leander Completed* (1598), and the long inset song in Jonson's *Hymenaei* (1606, lines 390–510) are all examples of the first type of marriage poem, and it is this 'lyric' mode of epithalamium

---

[15] On the genre of Claudian's epithalamia, see Guipponi-Gineste, 'Poésie, pouvoir et rhétorique' and 'L' "adlocutio sponsalis"'.

[16] Scaliger's essay on epithalamia is part of the *Poetices Libri Septem* (1561); a good English translation by Jackson Bryce is printed as an appendix to Dubrow, *Happier Eden*, 271–96.

which has attracted most critical attention.[17] The second, narrative, type is of greater relevance to this chapter and is largely its focus, though many examples in fact combine elements of both: both *Hymenaei* and *The Haddington Masque* (1608), for example, can be understood as dramatized versions of the narrative form, in both cases containing a 'marriage song' (that is, an example of the first type) within them, and Pontano's influential *Lepidina* (1496) combines pastoral with elements of a masque or pageant in order to celebrate the mythical marriage of Parthenope and Sebethus, which gave rise to the city of Naples.[18] Camden's *De Connubio Tamis et Isis* (1586) is an example of a purely mythological version of a narrative epithalamium (with a fashionable element of geography and aetiology), not tied to any contemporary marriage; Spenser's lost Latin *Epithalamion Thamesis* was apparently a similar project. His surviving *Prothalamion*, though nominally in celebration of the double marriage in 1596 of Elizabeth and Catherine, daughters of Edward Somerset, fourth Earl of Worcester, reaches London, and the marriage itself, only as an afterthought. The body of this poem, which belongs clearly to the second mythological narrative type of epithalamium, is taken up with the gathering of all the rivers.[19]

Early modern epithalamia, in both print and manuscript, frequently include marginal or prefatory references to the relevant classical authorities, and especially to Catullus and Claudian.[20] In his essay on the genre, however, Julius Caesar Scaliger includes in his list of exemplars also Musaeus' *Hero and Leander* – the model, as mentioned above, for Marlowe's poem on the same theme, and a poem which had been translated into Latin verse by the important Latin poet William Gager in

---

[17] Thomas M. Greene, 'Epithalamic Convention', traces only this type of poem from Catullus and Sappho onwards; subsequent scholarship has tended to follow his lead. Roland Greene, for instance, in a section on 'Epithalamium' in the *Oxford History of Classical Reception* dismisses the narrative tradition of Statius and Claudian by identifying the songs of Catullus and Sappho as 'the salient template for Renaissance epithalamia' ('Elegy, Hymn, Epithalamium, Ode', 329). Although not the focus here, there are plenty of contemporary Anglo-Latin examples of the Catullan song type of epithalamium, as for instance the 'Fescennine verses' composed by William Boswell for the marriage of John Holles, Lord Haughton in 1626 (BL MS Harley 6383, fol. 40ᵛ).
[18] Tufte groups Statius, Claudian and all the poems imitating them together as 'rhetorical epithalamia' (*Poetry of Marriage*). 'Narrative' is perhaps a more useful term.
[19] Spenser's *Prothalamion* is also indebted to Leland's *Cygnea Cantio* (1545) and Vallans' *A Tale of Two Swannes* (1590); in the preface to the latter work, Vallans reports having read Spenser's lost Latin *Epithalamion Thamesis* (sig. A2ʳ).
[20] Oxford University, *Epithalamia oxoniensia* (1625), an anthology of epithalamia for the marriage of Charles I and Henrietta Maria, for example, refers to Claudian's epithalamia on sig. E4ʳ.

the late 1570s, just before the emergence of the epyllion in English.[21] To my knowledge, none of the existing scholarship on Marlowe, Chapman or Gager has pointed out that Scaliger understood Musaeus' poem to be an example of epithalamium.[22] (By contrast, Scaliger does not use the term 'epyllion', which came into critical use only in the nineteenth century.)

In the notes attached to his early marriage masque for the Jacobean court, *Hymenaei* (1606), Ben Jonson cites Claudian as a model for courtly epithalamia. His annotations demonstrate his knowledge of contemporary scholarship, especially Scaliger's discussion; and the text draws upon Claudian and Catullus as well as contemporary sources including Spenser's English epithalamia and, strikingly, Chapman's additions to Marlowe's *Hero and Leander*, which include a formal wedding hymn in the fifth sestiad: Jonson's use of Chapman here is probably influenced by Scaliger's inclusion of Musaeus' poem in his list of models.[23]

Hymenaei includes a marriage 'song' (of the Catullan kind) within a frame of mythological and allegorical drama, in which personified Humours and Affections threaten to disrupt the marriage, only to be seen off by Reason. Tufte includes the presence of allegorical figures of this kind in her list of the conventional features of formal epithalamia deriving from Statius and Claudian. Claudian uses them in his epithalamium for Maria and Honorius to hint at the dangers and obstacles to married love:

> Nec cetera numina desunt;
> hic habitat nullo constricta Licentia nodo
> et flecti faciles Irae vinoque madentes
> Excubiae Lacrimaeque rudes et gratus amantum
> Pallor et in primis titubans Audacia furtis
> iucundique Metus et non secura Voluptas;
> et lasciva volant levibus Periuria ventis.

---

[21] Quotations of Scaliger are from the English translation by Jackson Bryce (in Dubrow, *Happier Eden*, 271–96, here 290). Scaliger also mentions Ausonius, *Cento Nuptialis*, a marriage poem constructed entirely from quotations of existing classical poetry. Other late antique examples include Sidonius, *Epithalamium Ruricio et Hiberiae* (very like Claudian though with some additional Christian elements) and Martianus Capellanus, *Nuptiis Philologiae et Mercurii*, an allegorical account of the marriage of the nymph Philology to Mercury.

[22] In her book on epithalamium, Virginia Tufte terms Musaeus' poem an 'anti-epithalamium', because it functions as a prelude to the tragedy of Leander's drowning and Hero's suicide (*Poetry of Marriage*, 52–6).

[23] *Hymenaei* 487–8 echoes Spenser, *Epithalamion* 385–7; echoes of Chapman, *Hero and Leander*, include *Hymenaei* 149 (5.320–2), 162–7 (5.340–6), 174 (5.322–40), 289 (5.365–9). In his note on line 354 of the marriage song in the *Haddington Masque* (1608), Jonson also cites Daniel Heinsius' Latin epithalamium for Otto Heurnius – Heinsius, *Laudatio* (1605), 158. *OED* credits *Hymenaei* 42 as the first use of 'zone' for girdle, though it also appears in Chapman, *Hero and Leander* (1598) 3.213.

quos inter petulans alta cervice Iuventas
excludit Senium luco.

(*Epithalamium*, 77–85)

Other deities are also present:
Licence dwells here, bound by no kind of restraint;
Anger, easily roused; Wakefulness dripping with wine;
Naïve tears, and the Paleness welcome to lovers;
Boldness trembling with excitement at his first stolen delights;
Pleasurable Fears and unreliable Desire;
And the Oaths of lovers, prey to the lightest breeze.
Among them all arrogant Youth, his neck held high
Bars Old Age from the grove.

The work on *Hymenaei* as an epithalamium has focused upon the inset marriage song (lines 390–510), an instance of the first kind of epithalamium;[24] but the masque as a whole can be understood as an example of the second, narrative or (here) dramatic mode in which, as in Statius and Claudian (and Catullus 64), the traditional stages and accoutrements of the wedding are held within the frame of a mythological story.

Catullus 64 is both an epithalamium *and* an epyllion, since it contains the story of Ariadne's abandonment by Theseus and rescue by Bacchus within the frame of an epithalamium for Peleus and Thetis.[25] This poem is therefore an important model for formal epithalamia and epyllia alike. Claudian's *Epithalamium* is very closely linked to Catullus 64: like Catullus' poem, Claudian uses the story of the wedding of Peleus and Thetis, at which Apollo sings of the future birth of Achilles and the tale of Troy, as the mythological frame for the main poem. Moreover, the 'frame' – in Claudian's case a separate 'praefatio' of 22 lines – intrudes into the 'core' when Maria's effect on the blushing Honorius is compared to that of Deidamia on the young Achilles (*Epith.* 16–19). But shorter and less complex examples of epithalamia also typically contain mythological material, such as recounting the role of Venus and Cupid in securing the match. Scaliger lists as appropriate mythological content for narrative epithalamia the stories of Peleus and Thetis; Bacchus and Ariadne; Hercules and Hebe; and the celebrations of the attendant gods, Venus, Apollo, Mars, Mercury, Diana, the Graces and the Muses; he recommends that Hymen, as god of marriage, may be addressed directly alongside Venus.[26] Virginia Tufte, in her analysis of the tradition of formal epithalamia, notes that Statius and

---

[24] Dubrow, *Happier Eden*, 214–21.
[25] On generic mixture and Catullus 64 as an epithalamium, see Blevins, *Catullan Consciousness*, 67.
[26] Bryce translation in Dubrow, *Happier Eden*, 276–7.

Claudian established a set of conventional features found in most later examples and from which Scaliger derives his principles, including a prominent role for Venus; a paradisal pastoral setting; the personified Hymen; a catalogue of water-nymphs and sea-deities; and the presence of allegorical figures such as Anger and Youth.[27]

In Catullus 64, the mythological epithalamium frames a short mythological epic (with an erotic theme); in Claudian, the mythological epithalamium frames a contemporary epithalamium, though with strong mythologizing elements (of which the structural parallel to Catullus is one). Moreover, lines 49–227 (out of a total of 341) of Claudian's *Epithalamium* are taken up with Venus' preparations for the wedding: a 'digression' but an entirely appropriate one, both because the tone and imagery of this passage are themselves intensely erotic, and because the extended *deferral* of the description of the actual wedding tropes the deferral and expectation of the consummation. In this sense, distinct from its content, the 'digression' is part of the erotics of the poem just as it is, so strikingly, in *Hero and Leander* or *Venus and Adonis*. The same is true, albeit on a smaller scale, of Claudian, *CM* 25 – in other words, both of Claudian's epithalamia are primarily mythological narratives.

It is uncomfortable to think of poems about sexual assault and rape, such as Campion's *Umbra* or indeed Shakespeare's *Venus and Adonis*, as standing generically and tonally alongside poems celebrating marriage. We generally do not associate marriage with assault or lament, though in fact there is almost always an element of lament and dramatized reluctance in formal epithalamia: the bride is typically depicted as anxious about the approaching sexual experience, and her mother as sorrowful to see her go. Scaliger recommends that poets should 'note [the bride's] fear of the coming wrestling-match and victory, how from tears come laughter and from hope, assured felicity'.[28] Claudian, *CM* 25 describes the tearful reticence of the young bride, Celerina, as Venus advises Palladius on how to overcome her reluctance (124–38). In his completion of Marlowe's *Hero and Leander*, Chapman, working in the same tradition, memorably compares Hero to Cadiz and Leander to the Earl of Essex:

> [Hero] was much like
> Th'*Iberian* citie that wars hand did strike
> By English force in princely *Essex* guide,
> When peace assur'd her towres had fortifide;
> (Sestiad 3, 203–6)

---

[27] Tufte, *Poetry of Marriage*, 66.   [28] Scaliger in Bryce translation, Dubrow, *Happier Eden*, 274.

In practice, many of the Elizabethan epyllia, like Marlowe's poem, combine both consensual and non-consensual sex and desire.

Nevertheless, there is a clear topical distinction between poems concerned, primarily, with celebrating marriage and stories of consensual but doomed love (as in *Hero and Leander*) or of hopeless, unwanted or evaded relationships (as in *Scillaes Metamorphosis* or Clapham's *Narcissus*). Catullus 64 has elements of both – the frame of the poem celebrates the marriage of Peleus and Thetis (a 'successful' story of marriage, though not without its tonal ambiguities) while the long central digression tells of Theseus' betrayal and abandonment of Ariadne. Claudian's *De Raptu Proserpinae*, usually described as 'mythological epic', also contains a 'dark' version of the epithalamium, since it describes at length how Hades, god of the underworld, longed for a wife. His kidnap of Proserpina is followed not by her disgrace, abandonment or transformation, but by a conventional marriage (at the end of Book 2) – even though the emotional focus of the fragment of this unfinished poem is on the distress of Proserpina's mother at finding her gone, and the poem breaks off in Book 3 as she embarks upon her own journey to the underworld in search of her. The poem also contains several other features typical of epithalamia, including a catalogue of Naiads, Proserpina's companions (*Rapt.* 2.55–70), and repeated lingering descriptions of the beauty of the landscape in which Proserpina is lured to pick flowers.

The *De Raptu Proserpinae* is unfashionable today, not often read or taught by classicists, but it was a core text of the medieval curriculum and retained an important place in early modernity.[29] Claudian's epithalamia and *Rapt.* are, I argue, important models alongside Catullus 64 for the erotic mythological narrative poems of the 1590s, marked by sexual themes (whether of consensual courtship or sexual violence): a poem such as Campion's strange *Umbra* (1595), for instance, combines a mythological story of divine rape, typical of epyllion, with a sensuous and lavishly described underworld setting, strongly reminiscent of the *Rapt.* Iole, the most beautiful of the daughters of Cybele (a goddess often conflated with Demeter, the mother of Proserpina), is raped by Apollo while unconscious, and gives birth to a beautiful black child, Melampus. Morpheus, god of sleep, falls in love with Melampus and having visited Proserpina's

---

[29] The poem was a consistent element of the so-called 'Liber Catonis', a set of standard medieval school texts, most of which remained staples in early modern England, updated by humanist commentaries. The humanist Angelo Poliziano made a philological study of the poem (see Charlet, 'La rose et le sang'). In 1620 Giambattista Marino relied on the first two books of the *Rapt.* in his fifth *Idillio favoloso* (see Felgentreu, 'Claudian').

underworld realm, filled with the ghosts of the most beautiful women, seduces him in his sleep in the form of a girl; Melampus, tormented by being unable to find her again, wastes away and is finally transformed into a shadow. In its first published form (from 1595) Campion's poem, like Claudian's, is a fragment, which breaks off incomplete – perhaps in conscious imitation of the *De Raptu Proserpinae*.[30]

Descriptive Style in Erotic Epyllia and Epithalamia: The Garden of Venus

There is a clear area of overlap between the themes and subject matter of early modern epithalamia, especially of the Claudianic narrative kind, and those of Elizabethan epyllia. Most striking, however, is the similarity of style. In late antique Latin authors, and in Claudian above all, we find many examples of highly sensuous and richly descriptive Latin poetry, replete with simile and metaphor, ravishing (but sometimes ultimately wearying) to read, and strongly associated, thematically, with the description of nature, of the beauty of divinities, and with eroticism; indeed, most typically of all, with all three of these things combined, as in the easily recognizable set-piece description of the 'Garden of Venus'. These scenes, a stock feature of epithalamia and, as we shall see, also found in various forms of epyllia in both Latin and English, points to the association of eroticism and an extravagant verse style; what Georgia Brown has described as the epyllion's characteristic concern 'with the representation of the aesthetic through the erotic'.[31] Brown takes this association of 'literariness, verbal fluency and imaginative facility ... with guiltiness and even with wantonness' to be an Ovidian phenomenon.[32] Ovid as a character was certainly associated with the erotically illicit in early modernity, but the signature sensuality of this descriptive style is not derived from Ovid.

In terms of ancient poetry, the most important and extensive model for verse in this style is found in Claudian, though many other late antique poets exhibit similar qualities, and Claudian's own style can be traced to passages in earlier Latin and Hellenistic Greek poets, most notably

---

[30] *Fragmentum Umbrae* in Campion, *Poemata* (1595); a completed version appeared in 1619 (Campion, *Epigrammatum Libri II. Umbra. Elegiarum liber vnus*). Modern editions with translations by Dana Sutton (www.philological.bham.ac.uk/campion/introduction.html) and Davis (ed.), *Works of Thomas Campion*. For a recent comparison with Shakespeare, see Garrison, 'Campion's *Umbra* and Shakespeare's *Venus and Adonis*'.
[31] Brown, *Redefining Elizabethan Literature*, 37.   [32] Brown, *Redefining Elizabethan Literature*, 40.

Catullus 64 (on the marriage of Peleus and Thetis). Gordon Braden, in his article on Claudian's 'Garden of Venus', describes Claudian's 'fondness for *ecphrasis*' as 'a distinguishing and for us almost unintelligible feature'; of *De Raptu Proserpinae*, he remarks that 'the ongoing narrative all but disintegrates into juxtaposed blocks – primarily static descriptions and formal speeches addressed to no one in particular'.[33] This is a strikingly similar comment to many of the attempts to summarize the style of Elizabethan epyllia.[34] In Claudian's *Epithalamium de Nuptiis Honorii Augusti*, for instance, the longer of his two formal epithalamia and probably the single most influential model for the long narrative epithalamium in early modernity, Cupid enters his mother's bower to find her sitting on a throne:

> Mons latus Ionium Cypri praeruptus obumbrat,
> invius humano gressu, Phariumque cubile
> Proteos et septem despectat cornua Nili.
> hunc neque candentes audent vestire pruinae,
> hunc venti pulsare timent, hunc laedere nimbi.
> Luxuriae Venerique vacat. pars acrior anni
> exulat; aeterni patet indulgentia veris.
> in campum se fundit apex; hunc aurea saepes
> circuit et fulvo defendit prata metallo.
> Mulciber, ut perhibent, his oscula coniugis emit
> moenibus et tales uxuorius obtulit arces.
> intus rura micant, manibus quae subdita nullis
> perpetuum florent, Zephyro contenta colono,
> umbrosumque nemus, quo non admittitur ales,
> ni probet ante suos diva sub iudice cantus:
> quae placuit, fruitur ramis; quae victa, recedit.
> vivunt in Venerem frondes omnisque vicissim
> felix arbor amat; nutant ad mutua palmae
> foedera, populeo suspirat populus ictu
> et platani platanis alnoque adsibilat alnus.
> (*Epith.*, 49–68)[35]

---

[33] Braden, 'Claudian and His Influence', 215 and 207.

[34] Lynn Enterline writes of Marlowe's 'ornamental and rhetorical self-consciousness', the 'ecphrasis which derails the poem's erotic plot' and 'the preference for sexually provocative material and excessive ornamentation' typical of epyllion ('Elizabethan Minor Epic', 259 and 263); Gerald Snare describes how despite differences all the Elizabethan epyllia are 'overlaid with the most precious, urbane, conceited and hyperbolic language any poet or rhetorician could imagine' ('Chapman's Ovid', 430).

[35] The scene continues until line 96, describing two fountains, one of sweet and one of bitter water; Cupid, his Brother Loves and various attendant personified qualities; and then the palace of Venus itself.

> *A steep mountain overshadows Cyprus, where it overlooks the Ionian plain:*
> *Unreachable by any human foot, it faces* [the island of] *Pharos,*
> *The home of Proteus and the seven mouths of the Nile.*
> *The silver hoar-frosts dare not clothe this mountain,*
> *The winds are afraid to beat upon it, the clouds fear to bother it.*
> *It is devoted entirely to indulgence and to Venus. The harsher part of the year*
> *Is banned from it; there the tender joy of an eternal spring lies spread.*
> *The mountain spills from the peak down into a plain; this plain is encircled*
> *By a golden hedge and defends the meadows with gleaming yellow metal.*
> *Mulciber, so they say, paid with this gift for his wife's kisses:*
> *The fortifications are the price offered by a devoted husband.*
> *The countryside inside gleams brightly; though never worked by hand*
> *It blooms continually, content with Zephyrus as husbandman,*
> *And no bird is allowed to enter the shady grove*
> *Unless the goddess* [Venus] *has first judged and approved its song:*
> *The birds which please her may enjoy the branches; any who do not pass*
>   *the test, must leave.*
> *The very branches live for love and every happy tree*
> *In turn experiences love: palms bend to join together*
> *The poplar sighs at the stroke of the poplar*
> *Planetree whispers to planetree, and alder to alder.*

In such a scene, almost every element has been sexualized: even the metal barrier around the garden turns out to be a payment for sex. It is hard to think of a better example of Brown's definition of the epyllion as 'the representation of the aesthetic through the erotic' or 'the wholesale sexualization of the processes and structures of late Elizabethan culture' which Brown attributes directly to the 'interest in Ovid'.[36] Although the plots of many of the English epyllia are indeed indebted to Ovid, the intense erotics of their style is much closer to that of Claudian.

The comparable scene in the shorter epithalamium is briefer though even more insistently sensuous. This time Venus has retreated in the midday heat to a shaded cave:

> Forte Venus blando quaesitum frigore somnum
> vitibus intexti gremio successerat antri
> densaque sidereos per gramina fuderat artus
> adclinis florum cumulo; crispatur opaca
> pampinus et musto sudantem ventilat uvam.
> ora decet neglecta sopor; fastidit amictum
> aestus et exuto translucent pectore frondes.

---

[36] Brown, *Redefining Elizabethan Literature*, 37.

Idaliae iuxta famulae triplexque vicissim
nexa sub ingenti requiescit Gratia quercu.
(*CM* 25, 1–9)[37]

By chance Venus had one day, in search of sleep in the enticing cool
Withdrawn into the interior of a cave overgrown with vines,
And had laid her star-like limbs on the thick grass,
Her head upon a cushion of flowers; the shadowed vine-tendril
Trembles and gently fans the grape-cluster oozing with juice.
Slumber suits her tumbled brow; such heat disdains any clothing
And the translucent leaves reveal the gleam of her bare breast.
All around lie her attendants, the nymphs of Ida, and beneath a great oak
Rest the three Graces, tangled together.

Claudian's description in both these passages borrows elements from Statius' epithalamium. Venus' 'starry' (*sidereos*) limbs, for instance, an unusually metaphorical phrase in Latin, is borrowed from *Silvae* 1.2.141, and in Statius as in Claudian the Nereids gather precious gifts from the sea.[38]

The many versions of the 'Garden of Venus' scene share multiple features: secrecy and remoteness, suggestive of erotic intimacy; the garden or grove walled or screened by dense vegetation or far distant from civilization; nature in its greatest fertility and abundance, often evoked as a kind of eternal spring or summer; a host of attendant nymphs, sometimes with details of their rural pursuits; the bower, throne or building itself of great beauty (in Statius, this is actually the palace of the bride, Violentilla, rather than of Venus herself). Often allegorical figures such as Youth and Desire are also present, a feature which originates in Claudian and is not found in the earlier classical examples but was much imitated by Renaissance and early modern poets: Braden describes Claudian's Garden of Venus as 'one of the most influential allegorical scenes in European literature'.[39] For Christian writers, this set piece often draws also upon biblical descriptions of Eden and (especially) the garden of the Song of Songs, itself a marriage poem.[40]

---

[37] The poem commemorates the marriage of Palladius and Celerina, of whom we know little, probably in 399 AD.

[38] Glaucus, Proteus and the Nereids search for pearl (*Silvae* 1.2.128–9); Nereids bring gifts of jewellery, pearls and freshly gathered coral (Claudian, *Epith.* 165–71).

[39] Braden, 'Claudian and His Influence', 223. Braden is particularly acute on the overlap in the imagery and sensiblity of Claudian with that of scripture, citing Revelation 21:18 and Isaiah 54:11–12.

[40] See also Homer's Garden of Alcinous (*Od.* 7.112–34); Eden in Dante, *Purgatorio* 28; and Nature's garden in Chaucer, *Parliament of Fowles*. Poliziano closely followed Claudian's description for his realm of Venus in the *Stanze per la giostra*.

Here for instance is the opening of Thomas Campion's version of this scene, in his 1595 Latin epyllion *Umbra*:

> Est in visceribus terrae nulli obvia vallis
> Concava, picta rosis, variaque ab imagine florum,
> Fontibus irrorata, & fluminibus lapidosis:
> Mille specus subter latitant, totidemque virenti
> Stant textae myrto casulae, quibus anxia turba
> Nympharum flores pingunt, mireque colorant.
> ...
>   Acclerant nymphae properata ex ordine matri
> Pensa ostentantes, quarum pulcherrima Iole
> Asportat gremio texturas mille colores.[41]
>   (*Umbra*, 17–22 and 39–41)

> *In the depths of the earth there is a deep valley,*
> *Unreachable, painted with roses and flowers of all kinds,*
> *Watered by fountains and by stony streams:*
> *A thousand caves are hidden beneath it, and the same number*
> *Of little huts or booths woven from green myrtle, which the solicitous band*
> *Of nymphs decorate with flowers and make wonderfully colourful.*
> ...
>   *The nymphs come rushing up, disheveled, eager to show*
> *Their mother [Cybele] the work they have done; Iole, the fairest of them*
> *Carries in her lap her weaving in a thousand colours.*

Or, to cast our net a little wider, the setting of Venus' intervention in Melchior Barlaeus' *De raptu Ganymedis liber* (1563), a poem indebted in particular to Claudian's *De Raptu Proserpinae*:

> Est prope magnificam fecundus floribus aulam,
> Arboribusque sacer non deficientibus hortus,
> Vna cui tantùm pars cognita totius anni,
> Perpetuùm veris floret fragrantis honore.
> Non Boreas fremit hîc austero flamine, solus
> Arboreos mota Zephyrus dat fronde susurros.
> Non torpor violauit eum, non exitialis
> Contristauit hiems: plantae genus omne virentis
> Languorem nescit: sunt germina nescia fati:
> Pendula depictos hîc vinea degrauat arcus.
> Hîc genus innumeris concentibus omne volucrum
> Personat, & rosidum testantur qualia Pestum
> Grata voluptificis descendunt flumina cliuis.
> Hîc Venus ad placidum consederat aurea fontem.[42]

---

[41] Campion, *Poemata* (1595), sig. Ci^{r–v}.   [42] Barlaeus, *De raptu Ganymedis liber* (1563), sig. A8^r.

Next to a magnificent hall is found, filled with flowers
A sacred garden, in which the trees never fail,
And to which only part of the full year's round is known:
It flowers constantly in the glory of a fragrant spring.
Boreas does not roar here with his harsh blast, only
Zephyrus makes the trees whisper and their branches stir.
No sluggish dullness has damaged this garden, and no deadly
Winter storm has afflicted it: every type of growing plant there
Knows nothing of weakness or fatigue; there are seeds which know nothing of death;
Here the pendulous vine hangs down in decorative loops.
Here every sort of bird sounds in uncountable concert
And the sorts of streams which are seen in Paestum, famous for its roses,
Flow beautifully down the slopes of pleasure.
Here golden Venus had sat down at the calm spring's head.

Despite such a reassuring beginning, this queasy work offers an extended, playful treatment of outright assault, not dissimilar to that of Shakespeare's *Venus and Adonis*: in a subsequent section in dialogue, Ganymede tries to talk his way out of being taken by Jupiter, insisting he'll be too annoying to be worth stealing, and that his constant talking will keep the god awake. Jupiter, undeterred, replies: go ahead, I'll enjoy that.[43]

In Phineas Fletcher's late example, *Venus and Anchises* (1628), Anchises happens upon the bower of Venus, another version of the 'Garden of Venus' motif. Stretched out on her bed of lilies and roses, Venus awakes and mistakes Anchises for Adonis, just as Neptune mistakes (or pretends to mistake) Leander for Ganymede in Marlowe's *Hero and Leander*. Even John Clapham's *Narcissus* (1591), though a supposedly moralizing poem about the dangers of self-love, employs related conventions at the start of the poem. Narcissus has grown up, it seems, in a very similar location, this time on a remote island, ruled over by a virgin Queen (transparently a version of England). The first half of the poem recounts how he visits the Palace of Cupid: this description, though borrowing in part from the (much briefer) description of the Palace of the Sun at the start of Ovid, *Met.* 2, is a version of the epithalamium motif of the palace of love. The two images described in detail in the ecphrasis of Cupid's Palace are of Hero and Leander, and Hercules: characters specifically suggested by Scaliger as appropriate myths for inclusion in epithalamia.

---

[43] Barlaeus, *De raptu Ganymedis liber* (1563), sig. Ciii[v]. Barlaeus' verse dialogues between Jupiter and Ganymede and Juno and Jupiter perhaps influenced the framing scene of Marlowe's *Dido, Queen of Carthage*.

Braden describes the 'overtly erotic' features of the scene in Claudian from which these passages are derived.[44] The sensual pleasure this poetry takes in lingering physical description, whether of the beauty of men and women or of the natural world, contributes to the strong erotic connotation. In poetry of this type, any narrative is secondary to the beauty of the poetry itself, and of the scenes it evokes, although the narratives to which such a style may be attached can be either celebratory or tragic (or with elements of both). It is a poetry of plenitude and also of a kind of imaginative self-sufficiency: 'a turning inward, partly toward psychological allegory, but more generally toward an activity of mimesis that is almost wholly literary ... Claudian's writing at times aspires to an unprecedented self-sufficiency in its depiction of worlds that could exist only in a poem.'[45]

Writing a formal epithalamium for friends in the 1640s, Payne Fisher, later Cromwell's poet, produced a version of just this kind of lush Claudianic verse. The poem marks the marriage of Col. Thomas Tomkins and Lucy Neale, which took place in 1643, though it was apparently not published until 1650.[46] In these passages, bold type has been used to indicate direct borrowings from Claudian:

> Et **Venerem** Vegetiva colunt,[47] **omnisque vicissim**
> **Felix arbor amat**, dum **mutua** brachia pandunt
> Nexibus implicitis, coeunt in chara *Cupressi*
> **Foedera**, **Populeae** succumbit *Populus* umbrae,
> Vitibus & Vites, **Alnoque assibilat Alnus**.[48]

Even the plants revere Venus, and every happy
Tree loves in its turn, as they spread out their branches together
In closely-woven embrace; the Cypresses enter together
The dear pledges [of marriage]; the Poplar succumbs to the Poplar's shade,
Vine to Vine, and Alder whispers to Alder.

---

[44] Braden, 'Claudian and His Influence', 222. [45] Braden, 'Claudian and His Influence', 226.

[46] Published in *Miscellania quaedam*, a volume with its own title page dated 1650, but only extant as the final part of the volume *Marston-Moor*; it was reprinted in Fisher's collected works (*Piscatoris Poemata*, 1656), where it contributes to the impression of an overall 'Claudianic' career. On Fisher, see esp. Chapter 9.

[47] This memorable phrase, literally 'Even vegetable things worship Venus', perhaps suggested the 'vegetable love' of Marvell's 'To His Coy Mistress' (11), thought to date from between the late 1640s and mid 1650s, a period in which Marvell was demonstrably reading Fisher with some attention.

[48] 'Epithalamium in Connubialia Avunculi Charissimi Col. Th. Tomkins, & Nobilissimae Luciae Neali', in *Piscatoris Poemata* (1656), sig. C2ᵛ.

This reworks Claudian's *Epith.* for Honorius and Maria:

> vivunt in **Venerem** frondes **omnisque vicissim**
> **felix arbor amat**; nutant ad **mutua** palmae
> **foedera, populeo** suspirat **populus** ictu
> et platani platanis **alnoque adsibilat alnus**.
> (Claudian, *Epith.*, 65–8)

> *The very leaves live for love and in his season every happy tree experiences love's power: palm bends down to mate with palm, poplar sighs its passion for poplar, plane whispers to plane, alder to alder.*

Fisher's dependence on Claudian is typical of neo-Latin epithalamium: earlier examples include, for instance, Sir Thomas Craig's *Henrici illustrissimi ... epithalamium* (1565), Hadrianus Junius, *Philippeis* (1554) and George Buchanan's epithalamium for Mary Queen of Scots and the future Francis II of France (1558).[49] Many presentation manuscript volumes of epithalamia have also survived.[50]

In Marlowe's *Hero and Leander* (before 1592) the ecphrastic tradition of the grove of Venus is transferred to Hero, a devotee of the goddess, whose robe itself depicts a version of the topos, including images of Venus and Adonis. Cupid, through whose eyes we encounter Venus in her grove in Claudian, here mistakes Hero for Venus herself:

> At Sestos Hero dwelt; Hero the faire,
> Whom young Apollo courted for her haire,
> And offred as a dower his burning throne,
> Where she should sit for men to gaze upon.
> The outside of her garments were of lawne,
> The lining, purple silke, with gilt starres drawne,
> Her wide sleeves greene, and bordered with a grove,
> Where Venus in her naked glory strove,
> To please the carelesse and disdainful eies
> Of proud Adonis that before her lies.
> Her kirtle blew, whereon was many a staine,
> Made with the blood of wretched Lovers slaine.
> Upon her head she ware a myrtle wreath,
> From whence her vaile reacht to the ground beneath.

---

[49] Buchanan's epithalamium was published as the fourth of his *Silvae*. Several of these are discussed briefly in Case, *English Epithalamies*. A brief account of the Claudianic elements of Buchanan's poem can be found in Felgentreu, 'Claudian'. Almost all the Pléiade poets also wrote epithalamia, some of which are discussed in Greene, 'Epithalamic Convention'. See also Wöhrmann, *Englische Epithalamiendichtung*; and Gaertner, *Englische Epithalamienliteratur*.

[50] Examples include BL MSS Royal 12 A XX (1554), 12 A XXVII (1613) and 12 A XXXV (1613), the latter by William Alabaster.

> Her vaile was artificial flowers and leaves,
> Whose workmanship both man and beast deceaves.
> . . .
> Some say, for her the fairest Cupid pyn'd,
> And looking in her face, was strooken blind.
> But this is true, so like was one the other,
> As he imagyn'd Hero was his mother.
> And oftentimes into her bosome flew,
> About her naked necke his bare arms threw,
> And laid his childish head upon her brest,
> And with still panting rockt there took his rest.
>
> (5–20 and 37–44)[51]

Shakespeare apparently had this passage in mind as he composed the end of *Venus and Adonis* (1593), a poem certainly influenced by Marlowe, which systematically ironizes the conventions of the epyllion:

> 'Here was thy father's bed, here in my breast;
> Thou art the next of blood, and 'tis thy right:
> Lo, in this hollow cradle take thy rest,
> My throbbing heart shall rock thee day and night:
> There shall not be one minute in an hour
> Wherein I will not kiss my sweet love's flower.'
>
> (1183–8)[52]

By his death Shakespeare's Venus forces Adonis to fit the erotic narrative which he constantly resisted while alive. Shakespeare's evasive poem consistently undercuts its own erotics, and actively sends up many elements of the tradition, not least by refusing to offer the luscious description of Venus' bower which the reader expects. Instead, the poem begins *in medias res*:

> Even as the sun with purple-colour'd face
> Had ta'en his last leave of the weeping morn,
> Rose-cheek'd Adonis hied him to the chase;
> Hunting he loved, but love he laugh'd to scorn;
> Sick-thoughted Venus makes amain unto him,
> And like a bold-faced suitor 'gins to woo him.
>
> (1–6)

The story of Venus and Adonis is told in the *Metamorphoses*, and alluded to routinely in depictions of Venus, including in Claudian's epithalamia

---

[51] Text from Donno (ed.), *Elizabethan Minor Epics*. For Cupid on Venus' breast, see for instance Statius, *Silvae* 1.2, 103–5.
[52] Text from Burrow (ed.), *Complete Sonnets and Poems*.

and his *Rapt*. Shakespeare's poem has wittily made Venus, conventionally the presiding deity of poems of this kind, into its beleaguered protagonist. The humorous elements of Shakespeare's poem, however, are not without precedent: in Claudian, too, Venus has a distinctive and amusingly self-centred personality.[53]

Spenser's *Faerie Queene* incorporates several versions of the 'garden' topos, and in one, the Garden of Adonis, he points out from his epic poem towards epithalamia and related forms:

> And in the thickest covert of that shade,
> There was a pleasant arbour, not by art,
> But of the trees own inclination made,
> Which knitting their rancke braunches part to part,
> With wanton yvie twine entrayld athwart,
> And Eglantine, and Caprifole emong,
> Fashioned above within their inmost part,
> That nether Phoebus beams could through them throng,
> Nor Aeolus sharp blast could worke them any wrong.
>
> And all about grew every sort of flower,
> To which sad lovers were transformd of yore;
> Fresh Hyacinthus, Phoebus paramoure,
> And dearest love,[54]
> Foolish Narcisse, that likes the watry shore,
> Sad Amaranthus, made a flower but late,
> Sad Amaranthus, in whose purple gore
> Me seemes I see Amintas wretched fate,
> To whom sweet Poets verse hath given endlesse date.
>
> There wont faire Venus often to enjoy
> Her deare Adonis joyous company,
> And reape sweet pleasure of the wanton boy;
> There yet, some say, in secrete he does ly,
> Lappéd in flowres and pretious spicery,
> By her hid from the world, and from the skill
> Of Stygian Gods, which doe her love envy;
> But she her selfe, when ever that she will,
> Possesseth him, and of his sweetnesse takes her fill
>   (3.6.44–6)[55]

---

[53] Coombe, *Claudian the Poet*, 171–6, comments on the elements of humour in the *Epith*. as a whole, including at the expense of Honorius as well as Venus. Tufte notes that Donne's epithalamia are also distinguished by their use of humour (*Poetry of Marriage*, 222).
[54] Compare Milton's similar use of a half-line in a flower catalogue, 'The glowing violet' (*Lycidas* 145).
[55] Text from Maclean and Prescott (eds.), *Edmund Spenser's Poetry*.

Lists of flowers of this kind, and the gathering of flowers, appear regularly in epithalamia.[56] They are strongly associated in Latin poetry with the rape of Proserpina, who was gathering flowers in a dark version of the epithalamium motif when she was snatched. Stephen Hinds has shown how Claudian's version of the scene (*Rapt.* 2.119–36) builds on Ovidian models (*Met.* 5.391–2 and *Fasti* 4.431–42) by adding to the violets, lilies and hyacinth already in Ovid also the narcissus, whose story is told in *Met.* 3.341–511 but who is not included in the list of flowers gathered by Proserpina.[57] Both Hyacinthus and Narcissus are, of course, men pursued sexually by gods, and their fate prefigures that of Proserpina herself. Moreover, in Claudian the scene is foreshadowed a few lines earlier by Venus, who is responsible for suggesting the flower-gathering expedition. Venus picks the flower 'marked with her own woe' (*Rapt.* 2.122–3) – that is, the anemone, into which Adonis was transformed in a scene which forms the end of Shakespeare's *Venus and Adonis*.

Spenser's highly self-conscious version of the scene replicates Claudian's extension to the Ovidian list by further adding Amaranthus ('made a flower but late') and Amintas ('To whom sweet Poets verse hath given endlesse date'). The amaranth appears as a flower in the *Fasti* 4 version of the Proserpina story (4.439), but without any attached myth, as is implied by 'made a flower but late'. Amyntas is the name of a shepherd in Virgil, *Eclogues* 3.66, but again, without a transformation story attached. The names Amaranthus and Amyntas here are usually taken to refer to Sidney, who died in 1586, and Thomas Watson, who died in 1592 and who published verse collections titled *Amyntas* (1585) and *Amintae gaudia* (1592), the latter of which includes a Latin epyllion on the death of Sidney, discussed further below.[58]

Watson is an important and still neglected figure in the development of the style of Latin and subsequently English narrative verse in the 1580s and 1590s. He experimented with various types of Latin verse narrative on erotic themes: the *Amyntas*, a sequence of the shepherd Amyntas' 'laments' for the

---

[56] Venus brings piles of various flowers to Celerina at Claudian, *CM* 25.116–23; Proserpina picks flowers before she is abducted in *Rapt*. There is a particularly extravagant example of a flower catalogue, also including the amaranthus among many others, in the epithalamium composed by Adrian Damman for the marriage of James VI and Anne of Denmark, and published in 1590 (Damman, *Schediasmata*, sig. B1^{r-v}).
[57] Hinds, *Displacing Persephone*, 23–5.
[58] The nymphs bind amaranth flowers with lilies and violets in Janus Dousa's *Daphnis Ecloga*, a poem also commemorating the death of Sidney. The amaranth appears also in Milton's *Lycidas*, where it is usually taken by commentators to recall Spenser, though might be alluding more generally to the laments for Sidney.

death of his beloved Phyllis, ends with Amyntas' own death and metamorphosis and has obvious links to epyllion as well as to pastoral (especially *The Shepherds' Calendar*). *Amyntas* was translated into English hexameters, without attribution, by Abraham Fraunce, as *The Lamentations of Amyntas* (1587), a work which went through multiple editions.

In 1586, Watson published a Latin verse translation of Colluthus' *Raptus Helenae*, which itself probably inspired a contemporary English translation (Richard Barnfield's *Hellens Rape* of 1594).[59] Watson's dedicatory poem to Henry Percy, Earl of Northumberland, introduces the language and mythology of the main poem, describing the Thames as a Naid, daughter of Nereus, and Percy himself as 'Perseus' (a pun on his name) who will go on to find his Andromeda and grow, in old age, to be a happy Nereus himself. Like both Catullus 64 and Claudian's *Epith.*, the *Raptus Helenae* uses the story of the marriage of Peleus and Thetis as a frame for the 'core' of the poem, in which Helen falls in love with Paris and is taken away by him:

> Thessalici celsis in regni montibus olim
> Cúm celebranda forent Phthii connubia regis,
> Pocula conuiuis Superûm pincerna ferebat.
> Illuc Caelicolûm conuênit plena corona,
> Ut pulchrae Thetidos facerent solennia taedis.
> Iupiter e summo caelo, Neptunus ab undis,
> Et rutilus vênit Musis comitatus Apollo,
> Quae dulces cecinere modos Helicone profectae.
> Hunc Iuno germana Iovis, coniuxque, sequuta est;
> Harmoniaeque parens haud lento Cypria passu
> Post illam gemini Chironis tecta subibat.
> Sponsales nectens aderat Suadela corollas,
> Quae teneri pictam pharetram gestabat Amoris;
> Et gravibus galeae cristis exuta Minerva
> Accessit, thalami quamuìs ignara iugalis;
> Nec Phoebi formosa soror Dictynna venire
> Distulit, incultis quantumuìs moribus esset;
> Et Mauors, qualis Vulcani sedibus hospes
> Successit, galeâque carens, longâque bipenni,
> Festiuas iniit, posito thorace, choraeas.
> Improba sola aberat tanto Discordia coetu,
> Nempè suis illam festis voluere deesse
> Peleus & Chiron, pacis studiosus vterque.
>   (17–39, sig. B1^{r-v})

---

[59] For the influence of Greek texts upon the Elizabethan epyllion, see Demetriou, 'Non-Ovidian Elizabethan Epyllion'. Barnfield's *Hellens Rape* is printed in *The Affectionate Shepheard* (1594).

> *Once upon a time, when in the high mountains of the Thessalian kingdom, the marriage of the king of Phthia was due to be celebrated, the cupbearer of the gods was bringing the glasses for the guests. A great circle of the Heaven-dwellers gathered there to complete with their torches the marriage rites for beautiful Thetis. Jupiter came from the highest part of heaven, Neptune from the waves, and shining Apollo came, accompanied by the Muses, who had set out singing sweetly from Helicon. And Juno, Jove's sister and wife, followed him; and Venus, the mother of Harmonia, came quickly after her into the house of the centaur Chiron. Persuasion was there too, weaving nuptial garlands, and it was she who carried gentle Love's painted quiver. Minerva came too, and took off the weighty crests of her helmet, even though she herself knows nothing of the marriage bed. Nor did Phoebus' lovely sister Dictynna delay her arrival, though her manners are unsophisticated. And Mars came too, like a guest in Vulcan's house, without his helmet, or his long spear, and he even took off his breastplate to join the festive dancing. Only wicked Discord was absent from the great assembly, for Peleus and Chiron, both eager to keep the peace, wanted her to keep away from their celebrations.*

Here the divine gathering for the marriage of Peleus and Thetis includes the allegorical personifications of Suadela ('Persuasion') and Discordia ('Discord', banished like the bad fairy in Sleeping Beauty only to cause trouble later). This motif is also traceable to a specifically Claudianic version of the 'Garden' motif, described by Braden as 'rigorous exclusivity': in Claudian's Garden of Venus, old age is shut out, and even the birds have to compete for admission.[60] In an interesting coda, set after Helen has been taken, Hermione, Helen's daughter, longing to know where her mother has gone, and sure that she has met with danger, eventually falls asleep and sees her mother in a dream. Helen tells her what has happened:

> Filia, moesta licet, passam infortunia noli
> Carpere me matrem: tecta quam fraude petîtam
> Iamdudum rapuit secum Priameïus haeros.
>
> (393–5, sig. D1ʳ)
>
> *Daughter, upset as you are, do not rail at me, your mother, who has suffered misfortune: that hero, the son of Priam [Paris], sought me out with treachery concealed in his heart, and now he has snatched me away with him.*

This is a concise version, with roles reversed, of Ceres' hopeless concern for her daughter in *De Raptu Proserpinae*, her sense of doom, and the dream vision in which Proserpina reveals that she has been taken down to the underworld as Pluto's bride. At 414 lines long, Watson's Latin version of

---

[60] Braden, 'Claudian and His Influence', 219–21.

Colluthus contains most of the elements, as well as many of the stylistic features, typical of the mythological epyllia of the 1590s.[61]

Marlowe, Gager and Musaeus

Hero and Leander is derived from a Greek rather than a Latin text, the late Greek poet Musaeus' *Hero and Leander*. Like Barnfield's *Hellen's Rape*, however, Marlowe was probably influenced as much by a contemporary Latin translation as the original Greek: William Gager's Latin version of *Hero and Leander*, though unpublished, dates almost certainly from 1578–80, making it one of the earliest examples of the epyllion in England.[62] Though largely forgotten by literary history, because he wrote only in Latin, Gager (1555–1622) was a prominent literary figure of the 1580s: the author of a strikingly innovative and ambitious series of Latin odes on the Parry plot of 1585 (discussed in Chapter 4), which became one of the first publications of the Oxford University Press, he also edited the important New College anthology on the death of Sidney (*Exequiae*, 1587), and has been described as 'arguably the best Latin playwright [in England] of the Tudor period'.[63] In the British Library manuscript in which it survives, *Hero and Leander* is accompanied by Gager's Latin play on Dido, Queen of Carthage (acted at Christ Church, Oxford in 1583), a second link to Marlowe, whose *Dido, Queen of Carthage* was published in 1594.[64]

---

[61] Barnfield's English poem *Hellens Rape* (1594), at only 75 lines, in English hexameters and an arch tone, is a different kind of poem: his version has stripped out all the mythological material and the marriage setting which precedes the abduction. Tania Demetriou, however, has nevertheless made an interesting case for its links to epyllia ('Non-Ovidian Elizabethan Epyllion'). Barnfield's poem of the following year, *Cassandra* (1595), has attracted comment only as evidence for the rapid imitation of Shakespeare's *Venus and Adonis*, and has oddly been left out of the standard lists of 1590s epyllia (the only exception of which I am aware is Campbell, *Divine Poetry*, 122). Nevertheless, this strange and tonally ambiguous poem is in most respects a typical epyllion, in which a well-known story of the doomed prophetess is told not in terms of her prophecy, or of her presence at the fall of Troy – which features memorably in Virgil – but only in relation to sex and marriage: her resistance to marriage, Apollo's thwarted attempt at seduction, and her eventual fate as a concubine of Agamemnon. The description of Cassandra herself, with which the poem begins and to which it constantly recurs, is, like that of Adonis in Shakespeare's poem, relentlessly eroticized.

[62] On the question of dating, see Sutton's introductory remarks to his online edition of the Latin text (www.philological.bham.ac.uk/gager/poetry/hero/intro.html).

[63] Sutton, preface to edition online, which also gathers some of the evidence of contemporary admiration (http://www.philological.bham.ac.uk/gager/pref.html).

[64] BL MS Add. 22583. The manuscript also contains Gager's Latin translation of the *Batrachomuomachia*, the biblical epyllion *Susanna* (a similar basic story to that of Chapman's *Ovids Banquet of Sence*), a Latin verse translation of the precepts of Isocrates, and a large quantity of occasional Latin verse. For editions, see Sutton (ed.), *William Gager: The Complete Works* and online (www.philological.bham.ac.uk/gager/poetry); and Tucker Brooke, 'William Gager to Queen Elizabeth'. Unlike in the *Aeneid*, Anna kills herself at the end of both Gager's and Marlowe's plays.

In Musaeus, Gager and Marlowe alike, Hero, as the devotee of Venus, stands in for Venus herself, and the description of her beauty is 'interchangeable' with that of the goddess: in Musaeus' original, as in Gager's (somewhat expanded) Latin version, she is twice described as appearing to be a 'second' or 'new' Venus.[65] Marlowe develops a much more sustained and self-conscious conceit in which Hero both takes the place of, depicts (on her clothing) and is mistaken for the goddess, even by her son, Cupid (as quoted above). In both cases, the collapse of the beloved female protagonist with Venus herself recalls the conventions of narrative epithalamia, in which Venus' beauty and careful preparation for the ceremony commonly function as a doubling device for that of the bride herself.[66]

Dating from slightly before Marlowe's *Hero and Leander*, Scipio (or Scipione) Gentili's *Nereus* was written to commemorate the birth of Philip Sidney's daughter Elizabeth in 1585, though it is largely taken up by a prophecy of Elizabeth's own eventual marriage and birth of a son. Though nominally a genethliacon (a poem celebrating a birth), it displays many of the shared stylistic features of the epyllion-epithalamium.[67] The poem begins in the grotto not this time of Venus, but of Father Thames, who wears an embroidered cape similar to Hero's garment in Marlowe's poem:

> Ergo hilaris, certusque suo se reddidit antro
> Spumeus. Hîc illi chlamydem noctes diesque
> Vrgebant hyalo nymphae, muscoque virenti:
> Grandiaque intextis ornabant fila smaragdis.
> Inter quas curâ melior Nesaeis, & arte,
> Conatur varias per lusum inspergere formas.
> Et iam cognatos Troiae depinxerat amnes:
> Iam Simois, Xanthusque fluunt: nemorosaque sacro
> Iminet Ida iugo: et fulvâ puer alite raptus
> Aetherias cursu nubes tranare videtur.
> Suspiciunt pauidi comites, atque inscia pubes
> Venantum: effusi manibus labuntur & arcus
> Et calami, coelumque canes latratibus implent.
> Omnia quae Tamesis tolli iubet, atque ita fatur.
>
> (16–29)[68]

---

[65] Gager, 48 and 88; Musaeus, 33 and 68.
[66] On this motif in Claudian, see Coombe, *Claudian the Poet*, 171–7; as a feature inherited from Statius and subsequently standard in epithalamia, see Roberts, 'Use of Myth', esp. 324.
[67] Text, translation and some biographical information on Gentili in Pallant, 'Printed Poems of Scipione Gentili', 17–34 and 143–50. Elizabeth Sidney went on to become Countess of Rutland, addressee of several poems by Jonson and Donne.
[68] Gentili, *Nereus* (1585), sig. B1^{r-v}.

> *So joyful and reassured* [the signs of celebration indicating an imminent birth], [Father Thames] *foamily returned himself to his cave. Here for days and nights the nymphs had industriously been working on a mantle of glass and greeny moss for him, decorating its great fabric with embroidered emeralds, among which Nesaeis, both more careful and more artistic than the rest, playfully sought to sprinkle varied images. Now she painted the twinned streams of Troy: now flows Simois and Xanthus, now Ida with her groves towers with its holy peak, and the boy snatched away on dusky wing* [Ganymede] *seems to swim on his course through the heavenly clouds. His fearful companions look up, and the rest of the oblivious crowd of young men out hunting: their bows and arrows, dropped, slide from their hands, and the dogs fill the sky with their yaps. All this Thames ordered to be removed, and spoke thus ...*

The embroidered garments such as this cape, and Hero's mantle depicting Venus and Adonis, echo the woven coverlet at the marriage of Peleus and Thetis in Catullus 64 (which depicts the story of Ariadne), but also the cloth Proserpina is weaving for her mother in *Rapt.* 1.246–70 (depicting the whole world) and the dress she is wearing before her abduction in *Rapt.* 2.41–54 (depicting the birth of the infant sun and moon, children of Tethys and Hyperion). *Hero and Leander*, like many of these poems, includes multiple ecphrases: the images on the walls of the temple of Venus are also described at length and it is often hard to keep track of where ecphrasis ends and narrative resumes. In Latin, such insistent ecphrasis is the signature of Claudian's style above all, described by Braden as 'a distinguishing and for us almost unintelligible feature'.[69]

Gentili's lovely poem has several original elements. Although it is standard for an epithalamium to hope children of the marriage, this poem celebrates a birth and uses that as an opportunity to look towards the child's future marriage. Again, however, there are points of contact with Claudian in this blending of present and future: Honorius and Maria were very young at the time of their marriage in 398, Honorius only 13 and Maria possibly only 12.[70] Claudian's choice of the marriage of Peleus and Thetis as the frame for the poem both alludes to Catullus 64 and places a particular emphasis upon the likely offspring of the marriage – since the son of Peleus and Thetis, Achilles, was of course much more famous than either of his parents. The structure of the poem suggests that Honorius and Maria will have a great warrior as a son, though it also, somewhat

---

[69] Braden, 'Claudian and His Influence', 215.   [70] See Coombe, *Claudian the Poet*, 157–8.

ambiguously, depicts Achilles as a lover (on Skyros), an aspect of his myth which is clearly meant to reflect Honorius' courtship of Maria.[71]

The typically English genre of the Elizabethan mythological epyllion, then, emerges as a bilingual, not a monolingual, phenomenon: Marlowe's *Hero and Leander* tells a story which is not found in Ovid and which, like Barnfield's *Hellens Rape*, is traceable to Greek texts which were available in the 1580s in good Latin verse translations by two of the most important, accomplished and influential Latin poets of that decade, Thomas Watson and William Gager. In addition to those translations, a penumbra of poems closely resembling the Elizabethan epyllia, but written in Latin, includes Barlaeus' *De raptu Ganymedis* (1563), Gentili's *Nereus* (1585) and Campion's *Umbra* (1595), as well as a relatively large number of Latin epithalamia in a very similar style. All of these works, in both Latin and English, look towards Claudian in particular for their lavish descriptive mode, and the erotics of ecphrasis.

The story of Thomas Lodge's *Scillaes Metamorphosis* (1589), generally considered the first English example of the form, can be traced to Ovid, who tells how Circe, jealous of Glaucus' love for Scilla, transformed her into a monster (*Met*. 13.898–14.74). Venus and Cupid play a prominent role in Lodge's poem, with the arrival of the Queen of Love a lavish centrepiece (quoted at the start of this chapter). *Scillaes Metamorphosis* also includes allegorical figures of the kind we saw in Claudian, Jonson and Watson:

> Furie and Rage, Wan-hope, Dispaire, and Woe
> From Ditis den by Ate sent, drewe nie:
> Furie was red, with rage his eyes did gloe,
> Whole flakes of fire from foorth his mouth did flie,
> His hands and armes ibath'd in blood of those
> Whome fortune, sinne, or fate made Countries foes.
>
> Rage, wan and pale upon a Tiger sat,
> Knawing upon the bones of mangled men;
> Naught can he view, but he repinde thereat:
> His lockes were Snakes bred foorth in Stigian den,
> Next whom, Dispaire that deepe disdained elf
> Delightlesse livde, still stabbing of her self.
>
> Woe all in blacke, within her hands did beare
> The fatall torches of a Funerall,

---

[71] On the possible political implications of the allusions to the *Achilleid*, see Coombe, *Claudian the Poet*, 159–71.

> Her Cheekes were wet, dispearsed was hir heare,
> Her voice was shrill (yet loathsome therewith all):
> Wan-hope (poore soule) on broken Ancker sitts,
> Wringing his armes as robbed of his witts.
>
> (stanzas 120–2)[72]

Douglas Bush comments on the 'remarkable ... combination of an Ovidian metamorphosis with figures from medieval allegory' in this passage.[73] Such a combination is indeed neither Augustan nor Ovidian, but the presence of these 'medieval' allegorical figures in an erotic context is, as we have seen, typical of Claudianic epithalamia. Similarly, the choice of Glaucus as protagonist is indebted, I argue, not primarily to Ovid, but to a Claudianic (and ultimately epithalamic) tradition in which he appears repeatedly in association with sea-nymphs in the retinue of Triton, Neptune or Venus.

The retinue of nymphs in Claudian derives from models in Virgil and Homer, especially *Iliad* 18.39–49, listing the nymphs who comfort Thetis, the mother of Achilles.[74] Virgil has a concise version of the motif at *Aen.* 5.823–6:

> et senior Glauci chorus Inousque Palaemon
> Tritonesque citi Phorcique exercitus omnis;
> laeva tenet Thetis et Melite Panopeaque virgo,
> Nisaee Spioque Thaliaque Cymodoceque.[75]
>
> *Glaucus' ancient company, and Ino's son, Palaemon;*
> *the nimble Tritons, and all of Phorcus' troop;*
> *Thetis, Melite, and virgin Panopea were on the left,*
> *Along with Nesaea, Spio, Thalia and Cymodoce.*

Glaucus and Nereus appear at Claudian, *Rapt.* 3.11–12, accompanied by sea-nymphs, but the most extensive such catalogue in Claudian is at *Epith.* 155–71:

> Cadmeia ludit
> Leucothoë, frenatque rosis delphina Palaemon;
> alternas violis Nereus interserit algas;
> canitiem Glaucus ligat immortalibus herbis.
> nec non et variis vectae Nereides ibant
> audito rumore feris (hanc pisce voluto

---

[72] Text from Donno (ed.), *Elizabethan Minor Epics*.
[73] Bush, *Mythology and the Renaissance Tradition*, 87.
[74] Homer's list is repeated by Boccaccio in his note on nymphs in *Genealogia deorum Gentilium* VII.14.
[75] See also *Georgics* 4.334–41, a very similar list.

> sublevat Oceani monstrum Tartesia tigris;
> hanc timor Aegaei rupturus fronte carinas
> trux aries; haec caeruleae suspensa leaenae
> innatat; haec viridem trahitur complexa iuvencum)
> certatimque novis onerant conubia donis.
> cingula Cymothoë, rarum Galatea monile
> et gravibus Psamathe bacis diadema ferebat
> intextum, Rubro quas legerat ipsa profundo.
> mergit se subito vellitque corallia Doto:
> vimen erat dum stagna subit; processerat undis:
> gemma fuit.

> *Leucothoë, daughter of Cadmus, is playing there, and Palaemon drives his dolphin with reins of roses. Nereus sets violets here and there among the seaweed and Glaucus wreathes his grey hair with deathless flowers. Hearing what is happening, the Nereids, too, came mounted on various beasts: one (maiden above, but fish below) rides the dread sea-tiger of Tartessus; another is carried by that fierce ram, the terror of the Aegean, who shatters ships with his forehead; a third bestrides the neck of a sea-lion; another is borne along by the sea-calf to which she clings. They vie with one another in bringing gifts to the newly wedded pair. Cymothoë presents a girdle, Galatea a precious necklace, Psamathe a diadem heavily encrusted with pearls gathered by herself from the depths of the Red Sea. Doto suddenly dives to gather coral, a plant so long as it is beneath the waves – but once brought forth, a jewel.*

Nereus is the subject both of Gentili's poem and also of Watson's dedication of the *Raptus Helenae*, which describes Percy as Nereus. Glaucus is the male protagonist of Lodge's *Scillaes Metamorphosis*. Here they appear together (157–8), while the nereids compete to bring presents (165), and Doto dives to gather fresh coral (169). Coral is offered as a gift by Glaucus to Scilla in Lodge's poem ('When midst the Caspian seas the wanton plaid, / I drew whole wreaths of corrall from the rockes: / And in her lap my heavenly presents laid', stanza 57). We find the same motif, alongside a catalogue of naiads, in Gentili:

> Ilicet omnes
> Sedibus exiluêre suis, Nereia Drymo,
> Et Metis & roseis Ciane spectanda lacertis
> Clióque, Clothóque, Pherusáque, Cymothoéque
> Candida populeis euinctae tempora sertis;
> Crisaee, Spioque, Ligeaque, Lamprothoeque,
> Asiáque, & Melite: quâ non est altera Nais
> Doctior herbosam iaculo contingere metam.
> Atque Ione, atque Halis, atque Idya Neptunine.

> Omnes caeruleae, Succinctae pellibus omnes,
> Omnes Assyrio perfusae membra liquore.
> Vnum omnes fecêre chorum, passisque feruntur
> Crinibus, & molles agitant per caerula lusus,
> Non tacitae: namque illae acrem super aurea Sydnen
> Astra ferunt, Sydnen ripae, collesque resultant.
> ...
>   pars gemmiferas non inscia conchas
> In mediis explorat aquis. pars gramina ponti,
> Aut imo euellit ramosa coralia saxo.
> Haec etiam scopulis muscum legit: illa virentes
> Querit, auens oculis, in parua monilia baccas.
>   (*Nereus*, 34–48 and 54–8, sig. B1^v-B2^r)

At once they all sprang from their seats, Dryo daughter of Nereus, and Metis, and Ciane, lovely with her rosy arms, and Clio, Clotho, Pherusa, and Cymothoe, their bright temples bound with garlands of poplar; Chrysaee, Spio, Ligea, and Lamprothoe, Asia and Melite (than whom there is no Naid more skilled at hitting the grass target with a dart). And Ione, Halis, and Neptune's daughter Idya. All dark blue, all clothed in skins, all with limbs soaked in Syrian perfume, they made a single chorus. They went along with their hair loosened, and played their gentle games across the dark waters; not in silence – for they bore their sharp cry of 'Sidney' above the golden stars, and the riverbanks and hills reechoed 'Sidney.'... A few of them, with the benefit of experience, go out into the mid-waters to look for gem-bearing shells. Others pull seaweed and branching coral from stones deep underwater. This one collects moss from the rocks, that one, searches eagerly with her eyes for fresh pearls to make little necklaces.

Spenser's *Prothalamion* – as we have seen, a rare English example from the 1590s of the 'narrative' type of epithalamium – includes the same scene:

> There, in a Meadow, by the Rivers side
> A Flocke of Nymphes I chauncéd to espy,
> All lovely Daughters of the Flood thereby,
> With goodly greenish locks all loose untyde,
> As each had bene a Bryde,
> And each one had a little wicker basket,
> Made of fine twigs entrayléd curiously,
> In which they gathered flowers to fill their flasket:
> And with fine Fingers, cropt full feateously
> The tender stalkes on hye.
> Of every sort, which in that Meadow grew,
> They gathered some; the Violet pallid blew,
> The little Dazie, that at evening closes,

> The virgin Lillie, and the Primrose trew,
> With store of vermeil Roses,
> To decke their Bridegromes posies,
> Against the Brydale day, which was not long:
>   Sweete Themmes runne softly, till I end my Song.
>   (19–36)

Hadrianus Junius' 1554 epithalamium for Mary I and Philip includes a highly Claudianic chorus of sea gods, in which Triton, Glaucus and Nereus appear together.[76] This association of the Nereids with epithalamium is evident also in manuscript verse: many similar features are found in Giles Fletcher the Elder's Latin epithalamium for the marriage of Anne Cecil and the Earl of Oxford in December 1571, and John Eston's (c.1625–90) Latin epithalamia of the 1640s include one titled 'Musae Pierides alloquuntur Nereidas Nymphas'.[77]

The strong generic link, if not identity, between formal epithalamia and Elizabethan epyllia has been concealed in part because of the lack of Anglo-Latin epithalamia in the late 1580s and 1590s: this absence is very marked also in the manuscript record compared to adjacent periods and is presumably a political phenomenon.[78] The aging queen, her succession unclear, made the composition of formal epithalamia even for non-royal addressees effectively impossible in England during the 1590s: Spenser's marriage poems of that decade are the obvious exception to this rule (though his *Epithalamion* was written for his own marriage in Ireland) and outside England the form continued to be produced routinely.[79]

Unable to compose formal epithalamia, English poets in the 1590s redeployed the highly fashionable Claudianic style of epithalamia in mythological epyllia. A particularly versatile example is found in Thomas Watson's *Amintae gaudia* (1592). Though a book of 'eclogues', most of

---

[76] Junius, *Philippeis* 311–30, sig. Biii^v–Biiii^r. This impressive poem also calls Aeolus 'Hippotades', as Milton does in a similar passage listing water nymphs and deities (*Lycidas* 96). The Claudianic features of Junius' poem are discussed briefly by Felgentreu, 'Claudian'.

[77] Preserved in Samuel Bellingham's collection, BL MS Sloane 608, fol. 201^r. There is good manuscript evidence that formal Latin epithalamia continued to be written to mark the marriages of friends and acquaintances throughout the seventeenth century.

[78] The *NLPEM* data at the time of writing strikingly includes no Latin epithalamia at all datable to the latter third of the sixteenth century, though 28 to the mid-sixteenth century, 17 to the early seventeenth century and 30 to the mid-seventeenth century. The resulting bar chart is unique among the generic analyses of the data, and suggests a tacit prohibition. Manuscript epithalamia are generally precisely datable (by reference to the wedding in question) and are relatively unlikely to circulate extensively long after the time of the marriage.

[79] Printed examples include Latin epithalamia on the 1589 marriage of James VI of Scotland to Anne of Denmark by Hercules Rollock, Adrianus Damman and A. Robertson.

the collection is not pastoral, and the fourth poem is a clear example of epyllion, though here applied inventively to the death of Sidney. In Watson's conceit, Amyntas recounts a dream in which Venus, anticipating the arrival of Sidney in heaven, wants to look her best, so heads to the ocean in search of appropriate cosmetics: a creative, if perhaps slightly tasteless version of the 'primping Venus', gift-gathering nymphs and marine motifs all found repeatedly in epithalamia and with roots in Claudian:

> Iamque domum redeunt primo sub uespere natae
> Doridis, & ueneri collectas undiquè gazas
> Contribuunt humiles:
> ...
> Prima Thoe, Cypri quem nuper legit in oris,
> Qualibet aërios referentem parte colores,
> Et Lemni tantum rotulis Adamanta secandum,
> Inclinata caput curuato poplite tradit.
> Hinc uiridem supplex offert Amathea smaragdum
> Littore quaesitum Libyco:
> ...
> Tumque aderant Glauceque Thaleiaque Cymodoceque,
> Donaque praebebant dudum explorata per altas
> Cycladas, Aegaei quas uerberat unda fluenti:
> ...
> Deniquè connexas in parua monilia baccas
> Dat Galataea Deae ...
>   (256–8, 266–71, 274–6 and 290–1, sig. I2ᵛ–I3ᵛ)

And now Doris' daughters came home in the twilight, and meekly presented Venus with the treasures they had gathered ... First Thoe bowed her head, bent her knee, and presented the stone she had just now picked from Cyprus' shores, reflecting the sky's color in its every facet, only to be cut by wheels made of Lemnos' adamant. Next Amalthea humbly offered a green emerald found on a Libyan beach ... Then appeared Glauce, Thalia, and Cymodoce, and gave her presents which they had long ago discovered in the high Cyclades, washed by Aegean currents ... And lastly Galataea gave the goddess pearls strung on a small necklace.

In this passage, the phrase 'in parua monilia baccas' (290) is apparently borrowed directly from Gentili's *Nereus* (58, quoted above). Although he does not comment on this specific borrowing, Dana Sutton in his edition notes the general similarity between the two poems, and suggests that Watson's fourth eclogue is a direct response to Gentili.[80] Similarly, in his

---

[80] www.philological.bham.ac.uk/watson/gaudia/intro.html.

edition of *Nereus*, Sutton wonders why the poem places such an emphasis upon marine imagery, suggesting that this perhaps alludes to Sidney's enthusiasm for marine exploration.[81] In fact, as we have seen, this imagery is a standard feature of formal epithalamium, noticeable also in the examples by Junius in the 1550s, Fletcher in the 1570s and Damman in the 1590s, as well as in Claudian from which this feature derives.

Epyllia and epithalamia share a distinctive erotics, in which sexual intercourse is continuously suggested, but deferred – as in Shakespeare, where Venus tells the story of her runaway horse to a trapped and wriggling Adonis, forced to listen. In Strada's 'Nightingale', a popular seventeenth-century mnemonic for Claudianic style quoted in Chapter 9, the same erotics of enforced ravishment are metaphorically transferred to the relationship between songbird and poet; and, implicitly, to that between the poet and the reader, subjected to the overwhelming aesthetic experience of this kind of verse.

Secondary Uses of the Conventions of Epyllia-Epithalamia

Chapman's *Ovids Banquet of Sence* (1595) has sometimes been described as an 'anti-epyllion', because of its employment of the stylistic features of the epyllion in the service of an essentially didactic project.[82] It is a marker of the familiarity of the literary conventions of the Latin epyllion – and perhaps also its particular association with the poetic tastes of young men – that Chapman's experiment is not unique. We find several examples in the 1590s of the genre being used in a 'secondary' way, for primarily didactic purposes. John Dickenson's poem, *Deorum Consessus* (1591), is oddly listed by several key reference works as an example of neo-Latin epyllion.[83] It is true that the opening pages of the poem are designed to give this impression:

> Nox erat, & moestus neglecto munere Phoebus
> Perpetuas misero tenebras indixerat orbi:
> ...
> Nereides madidae tepidis latuêre sub undis
> Caeruleusque senex redeuntia sidera cernens
> Flumine tam serò miratur mersa profundo.
> ...

---

[81] www.philological.bham.ac.uk/nereus/intro.html.
[82] Weaver, 'George Chapman's Anti-Epyllion'.
[83] IJsewijn and Sacré, *Companion to Neo-Latin Studies, Part II*, 31; and Korenjak, 'Short Mythological Epic', 529.

> Iupiter in thalamo curis & amore solutus
> Immotus iacuit: quem iuxta regia coniux
> Indulsit somno: liquefecit in igne metalla
> Vulcanus: Martemque ferum formosa Dione
> Sustinuit gremio: coelum terrasque tenebat
> Alta quies: auxit concentus gaudia suauis:
> Namque per ardentes caelestia corpora sphaeras
> Fecerunt gyros, currentia passibus aequis.
> (1–2, 10–12, 17–24, sig. A3ʳ)
>
> *It was night, and Phoebus, the gift of his light cast aside in his sorrow*
> *Had cursed the wretched world with endless darkness:*
> ...
>
> *The damp Nereids had hidden beneath the warm waves*
> *And the old blue-green man [Proteus], watching the returning stars*
> *Was surprised to see them sunk still so late in the deep river.*
> ...
>
> *Jupiter lay motionless in his bedchamber*
> *Lost to pain and love: next to him his royal wife*
> *Relaxed in sleep: Vulcan liquified metal in fire;*
> *Beautiful Dione cradled ferocious Mars*
> *In her lap: deep peace held the heaven and the earth*
> *And a sweet harmony added to their joys:*
> *For the celestial bodies drew circles*
> *Through the blazing spheres, running in steady pace.*

The first section even includes a lingering ecphrasis of the beauties of the divine palace. Despite this alluring overture, however, the poem is in fact a treatise on logic and rhetoric, in which the grammarian Lily and rhetorician Ramus eventually put in an appearance. Dickenson exploits the enticing poetics of the epyllion to 'seduce' his readers into a work of polemical didactic. He was probably aware of the allegorical and didactic model for this use of epithalamium provided by Martianus Capellanus, whose *Nuptiis Philologiae et Mercurii* is mentioned by Scaliger and also cited repeatedly by Jonson in his notes on *Hymenaei* (1606).

Similarly, though with a much more sophisticated and successful execution, the connection between epyllia, epithalamia and sex is literalized to didactic effect by David Kinloch (c.1559–1617), a Franco-Scottish poet and doctor, probably only recently released from imprisonment by the Inquisition.[84] Kinloch's extraordinary *De hominis procreatione, anatome, ac*

---

[84] See Yagüi-Beltrán and Adam, 'Imprisonment of David Kinloch'. Kinloch's poem includes a vivid description of incarceration, including as a simile describing the baby at the end of pregnancy,

morbis internis ('On human procreation, anatomy and internal diseases', 1596) combines Lucretian elements with many of the standard features of epithalamium to introduce an eye-wateringly explicit, and unforgettable, explication of the processes of and obstacles to human reproduction.[85]

Kinloch's poem makes particularly creative use of the 'Grove of Venus' motif. After an initial panegyric dedication to King James VI, Kinloch introduces his theme, relating how the primeval chaos was ordered by God in a summary of the creation narrative from Genesis (a fashionable theme for poetry at this date, given the enormous popularity of Du Bartas' *Sepmaines*). At this point he breaks off and begins what is immediately recognizable as a version of the 'Garden of Venus' scene:

> Hic in secessu longo convallis, & antrum
> Vndique succinctum densae velamine sylvae
> Occulitur, circumque virent placidissima Tempe:
> Tempe colliculis leviter surrecta gemellis.
> Argenti puri è sulcis plantaria surgunt
> Aurea, quae tenues ramos, & mollia crispant
> Brachia, bombycis nusquam cedentia telis.
> Purpureo emergunt amaranthi vellere dulces
> Fragrantes violae, praemollis amaracus, iris
> Purpureas depicta genas, & labra, hyacinthus
> Caeruleo quoque flore micans, atque aemula lactis
> Lilia, pulegium, nardus, libanotis, amomum,
> Cinnama, malabathrum, costus, thus, cassia, myrthus,
> Balsama, lignum aloes, moschus, triasantala, myrrha:
> Caeteraque, Assyrios latè spirantia odores,
> Sponte sua nascuntur, & omni tempore florent.
>
> (*DPS*, 8)
>
> *Here in the long fold of a valley, there is a cave hemmed in on each side by a veil of dense woodland, and around it flourishes wonderfully peaceful countryside like that of Tempe: a valley, undulating gently with two small hills. Golden nurseries rise from furrows of purest silver, curling*

---

longing to be born. Set specifically in Spain, the passage probably recalls Kinloch's own experience (Johnston, *Delitiae Poetarum Scotorum*, 28, see note 84).

[85] Though it has been described as a single poem in two books, several topics are treated in both, suggesting that they were originally conceived as separate works. The poem was reprinted in Johnston's *Delitiae Poetarum Scotorum* (*DPS*) (1637), II.3–66, though without the marginal annotations of the 1596 edition. Quotations and parenthetical page references are to the *DPS*, as images of this edition can be found online. I am not aware of any commentary upon this poem, aside from a single page in Bradner, *Musae Anglicanae*, 126–7. It is also discussed briefly in Moul, 'Didactic Poetry'. BL MS Sloane 499, apparently mid-seventeenth-century, contains two manuscript extracts from Kinloch's poem, indicating at least some near-contemporary readership, and it is also mentioned in Bartholin, *De medicis poetis* (1669), 139–40.

> with slender boughs and gentle arms, never attacked by the barbs of bees. From an enveloping fleece of purple amaranthus emerge sweet-smelling violets, intensely soft marjoram, the iris showing her purple-stained cheeks and lips, also the hyacinth glittering with its heavenly flower, the lily which resembles milk, pennyroyal, nard, rosemary, *amomum* [an aromatic shrub, cf. Virg., Ecl. 4.25], *cinnamon, malobathron* [an aromatic Indian plant], *costum* [an Oriental aromatic plant, mentioned in Hor., Odes 3.1.44], *frankincense, wild cinnamon, myrtle, balsam, the aloe tree, moschus* [unidentified, though perhaps chosen to recall Moschus, the Hellenistic Greek poet], *triasantala* [unidentified], *myrrh; and all the rest, breathing their Assyrian scents far and wide, each arising quite naturally, and continuously in flower.*

The extensive list of sweet-smelling plants here is similar to the opening of Adrian Damman's 1590 epithalamium for James VI which Kinloch, a Scot, may well have read.[86] Like all such examples, from Claudian onwards, Kinloch's grove of Venus is densely protected, thick with flowers, and geographically remote – in this case on a distant island, in a kind of perpetual spring. Venus' temple, we are told, displays the 'superba trophaea' ('proud trophies') of Mars, who had attempted to desecrate the temple, but was bound and forced to hand over all his 'spectacula' ('wonders'). As in *Hero and Leander*, the temple itself is adorned with images (9).

Here in the Garden of Love the poet sings a lavish hymn to Hymen (11–12), the god of marriage. Hymen appears as a character both in the shorter of Claudian's two epithalamia, *CM* 25, and in Chapman's completion of Marlowe's *Hero and Leander* (Sestiad 5, 251–60, the marriage of Hymen and Eucharis); as we saw above, Scaliger considered direct address to Hymen to be appropriate to formal epithalamia. Even Jupiter visits the shrine to pray for help, and the imagery returns repeatedly to the young men who attempt, but fail, to enter illicitly – a version of the Claudianic 'exclusivity' noted by Braden, played to insistently erotic effect. Any reader skimming the poem in search of risqué material finds their eye constantly caught by various forms of the verb 'penetrare'. Finally, the personified book itself makes erotic overtures in an attempt to win over Venus (12), and at this point the real didactic content – the 'interior' of the poem – begins.

The rest of the first book is concerned with the mechanics of human reproduction, describing all the obstacles that may impede conception,

---

[86] Damman, *Schediasmata* (1590), sig. B1 r–v.

including both male and female causes of infertility, and then the possible problems encountered during pregnancy and birth. Kinloch uses a range of Latin literary associations to make his content memorable: the narrow hard neck of the womb, for instance, is compared to hard earth which must be worked over gradually – that is, by frequent intercourse – in order to become fertile (13), while failures of conception are explained in relation to seeds which, planted in unsuitable soil, fail to grow (15). These passages recall the language of Virgil's *Georgics* on agricultural *labor*, while a subsequent section exploits the associations in the *Georgics* between horses and sexual passion. Kinloch, reminding the reader of the strange 'hippomanes' (a magical fluid supposedly produced by fertile mares, and mentioned at *Georgics* 3.282), remarks that women too produce fluid ('lac genital') when sexually aroused ('laxisque effundit habenis'; literally 'and it pours fourth when the reins are held slack'), and that this fluid is crucial to conception (13). In such imagery the woman is both field, furrow and female horse, while the phrase 'laxis ... habenis' is borrowed from Virgil's description of the young growing vine (*G.* 2.364). Elsewhere the woman's body is the enclosed garden itself.

This poem which begins with a hymn to Hymen, the god of love, is apparently sceptical about the existence of the anatomical hymen. In both books, Kinloch comments in an autobiographical aside that, though all the authorities describe the membrane named after the god of marriage, in his own experience of dissection he has never seen it.[87] The tone of this intervention is hard to assess, but probably comprises a genuine concern with scientific precision; a routine kind of misogynistic joke (suggesting that many girls who say they are virgin are not); and perhaps also a sidelong puncturing of his own opening myth. There are links here to the well-known tension between Lucretius' opening hymn to Venus and his attitude to the gods in the body of the poem.

Kinloch repeatedly exploits the conventional imagery of epithalamia and epyllia to make his content memorable. In poems of this type, sex is linked strongly with the sea – Venus is born from the sea-foam; Leander is memorably fondled by Neptune in Marlowe's *Hero and Leander*; Neptune must be distracted from pursuing a nymph in order to convey Venus in Claudian's *Epith.* 136–9; Buchanan's 1558 epithalamium for the marriage of Mary Queen of Scots and the Dauphin François, son of Henry II of France, compares sexual intercourse explicitly to the action of the

---

[87] *DPS*, 13 and 64. He describes also the anatomy of the clitoris and of the male foreskin.

ocean.[88] In one passage, Kinloch links an invocation of Venus, born of the sea-foam, to a very explicit description, a page later, of how semen thickens and changes colour after ejaculation:

> Alma Venus, levibus scopulis quam concita quondam
> Spuma maris niveo pollens candore, poëtis
> Progenuit: mihi spuma maris, spumansque maritae
> Seminium coiisse, tuis pulchramque puellam
> Auspiciis potuis peperisse Hymenaee videntur.
> ...
>   vagis anfractibus albos
> Cunctando in vultus se convertere: liquentem
> Crassities sensim mutavit spumea succum:
> ...
>   Quocirca albescit, quodcunque est aptum Hymenaeo
> Seminium, turgensque, suis sine pondere cellis
> Erumpit: nusquam rivi subtile liquentis
> More fluit, sed concoctum, crassumque rotundae
> Grandinis effigie, guttatim prosilit.[89]

Loving Venus, whom sea-foam powerful in its gleaming whiteness
Once produced from the light rocks, so was she brought
To birth by poets: to me the foam of the sea, and the foaming seed
Of a married woman seem to come together, and by your potent blessing,
   Hymen, apparently,
A beautiful girl can be born.
...
   As it [the semen] *lingers in the winding by-ways*
It changes its appearance and becomes white: bit by bit
A foamy thickness has transformed the running liquid:
...
For this reason it turns white, and as is required by Hymen for procreation
Thickens, and without weight bursts out of its chambers: nowhere
Does it flow like running water, but sticky, thick, like rounded
Hailstones, it bursts out drop by drop.

Kinloch's poem is a remarkable achievement, which deserves serious attention in its own right. For a reader interested more generally in the poetry of the period, however, his witty didactic use of the conventions of erotic mythological verse demonstrates how widely they were understood

---

[88] Buchanan, *Elegiarum, Sylvarum, Endecasyllabon* (1567), sig. Dvi[r]. Tufte describes Buchanan's poem as 'one of the best Latin epithalamia after Claudian' (*Poetry of Marriage*, 92–3), though Buchanan's Latin style, a product of the mid-sixteenth century, is plainer (in fact, more like Ovid and less like Claudian) than most of the poems discussed in this chapter.

[89] *DPS*, 11–13.

by the mid-1590s, and how closely this style was connected to matters of sex and marriage.

Conclusion

The Elizabethan epyllion was a form which developed in both Latin and English, with the Latin phenomenon in general slightly preceding the earliest English examples. Though undoubtedly containing Ovidian elements, it is not primarily Ovidian in form, tone or style. Tonally and stylistically, the lush extravagance of these poems and their association with the erotics of poetry as much as of actual sex derive from the late antique style of Claudian, especially the Claudian of the epithalamia and the *Rapt.*, and the reception history and understanding of that style in the period. Formally, they are indebted also to Catullus 64 (itself a blend of epithalamium and mythological short-epic) and to the Hellenistic literary tradition of Moschus, Musaeus and Colluthus.

Indeed, epyllia and epithalamia are so closely related as to belong together in any survey of sixteenth-century poetry: a fact which has been obscured largely because of the relative lack of formal epithalamia in late Elizabethan England, and because the many Latin examples from both before and after this period have not been connected to the stylistics of the Latin and English epyllia. Poets turned with particular enthusiasm to mythological epyllia in the 1590s in response to the tacit shutting down of formal epithalamia in England at this period. With the Queen so old, well past child-bearing age, and her succession uncertain, the mythological erotic epyllion emerged as an (at least somewhat) legitimate vehicle for the particular pleasures of erotic ecphrasis.

CHAPTER 11

Palingenian Epic
Allegory, Ambition and Didacticism

The primary epic model of *Paradise Lost* is widely acknowledged to be Virgil's *Aeneid*, though with elements derived from other classical epics as well as more recent works, such as Sannazaro's *De partu virginis* and Cowley's *Davideis*. Epic verse of the kind composed by Homer, Virgil, Statius and Lucan was not, however, the only or even the most obvious model for Christian 'didactic epic'. Late antique poets offered, for instance, examples of entirely allegorical works, such as Prudentius' *Psychomachia*, and *Paradise Lost* itself contains, as has often been pointed out, elements drawn from a wide range of genres, including, in the speech of Michael in Books 11 and 12, what Sarah Ross has termed 'the episodic, discursive, and emblematic structure' typical of scriptural verse paraphrase.[1] The tradition of consciously *un*classical scriptural paraphrase, such as that found in Guillaume de Salluste Du Bartas' (1544–90) *Sepmaines* and Lucy Hutchinson's *Order and Disorder*, has attracted some thoughtful critical attention in recent years.[2] Ross has suggested how works of this kind, in which women writers are particularly well represented, and many examples of which were never published in print, 'suggest a rich culture of sub-canonical biblical poetry in seventeenth century England, one in which women as well as men engaged'.[3] But Du Bartas' work was itself modelled – albeit with elements of contention – on a type of epic, exemplified by Palingenius' *Zodiacus Vitae*, which was the very opposite of 'sub-canonical' in the seventeenth century.

For the modern reader, approaching Milton via Virgil and Homer, the digressive mode of Du Bartas and Hutchinson – and with it the unclassical

---

[1] Ross, 'Epic, Meditation, or Sacred History?', 495. Ross discusses parallels between Milton and the work of Lucy Hutchinson and Anne Southwell among others. Barbara Lewalski has noted that the genre of these books has remained relatively underexplored in comparison to that of the rest of the poem ('Genres of *Paradise Lost*', 114).
[2] See Ross, 'Epic, Meditation, or Sacred History?'; and Norbrook, 'John Milton'.
[3] Ross, 'Epic, Meditation, or Sacred History?', 497; see also Auger, *Du Bartas' Legacy*.

447

elements of *Paradise Lost* – seems anomalous. Historically, however, this is almost exactly the wrong way round: early modern poets and readers alike prioritized scripture over the classics, and were taught to approach the classical authors *via* approved Protestant or quasi-Protestant works composed by near contemporaries. Of these, Palingenius' *Zodiacus Vitae*, though now largely forgotten by scholars and when remembered, almost universally misrepresented, was in England among one of the most ubiquitous and influential. This chapter takes the achievement and allure of Palingenius' remarkable work seriously as a source, model and catalyst in examining some of the very large number of examples of 'unclassical epic' read and composed by English authors in the sixteenth and seventeenth centuries.

Although there are notably few examples, in either English or Latin, of thoroughly classicizing 'epic' produced in early modern England, there are many examples of very long poems in a markedly *un*classical style. Many of these poems (though not all) either retell scripture in whole or in part or offer a more discursive or diffuse treatment of moral, religious or philosophical material. Of such poems which are not directly scriptural, many, like Prudentius' *Psychomachia*, Spenser's *Faerie Queene* and Palingenius' *Zodiacus Vitae*, are characterized primarily by allegorical drama rather than the retelling of pagan myths or martial heroism.[4] The canonical pre-eminence of Homer, Virgil and Milton has left the quantity and popularity of this type of writing in the shadows of literary history. Several examples, however – including Du Bartas' *La Sepmaine* (1578) in French, Latin and, especially following the publication of Sylvester's translation in 1605, also in English, and Maurice Ewens' *Votum Candidum* (first edition 1665) as well as Palingenius' *Zodiacus Vitae* itself (c.1535) – were demonstrably popular.[5] Despite the currency and appetite for poems of this sort, criticism has found various reasons for sidelining even the most undeniably widely read: as school texts (Palingenius), or as 'scriptural paraphrase' (Du Bartas among others), an apparently neutral term which has nevertheless acquired a derogatory implication, suggestive of a lack of literary ambition,

---

[4] The 'epic energy' of the period was also expressed in panegyric epic of the Claudianic type, discussed in Chapter 9, another literary mode that has been ignored by literary criticism and 'classical reception' alike.

[5] Du Bartas' poem has been described as 'one of the most celebrated and widely read contemporary poetic works in early modern Europe' (Auger, *Du Bartas' Legacy*, 4); on the print history of Du Bartas' works, see Bellenger and Ternaux, *Du Bartas*, 21–36. Ewens' *Votum Candidum* went through four editions between 1665 and 1679. Palingenius' work had appeared in at least 30 editions by 1600.

of piety (as if this were incompatible with literary quality), and often, also, an implicit acknowledgement of wide readership including or especially among women.[6]

Other poems in this category have been wholly or largely ignored because they are so stubbornly resistant to canonical ideas about what epic poetry should be like in terms of style and language, as well as the topics it should cover. Sir Thomas Chaloner's *De Republica Instauranda* (1579), Phineas Fletcher's *Purple Island* (1633, though probably written before 1610), Ewens' (1611–87) *Votum Candidum* (first edition 1665) and Abraham Cowley's *Plantarum Libri Sex* (1668) come into sharper focus when read within this broader generic context of unclassical epic; and indeed, the relatively unpopular Books 11 and 12 of Milton's own *Paradise Lost*, made up largely of scriptural paraphrase, themselves owe much to this tradition. Alastair Fowler has described those books as 'Bartasian' epic (for the versifying of scripture in the style of Du Bartas), though we could also consider them 'Palingenian', invoking the poet from whom Du Bartas probably derived the style and genre, though not the scriptural element, of his poem.[7]

These works are held together by several shared elements: considerable length, subdivided into books or sections; the use of the hexameter in Latin; a discursive, digressive and explicitly didactic style, with a tendency towards, as it were, 'factual' as well as moral or political didactic; an inclination to allegory; and the incorporation of classically epic elements (such as the invocation of the Muse and self-conscious ambition) in nevertheless unclassical poems. Several have elements of scriptural paraphrase. Most (though not all) examples of verse in this tradition have a marked Protestant identity: the shadowy 'Palingenius' had his work posthumously condemned by the Catholic Church, and he was widely believed to have been an early Protestant by his English readers in the sixteenth century.[8]

---

[6] 'Many or most anglophone critics still regard Du Bartas as an author of derivative, dull, and reductively systematic verse who was at best an inferior precursor to Milton' (Auger, *Du Bartas' Legacy*, 7). See also Prescott, 'Reception of Du Bartas'. Kevin Killeen remarks: 'With some splendid exceptions, the scriptural in early modern political writing, the resort to Old Testament example, is treated as a kind of biblical Tourette's syndrome, blurted out without its having much substantive content and without much tonal subtlety' (Killeen, *Political Bible*, 3). Similar assumptions are often made about the literary quality of scriptural works.
[7] Fowler, *Kinds of Literature*, 175.
[8] 'Palingenius' was for some time believed to be a pseudonym for Pietro Angelo Manzoli of Stellata, near Ferrara, active in the 1530s; more recent Italian scholarship has however debunked this identification, and suggested that he was probably a grammar school master in Campania, possibly with some medical training (see Bacchelli, 'Note'; and (in English) Haskell, 'Poetic Flights', 91).

Palingenius and His Readers in Early Modern England

The educational importance of Palingenius' *Zodiacus Vitae* (c.1535), in 12 books of between 287 and 1,079 hexameters, has been widely acknowledged in scholarship on the school curriculum, but with almost no further discussion: although we know that this text was frequently read in Latin in the first three years of a grammar school education, typically before reading Virgil's *Aeneid* or Ovid's *Metamorphoses*; that it was printed at least 10 times in England (and even more frequently in France) in the latter half of the sixteenth century; and that Shakespeare borrows from it directly, there is no modern English translation or edition of the Latin text.[9] The only English translation remains that made by a very young Barnabe Googe in the first half of the 1560s, and there is no modern edition of this translation either.[10]

Moreover, Googe's translation, in fourteeners, of an already expansive text has perhaps contributed to a general impression among English readers of a ramblingly didactic and essentially late medieval poem, concealing from view the clarity, confidence, poetic ambition, visionary coherence and sheer strangeness of Palingenius' work. (Whereas Sylvester's stylish and mature translation of Du Bartas has done much to popularize it, not only in the seventeenth century, but also amongst Anglophone scholars today.) Some very useful and much more nuanced recent scholarship on Palingenius has been written by classicists and neo-Latinists, mostly in Italian.[11] This work, correctively emphasizing the radical elements of the poem and interpreting its philosophical interests as a product of the Italy of the 1530s, has

---

[9] Beckwith reports 19 French editions, 16 in Switzerland, 7 in Holland, 13 in Germany and even 2 in Sweden in addition to the original first Italian edition (undated, but probably c.1535) and 10 in England (Beckwith, 'Study of Palingenius' *Zodiacus Vitae*', 4). There is a good modern French edition with Latin text and facing French translation, Chomarat (ed.), *Zodiaque de la vie*. Shakespeare, *As You Like It* II.vii ('All the world's a stage') is well known to derive from Palingenius, Book VI ('Virgo'), lines 644–725, though in fact Palingenius uses this image repeatedly, including in the dedication of his poem. Other possible parallels to Palingenius in Shakespeare include *Merchant of Venice* I.i.77–8 and *King Lear* IV.vi.183–4, on which see Gillespie, *Shakespeare's Books*, 326–8. Like most critics, Gillespie assumes Shakespeare's use of Googe rather than familiarity with the Latin text. Baldwin, *Small Latin*, vol. 1, 642–80 offers a detailed discussion of the combination of Palingenius with elements derived from Ovid and Horace in the single scene in *AYLI* but no more general overview. Watson, '*Zodiacus Vitae*', summarises each book and includes a useful appendix of English references to Palingenius.

[10] Barnabe Googe's translation, which describes Palingenius as 'the most Christian poet', appeared in stages in 1560, 1561 and (the first complete translation) 1565. Evidently there was a market for it: it was reprinted in 1576 and again in 1588.

[11] Yasmin Haskell is almost alone among Anglophone scholars in her serious attention to the poem ('Masculine Muse', 'Between Fact and Fiction' and 'Poetic Flights').

understandably not been much concerned with what difference such a reappraisal might make to our sense of its influence upon many generations of Protestant English schoolboys. Overall, it has become difficult even for scholars to access a text which we know for sure had been read by most if not all educated male adults in England in the late sixteenth and early seventeenth centuries, and which many others, including educated women, may have read in part either in Latin or in translation. To be plain: Palingenius' Latin is unclassical in style but pacey and straightforward to read. His syntactically simple Latin must have made the *Zodiacus Vitae* accessible to many readers who, for instance, had started but not finished grammar school or had an equivalent level of Latin education.

The *Zodiacus Vitae* was proscribed by the Catholic Church in 1558, a point which surely contributed to its popularity in Protestant countries, and there is extensive evidence for the reading and admiration of the work in England. Roger Ascham (in *The Scholemaster*, 1570), William Webbe (*A Discourse of English Poetrie*, 1586), Gabriel Harvey and Francis Meres (*Palladis Tamia*, 1598) all praise it or recommend it for school use.[12] Matthew Parker quoted from it on the title page of the second edition of his *Flores historiarum* (1570); still in the 1630s or 1640s it is included in a list of texts recommended by Alexander Ross to the teenage or student Henry Oxinden.[13] It appears frequently in personal book lists and is widely excerpted in commonplace books and manuscript miscellanies at least until the end of the seventeenth century – usually in Latin rather than Googe's translation.[14] Hankins has commented that the Elizabethans 'ranked Palingenius high among the minor Latin poets', but this plainly remained true well beyond the Elizabethan period.[15]

Most of the editions produced in the latter half of the sixteenth century are clearly designed with school use in mind: the 1574 Basel edition, for

---

[12] See Beckwith, 'Study of Palingenius' *Zodiacus Vitae*', 128–30. On the reading of Palingenius elsewhere in Europe, see Borgiani, *Marcello Palingenio Stellato*; and Bacchelli, 'Palingenio Stellato'.

[13] BL MS Add. 28010, fol. 66^r.

[14] The most frequently excerpted books are Book 1 (Aries) and 10 (Capricorn). Among many examples, see for instance extracts at BL MSS Sloane 319, fol. 35^r; Sloane 1255, fol. 153^v; Egerton 3880, fols. 132^v and 135^r; Harley 3354, fol. 34^r; Harley 3638, fol. 67^r; Bod. MSS Ashmole 1492, pp. 221–2; Fairfax 40, pp. 609–10 (with translation); Trinity College, Cambridge, MS R. 14. 18, fol. 94^r; CUL MSS Ff. V. 14, fol. 7^r; Dd. II. 43, pp. 119–22 (39 extracts with page references); Society of Antiquaries, MS SAL 437, p. 133. These manuscripts date from between the mid-sixteenth and the late seventeenth century. In addition, BL MS Add. 61822 (late sixteenth century) contains nine extracts from Googe's translation (fols. 84^{r-v}). I am grateful to the other members of the *NLPEM* team, especially Bianca Facchini, for their assistance in surveying and describing these manuscripts.

[15] Hankins, *Shakespeare's Derived Imagery*, 14.

instance, and after it most of the English editions, is prefaced by a liminary verse addressed specifically to schoolteachers; the 1575 London edition, and most that followed, include a substantial thematic index allowing precise location of very many passages, and line numbers which begin again at 1 on each page, rather than continuing for an entire poetic book. This unusual feature tends to confirm the point made by Baldwin and Green, that this was a text read at a relatively early stage of Latin learning, when boys would be reading slowly, and unlikely to cover more than a page in a lesson.[16] Several surviving copies are heavily marked up, with many words glossed in English, again suggesting that it was used at an early stage of Latin schooling. Extant copies also testify to its continued educational use throughout the seventeenth century.[17]

The *Zodiacus Vitae* is arranged in 12 books corresponding to the signs of the zodiac (and also, of course, to the *Aeneid*). The standard description of the poem, repeated more or less identically by a series of scholars, calls it 'a verse compendium of astronomical, moral and philosophical thought couched in the form of a dialogue and in a "vision" framework'.[18] A term like 'compendium' makes the work sound dully encyclopaedic, and both the subsequent descriptors are misleading: most (though not all) of the individual books feature dialogue, but the poet-narrator-protagonist encounters a wide range of different characters over the course of the work, not a single one as 'a dialogue' tends to suggest. Similarly, the poem contains remarkable visions or experiences – such as the journey of the poet to the moon in Book 9 (Sagittarius) – but the work as a whole is not a dream vision.[19] It features multiple allegorical personifications, such as encounters with 'Arete', personified virtue, in Book 3 (Gemini), with her son Timalphes in Book 4 (Cancer) and with Death in Book 6 (Virgo), but the poet also encounters Epicurus (in Book 3), with whom he discusses pleasure as a the highest good, several Muses (Calliope and Urania) and many other characters.

Above all, none of the existing descriptions of the work available in English mentions the clarity, strength, literary ambition and artistic

---

[16] Baldwin, *Small Latine*, vol. 1, 387, 413, 424, 433, 643–53.
[17] See for instance the 1579 edition digitized by *EEBO*, and apparently owned in 1655 by Sir Dudley North (1641–91), the fourth son of Dudley North, fourth Baron North, later an English merchant, politician and economist.
[18] This summary (Gillespie, *Shakespeare's Books*, 326) is typical, though some scholarly descriptions are even more misleading. Green describes it as '12 books of poems', as if it were a kind of anthology (Green, *Humanism and Protestantism*, 220).
[19] For the journey to the moon, compare the Ascent of Mutabilitie to the circle of the moon in Spenser, *FQ* VII.vi.8.

self-consciousness of the authorial voice. Palingenius himself, addressed as 'Stellatus' by a heavenly voice at the start of Book 9 (Sagittarius), is by far the most dominant and striking character, and the journey of the work is his quest to understand the life of man and (above all) the glory of the universe. The poem is both forcefully direct and passing strange: profoundly religious and yet only barely Christian. It is no surprise that it acted as a spur, challenge and provocation to so many of its early schoolboy readers; it is perhaps more surprising that they were allowed to read it at all.

The poem is much more obviously and self-consciously an *epic* poem than any of the existing critical descriptions by early modernists allows.[20] The poem has repeated invocations to variants of the epic Muse or presiding divinities, including Apollo (in Book 1 and 4), Calliope (6), the 'Muse' (7, 8, 9 and 11), Urania (11) and God himself (12). The invention of Urania as a Muse specifically for Christian epic – taken up by Milton who invokes her for the second half of *Paradise Lost* – is usually attributed to Du Bartas, glancing back at Pontano's *Urania* (a Latin cosmological poem written around 1480). But both Milton and Du Bartas were almost certainly influenced by Palingenius' intensely spiritual poem. Palingenius makes it clear, both in Book 1 and again in the second proem to Book 7, that his poem is epic in scale and ambition, and also a rejection of pagan mythological epic, especially the model offered by Ovid's *Metamorphoses*:

> An laudabo aliquem dictis mendacibus, vt pars
> Magna solet vatum, et coruum phoenica vocabo?
> Num melius plumis Iunonia regna secantem
> Daedalon, Icariosque ausus et fata gementem,
> Mutatasque deûm atque hominum memorare figuras?
> Et vacuas aures nugis mulcere canoris?
> Num melius iuuenum lasciuos dicere amores?
> Quodque nefas maius, dictis temerare prophanis
> Coelicolas? quid enim dementia nostra veretur?
> Concumbunt, rapiunt pueros, vitiantque puellas;
> In coelo est meretrix, in coelo est turpis adulter.
> Pro pudor! haec pietas? hoc fas? haec debita diuis
> Gratia, thura, foci, pecudes, altaria, laudes?[21]
>
> (Book 1, Aries, 111–23)

---

[20] Yasmin Haskell has used the term 'cosmological epic' ('Poetic Flights', 94). Neither Green, *Humanism and Protestantism*, nor Gillespie, *Shakespeare's Books*, probably the reference works most likely to be consulted by scholars of early modern literature, uses the term 'epic' at all.

[21] The Latin text of Palingenius is quoted throughout from Chomarat (ed.), *Zodiaque de la vie*.

> *Shall I praise some man with dishonest words (as the greater part*
> *Of poets tend to do); shall I call a crow a Phoenix?*
> *Surely it isn't better to tell yet again the story of Daedalus, cutting across*
> *The realm of Juno with his feathers, and of how he lamented*
> *Icarus' daring and his death; or to relate how the shapes of men and*
>   *of gods were transformed?*
> *To soothe empty ears with such mere trifles of song?*
> *Surely it's not better to tell of the young men's improper love affairs?*
> *And – even worse – to dishonour with prophane stories*
> *Those who dwell in heaven? Why should anyone revere such insanity?*
> *They sleep together, rape boys, defile girls:*
> *That [i.e. pagan] heaven is inhabited by a prostitute and a foul adulterer.*
> *For shame! Is this piety? Is that what is right? Do we owe those deities*
> *Gratitude, incense, sacred hearths, animal sacrifices, altars, and praise?*

He revisits this point at much greater length at the start of Book 7 (Libra), opening the second ('heavenly' rather than 'earthly') half of the work. His objections are echoed by many Elizabethan Protestant poets and critics. Lily Campbell quotes John Wharton, in his address 'To the Christian Reader' prefaced to Jud Smith's 1575 volume of scriptural verse paraphrases: 'For surely (gentle Reader) if thou covet to heare anye olde bables, as I may terme them, or stale tales of Chaucer, or to learne how Aeteon came by his horned head? If thy mynde be fixed to any such metamorphocall toyes, this booke is not apt nor fit for thy purpose.'[22]

Palingenius rejects erotic pagan mythology, but endorses the power and glory of poetry and of poetic fame in the strongest possible terms, remarking, for instance, that fame is a spur to virtue:

> Et vos Castalides Nymphae, si pectore puro
> Limina vestra adii, si non contagia caecae
> Luxuriae iuuenem potuêre auertere vestro
> A cultu, nec me vicit vesana libido,
> Tradite me famae, ne prorsus inutilis olim
> Vixisse hîc videar, pereámque in funere totus.
> Spes famae solet ad virtutem impellere multos.
>   . . .
> Adsis, & placido vultu dignare poëtam
> Aspicere, insolitas intentasque volentem
> Ire vias, vatum quas non vlla orbita signat
> Hactenus . . .
>   (Book 1, Aries, 23–9 and 41–4)

---

[22] Smith, *A Misticall Deuise* (1575), sig. aii^r, quoted by Campbell, *Divine Poetry*, 59. Campbell's important and perceptive book rightly continues to be frequently cited, though many of its modestly presented observations have not been fully digested by subsequent critics.

And you, Castalian nymphs, if I draw near
Your doors with a pure heart; if no taint of blind
Luxury could distract me, young man though I am, from your worship,
And no blind lust overwhelm me, hand me over
To fame, so that I may not seem to have lived here in vain, and perish entirely in death.
The hope of fame may spur many to virtue.
...

Come to me, please, and consider me worthy to be looked upon by you
With your gentle face, as a poet, one who longs to travel
By unfamiliar and untested paths, which no poet's cart-track
Has ever marked before:

A passage to which we could compare Milton's:

> Alas! what boots it with incessant care
> To tend the homely, slighted shepherd's trade,
> And strictly meditate the thankless Muse?
> Were it not better done, as others use,
> To sport with Amaryllis in the shade,
> Or with the tangles of Neæra's hair?
> Fame is the spur that the clear spirit doth raise
> (That last infirmity of noble mind)
> To scorn delights and live laborious days;
> But the fair guerdon when we hope to find,
> And think to burst out into sudden blaze,
> Comes the blind fury with the abhorred shears,
> And slits the thin-spun life. But not the praise,
> Phoebus replied, and touched my trembling ears ...
> (Milton, *Lycidas*, 64–77)

Structurally, the *Zodiacus Vitae* recalls the *Aeneid* – a poem itself frequently read as an allegorical version of the pursuit of wisdom. Book 4 (Cancer) is devoted to love, just as *Aeneid* 4 relates the love story (and tragedy) of Dido and Aeneas; in Book 6 Palingenius is conveyed to hell by Calliope, and forced to encounter Death, recalling Aeneas' visit to the underworld in the corresponding book of the *Aeneid*. As in the *Aeneid*, the work is divided clearly into two halves. The 'Odyssean' Books 1–6 of the *Aeneid* correspond to the 'earthly' first six books of Palingenius' poem, concerned primarily with human life, the question of true human flourishing, and a man's proper relation to other men. The 'Iliadic' second six books of the *Aeneid* correspond to the second half of the *Zodiacus Vitae*, concerned with the celestial and supra-celestial spheres, and the beings that inhabit them, including (according to Palingenius) angels both mortal (celestial) and immortal (supra-celestial). As in Virgil, Book 7 begins with a second proem and a self-consciously marked 'raising' of the poetic register:

> Musa, agedum, surge et melioribus vtere pennis:
> Alta pete atque humiles iamdudum despice curas:
> Rebus in excelsis decus est et gloria maior.
> Contemplare Deos totumque per aethera curre ...
> (Book 7, Libra, 1–4)

> *Come now Muse, rise up, and try some better wings:*
> *Seek the heights, and despise lowly concerns:*
> *In lofty themes there is greater glory and honour.*
> *Contemplate the gods, and take your path through all the heavens.*

> Nunc age, qui reges, Erato, quae tempora, rerum
> quis Latio antiquo fuerit status, advena classem
> cum primum Ausoniis exercitus appulit oris,
> expediam, et primae revocabo exordia pugnae.
> ...
>   maior rerum mihi nascitur ordo,
> maius opus moveo.
> (Virgil, *Aen.* 7.37–40, 44–5)

> *Come now, Erato, so I may tell of kings, and times*
> *and of the state of things in ancient Latium, when the invaders*
> *first brought their fleet to shore on the coast of Ausonia,*
> *and I shall tell how battle first began.*
> ...
>   *A greater theme is born for me;*
> *I undertake a greater task.*

In *Paradise Lost*, Milton invokes Urania – the name of Du Bartas' specifically Christian Muse and also the Muse of Palingenius' final two, highest-flown books – at the equivalent moment of transition, the start of Book 7:

> Descend from Heaven, Urania, by that name
> If rightly thou art called, whose voice divine
> Following, above the Olympian hill I soar,
> Above the flight of Pegasean wing.
> The meaning, not the name, I call: for thou
> Nor of the Muses nine, nor on the top
> Of old Olympus dwellest; but, heavenly-born,
> Before the hills appeared, or fountain flowed,
> Thou with eternal Wisdom didst converse,
> Wisdom thy sister, and with her didst play
> In presence of the Almighty Father, pleased
> With thy celestial song. Up led by thee

> Into the Heaven of Heavens I have presumed,
> An earthly guest, and drawn empyreal air,
> Thy tempering: with like safety guided down
> Return me to my native element:
> Lest from this flying steed unreined, (as once
> Bellerophon, though from a lower clime,)
> Dismounted, on the Aleian field I fall,
> Erroneous there to wander, and forlorn.
> Half yet remains unsung, but narrower bound
> Within the visible diurnal sphere;
> Standing on earth, not rapt above the pole,
> More safe I sing with mortal voice, unchanged
> To hoarse or mute, though fallen on evil days,
> On evil days though fallen, and evil tongues;
> In darkness, and with dangers compassed round,
> And solitude; yet not alone, while thou
> Visitest my slumbers nightly, or when morn
> Purples the east: still govern thou my song,
> Urania, and fit audience find, though few.
> (Milton, *Paradise Lost*, 7.1–31)

The Miltonic poet moves in the reverse direction from the Palingenian one, insisting that for this second half of the work he must be led down from the heavens, where he has been guided by Urania, to remain 'Standing on earth, not rapt above the pole' (23). In that phrase 'not rapt above the pole', Milton defines how his project differs from that of Palingenius. As we shall see, Du Bartas, similarly, uses the overture to his poem to define his project in relation to the *Zodiacus Vitae*.

Palingenian Style and Tone

Stylistically, Palingenius' Latin is unclassical compared either to Virgil or to the humanist poets who were his contemporaries. This point is usually made only in a negative sense, or implicitly so, suggesting that his verse is workmanlike but unpoetic. But Palingenius' Latin is attractive and highly readable, filled with excerptable gnomic remarks and vivid comparisons. Indeed it is readable and engaging in very much the same way as Sylvester's hugely popular translation of Du Bartas.[23] Although discursive and sometimes repetitious, the poem as a whole is very clearly structured both thematically and 'dramatically': each book is a self-contained unit with a

---
[23] A work acutely described by Peter Auger as seeming at first encounter 'too easy to read' for serious literary analysis (*Du Bartas' Legacy*, 1).

distinct theme, and these themes themselves build on each other in a comprehensible 'ascent' from basic ethical questions to the supra-celestial cosmogony of the final book.

Moreover, the work has a distinctive tone: Palingenius' use of classical material, as in his structural allusions to the *Aeneid* or (in the pastoral sections of Book 5) to the *Eclogues* of Virgil and Mantuan, gives an impression of profound familiarity with classical commonplaces, combined with a relaxed approach to them. In the first book for instance, setting out his poetic manifesto, he remarks:

> Ergo sic scribere oportet,
> Vt quicquam inde boni valeant haurire legentes,
> Ne frustra tempus sese triuisse querantur,
> Fallaces nugas et inania monstra legendo.
> Atqui scire opus est, triplex genus esse bonorum,
> Vtile, delectans, maiusque ambobus honestum.
> Horum aliquod, vel plura ferat quodcunque poëma …
> (Book 1, Aries, 139–45)

> *Therefore we must write in such a way*
> *That as men read our work they can draw from it something good,*
> *And not complain that they have spent their time in vain*
> *Reading deceptive trifles and empty horrors.*
> *And it is important to know that there are three types of good:*
> *The useful, the delightful, and, greater than either, the virtuous.*
> *Each poem should offer one, or more than one of these.*

Palingenius' declaration here of the 'threefold' types of a good poem alludes plainly to one of the most widely known and cited precepts of literary criticism in early modernity, formulated twice in close proximity in Horace's *Ars poetica*, in which there are *two* criteria by which to assess a poem:

> Aut prodesse volunt, aut delectare Poëtae,
> Aut simul et iucunda, & idonea dicere vitae.
> (*AP*, 333–4)

> *Poets wish either to improve, or to delight –*
> *Or to speak words which are at once both pleasing and useful for life.*

> Omne tulit punctum qui miscuit utile dulci,
> lectorem delectando pariterque monendo …
> (*AP*, 343–4)

> *He who mixes the useful and the sweet hits the mark perfectly,*
> *By delighting and instructing the reader to the same extent.*

Palingenius' memorable passage summarizes an ubiquitous classical topos deriving ultimately from Horace, while also quite cheerfully and authoritatively adding to it. The educational utility is obvious. A master reading this page painstakingly with a group of 11-year-old boys could take the opportunity to point out the reference to Horace, and perhaps look at a related adage (such as Erasmus, *Adagia*, 4.7.93, 'Quod utile honestum'). The boys would copy out the lines into a commonplace book and memorize them. The Latin is straightforward and serves a double purpose, encoding both a classical tradition and a Christian commentary upon that tradition – pleasure and utility are both important though not sufficient; virtue is a greater good than either. But such an experience doesn't end there: the attentive child who first encounters this famous fragment of the *Ars poetica* via Palingenius is likely always to remember Palingenius' rider. Poetry should profit or delight – or, as Jonson has it:

> Poëts would either profit, or delight,
> Or mixing sweet and fit, *teach life the right*.
> (Jonson, *Horace his Art of Poetry*, 477–8, italics mine)

Jonson is here translating Horace, *AP* 333–4, in a version often cited (and criticized) as the most deadening kind of 'word for word' translation. Even in such a text, though, we hear Jonson strike a note that does not come entirely from Horace. 'Mixing sweet and fit, teach life the right' is an expansion of *Aut simul et iucunda, & idonea dicere vitae* ('or, taking the two together, speak of what is both pleasant and useful for life'). 'Teach life the right' is a stronger, more abstract, more general and more morally insistent phrase than anything in Horace's Latin, and it comes close to the force of Palingenius' *honestum*. Jonson here, like so many ex-schoolboys before him, perhaps finds himself hearing Palingenius as he reads Horace.[24]

Palingenius' discursiveness and variety of material, again usually mentioned rather deprecatingly, as if it implies carelessness, or at least a prioritization of didactic purposes over artistic control, are clearly signalled by Palingenius himself as part of a self-conscious aesthetic of variety, in a passage which recasts the opening of Ovid's *Metamorphoses*:

> Scribere fert animus multa et diuersa, nec vno
> Gurgite versari semper: quo flamina ducent
> Ibimus, et nunc has, nunc illas nabimus vndas,
> Ardua nunc ponti, nunc littora tuta petemus.
> Et quanquam interdum, fretus ratione, latentes

---

[24] For discussion of Jonson's translation in general, see Moul, *Jonson, Horace*, 182–5.

> Naturae tentabo vias, atque abdita pandam,
> Praecipue tamen illa sequar quaecumque videntur
> Prodesse, ac sanctos mortalibus addere mores,
> Heu penitus (liceat verum mihi dicere) nostro
> Extinctos aeuo, quo non obscoenius vllum
> Aut fuit, aut posthac erit; et quaecunque nocentes
> Languenti valeant animo detrudere morbos.
> (Book 1, Aries, 62–73)

> *The mind makes us write many various things, and we are not*
> *Turned always in the same whirlpool: we shall go wherever the wind*
> *Blows us, and we'll swim first through these waters, now those,*
> *Seeking now the steep seas, now safe shores.*
> *And although from time to time, trusting to my reason, I shall attempt*
> *To enter Nature's hidden paths, and open her secrets,*
> *Most of all I shall follow whatever seems*
> *To be good, and to improve men's morals –*
> *Though alas! (but I must confess it) morality*
> *Is extinguished in our time, for there has never, and will never after*
> *Be an age more corrupt than ours – and I'll write whatever might have the power*
> *To drive out harmful afflictions from a suffering soul.*

Here the opening explicitly echoes the first line of Ovid's *Metamorphoses* ('in nova fert animus mutates dicere formas'), but transfers the image: the many transformations of Palingenius' poem are not the literal ones of Ovid, but the emotional and intellectual transformations of the poet himself, as he ranges adventurously wherever his mission of moral improvement might take him. The emphasis upon morality is not just different from Ovid, but in direct opposition to him, as we saw in the passage on the pagan gods discussed above.

Finally, this rich and strange poem offers a powerfully coherent vision of the grandeur and glory of the universe and all its inhabitants, particularly of the heavenly and supra-celestial realms, and a markedly positive declaration of the possibility of human contact with the divine and the quasi-divine, especially in the form of angels. In Milton's *Paradise Lost*, the extensive didactic material in Books 11 and 12 is delivered by the archangel Michael. This part of the poem incorporates scriptural paraphrase without itself being based in scripture. (Michael does not instruct Adam in this way in Genesis.) Although there is surprisingly little mention of Christ in Palingenius' poem, the work is strongly monotheistic, and suffused with awe and longing for the grandeur of God. The 'answer' to Palingenius' question, the true *summum bonum* for man, is to walk and talk with angels in this life and after death, just as Adam does in *PL* 11 and 12:

> Quod reor esse bonum summum finemque bonorum
> Cunctorum quaecunque homini contingere possunt,
> Donec praesentis vitae freta turbida sulcat,
> Cum vero elapsus mortali carcere abibit
> Spiritus, abducens secum hae tria, quae sibi semper
> Sunt propria, mentem, sensum, motum, aetheris oras
> Exultans petet et foelix perfecte erit illic;
> Quippe habitans cum Diis, Deus efficietur et ipse.
> O coelum immensum! o pulcherrima regia Diuum!
> Quam pura es, quam perspicua et mirabilis, et quot
> Vndique sideribus variis ornata renides,
> Regia cunctarum plenissima deliciarum!
> (Book 12, Pisces, 520–31)

> *This is what I take to be the greatest good, and the end of all*
> *Those goods which a man could attain*
> *As long as he ploughs the stormy straits of this life.*
> *But when his spirit, escaped from its mortal prison,*
> *Departs, he takes with him these three things, which always*
> *Are his own: his mind, his sense, his emotions: in joy he shall head*
> *For the shores of heaven, and there he shall be perfectly happy:*
> *Dwelling with divine beings, he shall be made into a god himself.*
> *O measureless heaven, o the beautiful realm of the celestial beings,*
> *How pure you are, how clear and marvellous, and how you shine*
> *Studded on every side with various stars,*
> *A realm filled with all the pleasures one can imagine!*

Palingenius, Du Bartas and Christian Didactic Epic

The manifesto for a Christian poetry laid out by Cowley in his 1656 *Poems* echoes that of Du Bartas in *L'Uranie: La Muse Chrestienne* (1574), Philip Sidney in the *Defence of Poesie* (c.1580, printed 1595) and even Ben Jonson in *Timber* (pub. 1640). All insist on the heavenly origin of poetry; that the poetry of the Old Testament is both older and ultimately better than that of the inspired classical poets, though closely related to it; and that Old Testament themes are superior subjects to classical mythology.[25] Du Bartas' *Sepmaines* and *L'Uranie*, though praised and translated by James VI/I in the sixteenth century, and demonstrably very widely read

---

[25] For a particularly important summary of this attitude, including a discussion of the relationship between Sidney and Du Bartas, see Campbell, *Divine Poetry*, 55–91. For the link between Cowley and Du Bartas, see Dykstal, 'Epic Reticence'.

in England in the seventeenth century following the appearance and frequent reprinting of Josuah Sylvester's translations, have been neglected until recently as a literary source and model. In a very recent book, Peter Auger has finally provided a full-length study of the considerable evidence for the importance of this work for our understanding of a very wide range of seventeenth-century English poetry.[26]

Du Bartas frequently appears in miscellanies, however, in proximity to Palingenius' *Zodiacus Vitae*. In an often-quoted marginal note, Gabriel Harvey associates Spenser's love of Du Bartas with Thomas Digges' admiration for Palingenius:

> M. Digges hath the whole Aquarius [Book 11] of Palingenius bie hart: & takes mutch delight to repeate it often. M. Spenser conceiues the like pleasure in the fourth day of the first Weeke of Bartas. Which he esteems as the proper profession of Urania.[27]

Digges' enthusiasm for Palingenius and Spenser's for Du Bartas seem to 'belong' together ('M. Spenser conceives the **like** pleasure'). Peter Auger, who also cites this passage, takes the connection between Palingenius and Du Bartas (and Buchanan's *Sphaera*, mentioned afterwards) to be thematic, because of the cosmological element in Du Bartas' creation poem.[28] This is obviously correct, but Palingenius and Du Bartas belong together also in more general ways. Although the *Sepmaines* is based on scripture and Palingenius' work is a philosophical poem, insistently monotheistic and in that sense compatible with Christianity but not an exposition of specifically Christian doctrine, there are many stylistic and structural similarities: both poems are written in an accessible and straightforward style; both are explicitly didactic; both are highly discursive; both are also profoundly religious and pervaded by awe at the majesty and complexity of creation. In a commonplace book kept by a boy at Kingston Grammar School in 1607, Palingenius, Mantuan and Du Bartas (in a Latin verse translation) are grouped together in consecutive pages. Though much more is taken from Palingenius than the others, the content chosen from all three is very similar: brief moralizing quotations on fate, death, time, fame and the vanity of human wishes.[29] Mantuan

---

[26] Auger, *Du Bartas' Legacy*. See also Prescott, 'Reception of Du Bartas', and (for the earlier period) Campbell, *Divine Poetry*.
[27] Moore Smith (ed.), *Gabriel Harvey's Marginalia*, 161.   [28] Auger, *Du Bartas' Legacy*, 89–90.
[29] BL MS Sloane 833, commonplace book of John Wrighte, fols. 14ʳ–15ʳ: 14 quotations from Mantuan, 5 from Du Bartas and 45 from Palingenius. By 1607 three separate Latin verse translations of Du Bartas were available; the Latin quoted by Wrighte is that of Gabriel Lermaeus, *Hebdomas*, a translation published in London in 1591 but also available in many

and Palingenius are two of the most frequently excerpted 'modern' (rather than classical or late antique) authors in sixteenth- and seventeenth-century commonplace books.[30]

Work on Du Bartas has occasionally acknowledged in passing an association with Palingenius, but has not pointed out or explored the many points of contact between the two texts. In the opening pages of Du Bartas' *Sepmaines*, before he begins the narration of creation, he works through a series of literary and moralizing motifs, all themselves conventional, the combination of which strongly recalls Palingenius in particular. Moreover, this series of correspondences is chosen and presented in such a way as to distinguish Du Bartas' project carefully from its Italian exemplar.

In the opening sequence, Du Bartas speaks as a sailor to his Muse (First Day of the First Weeke, 97–106), an image found repeatedly in Palingenius (Aries 62–5; Taurus 1–21 and 568–76 (end); Sagittarius 10–15). Du Bartas' poet-sailor, though, prudently coasts the shores of faith – that is, stays at least within sight of a scriptural source rather than heading out into the deep ocean. Du Bartas describes those who, like eagles, soar 'Beyond the Worlds walls' (First Day of the First Weeke, 129) to gaze upon the majesty of the heavens (recalling especially Palingenius, Gemini 529–53), but makes it clear that his own Muse 'trayned in true Religion, / Devinely-humane keepes the middle Region' (First Day of the First Weeke, 135–6).[31] Milton will explicitly reject Du Bartas' 'middling' course in the opening of *Paradise Lost*, his 'adventurous song / That with no middle flight intends to soar' (1.13–14).[32]

Du Bartas' versions of both these images evoke the moralizing topos of the dangers of high office and the virtues of the mean; Sylvester perhaps acknowledges this tradition by echoing Wyatt's translation of Seneca in his

---

continental editions, the earliest of which I'm aware having been printed in Paris in 1583. The other Latin translations available by 1607 were Damman, *Bartasias* (1600) and a parallel French–Latin edition of *L'Uranie* by Robert Ashley, *L'Uranie – Urania sive Musa Coelestis* (1589). Ashley and Sylvester were both educated at Southampton grammar school in the 1570s under Hadrianus Saravia, a Belgian Protestant émigré; very unusually for the period, this school specialized in French.

[30] Auger has described Du Bartas' work as 'poems of commonplaces' (*Du Bartas' Legacy*, esp. 9–17). His neat description of the *Sepmaines* as 'epic poems that do not need to be read in sequence' (16) is in part applicable also to Palingenius, though there is a clearer narrative and philosophical development in Palingenius' poem.

[31] Du Bartas is quoted throughout in Sylvester's translation, in Snyder (ed.), *Divine Weekes and Works*.

[32] Both of these images – of sailing and the eagle's gaze – have their classical source in the verse prefaces of Claudian. The poet as an intrepid sailor in the preface to *Rapt.*; eagles who can gaze at the sun in the preface to *III Cons*. For the use of Claudian as a model at this period, see Chapters 9 and 10.

translation of Du Bartas.[33] The sequence of images also makes a concrete point about what to expect: his poem is concerned with the worldly realm, the 'middle' – neither death and the underworld (visited by Palingenius in Book 6, Virgo, and from which he hears further reports in Book 10, Capricorn), nor the heavens or the realm beyond the heavens (the general subject of the second half of the *Zodiacus Vitae*). He is focused on perceiving the reflection of God in the creation of *this* world, not in the celestial or supra-celestial spheres with which Palingenius is most concerned.[34] Du Bartas, in other words, does not reject the validity or importance of Palingenius as a model, but uses the opening pages of his work to set out how his subject differs from that of the *Zodiacus Vitae*.

Du Bartas offers a series of images for the world that is the subject of his poem: as a school, a staircase, a palace or shop, a cloud, a stage and a book. This list both echoes Palingenius – who also, in a much-excerpted passage used by Shakespeare, calls the world a stage and all its people merely players – and challenges him. For Palingenius, the world we inhabit is a deceptive underworld, and our knowledge of God comes primarily from contemplation of what is above it – the heavens, the supra-celestial regions and their inhabitants. Du Bartas insists that the world itself, paid due attention, also reveals God in his majesty, as his reworking of one of the most memorable parts of Palingenius indicates:

> The World's a Stage, where God's Omnipotence,
> His Justice, Knowledge, Love, and Providence,
> Doo act their parts; contending in their kindes,
> Above the Heav'ns to ravish dullest mindes.
> (First Day of the First Weeke, 169–72)

The enthusiastic reception of Du Bartas' work in England arose in part because he applied to scriptural material a generic model already familiar from Palingenius, and demonstrated how a Palingenian style of poetic self-consciousness, authority and epic aspiration could be merged with the distinctively Protestant enthusiasm for the verse paraphrase of the Old Testament.

---

[33] 'Climbe they that list the battlements of Heav'n' (127), echoing Wyatt's 'Stand whoso list upon the slipper top'.

[34] This image of the intrepid thinker who climbs 'the battlements of Heav'n' is traceable ultimately to Lucretius' description of Epicurus (*De rerum natura* 1.62–79); the combination, however, of travel to the boundaries of the universe with the eagle's rapt gazing upon the divine sun is unique to Palingenius. Palingenius encounters Epicurus, whose philosophy is ultimately rejected but not mocked, in Book 3. The question of Palingenius' debt to Lucretius has been taken up by Yasmin Haskell in a series of essays ('Poetic Flights', 'Masculine Muse' and 'Between Fact and Fiction').

Moreover, while Du Bartas was demonstrably popular in the seventeenth century, and probably – given the evidence of John Wrighte's commonplace book – already absorbed into at least some English school curricula in its Latin form before 1600, Palingenius had been a standard school text from the 1560s, read within the first three years of grammar school, typically *before* the *Aeneid*.[35] Boys' sense of what epic is or should be was mediated by this first experience of epic verse, and such a reading order must have much encouraged the strongly allegorical readings of Ovid and Virgil which were in any case common. Similarly, early modern schoolboys typically read Virgil's *Eclogues* for the first time having already read the more insistently allegorical, and markedly anti-papal late fifteenth-century pastoral collection, the *Adulescentia* of Mantuan (Giovanni Baptista Spagnuoli, a Carmelite monk). The fourth book of Palingenius' poem (Cancer) also includes a pastoral section, strikingly similar to that of Mantuan, in which two shepherds sing in turn of their beloved, first of a boy Philetus, then of a girl, Mellina (4.70–197). Indeed, Mantuan's *Adulescentia* and Palingenius' *Zodiacus Vitae* are similar texts in several ways: both write clear, easily readable, and highly quotable Latin; both are prone to explicitly didactic asides; both were Italian Catholic poets hostile to the papal curia, and, as such, functioned as proto-Protestants for subsequent Protestant readers. As we saw, John Wrighte's commonplace book groups Mantuan, Palingenius and Du Bartas together.

In Milton's *Lycidas*, the 'grim wolf with privy paw' who 'Daily devours apace, and nothing said' (128–9) is usually taken to refer to the corruptions of Catholic clergy, and has most frequently been related to a similar passage in Spenser's *Shepherds' Calendar* (September, 148–60), and, behind him, to Mantuan (*Adulescentia* 9).[36] There is also, however, a very similar passage in Palingenius. In Book 4 (Cancer) on love, the pastoral singing contest between two lovelorn shepherds is interrupted when seven wolves invade the sheepfold, and the poet is left alone:

---

[35] The teaching of Mantuan, Palingenius and Mancini is discussed briefly by Green, *Humanism and Protestantism*, 219–22. Green remarks that the view that Christian poets should be read *rather* than pagan ones, as advocated for instance by John Colet who founded St Paul's, 'never achieved anything like majority support' but that nevertheless 'at grassroots level there was also some support for works by Christian authors like Mancini, Palingenius, and above all "Mantuan"', 219). Green is right to imply that very few schools if any avoided pagan authors entirely; but he underestimates I think the number who took pains to read Christian authors *first*. 'Some support' also much downplays the quantity of extracts from Palingenius and Mantuan (vastly more than Mancini) in surviving commonplace books and miscellanies. It matters what you read first, not least in shaping ideas of a genre, and especially given that plenty of boys started but did not complete grammar school.

[36] On Spenser's use of Mantuan, see Piepho, *Holofernes' Mantuan*, 113–21.

> Ecce autem veniunt per saxa crepidinis, inter
> Pendentes frutices, angusto calle, latenter
> Septem forte lupi, stimulante cupidine pastus,
> Inuaduntque greges, nunc has, nunc morsibus illas
> Dilaniant pecudes mersantque in sanguine rictus.
> Contra, conatur magnis latratibus hostes
> Pellere turba canum, ferro circumdata collum.
> Ingens fit strepitus; valles resonare boatu:
> Consurgunt trepidi, posito certamine cantus,
> Pastores ...
>
> (Book 4, Cancer, 198–207)

> *But look, they come through the rocks of the bank, among*
> *Dangling bushes, on a narrow path, unnoticed,*
> *Seven wolves, driven by their desire to feed:*
> *And they invade the flock, snapping on this side and that*
> *They tear apart the livestock, and soak their grins in gore:*
> *In response, a crowd of dogs, collared with iron*
> *And in a storm of barking attempts to drive the enemy off.*
> *As the noise is so great, the valleys echo with the tumult:*
> *So the shepherds, afraid, jump up, and their singing contest*
> *Is abandoned ...*

In Book 5 (Leo), the wolves return, this time identified explicitly with corrupt monks and clergy in a very frequently excerpted passage:

> Sed tua praecipue non intret limina quisquam
> Frater, vel monachus, vel quauis lege sacerdos.
> Hos fuge: pestis enim nulla hac immanior; hi sunt
> Fex hominum, fons stultitiae, sentina malorum,
> Agnorum sub pelle lupi, mercede colentes
> Non pietate Deum, falsa sub imagine recti
> Decipiunt stolidos ac relligionis in vmbra
> Mille actus vetitos et mille piacula condunt:
> Raptores, moechi, puerorum corruptores,
> Luxuriae atque gulae famuli, coelestia vendunt.
> Heu quas non nugas, quae non miracula fingunt,
> Vt vulgus fallant, optataque praemia carpant?
>
> (Book 5, Leo, 586–97)

> *But be especially careful that there should not cross your threshold*
> *Any brother, or monk, or any priest in holy orders.*
> *Avoid them at all costs: for no plague is more dreadful; those men are*
> *The very dregs of humanity, the fount of stupidity, the foul bilge-water of evils,*
> *Wolves in lambskins, worshiping God not with piety*
> *But with cash, under the false trappings of decency*
> *They trick the foolish, and under the shadow of religion*

Perform a thousand forbidden acts and a thousand outrages:
They rape, commit adultery, abuse children,
Slaves of luxury and greed, they sell what belongs to heaven.
Alas! What distractions, what miracles will they not invent
To trick the people and take what they long to have?

The image of monks or clergy as wolves among lambs, as found in Palingenius, Mantuan, Spenser and Milton, recalls and reverses the words of Jesus to his apostles at Matthew 10:16 ('mitto vos sicut agnos inter lupos', 'I send you as lambs among wolves'): rather than following the apostles as lambs, the clergy have become the wolves themselves.

A manuscript dating from after 1650 and consisting mostly of scriptural paraphrase, includes a copy of this passage headed 'Palingenius a Papist thus describes the monstrous Corruptions of the Romaine Clargie' and adds a translation (which is not that of Googe):

> Within thy doors noe Frier or Munck let in
> Then this a greater mischeife none can bring
> They wolves in sheepe skins are yitt none regards
> Not for deuotion serues but for rewards
> Wth fained shewes of Truth weake consience binds
> Vaild wth Religion Acts a thousand crimes
> Those that should be chast are such euell doers
> As sells things Holy to spend on ther whores
> What shame itt is the church should thus endure
> Such bease as these yitt would be thought tis pure.[37]

Palingenius and Milton

Palingenius, like Mantuan, was plainly very widely read. But an overemphasis on the mere fact of familiarity risks losing sight of – or failing to acknowledge – what goes without saying about Spenser or Milton. These are also very *good* poets: poets writing in a style which is not classical, but which is moving, effective, serious and highly memorable. Here, for instance, is Timalphes, the son of Arete (personified virtue), taking leave of the poet at the end of Book 4 in order to return to heaven, and describing the view of earth from above:

---

[37] Bod. MS Fairfax 40, pp. 609–10; immediately following an extract from Mantuan, *Eclogue* 5, also on corruption at Rome.

> Nunc tempus remeare monet locaque infima mundi
> Deserere et superas volitando reuisere sedes,
> Vnde ego tellurem soleo spectare frequenter,
> Admirans adeo paruam minimamque videri,
> Exiguique instar pomi pendere rotundam
> Aëris in medio, fultam molimine nullo,
> Atque suo tantum libratam pondere; cerno
> Inde etiam Oceanum totas circundare terras,
> Perque ipsas flexo, velut anguis, serpere cursu
> Nerea coeruleum, modici sub imagine riui.
>
> (Book 4, Cancer, 835–44)
>
> *Now the time warns me to return, to abandon the lower regions*
> *Of the world, and to regain by flight the upper realm:*
> *From there I often look down upon the earth,*
> *Wondering at how very tiny it seems,*
> *Like the sphere of a small apple hanging*
> *In the midst of the air, with no structure holding it up,*
> *And balanced only by its own weight; I see*
> *From that vantage point also the Ocean encircling all the lands:*
> *How, like a snake, it creeps around them in a curved shape,*
> *Blue-green Nereus, looking like a modest river.*

It is hard not to link such a striking passage with the famous portion of *Paradise Lost* in which Satan, winging his way to earth, sees it in the distance:

> But now at last the sacred influence
> Of light appears, and from the walls of heaven
> Shoots far into the bosom of dim Night
> A glimmering dawn; here nature first begins
> Her farthest verge, and Chaos to retire
> As from her outmost works a broken foe
> With tumult less and with less hostile din,   1040
> That Satan with less toil, and now with ease
> Wafts on the calmer wave by dubious light
> And like a weather-beaten vessel holds
> Gladly the port, though shrouds and tackle torn;
> Or in the emptier waste, resembling air,
> Weighs his spread wings, at leisure to behold
> Far off the empyreal heaven, extended wide
> In circuit, undetermined square or round,
> With opal towers and battlements adorned
> Of living sapphire, once his native seat;   1050
> And fast by hanging in a golden chain
> This pendent world, in bigness as a star

Of smallest magnitude close by the moon.
Thither full fraught with mischievous revenge,
Accursed, and in a cursed hour he hies.
        (2.1034–55, final lines of the book)[38]

Palingenius' version is both more homely – an apple hanging in space – and perhaps actually *more* memorable than Milton's scene. It is also highly suggestive: although it includes no explicitly Christian content, this apple, ripe for the picking, around which coils the ocean, 'velut anguis', 'like a snake', reminds the reader inevitably of the temptation of Adam in the Garden of Eden. Such an association is contextually appropriate for the end of a book about distinguishing between virtuous and sinful love, and the links to Milton's version of the image are obvious: Palingenius' angel-eye view of the world uses imagery that hints at its corruptibility. It is not implausible that this set of associations combined to prompt Milton's transfer of the image to the 'devil's eye' perspective of Satan himself, as he heads to earth to take the form of a serpent in the garden.

In fact, Milton in this passage, like Du Bartas at the opening of his work though to rather different effect, combines several elements all found also in the opening pages of Palingenius' poem. Satan is like a weather-beaten ship, an admittedly common image for the epic poet, traceable in particular to the preface to Claudian's *De Raptu Proserpinae*, but found repeatedly in Palingenius, as noted above. As, near earth, Milton's Satan relaxes and spends a while gazing back on heaven from which he has been cast out (1046–53), he recalls Palingenius' description of the soul of man like the eagle of Zeus:

        postquam alta polorum
Culmina conscendit, miratur clara pyropis
Moenia coelicolum, atque aliis splendentia gemmis,
Et stupet auratas aedes stellisque micantes,
Aspicit et solido factas adamante columnas,
Et constructa videt laquearia dentibus Indis;
Miratur latos campos lucemque perennem,
Deliciasque Deum, quales nec lingua referre
Vlla nec humanum pectus comprendere posset.
        (Book 3, Gemini, 536–44)

---

[38] Quotations of Milton from Carey and Fowler (eds.), *Poems of John Milton*.

> *Then he climbs the lofty*
> *Gables of the skies, and gazes in wonder at the walls*
> *Of heaven, bright with bronze, and gleaming with other jewels;*
> *He is stupefied at the sight of the golden structures glittering with stars,*
> *Looks upon the columns wrought of solid adamant,*
> *And sees coffered ceilings made of Indian ivory;*
> *He wonders at the broad plains, the everlasting light,*
> *And the delights of the gods – such pleasures as no tongue can tell,*
> *Nor human heart can compass.*

Milton, who in the second half of his work returns from the heavens to the earth, seems to link the grandeur and aspiration of Palingenius' poetic and philosophical voyage with Satan himself.

If we take Palingenius' *Zodiacus Vitae* seriously, both as a widely read and broadly influential generic model for epic, and as an excellent and highly memorable work of art, then a series of other poems, some of which are usually read only from a classical perspective and others which have tended not to be read at all, fall into a generic formation recognizable as 'Palingenian', running from Sir Thomas Chaloner's *De Republica Instauranda* (1579) down at least to Abraham Cowley's *Plantarum Libri Sex* (1668) and, as we have already seen, Milton's *Paradise Lost* (1667/1674).

Political Allegory and Didactic Epic in the Seventeenth Century: Phineas Fletcher, *The Purple Island*

In 1633, Phineas Fletcher published *The Purple Island*, a long allegorical poem which has a claim to be one of the most plainly 'didactic' English poems of the seventeenth century. Composed in 12 cantos of between 33 and 89 stanzas of 7 lines each, it is generally described as Spenserian.[39] Fletcher himself acknowledges the debt to Spenser, alongside prominent nods to Sannazaro, Mantuan and Du Bartas, each of whom is named in the poem or identified in marginal references.[40] The style, scale and use of allegory all link the poem to the Spenserian tradition, though it differs from Spenser's work in various respects including in its serious attempt, in the first half, to incorporate contemporary science, here anatomy.

Fletcher's unusual, but very readable poem, is an extended allegory in a pastoral frame. At the start of the poem Thirsil (that is, Fletcher) is elected

---

[39] Mitchell, *Purple Island and Anatomy*, for example, reads the poem in relation to *The Faerie Queene* as well as Du Bartas' *Sepmaines*. For a recent edition with notes, see Pope (ed.), *Purple Island*.
[40] Sannazaro is identified in a marginal note to Canto 1, stanza 13; 'Bartas' against stanza 14 and 'Spencer' alongside stanza 19. Mantuan is named in Canto 6, stanza 5.

Political Allegory and Didactic Epic 471

lord of the shepherds, and in response he sings an epic account of the human body and mind (Cantos 2–6), followed by its threat by and defence against the forces of evil (Cantos 7–12). The 'purple island' of the title is described in geographical detail, but each physical feature of the realm corresponds to different organs of the human body. Cantos 2 to 5, concerned with this physical description, are accompanied by marginal notes indicating to which features they refer. Canto 6 covers the government of the realm by its Prince (the intellect), his Queen (the will) and their maiden daughter ('Eclecta', the Church). The rest of the poem is taken up with the threat to this realm posed by the forces of evil, the personified qualities (such as worldliness and humility) on each side, and the ensuing battle. The poem ends, after the intervention of an Angel-King suggestive both of Christ and King James I, with the triumph of good and the marriage between Eclecta and the Angel, a version of the biblical Song of Songs.

Most of the poem, then, is the song of Thirsil, a shepherd proxy for Fletcher himself, who reappears mostly in a rather token way at the beginning and end of each canto as he restarts and then breaks off his didactic poem. These self-conscious and sometimes awkward closural and opening motifs are similar to those found in Palingenius. The division into 12 books of rather unequal length also strongly resembles the structure of the *Zodiacus Vitae*, as well as (more remotely) that of the *Shepherds' Calendar* (1579). Thirsil's recitation itself, however, takes place over seven days, creating a link to the seven days of creation as described by Du Bartas. The scientific content of the poem is framed and explained religiously: the purple isle is both every human body and all the people, the 'body' of the Church, and the focus on the human body is justified both (as in Du Bartas) by the idea that God's goodness is revealed in his creation, and, more specifically, by the theology of the Incarnation (Canto 6, stanzas 71–4).

Although mostly remarked for its element of anatomical didactic, the poem divides, like the *Aeneid*, the *Zodiacus Vitae* and, indeed, *Paradise Lost*, into two sets of six: the description of the purple island, the body of man itself, is confined to the first half, dealing with physical features in Cantos 2 to 5 and the 'government' of the body by the intellect and will in Book 6.[41] The allegorical figures introduced in that book, of Prince, Queen and Princess ('Eclecta', the Church), set the stage for the second half of the poem, concerned with the threat to this realm – which is both

---

[41] For Fletcher and anatomy, see Sawday, *Body Emblazoned*, 141–82; and Mitchell, *Purple Island and Anatomy*. Sawday (142) also briefly mentions Kinloch, discussed in Chapter 10.

the human body and, increasingly, England – by evil from outside it. This corresponds quite closely to the shift from human ethical and relational matters in *Zodiacus Vitae* 1–6 to cosmography in Books 7–12 (and also, as noted above, to a common allegorical interpretation of the distinction between the two halves of the *Aeneid*). Fletcher marks this transition with some self-consciousness, asserting the vanity of earthly satisfaction ('Fond man, that looks on earth for happinesse, / And here long seeks what here is never found!', 7.2). This passage is followed by a second invocation (of Thesio, 7.9).

The start of Book 11 sees a strongly marked transition to the most 'epic' section of the poem ('Who now shall teach to change my oaten quill / For trumpet 'larms?', 11.2). This further heightening is followed by an invocation not of any Muse (even a sacred one), but of the Holy Spirit itself ('Ah thou dread Spirit, shed thy holy fire', 11.3). Fletcher aligns himself explicitly with King David, 'that thrice famous Poet-Shepherd-King' (11.4). Both the content of this passage, and its position, recall how Palingenius, lost in awe at the glory of the heavens, invokes Urania, the Muse of holy poetry, also in Book 11 (Aquarius, 11.320–1). This is the book that Harvey notes Digges knew by heart.

In stanza 37 of the first canto, Fletcher makes use of the same passage of Palingenius as does Shakespeare in *As You Like It*:

> How like's the world unto a tragick stage!
> Where every changing scene the actours change;
> Some subject crouch and fawn; some reigne and rage:
> And new strange plots brings scenes as new & strange,
>   Till most are slain; the rest their parts have done:
>   So here, some laugh and play; some weep and grone;
> Till all put off their robes, and stage and actours gone.[42]
>
>   (1.37)

As in Palingenius and Du Bartas (and later in Cowley and Ewens, discussed below), Fletcher's religious awe at the mystery of creation is sincere, though focused on the extraordinary perfection of the human body rather than (as in Du Bartas) the world as a whole or (as in Palingenius and to a lesser extent Du Bartas) on the pre-Copernican cosmogony which was increasingly subject to dispute. Fletcher glosses over the genitals at the end of Canto 3, but is not ashamed to describe the

---

[42] A recurrent motif in Palingenius, found most extensively at 6.644–725 ('Virgo') but also e.g. at 5.24–5 as well as in the dedicatory preface to the work. Quotations of *The Purple Island* are from Pope (ed.), *Purple Island*.

urinary system (2.26) or the rectum and anus (2.43) in some detail. The 'chiefest Citie, and Imperiall' of the realm, however, is 'fair *Kerdia*' – that is, the heart (4.14).

The island's prince is the intellect, his wife Voletta represents will and his daughter Eclecta stands for the Church. The second half of the poem (Cantos 7–12) is taken up with the preparations for, and fighting of, a battle between the worldly forces of the dragon Caro (the flesh) and his attendant sins, and the virtuous forces of Humility, Faith, Love and other virtues. Finally, in the twelfth Canto, a descending angel suggestive of Christ but identified also with James I defeats the dragon.[43]

Though unpublished until 1633, Fletcher's poem was almost certainly written largely at Cambridge in the first decade of the seventeenth century. Thomas Healy has argued that the work was part of a Protestant campaign to persuade James I to play the part of a devout Calvinist monarch, robustly resisting Catholic elements: if so, its publication, under the patronage of the convinced Protestant and opponent of Laud, Edward Benlowes (1602–76), in 1633, the year in which Laud finally became archbishop of Canterbury, may have had a political force.[44]

The poem ends with a marriage song, a version of the scriptural Song of Songs, in which the union of the Angel-King and Eclecta suggests that of King James and his English Church, as well as all the traditional allegorical interpretations of the scriptural text: Christ and the soul, the soul and the body, Christ and his Church. The allegorical reading of the Songs of Songs is ancient; but contemporary commentaries offered political as well as spiritual interpretations. Jacob Durfeld's commentary, for instance, published like *The Purple Island* in 1633, glosses the 'sealed garden' of verse (4:12, 'hortus conclusus') under three allegorical headings: as a natural allegory (that is, a comparison to the beauties, pleasures and implied fertility of an actual garden), a political allegory (representing a flourishing and well-governed kingdom), and finally 'metaphorically, standing for the Church'.[45]

---

[43] The Angel has three crowns, descends 'from Northern coast' and God 'from supplanting gave his [the Angel's] ominous name' (Canto 12, stanza 55). In the 1633 print edition a marginal note identifies the Angel as 'Our late most learned Soveraigne'. One of the etymologies for the Hebrew name 'Jacob' is from the verbal stem '*qb* meaning 'follow' or 'supplant, overcome'; 'from supplanting gave his ominous name' is therefore a gloss of 'Jacobus', the standard Latin form of James, as at least one early reader appreciated: the British Library copy digitized by *EEBO* has a handwritten gloss 'Jacob.' at this point (p. 172).

[44] Healy, 'Sound Physic', 345. Healy does not note the reference to the etymology of 'Jacobus', though it certainly supports his interpretation. See also Bayer, 'Distribution of Political Agency'; and Pope (ed.), *Purple Island*, 4–5.

[45] Durfeld, *Commentarius Accuratus*, 527–9. On the paraphrase and imitation of the Song of the Songs, see Chapter 6.

Scriptural Paraphrase and Political Allegory in the Mid-Seventeenth Century

Scriptural paraphrase with a strongly political cast, or political allegories drawing heavily upon scriptural imagery, became a characteristic feature of mid-seventeenth-century Latin verse in England, though these works have been very little studied, and nowhere surveyed together. The preface to Abraham Cowley's 1656 *Poems* makes a point of the poet's formal originality in composing a (fragment of) biblical epic, the unfinished *Davideis* – Cowley mentions only Quarles and Heywood as (vernacular) examples of works he is aiming to surpass.[46] Despite this assertion of originality, the publication of the *Davideis* follows closely upon a flurry of Latin and Greek scriptural verse paraphrases published in the previous decade, most of which are sharply (if somewhat variously) political. These include Robert Hatcher, *Institutio, epithalamium, & militia viri* (1645) and *Paideutica* (1646); Robert Horsman, *Sionis certamina et triumphus* (1651, reprinted in 1653); Henry Oxinden, *Iobus triumphans. Vincit qui patitur* (1651); Patrick Panter, *Metamorphoseon Quae In S. Scriptura extant, Libri VI* (1651); and, in Greek, James Duport, Σολομῶν Ἔμμετρος (1646, a paraphrase of the Song of Songs, Proverbs and Ecclesiastes); Henry Stubbe, *Horae subsecivae* (1651, a paraphrase of Jonah and Susannah in Greek verse with parallel Latin prose); and John Ailmer, *Musae Sacrae* (Oxford, 1652, paraphrases in Greek of Jonah, Lamentations, Daniel and of David's lament over Saul and Jonathan). Cowley's poem, the political connotations of which – given its theme of anointed kingship – have often been debated, appears more rather than less politically suggestive when read alongside such contemporary Latin material.[47]

The allegiances of these authors are varied, but almost all the works themselves are politically inflected, and, as the preference for biblical texts concerned with personal and national suffering suggests, marked by lament: Hatcher, Stubbe and Ailmer, for instance, all present their work explicitly as a consolation in troubled times. Horsman's *Sionis certamina et triumphus*, published anonymously in 1651, without place or printer, and reprinted in 1653, is a curious combination of thematically arranged scriptural verse paraphrases and interpretations, in four sections – the first identifying the 'morbi', diseases or illnesses which afflict the Church; the second the means of cure (such as faith and repentance); the third the

---

[46] Cowley, *Poems* (1656), sig. (b)3ʳ for mention of Heywood and Quarles.
[47] See Moul, 'Cowley's 1656 *Poems* in Context'.

process of cure itself; and the fourth hymns celebrating the outcome. Though Horsman praises Cromwell and includes a paraphrase of Psalm 125 titled 'Ecclesiae Stabilitas, & Securitas' ('The Stability and Security of the Church'), the shape and tone of the work emphasize suffering. Its reliance upon a bodily allegory of the Church as subject to disease relates it to Fletcher's poem.

Henry Oxinden's *Iobus triumphans*, published like Horsman's work anonymously and without place or printer, is the most straightforwardly royalist of these volumes.[48] A series of commendatory poems is prominently dated at the end '8th July 1649', setting the collection in the immediate aftermath of the regicide. Oxinden's own brief prose dedication is addressed not to any single patron, but 'Oppressis Terrarum Dominis' ('to the oppressed Lords of the Earth'). Oxinden writes:

> Egregiam Jobi patientiam olim Regis totius Orientis ... Regibus procellis hujus seculi vehementioribus expositis imitandam proposui; Quibus enim potius quàm Principibus legenda & meditanda sunt heroica magnorum Principum gesta? (sig. A7ʳ)
>
> *I have set out the extraordinary suffering of Job, once King of all the East ... for imitation by Kings exposed to the still more violent storms of this age; for what could be more appropriate for Princes to read and meditate upon than the heroic deeds of great Princes?*

Cowley's comments upon his choice of King David as the subject of his poem are framed in a similar way:

> For what worthier *subject* could have been chosen among all the *Treasures* of past times, then the *Life* of this young *Prince*; who from so small beginnings, through such infinite troubles and oppositions, by such miraculous virtues and excellencies, and with such incomparable variety of wonderful actions and accidents, became the greatest *Monarch* that ever sat upon the most *famous* Throne of the whole Earth?[49]

Oxinden praises true kingship as a conqueror of tyrants (in Fletcher's *Purple Island*, the armour of the Angel-King is 'dy'd ... In purple bloud of thousand rebell Kings', 12.62) and compared to a phoenix, light shining in the darkness (as in John 1), Hercules, and Christ. The poem is filled with

---

[48] Oxinden's biblical paraphrases are probably influenced by those of Alexander Ross, whose work he praises. The *ODNB* entry for Oxinden describes him as politically neutral, with friends on both sides (Hingley, 'Oxinden [Oxenden], Henry'). Nevertheless, both *Iobus triumphans* (1651) and *Religionis funus, et hypocritae finis* (1647) are plainly supportive of Charles I, and Oxinden published *Charls Triumphant* heralding the Restoration in 1660.

[49] Cowley, *Poems* (1656), sig. (b)2ʳ.

the same sets of images – comparing Job's suffering to a ship in a storm, or a tree in a gale – that we find insistently in political verse of the period.[50] The poem nominally celebrates the suffering and final vindication of Job, but in a diffuse and digressive way, and the political application of the piece is transparent. A lengthy summary of Job's sufferings ends as follows:

> Nam si Rex tantus solio dejectus avito,
> Inque fimo sedeat: Rex, quo non ditior alter,
> Nec pietatis erat quisquam, nec amantior aequi,
> Et Rex qui flatus irarum pertulit omnes
> Caelitus emissos, pestesque Acheronte recluso
> Quas Stygiae regnator aquae de faucibus atris
> Turpiter evomuit, pedibus subjecit, & hostes
> Prostravit, meritósque tulit de Dite triumphos,
> Si Rex tantae inquam virtutis pertulit omnes
> Insultus Satanae sine murmure, nonne ministros
> CHRISTI ferre decet moderato pectore clades?[51]

> *For if even so great a King can be cast out of his ancestral throne*
> *And be seated amid the mire; a King, than whom no other is more richly endowed*
> *In piety, nor is any other a greater lover of justice;*
> *A King who has endured all blasts of fury*
> *Sent down from heaven, and crushed beneath his feet the plagues*
> *Which the ruler of the Stygian waters has unleashed from Acheron and foully*
> *Vomited forth from his black jaws; he has laid waste*
> *His enemies, and carried back well-deserved triumph from hell itself;*
> *If – I say – a King of such virtue has borne all these*
> *Attacks of Satan without complaint, surely it is only fitting*
> *That ministers of CHRIST should endure disaster with temperance and restraint?*

The poem merges the sufferings of the scriptural Job – who was not in fact a king, though a wealthy and prosperous man – with those of Christ as well as Charles I, to comfort royalists in their distress with assurances of eventual justification. The discursive structure and didactic tone, as well as the style of the Latin, link Oxinden's verse to the Palingenian tradition: as noted above, one of Oxinden's own surviving manuscripts records that Alexander Ross recommended to him the reading and imitation of Palingenius.

These works can all be described as instances of biblical poetry in which the scriptural content is deployed to suggest political as well as personal or spiritual allegory, even if several of them (as in Oxinden) do not track the

---

[50] On political imagery in the English and Latin verse of this period, see Moul, 'Marvell and Fisher'.
[51] Oxinden, *Iobus triumphans* (1651), sig. C1ᵛ.

scriptural text systematically or (as in Horsman) add considerable commentary to a series of paraphrases. Sarah Ross's terminology of the poetry of 'meditation', of works that dwell on and respond to a piece of scripture in various ways and sometimes with repeating or circling structures, fits poetry of this kind well, though both these examples are, in their interpretation, much more sharply political than any of the instances Ross describes.[52]

Closely related to this are a cluster of poems which, like Fletcher's *Purple Island*, are not themselves scriptural paraphrases but which draw closely upon scriptural allegory, especially of the Song of Songs, for political purposes. Many of the same authors composed examples of this type of poem, such as Hatcher's *Paideutica* (1646), an explicitly didactic poem on true wisdom, strongly in the Palingenian tradition, which incorporates inset sections of scriptural paraphrase, and Oxinden's own *Religionis funus* (1647), a plainly royalist allegorical poem on the death of true religion. *Religionis funus* ends with the poet in London, searching desperately for his 'bride', true religion, only to be confronted with her tomb:

> Illicque incerto sepelivit & IPSA sepulchro.
> RELLIGIO valeas, valeas dixi inde, priusquam
> CAROLUS ADVENIET, non expectanda resurget.[53]
>
> *Interred there was SHE HERSELF* [personified Religion] *in an anonymous tomb:*
> *Farewell RELIGION, farewell I said then, until*
> *CHARLES ARRIVES, she is not expected to rise again.*

Here as in Fletcher the true Church, the Bride of the Song of Songs, cannot be restored unless or until the King, like Christ the Bridegroom, returns.

Also dating from the 1640s, though written from an entirely different political perspective, is Peter Smart's (1568/9–c.1652) long poem of 1,290 hexameters, divided into five short books and dated in its published form 16 February 1643, attacking John Cosin (1594–1672) and the style of worship he oversaw at Durham Cathedral. Smart, an unflinching Calvinist and previous prebend of Durham Cathedral, spent much of the 1620s opposing the Arminianism (as he saw it) of the bishop of Durham and other cathedral colleagues including Cosin, resulting eventually in being stripped of his position and even imprisoned. Smart was already 76 in

---

[52] Ross, 'Epic, Meditation or Sacred History?'.
[53] Oxinden, *Religionis funus* (1647), p. 18 (sig. D1ʳ), final lines of the poem. Capitals and italics as in original.

1643 and this is a striking example of a highly conservative poem employing, though satirically, the then fashionable language of the Song of Songs. The printed version of the work is titled *Septuagenarii senis itinerantis cantus epithalamicus* (*Marriage Song of a Wandering Old Man of Seventy Years*), though it survives also in a manuscript copy in the Durham Cathedral archive.[54] It is an elaborate allegory of the Laudian period in which the English Church, corrupted by Catholic splendour and ritual, is described grotesquely as an old woman desperately attempting to disguise her age and appear as a youthful bride for marriage, not to Christ, but to anti-Christ (that is, Catholicism and Arminianism), before the eventual purging and restoration of the true Church by the events of 1642. The elaborate accoutrements intended to disguise the Church's age and corruption correspond to the elaborate music, liturgy, vestments and ceremonies to which Smart objected, and recall the standard scene in formal epithalamia in which first Venus, and then the bride herself, adorn themselves for the ceremony:

> Nempe puellascens canis matrona capillis
> Fastidit quodcunqe vetus ...
> Nec nova sufficiunt, quae terra domestica profert,
> Extremis peregrina volens accersit ab Indis.
> Horum, dentis egens, dentes mercatur eburnos,
> Ore suo figens Elephantis ab ore revulsos.
> Cursitat huc, illuc: agros, urbesque pererrat.
> Undique rara legens. Loculos scrutatur & arcas
> Siqua latent ubicunque medendae commoda formae,
> Arripit haec avidè. Sic irreparabile damnum
> Vultus ingenio restaurat, & arte resarcit.[55]

> *So a married woman with grey hair becomes a girl again*
> *And despises anything old ...*
> *But new things alone, of the kind which the domestic realm offers, do not suffice,*
> *She desires and sends for exotic items from the farthest Indies.*
> *Being without teeth herself, she pays for ivory dentures instead,*
> *Fixing in her own mouth teeth torn from that of an Elephant.*
> *She rushes hither and yon – ranging round the fields and cities.*
> *Everywhere she picks up unusual items. She pries into boxes and chests*
> *In case anything might be hidden there which could help to improve her appearance,*
> *And anything she finds she seizes on greedily. In this way she cunningly repairs*
> *The irreparable loss of her beauty, and artfully patches it over.*

---

[54] Durham Cathedral Library, MS Cath. Add. 352.   [55] Smart, *Cantus epithalamicus* (1643), 21.

Scriptural Paraphrase and Political Allegory 479

A third example, and one of the most ambitious and effective, is the opening and eponymous poem of Peter du Moulin's *Ecclesiae Gemitus*, first published anonymously in 1649.[56] Composed largely in iambic trimeters with an inset ode in alcaics (the same metre as Cowley uses for the Latin inset ode of *Davideis* 1), and a further inset speech in dactylic hexameter, Du Moulin's work is a very strange and memorable allegorical poem, in which the beleaguered Church of England is represented by a nymph threatened by violence and (it is implied) rape by a rabble of soldiery representing Parliamentarian forces.[57] Like Hatcher's *Paideutica*, Oxinden's *Iobus Triumphans* and Smart's *Cantus epithalamicus*, it is divided into short books (here called *metra*) and draws the imagery of its religio-political allegory from the same sources:

> Hunc Sponsa Christi, quâ nihil venustius
> Viget Orbe, Pulcra, sed perusa Solibus,
> Intenta rectis Totum ocellis accipit;
> Qualis Tonantis aquila Titanem solet
> Fixa irretorto contueri lumine.
> ...
>
> Extorris, exul, improbae tyrannidis
> Opima nuper praeda, nunc ludibrium;
> Decora largis ora fletibus rigans,
> Cruore stillans, ictibúsque lurida,
> Scissam vepretis in fugâ pallam trahens,
> Lacerósque crines; per loca aspera, squallida,
> Nudo pede errat, sola, deserto avio,
> Desertior Ipsa: Fessa tandem humi sedet,
> Ad veteris orni caudicem retorridum ...[58]

---

[56] Though published anonymously (and pointedly dated 'in the first year of the era of the martyrdom of Charles I, King of Britain'), at least some readers were evidently aware of its authorship: the Thomason Tracts copy has been annotated 'Du molin' on the title page. (The Bodleian copy of Birkhead's *Poematia* (1645), also published anonymously and without place of preparation, has a similar annotation on the title page: 'Scripsit Henricus Berket è Coll. Omn. Anim. Oxon.' Henry Birkhead was a fellow of All Souls, Oxford.) Du Moulin seems to have been chiefly responsible for a second anonymous tract against the regicide (and John Milton) designed for European circulation, *Regii sanguinis clamor ad coelum adversus paricidas Anglicanos* (1652). He also composed Latin verse invective against Milton, and his Latin poetry survives in several manuscript sources. There is no modern edition or translation of *Ecclesiae Gemitus*. This poem is discussed also in Chapter 5.

[57] This feature of metrical variety created by inset lyrics or verse speeches is found also in Hatcher's *Paideutica* (1646) and seems to have been highly fashionable at this point. It is discussed further in Chapter 5.

[58] Text from *Ecclesiae Gemitus* (1649), though with typographical errors corrected with reference to the 1670 edition.

> *The Bride of Christ, than whom nothing more chaste*
> *Flourishes on the earth, Beautiful as she is, but burnt by the Suns,*
> *Stares fixedly at the sun and welcomes it Whole with a straight gaze;*
> *Just as the eagle of the Thunderer is accustomed*
> *To behold the Titan straight, no eye turned aside.*
> ...
>
> *Now banished, exiled, recently the rich prey*
> *Of a wicked tyranny, now a laughing-stock;*
> *Bedewing her beautiful face with generous tears,*
> *Dripping with gore, bruised by blows,*
> *Dragging a cloak torn on the brambles in her flight,*
> *Her hair torn; through harsh places, dirty*
> *She wanders with a bare foot, alone, more deserted*
> *Than the trackless desert; at length, exhausted, she sits on the ground,*
> *At the parched foot of an ancient mountain-ash*

Du Moulin's Bride of Christ can, uniquely, gaze directly at the sun: an image linked to the eagle-poet-angel imagery found in Palingenius and Milton, and, as noted above, traceable to Claudian. The bedraggled female figure as a political allegory is probably also indebted to Claudian in particular: at the opening of *De Bello Gildonico*, a poem about the repression of Gildo's rebellion in 398 AD, Rome, cut off from the grain supply in Africa, appears as a starving goddess.[59] It was well established, however, in modern poetry: the beginning of Thomas Chaloner's *De Republica Instauranda* (published 1579, though composed before 1565) contains one of the most memorable Anglo-Latin versions. A didactic epic on good government in 10 books, Chaloner's poem is itself strongly influenced by Palingenius, and was probably known to all the authors discussed in this chapter.[60] Chaloner died in 1565, and by the time of its publication his poem, like Fletcher's *Purple Island*, related to the political context of the previous generation. In the first scene, Chaloner's 'mother' (that is,

---

[59] *Gild.* 1.17–27. Africa subsequently makes a very similar appearance, though depicted as wounded rather than starving (*Gild.* 1.134–9).

[60] Sir Thomas Chaloner (1521–65), who was one of the seven contributors to *A Mirror for Magistrates* (1559), composed the poem while ambassador to the court of Philip II of Spain (see O'Sullivan, *Reluctant Ambassador*). *De Republica Instauranda* was edited by William Malim (or Malym, 1548–94), headmaster of Eton (until 1573) and then of St Paul's. Book 1 is concerned with true religion (i.e. Protestantism); Book 2 with the preservation of an orderly society; Book 3 with the dangers of revolution; Book 4 with agriculture; Books 5 and 6 with the preparations for war. At the end of Book 6, the poet finds himself on an island of the Hesperides, told of the greatness of England to where he must sail. Book 7 describes society on the island; Book 8 clothing; Book 9 the education of women; and Book 10 the political constitution of England. National Archives, MS SP 9/36/8, part of the Williamson collection, contains a late sixteenth-century manuscript fragment from Book 6 (fol. 30), with corrections. Binns has called it 'probably the longest Elizabethan Latin poem' ('Humanist Latin Tradition', 188); see also Binns, *Intellectual Culture*, 26–9.

England herself) appears to the poet in a dream in a grotesque state, bedraggled, scrofulous and half-naked, though with breasts incessantly pouring milk (a reference to England's neglected natural fertility). Chaloner's dream has a wayward satiric energy of its own, drawing on Claudian's political allegory as well as epic scenes in which the hero encounters and consults with his own mother (Achilles and Thetis in *Iliad* 1; Aeneas and Venus in *Aeneid* 1).[61] Du Moulin's bedraggled nymph-of-the-national-church, by contrast, derives from a combination of Claudian and the eroticized imagery of the Song of Songs. Whereas the *sponsa* (Bride) of the Song of Songs is paradigmatically beautiful and desired, the beauty of the personified Church in Du Moulin's poem is besmirched and neglected, left to wander alone.

Later in *Ecclesiae Gemitus* the implied sexual threat becomes more explicit, and at this moment of greatest danger, collapsed at the foot of a tree and bleeding heavily, with the soldiers now right upon her, the nymph cries out for rescue. By divine intervention, her wounds are healed by the blood and tears of Christ, and she is saved from death.[62] The scenario here is markedly similar to that of Parthenia (literally, 'Maidenly') in Phineas Fletcher's *The Purple Island*. In the second, allegorical half of that poem, Parthenia represents chaste, unmarried love, who easily overcomes and kills Porneois (representing fornication) when he tries to assault her. She is in her turn, however, bested by false delight, whom she mistakenly considers virtuous, and has to be rescued by the arrival of the angel-king. It is this scene which is a close parallel for Du Moulin's poem:

> Th'undaunted Maid, feeling her feet denie
> Their wonted dutie, to a tree retir'd;
> Whom all the rout pursue with deadly crie:
> ...
>
> And now perceiving all her strength was spent,
> Lifting to listning heav'n her trembling eyes,
> Thus whispering soft, her soul to heav'n she sent;
> Thou chastest Love, that rul'st the wandring skies,
>   More pure then purest heavens by thee moved;
>   If thine owne love in me thou sure hast proved;
> If ever thou myself, my vows, my love hast loved.
>   (11.31–2)

---

[61] Chaloner describes himself as a satirist at several points (e.g. 1.185 and 10.816). The Book of Job, which contains an account of creation of importance for many of the didactic poems discussed in this chapter, was also sometimes described as satire. Scaliger calls Palingenius' *Zodiacus Vitae* 'sober' satire: 'Palingenii poema totum Satyra est: sed sobria, non insana, non foeda' – Scaliger, *Poetices* (1561), 306.

[62] Du Moulin, *Ecclesiae Gemitus* (1649), 39–40. The inset lyric at this point is discussed in Chapter 5.

In Fletcher's allegory, Chastity (Parthenia) and the Church-as-Bride-of-Christ (Eclecta) are separate characters. In Du Moulin, victimized Chastity has become the suffering of the Church itself in a time of civil war. But what is most striking about this cluster of texts is their shared use of a scripturally informed allegorical erotics across considerable differences of political and religious allegiance: ranging from the fiercely Calvinist and anti-Laudian Smart, via Horsman and Oxinden, to poetry as plainly royalist as Du Moulin. Such intense overlap in imagery recalls Nicholas McDowell's comment on the similarities, in their imaginative use of scripture in the 1640s, between poets as theologically distant as John Saltmarsh and Richard Crashaw.[63]

Under the pressure of events in the 1640s and 1650s, multiple poets combined the fashionable 'scriptural erotics' of the Song of Songs with the well-developed tradition of allegorical epic found in Palingenius, Chaloner, Spenser and Fletcher, to express deep concerns – from both sides of the debate – for the fate of the Church and the state. Whereas Milton achieved prominence in the 1650s for his prose writing for the Protectorate, his royalist contemporary Abraham Cowley, famous as a poet since adolescence, was renowned for his 1656 *Poems*. Indeed, at the Restoration it was Cowley, not Milton, who looked like the nation's great scriptural poet, and whose work of the 1650s most self-consciously furthered the project of a Protestant poetics as set out in the 1580s by Sidney and his contemporaries. The final section of this chapter offers a reading of the late work of Cowley and his contemporary and admirer, Maurice Ewens, within this 'Palingenian' (rather than Virgilian) tradition of didactic epic.

Maurice Ewens (Newport), *Votum Candidum* (1665 and Subsequent Editions)

One of the most lavish early testimonies to Cowley's importance, written during his lifetime, is found in the opening pages of a long Latin poem, *Votum Candidum*, by the English Jesuit poet Maurice Newport (1611–87).[64] In what amounts to almost the sum total of comment on Newport's work, Leicester Bradner noted that the description of Boscobel

---

[63] McDowell, 'Beauty of Holiness'.
[64] Newport, *Votum Candidum* (1665). Newport, born Maurice Ewens, studied at St Omer (c.1623–8) and entered the English College at Rome; ordained in Rome in 1634, he left to join the Society of Jesus in Belgium, where he was admitted under the assumed name of Maurice Newport. He was apparently teaching at St Omer in the 1630s and 1640s, and came to England in 1644. He was resident in Hampshire (1644), Devon (1645–9), Oxfordshire (1651–2) and finally London (from

wood in *Votum Candidum* is similar to Cowley's in the sixth book of his *Plantarum Libri Sex* (1668), suggesting that Cowley knew Newport's poem.[65] This is unsurprising: Newport praises Cowley by name in the opening pages, singling him out as 'Pindarica fidens, & versicolore Camoena' ('loyal to a Pindaric and versicoloured Muse'), alongside briefer tributes to Denham, Waller and D'Avenant.[66] The *Votum Candidum* was, moreover, apparently markedly popular, going through five editions between 1665 and 1679, with a partial translation published in 1695.[67] Despite this, Newport's poem has been ignored by critics. This is largely, no doubt, because there is no available translation, but also because in common with many of these 'Palingenian' epics, the poem is markedly hard to define in modern critical terms, including as it does elements of myth, medieval history, recent events (such as the Battle of Worcester), allegory, scriptural paraphrase and contemporary science.

Though a poem of praise, prayer for and celebration of the restored king, Charles II, Ewens' work is hedged and haunted by death: by the inevitability of death for us all, and more locally by the bloodshed of the Civil War and the execution of Charles' father in 1649. The certainty of death is his first point, and the one to which he constantly recurs. This is straightforward, memorable and explicitly didactic Latin verse in the Palingenian tradition:

> Verùm agesis, aciemque aliò mentemque retorque.
> Qui fato non cessuros promiserit annos,
> Nemo sit. aeterna pendentem ex arbore vitam
> Non opis est nostrae contingere. *flammeus* arcet
> Excubitor, telique minax *versatilis* ira.
> Debemur morti, qui nascimur; ex uteroque
> Addicti dominae nomen transcribimus urnae.
> . . .

1653), becoming rector of the London district in May 1666. See Clancy, 'Ewens [*alias* Newport], Maurice'.

[65] Bradner, *Musae Anglicanae*, 202. Newport's poem includes footnotes, a feature probably also imitated from Cowley.

[66] Newport, *Votum Candidum*, 2–3. Quotations throughout are from the 1665 edition. The text is unlineated; references are to page numbers.

[67] After the initial 1665 edition, the work was reprinted in 1669, 1674, 1676 and 1679. The first three are essentially the same, barring minor corrections and alterations. The 1676 edition, however, divides the third book differently, and adds a fourth, most of which is new, as well as an extensive index, referring in particular to the notes. The 1679 edition reverts to the earlier three-book version, without index. An English translation of a short portion of the poem was published in 1695 as *The Double Eternity, or, The Inevitable Choice*.

> Et quamvis meritorum alis subvecta tuorum
> Fama tuum portat super aurea sidera nomen,
> Quamvis densa fores obsidunt arma, tuumque
> Terra equitem tremit, & Neptunia marmora Typhin,
> Quamvis Atlantea sinus illabitur auro
> Unda tuos, & Gange, tuo modò, gemmeus exis,
> Pulvis es. ille tuas & opes, titulosque, minasque
> Excipit; extrema est in pulvere linea rerum.
> (*Votum Candidum*, 7–8)

> *But come now, turn your gaze and mind elsewhere.*
> *There is no one who can promise that their years will not*
> *Give way to death. It is not for us to touch*
> *Life that hangs from an eternal tree. A flaming guard*
> *Wards us off, and the menacing fury of his whirling weapon.*
> *We who are born are owed to death; from the very womb*
> *We are pledged like slaves to the urn on which we write our name.*
> ...
>
> *Although Fame, borne aloft on the wings of all your great deeds,*
> *Carries your name above the golden stars,*
> *Although your troops are drawn up in dense ranks outside your door;*
>   *although the earth*
> *Trembles at your calvary, and the marble surface of Neptune's*
>   *realm fears Typhis* [Tiphys was the pilot of the Argo];
> *Although the Atlantic wave floods your bays with gold,*
> *And you leave encrusted with gems from the Ganges*
>   *which is yours alone –*
> *Still, you are dust. Death takes all your wealth, all your titles*
> *All your threats – and the final line in the ledger is a line in the dust.*

Seeking the source of the uncertainties of life, the poet takes the reader on a tour of the body: *Vati / Adde gradum comes, & mecum interiora recede / Corporis in spatia humani* ('Follow / The poet closely, and draw with me far into / The deep spaces of the human body', *Votum Candidum*, 13). This is both the actual human body, as newly understood by medical science, and (as in Fletcher) the body of the state. The tour begins in the head, the body's Queen; but the most detailed and arresting section concerns the blood and the heart, with an especial emphasis upon the relation of the arterial and the venous systems, as discovered by William Harvey. (Cowley's enthusiasm for this topic is evident both in his ode on Harvey and in the treatment of the subject in the *Plantarum Libri Sex.*)

The passage builds to a climax in which Harvey, who died in 1657, is addressed in heaven. Newport includes a kind of infancy narrative, comparing Harvey to the baby Aesclepius, visited in his cradle by snakes, with links also to the Hercules myth as it is told in Pindar, *Nemean* 1 (one of the odes translated by Cowley and published in 1656).⁶⁸ Newport's mythologizing of Harvey follows an earlier description of the philosophical meditations of Prince Charles, the future Charles II, as a child of six by the river at Chelsea: the juxtaposition is probably intended to associate Harvey's long period of scientific exile before his ideas were accepted with the real-life exile (and eventual return) of Charles II.⁶⁹

As in Palingenius, the poet has a strong personality, and narrates his own adventures: into the body in Part I, and up to heaven (before later descending to hell) in Part II, in one of the most strongly Palingenian sections:

> Hìc lentus circumspexi, jam mente recepta,
> Convexos orbes, scenamque patentis Olympi,
> Palantesque aulae per caerula pensilis ignes;
> Ignibus & dixi proh quantùm dividor illis!
> . . .
>
> Et dixi quàm saepe, pedi talaria lento,
> Quis pennas humero nectat, queis nubila supra,
> Supra ignis lunaeque domos impervia terris
> Lumina tranem illa, empyrias & praepes ad arces
> Sistar, inaccessas ubi caeli filia gazas
> Incolit, indigetesque beat Macaritis alumnos?
> Sola moras omnes superat, mortalibus aptat
> Hanc humeris alam, haec pedibus talaria virtus.
>   (*Votum Candidum*, 49)

Here [in heaven] *I looked slowly around, and took in*
The globes of the planets, and heaven like a great stage-scene,
And the fires [of the stars] *wandering among the blue-green expanses*
    of this pendant court;
And I said, 'Oh how far am I divided from those fires!'
. . .

And then how often did I say: 'Who is it that fits winged sandals
To my sluggish foot, attaches feathers to my shoulder; how is it that I
Can sail above the clouds, above the realms of fire and
    of the moon, and fly past
Those lights unreachable from land and, winged like a bird,
    stop before
The citadels of fire, where the daughter of heaven inhabits

---

⁶⁸ Newport, *Votum Candidum*, 16–18. Hera sent two snakes to kill Hercules in his cradle, but he strangled them before they could harm him. Cowley's version of *Nemean* 1 is central to Stella Revard's argument about the implicit royalism of Cowley's Pindarics (Revard, 'Cowley's *Pindarique Odes*').
⁶⁹ Newport, *Votum Candidum*, 11. For the royalist associations of Harvey and his work, see Sawday, 'Chief Mystery'.

> *Her unreachable treasuries, and blesses the heroes, adopted*
>   *children of Bliss?*
> *One thing only overcomes all delays, and fits this wing*
> *To mortal shoulders, these winged sandals to mortal feet – virtue.'*

Part II contains also a long inset ecphrasis, presented by a figure of divine Justice, depicting what is effectively a miniature *Paradise Lost:* the fall of the angels (68); the temptation and expulsion of Adam and Eve from the Garden of Eden (68–9); the flood (69–71); the destruction by fire of the five cities (71); Aaron (72); Moses (72–3); and – departing from scripture – the whole variety of nations (73–4), culminating in England (74). Later, hosted in the forest, the poet hears of the Battle of Worcester, and visits Boscobel, where Charles II famously hid in an oak tree in the aftermath of the battle.

Overall, Newport's poem combines in a single work almost all the elements identified in this chapter: moral, religious, historical, political and scientific didactic; political and religious allegory; a version of the 'tour of the body' as in Fletcher; and the use of classical myth and reference in a work which, taken as a whole, is generically, stylistically and tonally markedly *un*classical. The didactic focus of the poem is moral – with lengthy Palingenian digressions on pleasure, good and glory – as well as religious and, plainly, political. But there is also a pioneering openness to new discoveries which links Newport's strange poem to the philosophical radicalism of Palingenius, the unflinching physiological detail of Fletcher and Kinloch (the latter discussed in Chapter 10), and the medical and herbal subjects of Cowley's *Plantarum Libri Sex*, first published in its complete form in 1668.

Cowley, *Plantarum Libri Sex* (1668)

The opening pages of Ewens' poem praise Cowley in lavish terms. It is unsurprising, therefore, that Cowley read Ewens' work and was almost certainly influenced by it as he worked on his magnum opus of the 1660s. Following the Restoration, it was not Cowley but Milton who pursued the logic of the scriptural-political allegory into a full-scale, complete biblical epic. Cowley, by contrast, only wrote one Latin and three English books of his *Davideis*, and the preface in the 1656 *Poems* indicates that he had abandoned the project by the time of publication. But Cowley, too, completed a major work in the 1660s: an epic of an entirely different kind. The *Plantarum Libri Sex* (*Six Books of Plants*) is an episodic didactic epic about the medicinal, herbal and cultural uses of plants, arranged in six books of escalating seriousness, which is also strikingly, though sometimes ambiguously, political in its celebration of the Restoration, condemnation of the Civil War, and its scientific optimism.[70] The poet-narrator appears as a character throughout, though frequently functioning largely as a framing device. In these as well as several other respects the poem belongs to the tradition of didactic epic associated with Palingenius.

The *Plantarum Libri Sex* has, however, some obvious formal differences from most of the poems considered in this chapter. The first two books, on herbs, initially published alone in 1662, were almost certainly begun before the Restoration.[71] Both of these books are in elegiac couplets. In the first, a miscellany of (female) herbs speak, relating stories which act as *aides-mémoires* for their medicinal uses, accompanied by dense footnotes. Several of the plants relate, or allude to, stories of their own metamorphosis, either derived from Ovid or of a recognizably Ovidian type, in what amounts to a kind of guying of Ovid for didactic effect. Whereas in the *Metamorphoses* almost every female protagonist is rendered mute by her transformation, Cowley's herb-women are positively loquacious, and on three occasions (assisted by the poet's notes) refer the reader to Ovid themselves. Mint ('Mentha'), for instance, tells how as a girl she was raped by Pluto, who was caught in the act by Proserpine. Apparently worried that she might not be believed, she cites Ovid as evidence of the truth of her story: 'Nè quis mentiri me fortè existimet, ore / *Veridico* meminit *Naso* Pöeta mei' ('Lest anyone should think that I am lying / The poet Ovid, who does not lie, has told my story').[72] The accompanying footnote gives the reference and quotes a line and a half from Ovid, *Met.* 10.729–30.

In their eloquence, these female plants more closely resemble the untransformed heroines of the *Heroides*, who are eloquent in their suffering. But Cowley's Ovidian herbs are no longer suffering at all: on the contrary, they are upbeat about their transformation and in many cases

---

[70] Unfortunately, there remains no modern translation of the *PLS*, first published in full within Cowley's *Poemata Latina* of 1668. Sutton's online edition includes a Latin text (based on the 1678 edition, though with some errors of transcription), keyed to the interesting but far from literal English translation of 1689, with contributions by Nahum Tate and Aphra Behn among others – Sutton (ed.), 'Abraham Cowley, *De Plantis Libri VI*'. Critical discussion remains fairly limited, though see Bradner, *Musae Anglicanae*, 118–22; Hinman, *Abraham Cowley's World of Order*, 267–96; Hofmann, 'Columbus in Neo-Latin Epic Poetry'; Ludwig, 'Neulateinische Lehrgedichte'; Monreal, *Flora Neolatina*; Spearing, 'Fruits of Retirement'. I have discussed various aspects of the poem in a series of chapters and articles, including 'Politics and Religion'; 'Ovidian Transformations'; 'Horatian Odes '; 'Latin and English Elegies'; and 'Introduction to *Abrahami Couleij Angli*'.

[71] Cowley, *Plantarum Libri duo* (1662).

[72] Text throughout from the 1668 edition of Cowley's *Poemata Latina*, here 60.

there is a memorable link between the reason for their metamorphosis and the use of the herb they have become. Nymphea (the water lily), for instance, tells towards the end of Book 1 how as a beautiful nymph she was seduced and then abandoned by Hercules:

> *Nympha* fui, *Dea* postremae non infima classis;
>   Venit *Amor*; quid tum profuit esse *Deam*?
> *Flammipotens* iubet *Ille*: accendor in *Hercule* viso,
>   Tótque *Triumphorum* pars *Dea* parva fui.
> ...
>
> Ille meos (quid multa?) ferus decerpsit honores
>   Ille meae *Florem Virginitatis* habet.[73]
>
> (5–8, 17–18)
>
> *I was a nymph, a goddess of no small rank; but then Love came: what good was my godhead then? In his flaming power he commanded me: I took fire at the sight of Hercules, and I a goddess was but a small part of his total triumphs ... For he (what more is there to say?) fiercely plucked my honour and took the flower of my virginity.*

In her shame and misery, she wishes to die; but, being divine, cannot. At this stage, we are still in plainly elegiac territory, and Cowley signals as much. The pool created by her ceaseless weeping is described, at line 42, with a phrase that echoes the abandoned Ariadne of Catullus 64, the bereft Cornelia of Propertius 4.11 and finally Gallus, addressed by Propertius in a poem that compares Gallus' beloved to Hylas, whom Hercules loved.[74]

Here, however, the poem takes a surprising turn. Jupiter, taking pity on Nymphea, turns her into a plant, the water lily, that grows in wet conditions with a sturdy root, the so-called 'club of Hercules'. In her new form, Nymphea is no longer sorrowful, but, on the contrary, considers herself fortunate and, above all, useful – because her suffering has seen her transformed into a plant with the power to ease exactly that painful experience by which she was defeated. As Cowley's detailed footnote makes clear, preparations made from the water lily are believed to assuage lust and fevers of various kinds. This metamorphosed woman-cum-herb not only has the power to speak and (unlike in the *Metamorphoses*) retains it after her transformation, she is able to be positively constructive – her typically elegiac suffering functions as a source of (and *aide-mémoire* for) her scientific usefulness.

---

[73] Cowley, *Poemata Latina* (1668), 29–30.
[74] Nymphea says 'Et collecta meos alluit unda pedes' (42, p. 30), with echoes of Catullus 64.68, and Propertius 4.11.16 and 1.20.8.

This is a very different kind of challenge to Ovid from the explicit rejection of pagan myths that we find in Palingenius, Du Bartas, or, indeed, in Cowley's own preface to his 1656 *Poems*. In some ways, though, it is a more robust one: Cowley harnesses his readers' knowledge of classical authors to make more memorable the points he has to teach about the marvellous variety and medicinal utility of the natural world. The overall impression is one of wonder at creation and a kind of purposive benevolence: Cowley's scientific interests are real, and the dense notes to the first five books show that he was up to date in his reading of botanical and medical material, but his imaginative engagement with emergent science has no assumption of impersonality. On the contrary, he infuses nature as a whole with individual personalities and suggests that these plants wish to be curative. Cowley's poem – like that of Palingenius – includes no explicitly Christian teaching; but his belief in the legibility, benevolence and coherence of creation is of course a religious one, and it has much in common with the combined pleasure and reverence with which Du Bartas describes nature, Fletcher or Kinloch the human body, or Palingenius the cosmic order.

It is only in Book 2 that the kind of narrative coherence typical of the later books starts to emerge: though also concerned with herbs, Book 2 has a dramatic setting, in the herb garden at Oxford, at night. These female herbs, all of them useful for specifically gynaecological problems, such as the regulation of menstruation, pregnancy and childbirth, discuss a series of fashionable scientific topics related to their areas of expertise, including the ethics of abortion and (a hot topic in the medicine of the period) the cause and purpose of menstruation.

This is a quite remarkable scene. Here personified female plants, alluding in several cases to their own experiences of seduction or sexual assault, recast the female lament. We have seen this motif, in this chapter, in the tradition which links dishevelled, lamenting Rome (in Claudian) to a poorly administered England in similar distress (in Chaloner) to the rescue of Eclecta (in Fletcher, drawing also on scriptural allegory) and of the nymph who represents the English Church in Du Moulin's *Ecclesiae Gemitus*. Shortly after the first publication of Cowley's work, several of the poems about the Fire of London depict London herself in the same terms.[75] But Cowley's plants are not rescued by anyone – on the contrary, they are merely interrupted by the gardener who bursts in at the end of Book 2, seeking treatment for his wife in

---

[75] E.g. Crouch, *Londinenses Lacrymae* (1666); [Anon.], *In tristissimum ... Carmen Lugubre* [1666].

labour. In their medicinal utility and high-level intellectual debate, they have found purpose and satisfaction; and the remedies they offer threaten to disrupt the ancient narrative: abortificients, as the herb Savin remarks, get raped and seduced girls out of trouble; but (Mugwort comments) if the nymphs and girls of myth had known how to use them, many great heroes would not have existed at all.[76] In this sense, Cowley's poem belongs to the same disruptive vein as the *Zodiacus Vitae*: a work which is characterized by reverence for divine creation, and in that respect not only compatible with Christianity but actively religious; but at the same time at a sharp angle to political and cultural orthodoxy, and serious about the development of knowledge.

As Cowley continued his poem in the subsequent four books, it became increasingly political and more complexly allegorical. At some point, he decided to expand the work not by continuing the essentially Ovidian form of women speaking in elegiac couplets, but to construct a work of epic length and scale which contains within it a kind of ascending hierarchy of Latin verse forms, developing from the elegiac speeches of the first two books, into a chain of Latin lyric poems linked by narrative sections in elegiacs (Books 3–4), and incorporating also what is effectively a set of epigrams (at the start of Book 4). The final two books are in the epic metre, hexameter. Moreover, this formal 'ascent' corresponds to an increase in botanical scale: the first two books are concerned with herbs; the third and fourth with flowers; and the fifth and sixth with trees, themselves divided between the smaller cultivated fruit and nut trees of an orchard (Book 5) and the great trees of a forest (Book 6). In this way, Cowley's didactic epic contains within it the full range both of plants and of standard Latin verse forms, to create a fully stocked garden which represents the 'garden-state' of England herself.

The political allegory of Cowley's poem becomes clear in Book 3: here Flora, newly returned with the Restored King Charles II in May of 1660, celebrates the Restoration on the bank of the Thames, and gathers the flowers to choose a ruler for their realm.[77] (This motif somewhat resembles that of Fletcher's *Purple Island*, in which the pretext for Thirsil's song is that he has been chosen as ruler of the shepherds.) Each of the inset lyrics is a kind of manifesto, as the flowers in turn make their case to be of greatest beauty and utility – not all of these flowers are female, but most are. In a

---

[76] For further discussion, see Moul, 'Ovidian Transformations'.
[77] Caroline Spearing has argued that the menstruation debate of Book 2 also refers, allegorically, to the bloodshed of the Civil War ('Fruits of Retirement', 187).

surprising conclusion, however, Flora decides not after all to create a monarch, but rather a pair of consuls, elected each year:

> Ut verum vobis fatear, *Romana*, Quirites,
>   Sum *Dea*, nec Regem jura creare sinunt.
> *Tarquinium* ne Hortis potero regnare Superbum,
>   *Romuleâ* factum Numen in urbe, pati?
> Et benè si memini gavisa est vestra Tyranni
>   Sacrilegi justâ Natio tota fugâ.
> Ille *Gabinorum* praeludens caedibus, Horto
>   Messuit infoelix *Lilia summa* suo.
> Non Hominum, *Florum capiti* non ille pepercit,
>   Abscidit horribili saevus utrumque joco.
> Vos quoque terrarum Dominos imitarier aequum est,
>   Florigenâ ductum nobile *Marte* genus,
> Esto igitur, sempérque mane, *Respublica Florum*,
>   Ordine plebeio patricióque potens.
> Quod foelix faustúmque fiet Vobísque Mihíque,
>   Jucundúmque *Hominum* sensibus atque *Deûm*,
> Tu, *Rosa*, sis Consul, Collegam *Lilia* sume[78]

> *To speak the truth, O descendants of Quirinus, I am a goddess of Rome, and the Roman laws do not allow us to create a king. How could I allow a proud Tarquin to rule the gardens, once I had been made a divinity in the city of Romulus? Indeed, if I remember correctly, your whole Nation rejoiced when that sacrilegious tyrant was deservedly put to flight. That man who, as a prelude to the slaughter of the Gabines, cut down in a sinister fashion the tallest lilies in his garden. The savage spared the heads neither of men nor of flowers, but cut off them both alike, as a kind of dreadful joke. So it is right that you too should imitate those lords of the earth, the noble race [i.e. of Romans] descended from Mars, himself born of a flower. Therefore establish yourself as, and always remain, a Republic of the Flowers, powerful in both the plebeian and the patrician order. May this arrangement bode well for you and for me, and please the senses of both men and gods: namely that you, Rose, should be consul, and take Lily as your fellow-consul.*

The rose and lily were the emblems of Charles I and Queen Henrietta Maria; they also appear together in the Song of Songs ('I am the rose of Sharon, and the lily of the valleys', 2:1). Cowley's own note on Tarquin quotes Livy, Pliny and Ovid, but there are surprising resonances too between this passage and the poetry of the previous decade. In Cromwellian propaganda of 1650, Tarquin was Charles Stuart – the son

---

[78] PLS 4.1048–64; Cowley, *Poemata Latina* (1668), 247–8.

of the executed Charles I, and the King in waiting, who was linked to Tarquin for a supposed inclination to tyranny and for his sexual appetite.[79] In the passage from Livy 19 quoted by Cowley in his footnote, Tarquin cuts down the tallest of the poppies in the garden; Flora's substitution of lilies ('lilia summa', 1055) for these poppies suits her rhetorical purpose – she is about to appoint the Lily as a consul – but also activates the language of royalist elegy.[80] The flower imagery also links this passage, the resolution of a debate which stretches over Books 3 and 4, to the description of the late medieval civil wars known as the 'Wars of the Roses' at the end of Book 3 (*PLS* 3.1102–15).[81] Like *Paradise Lost* and Ewen's *Votum Candidum*, Cowley's poem responds directly to the history of the previous decades. Although for Cowley, unlike Milton, the Restoration meant the fulfilment of his political hopes, this device by which the realm of flowers marks the Restoration by deciding *against* a monarchy is, at least, somewhat surprising. Rather as in Ewens' poem, the celebration of peace is haunted by imagery which recalls the trauma of civil war.

In Book 5, Pomona, goddess of the Orchard, summons to her autumn feast the country gods of the both the Old and the New World. Set on one of the Fortunate Isles, between Europe and America, she stages a contest in which the fruit and nut trees of Europe appear in procession and sing of their origins and virtues, followed by those of the New World, including coca, plantain, avocado, agave and coconut. Chaloner's poem also uses the Fortunate Isles: at the end of Book 6 of *De Republica Instauranda*, the poet makes landfall on one of these islands, only to discover there a perfect community, in which the Golden Age has never ended. Chaloner's island is a transparently allegorical version of England, or the England that could be if the advice of the poem were to be followed.

In his version of this motif, Cowley makes considerable use of recent work on the botany of the Americas, include de Laet's *Novus Orbis* (1633), and even includes an hexameter in Aztec-Nahuatl (*Oi Camacalli, camatli*,

---

[79] [Anon.], *Mercurius Politicus* 1 (6–13 June 1650), 12.
[80] E.g. Fisher's simile evoking the suffering of the inhabitants of York during the siege of 1644 – 'Labitur, & coctis arescit flosculus hortis, / Lilia deciduis, languéntque Rosaria capsis', 'The flower falls and dries up in scorched gardens, / The Lily and Rose-bushes droop as their seed-cases fall', *Marston-Moor* (1650), 34 – and Marvell's intensely elegiac, albeit enigmatic, 'The Nymph Complaining for the Death of her Fawn': 'I have a garden of my own / But so with roses overgrown, / And lilies, that you would it guess / To be a little wilderness' (71–5), tentatively attributed by Smith to the immediate aftermath of the execution of Charles I in 1649 – Smith (ed.), *Poems of Andrew Marvell*, 65. Mildmay Fane includes a Latin epigram on the lily and rose in his 1648 collection, *Otia Sacra* (164).
[81] For further discussion of classical, historical and scriptural sources in this passage, see Moul, 'Politics and Religion'.

natastlits, Intelolocti, 5.1010).⁸² But his conclusion is, again, surprising: finding the American plants superior, a quarrel breaks out between Bacchus and Omelichilus, the Mexican wine god, which is calmed by Apollo who delivers a remarkable speech foretelling the collapse of Europe, corrupted by greed for gold, and the subsequent rise of America, first as a haven for science and the arts (1153–91) and finally as a great empire, akin to that of Rome. These are the final lines of the prophecy, and of the book:

> Imperia hîc serae statuent tum maxima *Parcae*,
> Non numero ingenti Servorum & inutilis Auri
> *Barbarico* tantùm *fulgore* potentia vulgi
> Sensibus attoniti, vidistis qualia nuper
> Regna *Motezumae*, vel ditis *Guanacapaci*,
> Qualia *Romano* quondam sed vidimus *Orbe*,
> Et Domina his *Virtus* erit, & *Fortuna* Ministra.⁸³

> *Then the fates will belatedly found here*
> *the greatest of empires, mighty not by the measure*
> *of their many slaves, or as valued by vulgar minds*
> *dazzled with useless gold's barbarous gleam, such*
> *as you lately saw in the realms of Montezuma or rich*
> *Guanacapac, but such as we once saw in the Roman world,*
> *states in which Virtue will rule, with Fortune her attendant.*

Book 6 returns to England but shifts gear again, to penetrate into the deep forest. At this point, also, the footnotes drop away and the poem moves into straightforward narrative epic: a speech delivered to the poet by the Dryad of the oak tree relating the events of the Civil War, regicide, Protectorate and Restoration, culminating in a description of the Battle of Lowestoft against the Dutch in 1665 which is plainly intended to recall descriptions of Actium. Cowley's description of Boscobel, as Bradner noted, resembles a parallel passage in Ewens' *Candidum Votum*.⁸⁴

Charles II emerges here as a type of both doctor and gardener, replanting the forests, tending to the garden of England and binding the wounds of civil war while also looking outward, and preparing, as Chaloner had urged Elizabethan England to do, for foreign war:

> ... sed & haec quoque respicis inter
> Nonnullis Sylvas oculis; succurris earum
> Accisis inopum rebus, populatáque regna
> Arboreae gentis suffectâ pube novellâ

---

[82] See Monreal, *Flora Neolatina*, 274–6.
[83] *PLS* 5.1194–1200; Cowley, *Poemata Latina* (1668), 312. [84] Bradner, *Musae Anglicanae*, 202.

> Integras augésque, futurum extendis in aevum
> Imperium sylvestre, tuísque beata jacebit
> (*Optime Protector*) pronepotum turba sub Umbris.[85]
>
> *And yet even in these circumstances you*
> *Have regard for the Woodlands; you move to help*
> *Them in their torn and impoverished state, and you*
> *Restore and improve with fresh young stocks*
> *The ravaged realms of the race of trees: you extend into the future*
> *The woodland empire, and a blessed host of descendants*
> *(Best of Protectors) will lie in your Shade.*

The 'Imperium sylvestre' ('woodland empire') here refers both to the literal replanting of forests to provide timber for an ambitious navy, and to the imperial ambitions that navy will pursue.[86] The role of the Dryad of the oak recalls the confident female plants of the opening books, and also, in speaking for and in some sense embodying the nation as a whole, contrasts with the persecuted and suffering allegorical female figures we saw in the poems by Fletcher, Smart and Du Moulin. The poet's encounters with multiple voices and figures, none of whom is dominant, recalls the structure of Palingenius' epic – though the Dryad of Book 6, like Urania of Books 11–12 of the *Zodiacus Vitae*, marks out the most serious content.

Cowley's poem is didactic in multiple dimensions: scientifically, politically, philosophically; in its serious attention to nature; and probably also in how he envisaged his text being used – in his proposal for a new educational institution, which was never realized, Cowley specifically lamented the lack of good quality Latin poetry on scientific subjects.[87] If Palingenius was indeed a schoolmaster, he may similarly have intended that his work be taught. But the *Plantarum* is also didactic in the traditional, moralizing mode which we recognize from all the texts discussed in this chapter, and with which, indeed, this book began. The opening of Book 4, for instance, on the true happiness of modest aspirations and self-contained simplicity is easily paralleled many times over in the texts under discussion:

> Foelix, quem miserâ procul ambitione remotum
> Parvus Ager placidè, parvus & Hortus, alit.
> . . .

---

[85] *PLS* 6.1105–11; Cowley, *Poemata Latina* (1668), 359.
[86] John Evelyn, the author of a landmark work on forestry, *Sylva, or A Discourse of Forest-Trees, and the Propagation of Timber* (1664), was a friend of Cowley.
[87] Cowley, *Proposition for the Advancement of Experimental Philosophy* (1660).

> Talis, magne Deus (si te mihi dicere fas sit
>   Ridiculorum inter nomina vana Deûm)
> Talis, Vere Deus, nunc inclinantibus annis
>   Sit, precor, aetatis Scena suprema meae,
> Finis inutilium mihi sit precor illa laborum,
>   Jactatae statio firma sit illa rati.
> Sic mea coelestem praegustet Vita quietem;
>   Dormiat, & Mortem discat amare suam.[88]
>   (4.1–2 and 41–8)

> *Happy the man, who, far removed from wretched ambition, is sustained in peace by a small field and little garden ... Such a life as this, great God (if it's permissible for me even to name you amidst the empty titles of ridiculous pagan gods) – may such a life as this, True God, I pray, form the last act of my mortal life, in my now declining years; may such an end of my feeble labours, I pray, be granted me, and that firm harbour for my storm-tossed boat. May my life thus taste the peace of heaven; may it sleep, and learn to love its own death.*

Fletcher includes a very similar moralizing poem on the blessedness of the poor at the opening of his final canto (12.2–6); in the British Library copy, this passage has been marked as gnomic. Similarly, Palingenius' *Zodiacus Vitae* includes many examples, several of which are frequently excerpted. An expansive version of the motif from near the end of Book 2 (Taurus) includes this passage:

> Felix qui didicit contentus viuere paruo;
> Nec spem vllam in rebus ponit, quas linquere cogit
> Parca ferox, tanquam nostri non iuris; et aeui
> Quam breue sit spatium reputat; quam friuola demum
> Omnia quae in terris longe lateque creantur;
> Qui minor aduersis non fit maiorue secundis,
> Minoisque vrnam spernit, Stygiosque furores,
> Securus quodcumque ferat fortuna, tenere.
>   (474–81)

> *Lucky the man who has learnt to live content with a little;*
> *He places no hope in material goods, which a fierce Fate*
> *Can force him to leave behind, for she does not operate by our laws;*
>   *such a man*
> *Knows well how short his time might be; how worthless therefore*
> *Are all those things created in the world, however far and wide;*
> *Such a man is not made less by adversity, or puffed up by success –*
> *He rejects Minos' urn, and the furies of hell,*
> *Happy to take whatever fortune brings.*

---

[88] *PLS* 4.1–2 and 41–8; Cowley, *Poemata Latina* (1668), 192 and 194.

Both Cowley's and Palingenius' versions borrow from multiple sources, including Virgil's description of rural piety and the philosophical life, at *Georgics* 2.458–540. Cowley understood Virgil as a religious poet, as his remarks in *Of Agriculture* (which refer in particular to the *Georgics*) make clear:

> The first wish of Virgil (as you will find anon by his verses), was to be a good philosopher; the second, a good husbandman; and God (whom he seemed to understand better than most of the most learned heathens) dealt with him just as he did with Solomon: because he prayed for wisdom in the first place, he added all things else which were subordinately to be desired. He made him one of the best philosophers, and best husbandmen, and to adorn and communicate both those faculties, the best poet. He made him, besides all this, a rich man, and a man who desired to be no richer, *O fortunatus nimium et bona qui sua novit*. To be a husbandman, is but a retreat from the city; to be a philosopher, from the world; or rather, a retreat from the world, as it is Man's – into the world, as it is God's.[89]

Virgil (and to a lesser extent Lucretius) are important for many of the poets discussed in this chapter; but nevertheless none of these Palingenian poems is *in extenso* much like either Virgil or Lucretius to read: the characterful voice of the narrator-poet, the episodic structure and varied encounters, the intense though highly varied allegoresis, as well as the explicit moralizing and religious wonder all mark out a didactic epic tradition distinct from that of either the *Aeneid* or the *Georgics*. In these respects, Cowley's poem is best understood as a Palingenian epic.

---

[89] On Cowley's *Essays* as a religious work, see especially Major, 'Sacred and Secular'.

Afterword

I have tried to write the book I would have liked to read when I first found myself, fascinated but more or less baffled, attempting to make sense of some of that great majority and vast expanse of early modern Latin poetry that does not conform to modern expectations of 'classical' Latin style, form and genre. Latin poetry of the sixteenth and seventeenth centuries is hugely various – of course in quality as well as style, tone and form – but above all it is *strange* and so often barely legible in multiple dimensions: linguistically, if you are not a very confident reader of Latin; but also metrically, formally, generically, tonally – over and over again one encounters works which are arrestingly odd, even where they are also arrestingly good.

One of my most memorable experiences of this kind of encounter was the first time I read Payne Fisher's *Marston-Moor*, an astonishingly good poem which I found myself reading in bed on a muddy PDF downloaded from *EEBO*, so gripping was its pacey narrative, while also repeatedly asking myself: what is this style? The style is, more or less, Claudian, as I eventually worked out: ten years ago, in common I imagine with many British Latinists, I had not read any Claudian. For the first weeks that I was reading Fisher all I could have told you is what his style was not: not at all Virgilian, but also – more surprisingly given the convention about Virgil for royalists and Lucan for Parliamentarians – not deeply or meaningfully Lucanian either.

Not all of Fisher is of such high quality as *Marston-Moor*, which is surely his best work. But much of it is very good, and at its best it is unforgettable: Cromwell as an armoured elephant, the weaponry bouncing off his iron flanks (blending passages from Lucan and Prudentius); the city of York, after the raising of the siege, like a bride adorned for her husband; the death of Posthumus Kirton – in fact Fisher's half-brother, though he partly conceals this fact, probably for political reasons:

> Quàm vaga deciduis vergunt *Colocasia* capsis,
> Pubentésque Rosae primos moriuntur ad *Ortus* ...[1]
>
> *As the spreading Egyptian lily bends with its dropping seed-cases*
> *And the young men are dying at the first risings of the Rose ...*

I have had similarly intense experiences on encountering, among others, Beza's psalms, Sarbiewski's lyric poems, and Palingenius' *Zodiacus Vitae*. These are the works I would recommend to anyone who wanted to develop a real feel for what early modern Latin poetry could do: worthy companions to stand alongside Mary Sidney, George Herbert, John Milton, Andrew Marvell and Abraham Cowley.

I have finished this study at a strange and uncertain time, while libraries around the world are shut and the ordinary routines of academic and domestic life transformed or suspended. This book depends in large part on many years of scholarship of the painstaking, archival kind; that work was a great pleasure and I am extremely grateful for the funding and institutional support that allowed it, and very fortunate to have completed it before all those libraries closed. But this is finally a book about poetry, not scholarship. I hope one or two readers may, as a result of what I have written, seek out one or two of these poems and find themselves thereby consoled.

---

[1] Fisher, *Marston-Moor* (1650), 60.

Metrical Appendix: Latin Metres

The conventions governing the composition of Latin verse in the classical (rather than medieval) tradition were well understood in early modern England, but they are quite different to the principles of scansion in English verse. English poetry is usually described in terms of beats or stresses, and the patterns of, for instance, an iambic pentameter, are created by the juxtaposition of stressed and unstressed syllables. The patterns of Latin poetry, by contrast, are constructed not primarily according to whether or not a syllable is stressed in speech, but rather by how long it takes to pronounce.

This is not the place to offer a detailed account of the distinctions between long and short syllables in Latin, but the basic principles are easy to grasp. The syllables of words have a natural length (for instance, the common word *dominus* ('lord' or 'master') is three short syllables. A cluster of two or more consonants tends to make the preceding vowel long, and this is true whether the consonant cluster is part of the same word or starts a new one. For instance, in the word *Christus* ('Christ' in Latin), the cluster of *s* and *t* makes the first syllable long. In the phrase *Christum callidum*, the combination of the *m* at the end of the *Christum* and the *c* at the beginning of *callidum* make the final syllable of *Christum* long. The final syllable of each line is lengthened by its position – because it is natural to pause at the end of the line. For this reason a syllable which is naturally short can stand in this position, where it 'counts' as a long syllable. Many 'quantities' – that is, whether a syllable is long or short – can be deduced from applying a small set of rules of this sort, while some others have to be learnt alongside vocabulary on an individual basis.

In addition, where one word ends with a vowel and the next word begins with a vowel – as we find twice in the phrase *ex praelio undae ignisque* (*Musae Responsoriae* 27) – the two words are 'elided', that is, the *o* of *praelio* and the *u* of *undae* are merged to form a single syllable, and the same thing happens in this line between *undae* and *ignis*.

Conventionally, this effect is not represented in written Latin (though it is pronounced in reading poetry aloud), unlike in Greek poetry, and indeed in English: the poetic form '*Twas* (for 'it was') is an example of a similar phenomenon.

In order to describe the patterns of long and short syllables in Latin metres, we use a conventional notation: – denotes a long syllable, and ∪ a short syllable. So two longs is shown as: – –, two shorts as ∪ ∪ and so on. Where a syllable may be either long or short, this is indicated by an 'x'. The following notes describe using these symbols for the patterns of longs and shorts. Where the poet has a choice – for instance between a long and a short syllable, or a long and two shorts – this is represented by printing both options, one above the other. Latin verse lines are conventionally divided into 'feet', internal divisions marked here by | .

In these notes I have avoided as much as possible the technical terms used by scholars of Latin metre, and in some of the more complex forms I have also simplified to a small degree the range of options available. Almost every thorough Latin grammar offers more detailed explanation of the principles of Latin metre for readers who are interested.

Dactylic Hexameter

The hexameter line is the metrical form used in both Greek and Latin epic poems, but also in a wide range of other long, medium and (especially in the earlier part of the period covered by this book) also short Latin verse. The hexameter line is also the first line in each elegiac couplet: elegiac couplets are the single most common metre in early modern Latin. The word 'dactylic' refers to the basic pattern of a long followed by two shorts (– ∪∪, also called a dactyl).

The basic pattern of a hexameter line in Latin is as follows:

$$- \overline{\cup\cup} \mid - \overline{\cup\cup} \mid - \overline{\cup\cup} \mid - \overline{\cup\cup} \mid - \cup\cup \mid - x$$

This is a flexible metre. In each of the first four feet the poet can choose between the basic dactylic pattern – ∪∪ or two longs – –.

Elegiac Couplets

Elegiac couplets are composed of a hexameter line (see above) followed by a pentameter (that is, a shorter line of five feet). In this second shorter line, there is a strong break half way through (indicated by | |):

– ŪŪ | – ŪŪ | – ŪŪ | – ŪU | – UU | – x

– ŪŪ | – ŪŪ | – || – UU | – UU | – x

The second line of each couplet (the pentameter) is less flexible than the first (the hexameter), since in this second line the poet may choose between – UU and – – only in the first two feet. Accordingly, in a poem composed in elegiac couplets each even-numbered line (the pentameters) sounds more alike than the odd-numbered lines. Conventionally, there is also often a distinction in sense or tone between the hexameter and the pentameter lines. In epigrams, this can be used to point a contrast or present alternative perspectives. Elegiac couplets are the most common early modern Latin metre, and the first mastered at school.

Iambic Trimeters

Iambic trimeters become particularly popular as a non-dramatic metre in the early seventeenth century. The basic pattern is as follows:

Ū – U – | Ū – U – | Ū – U x

The iambic metres (including iambic trimeters and iambic distichs) also allow 'resolution': this is where a syllable that is long (–) in the basic pattern may be substituted for two shorts (UU). In combination with the existing short syllables in the metrical pattern, this allows for runs of several short syllables in a row. This makes iambic forms some of the most flexible in Latin poetry, leading to a large range of possible rhythmic effects.

Iambic Distichs

These are couplets formed from an iambic trimeter (see above) followed by an iambic dimeter – that is, a short two-foot version of the iambic line.

x – U – | x – U – | x – U x
x – U – | x – U x

This alternation of a longer followed by a shorter line creates a similar effect to the elegiac couplet. Like iambic trimeters, 'resolution' is allowed (see **iambic trimeter** above).

Phalaecian Hendecasyllable

This eleven-syllable line is associated particularly with Catullus and the neo-Latin imitators of Catullus (from Pontano onwards). It is often used for epigrams, and in Anglo-Latin verse is most popular in the seventeenth century.

x x – ∪∪ – ∪ – ∪ – x

Sapphics

This is a Latin adaptation of a Greek lyric metre used (among others) by Sappho. The form in which is it most commonly written in early modern Latin is modelled upon Horace's sapphic stanza. A poem in sapphics is composed of four-line stanzas or verses, and each stanza follows a rigid metrical scheme. The first three lines of each stanza follow an identical pattern, with a different form in the shorter final line (called an 'adonean', and sometimes understood as an extension of line three):

– ∪ – – – ‖ ∪∪ – ∪ – x
– ∪ – – – ‖ ∪∪ – ∪ – x
– ∪ – – – ‖ ∪∪ – ∪ – x
– ∪∪ – x

As the poet has very few options in this metrical form, sapphics – like the other lyric metres – are particularly challenging to compose. The particular popularity of sapphic metres in the sixteenth century is discussed in Chapter 4.

Alcaics

Like sapphics, these four-line stanzas use a form inherited from Greek poets (the name refers to the archaic Greek poet Alcaeus), but adapted for Latin by Horace.

x – ∪ – – ‖ – ∪∪ – ∪ –
x – ∪ – – ‖ – ∪∪ – ∪ –
x – ∪ – – – ∪ – –
– ∪∪ – ∪∪ – ∪ – ∪

As most of the quantities in this metre are fixed, each stanza sounds rhythmically similar. In particular, this metre is marked by the 'slower' third line (with three long syllables in a row in the middle) and the 'quicker' final line (with a large proportion of short syllables).

Choriambic Metres

Several lyric metres widely used in early modernity are constructed from different versions of an essentially 'choriambic' line. A 'choriamb' is a sequence of four syllables, two longs surrounding two shorts: – ∪∪ –. Various different lyric lines are constructed around one or more choriambs. One of the most frequently encountered is the **glyconic** line (sometimes called a 'choriambic trimeter'). Neither Horace nor Catullus used a sequence of pure glyconics in a poem, but we do find the line used in this way in some of Seneca's tragic choruses, and also in neo-Latin verse:

– – | – ∪∪ – | ∪ –

An expanded glyconic line with an additional choriamb is used stichically (that is, as a single repeated metrical line) by Horace and many early modern Latin poets. This metre is sometimes called the **'lesser' asclepiad, the 'first' asclepiad** or the **choriambic tetrameter:**

– – |– ∪∪ – | – ∪∪ – | ∪ –

Couplets of alternating glyconics and lesser asclepiads are found in Horace, *Odes* 1.3 and also, for instance, in Buchanan's Latin *Psalms* (14, 35, 43) and Herbert's *Musae Responsoriae* (40):

– – | – ∪∪ – | ∪ –
– – | – ∪∪ – | – ∪∪ – | ∪ –

Confusingly, different reference works number the asclepiad metres differently, and this combination is variously referred to as the 'second', 'third' and 'fourth' asclepiad.

Other less common metres are described in Chapter 2.

Bibliography A: Manuscripts

Arundel Castle (Duke of Norfolk)

Harington 311

Beinecke Library, Yale University

Osborn Manuscripts

Osborn b. 4
Osborn b. 52
Osborn b. 136

Biblioteca Nacional, Madrid

23888

Bodleian Library, Oxford

Additional Manuscripts

Add. A. 276
Add. B. 5
Add. B. 109

Ashmole Manuscripts

Ashmole 36/37
Ashmole 826
Ashmole 1492
Ashmole 1730

Ballard Manuscripts

Ballard 50

Barlow Manuscripts

Barlow 10

Cherry Manuscripts

Cherry 1
Cherry 5
Cherry 37

Douce manuscripts

Douce 280
Douce 357
Douce 387

Eng. poet.

Eng. poet. f. 13
Eng. poet. f. 16
Eng. poet. f. 17

Fairfax Manuscripts

Fairfax 40

Firth Manuscripts

Firth c. 1
Firth c. 3

Lat. misc.

Lat. misc. c. 19
Lat. misc. e. 19
Lat. misc. e. 23
Lat. misc. e. 32
Lat. misc. e. 38

Malone Manuscripts

Malone 14
Malone 15
Malone 19

Rawlinson Manuscripts

Rawl. C. 580
Rawl. D. 237
Rawl. D. 345
Rawl. D. 383
Rawl. poet. 25
Rawl. poet. 26
Rawl. poet. 31
Rawl. poet. 42
Rawl. poet. 57
Rawl. poet. 62
Rawl. poet. 63
Rawl. poet. 65
Rawl. poet. 72
Rawl. poet. 85
Rawl. poet. 94
Rawl. poet. 114
Rawl. poet. 142
Rawl. poet. 148
Rawl. poet. 154
Rawl. poet. 166
Rawl. poet. 171
Rawl. poet. 173
Rawl. poet. 209
Rawl. poet. 215
Rawl. poet. 246

Tanner Manuscripts

Tanner 306
Tanner 330
Tanner 406
Tanner 465
Tanner 466

Sancroft Manuscripts

Sancroft 26
Sancroft 28

Sancroft 53
Sancroft 89

Wood Manuscripts

Wood D 19

Bradford Archives (West Yorkshire Archive Service)

32D86/17

British Library

Additional Manuscripts

Add. 4456
Add. 4457
Add. 10418
Add. 10446
Add. 11723
Add. 12067
Add. 15227
Add. 15228
Add. 18044
Add. 18220
Add. 19863
Add. 22472
Add. 22583
Add. 23719
Add. 23723
Add. 23904
Add. 27447
Add. 28010
Add. 28644
Add. 29241
Add. 36529
Add. 37719
Add. 43410
Add. 44963
Add. 47111
Add. 48180
Add. 53726
Add. 61744
Add. 61822

Add. 62138D
Add. 70492
Add. 71125
Add. 72439
Add. 72899
Add. 73542
Add. 74231

Burney Manuscripts

Burney 370
Burney 390

Cotton Manuscripts

Cotton Faustina E. V.
Cotton Julius C. V.
Cotton Titus A XIII
Cotton Titus A XXIV

Egerton manuscripts

Egerton 2642
Egerton 3880

Harley Manuscripts

Harley 121
Harley 389
Harley 532
Harley 791
Harley 913
Harley 1221
Harley 1823
Harley 3258
Harley 3354
Harley 3496
Harley 3638
Harley 3831
Harley 3910
Harley 4484
Harley 4933
Harley 4935
Harley 5029

Harley 5110
Harley 5365
Harley 6038
Harley 6054
Harley 6211
Harley 6350
Harley 6383
Harley 6396
Harley 6637
Harley 6914
Harley 6922
Harley 6925
Harley 6932
Harley 6947
Harley 7315
Harley 7316
Harley 7363
Harley 7371

Lansdowne Manuscripts

Lansdowne 15
Lansdowne 104
Lansdowne 388
Lansdowne 695
Lansdowne 722
Lansdowne 762
Lansdowne 846
Lansdowne 852

Royal Manuscripts

Royal 2 D II
Royal 2 D XIV–XIX
Royal 12 A VII
Royal 12 A XX
Royal 12 A XXIII
Royal 12 A XXVII
Royal 12 A XXX
Royal 12 A XXXIII
Royal 12 A XXXV
Royal 12 A XXXVI
Royal 12 A XXXVII
Royal 12 A XLI

Royal 12 A XLIII
Royal 12 A XLVII
Royal 12 A LV
Royal 12 A LVI
Royal 12 A LVII
Royal 12 A LXI
Royal 12 A LXX
Royal 12 D VIII
Royal 14 B XVI

Sloane Manuscripts

Sloane 319
Sloane 499
Sloane 608
Sloane 833
Sloane 1249
Sloane 1255
Sloane 1458
Sloane 1466
Sloane 1479
Sloane 1710
Sloane 1766
Sloane 1768
Sloane 1867
Sloane 2287
Sloane 2764
Sloane 2832
Sloane 2870

Stowe Manuscripts

Stowe 305

Cambridge University Library

Add. 11
Add. 24 (D)
Add. 79
Add. 3873
Add. 4138
Add. 8861/1
Add. 8861/2
Add. 8915

Dd. II. 43
Dd. III. 73
Dd. III. 78
Dd. V. 75
Dd. V. 77
Dd. VIII. 28
Dd. IX. 59
Dd. XI. 80
Dd. XIV. 8
Ff. V. 14
Gg. I. 29
Kk. V. 14
Mm. I. 36
Mm. IV. 39

Cheshire Archives

DBC 2309/2/3

Chetham's Library, Manchester

Mun. A. 2.91
Mun. A. 4.15

Corpus Christi College, Oxford

258
266
294
309
311
317
324

Durham Cathedral Library

Cath. Add. 352
Hunter 27
Hunter 96

Durham PG Library

P 29

East Sussex Record Office

FRE/599

Emmanuel College, Cambridge

105

Essex Record Office

D/DL F106
D/DW Z3

The Family Album, Glen Rock, Pennsylvania

[Wolf MS]

Folger Shakespeare Library

V.a.103

Hertford County Record Office

Panshanger D/EP/F.36
Panshanger D/EP/F.48

Houghton Library, Harvard University

Eng. 645
Eng. 1544

Huntington Library

HM 904

Kent History and Library Centre

U275/C1/12

Lambeth Palace Library

113

Leeds University Library, Brotherton Collection

BC Lt 13
BC Lt 25
BC Lt 40
BC Lt 55
BC Lt 71
BC Lt q 18
BC Lt q 38

Manchester John Rylands Library

Eng. 410

National Archives

SP 9/36/8
SP 78/94/56

Nottingham University Library

117
Cl LM 59/1

Portland Manuscripts

PwV 47/31/1
PwV 48/31
PwV 518
PwV 929
PwV 1343
PwV 1345
PwV 1347
PwV 1456

The Queen's College, Oxford

284
347

Rosenbach Museum and Library

232/14

Society of Antiquaries (London)

SAL 437
SAL 330

Society of Friends Archive

Vol S 80
Vol S 193/5

Somerset Heritage Centre

DD\SF/18/2/8
DD\WO/57/1/1

Staffordshire County Record Office

D1287/19/6/50
D(W)1721/3/248

St John's College, Cambridge

O.65

Stonyhurst College, Lancashire

A. v. 4

Surrey History Centre

LM/1327/41

Trinity College, Cambridge

O. 6. 1
R. 3. 60
R. 7. 23
R. 14. 18

Westminster Abbey Muniments Room

31

West Yorkshire Archive Service (Leeds)

WYL 115/F6/2
WYL 156/237

William Clark Memorial Library

W2485M3

Bibliography B: Early Printed Books

[Anon.], *Ad Carolum Secundum, Britanniae Regem, Protrepticon* ([London: s.n.], 1649)
[Anon.], [Bodenham, John (ed.)?], *Englands Helicon* (London: I. R. for Iohn Flasket, 1600)
[Anon.], *Epigrammatum Delectus ex omnibus tum veteribus tum recentioribus Poetis* (London: Mosis Pitt, 1683; several subsequent editions)
[Anon.], *Ex Spinosa Anonymi Sylva, Folia quaedam; Sibyllinis licet veriora, Procellosis forte tamen ludibria hîc evolant ventis jactanda* ([Edinburgh?: s. n.], 1649)
[Anon.], *In illustrissimi comitis Leicestrensis, Oxoniensis Academiae cancellarij ... carmen gratulatorium* (Oxford: Josephus Barnes, 1585)
[Anon], *In tristissimum immanissimumque Urbis Londinensis Nonas Circiter Sept. LXVI Incendium, Carmen Lugubre* [London: s.n., 1666]
[Anon.], *Jonsonus Virbius* (London: E. P. for Henry Seile, 1638)
[Anon.], *Mercurius Politicus* (London: Robert White, 1650–60)
[Anon.], [Stapleton, Richard?], *The phoenix nest* (London: Iohn Iackson, 1593)
[Anon.], *Poems on Affairs of State* ([London: s.n.], 1702–7)
[Anon.], *Preces matutinae* (London: Thomas Vautrollerius, 1578)
[Anon.], *Satyra in poetastros O——C——enses* (London: [s.n.], 1702)
[Anon.], *Threnodia, sive Elegia In Injustissimam trucidationem sanctissimi, Prudentissimique Principis, Caroli Primi, Magnae Britanniae, Galliae, & Hiberniae, nuperrimè Regis* ([s.l.: s.n.], 1649)
[Anon.], *Umbritii Cantiani poemata* (London: Joannis Graius, 1729)
A Quercu, Leodegarius [Léger Duchesne], *Flores Epigrammatum*, 2 vols. (Paris: Petrus Beguin, 1555–60)
Adamson, Patrick, *Catechismus Latino carmine redditus et in libros quatuor digestus* (Edinburgh: Robertus Lekpreuik, 1581)
Poëmata sacra (London: Ioannes Billius, 1619)
Ailmer, John, *Musae Sacrae: seu Jonas, Jeremiae Threni, & Daniel. Graeco redditi carmine* (Oxford: L. Lichfield, 1652)
Ainsworth, Henry, *Solomon's Song of Songs. In English metre* ([Amsterdam?: s.n.], 1623)
Alites Carnutensis, Petrus, *De Utroque Jesu Christi Adventu* (Paris: Andreas Wechelus, 1561)

Allen, Nicholas, *Carmen encomiasticum Reginae Elizabethae* (London: Thomas Vautrollerius, 1571)
Allibond, John, *Rustica academiae oxoniensis Nuper Reformatae descriptio* ([London?: s.n.], 1648)
Alvarez, Emmanuel, *De Institutione Grammatica Libri Tres* (Venice: Society of Jesus, 1585)
Ashley, Robert (trans.) / Guillaume Du Bartas, *L'Uranie – Urania sive Musa Coelestis Roberti Ashelei de Gallica G. Salustii Bartasii delibata* (London: Johannes Wolfius, 1589)
Ashmore, John, *Certain Selected Odes of Horace, Englished; and the Arguments annexed. With poems (antient and modern) of divers subiects, translated. Whereunto are added, both in Latin and English, sundry new Epigrammes. Anagrammes. Epitaphes* (London: H[umphrey] L[ownes] for Richard Moore, 1621)
Aylett, Robert, *David's Troubles Remembred* (London: Richard Hodgkinsonne, 1638)
  Divine, and Moral Speculations in Metrical Numbers (London: Abel Roper, 1653)
  Joseph, or, Pharoah's Favourite (London: B. A. for Matthew Law, 1623)
  The Song of Songs, which was Salomons, Metaphrased in English heroiks by way of dialogue (London: William Stansby, 1621)
  Susanna: or, The Arraignment of the Two Unjust Elders (London: Iohn Teage, 1622)
Baker, Daniel, *Poems upon Several Occasions* (London: J. Jones, 1697)
Baldwin, William, *The canticles or balades of Salomon* (London: William Baldwin, 1549)
  A treatise of Morall phylosophie (London: [s.n.], 1547)
Ball, William, *Europa Lachrymans: Poema Heroicum* (London: Thomas Harper, 1650)
Bancroft, Thomas, *Two Bookes of Epigrammes, and Epitaphs. Dedicated to two top-branches of Gentry: Sir Charles Shirley, Baronet, and William Davenport, Esquire* (London: I. Okes for Matthew Walbancke, 1639)
Barberini, Maffeo [Pope Urban VIII], *Poemata* (Paris: Antonius Stephanus, 1623)
Barclay, John, *Argenis* (Paris: Nicolas Buon, 1621)
  Euphormionis Lusinini satyricon (Paris: Franciscus Huby, 1605)
Barlaeus, Caspar, *Britannia Triumphans* (Leiden: Godefrid Basson, 1626)
  Panegyris de laudibus Eminentissimi Cardinalis, Armandi Ioannis Plessiaci, Richelii Ducis, Franciae Patris (Amsterdam: J. et C. Blaeu, 1641)
  Poematum Editio Nova (Leiden: Elzevir, 1631)
Barlaeus, Melchior, *De raptu Ganymedis liber* (Antwerp: Gillis Coppens van Diest, 1563)
Barnfield, Richard, *The Affectionate Shepheard* (London: John Danter for T. G. and E. N., 1594), contains *Hellens Rape*.
  Cynthia. With Certaine Sonnets, and the Legend of Cassandra (London: Humfrey Lownes, 1595)

Bartholin, Thomas, *De medicis poetis dissertatio* (Copenhagen: Danielis Paullus, 1669)
Bastard, Thomas, *Chrestoleros* (London: Richard Bradocke for I[ohn] B[roome], 1598)
Bauhusius, Bernardus, *Epigrammata* (Antwerp: Plantijn, 1616)
Bellehachius, Ogerius, *Sacrosancta bucolica* (London: Henricus Midletonus for Guilielmus Ponsonbius, 1583)
Bettini, Mario, *Florilegium Variorum Poematum* (Leiden: Franciscus de la Botiere, 1633)
Beveridge, John, *Epistolae Familiares* (Philadephia: John Beveridge, 1765)
Beza [de Bèze], Theodorus, *Canticum Canticorum Solomonis, Latinis versibus expressum* ([Geneva]: Eustathius Vignon, 1584)
  Iobus ... cui etiam additus est Ecclesiastes (London: Georgius Bishop, 1589)
  Poemata juvenilia (Paris: Conrad Badius, 1548)
  Psalmorum Davidis et aliorum prophetarum, libri quinque (London: Thomas Vautrollerius for Hercules Franciscus, 1580)
Bidermann, Jacob, *Epigrammatum Libri Tres* (Antwerp: Heredes Martini Nutii, 1620)
[Birkhead, Henry,] *Poematia* ([Oxford?], 1645)
  Poematia in Elegiaca, Iambica, Polymetra, Antitechnemata et Metaphrases Membratim Quadripertita (Oxford: L. Lichfield, 1656)
Blount, Sir Thomas Pope, *De re poetica: or, Remarks upon Poetry with Characters and Censures of the Most Considerable Poets* (London: Ric. Everingham for R. Bently, 1694)
Boyd, Andrew, *Ad augustissimum monarcham Carolum ... carmen panegyricum* (Edinburgh: R. Junius, 1633)
Braithwait, Richard, *Barnabae Itinerarium* (London: J. Haviland, 1636)
Bridges, John, Bishop of Oxford, *Sacro-sanctum Novum Testamentum* (London: Valentinus Simsius, 1604)
Brinsley, John, *The posing of the parts. Or, A most plaine and easie way of examining the accidence and grammar, by questions and answeres, arising directly out of the words of the rules Whereby all schollars may attaine most speedily to the perfect learning, full understanding, and right use thereof; for their happy proceeding in the Latine tongue* (London: H. Lownes for Thomas Man, 1615)
Brome, Richard (ed.), *Lachrymae Musarum; The Tears of the Muses: Exprest in Elegies* (London: Tho: Newcomb, 1649)
  The Poems of Horace, Consisting of Odes, Satyres, and Epistles, Rendred in English Verse by Several Persons (London: Henry Brome, 1666)
Brownswerd, John, *Progymnasmata quaedam poetica*, ed. Thomas Newton (London: Thomas Woodcokus, 1589)
Buchanan, George, *De prosodia libellus* (Edinburgh: Andreas Hart, 1621)
  Elegiarum, Sylvarum, Endecasyllabon (Paris: Rob. Steph., 1567)
  Franciscanus et fratres (Basel: Thomas Guarinus Nervius, 1568)
  Paraphrasis Psalmorum Davidis Poetica, multo quam ante hac castigatior (London: Thomas Vautrollerius, 1580)

Buckley, William, *Arithmetica memorativa, sive Brevis, et Compendiaria Arithmeticae tractatio* (London: [s.n.], 1567)

Busby, Richard, *Grammatica Busbeiana Auctior & Emendatior, i.e. Rudimentum Grammaticae Graeco-Latinae Metricum in usum Nobilium Puerorum in Schola Regia Westmonasterii Opus Posthumum* (London: Eliz. Redmayne, 1696)

Calderwood, David, *Parasynagma Perthense et Iuramentum Ecclesiae Scoticanae et A. M. Antitamicamicategoria* ([Holland?: s.n.], 1620)

Calvin, Jean, *The Psalmes of David and others. With M. John Caluins Commentaries*, trans. Arthur Golding (London: Thomas East and Henry Middelton: for Lucas Harison, and George Byshop, 1571)

Cambridge University, *Academiae Cantabrigiensis ΣΩΣΤΡΑ. Sive, Ad Carolinum II reducem, de regnis ipsi, musis per ipsum feliciter resitutis gratulatio* (Cambridge: Joannes Field, 1660)

Anthologia in Regis Exanthemata: seu gratulatio musarum Cantabrigiensium de felicissimè conservata Regis Caroli valetudine (Cambridge University Press, 1633)

Irenodia Cantabrigiensis: Ob paciferum Serenissimi Regis Caroli è Scotia reditum Mense Novembri 1641 (London: Roger Daniel, 1641)

Lachrymae tumulo Philippi Sidnaei sacratae per Alexandrum Nevillum (London: Ioannis Windet, 1587)

Oliva Pacis. Ad illustrissimum celsissimumque Oliverum, Reipub. Angliae, Scotiae, & Hiberniae Dominum Protectorem: de pace cum Foederatis Belgis feliciter sancita, carmen Cantabrigiense (Cambridge University Press, 1654)

Sorrowes Ioy. Or, A Lamentation for our late deceased Soveraigne Elizabeth, with a triumph for the prosperous succession of our gratious King, James, &c. (Cambridge: John Legat, 1603)

Threno-thriambeuticon. Academiae Cantabrigiensis ob damnum lucrosum, & infoelicitatem foelicissimam, luctuosos triumphus (Cambridge: Iohannis Legat, 1603)

True Copies of all the Latine Orations, made and pronounced at Cambridge, on Tuesday and Thursday, the 25. and 27. of Februarie last past 1622 (London: W. Stansby for Richard Meighen, 1623)

Συνῳδία Sive Musarum Cantabrigiensium Concentus et Congratulatio, ad serenissimum Britanniarum Regem Carolum, de quinta sua sobole, clarissima principe, sibi nuper felicissimè nata (Cambridge University Press, 1637)

ΣΩΣΤΡΑ Sive, Ad Carolinum II reducem, de regnis ipsi, musis per ipsum feliciter resitutis gratulatio (Cambridge: Joannes Field, 1660)

Campion, Thomas, *Epigrammatum Libri II. Umbra. Elegiarum liber vnus* (London: E. Griffin, 1619)

Poemata (London: Richard Field, 1595)

Chapman, George, *Andromeda Liberata* (London: Laurence Lisle, 1614)

The Divine Poem of Musaeus (London: Isaac Iaggard, 1616)

Hero and Leander: Begun by Christopher Marloe; and finished by George Chapman (London: Felix Kingston for Paule Linley, 1598)

The Memorable maske of the two Honorable Houses or Inns of Court; the Middle Temple, and Lyncolns Inne (containing also *A Hymne to Hymen for the most time-fitted Nuptialls of our thrice gracious Princesse Elizabeth*) (London: G. Eld for George Norton, 1613)

Ovids Banquet of Sence (London: I. R. for Richard Smith, 1595)

Cheke, John, *De obitu doctissimi et sanctissimi theologi doctoris Martini Buceri* (London: [in officina Reginaldi Vuolfij], 1551)

Claudian, *Cl. Claudianus*, ed. Theodorus Pulmannus [Poelmann] (Antwerp: Plantin, 1585)

Claudii Claudiani Opera, ed. Daniel Heinsius et al. (Amsterdam: ex officina Schouteniana, 1760)

Clemens, Venceslaus, *Gustavidos Libri IX, quibus Gustavi II verè Magni & Augusti, Suecor. Gothor. Vandalor. &c. Regis Serenissimi, Victoriarum heroicarum, rerumquè per Germaniam Gestarum series carmine Heroico narratur* (Leiden: Franciscus Hegerus, 1632)

Cotton, John, *A brief exposition of the whole book of Canticles, or Song of Solomon* (London: Philip Nevil, 1642)

Cowley, Abraham, *The Mistresse, or Seuerall Copies of Love-Verses* (London: Humphrey Moseley, 1647)

Plantarum Libri duo (London: J. Flesher, 1662)

Poem on the Late Civil War (London: [s.n.], 1679)

Poemata Latina. In quibus Continentur, Sex Libri Plantarum, viz. Duo Herbarum. Florum. Sylvarum. Et Unus Miscellaneorum (London: T. Roycroft and Jo. Martyn, 1668)

Poems (London: Humphrey Moseley, 1656)

Poetical Blossomes (London: B. A. and T. F. for Henry Seile, 1633)

A Proposition for the Advancement of Experimental Philosophy (London: J. M. for Henry Herringman, 1660)

Craig, Thomas, *Henrici illustrissimi ducis Albaniae comitis Rossiae, &c. et Mariae serenissimae Scotorum reginae epithalamium* (Edinburgh: Robert Lekprevik, 1565)

Crashaw, Richard, *Carmen Deo Nostro* (Paris: Peter Targa, 1652)

Epigrammatum sacrorum liber (Cambridge: Thomas Buck and Roger Daniel, 1634)

Steps to the Temple. Sacred Poems, with other Delights of the Muses (London: T. W. for Humphrey Moseley, 1646)

Steps to the Temple, Sacred Poems. With The Delights of the Muses (London: Humphrey Moseley, 1648)

Crouch, John, *Londinenses Lacrymae. Londons Second Tears mingled with her Ashes* (London: T. Palmer, 1666)

Crowley, Robert, *One and Thyrtye Epigrammes* ([London]: Robert Crowley, 1550)

The Psalter of David newely translated into Englysh Metre ([London]: Robert Crowley, 1549)

Curio, Caelius Secundus (ed.), *Pasquillorum tomi duo* (Basel: Io. Oporinus, 1544)

Bibliography B: Early Printed Books 521

Pasquillorum versus aliquot ex diversis auctoribus collecti, ad exhilarandum, confirmandumque; hoc perturbatissimorerum statu pii lectoris animum, apprimè conducentia (Edinburgh: Robertum Lekpreuik, 1565)

Damman, Adrianus, *Schediasmata* (Edinburgh: Robertus Walde-grave, 1590)

(trans.) *Bartasias; qui de mundi creatione libri septem; è Gulielmi Sallustii Dn. de Bartas Septimana, poemate Francico liberius tralati, et multis in locis aucti* (Edinburgh: Robertus Walde-graue, 1600)

Dawson, John, *Summa moralis theologiae sive Exegesis tripartiti operis Solominici metris conscripta* (London: Johannes Norton for Richard Thrale, 1639)

de la Cerda, Juan Luis., *P. Virgilii Maronis Bucolica et Georgica Argumentis, Explicationibus, et Notis illustrata* (Cologne: Bernardi Gualteri, 1628)

De Laet, Joannes, *Novus Orbis, Seu Descriptionis Indiae Occidentalis Libri XVIII* (Leiden: Elzevier, 1633)

Dempster, Thomas, *Panegyricus, augustiss. potentiss. Q. principi Jacobo I. Britanniar. Franciae, et Hiberniae Regi, &c. domino suo clementiss* (London: Iohannes Billius, 1615)

Dethick, Henry, *Feriae Sacrae octo libris comprehensae, in quibus, naturae, tabularum, & gratiae leges exprimuntur* (London: per T. E. pro Humfredo Toy, 1577)

Dickenson, John, *Deorum consessu, Siue Apolinis ac Mineruae querela summam legentibus voluptatem nec minorem vtilitatem praebens* (London: Eduardus Allde, 1591)

Donne, John, *Paradoxes, Problemes, Essayes, Characters ... to which is added a Book of Epigrams: Written in Latin by the same Author; translated into English by J. Maine* (London: T. N. for Humphrey Moseley, 1652)

Dornavius [Dornau], Caspar, *Amphitheatrum sapientiae socraticae joco-seriae*, 2 vols. (Hanau: Typis Wechelianis, Impensis Danielis ac Davidis, 1619)

Dousa, Janus, *Odarum Britannicarum Liber* (Leiden: Plantin Press, 1586)

Drant, Thomas, *Epigrams and sentences spirituall* (London: Thomas Marshe, 1568)

In Selomonis regis et praeconis illustriss. Ecclesiasten, seu de vanitate mundi, concionem sapientissimam, et celeberrimam, paraphrasis poetica (London: Iohannes Daius, 1571)

A Medicinable Morall, that is, the two Bookes of Horace his Satyres, Englyshed accordyng to the prescription of saint Hierome ... The Wailyngs of the Prophet Hieremiah, done into Englyshe verse. Also Epigrammes (London: Thomas Marshe, 1566)

Drayton, Michael, *The Harmonie of the Church* (London: Richard Ihones, 1591)

Poemes Lyrick and pastorall. Odes, Eglogs, The man in the Moone (London: R. B. for N. L. and I. Flasket, 1606)

Dryden, John, *Astraea Redux. A Poem On the Happy Restoration & Return Of His Sacred Majesty Chares the Second* (London: Herringman, 1660)

Ovid's Epistles, Translated by Several Hands (London: Jacob Tonson, 1680)

Du Bartas, Guillaume, *Bartasias; qui de mundi creatione libri septem, è Gulielmi Sallustii Dn. de Bartas Septimana, poemata Francico liberius tralati, et multis*

in locis aucti, trans. Adrian Damman (Edinburgh: Robertus Walde-graue, 1600)
 Hebdomas ... latinitate donata, trans. Gabrielus Lermaeus (London: [John Windet?], 1591)
 La Sepmaine; ou Creation du monde (Paris: Jean Febvrier, 1578)
 L'Uranie – Urania sive Musa Coelestis Roberti Ashelei de Gallica G. Salustii Bartasii delibata, trans. Robert Ashley (London: Johannes Wolfius, 1589)
Du Moulin, Peter, *Carmen heroicum ad regem* (London: Ioannes Billius, 1625)
 Ecclesiae Gemitus sub Anabatpisticâ Tyrannide ([London: s.n.], 1649)
 Regii sanguinis clamor ad coelum adversus paricidas Anglicanos (The Hague [=London?]: Adrianai Vlac., 1652)
 Πάρεργα *Poematum Libelli Tres* (Cambridge: Joann. Hayes, 1671)
Duport, James, Σολομῶν Ἔμμετρος (Cambridge: Roger Danielis, 1646)
Duppa, Brian (ed.), *Jonsonus Virbius* (London: E. P. for Henry Seile, 1638)
Durfeld, Jacob, *Commentarius Accuratus in Canticum Canticorum Salomonis* (Rostock: Johan Hallervordius, 1633)
Echlin, John, *De regno Angliae, Franciae, Hiberniae ... panegyricon* ([Edinburgh]: Robertus Walde-graue, 1603)
Eleutherius, N. [pseudonym], *Triumphalia de victoriis Elizabethae regina Angliae* ([s.l. (Germany): s.n.], 1588)
Elyot, Sir Thomas, *The boke named the Gouernour* (London: in aedibus Tho. Bertheleti, 1531)
Elys, Edmund, *Dia poemata: Poetick Feet standing upon Holy Ground: or, Verses on certain Texts of Scripture* (London: J. G. for Philip Briggs, 1655)
 Miscellanea (Oxford: Hen. Hall for Tho: Robinson, 1662)
Evelyn, John, *Sylva, or A Discourse of Forest-Trees and the Propagation of Timber* (London: Jo. Martyn and Ja. Allestry, 1664)
Falckenburg, Jakob, *Ara et focus* (London: Rich. Grapheius, 1578)
 Ara et focus, pro ecclesiae, causaeque, bonae triumpho (London: Rich. Grapheius [i.e. R. Schilders], 1579)
 Britannia, siue De Apollonica humilitatis, virtutis (London: Richardus Grapheius, 1578)
 De expeditione Palaestinorum in Hebraeos. Pro Ecclesiae Victoria (London: Richardi Graphei, 1579)
Fane, Mildmay, *Otia Sacra* (London: Richard Cotes, 1648)
Fanshawe, Richard, *Il pastor Fido* (London: Humphrey Moseley, 1648)
 Selected Parts of Horace (London: M. M. Gabriel Bedel and T. Collins, 1652)
Farnaby, Thomas, *Florilegium epigrammatum Graecorum* (London: Felix Kyngstonius, 1629)
Fenner, Dudley, *The Song of Songs* (Middleburgh: Richard Schilders, 1587)
Filmer, Robert, *Anarchy of a limited or fixed Monarchy* ([London: s.n.], 1648)
Fisher, Payne, *Apobaterion* (London: Newcomb, 1655)
 Epinicion, vel elogium faelicissimi, serenissimi, fortitissimi Lodovici XIIII galliae, & navarae regis ([London: s.n.], 1658)
 In celeberrimam naumachiam (London: Tho. Newcomb, 1650)

In celeberrimum naumachiam, faelicissimámque serenissimae Venetiarum reipublicae victoriam contra numerosam stupendámque Turcarum classem 26 Junii, KDCLVI. Epincion (London: Tho. Newcomb, 1656)
Inauguratio Olivariana, sive pro praefectura Serenissimi Principis Angliae, Scotiae & Hiberniae, Dom. Protectoris Olivari: Carmen Votivum (London: Thomas Newcomb, 1654)
Irenodia Gratulatoria (London: T. Newcomb, 1652)
Marston-Moor, sive de Obsidione Praelioque Eboracensi Carmen (London: Thomas Newcomb, 1650)
Oratio Secunda Anniversaria (London: J. G. per Edoardum Blackmore, 1657)
Paean Triumphalis in secundum inaugurationem serenissimi nostri principis Olivari (London: Roger Daniels, 1657)
Patriarcha, or the Natural Power of Kings (London: Walter Davis, 1680)
Piscatoris Poemata (London: Thomas Newcomb, 1656)

FitzGeffrey, Charles, *Affaniae: sive epigrammatum libri tres* (Oxford: Josephus Barnesius, 1601)
Flatman, Thomas, *Poems and Songs* (London: S. and B. G[riffin] for Benjamin Took, 1674)
Fletcher, Phineas, *The Purple Island, or The Isle of Man, together with Piscatorie Eclogs and other Poeticall Miscellanies* (Cambridge University Press, 1633)
Fraunce, Abraham (trans.), Thomas Watson, *Amyntas. The lamentations of Amyntas for the death of Phillis, paraphrastically translated out of Latine into English hexameters* (London: John Wolfe, for Thomas Newman, and Thomas Gubbin, 1587)
Gager, William, *In Catilinarias Proditiones, ac Proditores Domesticos, Odae 6* (Oxford: Joseph Barnes, 1586)
  In Catilinarias Proditiones, ac Proditores Domesticos, Odae 9 (Oxford: Joseph Barnes, 1586)
  In Guil. Parry Proditorem. Odae & Epigrammata (Oxford: Joseph Barnes, 1585)
[Gager, William (ed.)], *Exequiae Philippi Sidnaei* (Oxford: Iosephi Barnesii, 1587)
Gauden, John, *Eikon Basilike* ([London: s.n.], 1649; many editions)
Gazet, Angelin, *Pia hilaria* (Amsterdam: Baltazar Bellerus, 1618)
  Pia hilaria Angelini Gazaei (London: Guil: Morden, 1657)
Gentili, Scipio, *In XXV. Davidis Psalmos Epicae Paraphrases* (London: Iohannes Wolfius, 1584)
  Nereus siue De natali Elizabethae illustriss. Philippi Sydnaei filiae (London: Iohannes Wolfius, 1585)
  Paraphrasis Aliquot Psalmorum Davidis, carmine heroico (London: Thomas Vautrollerius, 1581)
  Plutonis concilium, Ex initio quarti libri Solymeidos (London: Iohannes Wolfius, 1584)
  Solymeidos liber primus Latinis numeris expressus (London: Iohannes Wolfius, 1584)
  Solymeidos libri duo priores de Torquati Tassi (London: Iohannes Wolfius, 1584)

Gilbie, Anthonie, *The Psalmes of David truley opened and explaned by paraphrasis, according to the right sense of every Psalme* (London: Harison and Middleton, 1580)

Gill, Alexander, *Gratulatoria dicata sereniss. ac potentiss. Carolo regi* (London: Ioh: Waterson, 1641)

Goad, Thomas, *Cithara Octochorda Pectine Pulsata Horatiano* (London: E. A[llde] for Na: Fosbroke, 1605)

In homines nefarios (Cambridge: Iohannes Legat, 1605)

Proditoris Proditor. Sive Decachordon, plectrum admouente Horatio, concinens Liberationem Britannicam (London: Martin Clerk, 1606)

Gohaeus, Gulielmus, *Carmen Panegyrikon* (London: Guil. Iones, 1621)

Golding, Arthur (trans.) / Jean Calvin, *The Psalmes of David and others. With M. John Caluins Commentaries* (London: Thomas East and Henry Middleton: for Lucas Harison, and George Byshop, 1571)

Googe, Barnabe (trans.) / Marcello Palingenio Stellato, *The firste thre bokes of the most Christian poet Marcellus Palingenius, called the Zodyake of lyfe: newly translated out of latin into English* (London: Iohn Tisdale, for Rafe Newberye, 1560)

Greville, Fulke, *Certaine Learned and Elegant Workes of the Right Honorable Fulke Lord Brooke, Written in his Youth, and familiar Exercise with Sir Philip Sidney* (London: E. P. for Henry Seyle, 1633)

Grey, Nicholas, *Parabolae evangelicae Latinè redditae carmine paraphrastico varii generis. In usum scholae Tunbrigiensis* (London: J[ohn] S[treater] for Thomas Vnderhill, 1650)

Grotius, Hugo, *Poemata collecta & magnam partem nunc primùm edita à fratre Guilielmo Grotio* (Leiden: Andr. Clouquius, 1637)

Sacra: in quibus Adamus Exul Tragoedia, aliorumque eiusdem generis carminum Cumulus, consecrata Franciae Principi (Hague: Albertus Henricus, 1601)

Grove, Robert, *Carmen de sanguinis circuitu* (London: typis R. E[veringham] for Gualterus Kettilby, 1685)

Haddon, Walter, *Lucubrationes*, ed. Thomas Hatcher (London: Gulielmus Seresius, 1567)

Oratio Iesu Christi salvatoris nostri, qua populum affatus est, cum ascendisset in montem. Item, Epistola S. Iacobi. Ad haec, Psalmus Davidis, centesimus tertius (London: [s.n.], 1555)

Hall, John, *Paradoxes* (London: John Walker, 1653)

Hall, Joseph, *Virgidemiarum* (London: Thomas Creede, for Robert Dexter, 1597; further editions 1598, 1599, 1602)

Harmar, John, *Christologia metrikê, sive Hymnus ad Christum vitam ejus summatim ennarrans* (London: Joannis Macock, 1658)

Hartwell, Abraham, *Regina Literata* (London: [s.n.], 1565)

Hatcher, Robert, *Institutio, epithalamium, & militia viri* (London: T[homas] R[atcliffe] & E[dward] M[ottershead], 1645)

Paideutica, Sive Ascetica Quaedam ad Juventutis Cultum, & Subsidium Spectantia (London: R. Raworth, 1646)

Hawkins, Henry, *Partheneia Sacra: Or the Mysterious and Delicious Garden of the Sacred Parthenes* (Rouen: John Cousturier, 1633)
Heinsius, Daniel, *Crepundia Siliana* (Cambridge: R. Daniel, 1646)
   Laudatio Nobilissimi Amplissimi Clarissimique Viri Iani Dovsae ... Accedunt ejusdem Manes Dousici, Elegia item Funebris Josephi Scaligeri, & aliorum quaedam (Leiden: Iohannes Patius, 1605)
    et al. (eds.) / Claudian Claudianus, *Claudii Claudiani Opera* (Amsterdam: ex officina Schouteniana, 1760)
Herbert, George, *Musae Responsoriae*: see Vivian *et al.*
Herrick, Robert, *Hesperides* (London: John Williams and Francis Eglesfield, 1648)
   His Noble Numbers: Or, His Pious Pieces, Wherein (amongst other things) he sings the Birth of his Christ: and sighes for his Saviours suffering on the Crosse (London: John Williams and Francis Eglesfied, 1647) [final part of *Hesperides*, with separate title page]
Herring, Francis, *In foelicissimum serenessimi ac potentissimi principis, Iacobi primi ... poema gratulatorium* (London: Richardus Field, 1603)
Hessus, Eobanus, *Psalterium Davidis carmine redditum* (London: Thomas Vautrollerius, 1575)
Heywood, John, *An hundred epigrammes* (London: Thomas Berthelet, 1550)
Hill, Thomas, *Nundinae Sturbrigienses* (Dublin: A. Rhames for Jer. Pepyat, 1709)
H[ils], G. (trans.), *The Odes of Casimire. Translated by G. H.* (London: T. W. for Humphrey Moseley, 1646)
Hog, William, *Cato Divinus; sive Proverbia Solomonis Latine Carmine Reddita* (London: Thomas Cockerill, 1699)
   Comoedia Joannis Miltoni ... Paraphrastice Reddita (London: [s.n.], 1698)
   Paraphrasis in Jobum Poetica (London: Thomas Braddyll, 1682; 2nd edn London: Thomas Malthus, 1683)
   Paraphrasis poetica in tria Joannis Miltonis Poemata (London: John Darby, 1690)
   Satyra Sacra Vanitatem Mundi ... Paraphrasis Ecclesiasten Poetica (London: Typis Richardsonianis in usum Autoris, 1685)
   Solomonis Cantici Canticorum Paraphrasis Poetica (London: Fr. Collinii, 1699)
Holdsworth, Edward, *Muscipula* (London: E. Curll, 1709; many editions both in Latin and English this year)
Hoole, Charles, *An easie Entrance to the Latine Tongue* (London: Thomas Newcomb, 1651)
   A New Discovery of the old Art of Teaching Schoole (London: J. T. for Andrew Crook, 1661)
Horatius Flaccus, Quintus, *Poemata. Nouis Scholijs & Argumentis illustrata* (London: Guilelmus Nortonus, 1592)
Horsman, Robert, *Sionis certamina et triumphus* ([London: s.n.], 1651; repr. 1653)
Howel, James, *Epistolae Ho-Elianae. Familiar Letters Domestic & Forren* (London: Hum. Moseley, 1645)

Hume, David, *Lusus Poetici, in tres partes distincti* (London: Richardus Field, 1605)
I. A., *Gigantomachia huius saeculi, sive de rebellione Scotica contra regem* (London: [s.n.], 1659) [printed with Perrinchief, *Nuntius a mortuis* (1659), with separate title page]
Johnstoun, Arthur, *Canticum Salomonis* (London: Thomas Harper for Nathaniel Butter, 1633)
  Delitiae Poetarum Scotorum (Amsterdam: Joannes Blaeu, 1637)
Jonson, Ben, *His Part of King James his Royall and Magnificent Entertainement through his Honorable Cittie of London, Thurseday the 15. of March 1603* (London: V. S. for Edward Blount, 1604)
Julius, Alexander, *Paraphrasis prophetiae Chabakkuki poetica* (Edinburgh: Robertus Charteris, 1610)
  Paraphrasis prophetiae Maleaci poëtica (Edinburgh: Andreas Hart, 1611)
  Paraphrasis quinti capitis Ieschahiae (Edinburgh: Robertus Charteris, 1609)
  Poemata sacra (Edinburgh: Thomas Finlason, 1614)
Junius, Hadrianus, *Philippeis, seu, In Nuptias Divi Philippi ... & Heroinae Mariae* (London: [s.n.], 1554)
Kell, Samuel, *Carmen gratulatorium, ad serenissimum, potentissimum, et invictissimum monarcham, Iacobum* (Edinburgh: Andreas Hart, 1617)
King, Adam, *In Iacobum sextum Scotorum regem panegyris* (Edinburgh: Robertus Charteris, 1603)
King, Robert, *Catena, sive Elegiae Quatuor ... quibus accedit Satyra Aethiopica, sive Speculum Britannicum* (London: J. Y. & impensis A. B., 1647)
King, William, *Miltonis Epistola ad Pollionem* (London: T. Cooper, 1738)
  Sermo pedestris (London: T. Cooper, 1739)
Kinloch, David, *De hominis procreatione, anatome, ac morbis internis* (Paris: J. Mettayer et P. L'Huillier, 1596)
La Faye, Antoine de, *Emblemata et Epigrammata miscellanea* (Geneva: Petrus & Iacobus Chouët, 1610)
Langius, Josephus, *Anthologia sive Florilegium rerum et materarium selectarum* (Strasbourg: Typis Wilhelmi Christiani Glaseri, 1625)
Lauterbachius, Joannis, *Aenigmata* (Frankfurt: E collegio Paltheniano, 1601)
Leland, John, *Kykneion asma. Cygnea Cantio* (London: R. Wolfe, 1545)
Lermaeus, Gabrielus (trans.) / Guillaume de Salluste Du Bartas, *Hebdomas ... latinitate donata* (London: [John Windet?], 1591)
Leslie, John, *Libri duo: quorum uno, piae afflicti animi consolations, divináque remedia: altero, animi tranquilli munimentum & conservatio, continentur* (Paris: Petrus L'Huillier, 1574)
Lily, William, *Brevissima Institutio* (London: Reginald Wolf, 1558)
Littleton, Adam, *Dictionarium Latino-Barbarum* (London: J. C. for Johannis Wright & Richard Chiswel, 1677)
  Pasor metricus, sive Voces omnes Novi Tesamenti Primigeniae (in memoriae subsidium) Hexametris versibus comprehensae (London: Roger Daniels, 1658)
[Littleton, Adam,] *Tragi-Comoedia Oxoniensis* (Oxford: H. Hall, 1648)

Lock (or Lok), Ann, *Meditation of a Penitent Sinner* (London: Iohn Day, 1560)
Lovelace, Richard, *Lucasta* (London: Thomas Harper, 1649)
Maior, Georgius, *Sententiae veterum poetarum* (Magdeburg: Lotter, 1534)
Mameranus, Nikolaus, *Psalmi Davidis quinque* (London: Thomas Marshe, 1557)
Manley, Thomas, *Veni; Vidi; Vici. The Triumphs of the Most Excellent and Illustrious, Oliver Cromwell, &c* (London: John Tey, 1652)
Mantuan [Spagnuoli], Baptista, *Sylvarum F. Baptistae Mantuani, Carmeliate. Sex opuscula, quae prima ad nos perlata.* (Paris: Jehan Petit, 1503)
Markham, Gervaise, *Poem of Poems. Or, Sions Muse ... devided into eight Eclogues* (London: James Roberts for Matthew Lownes, 1596)
Marullus, Michael Tarchaniota, *Poetae tres Elegantissimi* (Paris: Denis Duval, 1582)
Melissus, Paulus [Paul Schede], *Oda Pindarica ad Serenissimam Potentissimamque Dominam Elisabetham Britanniae, Franciae, Hiberniaeque Reginam* (Augsburg: [s.n.], 1582)
   Schediasmata poetica (Paris: Arnoldus Sittartus, 1586)
Melville, Andrew, *Anti-Tami-Cami-Categoria*: see Vivian *et al*.
   Viri Clarissimi A. Melvini Musae et P. Adamsoni Vita et Palinodia ([Edinburgh?: s.n.], 1620)
Milton, John, *Poems* (London: Ruth Raworth for Humphrey Moseley, 1645)
Mirandula, Octaviano, *Illustrium Poetarum Flores* (Venice: [s.n.], 1507)
Mirandula, Octavius, *Illustrium Poetarum Flores* (London: Thomas Creed, 1598)
Neville, Alexander (ed.), *Academia Cantabrigiensis Lachrymae* (London: Ioannes Windet, 1587)
Newport, Maurice, *The Double Eternity, or, The Inevitable Choice* (London: M. Clark, 1695)
   Ob pacem toti ferè Christiano orbi mediante Carolo II. Mag. Brit. Fran. & Hib. Rege redditam ad eundem Sereniss. Principem carmen votivum (London: Robertus Carnius, 1679)
   Sereniss. Principi Carolo Secundo Mag. Brit. Fran. et Hib. Regi Votum Candidum Vivat Rex (London: Robertus Vitus, 1665)
   Sereniss. Principi Carolo Secundo Mag. Brit. Fran. et Hib. Regi Votum Candidum Vivat Rex (London: Newcomb, 1669)
   Sereniss. Principi Carolo Secundo Mag. Brit. Fran. et Hib. Regi Votum Candidum Vivat Rex (London: Robertus Vitus, 1674)
   Sereniss. Principi Carolo Secundo Mag. Brit. Fran. Et Hib. Regi Votum Candidum Vivat Rex (London: [s.n.], 1676)
Owen, John, *Epigrammatum Libri Tres* (London: John Legat for Simon Waterson, 1612)
Oxford University, *Academiae Oxoniensis pietas* (Oxford: Iosephus Barnesius, 1603)
   Bodleiomnema (Oxford: Iosephus Barnesius, 1613)
   Britannia Rediviva (Oxford: A. & L. Lichfield, 1660)

Carolus redux (Oxford: Iohannes Lichfield & Iacobus Short, 1623)
Epithalamia Oxoniensia. In auspicatissimum, potentissimi monarchae Caroli, Magnae Britanniae, Franciae, et Hiberniae Regis, &c. cum Henretta-Maria [sic], aeternae memoriae Henrici Magni Gallorum Regis Filia Connubium (Oxford: Iohannes Lichfield, & Guiliemus Turner, 1625)
Flos Britannicus (Oxford: Leonard Lichfield, 1637)
Musarum Oxoniensium charisteria (Oxford: Leonard Lichfield, 1639)
Musarum Oxoniensium Ἐλαιοφορία (Oxford: Leondardus Lichfield, 1654)
Oxoniensium στεναγμος sive carmina in obitum C. Hattoni (Oxford: Iosephus Barnesius, 1592)
Peplus, Illustrissimi Viri D. Philippi Sidnaei supremis honoribus dicatus (Oxford: Iosephus Barnesius, 1587)
Solis Britannici Perigaeum (Oxford: Iohannes Lichfield & Gulielmus Turner, 1633)
Oxinden, Henry, *Iobus triumphans. Vincit qui patitur* ([London: s.n.], 1651)
Religionis funus, et hypocritae finis (London: Tho. Whittaker, 1647)
Palingenio Stellato, Marcello, *The firste thre bokes of the most Christian poet Marcellus Palingenius, called the Zodyake of lyfe: newly translated out of latin into English*, trans. Barnabe Googe (London: Iohn Tisdale, for Rafe Newberye, 1560)
Panter, Patrick, *Metamorphoseon Quae in S. Scriptura extant, Libri VI* (London: R. I. for Tho: Vere, 1651)
Parker, Matthew (ed.), *Flores historiarum per Matthaeum Westmonasteriensem collecti* (London: Thomas Marshius, 1570)
Parmenius, Stephanus, *Paean Stephani Parmenii Budesi ad psalmum Davidis CIV* (London: Thomas Vautroullerius, 1582)
Perrinchief, Richard, *Nuntius a mortuis ... inter manes Henrici VIII & Caroli I. Angliae regum* (London: Guil. Palengenius Rolandus, 1659)
Pithou, Pierre, *Epigrammata et Poematia Vetera* (Paris: Denis Duval, 1590)
Playford, John, *Psalms & Hymns in Solemn Musick* (London: W. Godbid for J. Playford, 1671)
Pulmannus [Poelman], Theodorus (ed.) / Claudian, *Cl. Claudianus* (Antwerp: Plantin, 1585)
(ed.) / Boethius, *De consolatione philosophiae* (London: [s.n.], 1655)
Pyne, John, *Epigrammata religiosa, officioisa, jocosa. Anglo-latina, Latina, Anglica. Quibus miscentur Anagrammata eiusdem varietatis. In castam Seuerioiris Musae Recreationem* (London: William Stansby, 1626)
Quarles, Francis, *Divine Fancies* (London: M[iles] F[lesher] for Iohn Marriot, 1632)
Emblemes (London: G. M. for Iohn Marriot, 1635)
A Feast for Wormes: Set Forth in a Poeme of the History of Jonah (London: Felix Kyngston, for Richard Moore, 1620)
Hadassa: Or, the History of Queene Ester: With Meditations thereupon, Divine and Morall (London: Richard Moore, 1621)
The Historie of Samson (London: M[iles] F[lesher] for Iohn Marriott, 1630)

Job Militant: With Meditations Divine and Morall (London: Felix Kyngston for George Winder, 1624)
Memorials upon the Death of Sir Robert Quarles (London: Thomas Cotes, 1639)
Sions sonets. Sung by Solomon the King, and periphras'd by Fra. Quarles (London: W. Stansby for Thomas Dewe, 1625)
Randolph, Herbert, *Commercium ad mare australe* (London [Oxford?]: [s.n.], 1720)
Reusner, Nikolaus, *Icones sive imagines virorum literis illustrium* (Strasbourg: Bernardo Iobino, 1587)
Richardson, Augustine, *Ecloga Virgilii prima Sapphico carmine, reddita ab Augustino Richardsono in artibus Bacchalaureo* [s.l.: s.n., *ESTC* estimates c.1600]
Ross, Alexander, *Isagoge grammatica in gratiam illorum qui nolunt memoriam multis & longis regulis gravari, concinnata* (London: William Dugard for Jehos. Kirton, 1648)
Rerum Iudaicarum memorabiliorum. Ab exitu ex Aegypto ad ultimum usque Hierosolymitanum Excidium, liber quartus (London: Thomas Harperus, 1632)
Rerum Iudaicarum memorabiliorum. Ab exitu ex Aegypto ad ultimum usque Heirosolymitanum Excidium, liber quartus (London: Guilielmus Sheres, 1635)
Virgilii evangelisantis Christiados libri XIII (London: Iohannes Legate, for Richardus Thrale, 1638; subsequent editions in 1659 and 1769)
Virgilius evangelisans. Sive Historia Domini & Salvatoris nostril Iesu Christi (London: Iohannes Legatus for Richardus Thralus, 1634)
Ruggle, George, *Ignoramus* (London: Walter Burre, 1614)
Saltmarsh, John, *Poemata Sacra* (Cambridge: [s.n.], 1636)
Sandys, George, *A Paraphrase upon the Song of Solomon* (London: John Legatt, 1641)
Santeul, Jean-Baptiste, *Hymni Sacri et Novi* (Paris: Thierry, 1689)
Sarbiewski, Maciej Kazimierz [Casimir], *Lyricorum libri tres* (Cologne: Bernhard Wolter, 1625)
Lyricorum libri tres. Epigrammatum liber I (Vilnius: Acad. S. J., 1628)
Lyricorum libri tres. Epigrammatum liber I (Antwerp: Jan Cnobbaert, 1630)
Lyricorum lib. IV: Epodon lib. Unus altero Epigrammat. (Antwerp: ex officina Plantiniana, Balthasaris Moreti, 1630)
Lyricorum lib. IV. Epodon Lib. Vnus Alterque Epigrammatum (Antwerp: ex officina Plantiniana, Balthasaris Moreti, 1634)
Lyricorum Libri V. Epodon Liber Unus; Alterque Epigrammatum, cum Epicitharismate (Dijon: Petrus Palliot, 1647)
The Odes of Casimire. Translated by G. H. (London: T. W. for Humphrey Moseley, 1646)
Scaliger, Julius Caesar, *Poemata in duas partes divisas* ([Geneva]: Jacob Stoer for Gaspard de Hus, 1574)
Poetices libri septem (Geneva: Antonius Vincentius, 1561)

Poetices libri septem ([Heidelberg]: Commelinus, 1617)
Seton, John, *Panegyrici in Victoriam Illustrissimae D. Mariae, Angliae, Franciae, & Hiberniae Reginae &c. Item In Coronationem eiusdem Sereniss. Reginae, congratulatio* (London: Reginald Wolf, 1553)
Shaw, John, *Bibliorum summula* (London: Ricardus Field for Robert Mylbourne, 1623)
Shepreve, John, *Summa et synopsis Novi Testamenti distichis ducentis sexaginta* (Oxford: Iosephus Barnesius, 1586)
Sherburne, Edward, *Poems and Translations. Amorous, Lusory, Morall, Divine* (London: W. Hunt for Thomas Dring, 1651)
Shirley, James, *The Contention of Ajax and Ulysses* (London: T. W., 1659)
Grammaticae Latinae Institutiones (London: F. L. for R. L., 1654)
Sictor, Jan, *Compendium religionis Christiana his turbulentis temporibus Magnae Britanniae, in gratiam et usum studiosae juventutis paraphrase epicâ adornatum* (Cambridge: Roger Daniels, 1644)
Sictor, Ioannes, *Panegyricon britannicum* (London: [B. Norton and J. Bill], 1626)
Sictor, John, *Panegyricon inaugurale honoratissimi & amplissimi domini praetoris regii, sive maioris, nobilissimae & florentissimae reipublicae londinensis, Richardi Fenn* (London: Thomas Harper, 1638; and Cambridge: Roger Daniels, 1638)
Sidney, Philip, *The defence of poesie* (London: [Thomas Creede] for William Ponsonby, 1595)
Syr P. S. His Astrophel and Stella (London: Thomas Newman, 1591)
Simonidae, Simonis [Szymonowicz, Szymon], *Poematia Aurea* (Leiden: Iacobus Marcus, 1619)
Smart, Peter, *Septuagenarii senis itinerantis cantus epithalamicus* ([London: s.n.], 1643)
Smith, Henry, *Iurisprudentiae medicinae et theologiae dialogus dulcis* (London: I. Danter for Thomas Man, 1592)
Smith, Jud, *A Misticall Deuise of the Spirituall and Godly Love between Christ the Spouse, and the Church or Congregation* (London: H. Kirkham, 1575)
South, Robert, *Musica Incantans, sive Poema Exprimens Musicae Vires* (Oxford: Leon: Lichfield, 1655)
Spauter, Johannes, *Artis Versificatoriae Compendium* (Edinburgh: sumptibus haeredum Andreae Hart, 1631)
Spencer, Edward, *Boethius de consolatione, Anglo-Latine expressus* (London: [s.n.], 1654)
Spilimbergius, Bernadinus Parthenius, *Q. Horatii Flacci Carmina atque Epodos Commentarii quibus Poetae artificium, & uia ad imitationem, atque ad Poetice scribendum aperitur* (Venice: Dom. Nicolinus, 1584)
Stanley, Thomas, *Poems and Translations* (privately printed, 1647)
Stanyhurst, Richard, *The First Foure Bookes of Virgil His Aeneis Translated ... wyth oother Poëtical diuises theretoo annexed* (Leiden: Iohn Pates, 1582)
Strada, *Prolusiones academicae, oratoriae, historicae, poeticae* (Cologne: Ioannes Kinchius, 1617)

Stradling, John, *Epigrammatum libri quatuor* (London: George Bishop and John Norton, 1607)
Stubbe, Henry, *Horae subsecivae: seu Prophetiae Jonae et Historiae Susannae paraphrasis Graeca versibus heroicis* (London: Du-Gardianis, 1651)
Sweertius, Franciscus, *Selectae Christiani orbis deliciae* (Cologne: Agripp. rempt. Bern. Gualteri, 1608)
Swinnock, George, *The Christian-mans Calling: or a Treatise of Making Religion ones Business* (London: T. P., 1662)
Tesauro, Emanuele, *Caesares; et ejusdem varia carmina* (Oxford: L. Lichfield for William Webb, 1637)
   Il Cannocchiale Aristotelico (Venice: Paolo Baglioni, 1655)
   Il Cannocchiale Aristotelico (Turin: Bartolomeo Zavata, 1670)
   Poemata (Oxford: Hen. Hall for William Webb, 1651)
Thomas, Paul, *Poemata* (Paris: C. Morellus, 1627)
Tomkis, Thomas, *Lingua; or The combat of the tongue, and the fiue senses for superiority* (London: G. Eld for Simon Waterson, 1607)
Torrentius, Laevinus, *Poemata* (Antwerp: ex officina Christophe Plantin, 1579)
Tremellius, Immanuelis and Franciscus Junius, *Psalmi Davidis ex Hebraeo in Latinum Conversi* (London: Henricus Middletonus, 1580)
Turberville, George, *Epitaphes, Epigrams, Songs and Sonets* (London: Henry Denham, 1567)
Uthalmus, Lerimos, *Fasciculus Florum: or, A Nosegay of Flowers, Translated out of the Gardens of severall Poets, and other Authors* (London: A. M., 1636)
Vallans, W., *A Tale of Two Swannes* (London: Roger Ward for Iohn Sheldrake, 1590)
Vaughan, Henry, *Olor Iscanus* (London: T. W. for Humphrey Moseley, 1651)
   Silex Scintillans: or Sacred Poems and Private Eiaculations (London: T. W. for H. Blunden, 1650)
Vaughan, William, *Erotopaignion pium* (London: Richardus Iohnesus, 1597)
   Erotopaignion pium, pars secunda (London: G. Shaw, 1598)
Vaus, John, *Rudimenta puerorum in artem grammaticam* (Edinburgh: Robertus Lekpreuik, 1566)
Veen, Otto van, *Amorum Emblemata* (Antwerp: Henricus Swingenius, 1608)
Viccars, John, *England's Hallelu-jah* (London: Tho: Purfoot, for Henry Seile, 1631)
Vivian, John, James Duport, George Herbert and Andrew Melville, *Ecclesiastes Solomonis, Canticum Solomonis, nec non Epigrammata sacra. Accedunt ... Musae Responsoriae ad Andreae Melvini Anti-Tami-Cami-Categoriam* (Cambridge: John Field, 1662)
Walton, I. (ed.), *Reliquiae Wottonianae* (London: Thomas Maxey, for R. Marriot, G. Bedel, and T. Garthwait, 1651)
Waring, Robert, *Amoris effigies* (London: R. Daniel, 1664; several subsequent editions)
Wase, Christopher, *In mirabilem Caroli II ... Restitutionem Carmen Gratulatorium* (London: D. Maxwell and Charles Adams, 1660)

Watson, Thomas, *Amintae gaudia* (London: Gulihelmus Posonbeus, 1592)
   Amyntas (London: Henricus Marsh for Thomas Marsh, 1585)
   Coluthi Thebani Lycopolitani Poetae, Helenae Raptus Latinus, Paraphraste Thoma Watsono Londinensi (London: Iohannes Wolfius, 1586)
   The lamentations of Amyntas for the death of Phillis, paraphrastically translated out of Latine into English hexameters, trans Abraham Fraunce (London: John Wolfe, for Thomas Newman, and Thomas Gubbin, 1587)
Watts, Isaac, *Horae Lyricae. Poems, Chiefly of the Lyric Kind* (London: S. and D. Bridge, for John Lawrence, 1706)
   Horae Lyricae. Poems, Chiefly of the Lyric Kind (London: W. Wilkins, for S. Cliff, 1715)
   Horae Lyricae. Poems, Chiefly of the Lyric Kind (London: Richard Hett, 1737)
   Hymns and Spiritual Songs (London: J. Humfreys, for John Lawrence, 1707)
   The Psalms of David Imitated in the Language of the New Testament, and apply'd to the Christian state and worship (London: J. Clark and R. Ford, 1719)
Wedderburn, James, John and Robert, *Spirituall Sangis* (Edinburgh, 1567)
Willes, Richard, *Poematum liber* (London: Ex bibliotheca Tottellina, 1573)
Willet, Andrew, *Sacrorum emblematum centuria una* ([Cambridge]: Iohannes Legate, [1592?])
Wilson, Thomas (ed.), *Vita et obitus duorum fratrum Suffolciensium* (London: Richard Grafton, 1551)
Woodford, Samuel, *A Paraphrase upon the Canticles, and some select hymns of the New and Old Testament* (London: J. D. for John Baker, 1679)
   A Paraphrase upon the Psalms of David (London: R. White, for Octavian Pullein, 1667)
Wotton, Henry, *Reliquiae Wottonianae*, ed. Izaak Walton (London: Thomas Maxey for R. Marriot, G. Bedel, and T. Garthwait, 1651)
Wright, Abraham, *Delitiae delitiarum* (Oxford: Leonardus Lichfield for G. Webb, 1637)
Wyther [Wither], George, *A Preparation to the Psalter* (London: Nicholas Okes, 1619)

Bibliography C: Secondary Literature

[Anon.], 'Art. III. – 1. *A Latin Grammar, for the Use of Westminster School.* London: 1830. 2. *Graecae Grammaticae Compendium, in usum Scholae Regiae Westmonasteriensis.* London: 1830', *Edinburgh Review* 53 (March–June 1831), 64–82

[Anon.], 'The Autobiographies of Thomas Hobbes', *Mind* 48 (1939), 403–5

[Anon.], *Monumenta Germaniae Historica: Scriptores* 22 (Leipzig and Hanover: Hahn, 1879)

Alexander, Gavin (ed.), *William Scott: The Model of Poesy* (Cambridge University Press, 2013)

Allen, Don Cameron, *Image and Meaning: Metaphoric Traditions in Renaissance Poetry* (Baltimore, MD: Johns Hopkins University Press, 1960)

Allen, Elizabeth, 'Goade [Goad], Thomas (1576–1638)', *ODNB*, https://doi.org/10.1093/ref:odnb/10848

Allen, Richard C., 'Kelsall, John (1683–1743)', *ODNB*, https://doi.org/10.1093/ref:odnb/61965

Ancona, Ronnie, *Time and the Erotic in Horace's Odes* (Durham, NC: Duke University Press, 1994)

Arens, J. C., 'Sarbiewski's Ode Against Tears Imitated by Lovelace, Yalden and Watts', *Neophilologus* 47 (1963), 236–9

Attridge, Derek, *Well-Weighed Syllables: Elizabethan Verse in Classical Metres* (Cambridge University Press, 1974)

Auger, Peter, *Du Bartas' Legacy in England and Scotland* (Oxford University Press, 2019)

Austern, Linda, Kari Boyd McBride and David Orvis (eds.), *Psalms in the Early Modern World* (Farnham: Ashgate, 2011)

Bacchelli, Franco, 'Note per un inquadramento biografico di Marcello Palingenio Stellato', *Rinascimento* 25 (1985), 275–92

   'Palingenio Stellato e la sua fortuna europea', in M. Bosse and A. Stoll (eds.), *Napoli viceregno spagnolo: Una capital della cultura alle origini dall'Europa moderna (sec. XVI–XVII)* (Naples: Vivarium, 2001), 153–66

Baldick, Chris (ed.), *Oxford Dictionary of Literary Terms*, 3rd edn (Oxford University Press, 2008)

Baldwin, Barry, *The Latin and Greek Poems of Samuel Johnson* (London: Duckworth, 1995)

Baldwin, T. W., *William Shakspere's Small Latine and Less Greeke*, 2 vols. (Chicago: University of Illinois Press, 1944–50)

Bär, Silvio, 'The Elizabethan Epyllion: From Constructed Classical Genre to Twentieth-Century Genre Propre', in Silvio Bär and Emily Hauser (eds.), *Reading Poetry, Writing Genre: English Poetry and Literary Criticism in Dialogue with Classical Scholarship* (London: Bloomsbury, 2018), 138–50

Barker, William, 'Fraunce [France], Abraham (1559?–1592/3?)', *ODNB*, https://doi.org/10.1093/ref:odnb/10133

Barrett-Lennard, Thomas, *An Account of the Families of Lennard and Barrett* (London: Spottiswoode, 1908)

Barroway, Isaac, 'The Bible as Poetry in the English Renaissance', *JEGP* 32 (1933), 447–80

  'The Hebrew Hexameter: A Study in Renaissance Sources and Interpretation', *ELH* 11 (1935), 66–91

  'Tremellius, Sidney and Biblical Verse', *MLN* 40 (1934), 145–9

Bather, Philippa and Claire Stocks, *Horace's Epodes: Contexts, Intertexts, and Reception* (Oxford University Press, 2016)

Bayer, M., 'The Distribution of Political Agency in Phineas Fletcher's Purple Island', *Criticism* 44 (2002), 249–70

Beal, P., *Catalogue of English Literary Manuscripts 1450–1700*, www.celm-ms.org.uk

Beckwith, Marc Allan, 'A Study of Palingenius' *Zodiacus Vitae* and Its Influence on English Renaissance Literature', PhD thesis (Ohio State University, 1983)

Bellany, Alastair, 'Railing Rhymes Revisited: Libels, Scandals, and Early Stuart Politics', *History Compass* 5 (2007), 1136–79

Bellany, Alastair and Andrew McRae (eds.), 'Early Stuart Libels: An Edition of Poetry from Manuscript Sources', *Early Modern Literary Studies Text Series* 1 (2005), http://purl.oclc.org/emls/texts/libels

Early Stuart Libels, www.earlystuartlibels.net

Bellenger, Yvonne and Jean-Claude Ternaux, *Du Bartas*, Bibliographie des écrivains français 12 (Paris: Memini, 1998)

Bergmans, Paul, 'Les poésies manuscrites de François et Raphaël Thorius', in *Mélanges Paul Thomas: Recueil de mémoires concernant la philologie classique dédié a Paul Thomas* (Bruges: Imprimerie Sainte Catherine, 1930), 29–38

Berry, Lloyd E., 'Five Latin Poems by Giles Fletcher, the Elder', *Anglia* 79 (1961), 338–77, https://doi.org/10.1515/angl.1961.1961.79.338.

Bevington, D., M. Butler and I. Donaldson (eds.), *The Cambridge Edition of the Works of Ben Jonson*, 7 vols. (Cambridge University Press, 2012)

Binns, J. W., 'The Humanist Latin Tradition Reassessed', in Binns (ed.), *Latin Poetry of English Poets*, 186–96

  Intellectual Culture in Elizabethan and Jacobean England: The Latin Writings of the Age, ARCA Classical and Medieval Texts, Papers and Monographs 24 (Leeds: Francis Cairns, 1990)

  (ed.), *The Latin Poetry of English Poets* (London: Routledge & Kegan Paul, 1974)

Birrel, T. A., 'Sarbiewski, Watts and the Later Metaphysical Tradition', *English Studies* 37 (1956), 125–32
Bishop, Selma L., *Isaac Watts: Hymns and Spiritual Songs 1707–1748. A Study in Early Eighteenth Century Language Changes* (London: Faith Press, 1962)
Black, R., *Humanism and Education in Medieval and Renaissance Italy* (Cambridge University Press, 2005)
Blevins, Jacob, *Catullan Consciousness and the Early Modern Lyric in England: From Wyatt to Donne* (Farnham: Ashgate, 2004)
Bond, C., 'The Phoenix and the Prince: The Poetry of Thomas Ross and Literary Culture in the Court of Charles II', *RES* 60 (2009), 588–604
Booth, Ted, *A Body Politic to Govern: The Political Humanism of Elizabeth I* (Newcastle-upon-Tyne: Cambridge Scholars, 2013)
Borgiani, G., *Marcello Palingenio Stellato e il suo poema lo 'Zodiacus Vitae'* (Città di Castello: Lapi, 1912)
Braden, Gordon, 'Claudian and His Influence: The Realm of Venus', *Arethusa* 12.2 (1979), 203–31
Bradner, Leicester, 'The Latin Translations of Spenser's *Shepheardes Calender*', *MP* 33 (1935–6), 21–6
  Musae Anglicanae: A History of Anglo-Latin Poetry, 1500–1925 (New York: Modern Language Association of America, 1940)
  'Poems on the Defeat of the Spanish Armada', *JEGP* 4 (1944), 447–8
Brennan, M. G., 'The Date of the Countess of Pembroke's Translations of the Psalms', *Review of English Studies*, n.s., 33 (1982), 434–6
Brennan, Michael, Margaret Hannay and Noel Kinnamon (eds.), *The Collected Works of Mary Sidney Herbert*, 2 vols. (Oxford University Press, 1998)
Broadbent, J. B., 'The Nativity Ode', in Frank Kermode (ed.), *The Living Milton* (London: Routledge & Kegan Paul, 1960; repr. 1962), 12–31
Bromley, James, '"Let it Suffise": Sexual Acts and Narrative Structure in *Hero and Leander*', in Stephen Guy-Bray and Stephen Nardizzi (eds.), *Queer Renaissance Historiography: Backward Gaze* (Farnham: Ashgate, 2009), 67–84
Brown, Georgia, *Redefining Elizabethan Literature* (Cambridge University Press, 2009)
Brown, Marshall, 'Towards an Archaeology of English Romanticism: Coleridge and Sarbiewski', in Marshall Brown (ed.), *Turning Points: Essays in the History of Cultural Expressions* (Stanford University Press, 1997), 173–94
Bryan, Lynn and Robert C. Evans, 'Jonson's Response to Lipsius on The Happy Life', *Notes and Queries* 43.2 (June 1996), 181–2
Bunting, Basil, *Complete Poems*, ed. Richard Caddel (Newcastle-upon-Tyne: Bloodaxe, 2000)
Burrow, Colin, 'Horace at Home and Abroad: Wyatt and Sixteenth Century Horatianism', in Charles Martindale and David Hopkins (eds.), *Horace Made New: Horatian Influences on British Writing from the Renaissance to the Twentieth Century* (Cambridge University Press, 1993), 27–49
  (ed.), *Complete Sonnets and Poems*, The Oxford Shakespeare (Oxford University Press, 2002)

(ed.), 'Epigrams', in Bevington *et al.* (eds.), *Works of Ben Jonson*, vol. V, 101–98

(ed.), 'The Underwood', in Bevington *et al.* (eds.), *Works of Ben Jonson*, vol. VII, 69–296

Burrow, Colin and Charles Martindale 'Clapham's *Narcissus*: a pre-text for Shakespeare's *Venus and Adonis*?', *ELR* 22 (1992), 147–76

Burrzone, A., 'Il "concilium deorum" nella poesia panegiristica Latina da Claudiano a Sidonio Apollinare', in *Poesia Tardoantica e Medievale* (Alessandria: Orso, 2004), 129–41

Bush, Douglas, *Mythology and the Renaissance Tradition in English Poetry*, rev. edn (New York: W. W. Norton, 1963)

Cain, Tom (ed.), *The Poetry of Mildmay Fane, Second Earl of Westmorland: Poems from the Fulbeck, Harvard and Westmorland Manuscripts* (Manchester University Press, 2001)

Calhoun, Thomas O., Laurence Heyworth, Allan Pritchard and Ernest W. Sullivan II (eds.), *The Collected Works of Abraham Cowley*, vol. 1 (Newark: University of Delaware Press, 1989)

Calvert, Ian, 'Slanted Histories, Hesperian Fables: Material Form and Royalist Prophecy in John Ogilby's *The Works of Publius Virgilius Maro*', *The Seventeenth Century* 33 (2018), 531–55

Cameron, Alan, *Claudian: Poetry and Propaganda at the Court of Honorius* (Oxford: Clarendon Press, 1970)

Campbell, Lily B., *Divine Poetry and Drama in Sixteenth-Century England* (Cambridge University Press, 1959)

Cardini, Roberto and Donatella Coppini (eds.), *Il rinnovamento umanistico della poesia: l'epigramma e l'elegia* (Florence: Edizioni Pagliai Polistampa, 2009)

Carey, John and Alastair Fowler (eds.), *The Poems of John Milton* (London: Longman, 1968)

Carne-Ross, D. S., 'New Metres for Old: A Note on Pound's Metric', *Arion* 6 (1967), 216–32

Carne-Ross, D. S. and Kenneth Haynes (eds.), *Horace in English* (Harmondsworth: Penguin, 1996)

Case, Robert H., *English Epithalamies* (London: Bodley Anthologies, 1896)

Chamberlin, William J., *Catalogue of English Bible Translations: A Classified Bibliography of Versions and Editions Including Books, Parts, and Old and New Testament Apocrypha and Apocryphal Books* (Westport, CT: Greenwood Press, 1991)

Chappuis Sandoz, Laure (ed.), *Au-delà de l'élégie d'amour: Métamorphoses et renouvellements d'un genre latin dans l'Antiquité et à la Renaissance* (Paris: Classiques Garnier, 2011)

Charles, A. M., 'Touching David's Harp: George Herbert and Ralph Knevet', *George Herbert Journal* 2 (1978), 54–69

(ed.), *The Shorter Poems of Ralph Knevet: A Critical Edition* (Columbus: Ohio State University Press, 1966)

Charlet, L, 'La rose et le sang: Une note critique d'Ange Politien sur Claudien (misc. 11 et rapt. 2,122–123)', in G. Tarugi (ed.), *Homo sapiens. Homo*

humanus, vol. 1: *La cultura italiana tra il passato ed il presente in un disegno di pace universale* (Florence: Olschki, 1990), 3–15
Cheney, P. and P. Hardie (eds.), *The Oxford History of Classical Reception in English Literature*, vol. II: *1558–1660* (Oxford University Press, 2015)
Chomarat, Jacques (ed.), *Palingène: Le zodiaque de la vie* (Geneva: Droz, 1996)
Christiansen, Peder G., *The Use of Images by Claudius Claudianus* (The Hague and Paris: Mouton, 1969)
Clancy, Thomas H., 'Ewens [*alias* Newport], Maurice (c.1611–1687)', *ODNB*, https://doi.org/10.1093/ref:odnb/20036
Clarke, Elizabeth, *Politics, Religion and the Song of Songs in Seventeenth-Century England* (Basingstoke: Palgrave Macmillan, 2011)
Clarke, Susan A., 'Marvell in Royalist Gardens', *MSN* 2.2 (2010), www.st-andrews.ac.uk/marvellsociety/newsletter/susan-a-clarke-marvell-in-royalist-gardens
  'Royalists Write the Death of Lord Hastings: Post-Regicide Funerary Propaganda', *Parergon* 22 (2005), 113–30
Colclough, David, *Freedom of Speech in Early Stuart England* (Cambridge University Press, 2005)
  '"The Muses Recreation": John Hoskyns and the Manuscript Culture of the Seventeenth Century', *HLQ* 61 (1998), 369–400
Coombe, Clare, *Claudian the Poet* (Cambridge University Press, 2018)
Cooper, Charles Henry, *Memorials of Cambridge* (Cambridge University Press, 1861)
Copeland, R., 'The Curricular Classics in the Middle Ages', in R. Copeland (ed.), *The Oxford History of Classical Reception in English Literature*, vol. 1: *800–1558* (Oxford University Press, 2016), 21–34
Coronel Ramos, Marco Antonio, *La sátira latina* (Madrid: Editorial Síntesis, 2002)
Courtial, M.-Th., 'George Buchanan et la Saint-Barthélemy: La "Satyra in Carolum Lotharingum Cardinalem"', *BHR* 58.1 (1996), 151–63
Craigie, James (ed.), *The Basilikon Doron of King James VI* (Edinburgh and London: Scottish Text Society, 1944)
Crane, Mary Thomas, *Framing Authority: Sayings, Self, and Society in Sixteenth-Century England* (Princeton University Press, 1993)
  '*Intret Cato*: Authority and the Epigram in Sixteenth-Century England', in Barbara Kiefer Lewalski (ed.), *Renaissance Genres: Essays on Theory, History, and Interpretation* (Cambridge, MA: Harvard University Press, 1986), 158–86
Crawford, Julie, 'Sidney's Sapphics and the Role of Interpretive Communities', *ELH* 69 (2002), 979–1007
Cressy, David, 'Levels of Illiteracy in England, 1530–1730', *HJ* 20 (1977), 1–23
Cummings, Brian, *The Literary Culture of the Reformation: Grammar and Grace* (Oxford University Press, 2002)
Cummings, Robert, 'Andrew Melville, the "Anti-Tami-Cami-Categoria", and the English Church', in Reid and McOmish (eds.), *Neo-Latin Literature*, 163–81
  'Epigram', in Moul (ed.), *Guide to Neo-Latin Literature*, 83–97

Davidson, Peter, *The Universal Baroque* (Manchester University Press, 2007)
Davidson, Peter (ed.), *The Poems and Translations of Sir Richard Fanshawe*, 2 vols. (Oxford University Press, 1997–9)
Davidson, Peter and Anne Sweeney (eds.), *The Collected Poems of St Robert Southwell SJ* (Manchester: Carcanet, 2007)
Davie, Donald, 'Edward Taylor and Isaac Watts', in *Older Masters: Essays and Reflections on English and American Literature* (Manchester: Carcanet, 1992), 56–70
  A Gathered Church: The Literature of the English Dissenting Interest, 1700–1930 (Oxford University Press, 1978)
  (ed.), *Augustan Lyric* (London: Heinemann, 1974)
Davies, Ceri, *Latin Writers of the Renaissance* (Cardiff: University of Wales Press, 1981)
Davis, Walter R. (ed.), *The Works of Thomas Campion* (Garden City, NY: Doubleday, 1967)
de Beer, Susanna, Karl A. E. Enenkel and David Rijser (eds.), *The Neo-Latin Epigram: A Learned and Witty Genre*, Supplementa Humanistica 25 (Leuven University Press, 2009)
de Mourgues, Odette, *Metaphysical, Baroque and Précieux Poetry* (Oxford: Clarendon Press, 1953)
De Smet, Ingrid A. R., 'Satire', in Knight and Tilg (eds.), *Oxford Handbook of Neo-Latin*, 199–214
Degl'Innocenti Pierini, R. '*Aurea mediocritas*: La morale oraziana nei cori delle tragedie di Seneca', *QCTC* 10 (1992), 155–71
DeLapp, Nevada Levi, *The Reformed David(s) and the Question of Resistance to Tyranny: Reading the Bible in the 16th and 17th Centuries* (London: Bloomsbury, 2014)
Demetriou, Tania, 'The Non-Ovidian Elizabethan Epyllion: Thomas Watson, Christopher Marlowe, Richard Barnfield', in Janice Valls-Russell, Charlotte Coffin and Agnes Lafont (eds.), *Interweaving Myths in Shakespeare and His Contemporaries* (Manchester University Press, 2017), 41–64
Devos, Francis, 'François Thorius (Thooris) et son fils Raphaël médecins, poètes et mathématiciens de la Renaissance', https://meteren.pagesperso-orange.fr/FicheN16.htm
Dexter, Gary, *The People's Favourite Poems: Out and About with Kipling, Larkin and the Rest* (London: Old Street Publishing, 2019)
Dijk, Sharon van, 'The Eclogues of Giles Fletcher the Elder: Composition, Circulation and Reception, c.1560–1660', PhD thesis (University College London, 2021).
Doelman, James, 'The Contexts of George Herbert's *Musae Responsoriae*', *GHJ* 2 (1992), 42–54
  '"The Daring Pen of Sorrow": Elegies on the Death of Thomas Murray (1564–1623)', *The Seventeenth Century* 34.1 (2019), 27–63, https://doi.org/10.1080/0268117X.2017.1373258
  The Epigram in England, 1590–1640 (Manchester University Press, 2016)

'Herbert's Couplet?', *TLS* 5577 (2010), 15
'Herbert's *Lucus* and Pope Urban VIII', *GHJ* 32 (2008/9), 43–53
King James I and the Religious Culture of England (Woodbridge: Brewer, 2000)
'The Religious Epigram in Early Stuart England', *C&L* 54 (2005), 497–520
Dominik, W. J., C. E. Newlands and K. Gervais (eds.), *Brill's Companion to Statius* (Leiden: Brill, 2015)
Donaldson, Ian, 'Jonson's Ode to Sir Lucius Cary and Sir H. Morison', *SLI* 6 (1973), 139–52
—— (ed.), 'Informations to Drummond', in Bevington *et al.* (eds.), *Works of Ben Jonson*, vol. V, 351–91
Donno, Elizabeth Story (ed.), *Elizabethan Minor Epics* (London: Routledge & Kegan Paul, 1963)
Döpp, S., 'Claudian und die lateinische Epik zwischen 1300 and 1600', *RPL* 12 (1989), 39–50
Drury, John and Victoria Moul (eds.), *George Herbert: Complete Poems* (Harmondsworth: Penguin, 2016).
Dubrow, Heather, *A Happier Eden: The Politics of Marriage in the Stuart Epithalamium* (Ithaca, NY: Cornell University Press, 1990)
Duc, T., *Le 'De Raptu Proserpinae' de Claudien: Réflexions sur une actualization de la mythologie* (Frankfurt am Main: Peter Lang, 1994)
Duncan-Jones, Katherine (ed.), *Sir Philip Sidney: Selected Poems* (Oxford University Press, 1973)
Duncan-Jones, Katherine and Jan van Dorsten (eds.), *Miscellaneous Prose of Sir Philip Sidney* (Oxford: Clarendon Press, 1973)
Durand, Sylvain (ed.), *John Owen: Epigrammes / Epigrammata* (Paris: Les Belles Lettres, 2016)
Dykstal, Timothy, 'The Epic Reticence of Abraham Cowley', *SEL* 31 (1991), 95–116
Dzelzainis, Martin, '"A Greater Errour in Chronology": Issues of Dating in Marvell', in Martin Delzainis and Edward Holberton (eds.), *The Oxford Handbook of Andrew Marvell* (Oxford University Press, 2019), 317–36
Eckhardt, Joshua, *Manuscript Verse Collectors and the Politics of Anti-Courtly Love Poetry* (Oxford University Press, 2009)
Edwards, A. S. G., 'Surrey's Martial Epigram: Scribes and Transmission', *EMS* 12 (2005), 74–82
El-Gabalawy, S., 'Two Obscure Disciples of George Herbert', *N&Q* 222 (1977), 541–2
Ellis, Jim, *Sexuality and Citizenship: Metamorphosis in English Erotic Verse* (University of Toronto Press, 2003)
Enck, J. J., 'John Owen's *Epigrammata*', *HLB* 3 (1949), 431–4
Enenkel, Karl A. E., 'The Neo-Latin Epigram: Humanist Self-Definition in a Learned and Witty Discourse', in de Beer *et al.* (eds.), *Neo-Latin Epigram*, 1–22
Enenkel, Karl A. E. and Anita Traninger (eds.), *The Figure of the Nymph in Early Modern Culture* (Leiden: Brill, 2018)

Enenkel, Karl A. E. and Arnoud S. Q. Visser (eds.), *Mundus Emblematicus: Studies in Neo-Latin Emblem Books* (Turnhout: Brepols, 2003)
Enterline, Lynn 'Elizabethan Minor Epic', in Cheney and Hardie (eds.), *Oxford History of Classical Reception*, vol. II, 253–71
  Shakespeare's Schoolroom: Rhetoric, Discipline, Emotion (Philadelphia: University of Pennsylvania Press, 2012)
  (ed.), *Elizabethan Narrative Poems* (London: Bloomsbury, 2019)
Evans, J. M., 'The Text of Surrey's "The Meanes to Attain Happy Life"', *N&Q* 228 (1983), 409–11
Everett, Barbara, 'The Shooting of the Bears: Poetry and Politics in Andrew Marvell', in R. L. Brett (ed.), *Andrew Marvell: Essays on the Tercentenary of His Death* (Oxford University Press for the University of Hull, 1979), 62–103
Facchini, Bianca, 'The Reception of Italian Neo-Latin Poetry in English Manuscript Sources, c.1550–1720: Literature, Morality, and Anti-Popery', *The Seventeenth Century* 36.4 (2021), 527–60
  'Sannazaro's Latin Epigrams and Their Early Modern English Readers: From Venice to London', *HLQ* (forthcoming)
Felgentreu, F., 'Claudian (Claudius Claudianus)', in Christine Walde (ed.) in collaboration with Brigitte Egger, *Brill's New Pauly Supplements I, vol. V: The Reception of Classical Literature* (Leiden: Brill, 2012), 123–7
  Claudians Prefationes: Bedingungen, Beschreibungen und Wirkungen einer poetischen Kleinform (Stuttgart and Leipzig: Teubner, 1999)
Finkelpearl, P. J., 'Bastard, Thomas (1565/6–1618)', *ODNB*, https://doi.org/10.1093/ref:odnb/1656
Fitzgerald, William, *Agonistic Poetry: The Pindaric Mode in Pindar, Horace, Hölderlin, and the English Ode* (Berkeley: University of California Press, 1987)
  Martial: The World of the Epigram (University of Chicago Press, 2007)
Flinker, Noam, *The Song of Songs in English Renaissance Literature: Kisses of Their Mouths* (Cambridge: Brewer, 2000)
Ford, Philip, 'George Buchanan and the Satyra in Carolum Lotharingum Cardinalem', in I. D. McFarlane (ed.), *Acta conventus neo-latini sanctandreani. Proceedings of the Fifth International Congress of Neo-Latin Studies, St Andrew's, 1982* (Binghamton, NY: Medieval and Renaissance Texts and Studies, 1986), 43–50
  'Neo-Latin Prosody and Versification', in Philip Ford, Jan Bloemendal and Charles Fantazzi (eds.), *Brill's Encyclopaedia of the Neo-Latin World: Macropaedia* (Leiden: Brill, 2014), 63–74
Ford, Philip and Andrew Taylor (eds.), *Neo-Latin and the Pastoral*, Special Issue of *CRCL* 33 (2006)
Fordoński, Krzysztof, 'Maciej Kazimierz Sarbiewski and English Dissenting Poets of the early 18th Century: A Study in Reception of Neo-Latin Poetry in Great Britain', *Terminus* 13.2 (2011), 71–85
  'The Subversive Power of Father Matthias: The Poetry of Maciej Kasimierz Sarbiewski as Vehicle for Political Propaganda in England of the 17th

Century', in Jacek Fabiszak, Ewa Urbaniak-Rybicka and Bartosz Wolski (eds.), *Crossroads in Literature and Culture* (Heidelberg: Springer, 2013), 387–98

Fordoński, Krzysztof and Piotr Urbański (eds.), *Casimir Britannicus: English Translations, Paraphrases and Emulations of the Poetry of Maciej Cazimierz Sarbiewski* (London: Modern Humanities Research Association, 2010, rev. edn)

Fowler, Alastair, *Kinds of Literature: An Introduction to the Theory of Genres and Modes* (Cambridge, MA: Harvard University Press, 1982)
  Triumphal Forms: Structural Patterns in Elizabethan Poetry (Cambridge University Press, 1970)

Fry, Paul H., *The Poet's Calling in the English Ode* (New Haven, CT: Yale University Press, 1980)

Fuentes, M. C. G., 'Presencia horaciana en los coros de Séneca', *CFCEL* 16 (1999), 89–106

Fuhrmann, M., 'Claudian in der Neuzeit: Geschmackswandel und Übergang von der rhetorischen zur philologischen Betrachtungsweise', in W.-W. Ehlers *et al.* (eds.), *Aetas Claudianea: Eine Tagung an der Freien Universität Berlin vom 28. bis 3. Juni 2002* (Munich and Leipzig: K. G. Saur Verlag, 2004), 207–23

Gaertner, Adelheid, 'Die englische Epithalamienliteratur in siebzehnten Jahrhundert und ihre Vorbilder', dissertation (Coburg, 1936)

Gaertner, Johannes A., 'Latin Verse Translations of the Psalms, 1500–1620', *HTR* 49.4 (1956), 271–305

Gaisser, Julia Haig, *Catullus and His Renaissance Readers* (Oxford: Clarendon Press, 1993)

Garrison, James D., *Dryden and the Tradition of Panegyric* (Berkeley: University of California Press, 1975)

Garrison, John S., 'Love Will Tear Us Apart: Campion's *Umbra* and Shakespeare's *Venus and Adonis*', in Lynn Enterline (ed.), *Elizabethan Narrative Poems: The State of Play* (London: Bloomsbury, 2019), 167–88

Geiger, Jonathan, 'Strictness, Freedom, and Experimentation in Horatian and Senecan Metrics', in Martin Stöckinger, Kathrin Winter and Andreas T. Zanker (eds.), *Horace and Seneca: Interactions, Intertexts, Interpretations* (Berlin: De Gruyter, 2017), 159–84

Gibson, Lindsay G. 'James Leeke, George Herbert, and the Neo-Latin Contexts of *The Church Militant*', *HL* 67.2 (2018), 379–425

Gifford, William and Rev. Alexander Dyce (eds.), *The Dramatic Works and Poems of James Shirley*, 6 vols. (London: John Murray, 1833)

Gillespie, Stuart, 'After Strada: English Responses to Strada's Nightingale (*Prolusiones* 2.6) with texts of four previously unprinted versions', in C. W. Marshall (ed.), *Latin Poetry and its Reception: Essays for Susana Braund* (New York: Routledge, 2021), 192–214
  'Claudian's *Old Man of Verona*: An Anthology of English Translations with a New Poem by Edwin Morgan', *T&L* 2 (1993), 87–97
  'John Polwhele's Horatian Translations', *T&L* 30.1 (2021), 52–71

Newly Recovered English Classical Translations, 1600–1800 (Oxford University Press, 2019)
'Seneca ex Thyestes: A Collection of English Translations 1557–1800', *T&L* 24.2 (2015), 203–18
Shakespeare's Books: A Dictionary of Shakespeare Sources (London: Bloomsbury, 2016)
'Two Seventeenth-Century Translations of Dark Roman Satires: John Knyvett's Juvenal I and J. H.'s *In Eutropium* I', *T&L* 21 (2012), 43–66
Glover, Adam, 'Eros, Eucharist, and the Poetics of Desire', *Logos* 20.1 (2017), 17–44
Goldring, Elizabeth, Faith Eales, Elizabeth Clarke, Jayne Elisabeth Archer, Gabriel Heaton and Sarah Knight (eds.), *John Nichols's The Progresses and Public Processions of Queen Elizabeth I: A New Edition of the Early Modern Sources, volume I: 1533–1571* (Oxford University Press, 2014)
Gömöri, George, '"The Polish Swan Triumphant": The English Reception of Maciej Kazimierz Sarbiewski in the Seventeenth Century', *MLR* 106 (2011), 814–33
Grant, W. L., *Neo-Latin Literature and the Pastoral* (Chapel Hill: University of North Carolina Press, 1965)
Green, Ian, '"Hearing" and "Reading": Disseminating Bible Knowledge and Fostering Bible Understanding in Early Modern England', in Killeen *et al.* (eds.), *Oxford Handbook of the Bible*, 272–86
Humanism and Protestantism in Early Modern English Education (Farnham: Ashgate, 2009)
Green, Roger, 'Horace's Odes in the Psalm Paraphrases of Buchanan', in Revard *et al.* (eds.), *Acta Conventus Neo-Latini Guelpherbytani*, 71–80
'Poems and Not Just Paraphrases: Doing Justice to Buchanan's Psalms', in Dirk Sacré and Jan Papy (eds.), *Syntagmatia: Essays on Neo-Latin Literature in Honour of Monique Mund-Dopchie and Gilbert Tournoy* (Leuven University Press, 2009), 415–29
'Poetic Psalm Paraphrases', in Philip Ford, Jan Bloemendal and Charles Fantazzi (eds.), *Brill's Encyclopaedia of the Neo-Latin World* (Leiden: Brill, 2014), 461–9
(ed. and trans.), *George Buchanan: Poetic Paraphrase of the Psalms of David* (Geneva: Librairie Droz, 2011)
Greene, Roland, 'Elegy, Hymn, Epithalamium, Ode', in Cheney and Hardie (eds.), *Oxford History of Classical Reception*, vol. II, 311–43
'The Lyric', in G. P. Norton (ed.), *The Cambridge History of Literary Criticism, vol. III: The Renaissance* (Cambridge University Press, 1999), 216–28
'Sir Philip Sidney's Psalms, the Sixteenth-Century Psalter, and the Nature of Lyric', *SEL* 30 (1990), 19–40
Greene, Thomas M., *The Light in Troy: Imitation and Discovery in Renaissance Poetry* (New Haven, CT: Yale University Press, 1982)
'Spenser and the Epithalamic Convention', *CL* 9 (1957), 215–28

Greenwood, David Charles, *William King: Tory and Jacobite* (Oxford: Clarendon Press, 1969)
Griggs, Burke, 'South, Robert (1634–1716)', *ODNB*, https://doi.org/10.1093/ref:odnb/26048
Grosart, Rev. Alexander B. (ed.), *The Poems English and Latin of the Rev. Thomas Bastard, M.A. (1566–1618)* (privately printed, 1880)
Gruder-Poni, Gabriella, 'Cupid in the Garden', in Gilles Sambras (ed.), *New Perspectives on Andrew Marvell* (Université de Reims, 2008), 27–42
Guipponi-Gineste, M.-F., 'L' "adlocutio sponsalis" dans quelques épithalames de l'antiquité tardive, ou l'instrumentation du discours divin', in G. Abbamonte and L. Spinna (eds.), *Discorsi pronunciati, discorsi ascoltati: Contesti di eloquenza tra Grecia, Roma ed Europa* (Naples: Giannini, 2009), 483–502
  Claudien: Poète du monde à la cour d'occident (Paris: De Boccard, 2010), 281–331
  'Poésie, pouvoir et rhétorique à la fin du 4ᵉ siècle après J.-C.: Les poèmes nuptiaux de Claudien', *Rhetorica* 22.3 (2004), 269–96
Gwosdek, Hedwig, *Lily's Grammar of Latin in English* (Oxford University Press, 2013)
Haan, Estelle, *Andrew Marvell's Latin Poetry: From Text to Context* (Brussels: Latomus, 2003)
  'From Neo-Latin to Vernacular: Marvell's Bilingualism and Renaissance Pedagogy', in Gilles Sambras (ed.), *New Perspectives on Andrew Marvell* (Université de Reims, 2008), 43–64
  'Milton's *In Quintum Novembris* and the Anglo-Latin Gunpowder Epic', *HL* 41 (1992), 221–95; second part, *HL* 42 (1993), 368–93
Haber, Judith, *Desire and Dramatic Form in Early Modern England* (Cambridge University Press, 2009)
Hale, J. K., 'Milton and the Gunpowder Plot: *In Quintum Novembris* Reconsidered', *HL* 50 (2001), 351–66
  Milton's Cambridge Latin: Performing in the Genres 1625–1632 (Tempe: Arizona Center for Medieval and Renaissance Studies, 2005)
  'Thomas Hobbes' Poem of Exile: The Verse *Vita* and Ovid's *Tristia*', *Scholia* 17 (2008), 92–105
Hale, Sara, '"All Lingua's are to thee Vernaculus": The Bilingualism of Horatian Imitation in Early Eighteenth-Century Literary Culture', *HLQ* 81 (2018), 191–226
  'The "epistolary ode" in British Neo-Latin poetry, 1680–1765', PhD thesis (King's College London, 2018)
  'John Beveridge, the Neo-Latin Horatian Ode and the Narrative of British Colonialism in Eighteenth-Century North America', *IJCT* 27 (2020), 554–80
Hallyn, Fernand, '"A Light-Weight Artifice": Experimental Poetry in the 17th Century', trans. Rozanne Lapidus, *SubStance* 22.2–3 (1993), 289–305
Hamlin, Hannibal, *Psalm Culture and Early Modern English Literature* (Cambridge University Press, 2004)

Hamlin, Hannibal, Michael G. Brennan, Margaret P. Hannay and Noel J. Kinnamon (eds.), *The Sidney Psalter: The Psalms of Sir Philip and Mary Sidney* (Oxford University Press, 2009)

Hammond, M., '"Concilia Deorum" from Homer through Milton', *SP* 30 (1933), 1–16

Hammond, Paul (ed.), *The Poems Of John Dryden*, vol. 1: *1649–1681* (Harlow: Longman, 1995)

Hankins, John Erskine, *Shakespeare's Derived Imagery* (Lawrence: University of Kansas Press, 1953)

Hardie, Philip, 'Abraham Cowley, *Davideis. Sacri poematis operis imperfecti liber unus*', in Houghton and Manuwald (eds.), *Neo-Latin Poetry in the British Isles*, 69–86

  Celestial Aspirations: Reaching for the Heavens in Classical Antiquity and Early Modern Britain (Princeton University Press, forthcoming)

  'Epic Poetry', in Cheney and Hardie (eds.), *Oxford History of Classical Reception*, vol. II, 225–52

Hardison Jr, O. B., *The Enduring Monument: A Study of the Idea of Praise in Renaissance Literary Theory and Practice* (Westport, CT: Greenwood Press, 1962)

  Prosody and Purpose in the English Renaissance (Baltimore, MD: Johns Hopkins University Press, 1989)

Hardy, Thomas, *Collected Poems,* ed. Michael Irwin (Ware: Wordsworth, 2006)

Harries, Byron, 'John Owen the Epigrammatist: A Literary and Historical Context', *Renaissance Studies* 18 (2004), 19–32

Harris, J. and K. Sidwell (eds.), *Making Ireland Roman: Irish Neo-Latin Writers and the Republic of Letters* (Cork University Press, 2009)

Harrison, Stephen, 'The Reception of Horace in the Nineteenth and Twentieth Centuries', in Stephen Harrison (ed.), *The Cambridge Companion to Horace* (Cambridge University Press, 2007), 334–46

Haskell, Yasmin, 'Between Fact and Fiction: The Renaissance Didactic Poetry of Fracastoro, Palingenio and Valvasone', in Haskell and Hardie (eds.), *Poets and Teachers*, 77–103

  Loyola's Bees: Ideology and Industry in Jesuit Latin Didactic Poetry (Oxford University Press, 2003)

  'The Masculine Muse: Form and Content in the Latin Didactic Poetry of Palingenius and Bruno', in C. Atherton (ed.), *Form and Content in Didactic Poetry* (Bari: Levante, 1998), 117–44

  'Poetic Flights or Retreats? Latin Lucretian Poems in Sixteenth-Century Italy', in David Norbrook, Stephen Harrison and Philip Hardie (eds.), *Lucretius and the Early Modern* (Oxford University Press, 2016), 91–121

Haskell, Yasmin and Philip Hardie (eds.), *Poets and Teachers: Latin Didactic Poetry and the Didactic Authority of the Latin Poet from the Renaissance to the Present. Proceedings of the Fifth Annual Symposium of the Cambridge Society for Neo-Latin Studies, Clare College, Cambridge, 9–11 September, 1996* (Bari: Levante, 1999)

Haye, Thomas and Franziska Schnoor (eds.), *Epochen der Satire: Traditionslinien einer literarischen Gattung in Antike, Mittelalter und Renaissance* (Hildesheim: Weidmann, 2008)

Heale, Elizabeth, *Autobiography and Authorship in Renaissance Verse* (Basingstoke: Palgrave Macmillan, 2003)

Healy, Thomas, 'Sound Physic: Phineas Fletcher's *The Purple Island* and the Poetry of Purgation', *RS* 5 (1991), 341–52

'Crashaw, Richard, (1612/13–1648)', ODNB, https://doi.org/10.1093/ref:odnb/6622

Helander, Hans, 'The *Gustavis* of Venceslaus Clemens', in E. Kessler and H. C. Kuhn (eds.), *Germania Latina: Latinitas Teutonica. Politik, Wissenschaft, humanistische Kultur von späten Mittelalter bis in unsere Zeit*, Germania Latina (Munich: W. Fink, 2003), 609–22

Neo-Latin Literature in Sweden in the Period 1620–1720: Stylistics, Vocabulary and Characteristic Ideas, Acta Universitatis Upsaliensis; Studia Latina Upsaliensia 29 (Uppsala University Library, 2004)

Hinds, Stephen E., *Displacing Persephone: Epic between Worlds*, UCL Housman Lecture (limited circulation pamphlet) (University College London, 2013), 23–5

Hingley, Sheila, 'Oxinden [Oxenden], Henry, (1609–1670)', *ODNB*, https://doi.org/10.1093/ref:odnb/21053

Hinman, Robert B., *Abraham Cowley's World of Order* (Cambridge, MA: Harvard University Press, 1960)

Hintzen, Roswitha Simons (ed.), *Norm und Poesie: Zur expliziten und impliziten Poetik in der lateinischen Literatur der frühen Neuzeit* (Berlin: De Gruyter, 2013)

Hirst, Derek and Steven N. Zwicker, *Andrew Marvell, Orphan of the Hurricane* (Oxford University Press, 2012)

Hofmann, Heinz, '*Adveniat Tandem Typhis Qui Detegat Orbes:* Columbus in Neo-Latin Epic Poetry (15th–18th Centuries)', in Wolfgang Haase and Meyer Reinhold (eds.), *The Classical Tradition and the Americas: European Images of the Americas and the Classical Tradition* (Berlin: De Gruyter, 1994), 420–656

'Überlegungen zu einer Theorie der nichtchristlichen Epik der lateinischen Spätantike', *Philologus* 132 (1988), 101–59

Holberton, Edward, *Poetry and the Cromwellian Protectorate: Culture, Politics, and Institutions* (Oxford University Press, 2008)

Holton, A. and T. MacFaul (eds.), *Tottel's Miscellany: Songs and Sonnets of Henry Howard, Earl of Surrey, Sir Thomas Wyatt and Others* (London: Penguin, 2011)

Houghton, L. B. T., 'Renaissance Latin Love Elegy', in Thea S. Thorsen (ed.), *The Cambridge Companion to Latin Love Elegy* (Cambridge University Press, 2013), 290–305

Virgil's Fourth Eclogue in the Italian Renaissance (Cambridge University Press, 2019)

Houghton, L. B. T. and Gesine Manuwald (eds.), *Neo-Latin Poetry in the British Isles* (London: Bristol Classical Press, 2012)
House, Seymour Baker, 'Nicholas Grimald', in David A. Richardson (ed.), *Dictionary of Literary Biography, vol. 136: Sixteenth-Century British Non-Dramatic Writers*, second series (1994), 159–63
Hudson, Hoyt Hopewell, *The Epigram in the English Renaissance* (Princeton University Press, 1947)
  'Grimald's Translations from Beza', *MLN* 39 (1924), 388–94
Hughey, Ruth (ed.), *The Arundel Harington Manuscript of Tudor Poetry*, 2 vols., (Columbus: Ohio State University Press, 1960)
Hulse, Clark, *Metamorphic Verse: The Elizabeth Minor Epic* (Princeton University Press, 1981)
Hutchinson, F. E. (ed.), *The Works of George Herbert* (Oxford University Press, 1941)
Hutton, J., *The Greek Anthology in France and in the Latin Writers of the Netherlands to the year 1800* (Ithaca, NY: Cornell University Press, 1946)
  The Greek Anthology in Italy to the year 1800 (Ithaca, NY: Cornell University Press, 1935)
Ijsewijn, Jozef, *Companion to Neo-Latin Studies, Part I: History and Diffusion of Neo-Latin Literature*, 2nd edn (Leuven University Press, 1990)
  'Neo-Latin Satire: Sermo and Satyra Menippea', in R. R. Bolgar (ed.), *Classical Influences on European Culture A.D. 1500–1700* (Cambridge University Press, 1976), 41–55
Ijsewijn, Jozef and Dirk Sacré, *Companion to Neo-Latin Studies, Part II: Literary, Linguistic, Philological and Editorial Questions*, 2nd edn (Leuven University Press, 1998)
Jackson, Gordon (ed.), *Isaac Watts: Selected Poems* (Manchester: Fyfield, 1999)
Jackson Williams, Kelsey, 'Canon before Canon, Literature before Literature: Thomas Pope Blount and the Scope of Early Modern Learning', *HLQ* 77 (2014), 177–99
Jaeckle, Daniel, 'Bilingual Dialogues: Marvell's Paired Latin and English Poems', *SP* 98 (2001), 378–400
Jansen, Johannes, 'The Microcosmos of the Baroque Epigram: John Owen and Julien Waudré', in de Beer *et al.* (eds.), *Neo-Latin Epigram*, 275–99
Jantz, Harold, 'Baroque Free Verse in New England and Pennsylvania', in Peter White (ed.), *Puritan Poets and Poetics: Seventeenth-Century American Poetry in Theory and Practice* (University Park: Pennsylvania State University Press, 1985), 258–73
Jennings, Elizabeth, *Every Changing Shape* (Manchester: Carcanet, 1996)
Jerome, 'Preface to the Chronicle of Eusebius', trans. W. H. Fremantle, in Phillip Schaff and Henry Wace (eds.), *The Principal Works of St. Jerome, vol. VI: Nicene and Post-Nicene Fathers* (Edinburgh: T&T Clark, 1996)
Jeschke, Thomas, Andrew Pettegree and Malcolm Walsby (eds.), *Netherlandish Books*, 2 vols. (Leiden: Brill, 2010)
Jones, J. H., 'John Owen, Cambro-Britannus', *TCS* [no number] (1940), 130–43

'John Owen, the epigrammatist', *G&R* 10 (1941), 65–73
Kahn, Coppelia, 'Venus and Adonis', in Patrick Cheney (ed.), *The Cambridge Companion to Shakespeare's Poetry* (Cambridge University Press, 2007), 72–89
Kajanto, Iior, 'On Lapidary Style in Epigraphy and Literature in the Sixteenth and Seventeenth Centuries', *HL* 43 (1994), 137–72
Kaske, Carol V., 'Another Echo of the Tremellius-Junius *Libri Poetici* in Sidney's Biblical Poetics', *AN&Q* 5 (1992), 83–6
Kastner, L. E. (ed.), *The Poetical Works of William Drummond of Hawthornden*, 2 vols. (Manchester: Haskell House, 1913)
Kayachev, Boris, *Allusion and Allegory: Studies in the Ciris* (Berlin: De Gruyter, 2016)
Keach, William, *Elizabethan Erotic Narratives: Irony and Pathos in the Ovidian Poetry of Shakespeare, Marlowe, and Their Contemporaries* (New Brunswick, NJ: Harvester Press, 1977)
Kelliher, Hilton, 'John Dryden: A New Work from His Cambridge Days', *TCBS* 10.3 (1993), 341–58
Kelliher, W. H., 'The Latin Poetry of George Herbert', in Binns (ed.), *Latin Poetry of English Poets*, 26–57
Kellner, T., *Die Göttergestalten in Claudians 'De Raptu Proserpinae': Polarität und Koinzidenz als anthropozentrische Dialektik mythologischfornulierter Weltvergewisserung* (Leipzig: B. G. Teubner, 1997)
Key, Newton E., 'Littleton, Adam (1627–1694)', *ODNB*, https://doi.org/10.1093/ref:odnb/16780
Kilgour, Maggie, 'Cowley's Epic Experiments', in Philip Major (ed.), *Royalists and Royalism in 17th Century Literature: Exploring Abraham Cowley* (New York: Routledge, 2019), 93–123
Killeen, Kevin, 'My Exquisite Copies for Action: John Saltmarsh and the Machiavellian Bible', in Killeen *et al.* (eds.), *Oxford Handbook of the Bible*, 598–612
  The Political Bible in Early Modern England (Cambridge University Press, 2017)
Killeen, Kevin, Helen Smith and Rachel Willie (eds.), *The Oxford Handbook of the Bible in Early Modern England, c.1530–1700* (Oxford University Press, 2015),
Kilroy, Gerard, *Edmund Campion: Memory and Transcription* (Farnham: Ashgate, 2005)
  (ed.), *The Epigrams of Sir John Harington* (Farnham: Ashgate, 2009)
King, A. H., 'Some Notes on Andrew Marvell's "Garden"', *ES* 20 (1938), 118–21
Kinnamon, Noel, 'God's "Scholer": The Countess of Pembroke's Psalmes and Beza's *Psalmorum Davidis . . . Libri Quinque*', *N&Q* 44.1 (1997), 85–9
  'Notes on the Psalms in Herbert's *The Temple*', *GHJ* 4 (1981), 10–29
Kinney, J. Daniel, *The Abraham Cowley Text and Image Archive* (2007), https://cowley.lib.virginia.edu/index2.html
Kipling, Rudyard, *Collected Poems* (Ware: Wordsworth, 2001)

Knight, Sarah, 'Neo-Latin Literature and Early Modern Education', in Moul (ed.), *Guide to Neo-Latin Literature*, 52–65

Knight, Sarah and Stefan Tilg (eds.), *The Oxford Handbook of Neo-Latin* (Oxford University Press, 2015)

Knoppers, Laura Lunger, *Constructing Cromwell: Ceremony, Portrait, and Print, 1645–1661* (Cambridge University Press)

Knowles, R. (ed.), *The Entertainment of His Most Excellent Majestie Charles II ... by John Ogilby* (Binghamton, NY: Medieval and Renaissance Texts and Studies, 1988)

Korenjak, Martin, *Geschichte der neulateinischen Literatur: Vom Humanismus bis zur Gegenwart* (Munich: C. H. Beck, 2016)

  'Short Mythological Epic in Neo-Latin Literature', in Manuel Baumbach and Silvio Bär (eds.), *Brill's Companion to the Greek and Latin Epyllion and Its Reception* (Leiden: Brill, 2012), 519–37

Krautter, K., *Die Renaissance der Bukolik in der lateinischen Literatur des XIV. Jahrhunderts: Von Dante bis Petrarca* (Munich: Fink, 1983)

Kugel, James L., *The Idea of Biblical Poetry: Parallelism and Its History* (Baltimore, MD: Johns Hopkins University Press, 1998)

LaBranche, Anthony, 'The "Twofold Vitality" of Drayton's *Odes*', *CL* 15 (1963), 116–29

Laird, Andrew, *The Epic of America: An Introduction to Rafael Landívar and the 'Rusticatio Mexicana'* (London: Duckworth, 2006)

Larsen, Kenneth J., 'Richard Crashaw's *Epigrammata Sacra*', in Binns (ed.), *Latin Poetry of English Poets*, 93–120

Latham, Agnes M. C. (ed.), *The Poems of Ralegh* (London: Routledge & Kegan Paul, 1951)

Laurens, P., *L'abeille dans l'ambre: Célébration de l'épigramme de l'époque alexandrine à la fin de la Renaissance*. Collection d'études anciennes 59 (Paris: Les Belles Lettres, 1989)

  'Une situation de rivalité linguistique: La réussite tardive d'un Anacréon latin', in Jacques Jouanna and Jean Leclant (eds.), *La poésie grecque antique: Actes du 13e colloque de la Villa Kérylos* (Paris: De Boccard, 2003), 203–21

  (ed.), *Anthologie de l'épigramme de l'Antiquité à la Renaissance* (Paris: Gallimard, 2007)

Leach, A. F., *A History of Warwick School with Notices of the Collegiate Church, Gilds, and Borough of Warwick* (Edinburgh: T& A. Constable, 1906)

Lees, Charles J., S.M. (ed.), *The Poetry of Walter Haddon* (Mouton: The Hague and Paris, 1967)

Leishman, J. B., *The Art of Marvell's Poetry* (London: Hutchinson, 1966)

Lenihan, P. and K. Sidwell (eds.), *Poema de Hibernia: A Jacobite Latin Epic on the Williamite Wars (Dublin City Library and Archive, Gilbert MS 141)* (Dublin: Irish Manuscripts Commission, 2018)

Leonhardt, Jürgen, *Dimensio syllabarum: Studien zur lateinischen Prosodie- und Verslehre von der Spätantike bis zur frühen Renaissance* (Göttingen: Vandenhoeck & Ruprecht, 1989)

Lewalski, Barbara Kiefer, 'The Genres of *Paradise Lost*', in Dennis Danielson (ed.), *The Cambridge Companion to Milton*, 2nd edn (Cambridge University Press, 1999), 113–29
  Milton's Brief Epic: The Genre, Meaning, and Art of Paradise Regained (Providence, RI: Brown University Press, 1966)
  '*Paradise Lost*, the Bible, and Biblical Epic', in Killeen *et al.* (eds.), *Oxford Handbook of the Bible*, 546–60
  Protestant Poetics and the Seventeenth-Century Religious Lyric (Princeton University Press, 1979)
Lewis, C. T. and C. Short, *A Latin Dictionary* (Oxford University Press, 1879)
Li Vigni, A., *Poeta quasi creator: Estetica e poesia in Mathias Casimir Sarbiewski* (Palermo: Centro Internazionale Studi di Estetica, 2005)
Lindsay, Alexander, 'Cowley, Abraham (1618–1667)', *ODNB*, https://doi.org/10.1093/ref:odnb/6499
Liston, William T. (ed.), *Francis Quarles: Divine Fancies* (New York: Garland, 1992)
Livingstone, N. and G. Nisbet, *Epigram* (Cambridge University Press, 2010)
Lloyd Jones, G. *The Discovery of Hebrew in Tudor England: A Third Language* (Manchester University Press, 1983)
Lockie, D. M., 'The Political Career of the Bishop of Ross, 1568–80', *UBHJ* 4 (1954), 98–145
Loscocco, Paula, 'Royalist Reclamation of Psalmic Song in 1650s England', *RQ* 64 (2011), 500–43
Love, Harold, *English Clandestine Satire 1660–1702* (Oxford University Press, 2004)
  'Sir William Petty, the London Coffee Houses, and the Restoration "Leonine"', *The Seventeenth Century*, 22.2 (2007), 381–94
Ludwig, Walther, 'Horazrezeption in der Renaissance oder die Renaissance des Horaz', in Ludwig, Walther (ed.), *Horace, l'œuvre et les imitations: Un siècle d'interprétation* (Geneva: Fondation Hardt, 1993), 305–80
  'Neulateinische Lehrgedichte und Vergils *Georgica*', in D. H. Green, L. P. Johnson and Dieter Wuttke (eds.), *From Wolfram and Petrarch to Goethe and Grass: Studies in Literature in Honour of Leonard Forster* (Baden-Baden: Koerner, 1982), 151–80
  'Petrus Lotichius Secundus and the Roman Elegists: Prolegomena to a Study of Neo-Latin Elegy', in R. R. Bolgar (ed.), *Classical Influences on European Culture AD 1500–1700* (Cambridge University Press, 1976), 171–90
Lyne, Raphael, 'Writing Back to Ovid in the 1560s and 1570s', *T&L 13* (2004), 143–62
MacKellar, W., *The Latin Poems of John Milton* (New Haven, CT: Yale University Press, 1930)
Maclean, Hugh and Anne Lake Prescott (eds.), *Edmund Spenser's Poetry*, 3rd edn (New York: W. W. Norton, 1993)
Maddison, Carol, *Apollo and the Nine: A History of the Ode* (Baltimore, MD: Johns Hopkins University Press, 1960)

Main, C. F., 'Wotton's "The Character of a Happy life"', *The Library*, 5th ser., 10 (1955), 270–4
Major, Philip, 'Sacred and Secular in Cowley's *Essays*', in Philip Major (ed.), *Royalists and Royalism in 17th-Century Literature: Exploring Abraham Cowley* (London: Routledge, 2019), 202–28
Makin, Peter (ed.), *Basil Bunting on Poetry* (Baltimore, MD: Johns Hopkins University Press, 1999)
Maltby, Judith, *Prayer Book and People in Elizabethan and Stuart England* (Cambridge University Press, 1998)
Manley, Lawrence, 'Proverbs, Epigrams, and Urbanity in Renaissance London', *ELR* 15 (1985), 247–76
Marcus, Leah S., Janel Mueller and Mary Beth Rose (ed.), *Queen Elizabeth I: Collected Works* (University of Chicago Press, 2002)
Margoliouth, H. H. (ed.), *The Poems and Letters of Andrew Marvell*, 2 vols., 3rd edn with revisions by Pierre Legouis, with the collaboration of E. E. Duncan-Jones (Oxford University Press, 1971)
Marotti, Arthur F., *Manuscript, Print and the English Renaissance Lyric* (Ithaca, NY: Cornell University Press, 1995)
Marshall, Ashley, *The Practice of Satire in England 1658–1770* (Baltimore, MD: Johns Hopkins University Press, 2013)
Martin, L. C. (ed.), *The Poems English, Latin and Greek of Richard Crashaw* (Oxford: Clarendon Press, 1927; 2nd edn 1957)
  (ed.), *Poems of Humphrey Wanley* (Oxford University Press, 1928)
Martindale, C. and D. Hopkins (eds.), *Horace Made New: Horatian Influences upon British Writing from the Renaissance to the Twentieth Century* (Cambridge University Press, 1993)
Martindale, Joanna, 'The Best Master of Virtue and Wisdom: The Horace of Ben Jonson and His Heirs', in Martindale and Hopkins (eds.), *Horace Made New*, 50–85
Martyn, J. R. C., 'John Owen and Tudor Patronage: A Prosopographical Analysis of Owen's Epigrams', *HL* 28 (1979), 250–7
  (ed.), *Joannis Audoeni epigrammatum*, 2 vols., Textus Minores 69–70 (Leiden: Brill, 1976–8)
Maslov, Boris, 'Stella P. Revard, *Politics, Poetics, and the Pindaric Ode: 1450–1700*' (review), *MP* 110.4 (May 2013), E271–6
Mason, Tom, 'Abraham Cowley and the Wisdom of Anacreon', *CQ* 19 (1990), 103–37
May, Steven W., *Henry Stanford's Anthology: An Edition of Cambridge University Library Manuscript Dd. 5.75* (Abingdon: Routledge, 2019; first published 1988)
May, Steven W. and Alan Bryson, *Verse Libel in Renaissance England and Scotland* (Oxford University Press, 2016)
McBryde, John McLaren, 'A Study of Cowley's *Davideis* I', *JEGP* 2 (1898), 454–527
  'A Study of Cowley's *Davideis* II. Metre of the *Davideis*', *JEGP* 3 (1900), 24–34

McCabe, Richard, 'Elizabethan Satire and the Bishops' Ban of 1599', *YES* 11 (1981), 188–93

McCloskey, M. and P. Murphy, *The Latin Poetry of George Herbert: A Bilingual Edition* (Athens: Ohio University Press, 1965)

McDowell, Nicholas, 'The Beauty of Holiness and the Poetics of Antinomianiasm: Richard Crashaw, John Saltmarsh and the Language of Religious Radicalism in the 1640s', in Ariel Hessayon and David Finnegan (eds.), *Varieties of Seventeenth- and Early Eighteenth-Century English Radicalism in Context* (Burlington, VT: Ashgate, 2011), 31–50

'Marvell among the Cavaliers', in Laura Lunger Knoppers (ed.), *The Oxford Handbook of Literature and the English Revolution* (Oxford University Press, 2012), 253–72

Poetry and Allegiance in the English Civil Wars: Marvell and the Cause of Wit (Oxford University Press, 2008)

McFarlane, I. D., *Buchanan* (London: Duckworth, 1981)

McGaw, W. D, 'The Text of Surrey's "The Meanes to Attain Happy Life" – A Reply', *N&Q* 230 (1985), 456–8

McIlwain, Charles Howard (ed.), *James I: Political Works* (Cambridge, MA: Harvard University Press, 1918)

McOmish, David, 'A Community of Scholars: The Rise of Scientific Discourse in Early-Modern Scotland', in Reid and McOmish (eds.), *Neo-Latin Literature*, 40–74

'Scientia Demands the Latin Muse: The Authority of Didactic Poetry in Early Modern Scotland', in Lilah Grace Canevaro and Donncha O'Rourke (eds.), *The Didactic Poetry of Greece, Rome and Beyond: Knowledge, Power, Tradition* (Swansea: Classical Press of Wales, 2019), 249–74

'The Scientific Revolution in Scotland Revisited: The New Sciences in Edinburgh', *HU* 31 (2018), 153–72

McPherson, David, 'Ben Jonson's Library and Marginalia: An Annotated Catalogue', *SP* 71 (1974), 1–106

McQueen, William A., 'The Missing Stanzas in Marvell's "Hortus"', *PQ* 44 (1965), 173–9

McQueen, William A. and Kiffin A. Rockwell (eds.), *The Latin Poetry of Andrew Marvell* (Chapel Hill: University of North Carolina Press, 1964)

M'Crie, Thomas, *The Life of Andrew Melville*, 2 vols. (Edinburgh: William Blackwood, 1819)

McWilliams, John, '"A Storm of Lamentations Writ": "Lachrymae Musarum" and Royalist Culture after the Civil War', *YES* 33 (2003), 273–89

Medcalf, S., 'Horace's Kipling', in Martindale and Hopkins (eds.), *Horace Made New*, 217–35

Merchant, W. M., 'Ralph Knevet of Norfolk, Poet of Civill Warre', *ESMEA*, new ser., 13 (1960), 21–35

Miller, Anthony, *Roman Triumphs and Early Modern English Culture* (Basingstoke: Palgrave, 2001)

Miller, Edmund, 'Herbert's Baroque: The *Passio Discerpta*', *R&R* 3.2 (1979), 201–8
Miller, Paul W. 'The Elizabethan Minor Epic', *SP* 55 (1958), 31–8
Miller, W. E., 'Double Translation in English Humanistic Education', *SR* 10 (1963), 163–74
Miner, Earl, *The Cavalier Mode from Jonson to Cotton* (Princeton University Press, 1971)
Mitchell, Peter, *The Purple Island and Anatomy in Early Seventeenth-Century Literature, Philosophy, and Theology* (Cranbury, NJ: Associated University Presses, 2010)
Molekamp, Femke, *Women and the Bible in Early Modern England: Religious Reading and Writing* (Oxford University Press, 2013)
Money, David, 'Aspects of the Reception of Sarbiewski in England: From Hils, Vaughan, and Watts to Coleridge, Bowring, Walker and Coxe', in Piotr Urbański (ed.), *Pietas humanistica: Neo-Latin Religious Poetry in Poland in European Context* (Frankfurt: Peter Lang, 2006), 157–87
  The English Horace: Anthony Alsop and the Tradition of British Latin Verse (Oxford University Press, 1998)
  'Musarum Pueritia: Poetae Iuvenes in Schola Etonensi, sub Anglorum Regina Elizabetha Prima', *SUP* 25 (2005), 297–303
  'Owen, John [Joannes Audoenus] (1563/4–1622?), *ODNB*, https://doi.org/10.1093/ref:odnb/21013
  (ed.), 'BL MS Royal 12 A XXX', in Goldring *et al.* (eds.), *John Nichols's The Progresses and Public Processions*, vol. 1, 259–368
Monreal, Ruth, *Flora Neolatina: Die Hortorum libri IV von René Rapin S. J. und die Plantarum libri VI von Abraham Cowley. Zwei lateinische Dichtungen des 17. Jahrhunderts* (Berlin: De Gruyter, 2010)
Moore, O. H., 'The Infernal Council', *MP* 16 (1918), 1–25
Moore Smith, G. C. (ed.), *Gabriel Harvey's Marginalia* (Stratford-upon-Avon: Shakespeare Head Press, 1913)
Morgan, Edwin, 'Claudian's "Old Man of Verona": An Anthology of English Translations', *T&L* 2 (1993), 87–97
Morgan, Llewelyn, *Musa Pedestris: Metre and Meaning in Roman Verse* (Oxford University Press, 2010)
Moshenska, Joe, *A Stain in the Blood: The Remarkable Voyage of Sir Kenelm Digby* (London: Penguin, 2016)
Moss, Ann, *Printed Commonplace-Books and the Structuring of Renaissance Thought* (Oxford: Clarendon Press, 1996)
  Renaissance Truth and the Latin Language Turn (Oxford University Press, 2003)
Moul, Victoria, 'Abraham Cowley's 1656 *Poems* in context', in Philip Major (ed.), *Royalists and Royalism in 17th-Century Literature: Exploring Abraham Cowley* (London: Routledge, 2019), 150–79
  'Andrew Marvell and Payne Fisher', *RES* 68 (2017), 524–48

'Anglo-Latin Satiric Verse in the Long Seventeenth Century', in Cecilia Rosengren, Rikard Wingård and Per Sivefors (eds.), *Satire and the Multiplicity of Forms, 1600–1830: Textual and Graphic Transformations* (Manchester University Press, 2022), 60–87

'The Date of Marvell's *Hortus*', *The Seventeenth Century* 34 (2019), 329–51

'"Dazel'd Thus with Height of Place": An English Lyric in Two Latin Versions', in Gesine Manuwald, Lucy Nicholas and Luke Houghton (eds.), *An Anthology of British Neo-Latin Literature* (London: Bloomsbury, 2020), 167–77

'Didactic Poetry', in Moul (ed.), *Guide to Neo-Latin Literature*, 180–99

'Donne's Horatian Means: Horatian Hexameter Verse in Donne's Satires and Epistles', *JDJ* 27 (2008), 21–48

'England's Stilicho: Claudian's Political Poetry in Early Modern England', *International Journal of the Classical Tradition* 28 (2021), 23–50

'Grammar in Verse: Latin Pedagogy in Seventeenth-Century England', in Simon Coffey (ed.), *The History of Grammar in Foreign Language Teaching* (Amsterdam University Press, 2020), 113–32

'Horace', in Cheney and Hardie (eds.), *Oxford History of Classical Reception*, vol. II, 539–56

'Horace, Seneca and the Anglo-Latin 'Moralising' Lyric in Early Modern England', in K. Winter, M. Stöckinger and T. Zanker (eds.), *Horace and Seneca: Interactions, Intertexts, Interpretations* (Berlin: De Gruyter, 2017), 345–69

'Horatian Odes in Abraham Cowley's *Plantarum Libri Sex* (1668)', in Houghton and Manuwald (eds.), *Neo-Latin Poetry in the British Isles*, 87–104

'Introduction to *Abrahami Couleij Angli, Poemata latina. In quibus continentur, sex libri plantarum, viz. duo herbarum, florum, sylvarum, et unus miscellaneorum ... (1668)*', *EEBO Introductions*, http://eebo.chadwyck.com/intros/htxview?template=basic.htx&content=cowley.htm

Jonson, Horace and the Classical Tradition (Cambridge University Press, 2010)

'Latin and English Elegies in the Seventeenth Century', in Thea S. Thorsen (ed.), *The Cambridge Companion to Latin Love Elegy* (Cambridge University Press, 2013), 306–19

'*A Mirror for Noble Deeds*: Pindaric Form in Jonson's Odes and Masques', in Richard Rawles and Peter Agocs (eds.), *Receiving the Komos*, BICS Supplement 112 (London: Institute of Classical Studies, 2012), 141–56

'Neo-Latin Metrical Practice in English Manuscript Sources, c.1550–1720', in Stefan Tilg and Benjamin Harter (eds.), *Neulateinische Metrik: Formen und Kontexte zwischen Rezeption und Innovation* (Tübingen: Narr, 2019), 257–76

'Ovidian Transformations in Cowley's Herb Garden', in Peter Mack (ed.), *The Afterlife of Ovid* (London: Institute for Classical Studies, 2015), 221–34

'Politics and Religion in the Latin and English Garden Poetry of the Mid-Seventeenth Century', in Franziska Eickhoff and Stefan Tilg (eds.),

Mußeräume der Antike und der frühen Neuzeit (Tübingen: Mohr Siebeck Verlag, 2020), 97–129

'Revising the Siege of York: Payne Fisher's *Marston-Moor* and the Development of Cromwellian Poetics', *The Seventeenth Century* 31.3 (2016), 311–31

'Robert Duncan and Pindar's Dance', in Sheila Murnaghan and Ralph M. Rosen (eds.), *Hip Sublime: Beat Writers and the Classical Tradition* (Columbus: Ohio State University Press, 2018), 160–83

'A Satire on the Bishop of Salisbury: Anonymous (Thomas Brown?), *In Episcopum Quendam* (c.1689)', in Gesine Manuwald, Lucy Nicholas and Luke Houghton (eds.), *An Anthology of British Neo-Latin Literature* (London: Bloomsbury, 2020), 251–61

(ed.), *A Guide to Neo-Latin Literature* (Cambridge University Press, 2017)

Müllner, C., *De imaginibus similitudinibusque quae in Claudiani carminibus inveniuntur* (Vienna: C. Gerold, 1892)

Nethercot, A. H., *Abraham Cowley: The Muse's Hannibal* (London: Oxford University Press, 1931)

'Milton, Jonson, and the Young Cowley', *MLN* 49.3 (1934), 158–62

Netzley, Ryan, *Reading, Desire, and the Eucharist in Early Modern Religious Poetry* (University of Toronto Press, 2011)

Nevo, Ruth, *The Dial of Virtue* (Princeton University Press, 1963)

Newstok, Scott, *Quoting Death in Early Modern England: The Poetics of Epitaphs beyond the Tomb* (London: Palgrave Macmillan, 2009)

Nichols, F. J., 'The Development of Neo-Latin Theory of the Pastoral in the Sixteenth Century', *HL* 18 (1969), 95–114

Nisbet, Gideon, 'Epigrams – The Classical Tradition', in Philip Ford, Jan Bloemendal and Charles Fantazzi (eds.), *Brill's Encyclopaedia of the Neo-Latin World* (Leiden: Brill, 2014), vol. 1, 379–86

Norberg, Dag, *An Introduction to the Study of Medieval Latin Versification*, trans. Grant C. Roti and Jacqueline de La Chapelle Skubly, ed. Jan Ziolkowski (Washington, DC: Catholic University of America Press, 2004)

Norbrook, David, 'John Milton, Lucy Hutchinson and the Republican Biblical Epic', in Mark R. Kelley, Michael Lieb and John T. Shawcross (eds.), *Milton and the Grounds of Contention* (Pittsburgh, PA: Duquesne University Press, 2003), 37–63

Writing the English Republic: Poetry, Rhetoric and Politics 1627–1660 (Cambridge University Press, 1999)

Oates, Mary I., 'Jonson's "Ode Pindarick" and the Doctrine of Imitation', *PLL* 11 (1975), 126–48

Oberhelman, S. M. and J. Mulryan, 'Milton's Use of Classical Meters in the *Sylvarum Liber*', *MP* 81 (1983), 138–43

O'Brien, John, *Anacreon Redivivus: A Study of Anacreontic Translation in Mid-Sixteenth-Century France* (Ann Arbor: University of Michigan Press, 1995)

O'Connell, M. (ed.), 'The *Elisaeis* of William Alabaster', *SP* 76 (1979), 1–77

Ong, Walter, 'Latin Language Study as a Renaissance Puberty Rite', *SP* 61.2 (1959), 103–24

O'Sullivan, Dan, *The Reluctant Ambassador: The Life and Times of Sir Thomas Chaloner, a Tudor Diplomat* (Stroud: Anberly, 2016)
Paleit, E., 'Sexual and Political Liberty and Neo-Latin Poetics: The *Heroides* of Mark Alexander Boyd', *RS* 22.3 (2008), 351–67
Pallant, Anne, 'The Printed Poems of Scipione Gentili', MA thesis (University of Birmingham, 1983)
Panizza, L. (ed.), *Philosophical and Scientific Poetry in the Renaissance*, Special Issue of *RS* 5.3 (1991)
Parker, Holt N., 'Renaissance Latin Elegy', in Barbara K. Gold (ed.), *A Companion to Roman Love Elegy* (Malden, MA: Wiley-Blackwell, 2012), 476–90
Parker, Tom W. N., *Proportional Form in the Sonnets of the Sidney Circle: Loving in Truth* (Oxford University Press, 1998)
Partridge, E. B., 'Jonson's *Epigrammes*: The Named and the Nameless', *SLI* 6 (1973), 153–98
Patrides, C. A. (ed.), *George Herbert: The Critical Heritage* (London: Routledge, 1983)
Patterson, Annabel, *Fables of Power: Aesopian Writing and Political History* (Durham, NC: Duke University Press, 1991)
Marvell: The Writer in Public Life (Harlow: Longman, 2000)
Peacey, J. T., 'Fisher, Payne (1615/16–1693), Latin poet', *ODNB*, https://doi.org/10.1093/ref:odnb/9506
Pebworth, Ted-Larry, 'New Light on Sir Henry Wotton's "The Character of a Happy Life"', *The Library*, 5th ser., 33 (1978), 223–6
'Sir Henry Wotton's "Dazel'd Thus, with height of Place" and the Appropriation of Political Poetry in the Earlier Seventeenth Century', *PBSA* 71 (1977), 151–69
Perrelli, R., *I proemi Claudian: tra epica ed epidittica* (Catania: Centro di studi sull'antico cristianesimo, Università di Catanai, 1992)
Peterson, R. S., *Imitation and Praise*, rev. edn (Farnham: Ashgate, 2011)
Phillips, J. E., 'George Buchanan and the Sidney circle', *HLQ* 12 (1948–9), 23–55
Pieper, C., *Elegos redolere Vergiliosque sapere. Cristoforo Landinos 'Xandra' zwischen Liebe und Gesellschaft. Noctes Neolatinae*. Neo-Latin Texts and Studies 8 (Hildesheim: Georg Olms, 2008)
Piepho, Lee, *Holofernes' Mantuan: Italian Humanism in Early Modern England* (New York: Peter Lang, 2001)
Pigman, G. W., 'Neo-Latin Imitation of the Latin Classics', in Peter Godman and Oswyn Murray (eds.), *Latin Poetry and the Classical Tradition: Essays in Medieval and Renaissance Literature* (Oxford: Clarendon Press, 1990), 199–210
'Versions of Imitation in the Renaissance', *RQ* 33 (1980), 1–32
Platnauer, M. (ed.), *Claudian*, 2 vols. (Cambridge, MA: Harvard University Press, 1922)
Poole, W., 'Down and Out in Leiden and London: The Later Careers of Venceslaus Clemens (1589–1637) and Jan Sictor (1593–1652), Bohemian Exiles and Failing Poets', *The Seventeenth Century* 28 (2013), 163–85

Poole-Wilson, P. N., 'A Best-Seller Abroad: The Continental Editions of John Owen', in T. C. van Uchelen, K. van der Horst and G. Schilder (eds.), *Theatrum orbis librorum: liber amicorum presented to Nico Israel* (Utrecht: HES, 1989), 242–9

Pope, Johnathan H. (ed.), *Phineas Fletcher: The Purple Island: Or, the Isle of Man* (Leiden: Brill, 2017)

Potter, John M., 'Another Porker in the Garden of Epicurus: Marvell's "Hortus" and "The Garden"', *SEL* 11.1 (1971), 137–51

Potter, Lois, *Secret Rites and Secret Writing: Royalist Literature 1641–1660* (Cambridge University Press, 1989)

Pound, Ezra, *Poems and Translations*, ed. Richard Sieburth (New York: Literary Classics of the United States, 2003)

Powell, Jason, 'The Network behind *"Tottel's" Miscellany*', *ELR* 46 (2016), 193–224

Power, Henry, ' "Teares Breake off My verse": The Virgilian Incompleteness of Abraham Cowley's *The Civil War*', *T&L* 16 (2007), 141–59

Prancie, Antony, '"Ora pro me, sancte Herberte": James Duport and the Reputation of George Herbert', *GHJ* 24 (2000–1), 35–55

Prescott, Anne Lake, 'English Writers and Beza's Latin Epigrams: The Uses and Abuses of Poetry', *SR* 21 (1974), 83–117

 'The Reception of Du Bartas in England', *SR* 15 (1968), 144–73

 'A Year in the Life of King Saul: 1643', in Killeen *et al.* (eds.), *Oxford Handbook of the Bible*, 412–26

Prescott, Anne Lake with Lydia Kirsopp Lake, 'From "Amours" to *Amores*: Francis Thorius Makes Ronsard a Neolatin Lover', in Catherine Gimelli Martin and Hassan Melehy (eds.), *French Connections in the English Renaissance* (London and New York: Routledge, 2016), 161–78

Pritchard, Allan, 'Marvell's "The Garden": A Restoration Poem?', *SEL* 23 (1983), 371–88

Pugh, Syrithe, *Herrick, Fanshawe and the Politics of Intertextuality* (Farnham: Ashgate, 2010)

Putnam, Michael C. J., *Horace's 'Carmen Saeculare': Ritual Magic and the Poet's Art* (New Haven, CT: Yale University Press, 2000)

Putter, A., '*Cleanness* and the Tradition of Biblical Versificatio', in J. A. Burrow and H. N. Duggan (eds.), *Medieval Alliterative Poetry: Essays in Honour of Thorlac Turville-Petre* (Dublin: Four Courts Press, 2010), 166–84

 'Prudentius and the Late Classical Biblical Epics of Juvencus, Proba, Sedulius, Arator, and Avitus', in Rita Copeland (ed.), *Oxford History of Classical Reception in English Literature. vol. 1: 800–1558* (Oxford University Press, 2016), 351–76

 'Sources and Backgrounds for Descriptions of the Flood in Medieval and Renaissance Literature', *SP* 94 (1997), 137–59

Quitslund, Beth, *The Reformation in Rhyme: Sternhold, Hopkins and the English Metrical Psalter, 1547–1603* (Farnham: Ashgate, 2008)

Radzinowicz, M. A., 'Forced Allusions: Avatars of King David in the Seventeenth Century', in Diana T. Benet and Michael Lieb (eds.), *Literary Milton: Text, Pretext, Context* (Pittsburgh, PA: Duquesne University Press, 1994), 45–66

Raspa, A., *The Emotive Image: Jesuit Poetics in the English Renaissance* (Fort Worth: Texas Christian University Press, 1983)

Raven, D. S., *Latin Metre* (London: Bloomsbury, 2013)

Ray, Robert H., 'The Herbert Allusion Book: Allusions to George Herbert in the Seventeenth Century', *SP* 83 (1986), 1–182

Reid, Steven J., 'Melville's Anti-Episcopal Poetry: The *Andreae Melvini Musae*', in Roger A. Mason and Steven J. Reid (eds.), *Andrew Melville (1545–1622): Writings, Reception, and Reputation* (Farnham: Ashgate, 2014), 127–54

Reid, Steven J. and David McOmish (eds.), *Neo-Latin Literature and Literary Culture in Early Modern Scotland* (Leiden: Brill, 2016)

Revard, Stella P., 'Cowley's *Pindarique Odes* and the Politics of the Interregnum', *Criticism* 25 (1993), 391–418

  'The Latin Ode from Elizabeth I to Mary II: Political Approaches to Encomia', in Charles Burnett and Nicholas Mann (eds.), *Britannia Latina: Latin in the Culture of Great Britain from the Middle Ages to the Twentieth Century* (London: Warburg, 2005), 156–64

  'Pindar and Jonson's Cary-Morison Ode', in Claude J. Summers and Ted-Larry Pebworth (eds.), *Classic and Cavalier: Essays on Jonson and the Sons of Ben* (University of Pittsburgh Press, 1982), 17–29

  Pindar and the Renaissance Hymn-Ode: 1450–1700 (Tempe: Arizona University Press, 2001)

  Politics, Poetics, and the Pindaric Ode: 1450–1700 (Tempe: Arizona Center for Medieval and Renaissance Studies and Brepols, 2009)

Revard, S., F. Rädle and M. A. Di Cesare (eds.), *Acta Conventus Neo-Latini Guelpherbytani: Proceedings of the Sixth International Congress of Neo-Latin Studies* (Binghamton, NY: Medieval and Renaissance Texts and Studies, 1988), 353–63

Rhodes, Neil, *Common: The Development of Literary Culture in Sixteenth-Century England* (Oxford University Press, 2018)

Rienstra, Debra and Noel Kinnamon, 'Revisioning the Sacred Text', *SJ* 17 (1999), 53–77

Ringler, William A., *The Poems of Sir Philip Sidney* (Oxford University Press, 1962)

Ritter, Carolin, *Ovidius redivivus: Die Epistulae Heroides des Mark Alexander Boyd. Edition, Übersetzung und Kommentar der Briefe Atalanta Meleagro (1), Eurydice Orpheo (6), Philomela Tereo (9), Venus Adoni (15)*. Noctes Neolatinae 13 (Hildesheim: Georg Olms, 2010)

Roberts, Julian, 'The Latin Trade', in Maureen Bell, J. Barnard and D. F. McKenzie (eds.), *The Cambridge History of the Book in Britain, vol. IV: 1557–1695* (Cambridge University Press, 2002), 141–73

Roberts, M., 'The Use of Myth in Latin Epithalamia from Statius to Venantius Fortunatus', *TAPA* 119 (1989), 321–38

Robinson, Eloise (ed.), *The Minor Poems of Joseph Beaumont, 1616–1699* (London: Constable, 1914), 16–17
Rollins, Hyder, *Tottel's Miscellany*, 2 vols. (Cambridge, MA: Harvard University Press, 1965)
Ross, Sarah C. E., 'Epic, Meditation, or Sacred History? Women and Biblical Verse Paraphrase in Seventeenth-Century England', in Killeen *et al.* (eds.), *Oxford Handbook of the Bible*, 483–97
Røstvig, Maren-Sofie, 'Benlowes, Marvell, and the Divine Casimire', *HLQ* 18 (1954–5), 13–35
  'Casimire Sarbiewski and the English Ode', *SP* 51 (1954), 443–60
  The Happy Man: A Study in the Metamorphosis of a Classical Ideal, vol. 1: *1600–1700* (New York: Humanities Press, 1962; first published 1954)
  'Introduction', in *The Odes of Casimire. Translated by G. Hils (1646)*, Augustan Reprint Society 44 (Los Angeles: William Andrews Clark Memorial Library, 1953)
Rudenstine, N. L., *Sidney's Poetic Development* (Cambridge, MA: Harvard University Press, 1967)
Sacré, D., 'Ein übersehenes Epigramm des John Owen', *Wolfenbütteler Renaissance-Mitteilungen* 18 (1994), 74–6
Sawday, Jonathan, *The Body Emblazoned: Dissection and the Human Body in Renaissance Culture* (Abingdon: Routledge, 1996)
  'The Chief Mystery of the Seminall Business: Andrew Marvell, William Harvey, Abraham Cowley and the Politics of Fertility in the Seventeenth Century', *EJ* 56 (2007), 107–26
Schäfer, Eckart, *Deutscher Horaz: Conrad Celtis, Georg Fabricius, Paul Melissus, Jacob Balde. Die Nachwirkung des Horaz in der neulateinischen Dichtung Deutschlands* (Wiesbaden: Steiner, 1976)
  (ed.), *Sarbiewski: Der polnische Horaz* (Tübingen: Narr Francke Attempto Verlag, 2006)
Schindler, C., *Per Carmina Laudes: Untersuchungen zur spätantiken Verspanegyrik von Claudian bis Coripp* (Berlin: De Gruyter, 2009)
Schmidt, Gabriela, 'Realigning English Vernacular Poetics through Metrical Experiment: Sixteenth-Century Translation and the Elizabethan Quantitative Verse Movement', *LC* 7.5 (2010), 303–17
Schmitz, Thomas, 'L'ode latine pendant la Renaissance française: Un catalogue des odes publiées au seizième siècle', *HL* 43 (1994), 173–219
Schneditz-Bolfras, E., 'John Owen (Johannes Audoenus) als neulateinischer Epigrammatiker', thesis (Vienna, 1990)
Schnur, H. C., *Galle und Honig: Humanistenepigramme* (Leipzig: Philipp Reclam, 1982)
Schultheiss, Jochen, 'Zwischen philologischer Analyse und poetologischen Programm: Zur Metrik der neulateinischen Pindarischen Ode', in Stefan Tilg and Benjamin Harter (eds.), *Neulateinische Metrik: Formen und Kontexte zwischen Rezeption und Innovation* (Tübingen: Narr, 2019), 111–32

Scodel, Joshua, *The English Poetic Epitaph: Commemoration and Conflict from Jonson to Wordsworth* (Ithaca, NY: Cornell University Press, 1991)
  Excess and the Mean in Early Modern English Literature (Princeton University Press, 2002)
Scott-Warren, Jason, *Sir John Harington and the Book as Gift* (Oxford University Press, 2001)
Selden, Raman, 'Roughness in Satire from Horace to Dryden', *MLR* 66 (1971), 264–72
Shaaber, M. A., *Check-List of Works of British Authors Printed Abroad, in Languages other than English, to 1641* (New York: Bibliographical Society of America, 1975)
Shackleton Bailey, D. R. (ed. and trans.), *Statius: Thebaid, Books 1–7* (Cambridge, MA: Harvard University Press, 2004)
Shadduck, Gayle (ed.), *A Critical Edition of Abraham Cowley's Davideis* (New York: Garland, 1987)
Shankman, Steven, 'The Pindaric Tradition and the Quest for Pure Poetry', *CL* 40 (1988), 219–33
Sharp, Richard, 'King, William (1686–1763)', *ODNB*, https://doi.org/10.1093/ref:odnb/15606
Shepherd, W. G. (trans.), *Horace: Complete Odes and Epodes*, with an introduction by Betty Radice (London: Penguin, 1983)
Sidney, Sir Philip, *The Countess of Pembroke's Arcadia (The Old Arcadia)*, ed. Katherine Duncan-Jones (Oxford University Press, 2008)
Sidwell, K. and D. Edwards (eds.), *The Tipperary Hero: Dermot O'Meara's Ormonius (1615)* (Turnhout: Brepols, 2011)
Simeone, William, 'A Probable Antecedent of Marvell's Horatian Ode', *N&Q* 197 (1952), 316–18
Smith, Goldwin, 'Critical Introduction to Andrew Marvell', in Thomas Humphrey Ward (ed.), *English Poets*, vol. II (London: Macmillan, 1880), 382–4
Smith, Hallett, 'English Metrical Psalms in the Sixteenth Century and Their Literary Significance', *HLQ* 9 (1946), 249–71
Smith, Nigel, *Andrew Marvell: The Chameleon* (New Haven, CT: Yale University Press, 2012)
  'Cross-Channel Cavaliers', *The Seventeenth Century* 32.4 (2017), 433–53
  Literature and Revolution in England, 1640–1660 (New Haven, CT: Yale University Press, 1997)
  (ed.), *The Poems of Andrew Marvell* (London and New York: Routledge, 2007)
Smith, R. D., 'Lily, William (1468?–1522/1523)', *ODNB*, https://doi.org/10.1093/ref:odnb/16665
Smyth, Adam, 'Textual Transmission, Reception and the Editing of Early Modern Texts', *LC* 1 (2004), 1–9
Snare, Gerald, 'Chapman's Ovid', *SP* 75 (1978), 430–50
Snyder, Susan (ed.), *The Divine Weekes and Works of Guillaume De Saluste, Sieur Du Bartas, Translated by Josuah Sylvester* (Oxford: Clarendon Press, 1979)

Spalding, Ruth, 'Whitelocke, Bulstrode, Appointed Lord Whitelocke under the Protectorate (1605–1675)', *ODNB*, https://doi.org/10.1093/ref:odnb/29297
Spann, C. E. and M. E. Williams, Sr., *Presidential Praise: Our Presidents and Their Hymns* (Macon, GA: Mercer University Press, 2008)
Sparrow, John, *Visible Words: A Study of Inscriptions in and as Books and Works of Art* (Cambridge University Press, 1969)
Spearing, Caroline, 'The Fruits of Retirement: Political Engagement in the *Plantarum Libri Sex*', in Philip Major (ed.), *Royalists and Royalism in 17th-Century Literature: Exploring Abraham Cowley* (London: Routledge, 2019), 180–201
Spika, J. de, *Imitatione Horatiana in Senecae canticis chori* (Vienna: Staatsgymnasium Wien II, 1890)
Starke, Sue, '"The Eternal Now": Virgilian Echoes and Miltonic Premonitions in Cowley's "Davideis"', *C&L* 55 (2006), 195–219
Stawecka, Krystyna (ed.), *Sarbiewski: Dii Gentium Bogowie Pogan* (Warsaw: Zakład Narodowy im. Ossolińskich, 1972)
Stephens, M. (ed.), *The Oxford Companion to the Literature of Wales* (Oxford University Press, 1986)
Stevens, J. A. (1999), 'Seneca and Horace: Allegorical Technique in Two Odes to Bacchus (Hor. "Carm." 2.19 and Sen. "Oed." 403–508)', *Phoenix* 53 (1999), 281–307
Stevenson, Jane, *Women Latin Poets: Language, Gender, and Authority from Antiquity to the Eighteenth Century* (Oxford University Press, 2005)
Stogdill, Nathaniel, 'Abraham Cowley's "Pindaric Way": Adapting Athleticism in Interregnum England', *ELR* 42 (2012), 482–514
Stone, Lawrence, 'Literacy and Education in England, 1640–1900', *P&P* 42 (1969), 69–139
Streatfeild, Frank, *Latin Versions of the Book of Common Prayer*, Alcuin Club Pamphlet 19 (London: A. R. Mowbray, 1964)
Sullivan, J. P., 'Martial and English Poetry', *CA* 9 (1990), 149–74
  Martial: The Unexpected Classic. A Literary and Historical Study (Cambridge University Press, 1991)
    'Some Versions of Martial 10.47: The Happy Life', *TCO* 63 (1986), 112–15
Sullivan, J. P. and A. J. Boyle (eds.), *Martial in English* (Harmondsworth: Penguin, 1996)
Sutton, Dana (ed.), 'Abraham Cowley, *De Plantis Libri VI* (1668). A Hypertext Critical Edition', *The Philological Museum* (2006/7), www.philological.bham.ac.uk/plants
  (ed.), *William Gager: The Complete Works*, 4 vols. (New York: Garland, 1994), and online, www.philological.bham.ac.uk/gager/poetry
Sutton, Dana F. and Martin Wiggins, *The Philological Museum*, www.philological.bham.ac.uk/library.html
Swann, Joel, *Copying Epigrams in Manuscript Miscellanies*, in Joshua Eckhardt and Daniel Starza Smith (eds.), *Manuscript Miscellanies in Early Modern England* (Farnham: Ashgate, 2016), 151–68

Swedenberg, H. T., 'England's Joy: *Astraea Redux* in Its Setting', *SP* 1 (1953), 30–44
Tarrant, Richard, 'Ancient Receptions of Horace', in Stephen Harrison (ed.), *The Cambridge Companion to Horace* (Cambridge University Press, 2007), 277–90
 '*Custode rerum Caesare*: Horatian Civic Engagement and the Senecan Tragic Chorus', in Stephen Harrison (ed.), *The Cambridge Companion to Horace* (Cambridge University Press, 2007), 93–112
 (ed.), *Seneca's Thyestes. Edited with Introduction and Commentary* (Atlanta, GA: Scholars Press, 1985)
Thill, Andrée, Gilles Banderier and Marc Fumaroli, *La lyre jésuite: Anthologie de poèmes latins (1620–1730)* (Geneva: Droz, 1999)
Thomas, Richard F. (ed.), *Horace: Odes IV and Carmen Saeculare* (Cambridge University Press, 2011)
Thomson, Patricia, 'Wyatt's Boethian Ballade', *RES* 15 (1964), 262–7
Thomson, T., 'The Latin Psalm Paraphrases of Theodore de Bèze', in Revard et al. (eds.), *Acta Conventus Neo-Latini Guelpherbytani*, 353–63
Tilg, Stefan, 'Die "argute" Inschrift als barocke Form des freien Verses', in Stefan Tilg and Benjamin Harter (eds.), *Neulateinische Metrik: Formen und Kontexte zwischen Rezeption und Innovation* (Tübingen: Narr, 2019), 133–48
 'Neo-Latin Anacreontic Poetry: Its Shape(s) and Its Significance', in Manuel Baumbach and Nicola Dümmler (eds.), *Imitate Anacreon! Mimesis, Poiesis and the Poetic Inspiration in the Carmina Anacreontea* (Berlin: De Gruyter, 2014), 161–94
 'On the Origins of the Modern Term "Epyllion": Some Revisions to a Chapter in the History of Classical Scholarship', in Manuel Baumbach and Silvio Bär (eds.), *Brill's Companion to the Greek and Latin Epyllion and Its Reception* (Leiden: Brill, 2012), 29–54
Tilley, Morris Palmer, *A Dictionary of the Proverbs in England in the Sixteenth and Seventeenth Centuries* (Ann Arbor: University of Michigan Press, 1950)
Todd, Richard, '"So Well Attyr'd Abroad": A Background to the Sidney-Pembroke Psalter and Its Implications for the Seventeenth-Century Religious Lyric', *TSLL* 29 (1987), 74–93
Tomlinson, Charles (ed.), *The Oxford Book of Verse in English Translation* (Oxford University Press, 1980)
Traninger, Anita, 'Pleasures of the Imagination: Narrating the Nymph, from Boccaccio to Lope de Vega', in Karl A. E. Enenkel and Anita Traninger (eds.), *The Figure of the Nymph in Early Modern Culture* (Leiden: Brill, 2018), 15–52
Tucker Brooke, C. F., 'Some Pre-Armada Propagandist Poetry in England (1585–1586)', *Proceedings of the American Philosophical Society* 85.1 (1941), 71–83
 'William Gager to Queen Elizabeth', *SP* 29 (1932), 160–75
Tufte, Virginia, *The Poetry of Marriage: The Epithalamium in Europe and Its Development in England* (Los Angeles, CA: Tinnon-Brown, 1970)

Urban, Erich, *Owenus und die deutschen Epigrammatiker des XVII. Jahrhunderts* (Berlin: E. Felber, 1900)

Valdivia, Lucía Martínez, 'Psalms and Early Modern English Poetry', in Kristen Poole and Lauren Shohet (eds.), *Gathering Force: 1557–1623*, vol. 1 (Cambridge University Press, 2019), 287–305

Vallance, Edward, 'Samwaies [Samways], Peter (1615–1693)', *ODNB*, https://doi.org/10.1093/ref:odnb/24607

van Dorsten, J. A., *Poets, Patrons and Professors: Sir Philip Sidney, Daniel Rogers and the Leiden Humanists* (Leiden University Press and Oxford University Press, 1962)

Vine, Angus, *Miscellaneous Order: Manuscript Culture and the Early Modern Organisation of Knowledge* (Oxford University Press, 2019)

von Maltzahn, Nicholas, *An Andrew Marvell Chronology* (Basingstoke: Palgrave Macmillan, 2005)

  'Marvell's Restoration Garden', *MSN* 1.1 (2009), www.st-andrews.ac.uk/marvellsociety/newsletter/marvells-restoration-garden

Vredeveld, H., 'The Fairytale of Nicolas Denisot and the Seymour Sisters', *HL* 67.1 (2018), https://doi.org/10.30986/2018.143

Wall, Wendy, *The Imprint of Gender: Authority and Publication in the English Renaissance* (Ithaca, NY: Cornell University Press, 1993)

Wallace, Andrew, *Virgil's Schoolboys: The Poetics of Pedagogy in Renaissance England* (Oxford University Press, 2011)

Waquet, Françoise, *Latin, or the Empire of a Sign: From the Sixteenth to the Twentieth Centuries*, trans. John Howe (London: Verso, 2001); original publication, *Latin ou l'empire d'un signe* (Paris: Albin Michel, 1998)

Ware, C., 'Claudian: The Epic Poet in the Prefaces', in M. Gale (ed.), *Latin Epic and Didactic Poetry: Genre, Tradition and Individuality* (Swansea: Classical Press of Wales, 2004), 101–201

  Claudian and the Roman Epic Tradition (Cambridge University Press, 2012)

Warnke, Frank J., *European Metaphysical Poetry* (New Haven, CT: Yale University Press, 1961)

Warren, A., 'Crashaw's Epigrammata Sacra', *JEGP* 33 (1934), 233–9

Watson, Foster, *The 'Zodiacus Vitae' of Marcellus Palengenius Stellatus: An Old School-Book* (London: Philip Wellby, 1908)

Weaver, William P., 'The Banquet of the Common Sense: George Chapman's Anti-Epyllion', *SP* 111 (2014), 757–85

  '"O teach me how to make mine own excuse": Forensic Performance in *Lucrece*', *SQ* 59 (2008), 421–49

  Untutored Lines: The Making of the English Epyllion (Edinburgh: Edinburgh University Press, 2012)

West, Philip, 'Nathaniel Wanley and George Herbert: The Dis-Engaged and *The Temple*', *Review of English Studies*, New Series, 57.230 (2006), 337–58

Wheeler, S., 'The Underworld Opening of Claudian's *De Raptu Proserpinae*', *TAPA* 125 (1995), 113–34

Whipple, T. K., *Martial and the English Epigram from Sir Thomas Wyatt to Ben Jonson* (Berkeley: University of California Press, 1925)
White, P., *Renaissance Postscripts: Responding to Ovid's Heroides in Sixteenth-Century France* (Columbus: Ohio State University Press, 2009)
Whitlock, Baird W., 'The Authorship of the Couplet on Sir Albertus Morton and His Wife', *N&Q* 226 (December 1981), 523–4
  'The Baroque Characteristics of the Poetry of George Herbert', *Cithara* 7.2 (1968), 30–40
Whittington, Leah, 'Shakespeare's Grammar: Latin, Literacy, and the Vernacular', in Sean Keilen and Nick Moschovakis (eds.), *The Routledge Research Companion to Shakespeare and Classical Literature* (Routledge: London and New York, 2017), 78–106
Wickenheiser, Robert J., 'George Herbert and the Epigrammatic Tradition', *GHJ* 1 (1977), 39–56
Wilcher, Robert, '"Adventurous song" or "presumptuous folly": The Problem of "utterance" in John Milton's *Paradise Lost* and Lucy Hutchinson's *Order and Disorder*', *The Seventeenth Century* 21 (2006), 304–14
  'Lucy Hutchinson and Genesis: Paraphrase, Epic, Romance', *English* 59 (2010), 25–42
Wilcox, Helen, 'Puritans, George Herbert and "Nose-Twange"', *N&Q* 26 (1979), 152–3
  (ed.), *The English Poems of George Herbert* (Cambridge University Press, 2007)
Williamson, George, 'The Context of Marvell's "Hortus" and "Garden"', *MLN* 76 (1961), 590–8
Wilson, Penelope, 'Pindar and English Eighteenth-Century Poetry', in Richard Rawles and Peter Agocs (eds.), *Receiving the Komos*, BICS Supplement 112 (London: Institute of Classical Studies, 2012), 157–68
Winters, Yvor, 'The 16th Century Lyric in England: A Critical and Historical Reinterpretation: Part I', *Poetry* 53.5 (1939), 258–72
  'The 16th Century Lyric in England: A Critical and Historical Reinterpretation: Part II', *Poetry* 53.6 (1939), 320–35
  'The 16th Century Lyric in England: A Critical and Historical Reinterpretation: Part III', *Poetry* 54.1 (1939), 35–51
Wöhrmann, Kurt, *Die englische Epithalamiendichtung der Renaissance und ihre Vorbilder* (Leipzig: Universitätsverlag von Robert Noske, 1929)
Wong, Alex, *The Poetry of Kissing in Early Modern Europe: From the Catullan Revival to Secundus, Shakespeare and the English Cavaliers* (Woodbridge: Boydell & Brewer, 2017)
Woodhead, M. R. (ed.), *John Marston: What You Will* (Nottingham Drama Texts, 1980)
Woods, Suzanne, 'Ben Jonson's Cary-Morison Ode: Some Observations on Structure and Form', *SEL 1500–1900* 18 (1978), 57–74
Worden, Blair, *Literature and Politics in Cromwellian England: John Milton, Andrew Marvell, Marchamont Nedham* (Oxford University Press, 2007)
  'The Politics of Marvell's Horatian Ode', *HJ* 27 (1984), 525–47

Wright, F. A., *The Love Poems of Joannes Secundus* (London: Routledge, 1930)
Yagüi-Beltrán, Adam and Laura Adam, 'The Imprisonment of David Kinloch, 1588–1594: An Analysis of Newly Discovered Documents in the Archives of the Spanish Inquisition', *IR* 53.1 (2002), 1–39
Yoshinaka, Takashi, *Marvell's Ambivalence: Religion and the Politics of Imagination in Mid-Seventeenth-Century England* (Cambridge: Brewer, 2011)
Young, R. V., Jr, 'Jonson, Crashaw and the Development of the English Epigram', *Genre* 12 (1979), 137–52
Zim, Rivkah, *English Metrical Psalms: Poetry as Praise and Prayer 1535–1601* (Cambridge University Press, 1987)
Zwicker, Steven N., *Lines of Authority: Politics and English Literary Culture, 1649–1689* (Ithaca, NY: Cornell University Press, 1993)

Index

[Anon.]
  Carmen Lugubre, 489
  Commercium ad mare australe, 323
  Ex Spinosa Anonymi Sylva, 189, 336–7
  Gigantomachia, 189
  In illustrissimi comitis Leicestrensis Oxoniensis, 369–70
  Satyra in poetastros, 322–4
A Quercu, Leodegarius. *See* Duchesne, Léger
Abelard, Peter, 293
Aesop
  Fables, 14, 17, 296
Ailmer, John, 474
  Musae Sacrae, 208, 474
Alabaster, William, 40, 356, 393
  Elisaeis, 374–5, 378
    'Council in Hell' scene, 376
  epigrams, 274, 303, 313, 315, 318
  manuscript epithalamium, 425
Alciato, Andrea, 274
Alites, Petrus, Carnutensis
  De Utroque Jesu Christi Adventu, 148
allegorical verse, 189, 256, 330, 335, 337, 412, 414, 430, 435, 489
  and scriptural paraphrase, 474–82
  Ewens, *Votum candidum*, 486
  Fletcher, *Purple Island*, 470–4
  in mid-seventeenth century, 474–82
Allen, Nicholas
  Carmen encomiasticum, 368
Allibond, John
  Rustica academiae oxoniensis, 347
allusion, 20, 38
Alsop, Anthony, 10
Ambrose, 86, 108, 343
  use of iambic dimeter, 108
Anacreon, 47, 58
Anacreontea, 58, 60, 72
Andrewes, Lancelot, 233
Anglo-Saxon, 173

anthologies of Latin verse, produced by universities, 138–9, *See* Oxford university anthologies *and* Cambridge university anthologies
Aquinas, 343
Aramaic, 13
Archilochus, 181, 216, 332–3
Ascham, Roger, 68
  The Scholemaster, 451
Ashley, Robert, 9
  Latin translation of Du Bartas, 94
  L'Uranie – Urania, 463
Ashmore, John
  Certain Selected Odes of Horace, 50–3, 126, 313
Aston, John
  Latin poems in manuscript, 253–4
Atkinson, Thomas, 335
  'Melvinus Delirans', 331–5
Attridge, Derek, 114–15
Auger, Peter, 462
Augustine, 6
Ausonius, 6, 31, 73, 126, 288, 293, 310, 314, 326
  Cento Nuptialis, 414
Axon, William, 207
Aylett, Robert, 249
  David's Troubles Remembred, 193–4
  Divine, and Moral Speculations in Metrical Numbers, 193
  scriptural paraphrases, 193–4
Ayton, John
  epigrams, 313

Bacon, Francis, 54
Baker, Daniel
  poem on Thomas Burnet, 224
  poems of, 45–6, 246
  use of Pindarics, 221
Balde, Jakob
  satires, 320, 323

565

Baldwin, William
  Canticles or balades of Salomon, The, 249
  Treatise of Morall phylosophie, A, 33
Ball, William
  Europa lachrymans, 189
Bancroft, Thomas
  Two Bookes of Epigrammes, 237
Barberini, Maffeo, 184, 229
  Pindaric odes, 200–1, 203, 226
  Poemata, 195, 200–1, 307
  response to Herbert, 'Roma', 307–8
Barclay, John, 8–9, 285
  Argenis, 8
  epigrams, 301–2
  Euphormio, 40
  Satyricon, 9
Barlaeus, Caspar, 355, 360, 404
  assessment of Claudian, 366–7
  Britannia Triumphans, 372–3, 388
  Panegyris, 392
Barlaeus, Melchior
  De raptu Ganymedis liber, 422–3, 434
Barnfield, Richard
  Cassandra, 431
  Hellen's Rape, 429, 431, 434
baroque poetry, 224, 240–2
Barrow, Isaac, 176
Bartholin, Thomas
  De medicis poetis, 442
Bastard, Thomas, 142, 368
  Chrestoleros, 281
  epigrams, 273, 280, 288, 297–8
  ode on Philip Sidney, 158–60
Batrachomuomachia
  translation by Gager, 431
Bauhusius, Bernhard, 239–40, 247, 249, 308
  'Aspirat ad caelestem patriam', 255–6
  'Ecce Homo', 243–5
  Epigrammata, 225–6, 229, 242–5, 288
  'Homo Bulla', 245
  influence upon Herbert, 242–5
  paraphrase of Song of Simeon (Luke 2), 243
  'Roma' epigram, 305–7
Beal, Peter, 26
Beaumont, Francis
  Salmacis and Hermaphroditus, 406–7
Beaumont, Joseph
  'Jesus inter Ubera Maria', 251–2
Bede, 343
Bellehachius, Ogerius
  Sacrosancta bucolica, 249
Benlowes, Edward, 60, 368
  publisher of *Marston Moor*, 382
  publisher of *The Purple Island*, 473

Bettini, Mario, 239, 249
  anacreontic verse, 184
  imitation of Song of Songs, 252
  'Jesus lactens. Qui pascitur inter Lilia', 252
Beza, Theodorus. *See* Bèze, Théodore de
Bèze, Théodore de, 8, 10, 31, 38, 94, 97, 106, 109, 137
  Elegia 2, 36
  epigrams, 274, 313, 315
    translated into Scots, 315
  French psalter, 109
  influence upon Sidney psalter, 110–25
  Juvenilia, 71
  paraphrase of Job, 20
  paraphrase of Song of Songs, 93, 134–5, 248, 252
  praised by Melville, 324
  psalm paraphrases, 14, 20, 69, 74, 80, 86, 96–8, 101–6, 199, 224, 498
    metrical variety of, 105, 108, 115, 145
    Psalm 23, 133–4
    Psalm 41, 80
    Psalm 87, 92
    Psalm 96, 104–5
    Psalm 119, 80, 92
    Psalm 120, 117–18
    Psalm 140, 118–19
    use of rhyme in, 76, 118–19
    use of asclepiad metres, 87, 90
    use of iambic metres, 130
    use of iambic dimeter, 108
    use of pythiambic metres, 92
    use of trochaic metres, 93
Bidermann, Jacob, 229, 239
Binns, J. W., 1, 236
Birch, Thomas, 294, 299
  Christmas ode, 227
Birkhead, Henry, 393
  Poematia, 213, 378
Blount, Thomas Pope
  Remarks on Poetry, 127
Bodleian Library manuscripts
  Cherry 37, 300–3
  Eng. poet. f. 13, 317–18
  Eng. poet. f. 16, 44–5, 336–7
  Eng. poet. f. 17, 126
  Fairfax 40, 467
  Lat. misc. e. 32, 226
  Rawl. C. 580, 233
  Rawl. poet. 31, 47
  Rawl. poet. 57, 238–9
  Rawl. poet. 62, 252, 289
  Rawl. poet. 65, 208–11, 218, 226
  Rawl. poet. 173, 46

Index

Rawl. poet. 215, 233–4
Rawl. poet. 246, 337–9
Sancroft 28, 318–19
Sancroft 53, 203–4
Tanner 306, 190, 314–15, 332
Tanner 330, 253–4
Tanner 466, 206, 269–70, *See also* Sancroft, William, miscellany of
Boethius, 6, 12, 31, 36, 38–9, 41, 44, 50, 57, 62, 64, 67, 73–4, 84, 136, 138–9, 251, 293
  as metrical authority, 74
  as metrical model, 126
  Cons. 1 met. 2–7, 44
  Cons. 1 met. 4, 41–3, 63
  Cons. 1 met. 5, 44–5
  Cons. 1 met. 6, 53
  Cons. 1 met. 7, 84
  Cons. 2 met. 1–8, 44
  Cons. 2 met. 3, 77
  Cons. 2 met. 6, 84
  Cons. 2 met. 8, 53
  Cons. 2 pros. 2, 63
  Cons. 3 met. 1–6, 44
  Cons. 3 met. 3, 34
  Cons. 3 met. 4, 34
  Cons. 3 met. 5, 34–5
  Cons. 3 met. 6, 34, 41
  Cons. 3 met. 10, 76
  Cons. 3 met. 12, 35, 53
  Cons. 4 met. 2, 93
  Cons. 4 met. 3, 53
  Cons. 4 met. 7, 84
  Cons. 5 met. 4, 53
  lyric metres of, 35
  metra, 29, 33, 52, 64
  translation and imitation of, 34–6, 44, 129
  translation of, 36
  use of pythiambic metres, 92
Bonifacio, 31
Borbonius. *See* Bourbon, Nicholas
Bourbon, Nicholas, 280
  epigrams, 277
Boyd, Andrew
  Ad augustissimum monarcham, 368
Brackston, William
  commonplace book of, 8
Braden, Gordon, 419, 421, 423, 430, 433, 443
Bradner, Leicester, 1, 163, 482, 493
Braithwait, Richard
  Barnabae itinerarium, 346
Bridges, John, 20
  paraphrase of New Testament, 19
British Library manuscripts
  Add 11723, 246

Add 15227, 289
Add 19863, 379–82
Add 29241, 220
Add 36529, 128
Add 37719, 289–94
Add 61744, 313–14
Add 73542, 288–9
Cotton Titus A XXIV, 154–6
Egerton 2642, 34, 276–8
Harley 1221, 311–12
Harley 1823, 288
Harley 3258, 231–2
Harley 3910, 40–4, 46, 288
Harley 6038, 293, 302, 306, 308–12
Harley 6054, 314, 317–18
Harley 6211, 91
Harley 6350, 16
Harley 6383, 293
Harley 6637, 128
Harley 6932, 379–82
Harley 7316, 311
Lansdowne 695, 220–1
Lansdowne 846, 226
Royal 12 A XXIII, 148, 156–7
Royal 12 A XXX, 17, 76–8, 84, 146
Royal 12 A LVII, 365–6
Royal 12 A LXX, 129–31
Royal 12 D VIII, 364–5, *See also* Charles I, commonplace book of
Sloane 1768, 79–80
Sloane 833, 462
Sloane 2287, 15
Brome, Alexander
  Poems of Horace, 50
Brome, Richard
  Lachrymae Musarum, 60
Brotherton manuscripts, Leeds
  Lt 55, 65
  Lt q 18, 312–13
Brown, Georgia, 418, 420
Brown, Thomas
  poem on Bishop Burnet, 348–50
Brownswerd, John, 94
  Progymnasmata, 16, 79
Buchanan, George, 6, 8–9, 63, 71, 94, 103, 106, 226, 246, 343, 368, 383
  as metrical authority, 74, 97
  as metrical model, 126
  as model for Fisher, 355
  as religious poet, 230–1
  De prosodia libellus, 91, 94
  De Sphaera, 71
  epigrams, 274, 288, 294, 314

Buchanan, George (cont.)
    epithalamium for Mary Queen of Scots, 425, 444
    Franciscanus, 326, 332
    Iambi, 332, 339
    imitation of, 126–7, 129–30
    influence upon Sidney psalter, 109–14
    odes, 145
    paraphrase of Song of Simeon (Luke 2), 243
    Poemata, 230–1
    psalm paraphrases, 8, 12, 20, 66, 69–70, 73–5, 86, 96–8, 101, 106, 199, 224, 230, 270
        metrical variety of, 101, 108, 115, 145
        Psalm 1, 73
        Psalm 2, 92–3
        Psalm 5, 83
        Psalm 16, 90, 129–30
        Psalm 23, 132–3
        Psalm 28, 112
        Psalm 33, 77
        Psalm 68, 113–14
        Psalm 70, 77
        Psalm 80, 123–5
        Psalm 96, 103
        Psalm 120, 117
        Psalm 121, 77
        Psalm 142, 77
    use in schools, 100
    'Satyra in Carolum Lotharingum', 332
    Silvae, 71
    Sphaera, 462
    use of asclepiad metres, 87, 90, 108
    use of iambic metres, 130
        use of iambic dimeter, 108
    use of pythiambic metres, 92–3
    use of trochaic metres, 93
Bunting, Basil
    Odes 1.9, 77
    Odes 1.15, 88–9
    Odes 1.30, 89
Burnet, Thomas
    Telluris Theoria Sacra, 224
Burrus, John, 288
Burton, Robert
    Anatomy of Melancholy, 6, 251, 273
Busby
    Rudimentum Grammaticae Graeco-Latinae Metricum, 14
Bush, Douglas, 435
Butler, Samuel
    Hudibras
        translation into Latin, 318

Caesar, Charles, 26
Calfhill, James, 20

Callimachus
    Hecale, 409
    Iamboi, 332
Calvin, Jean, 232
    commentary on the psalms, 100, 109
Cambridge University anthologies
    Academiae Cantabrigiensis ΣΩΣΤΡΑ, 176, 214, 374, 397, 399
    Anthologia Regis in Exanthemata, 337
    Irenodia Cantabrigiensis, 171, 173–5
    Lachrymae, 86, 158
    Oliva Pacis, 139, 175
    Sorrowes Ioy, 150
    Threno-thriambeuticon, 143, 149–51, 188
    Συνῳδία, 150
Cambridge University Library manuscripts
    Add. 8861/2, 16
    Add. 8915, 146
    Dd. V. 75, 345
    Dd. V. 77, 221
    Dd. IX. 59, 6, 62–4, 251
    Dd. XI. 80, 8
    Kk. V. 14, 84–6
    Mm. IV. 39, 366
Camden, William, 15–16, 72, 79, 94, 220, 284
    Britannia, 72
    copy of Dousa, 158
    De Connubio Tamis et Isis, 413
    Remaines, 293
Camerarius, Philip
    Operae horarum subcisivarum, 52
Cameron, Alan, 363, 365
Campbell, Lily, 18, 454
Campion, Edmund, 232
Campion, Thomas, 10, 50, 68, 83, 298, 360
    Epigrammata, 72
    Epigrammatum Libri II, 72
    'Man of life upright', 48–50
    Umbra, 360, 410, 416–18, 422, 434
    use of asclepiad metres, 90
    'What faire pompe have I spide', 90
canon, Latin, in early modernity, 4–6, 10–12
Capellanus, Martianus
    Nuptiis Philologiae et Mercurii, 414, 441
Carleil, Christopher, 152
Carleton, George, 368
    Ad serenissimam Elizabetham
        'Council in Hell' scene, 376
Carne-Ross, Donald, 88
Carnutensis, Petrus Alites. *See* Alites, Petrus
Carr, Robert, Earl of Somerset, 54
Carter, Elizabeth
    extempore epigram, 299–300
Cartwright, Cartwright, 269
Cassiodorus, 34

Cato, distichs of. *See Cato's Distichs*
Cato's Distichs, 5–6, 12, 28, 282–7, 290–1, 296, 314, 319
Catullus, 52, 73, 129, 164, 274, 288, 293, 410, 412–14
  11, 50
  51, 49
  61, 412
  62, 412
  63, 41
  64, 412, 415–17, 429, 433, 446, 488
  use of hendecasyllable, 87, 138
Cecil, William
  ode to by Dousa, 158
centos
  Ausonius, *Cento Nuptialis*, 414
  Virgilian, 19–20, 78
Chaloner, Thomas, 482, 489
  contributor to *A Mirror for Magistrates*, 480
  De Republica Instauranda, 449, 470, 480–1, 492–3
Chapman, George, 409, 414
  Andromeda Liberata, 360, 411
  career of, 411–12
  Divine Poem of Musaeus, Hero and Leander, The, 411
  Hero and Leander Completed, 406, 411–12, 414, 416–17, 443
  Hymne to Hymen, 411–12
  Ovids Banquet of Sence, 187, 406, 411, 431, 440
Charles I
  commonplace book of, 6, 35, 358, 364–5
  Eikon Basilike, 356
Chatwin, John, 58
Chaucer, Geoffrey
  Boece, 34
  Parliament of Fowles, 421
Cheke, John
  De obitu Martini Buceri, 147, 152, 156
Cheney, Patrick, 359
Christiansen, Peder, 389
Chrytaeus, Nathan, 98
Churchyard, Thomas, 98
Cicero, 4
Clapham, John
  Narcissus, 409, 417, 423–4
Clarke, Edward, 84
Clarke, Elizabeth, 250
Claudian, 6, 11–12, 38–9, 46, 140, 293, 336, 355–405, 410, 413–15, 434, 489, 497
  as invective poet, 337
  as metrical authority, 74
  as school text, 359–60, 362–3
  Carmen Paschale, 358
Carmina Minora, 357, 364, 373, 380, 394
  epithalamium (*CM* 25), 412, 416, 420–1, 443
III. Cons., 154, 357, 365, 369–70, 377, 397
  preface, 463
IV. Cons., 357, 363, 365–7, 370, 395
VI. Cons., 357, 366, 370, 385–7, 389, 395
De sepulcro speciosae, 365
distinctive style of, 360–3
Epith., 357, 360, 393, 412, 414–16, 419–20, 424–5, 429, 433, 435–6, 444
  links to Catullus 64, 415–16
Eutr., 337, 357, 367, 385, 391–2
evidence for readership in early modern England, 363–7
Fescennine Verses, 357, 412
'Garden of Venus' scenes, 418–22
Get., 357, 395, 404
Gigantomachy, 357, 374
Gild., 357, 373, 389, 480
Goth., 389
his development of panegyric epic as a genre, 355
imitation of, 141, 175, 367–72, 378–97
Laus Christi, 358
Miracula Christi, 358
'Old Man of Verona', 29, 33, 35, 44, 357, 366
overlap of genres, 360
overview of Claudianic corpus, 356, 360
P&O, 357, 373
'Phoenix, The', 357, 391
polymetric sequence, 360
prefatory poems in elegiac couplets, 360
Rapt., 357, 359–60, 364, 419, 422, 427–8, 430, 433, 435, 446
  as model for epyllia, 417–18
  as school text, 417
  preface, 463, 469
  prefatory poem, 374–5
Ruf., 337, 357–8, 380–2, 391, 394
  imitated by Fisher, 383–4
  Ruf. 1 'Council in Hell' scene and imitations, 376–7
Stil., 357, 364, 366, 378, 389, 391, 394, 404
Stilicho, depiction of, 356, 371, 398, 401, 404
  as figure for Cromwell, 387–93
stylistic and generic influence in early modernity, 358–63
Theod., 357, 389, 391–2, 395
understood to have been a Christian, 12, 357–8, 360
use of gigantomachy, 337
use of rhyme, 360
use of similes, 361–2

Clemens, Venceslaus
  Gustavis, 373–4, 376
Cleveland, John
  epigrams, 317
  'The Rebel Scot', 338–40
Coleridge, Samuel Taylor, 247
Colet, John, 15, 465
Collinutio, 31
Colluthus, 446
  Raptus Helenae, 409
Commaundre, Robert, 280, 283
  miscellany of, 34, 276–8
commonplacing, 6
Coombe, Clare, 399
Cooper, Charles Henry
  Memorials of Cambridge, 238
Corpus Christi College Oxford manuscripts
  266, 234–5
  294, 303
  311, 303
  317, 345–6
  324, 278–9
Cotton, Charles, 34
Cotton, John, 249
Coverdale, Miles, 99
Cowley, Abraham, 2, 10, 13, 34, 45, 60, 69, 136,
    190, 246, 248, 267, 270, 294, 337, 404,
    472, 498
  Anacreontiques, 184, 252
  as scriptural poet, 184, 220
  Civil War, 185
  contribution to *Irenodia Cantabrigiensis*,
    173–5
  Davideis, 19, 183, 185, 187, 189, 195, 220,
    270, 385, 447, 474–5, 479, 486
  use of inset lyrics, 191–4
  Essays, 496
  'Extasie, The', 203, 256, 263–5, 270
  imitation of, 246
  influence of the 1656 *Poems*, 220
  Mistresse, The, 220
  ode on Harvey, 484
  ode on Hope, 217, 266
  'Ode upon the return of his Majestie', 171
  'Of Agriculture', 496
  Pindarique Odes, 1, 127, 131, 142, 183,
    195–222, 263–4, 270, 485
    Preface, 195
  'Plagues of Egypt, The', 270
  Plantarum Libri duo, 487
  Plantarum Libri Sex, 3, 187, 194, 294, 449,
    470, 484, 486–96
    Book 1, 487–9
    Book 2, 489–90
    Book 3, 490, 492
    Book 4, 490–2, 494–5
    Book 5, 490, 492–3
    Book 6, 483, 490, 493–4
    compared to the 1656 *Poems*, 194
    political allegory of, 490–6
    use of Ovid, 487–9
  Poems, 183–7, 190, 461, 482
    politics of, 184–7
    preface, 474, 486, 489
    Preface, 263
  Poetical Blossomes, 187
  Psalm 114, 270
  translated into Latin, 220, 318
  translation of Claudian, 357
  translation of Horace, *Odes* 4.2, 205
  translation of Pindar, *Olympian* 2, 217
  verse about, 221
  'Vision', 189
Cowper, William, 228
Craig, Thomas
  Henrici illustrissimi epithalamium, 425
Crane, Mary Thomas, 30, 283
Cranmer, Thomas, 99
Crashaw, Richard, 10, 13, 20, 223, 228, 248,
    265, 267, 482
  'Answer for Hope', 266
  'Bulla', 245
  Carmen Deo Nostro, 218
  circulation of epigrams, 238
  epigram on Luke 11
    27, 242
  metrical experiments of, 195, 217–19
  'Music's Duel', 363
  'On the Assumption', 218–19
  'On the Infant Martyrs', 242
  poem on the Assumption, 254–5
  psalm paraphrases, 217, 270
  scriptural epigrams, 233
  Steps to the Temple, 217, 245
Cromwell, Oliver, 247, 338, 361, 399–401, 404,
    475, 497
  as Stilicho, 356, 387–93
  as Typhoeus, 398–400
  depiction by Cowley, 337
  depiction by Fisher, 175–82, 214–17, 375–6,
    380–93
  depiction by Manley, 214–17
  depiction by Marvell, 171–3, 393–7
  depiction by Sprat, 203–4
  Latin verse for, 184
  Latin verse on, 211, 213–14, 256, 335–6, 355
Crouch, John
  Londinenses lacrymae, 489
Crowley, Robert
  One and Thyrtye Epigrammes, 281
  Psalter of David, 99
Cummings, Brian, 21

Index

Cummings, Robert, 324
Curio, Caelius Secundus
  Pasquillorum tomi duo, 278
  Pasquillorum versus aliquot, 278

D'Avenant, William, 483
D'Ewes, Simonds, 126
Damman, Adrianus, 438, 440
  Bartasias (Latin translation of Du Bartas), 463
  Schediasmata, 443
Daniel, Samuel, 127, 364, 371, 397
Dante, 421
David, as psalmist, 30, 73, 98, 142, 149, 193
Davidson, Peter, 9, 359
Davies, John, 310
  epigrams, 273, 280, 317
Davison, Francis, 83
Davison, William, 54
Dawson, John
  Summa moralis theologiae, 19, 126, 249
De Laet, Joannes
  Novus orbis, 492
Demetriou, Tania, 409
Dempster, Thomas
  Panegyricus, 368
Denham, John, 483
  translated into Latin, 318
Denisot, Nicolas, 368
Despauterius, Johannes
  Ars versificatoria, 91, 94
Dethick, Henry
  Feriae sacrae, 20, 236
Dickenson, John
  Deorum Consessus, 440–1
didactic verse, 71, 191, 231
Digges, Thomas
  admiration of Palingenius, 462, 472
Dillingham, William, 97
Disticha Catonis. See Cato's Distichs
Doelman, James, 280, 307
Dolman, Dorothy
  Latin notes by, 15
Donne, John, 6, 47, 99, 127, 246, 251, 269, 310
  as religious poet, 223
  as satirist, 321
  epithalamia, 427
  'Vota Amico Facta', 8
Dornavius, Caspar
  Ampitheatrum sapientiae, 39
Dousa, Janus, 72, 93, 97
  Daphnis Ecloga, 428
  Odarum Britannicarum Liber, 94–5, 157–8
  ode to William Cecil, 176
Drant, Thomas, 19, 130
  A Medicinable Morall
    metres of, 89–90

  Epigrams and sentences spirituall, 236
  Medicinable Morall, metres of, 80–2
  paraphrase of Ecclesiastes, 19
  translations of Gregory of Nazianzus, 236
Drayton, Michael, 6, 63, 72, 136, 141, 364, 371, 397
  Complaint of Rosamond, 406
  Eclogues, 82, 187
  Endimion and Phoebe, 406
  Harmonie of the Church, 249
  Odes, 46–7, 164, 170–1
  Piers Gaveston, 406
Drummond, William, 227
Dryden, John, 13, 144, 228, 359, 404
  'Absalom and Achitophel', 19
  Annus Mirabilis, 2, 400
  Astraea Redux, 355, 397, 401
  use of Claudian, 398–400
  commemorative poem for John Smith, 214
  'Heroic Stanzas', 392, 397, 400–1
  translations of Horace, 46
  translations of into Latin, 203
Du Bartas, Guillaume de Salluste, 9, 20, 447, 453, 456, 470–2, 489
  as school text, 465
  Latin translations of, 94, 462
  readership in England, 461–5
  relationship to Palingenius, 461–5
  Sepmaines, 442, 447–8, 461
    opening sequence, 463–5
  L'Uranie, 461
Du Moulin, Peter, 20, 294, 337, 482, 494
  Carmen heroicum, 368
  Ecclesiae gemitus, 191–2, 335–6, 478–82, 489
  invective verse against Milton, 335
  Poematum libelli tres, 268–9
  Regii sanguinis clamor, 191, 479
  religious poetry, 268–9
Duchesne, Léger
  Flores epigrammatum, 282–3
Duport, James, 236
  scriptural epigrams, 233
  Σολομῶν Ἔμμετρος, 249, 474
Duppa, Brian
  Jonson Virbius, 212–13
Durfeld, Jacob
  Commentarius accuratus in Canticum Canticorum Salomonis, 250, 257, 473
Durham University Library manuscripts
  Hunter MS 96, 288, 293
Dutch, 1, 9, 18, 109

Earthley, Edward, 152
Echlin, John
  De regno panegyricon, 368

eclogues, 71
  Nativity eclogues, 227
education, early modern, 3–7, 271, 319
  of women, 4, 15, 70, 85, 296–7
  role of paraphrase within, 13–21
Edwardes, Thomas
  dithyrambic verse, 208–11
Edwards, Thomas
  Cephalus and Procris, 406
Eikon Basilike, 291
elegy, love, 11
Eleutherius, N.
  Triumphalia, 372
Eliot, T. S., 87
Elizabeth I, 72, 76, 83, 94
  extempore epigram of, 298
  knowledge of Latin, 4
Ellwood, Thomas
  verse collection of, 314
Elyot, Thomas
  The Boke Named the Gouernour, 364
Emmanuel College Cambridge manuscripts
  105, 287–8
Enenkel, Karl, 279
Ennodius, 293
Enock, Richard
  miscellany of, 208
Enterline, Lynn, 359, 406, 408
epic, 11, 71
  allegorical, 2
  biblical, 19
  didactic, 2, 5, 447–96
    features of, 449–50
  Hellenistic short epic, 409
  Palingenian. *See* epic, didactic
  panegyric, 1, 154, 322, 355–405, 448
    after the Restoration, 397
    European context, 372–8
    in England, 1640-60, 378–97
    manuscript examples, 368–9
    produced in early modern England, 367–72
  'unclassical', 447–96
Epigrammatum delectus, 293
epigrams, 1–2, 5, 11, 71–2, 231, 237, 271–319, 322, 490
  accessibility of, 294–7
  aenigmata, 72, 79, 278, 296, 318
  and literary bilingualism, 271–319
  anthologies for school use, 293–4
  bilingual pairs of, 50, 312–17
  chronograms, 78, 273, 278
  classical, 280, 313
  created by excerpting, 273
  didactic, 28, 292, 319
  emblemata, 78, 238, 256, 273

  emergence in English, 1590-1610, 280–2
  epigram culture, 271–319
  exchange of, 28, 297–309, 319
  extempore, 298–300
  from Greek Anthology, 280
  humanist, 271, 273, 276, 279–81, 319
  in England before 1590, 276–80
  in manuscript record, 272–6
  moral, 276–7, 279, 282–7, 292, 319
  on Christmas, 225
  pasquils or pasquinades, 278
  relationship to moralizing distichs, 271
  religious, 228, 231, 240, 247–60, 267, 276
  satiric, 278, 281, 340–3, 351
  scriptural, 20, 223, 229, 232–40, 260, 279
  topical, 276–7, 279
  translation into Latin, 317–19
  types of epigram, 272, 274
epistles, 71
epithalamia
  disappearance in England in late sixteenth century, 411, 438
  'Garden of Venus' scenes, 410, 418–31
  lyric, 411–12, 414
  narrative, 410, 412–18
  relationship to epyllia, 410–12, 446
epyllia, 1–2, 322, 359, 405–7
  characteristics of Elizabethan epyllia, 406–10
  didactic epyllia, 440–6
  'Garden of Venus' scenes, 410, 418–31
  relationship to Claudian, 446
  relationship to epithalamia, 410–12, 446
  relationship to Ovid, 407–10, 446
Erasmus, Desiderius, 8, 15, 371
  Adagia, 459
  Gratulatorium Carmen, 368
  use of pythiambic metres, 92
Essex Record Office manuscripts
  D/DL F106, 296–7
Estienne, Henri
  Carmina Anacreontica, 72, 75
Eston, John, 438
Euripides, 34
Evelyn, John, 34
Ewens, Maurice, 10, 472
  praise of Cowley, 486
  Votum Candidum, 448, 482–6, 492–3

Fabricius, George, 343
Falckenburg, Jakob, 19
Fane, Mildmay, 60
  imitation of Horace, 137
  Otia Sacra, 57, 207, 260, 492
  parodia, 348, 352
  translation of Claudian, 357

Fanshawe, Richard, 36, 46, 136–7, 215
  Il pastor fido, 171
  'Ode Upon the occasion of His Majesties Proclamation in the year 1630', 171
  Selected Parts of Horace, 337
Farnaby, Thomas, 273
  Florilegium epigrammatum Graecorum, 63, 184, 251
Feckenham, John, 232
Fenner, Dudley
  Song of Songs, 249
figure poems, 78, 86, 131, 235
Filelfo, Francesco, 145
  Odes, 80
  polymetric verse, 80
  satires, 320
Fisher, Payne, 10, 359, 361, 374
  Anniversarium, 388–9, 396
  Apobaterion, 368, 389
  Cromwell, depiction during the Protectorate, 387–93
  Cromwell, early depiction of, 380–2, 387
  'De obsidione', 380–2
  early Latin poetry, 378–82
  Epinicion, vel elogium, 368
  Epithalamium, 424–5
  Inauguratio Olivariana, 356, 389, 393, 395–6
  influence upon Marvell, 393–7
  Irenodia Gratulatoria, 141, 175, 356, 389, 392, 395, 401, 404
  Marston-Moor, 176, 356, 360, 368, 377, 379, 382–7, 392, 395, 403–4, 492, 497–8
  models for his panegyric epic, 355–6
  ode to Cromwell, 175–82, 193, 214–17
  Oratio secunda anniversaria, 344
  Paean triumphalis, 375–6
  Piscatoris poemata, 213–14, 389, 392, 397
  Pro recuperata valetudine, 396
  use of Claudian, 404–5
    Stilicho for Cromwell, 356
  use of dithyrambics, 213–14
  use of poem for Ireton, 213–14
  use of steersman image, 395–7
FitzGeffrey, Charles
  Affaniae, 97, 127
  epigrams, 288, 298
Flaminio, Marc Antonio
  psalm paraphrases, 73, 106
Flatman, Thomas, 214
Fletcher, Giles, 10, 17, 77, 276, 438, 440
Fletcher, Phineas, 10, 482, 489, 494
  ode on death of Elizabeth I, 149–51, 156
  Purple Island, The, 2, 36, 47, 128, 449, 470–5, 477, 480–2, 484, 486, 489–90, 495
    similarities to Palingenius, 471–4
    version of the Song of Songs, 473
  Venus and Anchises, 406, 423
Flinker, Noam, 248
Ford, John
  The Lover's Melancholy, 363
Fortunatus, Venantius
  'Pangue lingua gloriosi', 93
Fraunce, Abraham, 68
  Countesse of Pembrokes Emanuel, The, 99, 107
  emblem collection for Sidney, 86
  Lamentations of Amyntas, The, 429
free verse, Latin, 2, 184, 211–14, 222, 248, 322, 344, *See also* inscription, literary
  satiric, 348–9, 352
French, 1, 9–10
Fulman, William
  notebooks of, 327

Gaertner, Johannes, 236
Gager, William, 10, 169–70, 434
  Exequiae, 86, 158, 431
  Hero and Leander
    relationship to Marlowe, 431–4
    relationship to Musaeus, 431–4
  In Catilinarias proditiones, 143, 163–9, 431
    Ode 1, 166
    Ode 2, 166
    Ode 3, 164–5
    Ode 4, 166
    Ode 7, 167–8
    Ode 8, 165, 168
  Latin translation of Musaeus, 413
  literary career, 431
  Susanna, 431
Gardiner, Stephen
  epigrams, 277
  poem on death of, 146
Garnet, James, 94
Garrison, James, 359, 371
Gascoigne, George, 28
Gawen, Thomas
  Latin translation of Cleveland, 'The Rebel Scot', 338–9
Gazet, Angelin
  Pia hilaria, 8, 339
genethliacon, 432
Geneva Bible, 100, 104, 109, 111, 119
Gentili, Alberico, 97
Gentili, Scipio, 10, 97
  nativity eclogue, 227
  Nereus, 432–4, 436–7, 439
  Plutonis concilium, 376
  psalm paraphrases, 96, 106, 108, 227
  Solymeidos liber primus, 376
  Solymeidos libri duo, 376

German, 278
Gibson, John
  prison notebook of, 289–94
Gibson, William, 297
Gilbie, Anthonie, 109
  translation of Beza, 101, 110, 120
Gill, Alexander, 239
  Gratulatoria, 368, 377–8
  'In Casabundum Colonellum', 339
Gillespie, Stuart, 44
Glanville, John, 46
  Articuli Christianae fidei, 15
Goad, Thomas, 239
  Proditoris proditor, 168–70
  use of polymetric verse, 188–9
Gohaeus, Gulielmus
  Carmen Panegyrikon, 368
Golding, Arthur
  Metamorphoses, 409
  translation of Calvin, 100, 109
Googe, Barnabe
  translation of Palingenius, 450–1
Gower, John, 34
  epigrams, 277
Graves, Robert
  'Love without hope', 272
Greek Anthology, 293
Greek, ancient, 1, 6–7, 9, 15, 86, 278
  epigrams, 63
  teaching of, 14, 19
Greene, Thomas, 38
Greville, Fulke, 68
  Caelica, 35
Grey, Nicholas, 20
  Parabolae evangelicae, 16
Grimald, Nicholas, 31, 36
Grotius, Hugo, 247, 270
  Adamus Exul, 95, 206–7, 270
  epigrams, 239, 274, 294, 313
  Inauguratio Regis Britanniarum, 372
  paraphrase of Psalm 104, 206–7, 270
  Sacra, 95
  use of dithyrambic, 206–7
Guilpin, Everard
  epigrams, 280
  Skialethia, 281
Gunpowder Plot poems
  'Council in Hell' scenes. See Claudian, *Ruf*, 'Council in Hell'
  short epic, 360, 379, 405
  'Council in Hell' scenes, 383

Haber, Judith, 408
Haddon, Walter, 20, 31, 34, 38, 235
  epigrams, 234, 277

Latin translation of the Book of Common Prayer, 99
Lucubrationes, 37, 82, 84, 148
Oratio Iesu Christi, 19, 75, 100
paraphrases of New Testament, 19
psalm paraphrases, 19
scriptural paraphrases, 234
Hall, John, 60, 393
Hall, Joseph
  Virgidemiarum, 333
Hamlin, Hannibal, 108
Hankins, James, 451
Hardie, Philip, 359
Hardy, Thomas
  'In Front of the Landscape', 88
Harington, John, 47, 128
  epigrams, 273, 280, 292
Harley, Richard, 311
Harley, Robert, 310–11
Harmar, John, 209
  Hymnus ad Christum, 15
Hartwell, Abraham
  Latin verse of, 235–6
Harvey, Gabriel, 68, 451, 472
  on Du Bartas and Palingenius, 462
Hatcher, Robert, 194, 474
  imitation of Sarbiewski, 256
  Institutio, epithalamium, & militia viri, 190–1, 256, 474
  Paideutica, 190–1, 256, 474, 477, 479
Healy, Thomas, 473
Hebrew, 1, 6–7, 9, 14, 86, 97, 100, 104–5, 111, 173, 473
  knowledge of, 100–1
  teaching of, 14, 19, 100, 224
Heinsius, Daniel
  Crepundia Siliana, 245
Heinsius, Nicolaas, 367
Helander, Hans, 7
Herbert, Edward, 47
Herbert, George, 10, 44–5, 69, 86, 99, 127, 223, 226, 228, 236, 252, 262, 267, 312, 327, 498
  'Agonie, The', 242
  as Latin poet, 228
  as religious poet, 228, 240–7
  as writer of epigrams, 228
  'Bag, The', 246
  'Charms & Knots'
    translated into Latin, 318–19
  'Christmas', 229–30
  'Church-Porch, The', 26–7, 319
  compared to Southwell, 229–30
  'Dum petit Infantem', 295–6
  epigrams, 274

figure poems, 78
'Good Friday', 82
  in Latin literary context, 240–7
'In Sacram Anchoram Piscatoris', 82
Lucus, 72, 228
  Lucus 1, 243–5
  Lucus 27, 307
  Lucus 28, 307
  Lucus 34, 241
  Lucus 35, 228
Memoriae matris sacrum, 10, 228
  Memoriae matris sacrum 7, 242
Musae Responsoriae, 147, 224, 228, 233, 239, 300, 308, 319, 323, 327, 332
  Musae Responsoriae 25, 53
  Musae Responsoriae 37, 334
Passio discerpta, 228, 237
  Passio discerpta 12, 240–1
'Pearl, The', 179–80
'Prayer (I)', 20–1
Psalm 23, 131–5, 229, 262
psalm paraphrases, 270
'Roma', 245, 303
  in BL Harley MS 6038, 306, 309
  in *Lucus*, 303, 307–8
  in *Musae Responsoriae*, 303, 306–8
'Sacrifice, The', 240–7
Temple, The, 2, 20, 68, 98, 129, 131–5, 187, 221, 223, 228, 241
  imitation of, 245–7
  translations into Latin, 246
Herbert, Mary. *See* Sidney, Mary
Herland, Bartholus, 7
Herrick, Robert, 61, 140
  anacreontic verse, 184
  Hesperides, 57, 237, 252
  'His Age, Dedicated to his Peculiar Friend, Mr John Wickes', 57
  His Noble Numbers, 237
Herring, Francis
  In foelicissimum, 368
  Pietas pontificia, 326
Hessus, Eobanus, 100, 106
  paraphrase of Ecclesiastes, 101
  psalm paraphrases, 101, 108
Heywood, John, 474
  An hundred epigrammes, 281
Heywood, Thomas
  Oenone and Paris, 406
Higges, G.
  use of polymetric verse, 189
Hill, Thomas
  Nundinae Sturbrigienses, 322
Hils, G.
  translation of Sarbiewski, 58, 62, 248, 250–1, 256

Hinds, Stephen, 428
Hobart, Miles, 81
Hogg, William, 10, 19
  Latin paraphrases of Milton, 19
  paraphrase of Proverbs, 19
  paraphrase of Song of Songs, 19
  Paraphrasis in Job, 19
  Satyra sacra vanitatem mundi, 19, 330
Holdsworth, Edward
  Muscipula, 323
Holland, Henry, 83
Holland, Hugh, 40
Homer, 358, 400, 447–8
  Iliad, 162, 400, 435, 481
  Odyssey, 162, 421
Hoole, Charles
  A New Discovery of the old Art of Teaching Schoole, 4, 9, 19, 126
  translations of *Cato's Distichs*, 291
Horace, 4, 6, 29–30, 35–6, 38, 41, 44, 46, 60, 62, 64, 73, 81, 98, 105, 126, 129, 236, 322, 330, 365
  Ars poetica, 44, 205, 458–9
  as metrical model, 126
  as writer of hymns, 30, 67, 149
  Carmen Saeculare, 140, 151, 156, 164
  imitation of, 145
  compared to Pindar, 141–2
  Epistles, 29, 63
    Epistles 1.10, 57
    Epistles 1.18, 44, 48
  Epodes, 29, 188, 325–7, 332, 339
    Epodes 2, 29, 32–3, 48, 51, 268, 339
    Epodes 3, 339
    Epodes 4, 333
    Epodes 5, 44, 334
    Epodes 7, 44, 336–7
    Epodes 8, 339
    Epodes 9, 332
    Epodes 12, 339
    Epodes 13, 58
    Epodes 16, 44, 92, 336–7
    Epodes 17, 325
    imitation of, 331–40
  metres of, 73
  pythiambic metres in, 91
  translation of, 36
  imitation of, 47
    by Sarbiewski, 247–63
  modern perception of, 29
  Odes, 12, 29, 39, 50–3, 55
    imitation of, 136–82
    metrical variety of, 87, 145
    Odes 1.1, 16, 32, 44, 51, 76, 79, 90, 108
    Odes 1.2, 140, 154, 166

Horace (cont.)
  Odes 1.4, 57, 93
  Odes 1.5, 51, 108
  Odes 1.9, 58
  Odes 1.10, 154
  Odes 1.12, 152
  Odes 1.13, 51
  Odes 1.14, 44, 336
  Odes 1.22, 48–51
  Odes 1.23, 51
  Odes 1.26, 51
  Odes 1.27, 181
  Odes 1.33, 44
  Odes 1.34, 176, 179
  Odes 1.35, 140, 179–80
  Odes 1.37, 140, 160, 348
  Odes Book 2, 29, 51
  Odes 2.2, 154
  Odes 2.3, 41–2, 63
  Odes 2.10, 30–3, 36, 51, 57, 63, 66
  Odes 2.13, 170
  Odes 2.14, 41, 44, 51, 57, 221
  Odes 2.15, 41, 51
  Odes 2.16, 51, 57
  Odes 2.18, 51, 57, 93
  Odes 2.19, 169, 206
  Odes 3.1, 56
  Odes 3.3, 40–1, 48
  Odes 3.4, 158, 175
  Odes 3.9, 51
  Odes 3.23, 41
  Odes 3.25, 206
  Odes 3.30, 51, 90
  Odes Book 4, 29, 51, 140
  Odes 4.1, 178
  Odes 4.2, 141, 163, 178, 205, 207, 216
  Odes 4.3, 51
  Odes 4.4, 140, 160, 176–7
  Odes 4.7, 41, 51, 57
  Odes 4.8, 51, 90, 158
  Odes 4.9, 41, 43–4, 67, 159–60, 163
  translation of, 36
  Odes, imitation of. *See also* metre, Horatian lyric metres
  Odes, metrical variety of, 73, 136
  parodia of, 168–70
  Satires, 29, 320–1, 324
    Satires 2.6, 57
  translation of, 44–5, 50–3
Horsman, Robert, 475, 477, 482
  Sionis certamina et triumphus, 474
Hoskyns, John, 10
  epigrams, 288
Housman, A. E.
  'Here dead lie we', 272

Howard, Henry, Earl of Surrey, 30, 99, 128, 277
  translation of Martial 10.47, 33–4
Hudson, Hoyt Hopewell, 36, 280
Hugo, Herman
  Pia desideria, 237, 250
Hulett, John, 209
Hume, David
  Lusus Poetici, 128
humorous verse, 320–52
Humphrey, Laurence, 152
Hutchinson, Lucy, 447
  Order and Disorder, 20, 447
hymns, 39, 71, 86, 343
  use of sapphics for, 147–52

imitation, 20, 30, 37, 39
  classical, 28, 38–40
inscription, literary, 2, 184, 211–14, 322, 344,
    See also free verse, Latin
  satiric, 348–51
intertextuality, 20, 38
invective, verse, 320–52
  use of iambics, 331–40
Isocrates, 431
Italian, 1, 9

James I
  Basilikon Doron, 364, 371
  epigram attributed to, 313
  translation of Du Bartas, 461
Jerome, 98
Johnston, Arthur
  Delitiae Poetarum Scotorum, 8, 273, 442
Johnston, John, 72, 94
Johnstoun, Arthur
  Canticum Salomonis, 19, 249
Jonson, Ben, 2, 10, 34, 43–4, 47, 67, 69, 72, 99,
    136, 141, 144, 172, 327, 397, 434
  as satirist, 321
  Cynthia's Revels, 151–2
  education of, 15
  Entertainment at Althorp, 372
  Epigrams, 2, 9, 28, 72, 273, 280
    Epigrams 2, 282
    Epigrams 5, 286
    Epigrams 133, 276
  moral seriousness of, 282–7
  preface, 282
  relationship to Cato and Owen, 282–7
  'Epode', 335
  'Execration upon Vulcan, An', 78
  Forest, 371
    Forest 3, 171
    Forest 12, 159, 171
    Forest 13, 171

Forest 14, 171
Forest 15, 229
Haddington Masque, 413
Hymenaei, 412, 441
  as epithalamium, 414–15
King's Entertainment, The, 372
library of, 8, 20, 52, 200, 231, 282, 284, 363
masques, 202
'Ode Allegorike', 142
'Ode to Himself', 196
on Southwell, 227
Panegyre, 360, 367, 370–2, 377
Pindaric odes, 131, 184, 196–7, 203, 205, 215–16, 371
Poetaster, 321, 324
'Queen and huntress, chaste and fair', 151–2
The King's Entertainment, 372
Timber, 461
'To the Memory of My Beloved the Author, Mr William Shakespeare', 204
translation of Horace, *Ars poetica*, 459
Underwoods, 371
  Underwoods 25, 142, 171, 196–7, 202
  Underwoods 70 (Cary-Morison ode), 196, 201–2
use of Claudian, 363–4
Jonson, Christopher, 83
Josephus, 98
Joyner, Robert
  Itys, 281
Julius, Alexander, 19
Junius, Franciscus
  Latin Bible of, 13, 100, 111
  use of Hebrew, 110
Junius, Hadrianus, 72, 440
  aenigmata epigrams, 318
  Philippeis, 425, 438
Juvenal, 6, 236, 322, 330
  Satires, 320–1

Kell, Samuel
  Carmen gratulatorium, 368
Kelsall, John, 67, 127
  epigrams, 303
Killeen, Kevin, 250
King, Adam
  In Iacobum sextum, 368
King, Robert
  Satyra Aethiopica, 330–1
King, William, 10, 330, 351
  Miltonis Epistola ad Pollionem, 327–30
  satires, 323
Kinloch, David
  De hominis procreatione, 2, 410, 441–6, 486, 489

Kinnamon, Noel, 100
Kipling, Rudyard, 61, 67
  'If –', 25
Knevet, Ralph
  A Gallery to the Temple, 246

Lactantius
  De Phoenice, 358
Landino, Christoforo
  Xandra, 71
Langius, Josephus
  Anthologia sive Florilegium rerum et materiarum selectarum, 39
Latin
  oral use of, 6–7, 13, 16
  publication of works in. *See* publication of Latin works
Lermaeus, Gabriel
  Hebdomas (Latin translation of Du Bartas), 462
Leslie, John, bishop of Ross
  odes to Mary Queen of Scots, 156
Lewis, Geoffrey
  poems for Elizabeth I, 148, 156–7
Lille, Alan of, 293
Lily, William, 441
  Lily's Grammar, 14–15, 296
Linus, 164
Lipsius, Justus, 57
  'Laus et vota vitae beatae', 51–3
literature, Latin, read in early modernity. *See* canon, Latin
Littleton, Adam
  Tragi-Comoedia-Oxoniensis, 190
Livy, 4, 17, 491–2
Llewelyn, Martin, 207, 269
Locke, John, 398
Lodge, Thomas, 98
  Scillaes Metamorphosis, 406–8, 417, 434–6
Loftus, Ann
  epigrams by, 4, 296–7
Loiseau, Pierre. *See* Alites, Petrus
Lok, Anne
  Meditation of a Penitent Sinner, 100
Love, Harold, 321
Lovelace, Richard, 57, 61, 67, 335
  'Grasse-hopper, The', 57–60, 64
  'Advice to my best Brother', 57
  Lucasta, 60
Lucan, 154, 236, 355, 358, 367, 381–2, 385, 400, 447, 497
Lucilius, 320
Lucretius, 5, 31, 464, 496
Luther, Martin, 232

lyric
  inset, 190, 193, 218, 335, 412, 479, 490
  moralizing, 21, 25–67, 69, 136
  panegyric. *See* odes, panegyric
  religious, 30, 223–32, 247–63
  satiric, 340

macaronic verse, 78, 346–7
Macrin, Jean, 145
  psalm paraphrases, 73
Maior, Georgius
  Sententiae veterum poetarum, 39
Malym, William, 76
Mameranus, Nikolaus
  Psalmi Davidis quinque, 100
Mancini, 465
Manley, Christopher, 237
Manley, Thomas
  version of Fisher's ode to Cromwell, 176, 214–17
mannerist poetry, 224
Mantuan, 5, 34, 273, 277, 291, 317–18, 355, 462, 465, 470
  Adulescentia, 5, 11, 71, 273, 458, 465, 467
  as school text, 465–7
  similarities to Palingenius, 465–7
manuscripts. *See* name of library, e.g. British library manuscripts
  circulation in, 27–8, 38, 44, 47
  quantity of Latin verse in, 1–2
Marino, Giambattista, 417
Markham, Gervase
  Poem of Poems, 249
Marlowe, Christopher, 414
  Dido, Queen of Carthage, 423, 431
  Hero and Leander, 406–8, 416–17, 423, 425–6, 434, 443–4
  relationship to Musaeus, 431–4
  use of Gager, 431–4
Marotti, Arthur, 27, 292
Marow, Edward, 207
Marston, John
  Jack Drum's Entertainment, 347
  What you Will, 15
Martial, 5, 12, 28, 31, 34, 36, 38, 41, 44, 50, 60, 273–4, 281–3, 288–9, 293, 312, 314
  2.90, 46
  9.17, 41
  10.47, 33–4, 41, 277
  11.40, 41
  as model for Jonson, 286
  prologue to Book 1, 282
  translation of, 36
Martindale, Joanna, 58

Marvell, Andrew, 10, 13, 20, 60, 144, 355, 359, 404, 498
  'Bludius et Corona', 315–18
  'First Anniversary', 1–2, 141, 355, 367, 389, 393–7
  'Garden, The', 256–60
  'Horatian Ode', 2, 57, 69, 136, 171–82, 211, 215, 392
    ambiguity of, 140
    Horatianism of, 136–9
    moralizing elements of, 142
    Pindaric features of, 141
  'Hortus', 256–60
  'Nymph Complaining for the Death of her Fawn, The', 492
  'Poem upon the Death of his Late Highness the Lord Protector, A', 397
  relationship to Fisher, 393–7
  'To his Coy Mistress', 424
  'Upon Appleton House', 260
  'Upon Blood's attempt to steal the Crown', 315–17
  use of Claudian, 393–7
Matthew, Robert
  commendatory verse by, 208
Mayne, Jasper, 310
McDowell, Nicholas, 248, 250, 482
Mead, Joseph
  letters of, 295, 319
Mead, Thomas, 270
Medcalf, Oswald, 152
Melissus, Paulus, 72, 94
  Pindaric odes, 158, 203
  Schediasmata poetica, 94–5, 200
  use of trochaic metres, 93
Melville, Andrew, 10, 19–20, 94, 306, 308, 319, 327, 334
  Anti-Tami-Cami-Categoria, 97, 146, 224, 228, 233, 308, 323–5, 331
  as religious poet, 231
  'Communis tecum mihi causa est', 302
  'Cur stant clausi', 301
  epigrams, 274, 297–8, 300–3, 311
  invective of, 331
  Melvini Musae, 302
  ode on the Gunpowder Plot, 143, 175, 325–7
  use of sapphics, 324
Meres, Francis
  Palladis Tamia, 451
metaphysical poetry, 27, 67, 223–4
Metcalf, Oswald, 147
metre
  adonean, 76, 83–7
  alcaics, 76, 82, 87, 93, 137, 144, 149, 160, 191–2, 227, 325–6, 479, 502–3

anacreontic, 79, 84, 86, 115, 252
anapaestic tetrameter, 105, 115–16
archilochian, 76, 251
asclepiad metres, 70, 76–7, 79, 82, 85–91, 94, 108, 118, 129–30, 137, 190, 251, 266, 503
choriambic. *See* metre, asclepiad
dactylic metres, 82, 86
  dactylic alcmanian, 126
  dactylic hexameter, 5, 75, 79, 94–5, 100, 285, 322–31, 479, 500
  dactylic tetrameter, 76
  elegiac couplets, 14, 71, 73, 75, 79, 91, 95, 101, 108, 332, 487, 500
  leonine hexameter, 75, 119, 344
dithyrambic, 95, 189, 204–11, 226, 266, 270, 348, *See* odes, Pindaric *and* odes, dithyrambic
glyconic, 53
hexameter, 65, 73
Horatian lyric metres, use of, 137–9
iambic metres, 71, 73, 76, 79, 82, 87, 91, 95, 138–9, 146, 226, 331–40
  galliambic, 79
  iambic dimeter, 75–6, 80, 86, 91, 105, 108, 115, 200
  iambic distichs, 76, 93–4, 106, 501
  iambic trimeter, 76, 79, 91, 105, 190–1, 211, 226, 331, 335–6, 338, 479, 501
  pythiambic, 83–4, 86, 91–3
  use during Civil War and Protectorate, 335
lyric metres, 28, 73, 75–6
phalaecian hendecasyllables, 71, 73, 75–6, 79, 87, 91, 94, 105, 115, 138–9, 200, 502
Pindarics, 95, 192, 195–222, 226, 248, 263, 265–6, 322, 348
  irregular Pindaric in English before Cowley, 214–17
polymetric, 78, 80–4, 86, 130–1, 184, 187–95, 211, 218, 256, 270, 322, 360
quantitative metre, introduction to, 499–503
quantitative, in English, 68, 83, 96, 107–8, 114–15
sapphics, 14, 65, 75–6, 79, 82–8, 91, 94, 108, 190, 200, 227, 279, 324, 502
  as closural tag, 80–1, 149, 200
  Elizabethan sapphic, 144–58, 164
  hymnic sapphic, 147–52, 162
  medieval use of, 147
  sapphic hendecasyllable, 76
stichic glyconic, 53
teaching of, 138
trochaic, 87, 93–5, 105, 133, 151, 252
variety of, 68–95
Miller, Edmund, 241

Miller, Paul, 409
Milton, John, 10, 19, 99, 126, 191, 265, 328–9, 331, 351, 355, 382, 404, 447–8, 482, 486, 492, 498
  'Ad Joannem Rousium', 204
  elegies, 72
  'In quintum Novembris', 316, 326, 376, 379
    alluded to by Fisher, 384–5
  Latin letters for Cromwell, 351
  Latin paraphrases of works by, 19
  Latin poetry of, 10
  Lycidas, 317, 427–8, 455, 465, 467
  'Nativity Ode', 198, 206, 225–7, 266, 269
  Paradise Lost, 8, 19–20, 183, 223, 376, 385, 448, 453, 456–7, 463, 486, 492
    Book 2, 468–9
    Book 3, 469–70
    Books 11–12, 449, 460
    'Council in Hell' scenes, 385
    models for, 447
    relationship to Palingenius, *Zodiacus Vitae*, 467–70
  Poems, 183, 195
  translated into Latin, 318
Mirandula, Octavius
  Illustrium poetarum flores, 39, 364
Moller, Heinrich, 110
  psalm translations, 102, 104, 109–11
Money, David, 288
Montaigne, Michel de, 9
More, Thomas, 232, 371
  Carmen Gratulatorium, 368
  epigrams, 274, 288, 314
Morton, Albertus, 239
Moschus, 446
  Europa, 409
Moss, Ann, 7
Mullyns, John, 152
Mundie, Francis
  translation of Alabaster, 315
Muret, Marc Antoine de, 31
Musaeus, 446
  Hero and Leander, 409, 411, 413–14, 431–4

Naogeorg, Thomas
  satires, 320, 323
Nazianzus, Gregory of, 236
Nedham, Marchamont, 393
neo-Latin, use of the term, 11
Nethersole, William
  dedicatory dithyrambic ode to Henry Oxinden, 213
Neville, Alexander
  Lachrymae, 158
Newcomb, Thomas, 393

Newport, Maurice. *See* Ewens, Maurice
Nicholson, William
  use of Pindarics, 205
Norbrook, David, 177
North, Dudley, 452

Ocland, Christopher
  Anglorum Praelia, 94
odes, 71–2
  dithyrambic, 183–211
  Horatian, 28, 47, 49, 55, 57
  panegyric, 29, 39, 69, 94–5, 136–82, 322, 355
    length of, 175
    moralizing elements in, 142–4
  Pindaric, 1–2, 45, 47, 69, 94, 128, 131, 136, 138, 142, 183–4, 195–222, 226, 246, 248, 263, 265, 270, 371
    irregular Pindaric in English before Cowley, 214–17
  political. *See* odes, panegyric
Origen, 98
Orpheus, 73, 101, 164
Ovid, 4, 6, 236, 290–1, 293, 359, 365, 372, 410, 418, 490–1
  Amores, 408
  Ex Ponto, 6, 64
  exile poetry, 64, 291
  Fasti, 428
  Heroides, 406, 487
  Metamorphoses, 292, 406–8, 423, 426, 428, 434, 450, 453, 460, 487–8
  Tristia, 6, 64, 291
Owen, Cadwallader, 311
Owen, John, 9–10, 237, 273, 291, 293
  as school text, 287, 291, 294
  epigrams, 8, 12, 28, 72, 283–9, 292, 296, 298, 313
    metres of, 285
  Epigrams, 72
    Epigrams 1.3, 288
    Epigrams 1.96, 288
    Epigrams 1.147, 291
    Epigrams 2.119, 304–5
    Epigrams 3.95, 285
    Epigrams Book 3, 285
    Epigrams 3.204, 289
    Epigrams 3.208, 300
    Epigrams 4.4, 286
    Epigrams 4.32, 285
    Epigrams 4.36, 285
    Epigrams 4.12, 285
    Epigrams 4.152, 288
    Epigrams 4.164, 286
    Epigrams 8.45, 286
    Epigrams 8.47, 286
    Epigrams 8.57, 286
    Epigrams 10.89, 291
    Epigrams 11.16, 300
  epigrams in manuscript record, 274
  evidence for readership in England, 287–9
  influence upon Jonson, 285
  poems about, 288, 294
Oxford University anthologies
  Academiae Oxoniensis pietas, 337, 369
  Bodleiomnema, 139, 189
  Britannia rediviva, 397
  Carolus redux, 207
  Exequiae, 86, 158, 431
  Musarum Oxoniensium charisteria, 207
  Musarum Oxoniensium Ἐλαιοφορία, 208
  Oxoniensium στεναγμος sive carmina in obitum C. Hattoni, 156
  Peplus, 86, 158
  Solis Britannici perigaeum, 207
Oxinden, Henry, 127, 451, 476, 482
  Charls Triumphant, 475
  Iobus triumphans, 213, 474–6, 479
  Religionis funus, 189, 475, 477

Paget, William
  manuscript verse of, 84–6
Palingenius, 5, 11, 317–18
  Palingenian epic. *See* epic, didactic
  Zodiacus Vitae, 5, 9, 11, 273, 447–96, 498
    as epic poem, 453–7
    as school text, 450–2, 465
    Book 1, 451, 453–5, 458–60, 463
    Book 2, 463, 495–6
    Book 3, 452, 463
    Book 4, 452–3, 455, 465–9
    Book 5, 466, 472
    Book 6, 450, 452–3, 455, 464, 472
    Book 7, 453–4, 456
    Book 8, 453
    Book 9, 452–3, 463
    Book 10, 451, 464
    Book 11, 453
    Book 12, 453, 460–1
    echoes in Milton, *Pardise Lost*, 467–70
    invocation of Urania, 453–6
    links with Du Bartas, 461–5
    proscribed by Catholic Church, 451
    readership in England, 450–7
    relationship to *Aeneid*, 455–8
    structure and contents of, 452–7
    style of, 451–3, 457–61
Paman, Clement, 270
Panter, Patrick
  Metamorphoseon, 474
paraphrase, 13–21, 30, 39–40

classical, 30–6
distinct from translation, 18
Latin paraphrases of works by Milton, 19
scriptural, 12–21, 28, 75, 79, 95, 189, 221,
    228–9, 231, 267, 279, 322, 330, 447,
    464, 477, *See also* scripture, literary use of
  Daniel, 208
  Ecclesiastes, 19, 101, 128, 233, 249, 270
  Epistle of St James, 75
  in mid-seventeenth century, 474–82
  Isaiah, 270
  Jeremiah, 208
  Job, 19, 191, 213, 256, 475–6
  Jonah, 208
  Judges, 270
  2 Kings, 263
  Luke, 231, 243
  Matthew, 75
  Proverbs, 19, 190, 249, 256
  Psalms. *See* psalm paraphrase
  relationship to allegorical verse, 474–82
  1 Samuel, 79
  2 Samuel, 193
  Song of Songs, 19, 128, 190, 218, 220,
    247–60, 471, 473
Parker, Matthew
  Flores historiarum, 451
Parmenius, Stephanus
  Psalm 104, 106, 108
parodia, 168–70, 348, 352
Parry plot, 158–69
Parry, William
  verse collection of, 317–18
pattern poems. *See* figure poems
Pebworth, Ted-Larry, 55
Pembroke, Mary, Countess of. *See* Sidney, Mary
Perrinchief, Richard
  Nuntius a mortuis, 189
Persius, 6, 320–2, 330
Petrarch, 31, 137
Philip II, of Spain
  extempore epigram, 298
Pindar, 6, 73, 98, 172, 181, 184, 216, *See also*
    metre, Pindaric; odes, Pindaric; odes,
    dithyrambic
  compared to Horace, 141–2
  Nemean 1, 484–5
  Nemean 6, 162
  Olympian 2, 217
  Pythian 12, 163
Plautus, 334
Pliny, 491
Poelman, Theodor, 64
poetics
  humanist, 46, 71–5, 95

Jesuit, 12, 223, 225–6, 228–9, 239–40,
    245–60
Protestant, 10, 12, 19, 74, 97, 105, 482
Poliziano, Angelo, 417, 421
Polwhele, John, 46
  manuscript verse, 44–5, 336–7
  response to Herbert's *Temple*, 245
  translations of Horace, 336–7
polymetric sequence. *See* metre, polymetric
polymetric verse. *See* metre, polymetric
Pontano, Giovanni, 71
  Baiae, 71, 73
  De amore coniugali, 71
  De laudibus divinis, 71
  De tumulis, 72
  Eridanus, 71
  Lepidina, 413
  Parthenopeus, 71, 73
  Pruritus, 73
  Urania, 453
  use of sapphics, 145
Pope, Alexander, 3, 299–300, 303, 323, 328
  Dunciad, 328
  Imitations of Horace, 321
Portland manuscripts, University of Nottingham
  PwV 1343, 346
  PwV 1456, 250–1
Posthius, Johannes, 93
Pound, Ezra, 87
  'The Return', 88
Propertius, 488
Protestantism, Latin poetry of. *See* poetics,
    Protestant
Prudentius, 6, 12, 73–4, 86, 89, 105, 137–9,
    326, 334, 343, 355, 382
  as metrical authority, 74, 126
  Cathemerinon, 93, 108, 129
  Dittochaeon, 20, 236
  Psychomachia, 384, 447–8
  use of iambic dimeter, 108
  use of pythiambic metres, 92
psalm paraphrase, 8–9, 19, 29–30, 36, 44, 50,
    66–8, 71, 92, 96–136, 193, 206–7, 217,
    220–1, 223, 229, 232, 246, 268, 270,
    279, 475
psalms, 19, 39, 96–135, *See also* psalm
    paraphrase
  liturgical use in England, 99–100, 142,
    228
  Psalm 1, 29, 50, 100, 217, 268, 270
  Psalm 2, 92
  Psalm 14, 100
  Psalm 36, 100
  Psalm 39, 100, 234, 279
  Psalm 44, 268

psalms (cont.)
  Psalm 45, 36, 156
  Psalm 51, 100, 193
  Psalm 68, 254
  Psalm 79, 100
  Psalm 90, 234
  Psalm 92, 162
  Psalm 98, 268
  Psalm 103, 75
  Psalm 104, 95, 270
  Psalm 114, 192, 270
  Psalm 119, 80
  Psalms 120–27, 114–15
  Psalm 125, 475
  Psalm 128, 246
  Psalm 137, 220, 268
psalms, paraphrase of. *See* psalm paraphrase
publication of Latin works, 7–9
Puttenham, George, 68
  Art of English Poesy, 343
Pyne, John
  Epigrammata, 237

Quarles, Francis, 249, 474
  Divine Fancies, 237–8
  Emblemes, 237, 250
  Memorials upon the Death of Sir Robert Quarles, 212
Queen's College Oxford manuscripts 284, 205

Rabelais, 347
Raleigh, Walter, 28, 54
  'E'en such is time', 25–7
  'Praisd be Diana's faire and harmless light', 152
Randolph, Herbert
  Commercium ad mare australe, 323
Randolph, Thomas, 34
  'Iam sileat Jack Drum', 346
  Latin translation of Jonson's 'Ode to Himself', 202
  translation of Claudian, 357
Rapin, René, 294
reception
  of classical literature, 2, 29, 38, 107, 351
  of Claudian, 357–60, 364, 446
  of Horace, 29, 339–40
  of Pindar, 141, 220
Reusner, Nicolas
  use of adoneans, 84
Revard, Stella, 141–2, 195
rhyme, use of in Latin verse, 11, 66, 74–5, 78, 118–19, 138, 360
  humorous and satiric rhyming verse, 343–8
Richardson, Augustine, 14

Ringler, William, 93, 112
Riparius, Julius, 372
Robertson, A., 438
Robinson, Matthew
  paraphrase of Song of Songs, 252
Rogers, Daniel, 79
Rollock, Hercules, 438
Ronsard, Pierre de, 72, 137, 142
  translation of, 79
Ross, Alexander, 19–20, 127, 451, 476
  Christados libri XIII, 20
  scriptural paraphrase of, 475
Ross, Sarah, 447, 477
Røstvig, Maren-Sofie, 53, 247
Ruggle, George
  Ignoramus, 346
Russell, John
  epigrams, 288–9

Saltmarsh, John, 218, 248, 482
  Poemata sacra, 237
Samways, Peter
  contribution to *Irenodia Cantabrigiensis*, 173–4
Sancroft, William, 332
  commonplace book of, 287–8
  miscellany of, 206, 246, 269–70
  translation of Alabaster, 315
Sandys, George, 249
Sannazaro, Jacopo, 31, 34, 71, 280, 470
  De partu virginis, 71, 447
  epigrams, 274, 277, 294, 313, 318
  Piscatoria, 71
Sappho, 145, 149, 413
  fr. 1, 147
Saravia, Hadrianus, 463
Sarbiewski, Casimir, 6, 8, 12, 29, 64, 67, 126, 137, 208, 222, 226, 229, 239–40, 246, 268, 498
  commendatory dithyrambic ode addressed to, 208
  Epigrams 4, 258–60
  Epodes, 333
    Epode 3, 61
  imitation of, 58–64, 66
  influence in England, 247–63
  influence upon Watts, 225
  Odes, 176
    Odes 1.19, 266
    Odes 2.1, 67
    Odes 2.5, 60, 255–6, 263–5, 269
    Odes 2.6, 63
    Odes 2.25, 188, 251
    Odes 3.4, 61–3
    Odes 4.3, 59, 63

Odes 4.13, 60, 63
Odes 4.21, 188, 251, 257–8
Odes 4.23, 58–60
Odes 4.34, 59–60
paraphrase of the Song of Songs, 247–60
Pindaric elements, 216
scriptural epigrams, 260
satire, verse, 11, 71, 320–52
  Augustan satire, 67, 321–2
  in Latin, 323
  bilingualism of, 340–8
  classical, 320
  in hexameter, 320, 351
    absence of in England before 1700, 322–31
  in Latin in England, 320–52
  of 1590s, 321, 333
  of Civil War and Protectorate, 335
  Restoration satire, 27, 321
  use of iambic metres, 351
  use of rhyme in Latin, 343–8, 352
Scaliger, Joseph, 31, 97
  epitaph on Buchanan, 127
Scaliger, Julius Caesar, 72, 184
  Ajax, 197
  definition of dithyrambic, 205
  'Natalia domini nostri Jesu Christi', 209
  on epithalamia, 412–14, 416, 423, 441, 443
  on Palingenius, *Zodiacus Vitae*, 481
  Poemata, 79, 197–9
  Poetices, 79, 197, 205–6, 412–14
  polymetric verse, 80
  use of iambics, 333
  use of Pindarics, 197–9, 203, 226
Schede, Paul. *See* Melissus, Paulus
Schoell, Adrian, 280
  epigrams, 278–9
  Latin verse of, 234–5
  use of sapphics, 146
Scott, William
  The model of Poesie, 333
scripture. *See also* paraphrase, scriptural *and* psalm paraphrase
  Acts, 238
  Ecclesiastes, 19, 110
  Genesis 1, 239
  Isaiah, 227
  Job, 19, 110, 234, 481
  John, 475
  literary use of, 12–17
  Luke, 236, 241–2
  Mark, 236
  Matthew, 311, 402, 467
  Proverbs, 19, 110
  Psalms. *See* psalms *and* psalm paraphrase, *See also* psalm paraphrase

Song of Songs, 110, 134–5, 162, 188, 249–50, 268, 290, 330, 412, 421, 477–82, 491
  translation of, 19
Sectanus. *See* Sergardi, Lodovico
Secundus, Johannes
  Basia, 73
Secundus, Petrus Lotichius
  Elegiarum liber, 72
Sedulius, 86
Selden, John, 209
Seneca, 6, 31, 34–6, 38–9, 44, 52, 57, 60, 62, 64, 67, 84, 136–8, 251, 293, 365
  Agamemnon, 41–3
  choruses of, 29, 36, 39, 50, 55, 80, 105, 139
  Herc. Oet., 63
  Hercules Furens, 32
  lyric metres of, 35
  Medea, 32, 41, 84
  Oedipus, 32, 53
  Phaedra, 33, 41, 52, 84
  Thyestes, 42, 48, 56
  kingship chorus, 31–4, 37, 41, 46, 53, 56, 59, 67, 143, 463
Serafino, 31
Sergardi, Lodovico
  satires, 320, 323
Seton, John
  Panegyrici, 75, 152–4
Shakespeare, William, 6, 137, 251
  As You Like It, 5, 450, 472
  Henry IV Part I, 15
  King Lear, 450
  Love's Labours Lost, 5
  Merchant of Venice, 450
  Merry Wives of Windsor, 14, 30
  Much Ado About Nothing, 15
  Rape of Lucrece, 406
  references to Palingenius, 450
  Richard II, 260
  Titus Andronicus, 15
  use of Palingenius, 464
  Venus and Adonis, 360, 406, 416, 423, 426–8, 431, 440
Shaw, John
  Bibliorum summula, 20
Sheffeld, John, 147
Shepreve, John
  scriptural epigrams, 234
  Summa et synopsis Novi Testamenti, 20
Sherburne, Edward
  Poems and Translations, 60
Shirley, James
  'Glories of our blood and state, The', 64–6
  Narcissus or The Self-Lover, 406

Sictor, John, 368
  Panegyricon, 368
Sidney circle. *See* Sidney, Philip, Sidney circle
Sidney Herbert, Mary. *See* Sidney, Mary
Sidney psalter, 2, 14, 20, 68–9, 96–8, 103–6, 108–25, 127, 227, 246
  Psalm 5, 113
  Psalm 16, 93
  Psalm 18, 117
  Psalm 28, 112–13
  Psalm 44, 119–22
  Psalm 68, 113–14
  Psalm 80, 123–5
  Psalm 96, 104
  Psalm 119, 80, 115
  Psalms 120–27, 114–15
  Psalm 120, 117–18
  Psalm 125, 83
  Psalm 126, 115–17
  Psalm 140, 118–19
Sidney, Mary, 14, 20, 68, 498
  knowledge of Hebrew, 111, 119–22
  Psalm 44, 119–22
  Psalm 68, 113–14
  Psalm 80, 123–5
  Psalm 96, 104
  Psalm 119, 115
  Psalms 120–27, 114–15
  Psalm 120, 117–18
  Psalm 125, 83
  Psalm 126, 115–17
  Psalm 140, 118–19
  psalm paraphrases, 96–8, 108–25
Sidney, Philip, 20, 68, 100, 106, 172, 227, 341, 428, 432, 440, 482
  Astrophel and Stella, 90, 93
  Defence of Poesie, 98, 109, 461
  'O sweet woods', 90, 108
  ode to by Dousa, 158
  Old Arcadia, 90, 115
  poem addressed to, 94
  poems on death of, 428, 439
  Psalm 5, 113
  Psalm 16, 93
  Psalm 18, 117
  Psalm 28, 112–13
  psalm paraphrases, 96–8, 108–14
  Sidney circle, 79, 86–7
  use of asclepiad metres, 90
  use of trochaic metres, 93–4
  verse collections on death of, 86–7, 138, 156, 158
Sidonius
  Epithalamium Ruricio et Hiberiae, 414
Silius Italicus, 6, 355, 382, 402–3
silva collections, 71–2

Sixtus, Pope, 293
Smart, Christopher, 228
Smart, Peter, 482, 494
  Cantus epithalamicus, 330, 477–9
Smet, Ingrid de, 330
Smith, Jud
  A Misticall Deuise, 249, 454
Smith, Nigel, 219
Smith, William
  Gemma fabri, 20
Society of Friends Archive manuscripts
  Vol S 80, 314
Some, Henry, 207
Somerset, Edward, 36
sonnets, 1–2, 79, 100, 137, 322
South, Robert
  Musica Incantans, 220–1, 363
  use of Pindarics, 220–1
Southwell, Anne, 447
Southwell, Robert, 231
  'Burning Babe', 225, 227, 229–30
  compared to Herbert, 229–30
Spagnuoli, Baptista. *See* Mantuan
Spauter, Jan de. *See* Despauterius, Johannes
Spencer, Edward, 64
Spenser, Edmund, 3, 414, 467, 470, 482
  admiration of Du Bartas, 462
  Epithalamion, 412, 438
  Faerie Queene, 427–8, 448, 452
  influence upon Cowley, 187
  lost works
    Epithalamion Thamesis, 413
    paraphrase of Ecclesiastes, 18
    paraphrase of Song of Songs, 18
  Muiopotmos, 406
  Prothalamion, 412–13, 437–8
  Shepherds' Calendar, 5, 71, 187, 317, 429, 465, 471
    Latin translation of, 199–200
Sprat, Thomas
  ode on the death of Cromwell, 203–4
St John's College Oxford
  Sors Caesarea, 189–90
Staffordshire County Record Office manuscripts
  D(W)1721/3/248, 17
Stanley, Thomas
  Poems and Translations, 128
Stanyhurst, Richard, 68, 90
  psalm paraphrases, 107–8, 125
Statius, 6, 129, 236, 355, 358, 413–15, 447
  Epithalamium in Stellam et Violentillam, 412
  Silvae, 73, 358, 421
  Thebaid, 381–2, 385

Index

Stellato, Marcello Palingenio. *See* Palingenius
Sternhold and Hopkins, 99, 132
Stilicho. *See* Claudian
Stogdill, Nathaniel, 219
Strada, Faminiano
   'The Nightingale' (*Prolusiones* 2.6), 362–3, 440
Stradling, John
   epigrams, 288, 298
Strode, William
   translation of Strada, 'The Nightingale', 362–3
Stubbe, Henry, 474
   Horae subsecivae, 474
Suckling, John
   religious epigrams, 233
Surrey, Earl of. *See* Howard, Henry
Sutton, Dana, 164, 287, 439
Sweerts, François
   letter to Camden, 284
Swinnock, George
   The Christian-Man's Calling, 246
Sylvester, Josuah, 9
   translation of Du Bartas, 448, 450, 457, 462–3
Syriac, 13
Szymonowicz, Szymon
   Poematia Aurea, 200

Talmud, 13
Tasso, Torquato, 106, 198
   Gerusalemme liberata, 376
Tertullian, 334
Tesauro, Emanuele, 184, 214, 348
   Caesares, 211–12
Theocritus, 126
Thomas, Paul, 20
   Poemata, 231
Thoor, Raphael de. *See* Thorius, Raphael
Thorius, Francis, 79
   Latin translations of, 79–80
Thorius, Raphael, 10, 239
   Hymnus Tabaci, 79
Tibullus, 126
Tollenarius, Joannes, 270
Tottel, Richard, 78
   Miscellany, 2, 25, 30–8, 43, 53, 61, 65
   Songes and Sonettes. *See* Tottel, Richard, *Miscellany*
Traherne, Thomas, 223, 245
translation, 15, 18, 20, 30, 36, 39, 271
   as distinct from paraphrase. *See* paraphrase, distinct from translation
   classical, 28, 38–40
   into Latin, 28, 34, 38, 53, 63, 65–6, 79, 227, 246, 317–19
   of scripture into the vernacular, 235

Tremellius, Immanuel
   Latin Bible of, 13, 96, 100, 111
   on Psalm 5, 113
   on Psalm 28, 112
   on Psalm 44, 121–2
   use of Hebrew, 109
Tufte, Virginia, 414–15
Turberville, George
   Epitaphes, Epigrams, Songs, and Sonets, 281

university anthologies of Latin verse, 138–9, *See also* Oxford University anthologies and Cambridge University anthologies
Urban VIII, Pope. *See* Barberini, Maffeo
Uthalmus, Lerimos
   Fasciculus Florum, 273, 313

Valdivia, Lucía Martínez, 132
Valerius Flaccus, 355, 382
van Dans, Adolpho
   Eliza, 372
Vaughan, Henry, 57, 67, 223, 228
   Olor Iscanus, 43, 60, 64, 245
   Silex Scintillans, 245
   translation of Claudian, 357
Vaughan, William
   Erotopaignion pium, 19, 231, 248–9
   Erotopaignion pium, pars secunda, 249
Vautrollerius, Thomas, 102, 106
Ventris, Thomas, 289
Verino, Michele, 284
verse, lapidary. *See* inscription, literary
verse, Latin, composition of, 4, 17
Viccars, John
   England's Hallelu-jah, 129
Vida, Marco Girolamo
   Christias, 376
Villiers, George, Duke of Buckingham, 54
Virgil, 4, 6, 11, 50, 181, 216, 236, 293, 305, 332, 355, 358–9, 361, 365, 367, 372, 383, 400, 447–8, 457, 496–7
   Aeneid, 14, 107, 302, 316, 396, 400, 435, 447, 450, 452, 455–8, 465, 471, 481, 496
   Eclogues, 11, 14, 221, 316, 428, 458, 465
   Eclogue 4, 227, 246
   Georgics, 444, 496
   parody of, 323
Vivian, John
   Ecclesiastes Solomonis, 233

Wallace, Michael
   In Serenissimi Regis Iacobi Liberationem, 326
Waller, Edmund, 220, 393, 400, 483
   'Of a War with Spain, and Fight at Sea', 397
   Panegyric, 393, 397
   'To My Lord of Falkland', 400

Walpole, Horace, 288
Walpole, Robert, 329
Walton, Izaak
   Reliquiae Wottonianae, 54
Wanley, Humphrey
   Scintullae Sacrae, 246
Waring, Robert
   poem on death of Ben Jonson, 212–13
Wase, Christopher
   definition of dithyrambic, 207–8
   'Hypotyposis est Resurrectionis', 207–8
   In mirabilem Caroli, 397
Watson, John, 65
Watson, Thomas, 10, 428–31, 434
   Amintae gaudia, 428, 438–40
   Amyntas, 428
   epyllion on death of Sidney, 428
   Raptus Helenae (translation of Colluthus), 429–31, 436
Watts, Isaac, 2, 10, 12, 20, 27, 60, 67, 69, 223, 228, 248, 260–7, 270
   'Breathing towards the Heavenly Country', 266–7
   'Church the Garden of Christ, The', 261
   'God Incomprehensible', 265–6
   Horae Lyricae, 66–7, 225, 261, 263, 266
   'Meditation in a Grove, 261–2
   Pindaric odes, 222, 263
   'Prospect of Heaven makes Death easy, The', 267
   Psalm 23, 135, 262
Watts, Thomas, 232
Webbe, William
   A Discourse of English Poetrie, 451
Weckherlin, Georg, 56
Wedderburn, David
   Meditationum campestrium, 293
Wedderburn, James, John and Robert
   Spirituall Sangis, 113
Weever, John
   Faunus and Melliflora, 406
Wesley, Charles, 67, 223, 228
Westminster Abbey manuscripts 31, 149, 368–9
Weston, Elizabeth Jane, 10
Whaley, John, 288
Wharton, John
   'To the Christian Reader', 454

Whipple, T. K., 280
Whitelocke, Bulstrode, 6, 393
Whitgift, John, archbishop of Canterbury, 16
Willes, Richard, 86
   Poematum liber, 76, 78–9, 81, 235, 344
Willet, Andrew
   Sacrorum emblematum centuria una, 78
Willis, Hugo
   commendatory verse by, 208
Wilson, Thomas
   Vita et obitus, 75, 152
Windle, Christopher
   psalm paraphrases, 129–30
Winters, Yvor, 28
Wither, George, 249
   Preparation to the Psalter, 73
women
   Latin poetry by, 296–300
Wood, Andrew
   scriptural epigrams, 238–9
Woodford, Samuel
   copy of Mary Sidney manuscript, 128
   paraphrase of Song of Songs, 128, 220
   psalm paraphrases, 128, 202–3, 220–1
   use of Pindarics, 202–3
Wotton, Henry, 65, 67, 246, 269
   'Character of a Happy Life, The', 25–6, 48, 53
   'Dazel'd thus, with height of place', 54–7, 65, 67
Wotton, John, 47
Wright, Abraham
   Delitiae delitiarum, 237, 239–40, 247, 252, 273, 313
Wrighte, John
   commonplace book of, 462, 465
Wyatt, George, 94
Wyatt, Thomas, 27, 30, 41, 44, 67, 128
   'He ruleth not though he raigne', 34, 41
   'Of the meane and sure estate', 32
   Penitential Psalms, 99
   'Stond who so list', 31–2, 463
   'Who lyst his welth and eas Retayne', 33

Yalden, Thomas, 60

Ziolkowski, Jan, 147
Zwingli, Huldrych, 232